Object Relations Theory and Practice

The Library of Object Relations

A Series of Books Edited By

David E. Scharff and Jill Savege Scharff

Object relations theories of human interaction and development provide an expanding, increasingly useful body of theory for the understanding of individual development and pathology, for generating theories of human interaction, and for offering new avenues of treatment. They apply across the realms of human experience from the internal world of the individual to the human community, and from the clinical situation to everyday life. They inform clinical technique in every format from individual psychoanalysis and psychotherapy, through group therapy, to couple and family therapy.

The Library of Object Relations aims to introduce works that approach psychodynamic theory and therapy from an object relations point of view. It includes works from established and new writers who employ diverse aspects of British, American, and international object relations theory in helping individuals, families, couples, and groups. It features books that stress integration of psychoanalytic approaches with marital, family, and group therapy, as well as those centered on individual psychotherapy and psychoanalysis.

Refinding the Object and Reclaiming the Self
David E. Scharff

The Primer of Object Relations Therapy
Jill Savege Scharff and David E. Scharff

Object Relations Couple Therapy
David E. Scharff and Jill Savege Scharff

From Inner Sources:
New Directions in Object Relations Psychotherapy
N. Gregory Hamilton, Ed.

Object Relations Family Therapy
David E. Scharff and Jill Savege Scharff

Projective and Introjective Identification and the Use of the Therapist's Self
Jill Savege Scharff

Foundations of Object Relations Family Therapy
Jill Savege Scharff, Ed.

The Practice of Psychoanalytic Therapy
Karl König

Repairing Intimacy:
An Object Relations Approach to Couples Therapy
Judith Siegel

Family and Couple Therapy
John Zinner

Close Encounters:
A Relational View of the Therapeutic Process
Robert Winer

The Autonomous Self:
The Work of John D. Sutherland
Jill Savege Scharff, Ed.

Crisis at Adolescence:
Object Relations Therapy with the Family
Sally Box et al., Eds.

Personal Relations Therapy: *The Collected Papers of H. J. S. Guntrip*
Jeremy Hazell, Ed.

Psychoanalytic Group Psychotherapy
Karl König and Wulf-Volker Lindner

Countertransference Analysis
Karl König

Object Relations Theory and Practice
David E. Scharff, Ed.

On Freud's Couch:
Seven New Interpretations of Freud's Case Histories
Iréne Matthis and Imre Szecsödy, Eds.

From Instinct to Self:
Selected Papers of W.R.D. Fairbairn, Volume I: Clinical and Theoretical Contributions
David E. Scharff and Ellinor Fairbairn Birtles, Eds.

From Instinct to Self:
Selected Papers of W.R.D. Fairbairn, Volume II: Applications and Early Contributions
Ellinor Fairbairn Birtles and David E. Scharff, Eds.

Object Relations Therapy of Physical and Sexual Trauma
Jill Savege Scharff and David E. Scharff

Object Relations Individual Therapy
Jill Savege Scharff and David E. Scharff

A Prophetic Analyst:
Erich Fromm's Contributions to Psychoanalysis
Mauricio Cortina and Michael Maccoby, Eds.

Intricate Engagements:
The Collaborative Basis of Therapeutic Change
Steven A. Frankel

A Primer of Kleinian Therapy
Irving Solomon

Containing Rage, Terror, and Despair:
An Object Relations Approach to Psychotherapy
Jeffrey Seinfeld

Object Relations Brief Therapy
Michael Stadter

Love and Hate in the Analytic Setting
Glen O. Gabbard

Cruelty, Violence, and Murder:
Understanding the Criminal Mind
Arthur Hyatt-Williams

Body and Soul:
The Role of Object Relations in Faith, Shame, and Healing
Harold E. Bronheim

How to Survive as a Psychotherapist
Nina Coltart

The Sexual Relationship:
An Object Relations View of Sex and the Family
David E. Scharff

Object Relations Theory and Practice

An Introduction

selected and integrated by
DAVID E. SCHARFF

A JASON ARONSON BOOK

ROWMAN & LITTLEFIELD PUBLISHERS, INC.
Lanham • Boulder • New York • Toronto • Oxford

A JASON ARONSON BOOK

ROWMAN & LITTLEFIELD PUBLISHERS, INC.

Published in the United States of America
by Rowman & Littlefield Publishers, Inc.
A wholly owned subsidiary of The Rowman & Littlefield Publishing Group, Inc.
4501 Forbes Boulevard, Suite 200, Lanham, Maryland 20706
www.rowmanlittlefield.com

PO Box 317
Oxford
OX2 9RU, UK

British Library Cataloguing in Publication Information Available

Library of Congress Cataloging-in-Publication Data

Scharff, David E., 1941–
Object relations theory and practice : an introduction / selected and integrated by David E. Scharff.
p. cm.
Includes bibliographical references and index.
ISBN 1-56821-419-7
1. Object relations (Psychoanalysis)
[DNLM: 1. Object Attachment. 2. Psychoanalytic Therapy. WM 460.5.02 S31086 1995]
RC455.4.023S33 1995
616.89'17—dc20 94-24240

Printed in the United States of America

∞™ The paper used in this publication meets the minimum requirements of American National Standard for Information Sciences—Permanence of Paper for Printed Library Materials, ANSI/NISO Z39.48-1992.

About the Editor

David E. Scharff, M.D., is Co-Director of the International Institute of Object Relations Therapy and Clinical Professor of Psychiatry at Georgetown University and at the Uniformed Services University of the Health Sciences. Dr. Scharff received his M.D. from Harvard and is board certified in adult and child psychiatry and certified by the American Psychoanalytic Association in psychoanalysis. He is a former President of the American Association of Sex Educators, Counselors, and Therapists.

Dr. Scharff has a national and international reputation as an author, editor, teacher, and therapist. Among his publications are *Object Relations Family Therapy, Object Relations Couple Therapy, Object Relations Individual Therapy, The Sexual Relationship, Refinding the Object and Reclaiming the Self, From Instinct to Self: The Selected Papers of W.R.D. Fairbairn*, and *The Primer of Object Relations Therapy.*

To
Arthur Hyatt Williams
and
the late John Derg Sutherland

CONTENTS

*excerpt or abridgement

Part IV
Melanie Klein

Part V
D. W. Winnicott

Part VI
Wilfred Bion

Part VII
Klein's Theory Elaborated

Part VIII
Early Contributions of the Independent Group

Part IX
Transference and Countertransference

The Relational Matrix of Growth and Change

Part XII
Treating Groups, Families, and Institutions

Part XIII
Suggestions for Further Reading

Preface and Acknowledgments

This collection is designed to give the reader a familiarity with the literature of each of the major contributors to object relations theory and practice, written in their own words, and to pave the way for the reader to pursue the areas that are of interest. The book can stand on its own as an introduction and overview, but I hope that it will lead to further exploration. In the table of contents, the reader will note asterisks indicating those selections which are excerpts or abridgements from longer works.

The reader who is unfamiliar with this field may be helped by first reading a book I previously wrote with Jill Savege Scharff, *Scharff Notes: A Primer of Object Relations Therapy* (Northvale, NJ: Jason Aronson, 1992). This primer is the equivalent of an introductory workshop on the ideas that are developed by the original contributors in this volume. However, the comments provided in this book should be an adequate guide in themselves, so that this volume can stand on its own.

This book grew out of my experience in object relations teaching, first in the program that I developed at the Washington School of Psychiatry in 1989, in other courses that I have taught over many years, and now full-time at the International Institute of Object Relations Therapy. Collecting the readings for such programs has always been a problem because the essential literature is scattered among many journals and books. As I began to select readings for inclusion here, I realized that these readings, accompanied by a suitable introductory framework, could provide the readings for a program in object relations theory and practice.

As always in such endeavors, I owe a considerable debt to teachers and colleagues who have taught me so much. This includes especially those many British colleagues who taught me during my time in London many years ago, and those who worked with my colleagues and me at the Washington School during my time there, and since then at the IIORT. Arthur Hyatt Williams, who has taught me so much for more than twenty years, was perhaps the most doggedly dedicated teacher among this wonderful group, and I am especially indebted to him. I am also grateful to my colleagues in the object relations programs at the Washington School and the IIORT for their encouragement and collaboration, and especially to Jill Savege Scharff, who has shared in the rewards and travails of the endeavor throughout. One learns most from students, and I am grateful to the many students who have persisted in studying and questioning concepts, and have taught me in the process.

I am also grateful to previous collectors of anthologies or writers of exegeses whose guidance I have used in part in making this selection, such as Juliet Mitchell for *The Selected Melanie Klein* (London: The Hogarth Press, 1986); Elizabeth Spillius for her account of the development of Klein's views and those of her English colleagues and students in several places, including especially her 1994 article, "Developments in Kleinian Thought: Overview and Personal View" *(Psychoanalytic Inquiry* 14(3). Particularly, I want to thank her for her close reading of much of my material, and the generosity of her comments on and contributions to this volume. In some places I have directly acknowledged her help, but there are many areas in which she helped sharpen my understanding and added immeasurably to the process of representing the Kleinian tradition. Among other influences are the written guidance provided by Masud Khan in his introduction to Winnicott's work reprinted in *The Maturational Processes and the Facilitating Environment;* Jock Sutherland, a mentor, for his 1980 article, "The British Object Relations Theorists: Balint, Winnicott, Fairbairn, Guntrip" (*Journal of the American Psychoanalytic Association* 28:829) and Eric Rayner for his survey of the Independent Tradition in his *The Independent Mind in British Psychoanalysis.* (Northvale NJ: Jason Aronson, 1991). But these are only representatives of my general indebtedness to the many who have tilled the soil before me and whose influence is surely evident, even if blended beyond specific recognition.

Finally, I am indebted to those who have specifically and generously helped in this project: to Jason Aronson, who suggested and supported it, to Judy Cohen, the editor, who slaved over it with me, to Nancy D'Arrigo, who designs such fine covers with such cheer. David Tuckett was enormously facilitating in obtaining permission for reprinting from the various trusts and the *International Journal of Psycho-Analysis* and the *International Review of Psycho-Analysis*. Ellinor Fairbairn Birtles, Elizabeth Bott Spillius, and Arthur Hyatt Williams also helped generously in this regard. Jo Parker, Anna Innes, and Zoe Scharff helped with the details of acquiring and checking resources. My wife Jill Savege Scharff, as always, stood by with encouragement and support. This has been a labor of love, but it is a labor that could not have been accomplished without their loving support and that of many others.

August 25, 1994
Nantucket, Massachusetts

I

THE ORIGINS OF OBJECT RELATIONS THEORY

1

The Major Trends in Object Relations Theory and Practice

The notion of "object relations" originated with Freud's discussion of the fate of the sexual instinct, libido, seeking an object or person by which to be gratified. However, a psychology of object relations that put the individual's need to relate to others at the center of human development first achieved prominence in the work of Ronald Fairbairn and Melanie Klein, who thought that the efforts of each infant to relate to the mother constituted the first and most important tendency in the baby. Winnicott's work, which began slightly later, soon became a central part of this legacy. These three were not alone in their efforts to establish elements of what has collectively come to be known as "object relations theory," but their work has continued to constitute the basic framework for the elaborations of others.

Each of these three major theoreticians is a complex thinker, whose work is difficult to digest without a teacher or a seminar group. Klein's writing has always been considered difficult. A native German speaker without scientific or philosophical training, she wrote descriptively of her observations and speculations. The writing is at once intuitive and confusing, but the power of her observation and thinking accumulates over time, and has come to be perhaps the greatest single force for psychoanalytic observation since Freud.

Fairbairn's writing is different. He had considerable training in philosophy during his first degree at the University in Edinburgh before he was a field officer in World War I, and he then went on to medical school. He is unique among the major contributors to psychoanalytic theory in this philosophical background, and in the rigor of his thought, which stems from the synthesis of philosophy and the scientific method. While his earliest published papers were full of intense clinical observation, his recently published early papers and lectures on analytic theory show his keen and inquiring attempts to make sense of the inconsistencies and potential strengths of Freud's work (Birtles and Scharff 1994, Scharff and Birtles 1994). His inquiries reached fruition in the papers written in the 1940s and 1950s, many of which are included in the only book he published himself, *A Psychoanalytic Study of the Personality* (Fairbairn 1952). The writing is a model of tight reasoning, condensed language, and rigor derived from the adherence to scientific and philosophical principles. The theory that emerged in this book, and that was elaborated upon and explained in later papers, which are now collected for the first time in Scharff and Birtles (1994), filled out the theory, linked it to the contemporary concerns of developing psychoanalytic theory, answered objections, and again considered his early concerns (Birtles and Scharff 1994) about methodological and scientific shortcomings in Freud's theory.

Fairbairn's contribution has emerged as the single most consistent theory of psychoanalysis we now have, the hub of a wheel to which the spokes can relate logically to add clinical and theoretical richness to our understanding. It is not that this theory replaces the others. The human condition is far too complex for any single theory to suffice. But Fairbairn's construction emerges as the most centered, the most logical, and the most helpful in organizing the others, including not only Klein and Winnicott, but also such current theories as attachment theory (Bowlby), self psychology (Kohut), and relational-conflict theory (Mitchell). Fairbairn's work also provides links between Freud, drive theory, ego psychology, and the relational theories. I describe some of these links in the introductions to each part of this book.

Winnicott's background was different. He was a pediatrician who fell in with a vibrant analytic group in London, but he maintained his grounding in pediatrics. His definition of his work was strongly influenced by his professional beginnings: the observation of the child, mother, and family. His writing is grounded in clinical and developmental observation, always given an idiosyncratic, imaginative twist. This then suddenly becomes a theory of development written in metaphorical and evocative language. Not surprisingly, the resulting language is like quicksilver: beautiful, suggestive, evanescent. Now you follow it, now you don't! The logical links are not always there, but always there is something powerfully and creatively convincing. The best experience of Winnicott comes with reading his work intuitively while letting go of logic and understanding, and slowly arriving at understanding from the inside by experiencing his words, which are powerful, magical, and confounding. There are some good guides to Winnicott's thought, which gradually began to build to a theory of development, but the summaries cannot offer clarity and still retain the magical creative confusion that his own words offer. Here, I will try to offer both: a bit of logic mixed in with a sturdy dose of the original magic.

Winnicott's magic covers the field: the child's coming into being, creating itself within the intimacies of the relationship with its mother, the mother's role in the child's development, and the implications of these observations for assessment and therapy with infants, children, and adults. His contributions on countertransference are among the most moving and evocative in the literature. His linking of technique with adults to what he has learned from dealing with children is original and valuable, and ranks with the work of Klein and her followers.

Fairbairn, Klein, and Winnicott came to analysis from different perspectives. I have chosen examples of their writings that highlight the centrality of each perspective, which gives the beginning reader a starting point. Because of the subtle shifts in their work, each has focused the analytic spotlight on different aspects of human development, and therefore has offered a different set of perspectives and techniques. Because of the partial nature of each view, they can be criticized. But I find it more useful to focus on the intense investigation they offer, each from their particular vantage. Then it is up to us to attempt a working synthesis.

FAIRBAIRN'S MODEL OF THE MIND

Fairbairn began his work with an intense scholarly interest in Freud, developing a thorough understanding of Freud's theory as demonstrated in the notes he used in the seminars he taught medical and other students at the University of Edinburgh (Birtles and Scharff 1994). He ended these early lectures with a series of questions about Freud's theoretical structure, questions that he could not fully answer until his own formulation in the 1940s, when he took up some of the objections from the standpoint of his new theory. However, he did not fully outline his differences with Freud and the reasons for them until the series of late papers (Scharff and

Birtles 1994). In his clinical reports written as early as 1927 (Fairbairn 1927), he considered the relationship of the patient to the family and others to be the central clinical matter, but he lacked a theoretical framework that differentiated such a perspective from the standard Freudian point of view.

Fairbairn followed the London scene and the work of Melanie Klein and her group closely, and was profoundly influenced by them, since their emphasis on the experience of the infant in relating to the mother fit well with his own ideas. However, he did not accept Klein's ideas without question. One can see him incorporate many of her ideas as his writing progresses, most notably in two papers he wrote on a psychology of art (Fairbairn 1936a, b) where the ideas represent an early, uncritical application of Klein's ideas of relating to the object, symbolism, and symbolic repair.

In his first original theoretical paper, written a few years after the papers on a psychology of art, the 1940 paper "Schizoid Factors in the Personality" (excerpted in Chapter 5), Fairbairn outlined the process of splitting of the ego in normal development and pathology. He amended Klein's early postulates of development, suggesting that splitting of the object and ego constituted an earlier position than the "depressive position" she had described as the infant's recognition of the mother as a whole person. She had, in the meantime, described the "paranoid position," involving early processes of projection of aggression. She now agreed with Fairbairn, and renamed this earlier position the "paranoid-schizoid position," to arrive at a description of an early position the infant takes in regard to its object that is characterized by the pairing of splitting and projection. Thus, for both theorists, splitting of the object came to represent an early and fundamental psychic defense against pain in relationships. Nevertheless, we can see the different emphasis already emerging in Fairbairn's work. Klein emphasized the infant's role in projection and splitting of the *object.* She thought the infant mainly tried to get unpleasant experience and affect outside the self by locating it in the mother. Fairbairn thought that the effect was to split the *ego*—or as we would now call it, the self—accompanied by repression, that is, disposing of unpleasant internalized relationships by splitting them off from the main core of the self and burying them. While for both theorists splitting of both object and ego is involved, the emphasis on ego or object says a good deal about each one's focus. Aspects of this interaction are mentioned in some of the papers excerpted in this volume.

Fairbairn (1943) suggested that the concept of "unconscious phantasy" that Klein had postulated as the fundamental link between the drives and reality should be replaced by his more useful concept of the "internal object." His point continues to make logical sense, but both terms remain in use.

Fairbairn's fundamental reorientation of analytic theory was published in 1944, in his paper on endopsychic structure that is excerpted in this volume (Chapter 7). In it he states that the infant is motivated, from the beginning, by a fundamental need for relationships, and that all development takes place and has meaning in the context of the relationship to the mother. (We can see here the origin of Winnicott's later, evocative statement: "There is no such thing as an infant without a mother.") The first defense against the inevitable disappointments in the relationship to the mother is to introject her as an internal object in an attempt to control the disappointment over rejection, but the infant is now saddled with an internalized rejecting object. The second defense is to split off the painful parts of that "bad" object and to repress them out of consciousness, leaving a relatively unencumbered central ego to relate to the remaining goodness of the object and the outside world. As the object is split, so a part of the ego splits, too, for since the idea of an object has no meaning without an ego (or a self) to relate to it, so each part of the object (or part-object) requires a part-ego or part of the self to be in relation with it.

We can now state the central orientation of Fairbairn's point of view, most of which had emerged by the time of this paper in 1944. The infant is born prepared (or "hard-wired") to take in experience with its object world. From the standpoint of psychology and psychoanalysis, this biological readiness to form relationships is the central fact of human experience. Fairbairn's model emphasizes that the internal world is organized by internalizing experience with the outer world. While he is specific about the influences the growing psyche adds to make a distinct inner world so that the psyche is not simply a carbon copy of the outer experience, nevertheless the model of the mind is one that is capable of blending outer influence with inner structuring throughout development. This balance makes his the most flexible of models, able to consider both the full influence of external reality and the inner forces that drive and modify development. For instance, Fairbairn's model can accept and understand the full force of external trauma such as physical or sexual abuse or the loss of a parent, but it also allows for the rich elaboration of the child's inner distortions and modifications of outer experience.

Fairbairn thought that the reorganization of internal structure during the oedipal phase is a creation of the child triggered by the experience of ambivalent relationships with both mother and father. The child tries to organize and simplify this complex situation, he said, by making one parent the good object and the other the bad, usually organized along sexual lines. It is this flexibility that warrants placing Fairbairn's model at the center of a comprehensive understanding of psychic development.

Fairbairn organized his theory into a brief statement in 1963, the year he died. It has the tight logical reasoning and spareness of a philosophical formulation. For this reason, it can also be captured in a diagram that I have used to explain the theory and that will allow us to consider graphically some of the major aspects of his theory and to relate them to Klein and Winnicott (Figure 1–1).

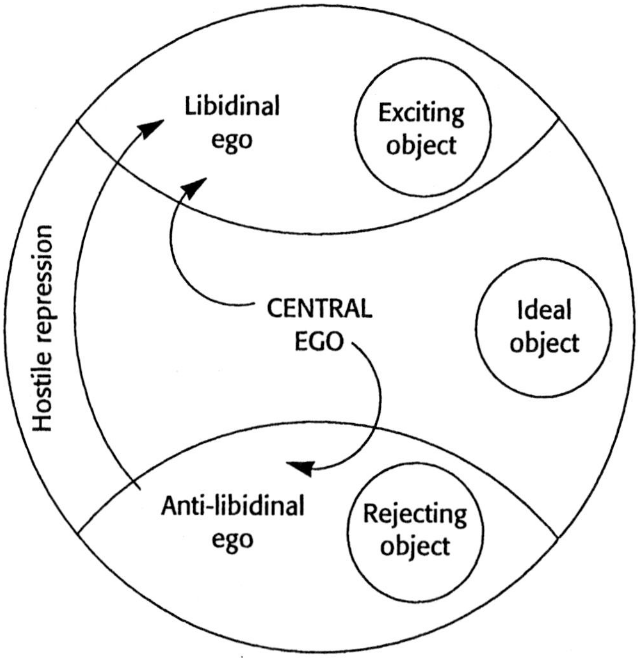

Figure 1–1. Fairbairn's model of psychic organization. From D. E. Scharff, (1982), *The Sexual Relationship: An Object Relations View of Sex and the Family,* London: Routledge and Kegan Paul. (Used by permission.)

In this model, the central ego and its ideal object are the relatively conscious and rational aspect of psychic functioning. Split off from the central ego, and repressed by it, are the "bad" internal objects (bad because they represent the internalization of painful interactions with the parents). In each case, an aspect of the ego or self is split off in relation to these split off and repressed objects. The frustrating or rejecting object is that image of the mother that is felt to be rejecting of need, and Fairbairn originally called the ego component attached to it the "internal saboteur" (Chapter 7). Later he used the term *anti-libidinal ego* for this subunit of the ego. Also associated with pain is the image of the mother who excessively excites needs, the "exciting object." The part-ego associated with this he called the "libidinal ego." While the central ego acts to repress both these constellations in order to avoid awareness of pain, there is also secondary repression carried out by the anti-libidinal ego on the libidinal ego and object in order to avoid the pain of unsatisfied longing. In describing this affect-laden interaction of internal structures, Fairbairn described the first example of "dynamic, internal object relations." We now understand that the dynamic quality works in all directions, so that the libidinal ego can, and does, act to repress the anti-libidinal ego and object in situations in which a person assumes an excessively sweet disposition to avoid the pain of experiencing rejection. The internal relations between self and object are subject to a dynamic flux in health, a system that is in open exchange with the environment. It is only in pathological situations that the internal relations become frozen in one or another static situation, forming then a fixed and closed internal system.

It is difficult to absorb the logic of Fairbairn's system on first reading. But this explanation and diagram can serve as a useful framework from which to read the articles in this book.

I have modified Fairbairn's system in my own work. In his later writing, and in the work of Guntrip and Sutherland that are excerpted in this volume, Fairbairn's model has been applied to the healthy development of the self, not only used in explanation of pathology. When it is used this way, it has to take into account the forces that the libidinal and anti-libidinal constellations represent for relating in both health and disease. Thus, I have come to see the libidinal ego as the part of the self that pulls toward the object, and the anti-libidinal ego as the part that stands for separation within the context of relationships. They represent the dominant trends in relating, and it is only the excesses of these trends that have to do with pathology. The exciting object and rejecting object also represent trends in the force of internal objects, and only the excesses represent the pathological object. Both aspects of the self–ego and object—are in dynamic internal relationship with each other, and these dynamics influence and are influenced by external object relations. Accordingly, I have modified the diagram of Fairbairn's theory to show the place of the libidinal and anti-libidinal constellations in development and pathology (Figure 1–2).

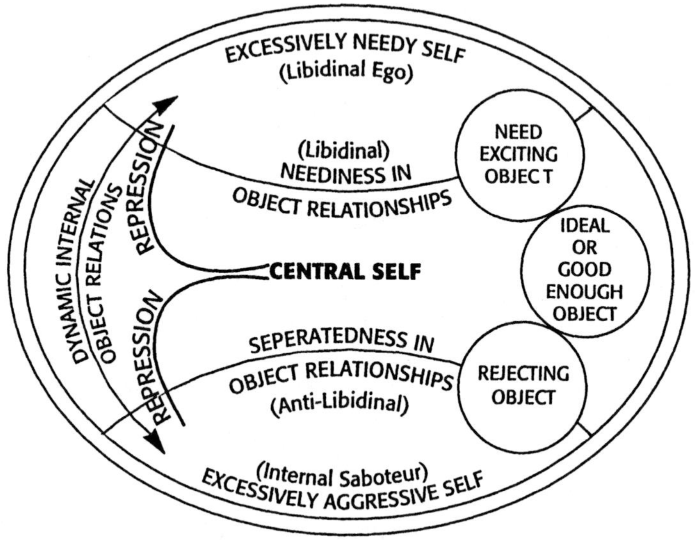

Figure 1–2. Revision of object relations theory. Neediness and separateness are aspects of the central self. Exciting and rejecting objects partly communicate with the ideal object and are partly repressed. All aspects of self and object are in dynamic relation. Used by permission.

KLEIN'S AND BION'S MODEL OF THE PSYCHE

Klein began forming her theory by observing and describing child development and psychopathology. She wrote with extraordinary clinical insight and imagination, using extensive clinical illustration of what she saw and said. She viewed things from the standpoint of the child's mind in relation to the mother, but not in relation to a real mother. She was aware of the role of mothers, and commented on it often, but her theory overlooks it. Fathers were overlooked too, except from the standpoint of the way the child felt and thought about them in the oedipal situation. But fathers do not figure prominently in the work of any of the theorists we are considering except in their oedipal role. It is not until the 1970s that they were considered, and even now it is often too commonly assumed that their role is secondary to whoever does the mothering, whether it is a woman or a man.

There is, however, a certain power in the singlemindedness of Klein's perspective that marked her observations. She saw things from inside the child's mind, and her view is that the child's development is driven by an unfolding of the drives that Freud had described. Freud had begun by describing sex as the fundamental drive motivating life toward pleasure. This, in brief, is his pleasure principle, which underlay his original dictum that dreams were always motivated by wish fulfillment. Later he broadened what he meant by sex to include a comprehensive life drive. Against this, he posited a death drive, or *thanatos*, that tended toward the disintegration and deterioration of life, toward the individual forces of self-destruction and the social forces of brutality and war.

Today, many analysts understand the drives as operating in more general ways. Rather than positing sex as a universal basis for positive human motivation, they see the tendency toward closeness in relatedness, toward the mastery of new situations, and toward growth as operating together, and that these situations include the positive aspects of physical and genital sexuality. The opposite pole of motivation is aggression, which, in its positive role, operates toward separateness in relationships and supports mastery of new situations, but, in its excesses, is part of human violence, war, and destruction. Thus tendencies toward affiliation and aggression can be understood to be the poles of behavior that Freud was first describing (see Figure 1–2).

Freud would not have necessarily agreed with this analysis, and certainly Klein would not have. She took his formulation of the life and death instincts seriously, and put them at the center of her orientation. Klein is both a drive and an object relations theorist. She differs from Freud in assuming that drives are immediately attached to objects, whereas he thought they became more or less fortuitously connected depending on the experiences of an individual. Her drives are more psychological, his more physiological (E. Spillius 1994). The infant she described is haunted by the death instinct and, because it is so concerned about the relationship to its objects, is motivated to undo the damage it believes it has caused from directing omnipotent phantasies of excessive aggression (biting, devouring, excreting) against its primary objects. She views the inner world from the orientation of an infant who might expect to have a competent mother *if the infant does not damage her or drive her away.*

Where Fairbairn saw an infant frustrated by the inevitability of being let down or rejected by its mother some of the time, Klein thought that the infant is terrified of its own death instinct, which it feels as a fear of annihilation. It deals with this by phantasies of projecting the aggression into its mother, and then feels she is bad. Klein emphasizes that this process originates with the baby, although she mentions in several places that bad experience contributes, too. For instance, she says that the inevitable trauma of birth contributes to the feeling of being annihilated. This anxiety is also felt from the beginning to be caused by the infant's objects. This problem represented the struggle the infant dealt with at the earliest stage of psychological life that Klein described, and she called the struggle represented by this constellation the "paranoid/schizoid *position*" to indicate that it was not a single developmental step, but a lifelong process. The word *paranoid* has to do with the projection of aggression outward, and was the process Klein first described as a "paranoid position." However, as we noted, she soon took Fairbairn's suggestion that splitting of the ego was involved in the projection process, and so renamed the process to reflect the pairing of splitting and projection. For Klein, however, the projection of an instinct is not exclusively the domain of the death instinct. It is equally important in the handling of the life instinct, where good external experience encourages the projection of love and the introjection of good objects. The fundamental point about the paranoid/schizoid position is that the life and death instincts are kept apart so that internal and external objects are not integrated but are felt to be either very good or very bad. Although Klein emphasized sadism in her early papers, by 1940 she had developed the idea of the depressive position in which the child strives to relate to an integrated object. She then came to emphasize the interplay of love and hate "from the beginning" (E. Spillius 1994). We can now see that projection of a part of the mental contents is only possible when that part has been split off from the core, so that indeed splitting and projection must operate together as the infant tries to manage its own anger and tendency to ruin things. (Klein saw projective processes as dominant, whereas Fairbairn saw repression. In fact, both processes operate at the same time, but some patients emphasize one more than the other.)

Later, the infant begins the lifelong job of understanding the situation of the mother who has had to put up with the difficult baby, and who, herself, while not perfect, is still the infant's loving mother. Klein called this internal struggle the "depressive position," making it clear that this position has nothing to do with clinical depression, but rather is part of the assumption of concern for the object, with the capacity for guilt. It leads to a desire to make reparation to the mother. The child in the paranoid/schizoid position envies the mother for having what the child needs and wants, embodied in the envy of her breast for having the milk the child needs and the pleasure of sucking the child craves, while the child in the depressive position is capable of gratitude for what the mother gives.

In her whole approach, Klein emphasized the dynamic role of the internal world in determining the quality of the developing personality and of external relations. Within this, the splitting into part objects, and the struggle to maintain relations to whole objects play a lifelong role.

Klein's concept of unconscious phantasy, which she first demonstrated so clearly in the play of the children she analyzed, characterized her writing from the beginning. She conceived of *un*conscious *phantasy* as the unconscious embodiment of the drives, those primitive organizations of mind that operate entirely unconsciously but act from underneath to determine everything that happens at more conscious and rational levels of organization. She then described many of the unconscious phantasies of the very young child, who, she felt, understood the essence of relational processes in bodily terms. She felt that the triangular oedipal situation that Freud (1905) had described many years earlier occurred in a primitive, essentially oral version in the 1-year-old child, and that the child's unconscious phantasy of the mother and father in intercourse, of the mother having orally and sadistically incorporated the father's penis inside her body, represented the prototype of a triangular situation to be envied. The conceptualization of unconscious phantasy as the expression of the drives was spelled out best by Isaacs (excerpted in this volume) but it was an essential element in Klein's own writing and clinical teaching long before Isaacs' paper.

The idea of *positions* that Klein introduced offered a fundamental shift from Freud's use of developmental *phases*. She felt that the characteristics of the paranoid/schizoid and depressive positions came into operation early, but then continued to organize experience throughout life. Although she implied the importance of dynamic flux between positions, it was Bion who stressed their constant interplay, thereby setting the stage for the later work of Joseph, Steiner, and others who have examined the fluctuations of position in personality development and in clinical sessions.

Perhaps the best known of Klein's concepts is that of *projective identification,* which should be paired with its counterpart, *introjective identification,* to make its usefulness more complete (J. S. Scharff 1992). In projective identification, the infant (or any person) unconsciously takes an aspect of its internal world–object or self–and projects it out and into the other person with whom it is in relationship, identifying the other person with that aspect of itself. This process is carried out by unconscious communication and supported by facial and bodily gestures, intonation, and context. It rides, as it were, piggyback on conscious communication. The other person introjectively identifies with these elements and, without knowing it, is partly taken over by the projected elements and acts in some ways to live them out. In a cycle of projective and introjective identification, this second person then re-projects aspects of herself (assuming this to be the mother) that the infant takes in through introjective identification. This cycle is the bedrock of unconscious communication, but in conditions of the pain of "bad object" relations, the infant projectively identifies with the painful aspects of itself that it locates in the mother in order to get them outside the self (in phantasy) so as to avoid their spoiling its internal world, and in the hope that after their sojourn in the mother they will come back detoxified. Alternatively, the infant projects out "good" aspects of its self for safe-keeping in the mother, or uses aspects of the personality to control her and keep her nearby when separation threatens.

Figure 1–3 depicts a situation of projective identification in which, for example, a child unconsciously seeks an exciting object form of relating to the mother, such as anxiously seeking a feed when no longer hungry. The mother rejects this unconscious initiative, for example by angrily shaking the child for being spoiled, and the child experiences a more severe rejection, introjecting an enlarged experience of the rejecting object relationship. A more thorough rejection or a refusal to take in the child's anxiety at all leaves the child to introject a feeling of nameless dread.

While Klein introduced the concepts of projective and introjective identification, it was Bion who elaborated the model and made it an interactive one with his concept of the *container/contained.* The infant's projected primitive anxieties are "the contained," to be taken in by the mother as "container"–that is by her active process of reception and digestion which he called her *reverie.* In this way, the mother, through her introjective identification and reverie, metabolizes and provides structure to the anxiety so it can be re-projected into the infant in detoxified and more tolerable form. Bion's elaboration transformed Klein's ideas into a cogent model of unconscious interaction.

Again, the reader new to these concepts will need to allow time for the growth of understanding while studying Klein's formulation of them, perhaps returning to these comments later.

Klein's early work analyzing children from the age of 2½ years was illustrated through the detailed descriptions of the clinical work, which came to be a hallmark of the British tradition. As with Freud's clinical writing, one may disagree with Klein but still know the data she used to draw her conclusions and what she meant clinically. This early work with young children gave her the conviction that the infant understood a great deal about the nature of sexuality and destruction. By extrapolation, the problem for the older patient in treatment becomes the disposal of forces deriving from these earliest struggles as the child or adult relives them in the analytic setting.

When Klein located these problems of the disposal of the drives of sexuality and death at the center of children's psychological development, she gave analysis a powerful way of understanding the difficulty we cause ourselves when excesses of anger, sexual feeling, longing, and rejection torment us. Her concept of inner phantasy organization has allowed us to see the richness of the inner world and its continuing influence on our lives through projective identification and other interactive processes. Her concept of positions has enriched many developmental theories that could be understood in relational terms for the first time.

What Klein does not offer is a similar richness of exploration of external influences on the child. Like Freud before her, she constructed a theory in which the growing child seemed like a flower, unfolding in a preset pattern so long as it was supported adequately by the sun, water, and nutrients of the ordinary environment. It is almost as though the mother is merely the provider of these elements, a benign but vague and impersonal figure who exerts no personal influence. Klein referred often to the theoretical effect of the environment, including the traumatic role of birth and the effect of bad experience—that is, experience with external objects—in exacerbating fear of annihilation, as well as that of good experience in promoting good internal objects. But, although she said the environment was important, she did not make it an integral part of her theory. It was Bion who later showed how the environment was important by building it into his model of container/contained. Nevertheless, even

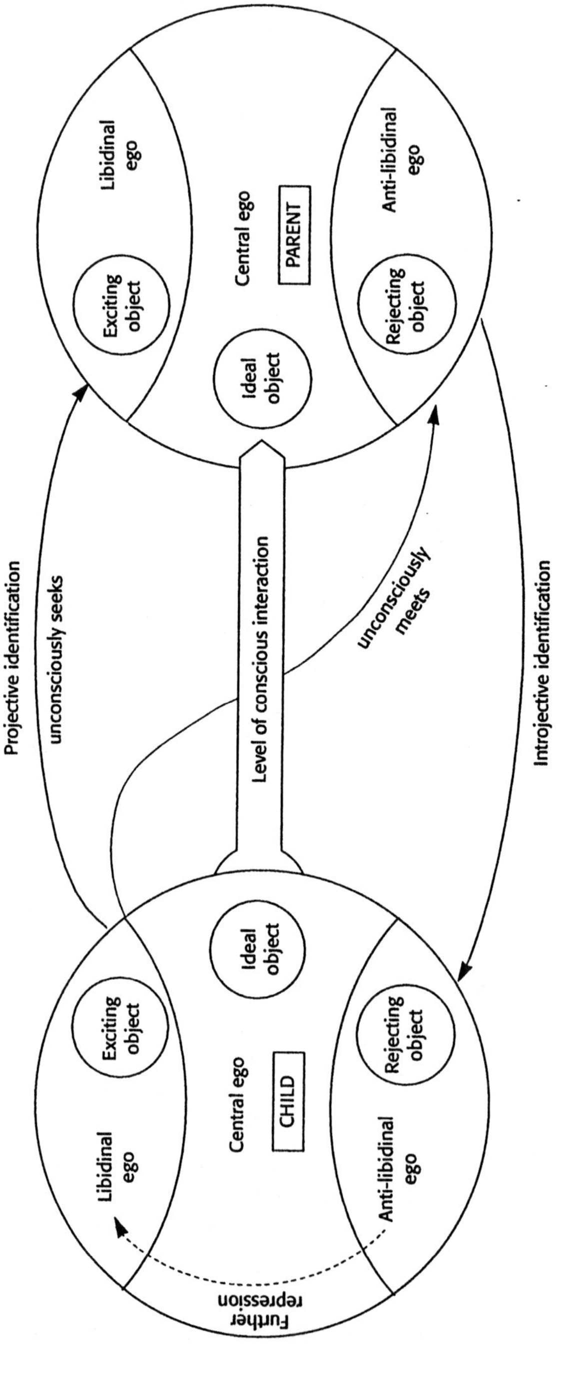

Figure 1–3. The mechanism here is the interaction of the child's projective and introjective identifications with the parent as the child meets frustration, unrequited yearning, or trauma. The diagram depicts the child longing to have his needs met and identifying with similar trends in the parent via projective identification. If he meets with rejection, he identifies with the frustration of the parent's own anti-libidinal system via introjective identification. In an internal reaction to the frustration, the libidinal system is further repressed by the renewed force of the child's anti-libidinal system. (From D. E. Scharff (1982), *The Sexual Relationship*. London: Routledge and Kegan Paul. Used by permission.)

he did not present a model of the primary influence of good and bad experience in shaping the child even before the child influenced its own experience with objects. This area of the primary influence of the external object is unique to Winnicott's work. While the lack of consideration of external influence has been held to be a shortcoming of Klein and the Kleinians, I believe it is more useful to examine their unparalleled offerings about the child's inner world, and then to look to other contributors—those in the tradition of Fairbairn and Winnicott—for ideas about the influence of the outer world. Fairbairn provided the theoretical structure that allowed full influence of the parents and significant others in fundamentally shaping the growing child, but it was Winnicott who first described the elements of the mother's (or mothering person's) treatment of the child that matter in this process.

WINNICOTT'S MODEL OF MOTHER AND BABY

Donald Winnicott came to analysis as a pediatrician, out of a lifelong interest in the development of babies and the care their mothers exercised of them. He was heavily influenced by Klein. Although he never became a formal member of her group, Klein considered Winnicott to be one of her supporters during the Controversial Discussions of the early 1940s. The centerpiece of his contribution is an evocative exploration of the mother–infant relationship. (He, too, had almost nothing to say about fathers.) Then he applied this growing understanding to the treatment of children and adults, seeing a reliving of processes of infant and child development in them.

For Winnicott, the adequacy of the maternal caregiving activity had a pervasive influence on the child's psychological development. Where Klein had put projection, and Fairbairn put the child's splitting and repression in response to frustration, Winnicott put developmental failure and the growth of the false self in response to maternal failures. He saw the ordinary mother as devoted to her infant's growth and well-being, but just as the "good-enough" mother's functioning facilitated development, so the mother's failures could be expected to handicap the child's maturational processes. The mother begins her task with a state of mind that he called "primary maternal preoccupation," representing an intense absorption with her infant and its well-being. This singlemindedness includes an openness to the infant's state of mind and its anxieties, and a willingness to be used by the infant for its own sake. His famous aphorism to the effect that there is no such thing as a baby (without a mother) captures the life-giving quality of the relationship between them.

Winnicott's contribution strongly implies a deficit model of psychopathology, that what is wrong with troubled children comes solely from deficiencies in their treatment by others, from inadequate supplies or security. His contribution is usefully applied to understanding the way shortcomings in the environmental provisions for a child are translated into psychic difficulty, in contrast with Klein, who largely ignored this area, and with Fairbairn, who did not supply any details about it. But it is inaccurate to say that Winnicott did not appreciate the child's own contribution to the development of a self. He insisted that the growth of a self and the realization of a true self was a joint matter. His view is, in many ways, closely balanced, particularly since there are several places in his writing in which he carefully and sensitively describes the state of mind and travails of the therapists and the parents, especially the mother. This is true, for instance, when he describes the need for the parents to survive the aggression of the infant without retaliation as a prerequisite for the child to have the experience of "I killed you and you survived." It is this reciprocal, enigmatic, and magical experience that allows the honing of aggression as a force for life.

The mother has two kinds of functions to offer. First, as the *environment mother,* she sets the context for growth by providing an envelope of safety and comfort to support the existence and growth of the child, a kind of "arms-around" relationship that holds the child safely and confidently. Within this envelope, she offers herself as an *object mother*—that is, she offers to be used as an object by the infant, as the focused subject of its love and hate, as the object of its experience, without being devoured or killed off. She offers to survive the experience of answering the infant's needs as a person and as a thing, and at many times does so without demanding anything in return. She survives the infant's love and hate, without dying, retaliating, or exploiting the child. In doing this, she reacts, and the infant learns to see itself as mirrored in her face, her reactions, and her treatment of the infant. As she becomes the first external object for the child, the child finds itself in her reaction and in her handling. And at the same time, the child internalizes the experience with her—that is, she becomes the material out of which the internal world is populated. In his concept of *the use of an object,* Winnicott describes the way the mother must offer herself as an object to be used, to be abused in the "ruthless" sense that the infant can make use of her with no obligation to have her experience in mind, and in that sense to be the subject of benign abuse. It is her own "ruth" or selfless concern for the infant that allows her to offer herself in this way.

Winnicott describes how the experience with the mother is taken in by the child. In his conception, the beginning has twin origins in the infant's core, expressed in the infant's own spontaneous gestures and in its exploration of the world around it, a taking in of outer experience and physical objects that parallels the process of taking in the experience with the mother. For instance, in his clinical invention of the spatula game Winnicott observes the way the child takes in an inert neutral object while doing so in the presence and with the support of the mother who holds the environment in which the infant can explore. The other beginning for the infant, mentioned above, is in the mother's mind, in her *primary maternal preoccupation* that holds the baby in mind, attends to its needs, moods, and being, and supports it psychologically. So the baby begins equally in itself and in its mother, simultaneously and paradoxically.

Winnicott conceived of the beginning relationship between mother and baby as a *psycho-somatic partnership,* that is, as a relationship equally grounded on the bodily and physical aspects of relating and the psychological partnership. Through the earliest months, this partnership becomes attenuated as a physical, bodily one, but the intense psychological partnership carries, throughout the rest of the child's life, the inheritance of its origin in the bodily closeness and communication that gave it the initial power and poignance and continue to characterize the way intense primary relationships penetrate the bodily being of the child. The mother takes care of her tasks through her holding and handling of the infant, conveying her environmental care so that the infant can become a going concern and receive the security of the capacity of "going on being" by being swaddled in the security of her arms and receiving her abiding, responsive concern.

As the mother–infant pair relate over time, they do so across a widening physical distance between parent and child that is echoed in a widening psychological separateness, which holds the essential potential for creativity and communication mediated by what Winnicott calls *transitional objects* and *transitional phenomena*. The transitional object is a physical article that the infant treats as though it were the mother, but that is completely under the control of the child. Thus the blanket, teddy bear, or other object is a tireless companion, an object to be used and abused, and a source of comfort. The child uses other phenomena in a similar way, perhaps at an early stage playing with the mother's face, breast, hair, or clothes, making use of an object of clothing in a habitual way even though the piece of clothing itself is interchangeable, and in adolescence by using other objects in such a way as to open a potential space—which we now also call a transitional space—in which internal issues and issues between people can be elaborated and experimented with in such a way that they represent simultaneously an internal experience of the child and the meeting of the child with another person. Whether the experience is internal or external is never quite clear, and this ambiguity is one of the sustained paradoxes Winnicott asks us to live with. The mother may put the object there for the child to find, but children must also have the experience of feeling that they invented it, while the parent agrees never to force the question, "Did the baby find this or invent it?"

Figure 1–4 summarizes some of these elements of Winnicott's formulation, but it does so by indicating that Fairbairn's formulation of internal organization can also be seen to be consistent with Winnicott's contributions. In constructing this diagram, I have called the functions performed by the environment mother those of "contextual" holding and relating to refer to the "arms-around" functions of the mother. Those of the object mother I have called "focused" relating, or "I-to-I" relating, to refer to the way mother and baby become each other's discrete objects of love and hate by looking into each other's eyes (eye-to-eye) and speaking and responding directly to each other (D. Scharff 1992).

Many of Winnicott's formulations are most evocative in their paradoxical and enigmatic quality, which makes it difficult to pin him down to precise formulations. He seems to have intended this, stating that it is in enigma and uncertainty that growth and creativity occur. This enigmatic quality also characterizes his terms *true self* and *false self*. The false self is a quality or state of the personality that is reactive to the mother's (and significant others') needs, which come to take precedence over those of the child itself. The true self, while hard to define, is a core of the child's being that is the center of the child's own personality, often covered by the social core of the false self that, in pathology, is overly responsive to the demands of others. The false self is not a bad thing, but rather the part of the self that is tuned to the outer reality, that protects the true self by doing so, and that facilitates relatedness to others.

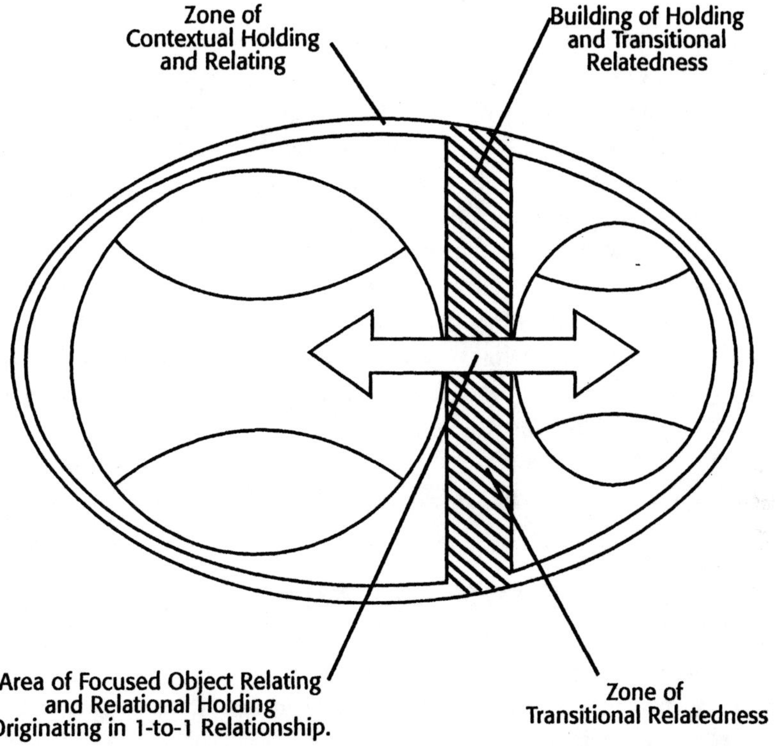

Figure 1–4. Diagram showing contextural and focused relationships. Focused (or centered or I-to-I) relating occurs in and across the transitional space. The transitional space is in contact with both contextual relating and focused relating, and is also the zone that blends the two. (From D. E. Scharff (1992), *Refinding the Object and Reclaiming the Self.* Northvale, NJ: Jason Aronson. Used by permission.)

Many of Winnicott's concepts are essentially clinical and developmental observations, given the evocative names and descriptions that have created his unique blend of clinical theory. Not surprisingly, his contributions have been uniquely applicable to the clinical situation with children and adults. His clinical concepts, like his developmental ones, center around the concept of play. It is in the child's ability to play in the gap between itself and the parent—in the transitional space—that growth and experimentation occur, and psychotherapy and psychoanalysis are conceived of as an experience of play in the area of overlap between patient and therapist. If the child cannot play, it is handicapped or ill in Winnicott's description. Like the well child, the adult must be able to play with ideas and with concepts of the relationship, with significant others, and with the therapist.

Because of his background as a pediatrician, and his orientation as a doctor to children with physical ills, Winnicott did some unconventional things as an analyst, such as encouraging some patients to walk around, placing a child outside the door during a temper tantrum, and physically holding some patients. While these acts, especially the physical contact, would be unacceptable to modern analytic therapists, it is in the *ideas* conveyed in these actions that Winnicott's most important clinical contributions have come. It is with the clinical concept of *holding* as a psychological state of mind of the therapist, or with *relating and mirroring,* that the therapist works, so that it is within this context that interpretation has an impact. Winnicott's (1949) description of his own countertransference activity with a boy who elicited feelings of hate during the treatment is the classic clinical description of the use of the analyst's unpleasant experience in the treatment of aggression (Chapter 16).

OTHER CONTRIBUTORS

Klein died in 1960, Fairbairn in 1963, and Winnicott in 1971. Even before their deaths, other contributors had picked up the threads of the rich tapestry they began. Such seminal writers as Michael Balint, Wilfred Bion, John Bowlby, Harry Guntrip, Herbert Rosenfeld, Hanna Segal, Masud Khan, Paula Heimann, Susan Isaacs, and Betty Joseph made central contributions to theory and clinical practice. They continued the tradition of applying rich, direct observation to clinical treatment of children and adults. This volume contains brief samples of their work in order to extend and fill in the themes begun by Fairbairn, Klein, and Winnicott, each of them introduced separately. Of this later group, the work of Bion has been most influential despite the difficulty of his writing, and is given the most space after those of Fairbairn, Klein, and Winnicott.

In the last two decades, the work has continued, increasingly on both sides of the Atlantic, throughout Europe and in North and South America. The spread of the tradition has become so rich that not all of the significant contributors can be represented in this volume. Object relations no longer resides solely in the British Isles. It has become a worldwide influence within the disciplines of psychoanalysis and psychotherapy, and the basis for work in psychotherapy, infant research and treatment, child and adult development, and groups and institutions. The relational paradigm first described by Fairbairn, Klein, and Winnicott has become the organizing set of ideas in modern psychoanalysis, and has influenced literature, philosophy, and organizational development. Within the clinical sphere, and beyond to wider fields of human endeavor, the opportunities offered by object relations theory have yet to be fully explored.

The chapters that follow consist of excerpts from original articles written by the contributors, beginning with the origin of object relations as term and theory in the work of Freud. After the writings of Fairbairn, Klein, and Winnicott, which occupy the first half of the volume, we explore other early contributors, including Bion, Balint, Guntrip, Isaacs, and Segal. Then we move on to subsequent elaborations and applications of object relations, ending with current contributors. It is my hope that after this introduction to object relations theory, the reader will wish to pursue further reading and study of these writers and their concepts.

REFERENCES

Birtles, E. F., and Scharff, D. E., eds. (1994). From *Instinct to Self: Selected Papers of W. R. D. Fairbairn,* vol. II. Northvale, NJ: Jason Aronson.

Fairbairn, W. R. D. (1927). Notes on the religious phantasies of a female patient. In *A Psychoanalytic Study of the Personality,* pp. 183–196. London: Routledge & Kegan Paul, 1952.

—— (1936). "Prolegomena to a psychology of art." and "The ultimate basis of aesthetic experience," in *From Instinct to Self,* vol. 2, ed. E. F. Birtles and D. E. Scharff, pp. 381–409. Northvale, NJ: Jason Aronson, 1994.

—— (1943). Phantasy and inner reality. In *From Instinct to Self,* vol. 2, ed. E. F. Birtles and D. Scharff, pp. 293–294. Northvale NJ: Jason Aronson, 1994.

—— (1952). *A Psychoanalytic Study of the Personality*. London: Routledge and Kegan Paul.

—— (1963). A synopsis of an object relations theory of the personality. *International Journal of Psycho-Analysis* 44:224–225.

Freud, S. (1905). Three essays on the theory of sexuality. *Standard Edition* 7:135–243.

Scharff, D. E. (1992). *Refinding the Object and Reclaiming the Self.* Northvale, NJ: Jason Aronson.

Scharff, D. E., and Birtles, E. F., eds. (1994). *From Instinct to Self: Selected Papers of W. R. D. Fairbairn,* vol. I. Northvale, NJ: Jason Aronson.

Scharff, J. S. (1992). *Projective and Introjective Identification and the Use of the Therapist's Self.* Northvale, NJ: Jason Aronson.

Spillius, E. B. (1994). Developments in Kleinian thought: overview and personal view. *Psychoanalytic Inquiry* 14(3) 324–364.

Winnicott, D. W. (1949). Hate in the countertransference. *International Journal of Psycho-Analysis* 30:69–74. (Excerpted in this volume, Chapter 16.)

II

SIGMUND FREUD

The term *object relations* originated with Sigmund Freud, who thought that instincts had an existence of their own that could be separated out from their aim, on the one hand, and their object, on the other. In this way he described the sexual instinct, or *libido,* which he felt was at the heart of all human motivation. Later he spoke more frequently of the "life instinct," a broader concept than libido, which balanced the death instinct, or *thanatos*—the drive that propels the organism toward disintegration and death. He placed the role of aggression within the domain of thanatos, a theme that would later be elaborated by Melanie Klein and her followers.

To introduce the terms *object, instinct,* and *aim* we begin with brief selections from his early paper "Three Essays on the Theory of Sexuality," published in 1905, in which he explored the relationship between the sexual instinct and its aims and objects. This essay includes his first description of the form of libido in the phases of psychosexual development, which he originally thought included oral, anal, and genital phases. He later added another pregenital phase—that is, the last of the phases before the genital or oedipal organization took hold—which he termed the phallic phase.

Freud wrote that the connection of the sexual aim to the object is fortuitous, almost a matter of indifference, to be shaped by a combination of the vicissitudes of an instinct searching for an object of gratification, like a missile seeking heat rather than a specific target. This point of view and even Freud's language of "instinct" and "object" de-emphasize the importance of the specific personal quality of relational bonds in children and adults. This insistence that the relationship is secondary and derivative of the experience of satisfying an impersonal drive forms an important difference from the emphasis Fairbairn and Winnicott would later place on the need of an infant for its own, specific parent, and even from Klein, who said that object relations were important from the beginning of life.

2

Three Essays on the Theory of Sexuality (1905)

It has been brought to our notice that . . . we have been in the habit of regarding the connection between the sexual instinct and the sexual object as more intimate than it in fact is. Experience of the cases that are considered abnormal has shown us that in them the sexual instinct and the sexual object are merely soldered together—a fact which we have been in danger of overlooking in consequence of the uniformity of the normal picture, where the object appears to form part and parcel of the instinct. We are thus warned to loosen the bond that exists in our thoughts between instinct and object. It seems probable that the sexual instinct is in the first instance independent of its object; nor is its origin likely to be due to its object's attractions. . . .

I am inclined to believe that it may be explained by the fact that the impulses of sexual life are among those which, even normally, are the least controlled by the higher activities of the mind.

Under a great number of conditions and in surprisingly numerous individuals, the nature and importance of the sexual object recedes into the background. What is essential and constant in the sexual instinct is something else.[1] . . .

---

1. [Footnote added 1910:] The most striking distinction between the erotic life of antiquity and our own no doubt lies in the fact that the ancients laid the stress upon the instinct itself, whereas we emphasize its object. The ancients glorified the instinct and were prepared on its account to honour even an inferior object; while we despise the instinctual activity in itself, and find excuses for it only in the merits of the object.

THE PHASES OF DEVELOPMENT OF THE SEXUAL ORGANIZATION

The characteristics of infantile sexual life which we have hitherto emphasized are the facts that it is essentially auto-erotic (i.e., that it finds its object in the infant's own body) and that its individual component instincts are upon the whole disconnected and independent of one another in their search for pleasure. The final outcome of sexual development lies in what is known as the normal sexual life of the adult, in which the pursuit of pleasure comes under the sway of the reproductive function and in which the component instincts, under the primacy of a single erotogenic zone, form a firm organization directed toward a sexual aim attached to some extraneous sexual object.

Pregenital Organizations

The study, with the help of psycho-analysis, of the inhibitions and disturbances of this process of development enables us to recognize abortive beginnings and preliminary stages of a firm organization of the component instincts such as this—preliminary stages which themselves constitute a sexual regime of a sort. These phases of sexual organization are normally passed through smoothly, without giving more than a hint of their existence. It is only in pathological cases that they become active and recognizable to superficial observation.

We shall give the name pregenital to organizations of sexual life in which the genital zones have not yet taken over their predominant part. We have hitherto identified two such organizations, which almost seem as though they were harking back to early animal forms of life.

The first of these is the *oral* or, as it might be called, *cannibalistic pregenital* sexual organization. Here sexual activity has not yet been separated from the ingestion of food, nor are opposite currents within the activity differentiated. The object of both activities is the same; the sexual aim consists in the incorporation of the object—the prototype of a process which, in the form of identification, is later to play such an important psychological part. A relic of this constructed phase of organization, which is forced upon our notice by pathology, may be seen in thumb-sucking, in which the sexual activity, detached from the nutritive activity, has substituted for the extraneous object one situated in the subject's own body.[2]

A second pregenital phase is that of the sadistic-anal organization. Here the opposition between two currents, which runs through all sexual life, is already developed: they cannot yet, however, be described as "masculine" and "feminine," but only as "active" and "passive." The activity is put into operation by the instinct for mastery through the agency of the somatic musculature; the organ which, more than any other, represents the passive sexual aim is the erotogenic mucous membrane of the anus. Both of these currents have objects, which, however, are not identical. Alongside these, other component instincts operate in an auto-erotic manner. In this phase, therefore, sexual polarity and an extraneous object are already observable. But organization and subordination to the reproductive function are still absent. . . .

In order to complete our picture of infantile sexual life, we must also suppose that the choice of an object, such as we have shown to be characteristic of the pubertal phase of development, has already frequently or habitually been effected during the years of childhood; that is to say, the whole of the sexual currents have become directed toward a single person in relation to whom they seek to achieve their aims. This then is the closest approximation possible in childhood to the final form taken by sexual life after puberty. The only difference lies in the fact that in childhood the combination of the component instincts and their subordination under the primacy of the genitals have been effected only very incompletely or not at all. Thus the establishment of that primacy in the service of reproduction is the last phase through which the organization of sexuality passes.[3] . . .

---

2. [Footnote added 1920:] For remnants of this phase in adult neurotics, cf. Abraham (1916). [Added 1924:] In another, later work (1924) the same writer has divided both this oral phase, and also the later sadistic-anal one, into two subdivisions, which are characterized by differing attitudes toward the object.

3. [Footnote added 1924:] At a later date (1923), I myself modified this account by inserting a third phase in the development of childhood, subsequent to the two pregenital organizations. This phase, which already deserves to be described as genital, presents a sexual object and some degree of convergence of the sexual impulses upon that object; but it is differentiated from the final organization of sexual maturity in one essential respect. For it knows only one kind of genital: the male one. For that reason I have named it the "phallic" stage of organization (Freud 1923.) According to Abraham (1924), it has a biological prototype in the embryo's undifferentiated genital disposition, which is the same for both sexes.

REFERENCES

Abraham, K. (1916). The first pregenital stage of the libido. In *Selected Papers*. London: 1927.

——(1924). A short study of the development of the libido. In *Selected Papers*. London: 1927.

Freud, S. (1923). The infantile genital organization of the libido. *Standard Edition* 19:141–145.

3

Mourning and Melancholia (1917)

In 1917, Freud advanced his contribution to object relations when he studied the process of object loss. Following Ferenczi's (1909) description of introjection, he noted the particular way the lost object was taken into the self through identification. The original description of this process centered around the pathological losses of depression–or melancholia, as he originally called depression. Here he noticed that the ego itself was altered by taking a lost object into the ego and then identifying with it, a process he thought occurred on the lines of the oral model of incorporation. Much of Melanie Klein's work on object relations took this essay as its starting point, and Fairbairn's model followed suit in designing a model of internal objects built through incorporation and identification.

REFERENCE

Ferenczi, S. (1909). Introjektion und Ubertragung (Introjection and transference). In *First Contributions to Psycho-Analysis*, trans. E. Jones, pp. 35–93. New York: Brunner/Mazel, 1952.

If one listens patiently . . . to a melancholic's many and various self-accusations, one cannot in the end avoid the impression that often the most violent of them are hardly at all applicable to the patient himself, but that with insignificant modifications they do fit someone else, someone whom the patient loves or has loved or should love. Every time one examines the facts this conjecture is confirmed. So we find the key to the clinical picture: we perceive that the self-reproaches are reproaches against a loved object which have been shifted away from it on to the patient's own ego.

The woman who loudly pities her husband for being tied to such an incapable wife as herself is really accusing her *husband* of being incapable, in whatever sense she may mean this. There is no need to be greatly surprised that a few genuine self-reproaches are scattered among those that have been transposed back. These are allowed to obtrude themselves, since they help to mask the others and make recognition of the true state of affairs impossible. Moreover, they derive from the pros and cons of the conflict of love that has led to the loss of love. The behaviour of the patients, too, now becomes much more intelligible. Their complaints are really "plaints" in the old sense of the word. They are not ashamed and do not hide themselves, since everything derogatory that they say about themselves is at bottom said about someone else. Moreover, they are far from evincing toward those around them the attitude of humility and submissiveness that would alone befit such worthless people. On the contrary, they make the greatest nuisance of themselves, and always seem as though they felt slighted and had been treated with great injustice. All this is possible only because the reactions expressed in their behaviour still proceed from a mental constellation of revolt, which has then, by a certain process, passed over into the crushed state of melancholia.

There is no difficulty in reconstructing this process. An object-choice, an attachment of the libido to a particular person, had at one time existed; then, owing to a real slight or disappointment coming from this loved person, the object-relationship was shattered. The result was not the normal one of a withdrawal of the libido from this object and a displacement of it on to a new one, but something different, for whose coming-about various conditions seem to be necessary. The object-cathexis proved to have little power of resistance and was brought to an end. But the free libido was not displaced on to another object; it was withdrawn into the ego. There, however, it was not employed in any unspecified way, but served to establish an *identification* of the ego with the abandoned object. Thus the shadow of the object fell upon the ego, and the latter could henceforth be judged by a special agency, as though it were an object, the forsaken object. In this way an object-loss was transformed into an ego-loss and the conflict between the ego and the loved person into a cleavage between the critical activity of the ego and the ego as altered by identification. . . .

We have elsewhere shown that identification is a preliminary stage of object-choice, that it is the first way—and one that is expressed in an ambivalent fashion—in which the ego picks out an object. The ego wants to incorporate this object into itself, and, in accordance with the oral or cannibalistic phase of libidinal development in which it is, it wants to do so by devouring it. Abraham is undoubtedly right in attributing to this connection the refusal of nourishment met with in severe forms of melancholia.[1] . . .

REFERENCES

Freud, S. (1915). Instincts and their vicissitudes. *Standard Edition* 14:117–140.

Jones, E. (1955). *The Life and Work of Sigmund Freud, vol. II: 1901–1919: Years of Maturity*. New York: Basic Books.

1. [Abraham apparently first drew Freud's attention to this in a private letter written between February and April, 1915. See Jones's biography (1955, p. 368).]

4

The Ego and the Id (1923)

In *The Ego and the Id*, Freud explored his mature ideas concerning object relations. The superego, which he also called the "ego ideal," is formed by renunciation of the erotic, oedipal relationship with the parent of the opposite sex and strengthened identification with the parent of the same sex. Through the process of mourning, the lost aspect of the parent is taken into the ego. In the process, the identification with the same-sex parent as ego ideal becomes the core of the superego, which is split off from the ego in the process. Freud described this process as a developmental one that is essential to the achievement of the final childhood organization. We notice here that this developmental step is unlike the ones he previously described—the oral, anal, and phallic stages. These were described by giving primacy to progressive stages of libido, with the object being a matter of relative indifference. But in the oedipal renunciation of the parent of the opposite sex and the development of the superego in identification with the same-sex parent, the process of development is given a new kind of explanation, tied to the fate of relationships to the specific parents. In this way, the oedipal phase became Freud's first formulation of development in specifically object relations terms.

When Fairbairn carefully studied *The Ego and the Id* five years after its publication in order to teach it to his students, he noticed a number of inconsistencies in Freud's formulation of the repression of the superego by the ego and the method Freud proposed for the installation of the renounced object and the birth of the ego ideal. These reservations led Fairbairn eventually to the development of his own theory of object relations (Fairbairn 1928, 1929).

REFERENCES

Fairbairn, W. R. D. (1928). Introduction: Working towards the theory of object relations. In *From Instinct to Self*, vol. II, ed. E. F. Birtles and D. E. Scharff, pp. xvii–xxiii. Northvale, NJ: Jason Aronson.

—— (1929). The superego. In *From Instinct to Self*, vol. II, ed. E. F. Birtles and D. E. Scharff, pp. 80–114. Northvale, NJ: Jason Aronson.

THE EGO AND THE SUPEREGO (EGO IDEAL)

. . . We succeeded in explaining the painful disorder of melancholia by supposing that (in those suffering from it) an object which was lost has been set up again inside the ego—that is, that an object-cathexis has been replaced by an identification. At that time, however, we did not appreciate the full significance of this process and did not know how common and how typical it is. Since then we have come to understand that this kind of substitution has a great share in determining the form taken by the ego and that it makes an essential contribution toward building up what is called its "character."

At the very beginning, in the individual's primitive oral phase, object-cathexis and identification are no doubt indistinguishable from each other. We can only suppose that later on object-cathexes proceed from the id, which feels erotic trends as needs. The ego, which to begin with is still feeble, becomes aware of the object-cathexes, and either acquiesces in them or tries to fend them off by the process of repression.[1]

When it happens that a person has to give up a sexual object, there quite often ensues an alteration of his ego which can only be described as a setting up of the object inside the ego, as it occurs in melancholia; the exact nature of this substitution is as yet unknown to us. It may be that by this introjection, which is a kind of regression to the mechanism of the oral

1. An interesting parallel to the replacement of object-choice by identification is to be found in the belief of primitive peoples, and in the prohibitions based upon it, that the attributes of animals which are incorporated as nourishment persist as part of the character of those who eat them. As is well known, this belief is one of the roots of cannibalism and its effects have continued through the series of usages of the totem meal down to Holy Communion. [Cf. *Totem and Taboo* (1912–13), *Standard Edition* 13, 82, 142, 154–55, etc.] The consequences ascribed by this belief to oral mastery of the object do in fact follow in the case of the later sexual object-choice.

phase, the ego makes it easier for the object to be given up or renders that process possible. It may be that this identification is the sole condition under which the id can give up its objects. At any rate the process, especially in the early phases of development, is a very frequent one, and it makes it possible to suppose that the character of the ego is a precipitate of abandoned object-cathexes and that it contains the history of those object-choices. It must, of course, be admitted from the outset that there are varying degrees of capacity for resistance, which decide the extent to which a person's character fends off or accepts the influences of the history of his erotic object-choices. In women who have had many experiences in love there seems to be no difficulty in finding vestiges of their object-cathexes in the traits of their character. We must also take into consideration cases of simultaneous object-cathexis and identification—cases, that is, in which the alteration in character occurs before the object has been given up. In such cases the alteration in character has been able to survive the object-relation and in a certain sense to conserve it.

From another point of view it may be said that this transformation of an erotic object-choice into an alteration of the ego is also a method by which the ego can obtain control over the id and deepen its relations with it—at the cost, it is true, of acquiescing to a large extent in the id's experiences. When the ego assumes the features of the object, it is forcing itself, so to speak, upon the id as a love-object and is trying to make good the id's loss by saying, "Look, you can love me too—I am so like the object." . . .

Although it is a digression from our aim, we cannot avoid giving our attention for a moment longer to the ego's object-identifications. If they obtain the upper hand and become too numerous, unduly powerful and incompatible with one another, a pathological outcome will not be far off. It may come to a disruption of the ego in consequence of the different identifications becoming cut off from one another by resistances; perhaps the secret of the cases of what is described as "multiple personality" is that the different identifications seize hold of consciousness in turn. Even when things do not go so far as this, there remains the question of conflicts between the various identifications into which the ego comes apart, conflicts which cannot after all be described as entirely pathological.

But, whatever the character's later capacity for resisting the influences of abandoned object-cathexes may turn out to be, the effects of the first identifications made in earliest childhood will be general and lasting. This leads us back to the origin of the ego ideal; for behind it there lies hidden an individual's first and most important identification, his identification with the father in his own personal prehistory.[2] This is apparently not in the first instance the consequence or outcome of an object-cathexis; it is a direct and immediate identification and takes place earlier than any object-cathexis. But the object-choices belonging to the first sexual period and relating to the father and mother seem normally to find their outcome in an identification of this kind, and would thus reinforce the primary one.

The whole subject, however, is so complicated that it will be necessary to go into it in greater detail. The intricacy of the problem is due to two factors: the triangular character of the Oedipus situation and the constitutional bisexuality of each individual.

In its simplified form the case of a male child may be described as follows. At a very early age the little boy develops an object-cathexis for his mother, which originally related to the mother's breast and is the prototype of an object-choice on the anaclitic model; the boy deals with his father by identifying himself with him. For a time these two relationships proceed side by side, until the boy's sexual wishes in regard to his mother become more intense and his father is perceived as an obstacle to them; from this the Oedipus complex originates. His identification with his father then takes on a hostile colouring and changes into a wish to get rid of his father in order to take his place with his mother. Henceforward his relation to his father is ambivalent; it seems as if the ambivalence inherent in the identification from the beginning had become manifest. An ambivalent attitude to his father and an object-relation of a solely affectionate kind to his mother make up the content of the simple positive Oedipus complex in a boy.

Along with the demolition of the Oedipus complex, the boy's object-cathexis of his mother must be given up. Its place may be filled by one of two things: either an identification with his mother or an intensification of his identification with his father. We are accustomed to regard the latter outcome as the more normal; it permits the affectionate relation to the mother to be in a measure retained. In this way the dissolution of the Oedipus complex would consolidate the masculinity in a boy's character.

---

2. Perhaps it would be safer to say "with the parents," for before a child has arrived at definite knowledge of the difference between the sexes, the lack of a penis, it does not distinguish in value between its father and its mother. In order to simplify my presentation I shall discuss only identification with the father.

In a precisely analogous way,[3] the outcome of the Oedipus attitude in a little girl may be an intensification of her identification with her mother (or the setting up of such an identification for the first time)—a result which will fix the child's feminine character.

These identifications are not what we should have expected, since they do not introduce the abandoned object into the ego; but this alternative outcome may also occur, and is easier to observe in girls than in boys. Analysis very often shows that a little girl, after she has had to relinquish her father as a love-object, will bring her masculinity into prominence and identify herself with her father (that is, with the object which has been lost), instead of with her mother. This will clearly depend on whether the masculinity in her disposition—whatever that may consist in—is strong enough. . . .

So long as we had to concern ourselves with the study of what is repressed in mental life, there was no need for us to share in any agitated apprehensions as to the whereabouts of the higher side of man. But now that we have embarked upon the analysis of the ego we can give an answer to all those whose moral sense has been shocked and who have complained that there must surely be a higher nature in man: "Very true," we can say, "and here we have that higher nature, in this ego ideal or superego, the representative of our relation to our parents. When we were little children we knew these higher natures, we admired them and feared them; and later we took them into ourselves."

The ego ideal is therefore the heir of the Oedipus complex, and thus it is also the expression of the most powerful impulses and most important libidinal vicissitudes of the id. By setting up this ego ideal, the ego has mastered the Oedipus complex and at the same time placed itself in subjection to the id. Whereas the ego is essentially the representative of the external world, of reality, the superego stands in contrast to it as the representative of the internal world, of the id. Conflicts between the ego and the ideal will, as we are now prepared to find, ultimately reflect the contrast between what is real and what is psychical, between the external world and the internal world. . . .

It is easy to show that the ego ideal answers to everything that is expected of the higher nature of man. As a substitute for a longing for the

3. [The idea that the outcome of the Oedipus complex was "precisely analogous" in girls and boys was abandoned by Freud not long after this. See 'Some Psychical Consequences of the Anatomical Distinction between the Sexes' (1925), p. 248]

father, it contains the germ from which all religions have evolved. The self-judgement which declares that the ego falls short of its ideal produces the religious sense of humility to which the believer appeals in his longing. As a child grows up, the role of father is carried on by teachers and others in authority; their injunctions and prohibitions remain powerful in the ego ideal and continue, in the form of conscience, to exercise the moral censorship. The tension between the demands of conscience and the actual performances of the ego is experienced as a sense of guilt. Social feelings rest on identifications with other people, on the basis of having the same ego ideal.

III

W. R. D. FAIRBAIRN

5

"Schizoid Factors in the Personality" (1952)

The opening paper in Fairbairn's book *Psychoanalytic Studies of the Personality* contains some of his most evocative clinical writing on the nature of the schizoid patients who retreat from relationships with others to their own interior realms. That paper was written a few years before Fairbairn formulated his object relations theory, but it describes the clinical situation that is the starting point for his evolving theory. This paper presents Fairbairn's original description of schizoid phenomena and the fundamental role of splitting of the ego in development and in psychopathology.

REFERENCE

Fairbairn, W. R. D. (1952). *Psychoanalytic Studies of the Personality.* London: Routledge.

Mental processes of a schizoid nature have latterly come to occupy my attention to an increasing degree, and cases in which such processes are sufficiently marked to impart a recognizably schizoid complexion to the personality now seem to me to provide the most interesting and fruitful material in the whole field of psychopathology. . . .

Among the various characteristics common to the apparently conglomerate group of individuals who fall under the schizoid category as now envisaged three are of sufficient prominence to deserve special mention. These are (1) an attitude of omnipotence, (2) an attitude of isolation and detachment, and (3) a preoccupation with inner reality. It is important, however, to bear in mind that these characteristics are by no means necessarily overt. Thus the attitude of omnipotence may be conscious or unconscious in any degree. It may also be localized within certain spheres of operation. It may be overcompensated and concealed under a superficial attitude of inferiority or humility; and it may be consciously cherished as a precious secret. Similarly the attitude of isolation and detachment may be masked by a facade of sociability or by the adoption of specific roles; and it may be accompanied by considerable emotionality in certain contexts. So far as the preoccupation with inner reality is concerned, this is undoubtedly the most important of all schizoid characteristics; and it is nonetheless present whether inner reality be substituted for outer reality, identified with outer reality or superimposed upon outer reality. . . .

The fundamental schizoid phenomenon is the presence of splits in the ego, and it would take a bold man to claim that his ego was so perfectly integrated as to be incapable of revealing any evidence of splitting at the deepest levels, or that such evidence of splitting of the ego could in no circumstances declare itself at more superficial levels, even under conditions of extreme suffering or hardship or deprivation (e.g., under conditions of grave illness, or of Arctic exploration, or of exposure in an open boat in mid-Pacific, or of relentless persecution, or of prolonged subjection to the horrors of modern warfare). The all-important factor here is the mental depth which requires to be plumbed before evidence of splitting of the ego declares itself. In my opinion, at any rate, some measure of splitting of the ego is invariably present at the deepest mental level—or (to express the same thing in terms borrowed from Melanie Klein) *the basic position in the psyche is invariably a schizoid position.* This would not hold true, of course, in the case of a theoretically perfect person whose development had been optimum; but then there is really nobody who enjoys such a happy lot. Indeed it is difficult to imagine any person with an ego so unified and stable at its higher levels that in no circumstances whatever would any evidence of basic splitting come to the surface in recognizable form. There are probably few "normal" people who have never at any time in their lives experienced an unnatural state of calm and detachment in face of some serious crisis, or a transient sense of "looking on at oneself" in some embarrassing or paralysing situation; and probably most people have had some experience of that strange confusion of past and present, or of phantasy and reality, known as déjà vu. And such phenomena, I venture to suggest, are essentially schizoid phenomena. There is one universal phenomenon, however, which proves quite conclusively that everyone without exception is schizoid at the deeper levels—viz. the dream; for, as Freud's researches have shown, the dreamer himself is commonly represented in the dream by two or more separate figures. Here I may say that the view which I myself have now come to adopt is to the effect that all figures appearing in dreams represent either (1) some part of the dreamer's personality, or (2) an object with whom some part of his personality has a relationship, commonly on a basis of identification, in inner reality. Be that as it may, the fact that the dreamer is characteristically represented in the dream by more than one figure is capable of no other interpretation except that, at the level of the dreaming consciousness, the ego of the dreamer is split. The dream thus represents a universal schizoid phenomenon. The universal phenomenon of the "superego" as described by Freud must also be interpreted as implying the presence of a split in the ego; for, in so far as the superego is regarded as an ego-structure capable of distinction from the ego as such, its very existence ipso facto provides evidence that a schizoid position has been established. . . .

The concluding section of this paper illustrates Fairbairn's ability to write about theoretical matters in a way that brings them close to everyday experience. It has been a hallmark of object relations theory that it is "experience-near"—that the theory can be readily applied to patients without much translation of terms or ideas. (D.E.S.)

EMPTYING OF THE OBJECT AS AN IMPLICATION OF THE LIBIDINAL ATTITUDE

Emptying of the object is an implication of the incorporative quality of the early oral attitude, and, when attention was drawn to this feature earlier, some account was given of its psychological consequences for the child. Thus, it was pointed out how, in circumstances of deprivation, the anxiety which arises in the child's mind over his own emptiness gives rise to anxiety over emptiness affecting his mother's breast. It was also pointed out how he comes to interpret any apparent or actual emptiness of his mother's breast as due to his own incorporative strivings, and how he thus comes to entertain anxiety over being responsible for the disappearance and destruction, not simply of his mother's breast, but of his mother herself—anxiety considerably increased by the effect of deprivation in imparting an aggressive quality to his libidinal need. Such anxiety finds a classic expression in the fairy tale of "Little Red Riding Hood." In the story, it will be remembered, the little girl finds to her horror that the grandmother whom she loves has disappeared, and that she is left alone with her own incorporative need in the form of a devouring wolf. The tragedy of Little Red Riding Hood is the tragedy of the child in the early oral phase. Of course, the fairy tale has a happy ending, as fairy tales do. And, of course, the infant does discover that the mother, whom he fears he has eaten up, does eventually reappear again. Nevertheless, in their infancy children, although they do not lack intelligence, yet lack the organized experience from which they might otherwise derive reassurance against their anxiety. In due course they acquire sufficient conscious knowledge to realize that in actual fact their mothers do not disappear in consequence of the apparent destructiveness of their incorporative needs; and the whole experience of the traumatic situation arising out of deprivation during the early oral phase becomes subjected to repression. At the same time the anxiety attached to this situation persists in the unconscious, ready to be reactivated by any subsequent experience of an analogous kind. In the presence of a marked fixation in the early oral phase, the traumatic situation is particularly liable to be reactivated if the child later comes to feel that he is not really loved and valued as a person by his mother, and that she does not really appreciate and accept his love as good.

It is important to bear in mind the distinction between the situation which arises in the early oral phase and that which arises during the late oral phase, when the biting tendency emerges and takes its place side by side with the sucking tendency. In the late oral phase there occurs a differentiation between oral love, associated with sucking, and oral hate, associated with biting; and the development of ambivalence is a consequence of this. The early oral phase is pre-ambivalent; and this fact is specially important in the light of the further fact that the oral behaviour of the child during this pre-ambivalent phase represents the individual's first way of expressing love. The child's oral relationship with his mother in the situation of suckling represents his first experience of a love relationship, and is, therefore, the foundation upon which all his future relationships with love objects are based. It also represents his first experience of a social relationship; and it therefore forms the basis of his subsequent attitude to society. Bearing these considerations in mind, let us return to the situation which arises when the child who is fixated in the early oral phase comes to feel that he is not really loved and valued as a person by his mother, and that she does not really appreciate and accept his love as good. What happens in these circumstances is that the original traumatic situation of the early oral phase becomes emotionally reactivated and reinstated; and the child then feels that the reason for his mother's apparent lack of love towards him is that he has destroyed her affection and made it disappear. At the same time he feels that the reason for her apparent refusal to accept his love is that his own love is destructive and bad. This is, of course, an infinitely more intolerable situation than the comparable situation which arises in the case of a child fixated in the late oral phase. In the latter case the child, being essentially ambivalent, interprets the situation in the sense that it is his hate, and not his love, that has destroyed his mother's affection. It is then in his hate that his badness seems to him to reside; and his love is thus able to remain good in his eyes. This is the position which would appear to underlie the manic-depressive psychosis, and to constitute the depressive position. By contrast the position underlying schizoid developments would appear to be one arising in the pre-ambivalent early oral phase—the position in which the individual feels that his love is bad because it appears destructive towards his libidinal objects; and this may be appropriately described as the *schizoid position.* It represents an essentially tragic situation; and it provides the theme of many of the great tragedies of literature, as well as providing a favourite theme for poetry (as in the case of the "Lucy" poems of Wordsworth). It is small wonder then that individuals with any considerable schizoid tendency experience such difficulty in showing love, for they always entertain the deep anxiety expressed by Oscar Wilde in *The Ballad of Reading Gaol* when he wrote, "Each man kills the thing he loves." It is small wonder too that they experience difficulty in emotional giving; for they can never entirely escape the fear that their gifts are deadly, like the gifts of a Borgia. Hence the remark of a patient of mine, who, after bringing me a present of some fruit, opened the next day's session with the question, "Have you been poisoned?"

We are now in a position to appreciate that the individual with a schizoid tendency has another motive for keeping his love inside himself besides that arising from the feeling that it is too precious to part with. He also keeps his love shut in because he feels that it is too dangerous to release upon his objects. Thus he not only keeps his love in a safe, but also keeps it in a cage. The matter does not end there, however. Since he feels that his own love is bad, he is liable to interpret the love of others in similar terms. Such an interpretation does not necessarily imply projection on his part; but, of course, he is always liable to have recourse to this defensive technique. It is illustrated, for example, in the fairy tale of "Little Red Riding Hood," to which reference has already been made; for although, as we have seen, the wolf does represent her own incorporative oral love, the story also tells us that the wolf takes her grandmother's place in the bed—which means, of course, that she attributes her own incorporative attitude to her libidinal object, who then seems to turn into a devouring wolf. So it comes about that the individual with schizoid characteristics is liable to feel driven to erect defences, not only against his love for others, but also against their love for him; and it was on this account that a rather schizoid young woman, who was a patient of mine, used sometimes to say to me, "Whatever you do, you must never like me."

When, accordingly, an individual with a schizoid tendency makes a renunciation of social contacts, it is above all because he feels that he must neither love nor be loved. He does not always rest content with a mere passive aloofness, however. On the contrary, he often takes active measures to drive his libidinal objects away from him. For this purpose he has an instrument ready to hand inside himself in the form of his own differentiated aggression. He mobilizes the resources of his hate, and directs his aggression against others—and more particularly against his libidinal objects. Thus he may quarrel with people, be objectionable, be rude. In so doing, he not only substitutes hate for love in his relationships with his objects, but also induces them to hate, instead of loving, him; and he does all this in order to keep his libidinal objects at a distance. Like the Troubadours (and perhaps also the dictators), he can only permit himself to love and be loved from afar off. This is the second great tragedy to which individuals with a schizoid tendency are liable. The first is, as we have seen, that he feels his love to be destructive of those he loves. The second arises when he becomes subject to a compulsion to hate and be hated, while all the time he longs deep down to love and to be loved.

There are two further motives, however, by which an individual with a schizoid tendency may be actuated in substituting hating for loving—

curiously enough one an immoral, and the other a moral, motive; and incidentally these would appear to be specially powerful motives in the case of the revolutionary and the Quisling. The immoral motive is determined by the consideration that, since the joy of loving seems hopelessly barred to him, he may as well deliver himself over to the joy of hating and obtain what satisfaction he can out of that. He thus makes a pact with the Devil and says, "Evil be thou my good." The moral motive is determined by the consideration that, if loving involves destroying, it is better to destroy by hate, which is overtly destructive and bad, than to destroy by love, which is by rights creative and good. When these two motives come into play, therefore, we are confronted with an amazing reversal of moral values. It becomes a case, not only of "Evil be thou my good," but also of "Good be thou my evil." This is a reversal of values, it must be added, which is rarely consciously accepted; but it is nonetheless one which often plays an extremely important part in the unconscious—and that this should be so is the third great tragedy to which individuals with a schizoid tendency are liable.

6

"A Revised Psychopathology of the Psychoses and Psychoneuroses" (1941)

This is Fairbairn's next major paper, in which he continued his description of schizoid mechanisms and the schizoid condition, and then formulated his ideas concerning the process of maturation from infantile dependency to "mature dependency." Between the *primary identification with the object*, which characterizes infantile dependency, and the achievement of mature dependency lies a series of intermediate *transitional methods* of relating to internal objects. Fairbairn's formulation provides a new understanding of character and psychopathology. A few years later, Winnicott made use of Fairbairn's idea of a transitional process in creating his contribution of transitional objects and transitional phenomena. The outline contained here for understanding maturation and an object relations view of pathology is one of Fairbairn's major clinical achievements.

It is now submitted that the norm for the development of object relationships conforms to the following scheme:

I. Stage of Infantile Dependence, characterized predominantly by an Attitude of Taking.
   (1) Early Oral—Incorporating—Sucking or Rejecting (Pre-Ambivalent).
   (2) Late Oral—Incorporating—Sucking or Biting (Ambivalent).
II. Stage of Transition between Infantile Dependence and Mature Dependence, or Stage of Quasi-Independence—Dichotomy and Exteriorization of the Incorporated Object.

III. Stage of Mature Dependence, characterized predominantly by an Attitude of Giving—Accepted and Rejected Objects Exteriorized.

The distinctive feature of this scheme is that it is based upon the nature of the object relationship, and that the libidinal attitude is relegated to a secondary place. What has convinced me of the paramount importance of the object relationship is the analysis of patients displaying schizoid characteristics; for it is in such individuals that difficulties over relationships with objects present themselves most clearly. During the course of analysis, such an individual provides the most striking evidence of a conflict between an extreme reluctance to abandon infantile dependence and a desperate longing to renounce it; and it is at once fascinating and pathetic to watch the patient, like a timid mouse, alternately creeping out of the shelter of his hole to peep at the world of outer objects and then beating a hasty retreat. It is also illuminating to observe how, in his indefatigable attempts to emerge from a state of infantile dependence, he resorts by turns to any or all four of the transitional techniques which have been described—the paranoid, obsessional, hysterical, and phobic. What emerges as clearly as anything else from the analysis of such a case is that the greatest need of a child is to obtain conclusive assurance (a) that he is genuinely loved as a person by his parents, and (b) that his parents genuinely accept his love. It is only insofar as such assurance is forthcoming in a form sufficiently convincing to enable him to depend safely upon his real objects that he is able gradually to renounce infantile dependence without misgiving. In the absence of such assurance his relationship to his objects is fraught with too much *anxiety over separation* to enable him to renounce the attitude of infantile dependence; for such a renunciation would be equivalent in his eyes to forfeiting all hope of ever obtaining the satisfaction of his unsatisfied emotional needs. Frustration of his desire to be loved as a person and to have his love accepted is the greatest trauma that a child can experience; and it is this trauma above all that creates fixations in the various forms of infantile sexuality to which a child is driven to resort in an attempt to compensate by substitutive satisfactions for the failure of his emotional relationships with his outer objects. Fundamentally these substitutive satisfactions (e.g., masturbation and anal erotism) all represent *relationships with internalized objects, to which the individual is compelled to turn in default of a satisfactory relationship with objects in the outer world.* Where relationships with outer objects are unsatisfactory, we also encounter such phenomena as exhibitionism, homosexuality, sadism, and masochism; and these phenomena should be regarded as in no small measure attempts to salvage natural emotional relationships which have broken down. Valuable as it is to understand the nature of these "relationships by default," such understanding is much less important than a knowledge of the factors which compromise spontaneous relationships. By far the most important of these factors is a situation in childhood which leads the individual to feel that his objects neither love him as a person nor accept his love. It is when such a situation arises that the inherent libidinal drive towards the object leads to the establishment of aberrant relationships and to the various libidinal attitudes which accompany them.

The scheme of development outlined in the preceding list has been based on the quality of dependence upon the object because there is reason to think that this is the most important factor in early relationships. It is desirable, however, to be clear as to the nature of the object appropriate to each stage of development. And here it is important to distinguish between the natural (biological) object and the incorporated object which is so largely substituted for it in psychopathological cases. Objects may, of course, be either part-objects or whole objects; and, when the biological history of early childhood is considered, it becomes plain that there is only one natural part-object, viz. the breast of the mother, and that the most significant whole object is the mother—with the father as rather a poor second. As has already been pointed out, feces is not a natural object. It is a symbolic object; and the same may be said of the genital organs insofar as these are treated as phallic objects, viz. part-objects. Thus, whilst the most important immediate factor in male homosexuality is doubtless a search for the father's penis, this search involves the substitution of a part-object for a whole object and is a regressive phenomenon representing a revival of the original (oral) relationship with the original part-object (the breast). The homosexual's search for his father's penis thus resolves itself, so to speak, into a search for his father's breast. The persistence of the breast as a part-object is well marked in the case of hysterics, for whom the genital organs always retain an oral significance. This is well illustrated in the case of a female hysterical patient, who, in describing her pelvic "pain," remarked: "It feels as if something wanted feeding inside." The frequency with which, as wartime experience has shown, hysterical soldiers complain of gastric symptoms is similarly significant.

In the light of what has just been said, the natural objects appropriate to the various stages of development may be indicated as follows:

I. Infantile Dependence.
   (1) Early Oral–Breast of the Mother–Part-Object.
   (2) Late Oral–Mother with the Breast–Whole Object treated characteristically as a Part-Object.

II. Quasi-Independence (Transitional).
   Whole Object treated characteristically as Contents.

III. Mature Dependence.
   Whole Object with Genital Organs.[1]

THE STAGE OF TRANSITION BETWEEN INFANTILE AND ADULT DEPENDENCE, ITS TECHNIQUES, AND ITS PSYCHOPATHOLOGY

It will be noticed that in the preceding lists the transition stage has been described as a stage of "Quasi-Independence," and the reason for the adoption of this description is of sufficient importance to demand special attention. It emerges clearly from the study of individuals with schizoid tendencies that the most characteristic feature of the state of infantile dependence is *primary identification with the object.* Indeed, it would not be going too far to say that, psychologically speaking, identification with the object and infantile dependence are but two aspects of the same phenomenon. On the other hand, mature dependence involves a relationship between two independent individuals, who are completely *differentiated* from one another as mutual objects.[2] This distinction between the

1. This list is intended to represent the norm of libidinal development, so far as this can be assessed; but it is important to bear in mind the distinction between such a norm and the actual process of development revealed by the analysis of a psychopathological case. Thus it must be explicitly recognized that the natural object during the early oral phase remains the *actual* breast of the mother quite irrespective of any process whereby the breast is *mentally* incorporated and established as an internal object, as also that during this phase the individual is in actual fact both physically and emotionally dependent upon the breast as an external object quite apart from any emotional dependence upon an internalized breast. It must also be recognized that the breast may persist as an internal object during later libidinal phases in which the natural object is other than the breast.

2. An important aspect of the difference between infantile dependence and mature dependence is that, whereas the former is a state which has not yet been abandoned, the latter is a state which has been already achieved.

two kinds of dependence is identical with Freud's distinction between the narcissistic and the anaclitic choice of objects. The relationship involved in mature dependence is, of course, only theoretically possible. Nevertheless, it remains true that *the more mature a relationship is, the less it is characterized by primary identification;* for what such identification essentially represents is failure to differentiate the object. It is when identification persists at the expense of differentiation that a markedly compulsive element enters into the individual's attitude towards his objects. This is well seen in the infatuations of schizoid individuals. It may also be observed in the almost uncontrollable impulse so commonly experienced by schizoid and depressive soldiers in wartime to return to their wives or their homes, when separated from them owing to military necessities. *The abandonment of infantile dependence involves an abandonment of relationships based upon primary identification in favour of relationships with differentiated objects.* In dreams the process of differentiation is frequently reflected in the theme of trying to cross a gulf or chasm, albeit the crossing which is attempted may also occur in a regressive direction. The process itself is commonly attended by considerable anxiety; and this anxiety finds characteristic expression in dreams of falling, as also in such symptoms as acrophobia and agoraphobia. On the other hand, anxiety over failure of the process is reflected in nightmares about being imprisoned or confined underground or immersed in the sea, as well as in the symptom of claustrophobia.

The process of differentiation of the object derives particular significance from the fact that infantile dependence is characterized not only by identification, but also by an oral attitude of incorporation. In virtue of this fact the object with which the individual is identified becomes equivalent to an incorporated object, or, to put the matter in a more arresting fashion, the object in which the individual is incorporated is incorporated in the individual. This strange psychological anomaly may well prove the key to many metaphysical puzzles. Be that as it may, however, it is common to find in dreams a remarkable equivalence between being inside an object and having the object inside. I had a patient, for example, who had a dream about being in a tower, and his associations left no room for doubt that this theme represented for him not only an identification with his mother, but also the incorporation of his mother's breast—and, incidentally, his father's penis.

Such then being the situation, the task of differentiating the object tends to resolve itself into a problem of expelling an incorporated object, i.e., to become a problem of expelling contents. Herein lies much of the rationale of Abraham's "anal phases," and it is in this direction that we must look for much of the significance of the anal techniques which play such an important part during the transition stage. It is important here as elsewhere to ensure that the cart is not placed before the horse, and to recognize that it is not a case of the individual being preoccupied with the disposal of contents at this stage because he is anal, but of his being anal because he is preoccupied at this stage with the disposal of contents.

The great conflict of the transition stage may now be formulated as a conflict between a progressive urge to surrender the infantile attitude of identification with the object and a regressive urge to maintain that attitude. During this period, accordingly, the behaviour of the individual is characterized both by desperate endeavours on his part to separate himself from the object and desperate endeavours to achieve reunion with the object–desperate attempts "to escape from prison" and desperate attempts "to return home." Although one of these attitudes may come to preponderate, there is in the first instance a constant oscillation between them owing to the anxiety attending each. The anxiety attending separation manifests itself as a fear of isolation, and the anxiety attending identification manifests itself as a fear of being shut in, imprisoned, or engulfed ("cribbed, cabined, and confined"). These anxieties, it will be noticed, are essentially phobic anxieties. It may accordingly be inferred that it is to the conflict between the progressive urge towards separation from the object and the regressive lure of identification with the object that we must look for the explanation of the *phobic state.*

Owing to the intimate connection existing between primary identification and oral incorporation, and consequently between separation and excretory expulsion, the conflict of the transition period also presents itself as a conflict between an urge to expel and an urge to retain contents. Just as between separation and reunion, so here there tends to be a constant oscillation between expulsion and retention, although either of these attitudes may become dominant. Both attitudes are attended by anxiety–the attitude of expulsion being attended by a fear of being emptied or drained, and the attitude of retention by a fear of bursting (often accompanied or replaced by a fear of some internal disease like cancer). Such anxieties are essentially obsessional anxieties; and it is the conflict between an urge to expel the object as contents and an urge to retain the object as contents that underlies the *obsessional state.*

The phobic and obsessional techniques are thus seen to represent two differing methods of dealing with the same basic conflict; and these two differing methods correspond to two differing attitudes towards the object. From the phobic point of view the conflict presents itself as one between flight from and return to the object. From the obsessional point of view, on the other hand, the conflict presents itself as one between expulsion and retention of the object. It thus becomes obvious that the phobic technique corresponds in the main to a passive attitude, whereas the obsessional technique corresponds in the main to an active attitude. The obsessional technique also expresses a much higher degree of overt aggression towards the object, for whether the object be expelled or retained, it is being subjected to forcible control. For the phobic individual, on the other hand, the choice lies between escaping from the power of the object and submitting to it. In other words, whilst the obsessional technique is predominantly sadistic in nature, the phobic technique is predominantly masochistic.

In the *hysterical state* we can recognize the operation of another technique for attempting to deal with the basic conflict of the transition period. In this case the conflict appears to be formulated as simply one between acceptance and rejection of the object. Acceptance of the object is clearly manifested in the intense love relationships which are so typical of the hysteric; but the very exaggeration of these emotional relationships in itself raises a suspicion that a rejection is being overcompensated. This suspicion is confirmed by the propensity of the hysteric to dissociative phenomena. That these dissociative phenomena represent a rejection of the genitals need not be stressed, but, as was pointed out earlier, analysis can always unmask an identification of the rejected genitals with the breast as the original libidinal object during the period of infantile dependence. This being so, it is noteworthy that what is characteristically dissociated by the hysteric is an organ or function in himself. This can only have one meaning—that the rejected object is an internalized object with which there is a considerable measure of identification. On the other hand, the hysteric's overvaluation of his real objects leaves little room for doubt that in his case the accepted object is an externalized object. The *hysterical state* is thus seen to be characterized by acceptance of the externalized object and rejection of the internalized object—or, alternatively, by externalization of the accepted object and internalization of the rejected object.

If the paranoid and the hysterical states are now compared, we are confronted with a significant contrast. Whereas the hysteric overvalues objects in the outer world, the paranoid individual regards them as persecutors, and whereas the hysterical dissociation is a form of self-depreciation, the attitude of the paranoid individual is one of extravagant grandiosity. The *paranoid state* must, accordingly, be regarded as representing rejection of the externalized object and acceptance of the internalized object—or, alternatively, externalization of the rejected object and internalization of the accepted object.

Having interpreted both the hysterical and paranoid techniques in terms of the acceptance and rejection of objects, we can now obtain interesting results by applying a similar interpretation to the phobic and obsessional techniques. The conflict underlying the phobic state may be concisely formulated as one between flight to the object and flight from the object. In the former case, of course, the object is accepted, whereas in the latter case the object is rejected. In both cases, however, the object is treated as external. In the obsessional state, on the other hand, the conflict presents itself as one between the expulsion and the retention of contents. In this case, accordingly, both the accepted and the rejected objects are treated as internal. If in the case of the phobic state both the accepted and the rejected objects are treated as external and in the obsessional state both are treated as internal, the situation as regards the hysterical and paranoid states is that one of these objects is treated as an externalized object and the other as an internalized object. In the hysterical state, it is the accepted object that is externalized, whereas in the paranoid state the object which is externalized is the rejected object. The nature of the object relationships characteristic of the four techniques may be summarized in the following table:

Technique	*Accepted object*	*Rejected object*
Obsessional	Internalized	Internalized
Paranoid	Internalized	Externalized
Hysterical	Externalized	Internalized
Phobic	Externalized	Externalized

The chief features of the stage of transition between infantile and mature dependence may now be briefly summarized. The transition period is characterized by a process of development whereby object relationships based upon identification gradually give place to relationships with a differentiated object. Satisfactory development during this period, therefore, depends upon the success which attends the process of differentiation of the object; and this in turn depends upon the issue of a conflict over separation from the object—a situation which is both desired and feared. The conflict in question may call into operation any or all of four characteristic techniques—the obsessional, the paranoid, the hysterical, and the phobic; and, if object relationships are unsatisfactory, these techniques are liable to form the basis of characteristic psychopathological developments in later life. The various techniques cannot be classified in any order corresponding to presumptive levels of libidinal development. On the contrary, they must be regarded as alternative techniques, all belonging to the same stage in the development of object relationships. Which of the techniques is employed, or rather to what extent each is employed, would appear to depend in large measure upon the nature of the object relationships established during the preceding stage of infantile dependence. In particular it would seem to depend upon the degree to which objects have been incorporated, and upon the form assumed by relationships which have been established between the developing ego and its internalized objects. . . .

The phenomenon of narcissism, which is one of the most prominent characteristics of infantile dependence, is an attitude arising out of identification with the object. Indeed *primary narcissism* may be simply defined as just such a state of identification with the object, *secondary narcissism* being a state of identification with an object which is internalized. Whilst narcissism is a feature common to both the early and the late oral phases, the latter phase differs from the former in virtue of a change in the nature of the object. In the early oral phase the natural object is the breast of the mother, but in the late oral phase the natural object becomes the mother with the breast. The transition from one phase to the other is thus marked by the substitution of a whole object (or person) for a part-object, but it is also characterized by the emergence of the biting tendency. Thus, whereas in the early oral phase the libidinal attitude of sucking monopolizes the field, in the late oral phase it is in competition with an accompanying attitude of biting. Now biting must be regarded as being essentially destructive in aim, and indeed as constituting the very prototype of all differentiated aggression. Consequently the late oral phase is characterized by a high degree of emotional ambivalence. The early oral phase has been well described by Abraham as "pre-ambivalent," but this does not preclude simple rejection or refusal of the object without any of that aggressive biting which characterizes the late oral phase. Such rejection does not imply ambivalence, and I consider that the early oral urge to incorporate is essentially a libidinal urge, to which differentiated and direct aggression makes no contribution. The recognition of this fact is of the greatest importance for an understanding of the essential problem underlying schizoid states. It is true that the incorporative urge is destructive in effect, in the sense that what is eaten disappears. Nevertheless the urge is not destructive in aim. When a child says that he "loves" cake, it is certainly implied that the cake will vanish, and, ipso facto, be destroyed. At the same time the destruction of the cake is not the aim of the child's "love." On the contrary, the disappearance of the cake is, from the child's point of view, a most regrettable consequence of his "love" for it. What he really desires is both to eat his cake and have it. If the cake proves to be "bad," however, he either spits it out or is sick. In other words, he rejects it; but he does not bite it for being bad. This type of behaviour is specially characteristic of the early oral phase. What is characteristic is that, insofar as the object presents itself as good, its contents are incorporated, and, insofar as it presents itself as bad, it is rejected; but even when it appears bad, no attempt is made to destroy it. At the same time, under conditions of deprivation anxiety arises lest the object itself should have been incorporated together with its contents and so destroyed, albeit not by intention. In the late oral phase the situation is different, for in this phase the object may be bitten insofar as it presents itself as bad. This means that differentiated aggression, as well as libido, may be directed towards the object. Hence the appearance of the ambivalence which characterizes the late oral phase.

In accordance with what precedes, it becomes evident that the emotional conflict which arises in relation to object relationships during the early oral phase takes the form of the alternative, "to suck or not to suck," i.e., "to love or not to love." This is the conflict underlying the schizoid state. On the other hand, the conflict which characterizes the late oral phase resolves itself into the alternative, "to suck or to bite," i.e., "to love or to hate." This is the conflict underlying the depressive state. It will be seen, accordingly, that the great problem of the schizoid individual is how to love without destroying by love, whereas the great problem of the depressive individual is how to love without destroying by hate. These are two very different problems. . . .

If loss of the real object were the only trauma of the schizoid state, the position of the schizoid individual would not be so precarious. It is necessary, however, to bear in mind the vicissitudes of the ego, which accompany loss of the object. Reference has already been made to the narcissism which results from an excessive libidinization of internalized objects, and such narcissism is specially characteristic of the schizoid individual. Accompanying it we invariably find an attitude of superiority which may manifest itself in consciousness to a varying degree as an actual sense of superiority. It should be noticed, however, that this attitude of superiority is based upon an orientation towards internalized objects, and that in relation to objects in the world of outer reality the basic attitude of the schizoid individual is essentially one of inferiority. It is true that the externally oriented inferiority may be masked by a façade of superiority based upon an identification of external with internalized objects. Nevertheless, it is invariably present, and it is evidence of a weakness in the ego. What chiefly compromises the integrity of the ego in the case of the schizoid individual is the apparently insoluble dilemma which attends the direction of libido towards objects. Failure to direct libido towards the object is, of course, equivalent to loss of the object, but since, from the point of view of the schizoid individual, libido itself seems destructive, the object is equally lost when libido *is* directed towards it. It can thus readily be understood that, if the dilemma becomes sufficiently pronounced, the result is a complete impasse, which reduces the ego to a state of utter impotence. The ego becomes quite incapable of expressing itself, and, insofar as this is so, its very existence becomes compromised. This is well exemplified by the following remarks of a patient of mine during an analytical session: "I can't say anything. I have nothing to say. I'm empty. There's nothing of me. . . . I feel quite useless; I haven't done anything. . . . I've gone quite cold and hard; I don't feel anything. . . . I can't express myself; I feel futile." Such descriptions well illustrate not only the state of impotence to which the ego may be reduced, but also the extent to which the very existence of the ego may be compromised by the schizoid dilemma. The last quoted remark of this patient is perhaps particularly significant as drawing attention to the characteristic affect of the schizoid state, for *the characteristic affect of the schizoid state is undoubtedly a sense of futility*. . . .

Loss of the ego is the ultimate psychopathological disaster which the schizoid individual is constantly struggling, with more or with less success, to avert by exploiting all available techniques (including the transitional techniques) for the control of his libido. In essence, therefore, the schizoid state is not a defence, although evidence of the presence of defences may be detected in it. It represents the major disaster which may befall the individual who has failed to outgrow the early oral phase of dependence.

If the great problem which confronts the individual in the early oral phase is how to love the object without destroying it by love, the great problem which confronts the individual in the late oral phase is how to love the object without destroying it by hate. Accordingly, since the depressive reaction has its roots in the late oral phase, it is the disposal of his hate, rather than the disposal of his love, that constitutes the great difficulty of the depressive individual. Formidable as this difficulty is, the depressive is at any rate spared the devastating experience of feeling that his love is bad. Since his love at any rate seems good, he remains inherently capable of a libidinal relationship with outer objects in a sense in which the schizoid is not. His difficulty in maintaining such a relationship arises out of his ambivalence. This ambivalence in turn arises out of the fact that, during the late oral phase, he was more successful than the schizoid in substituting direct aggression (biting) for simple rejection of the object. Whilst his aggression has been differentiated, however, he has failed in some degree to achieve that further step in development which is represented by dichotomy of the object. This further step, had it been adequately achieved, would have enabled him to dispose of his hate by directing it, predominantly at least, towards the rejected object, and he would have been left free to direct towards his accepted object love which was relatively unaccompanied by hate. Insofar as he has failed to take such a step, the depressive remains in that state which characterized his attitude towards his object during the late oral phase, viz. a state of ambivalence towards the incorporated object. The presence of such an inner situation is less disabling so far as outer adjustments are concerned than is the corresponding inner situation in the case of the schizoid, for in the case of the depressive there is no formidable barrier obstructing the outward flow of libido. Consequently the depressive individual readily establishes libidinal contacts with others, and if his libidinal contacts are satisfactory to him, his progress through life may appear fairly smooth. Nevertheless the inner situation is always present, and it is readily reactivated if his libidinal relationships become disturbed. Any such disturbance immediately calls into operation the hating element in his ambivalent attitude, and when his hate becomes directed towards the internalized object, a depressive reaction supervenes. Any frustration in object relationships is, of course, functionally equivalent to loss of the object, whether partial or complete, and since severe depression is so common a sequel to actual loss of the object (whether by the death of a loved person or otherwise), loss of the object must be regarded as the essential trauma which provokes the depressive state. . . . We find ourselves confronted with two basic psychopathological conditions, each arising out of a failure on the part of the individual to establish a satisfactory object relationship during the period of infantile dependence. The first of these conditions, viz. the schizoid state, is associated with an unsatisfactory object relationship during the early oral phase; and the second of these conditions, viz. the depressive state, is associated with an unsatisfactory object relationship during the late oral phase. It emerges quite clearly, however, from the analysis of both schizoid and depressive individuals that unsatisfactory object relationships during the early and late oral phases are most likely to give rise to their characteristic psychopathological effects when object relationships continue to be unsatisfactory during the succeeding years of early childhood. The schizoid and depressive states must, accordingly, be regarded as largely dependent upon a regressive reactivation, during subsequent childhood, of situations arising respectively during the early and late oral phases. The traumatic situation in either case is one in which the child feels that he is not really loved as a person, and that his own love is not accepted. If the phase in which infantile object relationships have been preeminently unsatisfactory is the early oral phase, this trauma provokes in the child a reaction conforming to the idea that he is not loved because his own love is bad and destructive, and this reaction provides the basis for a subsequent schizoid tendency. If, on the other hand, the phase in which infantile object relationships have been preeminently unsatisfactory is the late oral phase, the reaction provoked in the child conforms to the idea that he is not loved because of the badness and destructiveness of his hate, and this reaction provides the basis for a subsequent depressive tendency. Whether in any given case a schizoid or depressive tendency will eventually give rise to an actual schizoid or depressive state depends in part, of course, upon the circumstances which the individual is called upon to face in later life, but the most important determining factor is the degree to which objects have been incorporated during the oral phases. The various defensive techniques which characterize the transition period (i.e., the obsessional, paranoid, hysterical, and phobic techniques) all represent attempts to deal with difficulties and conflicts attending object relationships in consequence of the persistence of incorporated objects. These defensive techniques may now also be seen to resolve themselves into differing methods of controlling an underlying schizoid or depressive tendency, and thus averting the onset of a schizoid or depressive state, as the case may be. Where a schizoid tendency is present, the defensive techniques represent methods designed to avert the ultimate psychopathological disaster which follows from loss of the ego, and where a depressive tendency is present, they represent methods designed to avert the ultimate psychopathological disaster which follows from loss of the object. . . .

7

"Endopsychic Structure Considered in Terms of Object Relationships" (1944)

This paper is the culmination of Fairbairn's theory. The highlights of its rigorous model of the mind, psychopathology, and dreams are reprinted here. In the first excerpt, Fairbairn uses a dream from a hysterical patient to derive and illustrate the basic endopsychic situation. In the second excerpt, he makes the case that internal objects are themselves part of the ego and therefore capable of generating and organizing activity.

A MULTIPLICITY OF EGOS

Attention has already been drawn to the fact that, whereas the repressed was eventually described by Freud as consisting essentially of impulses, he found it necessary to fall back upon structural conceptions (the ego and the superego) when he came to seek an explanation of the agency of repression. Reduced to its simplest terms, Freud's conception of repression is to the following effect: (a) that the agency of repression is the ego, (b) that repression is instigated and maintained by the pressure of the superego (an internalized parental figure) upon the ego, (c) that the repressed consists essentially in libidinal impulses, and (d) that repression arises as a means of defence against impulses involved in the Oedipus situation and treated by the ego as "guilty" in terms of the pressure of the superego. That the agent and the instigator of repression should both be regarded as structures whilst the repressed is regarded as consisting of impulses involves a certain anomaly which appears so far to have escaped attention. The extent of this anomaly may perhaps best be appreciated in the light of the fact that the superego, which is described as the instigator of repression, is itself largely unconscious; for this raises the difficult question whether the superego itself is not also repressed. Freud himself was by no means oblivious to this problem, and he expressly envisages the possibility of the superego being in some measure subject to repression. Repression of the superego would, of course, represent the repression of a structure. It would thus appear that the general possibility of the repression of a structure is recognized by Freud, and, in the light of the considerations already advanced, it becomes reasonable to ask whether the repressed is not invariably and inherently structural. In this event the anomaly to which I have referred would be avoided.

That the repressed is essentially structural in nature is implicit in the view which I have already advanced (Fairbairn 1943) to the effect that repression is primarily directed against internalized objects which are treated as bad, for unless it is assumed that internalized objects are structures, the conception of the existence of such objects becomes utterly meaningless. In the light of further experience, my view that repression is primarily directed against bad internalized objects has proved to require considerable elaboration in a direction which has eventually led me to a revised conception of psychical structure. What actually provided the occasion of my chief step in this direction was the analysis of a dream recorded by one of my patients. This patient was a married woman who originally came to me for analysis on account of frigidity. Her frigidity was unquestionably a phenomenon of hysterical dissociation (hysterical anesthesia combined with hysterical paresis of the vagina), but, like all such phenomena, it represented but one part of a general personality problem. The dream itself was simple enough, but it struck me in the light of one of those simple manifestations which have so often in the history of science been found to embody fundamental truths.

The (manifest) dream to which I refer consisted in a brief scene in which the dreamer saw the figure of herself being viciously attacked by a well-known actress in a venerable building which had belonged to her family for generations. Her husband was looking on, but he seemed quite helpless and quite incapable of protecting her. After delivering the attack the actress turned away and resumed playing a stage part, which, as seemed to be implied, she had momentarily set aside in order to deliver the attack by way of interlude. The dreamer then found herself gazing at the figure of herself lying bleeding on the floor, but as she gazed she noticed that this figure turned for an instant into that of a man. Thereafter the figure alternated between herself and this man until eventually she awoke in a state of acute anxiety.

It came as no great surprise to me to learn from the dreamer's associations that the man into whom the figure of herself turned was wearing a suit closely resembling one which her husband had recently acquired, and that, whilst he had acquired this suit at her instigation, he had taken "one of his blondes" to the fitting. This fact, taken in conjunction with the fact that in the dream he was a helpless spectator of the attack, at once confirmed a natural suspicion that the attack was directed no less against him than against herself. This suspicion was amply confirmed by further associations which need not be detailed. The course followed by the associations also confirmed an additional suspicion that the actress who delivered the attack belonged as much to the personality of the dreamer as did the figure of herself against which the attack was delivered. In actual fact, the figure of an actress was well suited to represent a certain aspect of herself, for she was essentially a shut-in and withdrawn personality who displayed very little genuine feeling towards others, but who had perfected the technique of presenting facades to a point at which these assumed a remarkably genuine appearance and achieved for her a remarkable popularity. Such libidinal affect as she experienced had, since childhood, manifested itself predominantly in a secret phantasy life of masochistic complexion, but in the life of outer reality she had largely devoted herself to the playing of roles—e.g., the roles of good wife, good mother, good hostess, and good businesswoman. From this fact the helplessness attributed to her husband in the dream derived additional significance, for although she played the role of good wife with conspicuous success, her real personality was quite inaccessible to him, and the good wife whom he knew was for the most part only the good actress. This held true not only within the sphere of emotional relationships, but also within the sphere of marital relations, for whilst she remained frigid during intercourse, she had acquired the capacity of conveying the impression of sexual excitement and sexual satisfaction. Further, as the analysis revealed beyond all question, her frigidity represented not only an attack upon the libidinal component in herself, but also a hostile attitude towards her husband as a libidinal object. It is clear, therefore, that a measure of hidden aggression against her husband was involved in her assumption of the role of actress as this was portrayed in the dream. It is equally clear from the dream that, in a libidinal capacity, she was identified with her husband as the object of her own aggression. At this point it should be mentioned that, when the dream occurred, her husband was a member of one of the combatant services and was about to return home on leave. On the eve of his return, and just before the occurrence of the dream, she had developed a sore throat. This was a conjunction of events which had occurred so frequently in the past as to preclude coincidence on this occasion, and which accordingly served to confirm her identification with her husband as the object of her aggression. The situation represented in the dream is thus one in which the dreamer in one capacity, so far unspecified, vents her aggression directly against herself in another capacity, viz., a libidinal capacity, whilst, at the same time, venting her aggression indirectly against her husband as a libidinal object. At a superficial level, of course, this situation readily lent itself to being interpreted in the sense that the dreamer, being ambivalent towards her husband, had diverted the aggressive component in her ambivalent attitude from her husband to herself at the instance of guilt over her aggression in conformity with the melancholic pattern. Nevertheless, during the actual session in which the dream was recorded this interpretation did not commend itself to me as exhaustive, even at a superficial level.

It is obvious, of course, that the situation represented in the dream lent itself to a deeper interpretation than that to which reference has just been made. The situation was described a moment ago as one in which the dreamer in a capacity so far unspecified vented her aggression directly against herself in a libidinal capacity, whilst, at the same time, venting her aggression indirectly against her husband as a libidinal object. This description is, of course, incomplete in that it leaves unspecified the capacity in which she expressed her aggression, and it is when we come to consider the nature of this unspecified capacity that the deeper significance of the dream becomes a matter of moment. According to the manifest content of the dream, it was as an actress that she delivered the attack, and we have already seen how well suited the figure of an actress was to represent an aspect of herself hostile to libidinal relationships. However, abundant material had already emerged during the analysis to make it plain that the figure of an actress was at least equally well suited to represent the dreamer's mother—an artificial woman who had neither displayed any natural and spontaneous affection towards her children nor welcomed any such display on their part towards herself, and for whom the fashionable world provided a stage upon which she had spent her life in playing parts. It was thus easy to see that, in the capacity of actress, the dreamer was closely identified with her mother as a repressive figure. The introduction of her mother into the drama as an apparently superego figure at once raises the question whether the deeper interpretation of the dream should not be couched in terms of the Oedipus situation, and it becomes natural to ask whether her father is not also represented. In reality her father had been killed on active service during the war of 1914–18, at a time when she was only 6 years of age, and analysis had revealed the presence of considerable resentment towards him as a libidinal object who had proved at once exciting and rejecting (this resentment being focused particularly upon the memory of an early dressing-room scene). If then we are to look for a representation of her father in the dream, our choice is obviously limited to a single figure—the man who alternated with the figure of the dreamer as the object of attack. We have seen, of course, that this figure represented her husband, but analysis had already revealed how closely her husband was identified by transference with her father. For this, as well as for other reasons which need not be detailed, it was safe to infer that the man who was involved in the attack represented her father at the deeper level of interpretation. At this level, accordingly, the dream was capable of being interpreted as a phantasy in which both she and her father were portrayed as being killed by her mother on account of a guilty incestuous relationship. At the same time the dream was equally capable of being interpreted in terms of psychical structure, and thus as representing the repression of her libido on account of its incestuous attachment to her father at the instigation of a superego modeled upon her mother. Nevertheless, neither of these interpretations seemed to me to do justice to the material, although the structural interpretation seemed to offer the more fruitful line of approach. . . .

According to my present view, . . . the situations depicted in dreams represent relationships existing between endopsychic structures, and the same applies to situations depicted in waking phantasies. This conclusion is the natural outcome of my theory of object relationships taken in conjunction with a realization of the inescapable fact that internalized objects must be regarded as endopsychic structures if any theoretic significance whatever is to be attached to them. . . .

In the manifest dream the actual drama involves four figures: (1) the figure of the dreamer subjected to attack, (2) the man into whom this figure turns and who then alternates with it, (3) the attacking actress, and

(4) the dreamer's husband as a helpless onlooker. In our preoccupation with the actual drama, however, we must not forget our only witness of its occurrence—the dreamer herself, the observing ego. Including her, there are five figures to be reckoned with. At this juncture I venture to suggest that, if the dream had ended a few seconds earlier, there would only have been four figures, even on the assumption that the "I" of the dream is taken into account, for it was only in the fifth act, so to speak, that a man began to alternate with the figure of the dreamer as the object of attack. This is an interesting reflection, for we must conclude that, up to the point of the emergence of this man, the object of attack was a composite figure. The special interest of this phenomenon resides in the fact that, as we have seen, there is good reason to regard a second figure as composite, for the attacking actress undoubtedly represented both another figure of the dreamer and the dreamer's mother. I venture, therefore, to hazard a further suggestion—that, if the dream had lasted a few seconds longer, there might well have been six figures, instead of five. It is safe, at any rate, to infer that there were six figures in the latent content, and this, after all, is what matters for purposes of interpretation. Assuming then that six figures are represented in the dream, let us proceed to consider the nature of these figures. When we do so, our first observation is that the figures fall into two classes—ego structures and object structures. Interestingly enough there are three members of each class. The ego structures are (1) the observing ego or "I," (2) the attacked ego, and (3) the attacking ego. The object structures are (1) the dreamer's husband as an observing object, (2) the attacked object, and (3) the attacking object. This leads us to make a second observation—that the ego structures naturally lend themselves to be paired off with the object structures. There are three such pairs: (1) the observing ego and the dreamer's husband, who also figured as an observer; (2) the attacking ego and the attacking object representing her mother; and (3) the attacked ego and the attacked object representing her father (for at this point it is to the deeper level of interpretation that we must adhere).

Bearing these two main observations in mind, let us now consider the conclusions to which I was led in an attempt to interpret the dream to my satisfaction. They are as follows. The three ego figures which appear as separate in the dream actually represent separate ego structures in the dreamer's mind. The dreamer's "ego" is therefore split in conformity with the schizoid position, and it is split into three separate egos—a central ego and two other subsidiary egos which are both, relatively speaking, cut off from the central ego. Of these two subsidiary egos, one is the object of aggression on the part of the other. Since the ego which is attacked is closely related to the dreamer's father (and by transference to her husband), it is safe to infer that this ego is highly endowed with libido, and it may thus be appropriately described as a "libidinal ego." Since the attacking ego is closely related to the dreamer's mother as a repressive figure, its behaviour is quite in accord with that traditionally ascribed to the superego in the setting of the Oedipus situation. Since, however, the attack bears all the marks of being vindictive, rather than moral, and gives rise to an affect, not of guilt, but of plain anxiety, there is no justification (apart from preconceptions) for equating the attacking ego with the superego. In any case, as I have already indicated, there is reason to attach overriding psychopathological importance to a level beneath that at which the superego functions. At the same time, it was shown by the circumstances in which the dream occurred that the dreamer's libidinal relationship with her husband was severely compromised, and, so far as the dream is concerned, it is clearly to the operation of the attacking ego that we must look for the compromising factor. Consequently, the attacking ego may perhaps be most appropriately described as an "internal saboteur." In an attempt to discover what this dream was stating and to determine the structural significance of what was stated, I was accordingly led to set aside the traditional classification of mental structure in terms of ego, id, and superego in favour of a classification couched in terms of an ego-structure split into three separate egos—(1) a central ego (the "I"), (2) a libidinal ego, and (3) an aggressive, persecutory ego which I designate as the internal saboteur. Subsequent experience has led me to regard this classification as having a universal application.

THE OBJECT RELATIONSHIPS OF THE CENTRAL EGO AND THE SUBSIDIARY EGOS

Such being my conclusions regarding the ego structures represented in the dream, let us now pass on to consider my conclusions regarding the object relationships of these ego structures. As already indicated, each of the three egos in question naturally lends itself to being paired off with a special object. The special object of the central ego was the dreamer's husband, and it is convenient to begin by considering the nature of the attitude adopted by the dreamer's central ego towards him. Since the central ego was the observing "I" of the dream, who was felt to be continuous with the waking "I" by whom the dream was subsequently described, it is safe to infer that this ego is in no small measure preconscious–which is, in any case, what one would naturally expect of an ego deserving the title of "central." This inference gains further support from the fact that the dreamer's husband was a supremely important object in outer reality and was very much in the dreamer's conscious thoughts on the eve of the dream. Although the figure representing him in the dream must be regarded as an internalized object, this object must obviously occupy a much more superficial position in the psyche than the other objects represented (parental objects internalized in childhood), and it must correspond comparatively closely to the relative object in outer reality. Accordingly, the dreamer's attitude to her husband as an external object assumes considerable significance for our present purpose. This attitude was essentially ambivalent, especially where marital relations were concerned. Active manifestations of aggression towards him were, however, conspicuously absent. Equally, her libidinal attachment to him bore the marks of severe repression, and, in associating to the dream, she reproached herself over her lack of deep feeling towards him and her failure to give to him of herself, albeit her conscious capacity to remedy these deficiencies was restricted to an assumption of the role of "good wife." The question therefore arises whether, since her hidden aggression towards him and her hidden libidinal need of him do not declare themselves directly in the dream, they may not manifest themselves in some indirect fashion. No sooner is this question raised than we are at once reminded of the metamorphosis undergone by the figure of the libidinal ego after this was attacked by the figure of the internal saboteur. The libidinal ego changed into, and then began alternating with, a man who, whilst representing the dreamer's father at a deep level, was nevertheless closely associated with her husband. It is thus evident that, instead of being directed against her husband as an external object, a considerable proportion of her aggression was absorbed in an attack directed, not simply against the libidinal ego, but also against an internal object closely connected with the libidinal ego. It is likewise evident that this volume of aggression had come to be at the disposal, not of the central ego, but of the internal saboteur. What then of the libidinal component in her ambivalence? As we have seen, her libidinal attitude to her husband showed signs of considerable impoverishment in spite of good intentions at a conscious level. It is obvious, accordingly, that what held true of her aggression also held true of her libido. A considerable proportion had ceased to be at the disposal of the central ego. The object towards whom this volume of libido is directed can hardly remain in doubt. In terms of the dream, it must surely be the man who alternated with the libidinal self as the object of aggression. Unlike the aggression, however, this libido is not at the disposal of the internal saboteur. On the contrary we must regard it as being at the disposal of the libidinal ego, and indeed it is precisely for this reason that the term *libidinal ego* has come to commend itself to me for adoption. At this point it becomes desirable to formulate a suspicion which must be already present in the mind of the reader—that, although it is represented otherwise in the dream, the attack delivered by the internal saboteur is only secondarily directed against the libidinal ego and is primarily directed against the libidinal object which alternates with this ego. Assuming this suspicion to be correct, we must regard the ordeal to which the libidinal ego is subjected as evidence of a very complete identification with, and therefore a very strong libidinal attachment to, the attacked object on the part of the libidinal ego. It is evidence of the measure of "suffering" which the libidinal ego is prepared to endure out of devotion to its object. The anxiety experienced by the dreamer on waking may be interpreted in a similar sense, and indeed I venture to suggest that this anxiety represented an irruption into consciousness of such suffering on the part of the libidinal ego. Here we are at once reminded of Freud's original conception of neurotic anxiety as libido converted into suffering. This is a view which at one time presented the greatest theoretic difficulty to me, but which I have now come to appreciate in the light of my present standpoint, and substantially to accept in preference to the modified view which Freud later (and, as I think, rather reluctantly) came to adopt.

The position regarding the object relationships of the three egos represented in the dream has now been to some extent clarified, but the process of clarification is not yet complete. Up to date, the position which has emerged would appear to be as follows. The dreamer's preconscious attitude towards her husband is ambivalent, and this is the attitude adopted by her central ego towards its external object, as well as towards the internalized representative of this object. However, both the libidinal and the aggressive components in the object relationship of the central ego are predominantly passive. On the other hand, a considerable proportion of the dreamer's active libido is at the disposal of the libidinal ego and is directed towards an internalized object which, for purposes of nomenclature, may perhaps best be described as the "(internal) exciting object." At the same time, a considerable proportion of her aggression is at the disposal of the internal saboteur and is directed (1) towards the libidinal ego, and (2) towards the exciting object (i.e., towards the object of the libidinal ego). It cannot fail to be noticed, however, that this summary of the position leaves out of account certain endopsychic relationships which may be presumed to exist—notably (1) the relationship of the central ego to the other egos, and (2) the relationship of the internal saboteur to the internalized object with which it is so closely associated, and which is represented by the maternal component in the actress figure. Taking the latter relationship first, we have no difficulty in seeing that, since the actress in the dream was a composite figure representing both the dreamer's mother and herself, the internal saboteur is closely identified with its object and must therefore be regarded as bound to this object by a strong libidinal attachment. For purposes of description we must give the object a name, and I propose to describe it as the "(internal) rejecting object." I have chosen this term primarily for a reason which will emerge later, but meanwhile my justification will be that the dreamer's mother, who provided the original model of this internalized object, was essentially a rejecting figure, and that it is, so to speak, in the name of this object that the aggression of the internal saboteur is directed against the libidinal ego. As regards the relationship of the central ego to the other egos, our most important clue to its nature lies in the fact that, whereas the central ego must be regarded as comprising preconscious and conscious, as well as unconscious, elements, the other egos must equally be regarded as essentially unconscious. From this we may infer that the libidinal ego and the internal saboteur are both rejected by the central ego, and this inference is confirmed by the fact that, as we have seen, the considerable volume of libido and of aggression which has ceased to be at the disposal of the central ego is now at the disposal of the subsidiary egos. Assuming then that the subsidiary egos are rejected by the central ego, it becomes a question of the dynamic of this rejection. Obviously the dynamic of rejection cannot be libido. So there is no alternative but to regard it as aggression. Aggression must, accordingly, be regarded as the characteristic determinant of the attitude of the central ego towards the subsidiary egos.

I have now completed the account of my attempt to reconstruct, in terms of dynamic structure, the endopsychic situation represented in a patient's dream. The account has been cast in the form of a reasoned statement, and, as such, it should serve to give some indication of what is involved in my view that dreams are essentially "shorts" of inner reality (rather than wish-fulfillments). However, it is not primarily with the aim of substantiating my views on dreams in general that I have claimed so much of the reader's attention for a single dream. On the contrary, it is because the dream in question seems to me to represent an endopsychic situation of a classic order, and indeed of a basic character which entitles it to be regarded as the paradigm of all endopsychic situations. For convenience, the general features of this situation are illustrated in Figure 7–1.

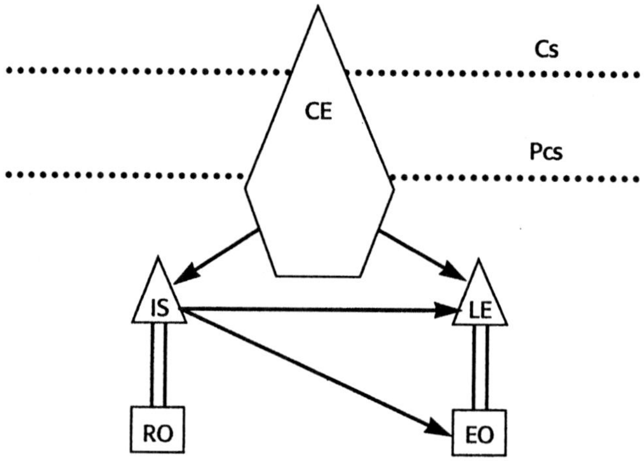

Figure 7–1. CE, central ego; IS, internal saboteur; LE, libidinal ego; RO, rejecting object; EO, exciting object. Cs, conscious; Pcs, preconscious; Ucs, unconscious. →, aggression; =, libido.

THE BASIC ENDOPSYCHIC SITUATION AND A REVISED THEORY OF MENTAL STRUCTURE FOUNDED THEREON

I myself feel convinced that the basic endopsychic situation above described is the situation underlying Freud's description of the mental apparatus in terms of ego, id, and superego. It is certainly the endopsychic situation upon which I deliberately base the revised theory of mental structure which I now submit, and which is couched in terms of central ego, libidinal ego, and internal saboteur. As it would, of course, be natural to expect, there is a general correspondence between Freud's concepts and those which I have now come to adopt. In the case of the *central ego,* the correspondence to Freud's *ego* is fairly close from a functional standpoint, but there are important differences between the two concepts. Unlike Freud's ego, the central ego is not conceived as originating out of something else (the *id*), or as constituting a passive structure dependent for its activity upon impulses proceeding from the matrix out of which it originated, and on the surface of which it rests.[1] On the contrary, the central ego is conceived as a primary and dynamic structure, from which, as we shall shortly see, the other mental structures are subsequently derived. The *libidinal ego* corresponds, of course, to Freud's id, but whereas according to Freud's view the ego is a derivative of the id, according to my view the libidinal ego (which corresponds to the id) is a derivative of the central ego (which corresponds to the ego). The libidinal ego also differs from the id in that it is conceived, not as a mere reservoir of instinctive impulses, but as a dynamic structure comparable to the central ego, although differing from the latter in various respects, e.g., in its more infantile character, in a lesser degree of organization, in a smaller measure of adaptation to reality and in a greater devotion to internalized objects. The "internal saboteur" differs from the superego in a number of respects. For one thing it is in no sense conceived as an internal object. It is wholly an ego structure, although, as we have seen, it is very closely associated with an internal object. Actually, the superego corresponds not so much to the internal saboteur as to a compound of this structure and its associated object (like the figure of the actress in the dream). At the same time, the internal saboteur is unlike the superego in that it is conceived as, in itself, devoid of all moral significance. Thus I do not attribute the affect of guilt to its activity, although this activity is unquestionably a prolific source of anxiety. Such anxiety may, of course, merge with guilt, but the two affects are theoretically distinct. Here it should be noted that, whilst

1. Freud's conception of the ego was, of course, borrowed from Groddeck, but, if there is any truth in the conclusions which will shortly be recorded, it is a conception based upon an endopsychic situation resulting from repression, and therefore is anomalous in terms of Freud's own views, since it implies that repression is responsible for the origin of the ego.

introducing the conception of the internal saboteur, I am not prepared to abandon the conception of the superego as I have now come to abandon that of the id. On the contrary, it seems to me impossible to offer any satisfactory psychological explanation of guilt in the absence of the superego; but the superego must be regarded as originating at a higher level of mental organization than that at which the internal saboteur operates. Exactly how the activities of the two structures are related must in the meantime remain an open question; but, for the most recent expression of my views regarding the origin and the function of the superego I must refer the reader to a previous paper (Fairbairn 1943). . . .

THE DYNAMIC QUALITY OF INTERNALIZED OBJECTS

The feature of Freud's theory of the mental apparatus presenting the greatest anomaly is one to which reference has not yet been made. It is this—that the only part of the psyche which he describes in terms at all approximating to those of dynamic structure is the superego. The id is, of course, described as a source of energy without structure, and the ego is described as a passive structure without energy except such as invades it from the id. By contrast, the superego is described as a structure endowed with a fund of energy. It is true that the energy in question is conceived as being ultimately derived from the id, but this in no way alters the fact that Freud attributes to the superego a considerable measure of independent functional activity. So much is this the case that he speaks of the superego and the id as diametrically opposed to one another in the aims of their activities, and of the ego as buffetted between these two endopsychic entities. The odd thing about all this is that the superego is really only a naturalized alien, as it were, within the realm of the individual mind, an immigrant from outer reality. Its whole significance resides in the fact that it is essentially an internalized object. That the only part of the psyche which Freud treats as a dynamic structure should be an internalized object is, to my mind, an anomaly sufficient in itself to justify my attempt to formulate an alternative theory of psychical structure. It will be observed that, in formulating such an alternative theory, I have so far followed a line opposite to that followed by Freud in that, whereas an internalized object is the only part of the psyche which Freud treats as a dynamic structure, the internalized objects which I envisage are the only parts of the psyche which I have *not* treated as dynamic structures. I have treated the internalized objects simply as *objects* of the dynamic ego structures, i.e., as endopsychic structures which are not themselves dynamic. I have done this deliberately, not only to avoid complications of exposition, but also to bring into focus the activity of the ego structures which I find it necessary to postulate, and to avoid all risk of underrating the primary importance of this activity, for, after all, it is only through this activity that objects ever come to be internalized. However, in the interests of consistency, I must now draw the logical conclusion of my theory of dynamic structure and acknowledge that, since internal objects are structures, they must necessarily be, in some measure at least, dynamic. In drawing this conclusion and making this acknowledgement, I shall not only be here following the precedent of Freud, but also, it would seem, conforming to the demands of such psychological facts as are revealed, e.g., in dreams and in the phenomena of paranoia. This further step will enhance the explanatory value of my theory of mental structure by introducing additional possibilities into the endopsychic situation by way of permutation and combination. It must be recognized, however, that, in practice, it is very difficult to differentiate between the activity of internalized objects and the activity of the ego structures with which they are associated, and, with a view to avoiding any appearance of demonology, it seems wise to err, if anything, on the side of overweighting the activity of the ego structures rather than otherwise. It remains true, nevertheless, that under certain conditions internalized objects may acquire a dynamic independence which cannot be ignored. It is doubtless in this direction that we must look for an explanation of the fundamental animism of human beings, which is none the less persistent under the surface even when it is hidden under the veneers of civilization and science, but which significantly betrays itself even in the most sophisticated forms of art. . . .

REFERENCE

Fairbairn, W. R. D. (1943). The repression and return of bad objects. In *Psychoanalytic Studies of the Personality*, pp. 59–81. London: Routledge, 1952.

8

"Observations on the Nature of Hysterical States" (1954)

This paper is the last of Fairbairn's great clinical theory papers, offering a review of the problems that had concerned both Freud and Fairbairn. It contains a review of the theoretical developments that differentiate object relations theory from Freud. The sections included here summarize Fairbairn's theoretical developments up to that time, establish the basis of the oedipal situation, postulate a new theory of conversion as the substitution of a bodily dysfunction for a problem in personal relations, and suggest that the basis for Freud's pleasure principle is itself a phenomenon of conversion in the realm of theoretical metaphor.

The basic outline of Fairbairn's conception of psychic organization is now clear: that the child is organized by its basic need to be related to others ("libido is essentially object seeking"). However, due to the inevitable frustration in all relationships, and therefore in the relationship to the mother, the child is confronted with a relationship to a rejecting, or emotionally "bad" object. To deal with this situation, the child incorporates a representation of that object, and, still finding this originally whole, unsatisfying object painful to relate to, splits off its unsatisfying part-objects, which are then repressed in order to clear the way for a central ego and object to have a less painful relationship. Whenever the object is split and repressed, so is a part of the ego (which in contemporary terms we consider to be the "self") that is in relationship to it, so that eventually there are a group of buried aspects of self and object that come to constitute the internal organization of the psyche. Fairbairn summarizes the intricacies of this situation here before he applies object relations theory to the specific nature of hysterical states.

A few elements of Fairbairn's theoretical outline remained to be clarified during the final years of his life. He came to call the ego attached to the rejecting object the *anti-libidinal ego* instead of his original term, the *internal saboteur,* which was first used in the 1944 paper on endopsychic structure and was more evocative in signifying that part of the person that is addicted to the bad object and is, therefore, repeatedly self-defeating. This was Fairbairn's explanation of the repetition compulsion, which Freud had ascribed to the action of the death instinct. By the mid-1950s, however, Fairbairn chose the term *anti-libidinal ego* to conform to the term *libidinal ego,* which he had been employing to refer to that part of the self craving the teasing and tantalizing relationship with the excessively exciting object.

In his final writings, Fairbairn also rethought the place of superego functions in his theory. He had begun his theoretical journey in his study of Freud's "The Ego and the Id" during the late 1920s, puzzled by the explanation of the origin of the superego in Freud's structural theory. Fairbairn recognized from the beginning that the superego represented a structure that Freud had said was itself repressed by the ego (Fairbairn 1994). This implied that, more than unpleasant content, mental structure itself could be split off and repressed. Fairbairn's research on the nature of the guiding functions of mental life continued until he arrived at a formulation of superego functions carried out by three of the subunits of his six-part endopsychic structure. The guiding and beckoning role played by Freud's ego ideal is taken in Fairbairn's terminology by the ideal object that is the object of the central ego. The punitive and archaic persecuting functions of the superego are subsumed in the relationship between the rejecting object and anti-libidinal ego (Fairbairn 1963).

These final theoretical formulations added rigor and completeness to Fairbairn's theoretical structure. As we come to further contributions to object relations theory in the rest of this volume, we can employ Fairbairn's framework to organize and integrate fundamental ideas from other contributors. It is interesting to contrast Fairbairn's spare and tight style and form, as evidenced in this paper, to the evocative language of Melanie Klein, to Bion's exploration of unconscious processes, and to the purposefully enigmatic expression of ideas through which Winnicott conveyed the intricacies of the earliest relationship between mother and child.

REFERENCES

Fairbairn, W. R. D. (1963). Synopsis of an object relations theory of the personality. *International Journal of Psycho-Analysis* 44:224–225. [Also in Fairbairn, W. R. D. (1994). In *From Instinct to Self*, vol. 1, ed. D. E. Scharff, and E. F. Birtles, pp. 155–156. Northvale, NJ: Jason Aronson.]

——(1994). The Superego. In *From Instinct to Self*, vol. 2, ed. E. F. Birtles and D. E. Scharff, pp. 80–114. Northvale, NJ: Jason Aronson.

OBSERVATIONS ON THE NATURE OF HYSTERICAL STATES

In addition to such intrinsic interest as hysterical states may be expected to possess for the psychopathologist, they must always assume a quite special significance for him owing to the fact that it was upon the intensive investigation of these states that modern psychopathology was founded. It was, of course, at the Salpêtrière in Paris that this investigation was originally set in motion by Charcot; but it is to Janet, his pupil and successor in research, that we owe the formulation of the concept of hysteria as a recognizable clinical state. Janet's achievement was not confined, however, to a classification and description of hysterical symptomatology. It included an attempt to provide a scientific explanation of the genesis of the phenomena displayed by the hysteric, and the explanatory concept which Janet formulated was, of course, the classic concept of *dissociation.* In terms of this concept the hysterical state is essentially due to inability on the part of the ego to hold all the functions of the personality together, with the result that certain of these functions become dissociated from, and lost to, the rest of the personality and, having passed out of the awareness and control of the ego, operate independently. The extent of the dissociated elements was described by Janet as varying within wide limits, so that sometimes what was dissociated was an isolated function such as the use of a limb, and sometimes a large area or large areas of the psyche (as in cases of dual and multiple personality), and the occurrence of such dissociations was attributed to the presence of a certain weakness of the ego—a weakness partly inherent, and partly induced by circumstances such as illness, trauma, or situations imposing a strain upon the individual's capacity for adaptation.

Dissociation as described by Janet is, of course, essentially a passive process—a process of disintegration due to a failure on the part of the cohesive function normally exercised by the ego. The concept of dissociation thus stands in marked contrast to the concept of *repression* formulated somewhat later by Freud in an attempt to provide a more adequate explanation of hysterical phenomena. Freud was familiar with the investigations conducted at the Salpêtrière, to which he himself paid an extensive visit. . . .

The fact of resistance has now become so familiar to psychopathologists that the very mention of it seems to demand an apology. What is not universally appreciated, however, is that the resistance of the hysterical patient is not so much a resistance to the psychotherapeutic process as a *resistance to the psychotherapist himself.* Be this as it may, it was to explain the resistance that Freud postulated the process of repression, and, since resistance is an active process, it was as an inherently active process that repression was conceived by Freud. It is largely for this reason that the concept of repression has come to supersede that of dissociation, for, being a dynamic concept, it lends itself, as the concept of dissociation does not, to providing the basis for a comprehensive investigation of the dynamics of the personality, and, in actual fact, it is the foundation stone upon which the whole explanatory system represented by psychoanalytical theory has been built. At the same time I must record the opinion that the eclipse of the concept of dissociation, which has accompanied the explanatory ascendancy of the concept of repression, has not been altogether an unmixed gain. According to Janet, as we have seen, the dissociative process characterizing hysteria was a manifestation of ego weakness, and, although it did not take Freud long to recognize that hysterical symptoms were the product of a defence springing from weakness of the ego, the presence of such a weakness is not inherent in the concept of repression as such. Further consideration reveals that the process of dissociation, as conceived by Janet, carries with it the implication of a *split in the personality,* variable in its extent and often multiple, and the view that such an underlying splitting of the personality is implied in hysterical phenomena is a view which I sought to substantiate in a paper written in 1944 ("Endopsychic Structure"). Such a view is one which Freud himself at one time entertained,[1] but

1. This is evident from the following statement in his paper entitled "On the Psychical Mechanism of Hysterical Phenomena," published in 1893: "Indeed, the more we occupied

which he subsequently allowed to pass into abeyance as he concentrated upon the development of the concept of repression. . . .

I have formulated a revised theory of repression, the nature of which may perhaps best be indicated by the following summary of the general views which I have come to adopt regarding the development and differentiation of the personality:

1. The pristine personality of the child consists of a unitary dynamic ego.
2. The first defence adopted by the original ego to deal with an unsatisfying personal relationship is mental internalization, or introjection, of the unsatisfying object.[2]

---

ourselves with these phenomena the more certain did our conviction become that splitting of consciousness, which is so striking in the well-known classical cases of double conscience, exists in a rudimentary fashion in every hysteria and that the tendency to dissociation . . . is a fundamental manifestation of this neurosis" (Freud 1924, p. 34).

2. Here it is perhaps necessary for me to explain that I can think of no motive for the introjection of an object which is *perfectly satisfying*. Thus, in my opinion, it would be a pointless procedure on the part of the infant to introject the maternal object if his relationship with his actual mother were completely satisfying, both within the emotional sphere and within the more specific sphere of the suckling-situation. As it seems to me, it is only insofar as the infant's relationship with his mother falls short of being completely satisfying that he can have any conceivable motive for introjecting the maternal object. This is a view which appears to present considerable difficulty for Melanie Klein and her collaborators, especially since the introjection of "good" objects plays such an important part in their theoretical system. The difficulty in question is perhaps in no small measure due to the fact that, in previous formulations of my views on this subject (Fairbairn 1952), I expressed the opinion that it was always "bad" objects that were introjected in the first instance. However, I have now revised my previous opinion to the effect (1) that the differentiation of objects into categories to which the respective terms good and bad can be applied only arises after the original (pre-ambivalent) object has been introjected, and (2) that this differentiation is effected through splitting of an internalized object which is, in the first instance, neither good nor bad, but in some measure unsatisfying, and which only becomes truly ambivalent after its introjection. The manner in which I conceive the process of splitting to occur is indicated in the summary provided in the text above. It should be added, however, that a completely satisfying relationship between the infant and his actual mother represents a contingency which is only theoretically possible, and which never materializes in actual fact. From a practical standpoint, therefore, it may be regarded as inevitable that circumstances will arise to provide the infant with a motive for introjecting the maternal object. Such circumstances may arise at any moment after the cessation of intrauterine existence, and indeed the disturbance of intrauterine bliss by the birth process itself may be regarded as representing such a circumstance.

It will not escape the notice of the reader that I describe introjection of the unsatisfying

3. The unsatisfying object has two disturbing aspects, viz. an exciting aspect and a rejecting aspect.
4. The second defence adopted by the ego is to reject and split off from the internalized object two elements—one representing its exciting aspect, and one representing its rejecting aspect.
5. The internalized object is thus split into three objects, viz. the exciting object, the rejecting object, and the nucleus which remains after the exciting and rejecting elements have been split off from it.
6. This residual nucleus represents the relatively satisfying, or at any rate tolerable, aspect of the internalized object, and is therefore not rejected by the ego, but remains actively cathected by it under conditions which render the term ideal object appropriate for its description.[3]
7. The rejection and splitting-off of the exciting and rejecting objects constitute and act of *direct and primary repression* on the part of the ego.
8. Since the exciting and rejecting objects remain cathected while in process of being repressed, their repression involves a splitting-off, from the substance of the ego, of two portions representing the respective cathexes of the two repressed objects.

---

object as a *defence*—"the first defence adopted by the original ego." This implies, of course, that I do not regard introjection of the object as the inevitable expression of the infant's instinctive incorporative needs—as something that just happens, so to speak; for, obviously, the aim of the instinctive incorporative need is not incorporation, whether physical or mental, of either the mother or her breast, but physical incorporation of the mother's milk. Nor can the process of introjection of the object (viz. the process whereby a *mental structure* representing an external object becomes established within the psyche) be regarded simply as a manifestation of that general perpetuation of experience which is described as "memory." It would appear, accordingly, that it is only when introjection is conceived as a defensive technique that this concept possesses any significant meaning. As it seems to me, the real problems lying behind the difficulty which my views regarding introjection present for Melanie Klein and her collaborators are the problems (1) of the form in which the child's experience of good and satisfying relationships is perpetuated within the psyche, and (2) of the manner in which the personality is moulded by such experience. These vital problems are hardly such as to lend themselves to discussion in a footnote which is perhaps already too long, but I can at least point out that, in terms of my theory of the development of the personality (as described in the summary appearing in the text above), the key to these problems is to be found in the relationship of the central ego to the ideal object.

3. I have previously employed the term *ego-ideal* to describe this internal object (Fairbairn 1952), but I now feel it desirable to adopt the term *ideal object* for its description, and so to emphasize its object-status and bring it into terminological alignment with the *exciting object* and the *rejecting object*.

9. The splitting-off of these two portions of the ego from its remaining central portion represents an act of *direct and secondary repression* on the part of the latter.
10. The resulting endopsychic situation is one in which we find a central ego cathecting the ideal object as an acceptable internal object, and two split-off and repressed ego structures each cathecting a repressed internal object.
11. The terms libidinal ego and anti-libidinal ego[4] have been adopted to describe, respectively, the repressed ego structure cathecting the exciting object and that cathecting the rejecting object.
12. The term anti-libidinal ego has been adopted on the grounds that the repressed ego structure so designated, being in alliance with the rejecting object, has aims inherently hostile to those of the libidinal ego in its alliance with the exciting object.
13. Being a dynamic structure, the anti-libidinal ego implements its hostility to the aims of the libidinal ego by subjecting the latter to a sustained aggressive and persecutory attack which supports the repression already exercised against it by the central ego, and which it thus seems appropriate to describe as a process of indirect repression.
14. Although direct and indirect repression of the libidinal ego are two processes of a very different nature, they are both included under the single term repression as understood by Freud; but it is to be noted that Freud took no account of direct repression of the anti-libidinal ego by the central ego, except in such incidental references as are contained in the passages in "The Ego and the Id" (Freud 1923), in which he raised the questions why the superego is unconscious, and whether, in the case of the hysterical personality at any rate, this instigator of repression is not itself subject to repression—questions to which the exigencies of his own theory did not permit of a satisfactory answer.
15. Although the anti-libidinal ego, the rejecting object, and the ideal object are all independent structures playing different roles in the economy of the psyche, they are all included by Freud in the

4. I have previously employed the term *internal saboteur* to describe this ego-structure (see Fairbairn 1952), but I now feel it desirable to adopt the term *anti-libidinal ego* for its description, and so to emphasize its ego-status and bring it into terminological alignment with the *central ego* and the *libidinal ego*.

comprehensive concept of the superego; and this source of confusion may be obviated by recognition of their independent character.

16. The endopsychic situation resulting from the twin processes of repression and splitting, which have just been described, is one which, in its general outlines, inevitably becomes established in the child at an early age, and in this sense may be regarded as normal; but, especially in its dynamic aspect, it contains within it the potentialities of all psychopathological developments in later life.
17. The conception of this basic endopsychic situation provides an alternative, couched in terms of personal relationships and dynamic ego structure, to Freud's description of the psyche in terms of id, ego, and superego, based as this is upon a Helmholtzian divorce of energy from structure no longer accepted in physics, and combined as it is, albeit at the expense of no little inconsistency, with a nonpersonal psychology conceived in terms of biological instincts and erotogenic zones.

Such then is the background of my approach to the problems of the hysterical state. So far as the hysteric is concerned, a characteristic feature of the basic endopsychic situation which I have just outlined is that the exciting object is excessively exciting, and the rejecting object excessively rejecting; and from this it inevitably follows that the libidinal ego is excessively libidinal, and the anti-libidinal ego excessively persecutory. These features seem to me to shed considerable light upon the nature of the hysterical state, for they go a long way to explain both (1) the intensity of the hysteric's repressed sexuality, and (2) the extent of the compulsive sacrifice of sexuality, which is such a characteristic hysterical phenomenon.

The inner situation prevailing in the case of the hysteric may be illustrated in classic form by the following dream. It was recorded by a patient, whom I shall call Louise—a patient of the hysterical type, who originally consulted me on account of conjugal difficulties, but who had a previous history of psychosomatic symptoms. In the dream she found herself as a child in a short passage with a door at either end and a window in one of the walls. In front of each door stood a figure of her father facing her with what appeared to be a stick in his hand. One of these figures held his stick in front of his genitals pointing towards her in such a manner as to indicate clearly that it symbolized an erect penis, whilst the other figure was holding his stick above his head like a whip with which he was about to punish her. Louise herself was standing immobilized between these two figures of her father, dancing from foot to foot in a state of excitement and anxiety. Meanwhile, she saw through the window a procession of couples of men and women, who cast superior and scornful glances upon her as they passed by and observed her predicament. Their glances conveyed to her the impression that they regarded her as just a "silly little thing," and this was exactly what she felt about herself, overwhelmed as she was by a sense of utter helplessness and hopeless inferiority as she stood immobilized between the two figures of her father in the passage. Such a sense of helplessness and inferiority is, of course, a familiar experience for the hysteric in waking life, as indeed was the case with Louise, and the source from which this experience springs is well illustrated by the dream scene. This scene represented an inner situation derived from the circumstances of Louise's actual relationship with her father in childhood, for her father was an erratic individual with manic-depressive characteristics who treated her at times with attentions which could not fail to be sexually provocative, and at other times with thoughtless indifference and neglect which conveyed to her a sense of rejection on his part.

The presence of a similar inner situation in the case of a male patient, whom I shall call Morris, was revealed during the course of analysis in his description of the position in which he felt himself to be placed in his relationship with his mother. This patient was also of a hysterical type, although his symptoms manifested themselves chiefly in the form of anxiety, and, significantly enough, it was upon his return home to his widowed mother with a wound after serving in the Army during the Second World War that he developed the acute anxiety symptoms which necessitated analytical treatment. The inner situation which emerged during the course of analysis was one in which he felt as if his mother were both holding down his erect penis and crushing his testicles with her hand, and he described himself as not only terrified that she would destroy his genitals if he struggled to get free, but also afraid that she would release her grip, since, if she did, it would put an end to the sexual excitement which her handling of his genitals provoked. Here again we find evidence of the simultaneous influence of an exciting and a rejecting object. It is true that Morris did not describe these two objects as separate in the imagined scene, but this may be accounted for not only on the grounds that his description was at a conscious level, but also on the grounds that, as is so characteristic a feature of hysterics, he sought a masochistic solution of his dilemma in the inner world. For he explained that, in spite of his fear of castration by his rejecting mother, he also felt that the excitement which she provoked in him could only be allayed if she squeezed his genitals to the point of destruction, and that this eventuality would constitute the only means of providing him with complete sexual satisfaction. The actual situation in his childhood was, briefly, one in which, as the only boy in a family otherwise composed of girls, he was the object of excessive solicitude on the part of a fussy and possessive mother, who not only bound him to her libidinally by her attentions, but also frowned upon any manifestation of sexuality on his part, forbade him to masturbate, and on one occasion inflicted upon him the trauma of slapping him for showing his penis to her. This situation, it may be added, was considerably aggravated by the fact that his father was a remote and inaccessible personality, and that he was thus deprived of a relationship which would otherwise have helped to rescue him from the toils of his mother and encourage him to develop an attitude of adult male independence.

The two pictures of the endopsychic situation which I have now described may be regarded as quite characteristic of the hysterical state; but it will be observed that, in both pictures, attention is focused almost exclusively upon the exciting and the rejecting objects. I propose in a moment to provide a picture in which attention is focused upon the three ego structures involved in the endopsychic situation. Before proceeding to do so, however, I should like to say a word regarding the third internal object, viz. the ideal object. This object is found to be less commonly represented in the dreams of hysterics than the exciting and rejecting objects, but it frequently finds a place in their conscious phantasies. Thus another of my hysterical patients, whom I shall call Jean, recorded that, for many years previous to the breakdown which finally brought her to analysis, she had sought consolation in daydreams about a sexless marriage to a wealthy and indulgent husband who provided her with a luxurious house, innumerable servants, splendid motor cars, elegant clothes, magnificent jewels, and sumptuous food. She also sometimes imagined his providing her with children, but these children just appeared mysteriously out of nowhere without any preliminary intercourse, pregnancy, or confinement. It will be noticed that such phantasies are characterized by a conspicuous absence of any element of sexual excitement on the one hand, or of frustration and rejection on the other. Both the exciting object and the rejecting object are thus excluded from such phantasies—as also, for that matter, are the libidinal ego and the anti-libidinal ego. In other words, such phantasies represent a relationship between the central ego and the ideal object—and it may be added that the nucleus of the ideal object is the mother insofar as she has proved satisfying and comforting in infancy. This incidentally is the type of relationship which the hysteric seeks to establish and maintain with the analyst in the analytical situation, and although under the pressure of transference the analyst also soon comes to assume the roles of both exciting object and rejecting object, conscious recognition of this fact commonly meets with extreme resistance on the part of the patient, who characteristically reacts with anxiety or bodily distress to the threatened invasion of the analytical situation by these repressed internal objects.

After this brief reference to the ideal object, I shall now describe a dream in which the endopsychic situation prevailing in the hysteric is represented exclusively in terms of the three ego structures. The dreamer in this case was the last-mentioned patient, Jean, and the dream was quite simple. It was about two dogs racing one another. One dog was white, and the other black, and the black dog won the race. Then Jean found herself comforting the white dog because it had lost the race, and while she was comforting it, the black dog came and attacked it. The interpretation of this dream will present little difficulty in the light of my introductory remarks—especially since Jean's own comment on the dream was "I suppose both the dogs are me," for obviously the white dog represents the libidinal ego, the black dog the anti-libidinal ego, and Jean herself the central ego. So far as the drama itself is concerned, the black dog's victory over the white dog in the race and its subsequent vicious attack upon the white dog provide a perfect picture of that dominance of the anti-libidinal ego over the libidinal ego and that relentless persecution of the latter by the former, which are such characteristic features of the hysterical state; for self-deprivation, self-sabotage, a compulsion to sacrifice sexuality, and a need to suffer are typical hysterical features.

Jean's concern over the plight of the white dog in the dream also provides a typical picture of the hysteric's tendency to self-pity, for although, as we have seen, the libidinal ego is repressed, the hysteric never ceases to lament the limitations, sacrifices, and sense of inferiority to which its repression gives rise, to long for its restoration, and to envy those in whose case its repression has been less drastic. In addition, the hysteric entertains a tremendous sense of grievance, nonetheless present even when it is unconscious, against those involved in the outer circumstances in which the endopsychic drama had its ultimate origin. And here it becomes apposite to remark that, whereas the libidinal ego is preeminently characterized by libidinal need, the antilibidinal ego is preeminently characterized by aggression. Considered in conjunction, these two repressed ego structures can thus be seen to reflect the early ambivalence of the child towards his objects. The child's aggression is, in my opinion, originally directed towards objects no less than is his libido (for I do not accept the concept of primary death instincts); but the process of development whereby this original aggression comes to be directed mainly against the libidinal ego through the agency of the anti-libidinal ego represents a very characteristic feature in the genesis of the hysterical state.

The pattern of circumstances which gives rise to such a development may be illustrated from the case of another hysterical patient, whom I shall call Olivia. This patient was sent to me primarily on account of anorexia nervosa. She could only eat the scantiest of meals, and when she went out anywhere she experienced intense nausea associated with a sensation of painful contraction in the epigastrium. Indeed, even the anticipation of going out was sufficient to precipitate these symptoms, which were always at their worst where social engagements were concerned. She was never actually sick, but was terrified of being so, and her special fear of being sick in public had given rise to a superadded phobia of going out. The pattern of circumstances which had led to these developments had its original source in infancy. Needless to say, she had no direct memory of the incidents in question, but they had become quite familiar to her as the result of conversation in the family circle. The position was that feeding difficulties developed at an early stage. Breast-feeding did not prove a success, and her mother found difficulty not only in inducing her to feed from a bottle in the first instance, but also in finding a suitable mixture for her once bottle-feeding had been established. As might be expected, she cried constantly, and since her crib was in her parents' bedroom, this disturbed her father, who, finally driven to desperation, adopted the expedient of holding her down until she stopped crying. His technique proved only too successful, for it initiated an internal process whereby she came to assume the role of, so to speak, holding herself down. In terms of the endopsychic situation which I have described, this internal process involved a relentless attack upon her libidinal ego by her anti-libidinal ego, identified as the latter was in the most intimate fashion with her father as a rejecting object, and the effects of this attack manifested themselves directly in the inhibition of her oral needs, with the result that she habitually refused food throughout her early childhood. Inhibition of need also came to be applied to other functions of her libidinal ego, for throughout her childhood she was both constipated and retentive of urine, and although as she grew up her constipation disappeared, her urinary retentiveness persisted, and she became sexually inhibited as well. The selective persistence of her urinary retentiveness was in no small measure bound up with the fact that her father reacted to it by constantly urging her to go to the lavatory to pass water, thus obviously playing the part of exciting object. By contrast, the management of her bowels remained in the hands of her mother, who, being less fussy and overprotective towards her than her father, constituted a less controversial figure for her. The fact that her father's fussiness and overprotectiveness extended to all spheres of her life still further complicated her relationship with him, for whilst, as we have seen, the resulting interference with her life on his part had its exciting side, it also constituted him a very frustrating and rejecting figure for her. Thus, in his anxiety to prevent her coming to harm, he was constantly imposing restrictions upon her spontaneous activities. For example, on the grounds that she was a girl, he discouraged her from engaging in many of the more adventurous activities which he permitted, and even encouraged, in the case of her brother, who was four years younger. This had the effect of intensifying an already existent jealousy of her brother and encouraging penis envy, and the guilt thereby engendered exacerbated the repression of her libidinal ego and left it all the more at the mercy of her persecuting anti-libidinal ego. Because she was a girl, her father also sought to protect her from sexual dangers by imposing considerable restrictions upon her freedom of movement and independence. In this respect, however, his efforts were not altogether successful, for she became the subject of several sexual traumata during childhood. Under the influence of guilt, these traumata led to further repression of her libidinal ego, especially where its genital component was concerned, and exposed it still further to persecution by her anti-libidinal ego. They also led to increased repression of the exciting object, and this was reflected in intense fear of, and hostility towards, men as sexual figures. The situation was further aggravated by the fact that the exciting effect of her father's solicitude was reinforced by his making her the constant object of provocative teasing. So far as the endopsychic situation was concerned, she was thus reduced to the state of helpless and hopeless immobility so well represented in Louise's dream of the two fathers. But whereas Louise was only partially immobilized in real life, Olivia had given up all effort and become almost completely passive by the time she came to me.

My account of Olivia's case, although of necessity very sketchy, should serve to illustrate the extent to which the development of hysterical symptoms depends upon the simultaneous experience of excitement, on the one hand, and frustration or rejection, on the other—all in the setting of object-relationships.[5] It also enables us to appreciate the pattern of circumstances which leads to the repressive splitting-off, first of the exciting and rejecting objects from the original internalized object, and second of the libidinal and anti-libidinal egos from the original ego. At the same time, it enables us to understand in some measure how the original ambivalence of the child towards an object who is both exciting and rejecting ultimately gives rise to an inner situation in which a repressed libidinal ego becomes the object of aggression on the part of a repressed anti-libidinal ego, and thus to that compulsive sacrifice of libidinal activity which is so characteristic of the hysteric.

In the case of Olivia it is obvious, in view of her infantile feeding difficulties, that her mother was the first object to combine in a big way the roles of exciting and rejecting object for her, and an infantile situation in which the mother plays both these roles would appear to provide the basic nucleus round which the hysterical personality is characteristically built. Hence the explanation of the fact that the libidinal ego of the hysteric is found to contain so powerful an oral component.[6]

---

5. I speak here of "frustration or rejection," but it is to be understood that, in terms of object relations psychology, frustration is always emotionally equivalent to rejection. It is only in terms of impulse psychology that frustration can have a meaning capable of differentiation from that of rejection, for if the child is essentially object-seeking, frustration is inevitably experienced as rejection on the part of the object. Further, since the child's primary objects are always personal, it follows that the child is inevitably animistic, and that the world of inner reality established during childhood is inevitably founded upon an animistic basis. This inherent animism of the human mind is, in my opinion, ineradicable, and remains unaffected by sophisticated conscious thinking. It would thus also appear to follow that solutions of deep-seated emotional conflicts can only be satisfactorily effected in animistic terms—a fact which, as it seems to me, has important implications for psychoanalytical therapy.

6. It was in the light of this fact that, on a previous occasion (Fairbairn 1952), I ventured to state (1) that "a sufficiently deep analysis of the Oedipus situation invariably reveals that this situation is built up around the figures of an internal exciting mother and an internal rejecting mother," and (2) that "I have yet to analyse the hysteric, male or female, who does not turn out to be an inveterate breast-seeker at heart" (p. 124).

Such a situation certainly arose in the infancy of Jean no less than in that of Olivia, for she likewise had been informed of early incidents arising out of an unsatisfactory relationship with her mother in the feeding situation, and it is significant in this respect that, later in her childhood, she was addicted both to stealing sweets and to stealing money to spend on sweets. As an infant, she reacted like Olivia in that she disturbed her parents by crying during the night, and, as in Olivia's case, it was her father who was moved to take repressive action. The action which he took was, however, quite different from that taken by Olivia's father, for instead of holding her down, he carried her to the drawing room in her crib and left her to cry there, out of earshot, until the morning. . . .

From my point of view, of course, the concept of the classical Oedipus conflict, couched as this is in terms of object relationships, provides a more acceptable type of explanation for the origin of hysterical states than the concept of a fixation at the earlier genital phase, but, from a comparatively early stage in the history of psychoanalysis, it has been customary to regard the emergence of such a phase as a precondition of the emergence of the classical Oedipus conflict, and thus to subordinate this latter concept to the requirements of the phase theory. However, this view has proved increasingly difficult to maintain in the light of more recent researches. Such researches, and conspicuously those of Melanie Klein, have drawn attention to the extent to which all psychopathological conditions are determined by conflicts arising long before the putative earlier genital phase develops, and even in infancy (Gitelson 1952, Heimann 1952, Lampl-de Groot 1952, van der Sterren 1952), and that the hysterical state proves no exception to this rule is borne out by the data which I have already provided from the cases of Jean and Olivia. The attempt of Melanie Klein and her school to meet the resultant difficulty assumes the general form of antedating the emergence of the Oedipus conflict; but there are other psychoanalysts who prefer to stress the determining importance of pre-Oedipal conflicts, e.g., Lampl-de Groot (1952). My own views on this particular subject, although independent, are perhaps more in line with the solution offered by the latter group, for in a paper written in 1944 I attempted to show that the Oedipus situation is not so much a causal phenomenon as an end product, and represents not so much an explanatory concept as a phenomenon to be explained—i.e., a derivative phenomenon. I also attempted to establish that the Oedipus situation is one which has its roots in the vicissitudes of infantile dependence.[7] In this connexion it is relevant to point out that, whereas Freud's description of the psyche as constituted by id, ego, and superego was framed in terms of the Oedipus conflict, my own concept of the basic endopsychic situation is framed in terms of the original relationship of the child to his mother and the ambivalence which develops out of it. Thus, in my view, the triangular situation which provides the original conflict of the child is not one constituted by three persons (the child, his mother, and his father), but one constituted essentially by the central ego, the exciting object, and the rejecting object. Also, as I have attempted to show, it is in the setting of the child's relationship to his mother that the differentiation of endopsychic structure is accomplished and repression originated, and it is only after these developments have already occurred that the child is called upon to meet the particular difficulties which attend the classical Oedipus situation. Regarded from this point of view, the Oedipus situation is one which develops in circumstances in which the child identifies one parent (usually of opposite sex) predominantly with the exciting object, and the other parent (usually of similar sex) predominantly with the rejecting object. This pattern of identification is, however, very far from being inevitable. Thus, although there was some evidence of the classical Oedipus situation in the case of Olivia, the rejecting, no less than the exciting, object was predominantly identified with her father—a fact which, incidentally, gave rise to an exceptionally stubborn resistance in the transference situation. Similarly in the case of Morris, for although a classical Oedipus situation manifested itself in the earlier stages of his analysis, the more basic situation which was later revealed was one in which both the exciting and the rejecting objects were constituted by his mother.

In the final section of the present study I propose to discuss some aspects of the characteristic hysterical process of conversion. Hysterical conversion is, of course, a defensive technique—one designed to prevent

---

7. It is a remarkable fact that psychoanalytical interest in the classical story of Oedipus should have been concentrated so preponderantly upon the final stages of the drama, and that the earliest stage should have been so largely ignored, for it seems to me a fundamental principle of psychological, no less than of literary, interpretation that a drama should be considered as a unity deriving its significance as much from the first act as from the last. In the light of this principle, it becomes important to recognize that the same Oedipus who eventually killed his father and married his mother began life by being exposed upon a mountain, and thus being deprived of maternal care in all its aspects at a stage at which his mother constituted his exclusive object.

the conscious emergence of emotional conflicts involving object relationships. Its essential and distinctive feature is the *substitution of a bodily state for a personal problem,* and this substitution enables the personal problem as such to be ignored. All personal problems are basically problems involving personal relationships with significant objects, and the objects involved in the conflicts of the hysteric are essentially *internal objects*—and more specifically the exciting and frustrating objects, albeit the ideal object also comes into the picture. The endopsychic situation in question involves ego structures, of course, no less than internal objects, but so long as successful repression can be maintained, there is no occasion for resort to the defence of hysterical conversion. This defence is only mobilized in circumstances in which repression can no longer be successfully maintained and phenomena of transference (understood in the broadest sense of the term) threaten to objectify the repressed situation in the individual's ordinary life. The deeper the exploration of the circumstances in which hysterical conversion occurs, the clearer is the evidence that this defence is a reaction to specific outer situations which are essentially traumatic to the individual concerned, and which favour a revival and reactivation of repressed situations in the inner world. Thus the psychosomatic symptoms from which Louise at one time suffered were a reaction to circumstances in her marriage favouring a revival of the inner situation depicted in her dream of the two fathers. Similarly, Olivia's anorexia and all the symptoms which accompanied it were a reaction to her return home at the age of 18 after several years' absence at a boarding school abroad—the effect of her return being to reactivate the original situation with her father which had been internalized and repressed at an early age. During the course of analysis this situation became closely bound up with her relationship to me at the instance of transference, and the variations which occurred in the severity of her symptoms could then be seen to be related to the vicissitudes of the analytical situation.

In the case of Olivia the gastric localization of her conversion symptoms was, of course, related to the fact that the original traumatic situation involving her father (viz. that in which he held her down in her crib until she stopped crying) was one involving the presence of intense oral need; but it is interesting to note that what actually precipitated the onset of her anorexia after her return home from school was a gastrointestinal infection such that her conversion symptoms presented the superficial appearance of sequelae of the infection itself. Her case thus serves to draw attention to the part often played by precipitating factors in determining the particular bodily localization of conversion symptoms. In the case of Jean, the complex of precipitating events was more general in character, comprising as it did in large measure the responsibilities of married life (for which she was ill-prepared), the deaths of both her parents, disagreements between her husband and her brother, the ill-health of her only child, and the compulsions of life during the Second World War. It is perhaps no coincidence, therefore, that her conversion symptoms assumed a form characterized by the absence of any narrowly focused bodily localization, for she was racked from head to toe by pains and other distressing sensations which she described in terms of pulling, tearing, twisting, squeezing, hammering, and the like. Incidentally, these various physical torments provide a good illustration of the effects of internally directed aggression, but it is on account of their generalized distribution throughout Jean's body that I cite them here. I should add that Jean also suffered from a psychosomatic disturbance in the form of psoriasis; but the affected areas of skin were so scattered that even this condition conformed to the pattern of a generalized distribution. It is commoner, however, for conversion symptoms to assume a more localized form. Frequently, as in the case of Olivia's anorexia, the precipitating circumstances involved a bodily organ, or bodily system, which was deeply involved in the original traumatic situation, but this is very far from being invariably the case. . . .

In general it would appear that, when the object relationships of the child are unsatisfactory, libidinal charges become, so to speak, dammed up in the organic systems which provide, in varying measure, available channels for libidinal expression, and indeed the same may be said of aggressive charges also. When this happens, the organic systems in question themselves assume the functional significance of objects, and thus become themselves libidinally cathected, and such a process would appear to be involved in the establishment of isolated erotogenic zones. In infancy the appetitive system which extends from the mouth to the stomach provides a natural focus for the operation of this process—as do the genital organs likewise at a later stage. These two systems represent, of course, instinctively determined channels for object seeking, but the same can hardly be said of the defecatory and urinary systems. At the same time, these latter systems are of such a nature as to readily acquire the function of channels of libidinal and aggressive expression, particularly in view of the extent to which parental figures participate in, supervise, and attempt to control the child's excretory activities. The vicissitudes of childhood thus provide conditions calculated to encourage the conversion of the defecatory and urinary systems into isolated erotogenic zones in the manner already indicated. At the same time, it must be recognized that, under appropriate conditions, any part of the body whatsoever may become the focus of the conversion process, and so become constituted into an erotogenic zone in which the dramas of disturbed personal relationships are localized. The factors which chiefly determine the choice of an apparently arbitrary part of the body as a focus for the conversion process would appear to be (1) traumatic experiences involving or having relevance to the part of the body concerned, (2) considerations of symbolization, and (3) motives for deflecting or displacing the incidence of the conversion process from one part of the body to another with a view to preserving or restoring the functions of the former.

The classic theory of erotogenic zones is, of course, bound up with the view that the original libidinal orientation of the child is inherently autoerotic, and that an alloerotic or object-seeking orientation is only acquired at a later stage in the process of development. The object relations psychology which I have come to adopt is, of course, in complete contradiction of this view, but I have tried to show how the concept of erotogenic zones may be assimilated into the system of object relations psychology in terms of the process of hysterical conversion.

As regards the nature of hysterical states in general, I am only too well aware of the limited nature of the present study. In this study, however, I have attempted to show how the special problems presented by hysterical states may be approached from the standpoint of the psychology of object relations and dynamic structure, and I have tried to indicate, in terms of this standpoint, some of the basic processes which appear to be involved in the development of hysterical symptoms.

REFERENCES

Fairbairn, W. R. D. (1944). Endopsychic structure considered in terms of object-relationships. *International Journal of Psycho-Analysis* 27(1,2):70–93.

——(1952). *Psychoanalytic Studies of the Personality.* London: Tavistock, with Routledge and Kegan Paul.

Freud, S. (1923). The ego and the id. *Standard Edition* 19:3–66.

——(1924). On the psychical mechanism of hysterical phenomena (1893). In *Collected Papers*, vol. 1. London: Hogarth.

Gitelson, M. (1952). Re-evaluation of the role of the Oedipus complex. *International Journal of Psycho-Analysis* 33:351–354.
Heimann, P. (1952). A contribution to the re-evaluation of the Oedipus complex – the early stages. *International Journal of Psycho-Analysis* 33:84–92.
Lampl-de Groot, J. (1952). Re-evaluation of the role of the Oedipus complex. *International Journal of Psycho-Analysis* 33:335–342.
van der Sterren, J. A. (1952). The "King Oedipus" of Sophocles. *International Journal of Psycho-Analysis* 33:343–350.

9

"The Nature and Aims of Psychoanalytic Treatment" (1958)

This classic paper is Fairbairn's statement on the therapeutic action of analysis, written in response to a paper by Thomas Szasz (1957) suggesting that analysis was more a form of scientific education than a form of treatment. Fairbairn thought that the curative agency in analytic treatment is the relationship between therapist and patient, and the force it exerts for synthesis of splits and for integration in personality. He was later followed in this view by Guntrip, Sutherland, and Winnicott.

It may seem strange that hitherto I have made only the scantiest reference in print to the implications of my theoretical formulations for the practice of psychoanalytical treatment. From this fact it might be inferred that, even in my own opinion, my views are of merely theoretical interest and their implementation in practice would leave the technique of psychoanalysis unaffected. Such an inference would be quite unwarranted—the fact being that the practical implications of my views have seemed so far-reaching that they could only be put to the test gradually and with the greatest circumspection if premature or rash psychotherapeutic conclusions were to be avoided. . . .

In terms of the object relations theory of the personality, the disabilities from which the patient suffers represent the effects of unsatisfactory and unsatisfying object relationships experienced in early life and perpetuated in an exaggerated form in inner reality; and, if this view is correct, the actual relationship existing between the patient and the analyst as persons must be regarded as in itself constituting a therapeutic factor of prime importance. The existence of such a personal relationship in outer reality not only serves the function of providing a means of correcting the distorted relationships which prevail in inner reality and influence the reactions of the patient to outer objects, but provides the patient with an opportunity, denied to him in childhood, to undergo a process of emotional development in the setting of an actual relationship with a reliable and beneficent parental figure. Theoretical recognition of the therapeutic importance of the actual relationship between patient and analyst is, of course, difficult to reconcile with a psychology conceived predominantly in terms of "impulse," as is the psychology represented by Freud's libido theory and his theory of instincts. It is quite compatible, however, with a psychology conceived in terms of object relations and dynamic structure, and, in my opinion, such a psychology not only promotes therapeutic aims more effectively than the predominantly impulse psychology formulated by Freud, but actually corresponds more closely to the psychological facts and possesses a greater explanatory value from a purely scientific standpoint. . . .

It must be remembered that, even within the field of pure science, the results obtained are partly conditioned by the method employed to obtain them, and therapeutic results are even more dependent upon the method used and may be limited by the limitations of the method. From this point of view, the validity of the various restrictions of the psychoanalytical technique becomes a matter for consideration. Thus I have come to entertain doubts regarding the validity of the requirement that the patient shall lie on a couch with the analyst out of view. This requirement seems to me partly a fortuitous inheritance from the hypnotic technique employed initially by Freud and partly a consequence of Freud's personal dislike of being looked at by patients all day long, and it becomes a question how far the stock arguments brought forward in favor of the couch technique are not largely rationalizations. Personally I have now abandoned the couch technique in the case of all comparatively recent patients—to great advantage in my opinion. This departure from the classic method on my part represents an attempt to put into practice the logical implications of the object relations theory. It may be added, however, that I do not favour the technique of the face-to-face interview advocated by such psychotherapists as H. S. Sullivan. In actual practice I sit at a desk, and the patient sits in a comfortable chair placed to the side of the desk, almost parallel to mine, but slightly inclined towards me. In terms of this arrangement, patient and analyst are not ordinarily looking at one another, but either may look at the other, if he so wishes. Thus the setting of an object relationship is maintained without undue embarrassment to either party. In this connexion it seems to me a question whether Freud's emphasis on the need to protect the patient from the influence of the analyst's personality is not largely a rationalization covering a need on the part of the analyst to be protected from the demands of the patient. However this may be, my personal experience is that the demands of the patient are actually less exacting when he is *not* isolated from the analyst on the couch and thus deprived of any semblance of a real relationship with him. It may be added that the traditional detachment of the analyst (which must be carefully distinguished from the necessary requirement of objectivity of interpretation) has obviously a very high defensive value for the analyst himself. So have such common features of psychoanalytical practice as the adoption of a standardized length of session irrespective of such considerations as the tempo of the patient and the situation prevailing when the session is due to terminate according to the clock. It would thus appear to be an obligation on the part of the analyst to ask himself how far such features of psychoanalytical technique are dictated by his own interests rather than by those of his patients, and, if so, to adjust his technique accordingly (as I myself have felt compelled to do). It would appear to be an elementary requirement that in a therapeutic situation the restrictions of the therapeutic method employed should be imposed primarily in the interests of the patient. This does not mean, however, that the interests of the analyst should be ignored. Indeed, the greater the importance attached to the actual relationship existing between the patient and the analyst as person, the greater the justification for recognizing the personal interests of both parties to the relationship. At the same time, if it is felt necessary to impose restrictions in the interests of the analyst, this fact should be explicitly acknowledged.

In general, I cannot help feeling that any tendency to adhere with pronounced rigidity to the details of the classic psychoanalytical technique as standardized by Freud more than half a century ago, is liable to defensive exploitation, however unconscious this may be, in the interests of the analyst and at the expense of the patient, and certainly any tendency to treat the classic technique as sacrosanct raises the suspicion that an element of such a defensive exploitation is at work. Further, it seems to me that a complete stultification of the therapeutic aim is involved in any demand, whether explicit or implicit, that the patient must conform to the nature of the therapeutic method rather than that the method must conform to the requirements of the patient. Such a demand would merely serve to lend substance to the old joke, "The operation was successful, but the patient died," and to illustrate the outlook of the French general who remarked at Balaclava, "C'est magnifique, mais ce n'est pas la guerre." It is certainly in complete conformity with these instances when the attitude is adopted that, if an analysed patient does not "get better," it is necessarily because he is unsuitable for psychoanalytical treatment, and that, if a patient "gets better" by means of some nonanalytical form of psychotherapy, it is all very well, but it is not psychoanalysis. Such purism resolves itself simply into an apotheosis of the method at the expense of the aims which the method is intended to serve.

In recent years, under the influence of an outlook based on the object relations theory, I have shed enough sophistication to enable me to ask myself repeatedly such naïve questions as, "If the patient does not make satisfactory progress under analysis, how far is this due to some defect in the psychoanalytical method?" This is a question to which there can be no adequate answer in the absence of prolonged investigation, but it seems to me beyond question that the couch technique has the effect of imposing quite arbitrarily upon the patient a positively traumatic situation calculated inevitably to reproduce such traumatic situations of childhood as that imposed upon the infant who is left to cry in his pram alone, or that imposed upon the child who finds himself isolated in his cot during the primal scene. If this view is correct, then it follows that the couch technique is very far from being as "natural" as it is supposed to be, and that the analyst, in employing this technique, is equally far from being "neutral." It also follows that the data provided by the patient who finds himself isolated upon the couch must be significantly influenced by the trauma thus arbitrarily imposed, and it is difficult to believe that the therapeutic result is not similarly influenced.

Amongst other naïve questions which I have felt constrained to ask myself are, "How does psychoanalysis work?" and "What is the analyst really trying to do in analysing a patient?" . . . In my own opinion, the really decisive factor is the relationship of the patient to the analyst. . . . In the absence of a therapeutic relationship with the analyst [other factors] simply do not occur. This opinion is, of course, in conformity with the object relations theory of the personality which

I have come to adopt. It should be added that what I understand by the "relationship between the patient and the analyst" is not just the relationship involved in the transference, but the total relationship existing between the patient and the analyst as persons. After all, it is on the basis of the relationships existing between the individual and his parents in childhood that his personality develops and assumes its particular form,. and it seems logical to infer that any subsequent change in his personality that may be effected by psychoanalytical treatment (or any other form of psychotherapy) must be effected primarily on the basis of a personal relationship. . . .

I consider that the term *analysis* as a description of psychoanalytical treatment is really a misnomer, and that *the chief aim of psychoanalytical treatment is to promote a maximum "synthesis" of the structures into which the original ego has been split, in the setting of a therapeutic relationship with the analyst.* Involved in the achievement of this aim are two further aims, viz. (a) a maximum reduction of persisting infantile dependence, and (b) a maximum reduction of that hatred of the libidinal object which, according to my theory, is ultimately responsible for the original splitting of the ego. Such aims, together with an aim to be mentioned, are, in my opinion, the chief aims of psychoanalytical treatment. The resistance on the part of the patient to the achievement of these aims is, of course, colossal, for he has a vested interest in maintaining the early split of his internalized object, upon which, according to my theory, the split of his ego depends, and which represents a defence against the dilemma of ambivalence. In addition, he has a vested interest in keeping his aggression internalized for the protection of his external libidinal object—with the result that his libidinal cathexis is correspondingly internalized. Implied in these various manifestations of resistance on the part of the patient is a further defensive aim which I have now come to regard as *the greatest of all sources of resistance—viz. the maintenance of the patient's internal world as a closed system.* In terms of the theory of the mental constitution which I have proposed, the maintenance of such a closed system involves the perpetuation of the relationships prevailing between the various ego structures and their respective internal objects, as well as between one another, and since the nature of these relationships is the ultimate source of both symptoms and deviations of character, *it becomes still another aim of psychoanalytical treatment to effect breaches of the closed system which constitutes the patient's inner world, and thus to make this world accessible to the influence of outer reality.*

The unconscious determination of the patient to preserve his inner world as a closed system at all costs would appear to be the phenomenon on the basis of which Freud was led to formulate the concept of the *pleasure principle* as the primary determinant of behavior. In my opinion, this formulation is a mistaken generalization from what is essentially a defensive phenomenon—one so highly defensive that it cannot be regarded as representing a primary principle of behavior. There can be no doubt, as it seems to me, (a) that the pleasure principle can only operate within a closed system, (b) that the maintenance of inner reality as a closed system is essentially a psychopathological phenomenon, and (c) that, insofar as inner reality is maintained as a closed system, behavior will be determined almost inevitably by the pleasure principle. Thus a patient of mine, whom I have described as "Gertrude" on a previous occasion (Fairbairn 1954) and in whose case the maintenance of inner reality as a closed system has declared itself in no uncertain terms, can only bring herself to have intercourse with her husband if she immerses herself in fantasies which patently represent an infantile sexual relationship with her father as an internal object, and becomes oblivious to the actual situation prevailing in outer reality. Such satisfaction as she obtains in intercourse is thus dependent upon relief of tension achieved exclusively within the confines of the inner world, i.e., within a closed system, and on the basis of the pleasure principle. If, by contrast, she were capable of having a genuine sexual relationship with her husband, her behavior would have the characteristics of behavior in a situation in outer reality, viz. in the setting of an open system, and would be determined by what Freud has described as the *reality principle.* Thus the distinction between the pleasure principle and the reality principle is not properly a distinction between a primary and a secondary principle of behavior, but represents a distinction between behavior originating within a closed system constituted by internal reality and behavior in an open system in which inner and outer reality are brought into relation.

It is to be noted that the phenomenon of transference constitutes another manifestation of behavior originating within a closed system. A real relationship with an external object is a relationship in an open system, but insofar as the inner world assumes the form of a closed system, a relationship with an external object is only possible in terms of transference, viz. on condition that the external object is treated as an object within the closed system of inner reality.[1]

The psychotherapeutic implication of these considerations is that the interpretation of transference phenomena in the setting of the analytical situation is not in itself enough to promote a satisfactory change in the patient. For such a change to accrue, it is necessary for the patient's relationship with the analyst to undergo a process of development in terms of which a relationship based on transference becomes replaced by a realistic relationship between two persons in the outer world. Such a process of development represents the disruption of the closed system within which the patient's symptoms have developed and are maintained, and which compromises his relationships with external objects. It also represents the establishment of an open system in which the distortions of inner reality can be corrected by outer reality and true relationships with external objects can occur. A movement in the direction of the substitution of an open for a closed system, or at any rate evidence of a breach in the closed system of internal reality, would appear to have been registered recently in the dreams of a recalcitrant patient of long standing, whom I shall call Karl. The dreams in question were as follows:

> 1. I was out walking with my father; and we met you. You handed me a book or paper. My father protested that I was neglecting or forsaking him, *but I did acknowledge you.*
>
> 2. I was talking to you, but at the same time I was in bed with my mother. I felt embarrassed, because my mother was listening to what I was saying to you. Sometimes my mother leaned over me and came in contact with me. This horrified me and made me shrink away from her. *But I did not stop talking to you.*

These dreams seem to me to be not so much transference dreams as dreams representing the impact of a realistic relationship with the analyst in the outer world upon Karl's relationships with the figures of his parents in the inner world, and thus indicating a breach in the closed system of inner reality. It is interesting to note that, more or less contem-

1. I take this opportunity to record my conception of the essential difference between a psychoneurosis and a psychosis. The distinction in question has been the subject of much debate, but in my opinion it is quite simple, viz. to the effect that, whereas the psychoneurotic tends to treat situations in outer reality as if they were situations in inner reality (i.e., in terms of transference), the psychotic tends to treat situations in inner reality as if they were situations in outer reality.

poraneously with these dreams, there occurred a dream in which Karl was exposing his erect penis to his mother. The interest of this dream lies in the fact, to which Karl himself drew attention, that in the past he had always sought "on principle" to deny having a penis where his mother was concerned. It would thus appear that the breach in the closed system of inner reality represented in the other dreams had had the effect of releasing repressed material. However, there were also contemporary dreams revealing a movement in the direction of restoring the closed system, e.g., the following:

> 1. I was with you, and while I was talking to you, I felt a compulsive urge to masturbate. I wondered if you would notice me doing this while I kept up the flow of talk. Then I found that you were in fact *in an adjoining room,* and I felt that I could probably masturbate without your noticing.
>
> 2. *I left here and walked away. My mother was walking several yards ahead of me.* I don't know if I thought she was leaving me behind, but *I thought I might attract her attention* by throwing gravel at her. Then I found that I was terribly worked up and was pelting her with stones.

These dreams, in contrast to those first quoted, appear to reflect a movement in the direction of maintaining relationships with objects in the inner world at the expense of a realistic and therapeutic relationship with the analyst, viz. a movement having the aim of preserving internal reality as a closed system. Such an aim on the patient's part seems to me to constitute the most formidable resistance encountered in psychoanalytical treatment, and it is difficult to see how it can be overcome except on the basis of a true relationship between patient and analyst as persons in outer reality. It must be recognized, of course, that it is always possible for the psychotherapist to exploit the patient's closed system for a therapeutic purpose, but such a procedure is essentially foreign to the principles of psychoanalytical treatment, although it may be suspected that a good deal of so-called sublimation is effected upon this basis.

Allied to the concept of the closed system of inner reality is another concept which I have recently come to adopt, viz. that of the *static internal situation.* The descriptive epithet "static," as applied to the situations in question, was suggested to me by the remark of a patient whom I shall call Ian. This patient in the course of his associations had frequently described a frustrating and rage-provoking type of situation about which he would say, "This is an impossible situation," adding characteristically, "And there is nothing to be done about it." For some time I construed this last remark in the sense that he felt the situation in question to be outside the influence of psychoanalytical therapy, but eventually I came to realize that when he said that there was nothing to be done about a situation, he was not talking about the therapeutic prospects, but describing a feature of the situation itself as he experienced it. These "impossible" situations, whether remembered or imagined, were characteristically conflictful situations involving himself and one or other or both of his parents. Such a situation he described one day in the following terms:

> I'm enraged with Daddy, because he gets Mummy and I don't. I try to be good—and he doesn't. I castrate myself to be good, but Daddy just despises me . . . He's privileged, although he is not good. I try to be good, and I'm not privileged. If I'm not good, I'm blamed and attacked, and if I'm good, I'm despised. I'm enraged about being despised, but I'm afraid of being blamed. The only hope is to be right, but with Daddy and Mummy . . . I'm compelled to be wrong . . . I don't know how to get away from this blame . . . Being blamed is death . . . There is nothing I can do if I'm rejected . . . This situation of being blamed and rejected by Mummy, and being enraged and unable to do anything about it is completely static.

It was this last remark of Ian's that suggested the employment of the term *static internal situation* to describe self-contained situations in inner reality, which persist unchanged indefinitely, and which are precluded from change by their very nature so long as they remain self-contained. "Frozen dramas" was the more colloquial description applied to such situations by the patient Karl, after I had had occasion to draw his attention to them. But let us allow Ian to continue his account of the static internal situation which he was describing:

> My dependence on my mother is so great, and she is so privileged in my eyes that it makes my rage more acute and more forbidden. Mummy is someone I cannot attack . . . My position with her is so precarious that I daren't risk upsetting the balance. I must try to placate her. I must not upset the status quo, the equilibrium of the moment . . . There is no possibility of my releasing that rage. She possesses me. I need her. She has me imprisoned. I can't release this rage until I've got away from this gaol.

It would be a mistake, however, to infer that it is necessarily one of the functions of the static internal situation to preserve the internal object from attack or destruction. Indeed, there are cases in which it would appear that one of the functions which it performs is rather to perpetuate the destruction of the internal object. Such a case is that of a female patient whom I shall call Annabel, and who was driven to seek analysis owing to the limitations imposed upon her by a phobia of coming across accidents on the road, particularly while driving her car in the course of her professional activities. The analytical material which she provided left it open to no doubt that the injured body which she was so afraid of coming across represented the corpse of her father as an internalized sexual object, and the maintenance of a static internal situation in which he figured as a corpse undoubtedly functioned for her as a defence against a situation of incestuous rape. Her phobia was, of course, itself a defence against the defensive murder implied in the static internal situation, and it thus conformed to the phobic pattern of a defence against a defence. There is considerable evidence, in my opinion, to the effect that the persistence of a static internal situation in which the incestuous object is reduced to the status of a corpse is a characteristic feature of the phobic state. . . .

I have already recorded my opinion that Freud's concept of the pleasure principle as a primary determinant of human behavior was a mistaken generalization about behavior on the basis of what is essentially a psychopathological phenomenon—this phenomenon being the obstinate tendency of patients undergoing psychoanalytical treatment to maintain their inner worlds as closed systems, and to resist every attempt to convert these systems into open systems and so render them amenable to change through the impact of influences in outer reality. Another concept of Freud's which I have come to regard as a similarly mistaken generalization about behavior on the basis of an essentially psychopathological phenomenon is his concept of the *death instinct.* In this case the particular phenomenon in question is an obstinate tendency on the part of the patient undergoing psychoanalytical treatment to keep his aggression localized within the confines of the closed system of the inner world. The operation of such a particular tendency, as well as of the general tendency to maintain the inner world as a closed system, is well illustrated in the case of a patient whom I have previously designated "Ivy" (Fairbairn 1954), and who, in a sequence of sessions, provided associative material of which the nature may be gathered from the quotations which follow. It should be added that the insights registered in this material were only achieved after prolonged and painstaking analysis.

> I have no words to describe how I hate you. But why can't I just hate you and get on with it? The only reason I can think of is that I need my hate for

some other purpose. It's too precious to waste on you. It is vital to my internal economy not to waste hate on you. I feel I need the hate for myself. I need the hate to run myself on . . .

My aim is to sail as near the wind as I can to killing myself. My aim is to carry out Mother's and Father's wishes . . . I do it partly to please them, and partly to annoy them. I'm going as near the wind as I dare to killing myself. I don't confine it to sexual things . . . I extend it to my whole life . . . I feel my life is interfering with my neurosis, instead of vice versa . . . My ordinary life is an interference with my neurosis . . . I feel my unconscious life is my true life, and it is a life of frustrated excitement, which I seem to regard as bliss. I feel I really have a strong urge to destroy myself . . . I want to see how near I can get to the edge of the cliff. There is a bit of me that keeps me alive, but my real purpose is directed to killing myself and frustration. I have trouble over you, for I don't want to tell you things. *If I have a relationship with you, it interferes with my death-circuit* . . . You interfere with my neurosis and my desire to destroy myself . . . Originally I was frustrated from outside; but now I impose frustration on myself, and that is to be my satisfaction . . . It is a terrible perversion.

The associative material contained in these quotations seems to me to provide convincing evidence in support of my opinion that what Freud described as the death instinct is really a psychopathological phenomenon representing an obstinate tendency on the part of the individual to keep his aggression localized within the confines of the inner world as a closed system. It also seems to me to provide convincing evidence of (a) an obstinate tendency on the part of the individual to keep his libido similarly confined, (b) a general tendency to maintain the inner world as a closed system at all costs, and (c) the central role played by this general tendency in the maintenance of psychopathological states and the resistance of the patient to psychoanalytical therapy. It suggests further that what drives the individual to seek such satisfaction as can be obtained within the closed system of internal reality is early experience such as to induce a sense of hopelessness over the possibility of obtaining satisfaction in relationships with the external objects upon whom he is dependent. In addition it reveals the central importance of the relationship between patient and analyst as a means of effecting a breach in the closed system of internal reality in which the patient's symptoms are entrenched. In the light of such evidence it would appear that, however neutral a role the psychoanalyst may assign to himself therapeutically, he cannot escape from the necessity of becoming an interventionist if he is to be therapeutically effective—and it must be recognized that every interpretation is really an intervention. Thus, in a sense, *psychoanalytical treatment resolves itself into a struggle on the part of the patient to press-gang his relationship with the analyst into the closed system of the inner world through the agency of transference, and a determination on the part of the analyst to effect a breach in this closed system and to provide conditions under which, in the setting of a therapeutic relationship, the patient may be induced to accept the open system of outer reality.* Whether such an aim on the part of the analyst is capable of fulfilment must, of course, depend in no small measure upon the extent to which internal reality has become entrenched as a closed system in the individual case, and an assessment of the extent to which this is so must be regarded as the real criterion of the suitability of a case for psychoanalytical treatment. In any event, however, it would appear that, if the foregoing considerations are well founded, the actual relationship between the patient and the analyst constitutes the decisive factor in psychoanalytical, no less than in any other form of psychotherapeutic, cure—even if in the case of psychoanalytical therapy it operates in a distinctive manner, as indeed it unquestionably does.

REFERENCES

Fairbairn, W. R. D. (1954). Observations on the nature of hysterical states. *British Journal of Medical Psychology* 27(3):106–125.

Szasz, T. (1957). On the theory of psycho-analytic treatment. *International Journal of Psycho-Analysis* 38:166–182.

IV

MELANIE KLEIN

10

"The Psychoanalytic Play Technique: Its History and Significance" (1955)

This paper was written late in Klein's career. It is a good place to begin with her ideas for several reasons. In her later years, her writing became more organized and easier to understand, less compromised by the difficult language of early psychoanalytic theory. It is interesting to follow the course of Klein's writing: While her earliest clinical material was easy to follow, the theoretical papers in which she was breaking new ground became difficult. Then, as she solidified her ideas, the writing clarified again. This sequence of alternating clarity and cloudiness in her writing is often confusing to the reader coming to her ideas for the first time.

This essay comes from the later writing for a more general audience, where her style is, once again, clear and direct. In it, she reviews her innovative play technique with its access to the psychology of the young child, and describes why this experience was central to all of her work. In reviewing play, she also mentions most of the ideas that became tenets of her contribution over the span of her long career between the early 1920s and her death in 1963.

The paper begins with her discovery of the access play gave her to children's concerns, especially those of their parents' life and relationship, along with children's sadism and aggression and the consequences in their relationship with parents and analyst through transference. From the beginning Klein thought that interpreting the transference relationship was crucial to obtaining the child's trust and understanding. Klein next reviews the early discoveries of the child's concerns with the parents' relationship and bodies, the examination of these in the treatment, and the importance of early symbol formation—by which she means the process through which these early concerns are progressively distanced from an unconscious literal preoccupation with primitive drives, affects, and relationships, and are progressively understood through the expression of them with toys and language, which stand for these processes and anxieties but are not the literal equivalent of them. Symbolizing frees the child to carry out mental manipulation of the concepts which she called *unconscious phantasies,* rather than having to treat fears and concerns as literal dangers.

In her discourse, we can see Klein's use of bodily processes and relations as a model for mental process that she had taken from Ferenczi. She sees children as preoccupied with their own bodily processes, which they then attribute to their parents through projection and introjection. It is of great interest to compare this way of understanding mental development with Winnicott's concept of the *psychosomatic partnership,* which we shall meet later, an idea that the baby and mother have at first a somatic, bodily partnership out of which their psychological partnership is born and through which the baby's mental processes are organized. The child understands the parents' physical and emotional relationship to be similarly intertwined because it attributes its own method of understanding to them. Winnicott's contribution clarifies why the baby is concerned with the consequences of its relationship to the mother in terms of her responsiveness to the child's bodily needs. He thought the actual psychosomatic partnership is the organizing center of the baby's growing psyche from the beginning. With this perspective, it is easier to see why the growing child would think of relationships in terms of bodily interactions beyond projection and introjection in phantasy, and to understand more clearly aspects beyond Klein's emphasis on the young child's preoccupation with its body and the body parts of its parents.

We might also keep in mind that Fairbairn described Freud's schema of psychosexual development in bodily terms as an example of a conversion phenomenon in the form of theory—that is, a substitution of bodily processes for emotional issues. Remembering this point lets us see the way that Klein's explorations provide specific language and examples of the way the young child deals with a human inborn tendency to conversion, of the lifelong interconvertability of bodily and emotional processes.

There are a number of other concepts introduced in this essay that we will encounter again. Klein describes the importance of the interactive processes of projection and introjection in the growth of mental organization, with a greater emphasis on the introjective side of this continuous feedback loop than has been commonly understood to operate both in development and in therapy. The emphasis in her model before her description of the depressive position was on the projection of aggressive and sadistic impulses, which she believed to originate in the child under the influence of the death instinct, and the consequences of this predominant projection for the child's developing psychology. Once she described the depressive position, she added the projection and introjection of love and the experience of gratitude as comparable processes emanating from the life instinct. In her description of projective processes, Klein teaches us much about the child's role in determining the nature of relationships. The active nature of the child's mind in organizing its own experience was less emphasized in Fairbairn's description, which did give credit to the organizing activity of the child's concerns, but which focused more actively on the introjection of actual experience with the mother as handled by the inherent splitting and repression of the psyche. Winnicott's emphasis too was on the effect of the external object relationship on the child's growth. So it is from Klein that we have learned the most about the child's role in building its own internal world and influencing relationships. It is only the later theorists who have emphasized the exquisite balance of factors in which it is *both* the parent and the infant who contribute to the growth of the infant and child's psyche (see Stephen A. Mitchell's excerpt in Chapter 55).

Chapter 10 gives extensive attention to the inhibition of the ability to play as a sign of illness. It illustrates Klein's treatment approach, and it resonates with Winnicott's later emphasis on the capacity to play as a sign of mental health and of the child's creative potential for growth. This chapter also gives a summary of Klein's concepts of the paranoid-schizoid and depressive positions—the bulwark of her developmental schema. Here she emphasized the reparative aspect of the depressive position. She was unique in the early analytic world in emphasizing the loving, growth-promoting side of development. She was later followed in this emphasis by Winnicott, and more recently in Bollas's (1992) concept of psychic genera—those relational nuclei that form the heart of growth and psychic healing (excerpted in Chapter 56).

My work with both children and adults, and my contributions to psychoanalytic theory as a whole, derive ultimately from the play technique evolved with young children. I do not mean by this that my later work was a direct application of the play technique; but the insight I gained into early development, into unconscious processes, and into the nature of the interpretations by which the unconscious can be approached, has been of far-reaching influence on the work I have done with older children and adults. . . .

My first patient was a 5-year-old boy. I referred to him under the name "Fritz" in my earliest published papers (Klein 1923, 1924, 1926).[1] To begin with I thought it would be sufficient to influence the mother's attitude. I suggested that she should encourage the child to discuss freely with her the many unspoken questions which were obviously at the back of his mind and were impeding his intellectual development. This had a good effect, but his neurotic difficulties were not sufficiently alleviated and it was soon decided that I should psychoanalyse him. In doing so, I deviated from some of the rules so far established, for I interpreted what I thought to be most urgent in the material the child presented to me and found my interest focusing on his anxieties and the defences against them. This new approach soon confronted me with serious problems. The anxieties I encountered when analysing this first case were very acute, and although I was strengthened in the belief that I was working on the right lines by observing the alleviation of anxiety again and again produced by my interpretations, I was at times perturbed by the intensity of the fresh anxieties which were being brought into the open. On one such occasion I sought advice from Dr. Karl Abraham. He replied that since my interpretations up to then had often produced relief and the analysis was obviously progressing, he saw no ground for changing the method of approach. I felt encouraged by his support and, as it happened, in the next few days the child's anxiety, which had come to a head, greatly diminished, leading to further improvement. The conviction gained in this analysis strongly influenced the whole course of my analytic work.

The treatment was carried out in the child's home with his own toys. This analysis was the beginning of the psychoanalytic play technique, because from the start the child expressed his phantasies and anxieties mainly in play, and I consistently interpreted its meaning to him, with the result that additional material came up in his play. That is to say, I already used with this patient, in essence, the method of interpretation which became characteristic of my technique. This approach corresponds to a

1. Fritz was in all likelihood Klein's youngest son Erich (Grosskurth 1956).

fundamental principle of psychoanalysis—free association. In interpreting not only the child's words but also his activities with his toys, I applied this basic principle to the mind of the child, whose play and varied activities—in fact his whole behaviour—are means of expressing what the adult expresses predominantly by words. I was also guided throughout by two other tenets of psychoanalysis established by Freud, which I have from the beginning regarded as fundamental: that the exploration of the unconscious is the main task of psychoanalytic procedure, and that the analysis of the transference is the means of achieving this aim.

Between 1920 and 1923 I gained further experience with other child cases, but a definite step in the development of play technique was the treatment of a child of 2 years and 9 months whom I psychoanalysed in 1923. I have given some details of this child's case under the name "Rita" in my book *The Psycho-Analysis of Children* (1932).[2] Rita suffered from night terrors and animal phobias, was very ambivalent towards her mother, at the same time clinging to her to such an extent that she could hardly be left alone. She had a marked obsessional neurosis and was at times very depressed. Her play was inhibited and her inability to tolerate frustrations made her upbringing increasingly difficult. I was very doubtful about how to tackle this case since the analysis of so young a child was an entirely new experiment. The first session seemed to confirm my misgivings. Rita, when left alone with me in her nursery, at once showed signs of what I took to be a negative transference: she was anxious and silent and very soon asked to go out into the garden. I agreed and went with her—I may add, under the watchful eyes of her mother and aunt, who took this as a sign of failure. They were very surprised to see that Rita was quite friendly towards me when we returned to the nursery some ten to fifteen minutes later. The explanation of this change was that while we were outside I had been interpreting her negative transference (this again being against the usual practice). From a few things she said, and the fact that she was less frightened when we were in the open, I concluded that she was particularly afraid of something which I might do to her when she was alone with me in the room. I interpreted this and, referring to her night terrors, I linked her suspicion of me as a hostile stranger with her fear that a bad woman would attack her when she was by herself at night. When, a few minutes after this interpretation, I

2. See also Rickman 1936 and Klein 1945.

suggested that we should return to the nursery, she readily agreed. As I mentioned, Rita's inhibition in playing was marked, and to begin with she did hardly anything but obsessionally dress and undress her doll. But soon I came to understand the anxieties underlying her obsessions, and interpreted them. This case strengthened my growing conviction that a precondition for the psychoanalysis of a child is to understand and to interpret the phantasies, feelings, anxieties, and experiences expressed by play or, if play activities are inhibited, the causes of the inhibition. . . .

Aggressiveness is expressed in various ways in the child's play, either directly or indirectly. Often a toy is broken or, when the child is more aggressive, attacks are made with knife or scissors on the table or on pieces of wood, water or paint is splashed about and the room generally becomes a battlefield. It is essential to enable the child to bring out his aggressiveness, but what counts most is to understand why at this particular moment in the transference situation destructive impulses come up and to observe their consequences in the child's mind. Feelings of guilt may very soon follow after the child has broken, for instance, a little figure. Such guilt refers not only to the actual damage done but to what the toy stands for in the child's unconscious, e.g., a little brother or sister, or a parent; the interpretation has therefore to deal with these deeper levels as well. Sometimes we can gather from the child's behaviour towards the analyst that not only guilt but also persecutory anxiety has been the sequel to his destructive impulses and that he is afraid of retaliation. . . .

It is an essential part of the interpretative work that it should keep in step with fluctuations between love and hatred, between happiness and satisfaction on the one hand and persecutory anxiety and depression on the other. This implies that the analyst should not show disapproval of the child having broken a toy; he should not, however, encourage the child to express his aggressiveness, or suggest to him that the toy could be mended. In other words, he should enable the child to experience his emotions and phantasies as they come up. It was always part of my technique not to use educative or moral influence, but to keep to the psychoanalytic procedure only, which, to put it in a nutshell, consists in understanding the patient's mind and in conveying to him what goes on in it. . . .

There are many children who are inhibited in play. Such inhibition does not always completely prevent them from playing, but may soon interrupt their activities.

The boy, aged 3 years 9 months, whom I described under the name "Peter" in *The Psycho-Analysis of Children* (1932), was very neurotic.[3] To mention some of his difficulties: he was unable to play, could not tolerate any frustration, was timid, plaintive, and unboyish, yet at times aggressive and overbearing, very ambivalent towards his family, and strongly fixated on his mother. She told me that Peter had greatly changed for the worse after a summer holiday during which at the age of 18 months he shared his parents' bedroom and had opportunity of observing their sexual intercourse. On that holiday he became very difficult to manage, slept badly, and relapsed into soiling his bed at night, which he had not done for some months. He had been playing freely until then, but from that summer onwards he stopped playing and became very destructive towards his toys; he would do nothing with them but break them. Shortly afterwards his brother was born, and this increased all his difficulties.

In the first session Peter started to play; he soon made two horses bump into each other, and repeated the same action with different toys. He also mentioned that he had a little brother. I interpreted to him that the horses and the other things which had been bumping together represented people, an interpretation which he first rejected and then accepted. He again bumped the horses together, saying that they were going to sleep, covered them up with bricks, and added: "Now they're quite dead; I've buried them." He put the motorcars front to rear in a row which, as became clear later in the analysis, symbolized his father's penis, and made them run along, then suddenly lost his temper and threw them about the room, saying: "We always smash our Christmas presents straight away; we don't want any." Smashing his toys thus stood in his unconscious for smashing his father's genital. During this first hour he did in fact break several toys.

In the second session Peter repeated some of the material of the first hour, in particular the bumping together of cars, horses, etc., and speaking again of his little brother, whereupon I interpreted that he was showing me how his Mummy and Daddy bumped their genitals (of course using his own word for genitals) and that he thought that their doing so caused his brother to be born. This interpretation produced more material, throwing light on his very ambivalent relation towards his

3. This child, whose analysis was begun in 1924, was another of the cases that helped to develop my play technique.

little brother and towards his father. He laid a toy man on a brick which he called a "bed," threw him down and said he was "dead and done for." He next reenacted the same thing with two toy men, choosing figures he had already damaged. I interpreted that the first toy man stood for his father whom he wanted to throw out of his mother's bed and kill, and that one of the two toy men was again the father and the other represented himself to whom his father would do the same. The reason why he had chosen two damaged figures was that he felt that both his father and himself would be damaged if he attacked his father.

This material illustrates a number of points, of which I shall only mention one or two. Because Peter's experience of witnessing the sexual intercourse of his parents had made a great impact on his mind, and had aroused strong emotions such as jealousy, aggressiveness, and anxiety, this was the first thing which he expressed in his play. There is no doubt that he had no longer any conscious knowledge of this experience, that it was repressed, and that only the symbolical expression of it was possible for him. I have reason to believe that if I had not interpreted that the toys bumping together were people, he might not have produced the material which came up in the second hour. Furthermore, had I not, in the second hour, been able to show him some of the reasons for his inhibition in play, by interpreting the damage done to the toys, he would very likely—as he did in ordinary life—have stopped playing after breaking the toys. . . .

I have said much about the importance of interpretations for play technique and have given some instances to illustrate their content. This brings me to a question which I have often been asked: "Are young children intellectually able to understand such interpretations?" My own experience and that of my colleagues has been that if the interpretations relate to the salient points in the material, they are fully understood. Of course, the child analyst must give his interpretations as succinctly and as clearly as possible, and should also use the child's expressions in doing so. But if he translates into simple words the essential points of the material presented to him, he gets into touch with those emotions and anxieties which are most operative at the moment; the child's conscious and intellectual understanding is often a subsequent process. One of the many interesting and surprising experiences of the beginner in child analysis is to find in even very young children a capacity for insight which is often far greater than that of adults. To some extent this is explained by the fact that the connections between conscious and unconscious are closer in young children than in adults, and that infantile repressions are less powerful. I also believe that the infant's intellectual capacities are often underrated and that in fact he understands more than he is credited with.

I shall now illustrate what I have said by a young child's response to interpretations. Peter, of whose analysis I have given a few details, had strongly objected to my interpretation that the toy man he had thrown down from the "bed" and who was "dead and done for" represented his father. (The interpretation of death wishes against a loved person usually arouses great resistance in children as well as in adults.) In the third hour Peter again brought similar material, but now accepted my interpretation and said thoughtfully: "And if I were a Daddy and someone wanted to throw me down behind the bed and make me dead and done for, what would I think of it?" This shows that he had not only worked through, understood, and accepted my interpretation, but that he had also recognized a good deal more. He understood that his own aggressive feelings towards his father contributed to his fear of him, and also that he had projected his own impulses on to his father.

One of the important points in play technique has always been the analysis of the transference. As we know, in the transference on the analyst the patient repeats earlier emotions and conflicts. It is my experience that we are able to help the patient fundamentally by taking his phantasies and anxieties back in our transference interpretations to where they originated—namely, in infancy and in relation to his first objects. For by reexperiencing early emotions and phantasies and understanding them in relation to his primal objects, he can, as it were, revise these relations at their root, and thus effectively diminish his anxieties.

In looking back over the first few years of my work, I would single out a few facts. I mentioned at the beginning of this paper that in analysing my earliest child case I found my interest focusing on his anxieties and defences against them. My emphasis on anxiety led me deeper and deeper into the unconscious and into the phantasy life of the child. This particular emphasis ran counter to the psychoanalytical point of view that interpretations should not go very deep and should not be given frequently. I persisted in my approach, in spite of the fact that it involved a radical change in technique. This approach took me into new territory, for it opened up the understanding of the early infantile phantasies, anxieties, and defences, which were at that time still largely unexplored. This became clear to me when I began the theoretical formulation of my clinical findings.

One of the various phenomena which struck me in the analysis of Rita was the harshness of her superego. I have described in *The Psycho-Analysis of Children* (1932) how Rita used to play the role of a severe and punishing mother who treated the child (represented by the doll or by myself) very cruelly. Furthermore, her ambivalence towards her mother, her extreme need to be punished, her feelings of guilt, and her night terrors led me to recognize that in this child aged 2 years and 9 months—and quite clearly going back to a much earlier age—a harsh and relentless superego operated. I found this discovery confirmed in the analyses of other young children and came to the conclusion that the superego arises at a much earlier stage than Freud assumed. In other words, it became clear to me that the superego, as conceived by him, is the end product of a development which extends over years. As a result of further observations, I recognized that the superego is something which is felt by the child to operate internally in a concrete way, that it consists of a variety of figures built up from his experiences and phantasies, and that it is derived from the stages in which he had internalized (introjected) his parents.

These observations in turn led, in the analyses of little girls, to discovery of the leading female anxiety situation: the mother is felt to be the primal persecutor who, as an external and internalized object, attacks the child's body and takes from it her imaginary children. These anxieties arise from the girl's phantasied attacks on the mother's body, which aim at robbing her of its contents, i.e. of faeces, of the father's penis, and of children, and result in the fear of retaliation by similar attacks. Such persecutory anxieties I found combined or alternating with deep feelings of depression and guilt, and these observations then led to my discovery of the vital part which the tendency to *make reparation* plays in mental life. Reparation in this sense is a wider concept than Freud's concepts of *undoing in the obsessional neurosis* and of *reaction formation,* for it includes the variety of processes by which the ego feels it undoes harm done in phantasy, restores, preserves, and revives objects. The importance of this tendency, bound up as it is with feelings of guilt, also lies in the major contribution it makes to all sublimations, and in this way to mental health.

In studying the phantasied attacks on the mother's body, I soon came upon anal- and urethral-sadistic impulses. I have mentioned above that I recognized the harshness of the superego in Rita (1923) and that her analysis greatly helped me to understand the way in which destructive impulses towards the mother become the cause of feelings of guilt and persecution. One of the cases through which the anal- and urethral-sadistic nature of these destructive impulses became clear to me was that of Trude, aged 3 years and 3 months, whom I analysed in 1924 (Klein 1932). When she came to me for treatment, she suffered from various symptoms, such as night terrors and incontinence of urine and faeces. Early on in her analysis she asked me to pretend that I was in bed and asleep. She would then say that she was going to attack me and look into my buttocks for faeces (which I found also represented children) and that she was going to take them out. Such attacks were followed by her crouching in a corner, playing that she was in bed, covering herself with cushions (which were to protect her body and which also stood for children); at the same time she actually wetted herself and showed clearly that she was very much afraid of being attacked by me. Her anxieties about the dangerous internalized mother confirmed the conclusions I first formed in Rita's analysis. Both these analyses had been of short duration, partly because the parents thought that enough improvement had been achieved.[4]

Soon afterwards I became convinced that such destructive impulses and phantasies could always be traced back to oral-sadistic ones. In fact Rita had already shown this quite clearly. On one occasion she blackened a piece of paper, tore it up, threw the scraps into a glass of water which she put to her mouth as if to drink from it, and said under her breath "dead woman" (Klein 1945, p. 404). This tearing up and soiling of paper I had at the time understood to express phantasies of attacking and killing her mother, which gave rise to fears of retaliation. I have already mentioned that it was with Trude that I became aware of the specific anal- and urethral-sadistic nature of such attacks. But in other analyses, carried out in 1924 and 1925 (Ruth and Peter, both described in *The Psycho-Analysis of Children* [1932]), I also became aware of the fundamental part which oral-sadistic impulses play in destructive phantasies and corresponding anxieties, thus finding in the analysis of young children full confirmation of Abraham's discoveries (1924). These analyses, which gave me further scope for observation, since they lasted longer than Rita's and Trude's,[5] led me towards a fuller insight into the fundamental role of oral desires and anxieties in mental development, normal and abnormal.[6]

4. Rita had eighty-three sessions, Trude eighty-two sessions.

5. Ruth had 190 sessions, Peter 278 sessions.

6. This growing conviction about the fundamental importance of Abraham's discoveries was also the result of my analysis with him, which began in 1924 and was cut short 14 months later through his illness and death.

As I have mentioned, I had already recognized in Rita and Trude the internalization of an attacked and therefore frightening mother—the harsh superego. Between 1924 and 1926 I analysed a child who was very ill indeed.[7] Through her analysis I learned a good deal about the specific details of such internalization and about the phantasies and impulses underlying paranoid and manic-depressive anxieties. For I came to understand the oral and anal nature of her introjection processes and the situations of internal persecution they engendered. I also became more aware of the ways in which internal persecutions influence, by means of projection, the relation to external objects. The intensity of her envy and hatred unmistakably showed its derivation from the oral-sadistic relation to her mother's breast, and was interwoven with the beginnings of her Oedipus complex. Erna's case much helped to prepare the ground for a number of conclusions which I presented to the Tenth International Psycho-Analytical Congress in 1925 (1928), in particular the view that the early superego, built up when oral-sadistic impulses and phantasies are at their height, underlies psychosis—a view which two years later I developed by stressing the importance of oral-sadism for schizophrenia (Klein 1930).

Concurrently with the analyses so far described I was able to make some interesting observations regarding anxiety situations in boys. The analyses of boys and men fully confirmed Freud's view that castration fear is the leading anxiety of the male, but I recognized that owing to the early identification with the mother (the feminine position which ushers in the early stages of the Oedipus complex) the anxiety about attacks on the inside of the body is of great importance in men as well as women, and in various ways influences and moulds their castration fears.

The anxieties derived from phantasied attacks on the mother's body and on the father she is supposed to contain, proved in both sexes to underlie claustrophobia (which includes the fear of being imprisoned or entombed in the mother's body). The connection of these anxieties with castration fear can be seen for instance in the phantasy of losing the penis or having it destroyed inside the mother—phantasies which may result in impotence.

I came to see that the fears connected with attacks on the mother's body and of being attacked by external and internal objects had a particular quality and intensity which suggested their psychotic nature.

7. Described under the name "Erna" in *The Psycho-Analysis of Children* (1932), Chapter 3.

In exploring the child's relation to internalized objects, various situations of internal persecution and their psychotic contents became clear. Furthermore, the recognition that fear of retaliation derives from the individual's own aggressiveness led me to suggest that the initial defences of the ego are directed against the anxiety aroused by destructive impulses and phantasies. Again and again, when these psychotic anxieties were traced to their origin, they were found to stem from oral-sadism. I recognized also that the oral-sadistic relation to the mother and the internalization of a devoured, and therefore devouring, breast create the prototype of all internal persecutors, and furthermore that the internalization of an injured and therefore dreaded breast on the one hand, and of a satisfying and helpful breast on the other, is the core of the superego. Another conclusion was that, although oral anxieties come first, sadistic phantasies and desires from all sources are operative at a very early stage of development and overlap the oral anxieties.[8]

The importance of the infantile anxieties I have described above was also shown in the analysis of very ill adults, some of whom were borderline psychotic cases.[9]

---

8. These and other conclusions are contained in the two papers I have already mentioned (Klein 1928, 1930). See also Klein 1929.

9. It is possible that the understanding of the contents of psychotic anxieties and of the urgency to interpret them was brought home to me in the analysis of a paranoiac-schizophrenic man who came to me for one month only. In 1922 a colleague who was going on holiday asked me to take over for a month a schizophrenic patient of his. I found from the first hour onwards that I must not allow the patient to remain silent for any length of time. I felt that his silence implied danger, and in every such instance I interpreted his suspicions of me, e.g., that I was plotting with his uncle and would have him certified again (he had recently been de-certified)—material which on other occasions he verbally expressed. Once when I had interpreted his silence in this way, connecting it with former material, the patient, sitting up, asked me in a threatening tone: "Are you going to send me back to the asylum?" But he soon became quieter and began to speak more freely. That showed me that I had been on the right lines and should continue to interpret his suspicions and feelings of persecution. To some extent a positive as well as a negative transference to me came about; but at one point, when his fear of women came up very strongly, he demanded from me the name of a male analyst to whom he could turn. I gave him a name, but he never approached this colleague. During that month I saw the patient every day. The analyst who had asked me to take over found some progress on his return and wished me to continue the analysis. I refused, having become fully aware of the danger of treating a paranoiac without any protection or other suitable management. During the time when I analysed him, he often stood for hours opposite my house, looking up at my window, though it was only on a few occasions that he rang the bell and asked to see me. I may mention that after a short time he

There were other experiences which helped me to reach yet a further conclusion. The comparison between the undoubtedly paranoiac Erna and the phantasies and anxieties that I had found in less-ill children, who could only be called neurotic, convinced me that psychotic (paranoid and depressive) anxieties underlie infantile neurosis. I also made similar observations in the analyses of adult neurotics. All these different lines of exploration resulted in the hypothesis that anxieties of a psychotic nature are in some measure part of normal infantile development and are expressed and worked through in the course of the infantile neurosis.[10] To uncover these infantile anxieties the analysis has, however, to be carried into deep layers of the unconscious, and this applies both to adults and to children.[11]

It has already been pointed out in the introduction to this paper that my attention from the beginning focused on the child's anxieties and that it was by means of interpreting their contents that I found myself able to diminish anxiety. In order to do this, full use had to be made of the symbolic language of play which I recognized to be an essential part of the child's mode of expression. As we have seen, the brick, the little figure, the car, not only represent things which interest the child in themselves, but in his play with them they always have a variety of symbolical meanings as well which are bound up with his phantasies, wishes, and experiences. This archaic mode of expression is also the language with which we are familiar in dreams, and it was by approaching the play of the child in a way similar to Freud's interpretation of dreams that I found I could get access to the child's unconscious. But we have to consider each child's use of symbols in connection with his particular emotions and anxieties and in relation to the whole situation which is presented in the analysis; mere generalized translations of symbols are meaningless.

---

was again certified. Although I did not at the time draw any theoretical conclusions from this experience, I believe that this fragment of an analysis may have contributed to my later insight into the psychotic nature of infantile anxieties and to the development of my technique.

10. As we know, Freud found that there is no structural difference between the normal and the neurotic, and this discovery has been of the greatest importance in the understanding of mental processes in general. My hypothesis that anxieties of a psychotic nature are ubiquitous in infancy, and underlie the infantile neurosis, is an extension of Freud's discovery.

11. The conclusions I have presented in the last paragraph can be found fully dealt with in *The Psycho-Analysis of Children* (1932).

The importance I attributed to symbolism led me—as time went on—to theoretical conclusions about the process of symbol formation. Play analysis had shown that symbolism enabled the child to transfer not only interests, but also phantasies, anxieties, and guilt to objects other than people.[12] Thus a great deal of relief is experienced in play and this is one of the factors which make it so essential for the child. For instance, Peter to whom I have referred earlier, pointed out to me, when I interpreted his damaging a toy figure as representing attacks on his brother, that he would not do this to his real brother, he would only do it to the toy brother. My interpretation of course made it clear to him that it was really his brother whom he wished to attack, but the instance shows that only by symbolic means was he able to express his destructive tendencies in the analysis.

I have also arrived at the view that, in children, a severe inhibition of the capacity to form and use symbols, and so to develop phantasy life, is a sign of serious disturbance (Klein 1930). I suggested that such inhibitions, and the resulting disturbance in the relation to the external world and to reality, are characteristic of schizophrenia.[13]

In passing I may say that I found it of great value from the clinical and theoretical point of view that I was analysing both adults and children. I was thereby able to observe the infant's phantasies and anxieties still operative in the adult and to assess in the young child what his future development might be. It was by comparing the severely ill, the neurotic, and the normal child, and by recognizing infantile anxieties of a psychotic nature as the cause of illness in adult neurotics, that I had arrived at the conclusions I have described above.[14]

In tracing, in the analyses of adults and children, the development of impulses, phantasies, and anxieties back to their origin, i.e., to the feelings towards the mother's breast (even with children who have not been breast-fed), I found that object relations start almost at birth and arise with the first feeding experience; furthermore, that all aspects of mental life are bound up with object relations. It also emerged that the child's experience of the external world, which very soon includes his ambivalent relation to his father and to other members of his family, is

---

12. In this connection, cf. Ernest Jones's important paper "The Theory of Symbolism" (1916).

13. This conclusion has since influenced the understanding of the schizophrenic mode of communication and has found its place in the treatment of schizophrenia.

14. I cannot deal here with the fundamental differences which, besides common features, exist between the normal, the neurotic and the psychotic.

constantly influenced by—and in turn influences—the internal world he is building up, and that external and internal situations are always interdependent, since introjection and projection operate side by side from the beginning of life.

The observations that in the infant's mind the mother primarily appears as good and bad breast split off from each other, and that within a few months, with growing ego integration the contrasting aspects are beginning to be synthesized, helped me to understand the importance of the processes of splitting and keeping apart good and bad figures (Klein 1929), as well as the effect of such processes on ego development. The conclusion to be drawn from the experience that depressive anxiety arises as a result of the ego synthesizing the good and bad (loved and hated) aspects of the object led me in turn to the concept of the depressive position which reaches its climax towards the middle of the first year. It is preceded by the paranoid position, which extends over the first three or four months of life and is characterized by persecutory anxiety and splitting processes (Klein 1935). Later on (Klein 1946), when I reformulated my views on the first three or four months of life, I called this stage (making use of a suggestion of Fairbairn's (1941), the paranoid-schizoid position, and, in working out its significance, sought to coordinate my findings about splitting, projection, persecution, and idealization.

My work with children and the theoretical conclusions I drew from it increasingly influence my technique with adults. It has always been a tenet of psychoanalysis that the unconscious, which originates in the infantile mind, has to be explored in the adult. My experience with children had taken me much deeper in that direction than was formerly the case, and this led to a technique which made access to those layers possible. In particular, my play technique had helped me to see which material was most in need of interpretation at the moment and the way in which it would be most easily conveyed to the patient, and some of this knowledge I could apply to the analysis of adults.[15] As has been pointed

---

15. The play technique has also influenced work with children in other fields, as for example in child guidance work and in education. The development of educational methods in England has been given fresh impetus by Susan Isaacs' research at the Malting House School. Her books about that work have been widely read and have had a lasting effect on educational techniques in this country, especially where young children are concerned. Her approach was strongly influenced by her great appreciation of child analysis, in particular of play technique, and it is largely due to her that in England the psychoanalytic understanding of children has contributed to developments in education.

out earlier, this does not mean that the technique used with children is identical with the approach to adults. Though we find our way back to the earliest stages, it is of great importance in analysing adults to take account of the adult ego, just as with children we keep in mind the infantile ego according to the stage of its development.

REFERENCES

Abraham, K. (1924). A short history of the development of the libido, viewed in the light of mental disorders. In *Selected Papers on Psycho-Analysis.* London: Hogarth, 1927.

Fairbairn, W. R. D. (1941). A revised psychopathology of the psychoses and neuroses. In *Psychoanalytic Studies of the Personality,* pp. 28–58. London: Routledge & Kegan Paul.

Grosskurth, P. (1986). *Melanie Klein: Her World and Her Work.* New York: Knopf.

Jones, E. (1916). The theory of symbolism. In *Papers on Psycho-Analysis.* London: Balliere.

Klein, M. (1921). The development of a child. In *Collected Works,* vol 1, pp. 1–53. London: Hogarth, 1975.

——(1923). Early analysis. In *Collected Works,* vol 1, pp. 77–105. London: Hogarth, 1975.

——(1924). The role of the school in the libidinal development of the child. In *Collected Works,* vol 1, pp. 59–76. London: Hogarth, 1975.

——(1928). Early stages of the Oedipus conflict. In *Collected Works,* vol 1, pp. 186–198. London: Hogarth, 1975.

——(1929). Personification in the play of children. *Collected Works,* vol 1, pp. 199–209. London: Hogarth, 1975.

——(1930). The importance of symbol-formation in the development of the ego. In *Collected Works,* vol 1, pp. 219–232. London: Hogarth, 1975.

——(1932). *The Psychoanalysis of Children.* London: Hogarth.

——(1935). A contribution to the psychogenesis of manic-depressive states. In *Collected Works,* vol 1, pp. 262–289. London: Hogarth, 1975.

——(1945). The Oedipus complex in the light of early anxieties. In *Collected Works,* vol 1, pp. 370–419. London: Hogarth, 1975.

Rickman, J., ed. (1936). *On the Bringing Up of Children.*

11

"Some Theoretical Conclusions Regarding the Emotional Life of the Infant" (1952)

"The Oedipus Complex in the Light of Early Anxieties" (1945) is an important but difficult paper that I will discuss without presenting an excerpt. In it, Klein presented two case histories of child analyses that gave the material supporting her contention that the Oedipus complex begins during the first year of life. She wrote that it began with the influence of the oral sadistic stage, which was soon mingled with urethral and anal sadistic elements. This hallmark of Kleinian theory moved the age at which children became concerned with the relationship between their parents to the first year of life instead of the third, as Freud had written. It has been controversial with other schools of analysis, but has remained a tenet of the Kleinians.

Writing the year before, Fairbairn (1944) did not move up the date of oedipal development as Klein did, but he did stress the importance of early development as the major determinant of the form of the Oedipus complex. In this regard, the two theorists were alike in stressing the importance of earlier aspects of development on the shape of the constellation, and of linking them to the earliest relationships.

Besides the controversy regarding the early stage of the appearance of elements and of the primitive beginnings of the superego, Klein made several other notable contributions in this paper. First, she briefly acknowledged the importance of external relations with objects, but focused her own comments on the infant and young child's modification of them in the internal world though the combined processes of introjection and projection, a never-ending feedback loop between internal and external reality. She described how body parts are understood by the infant to stand for the part-object relations that predominate, giving us language for the internalization of the psychosomatic partnership that

Winnicott later also described in part-object terms. She described more of the child's use of bodily experience in building the mind than any of the object relations theorists who followed.

Second, Klein briefly noted that it is the excesses of idealization and aggression in response to frustration experienced with the mother that lead to the modification of internal objects, agreeing with this fundamental way of organizing mind that Fairbairn (1944) had published the year before. He had placed this idea at the center of his theory, in the form of the libidinal ego and object (close to the idea of Klein's idealized object) and the anti-libidinal ego and frustrating object (close to Klein's internal persecutor). This is another instance of the mutual influence of Klein and Fairbairn on each other in these years.

There are several other noteworthy points covered in the paper. Klein, like Fairbairn, believed that the child's relationship of frustration with the father (which she expressed as the infant's concern about the father's penis) is carried over from an earlier relationship of frustration with the mother and her breast, which is primary—that experience with a second object and later the Oedipus complex itself are built on earlier experience. Although she does not say so explicitly, there is a clear implication that the girl has a feminine identity long before fears of castration or penis envy, which she holds to be secondary to envy of the mother. Klein's thorough discussion of envy is notable, in fact, for discussing the envy of both the boy and the girl toward both parents, and for stressing the roles of positive identification with each parent, of reparation and the positive trends in the resolution of the Oedipus complex that counterbalance envy and fear of retaliation for projected aggression. She implies that envy has a more central role than castration, and that the child is envious not only of each parent but also of a sexualized version of the combined relationship of mother and father, understood often to be going on inside the body (and we would now add, the mind) of the mother. Behind the complex language is the first description of the child's envy of the parental couple for having an intimate relationship to each other that excludes the child. Klein describes the child's phantasy as the mother capturing the father's penis inside her body, but we would now see it as her having captured also the whole father in a relationship desired by the child. This is a theme elaborated by Ogden (1989) many years later in his description that the child relates to the situation first through taking in the mother's mental image of her relationship to the father.

Throughout Klein's discussion run the themes of the relations of the Oedipus complex to the working through of the depressive position, of part-object relations to whole-object relations, of the building of the superego in relationship to real objects, and of the phantasy elaboration of oedipal issues in response to the fear of the child's own projection of aggression and of internal persecutors. This paper is a rich culmination and summary of many of Klein's early contributions.

"Some Theoretical Conclusions Regarding the Emotional Life of the Infant" (1952) presents a consolidation of ideas Klein had been developing over the previous years, including those on the early Oedipus. In it, she presents crystalized summaries of the development of good and bad in both paranoid/schizoid and depressive positions, the dynamics of greed, the internal world, the importance of the environment, and the method by which infants imbue the breast with their own qualities and anxieties.

The excerpt here conveys her ideas about the role and development of the early Oedipus in relation to superego development, which, she held, must go together. The recognition of the couple and of the object's separate identity and relationships with others is an intrinsic part of the development of the depressive position. Britton (1992) has elaborated on this theme recently.

REFERENCES

Britton, R. (1992). The Oedipus complex and the depressive position. In *Clinical Lectures on Klein and Bion,* ed. R. Anderson, pp. 34–45. London: Routledge.

Fairbairn, W. (1944). Endopsychic structure considered in terms of object relationships. *International Journal of Psycho-Analysis* 27 (1,2): 70–93.

Ogden, T. (1989). *The Primitive Edge of Experience*. Northvale, NJ: Jason Aronson.

In my paper on "Mourning and its Relation to Manic-Depressive States," I expressed the following view: "My experience leads me to conclude that, while it is true that the characteristic feature of normal mourning is the individual's setting up the lost loved object inside himself, he is not doing so for the first time but, through the work of mourning, is reinstating that object as well as all his loved *internal* objects which he feels he has lost." Whenever grief arises, it undermines the feeling of secure possession of the loved internal objects, for it revives the early anxieties about injured and destroyed objects—about a shattered inner world. Feelings of guilt and persecutory anxieties—the infantile depressive position—are reactivated in full strength. A successful reinstating of the *external* love object which is being mourned, and whose introjection is intensified through the process of mourning, implies that the loved *internal* objects are restored and regained. Therefore the testing of reality characteristic of the process of mourning is not only the means of renewing the links to the external world but of *re-establishing the disrupted inner world*. Mourning thus involves the repetition of the emotional situation the infant experienced during the depressive position. For under the stress of fear of loss of the loved mother, the infant struggles with the task of establishing and integrating his inner world, of building up securely the good objects within himself.

One of the fundamental factors in determining whether or not the loss of a loved object (through death or other causes) will lead to manic-depressive illness or will be normally overcome is, in my experience, the extent to which, in the first year of life, the depressive position has been successfully worked through and the loved introjected objects securely established within.

The depressive position is bound up with fundamental changes in the infant's libidinal organization, for during this period—about the middle of the first year—the infant enters upon the early stages of the direct and inverted Oedipus complex. I shall restrict myself here to the broadest outline only in giving an account of the early stages of the Oedipus complex.[1] These early stages are characterized by the important role which part-objects still play in the infant's mind while the relation to complete objects is being established. Also, though genital desires are coming strongly to the fore, the oral libido is still leading. Powerful oral desires, increased by the frustration experienced in relation to the mother, are transferred from the mother's breast to the father's penis.[2] Genital desires in the infant of either sex coalesce with oral desires and therefore an oral, as well as a genital, relation to the father's penis ensues. Genital desires are also directed towards the mother. The infant's desires for the father's penis are bound up with jealousy of the mother because he feels she receives this

1. See Heimann (1952), Part 2. I have given detailed accounts of the Oedipus development in my *Psycho-Analysis of Children* (particularly Chapter 8); also in my papers "Early Stages of the Oedipus Conflict" and "The Oedipus Complex in the Light of Early Anxieties."

2. Abraham writes (1924, p. 490), "Another point to be noted in regard to the part of the body that has been introjected is that the penis is regularly assimilated to the female breast, and that other parts of the body, such as the finger, the foot, hair, faeces and buttocks, can be made to stand for those two organs in a secondary way. . . ."

desired object. These manifold emotions and wishes in either sex underlie both the inverted and the direct Oedipus complex.

Another aspect of the early Oedipus stages is bound up with the essential part which the mother's "inside," and his own "inside," play in the young infant's mind. During the preceding period, when destructive impulses prevail (paranoid-schizoid position), the infant's urge to enter his mother's body, and take possession of its contents, is predominantly of an oral and anal nature. This urge is still active in the following stage (depressive position), but when genital desires increase it is directed more towards the father's penis (equated to babies and faeces) which, he feels, the mother's body contains. Simultaneously the oral desires for the father's penis lead to its internalization, and this internalized penis—both as a good and bad object—comes to play an important part in the infant's internal object world.

The early stages of the Oedipus development are of the greatest complexity: desires from various sources converge; these desires are directed towards part-objects as well as towards whole objects; the father's penis, both desired and hated, exists not only as a part of the father's body, but is also simultaneously felt by the infant to be inside himself and inside the mother's body.

Envy appears to be inherent in oral greed. My analytic work has shown me that envy (alternating with feelings of love and gratification) is first directed towards the feeding breast. To this primary envy jealousy is added when the Oedipus situation arises. The infant's feelings in relation to both parents seem to run like this: when he is frustrated, father or mother enjoys the desired object of which he is deprived—mother's breast, father's penis—and enjoys it constantly. It is characteristic of the young infant's intense emotions and greed that he should attribute to the parents a constant state of mutual gratification of an oral, anal and genital nature.

These sexual theories are the foundation for combined parent figures such as: the mother containing the father's penis or the whole father; the father containing the mother's breast or the whole mother; the parents fused inseparably in sexual intercourse.[3] Phantasies of this nature also contribute to the notion of "the woman with a penis." Furthermore, owing to internalization, the infant establishes such combined parent figures within himself, and this proves fundamental for many anxiety situations of a psychotic nature.

---

3. Cf. the concept of the combined parent figure in Klein 1932, Chapter 8.

As, gradually, a more realistic relation to the parents develops, the infant comes to consider them as separate individuals, that is to say, the primitive combined parent figures lose in strength.[4]

These developments are interlinked with the depressive position. In both sexes, the fear of the loss of the mother, the primary loved object—that is to say, depressive anxiety—contributes to the need for substitutes; and the infant first turns to the father, who at this stage is also introjected as a complete person, to fulfill this need.

In these ways, libido and depressive anxiety are deflected to some extent from the mother, and this process of distribution stimulates object relations as well as diminishes the intensity of depressive feelings. The early stages of the direct and inverted Oedipus complex thus bring relief to the anxieties of the child and help him to overcome the depressive position. At the same time, however, new conflicts and anxieties arise, since the Oedipus wishes towards the parents imply that envy, rivalry and jealousy—at this stage still powerfully stirred by oral-sadistic impulses—are now experienced towards two people who are both hated and loved. The working through of these conflicts, first arising in the early stages of the Oedipus complex, is part of the process of modification of anxiety which extends beyond babyhood into the first years of childhood. . . .

REFERENCES

Abraham, K. (1924). A short study of the development of the libido. In *Selected Papers on Psycho-Analysis*. London: Hogarth, 1927.

Heimann, P. (1952). Certain functions of introjection and projection in early infancy. In *Developments in Psycho-Analysis*, ed. M. Klein et al. London: Hogarth.

Klein, M. (1928). Early stages of the Oedipus complex. *International Journal of Psycho-Analysis* 9:(1).

——(1932). *The Psycho-Analysis of Children*. London: Hogarth.

——(1945). The Oedipus complex in the light of early anxieties. *International Journal of Psycho-Analysis* 26:(1).

---

4. The infant's capacity to enjoy at the same time the relation to *both* parents, which is an important feature in his mental life and conflicts with his desires, prompted by jealousy and anxiety, to separate them, depends on his feeling that they are separate individuals. This more integrated relation to the parents (which is distinct from the compulsive need to keep the parents apart from one another and to prevent their sexual intercourse) implies a greater understanding of their relation to one another and is a precondition for the infant's hope that he can bring them together and unite them in a happy way.

12

"Notes on Some Schizoid Mechanisms" (1946)

This paper begins with a clear summary of previous theoretical contributions, followed by a discussion of points of agreement and disagreement with Fairbairn. Klein accepted his ideas on splitting, renaming what she had previously called the *paranoid position* as the *paranoid-schizoid position*. While Klein stated her agreement on the importance of splitting in relationships to include both object and ego, she continued to emphasize the projection which is motivated by the child's own aggression and factors of the internal object relationship, while Fairbairn emphasized that splitting is a response to frustration at the hands of the object—the treatment of the child in the external object relationship. Thus, it takes both contributions to reach a view that includes the child's and the parent's contributions. Fairbairn's description of splitting emphasized the effects on the ego, the turning of the person to the internal world in the schizoid situation. Klein, in contrast, emphasized the way the external expression of splitting via projection of aggression or idealization results in the return of aggression through a phantasy of aggression returned by the object. Fairbairn had described the interrelationship of splitting and repression as internal mechanisms affecting the ego. Klein also emphasizes that splitting, projection, and introjection involving the object must also involve splitting of the ego. While clinically, Klein emphasized the splitting of the object, and Fairbairn emphasized the splitting of the ego or self, they were in agreement that a split in the object must also involve a splitting of the ego.

Klein noted that she did not agree with Fairbairn that the frustrating object is introjected first. She stated that the good object is taken in from the first as the nucleus of positive growth in development. This balance of good and bad is an essential feature of Klein's writing that is frequently overlooked.

The developmental schema of the move from the paranoid-schizoid to the depressive position that Klein had now described should be compared with Fairbairn and Winnicott's ideas. What Klein described as the concern for a whole object with the new role of guilt in the depressive position, Winnicott called a "capacity for concern" for the other. Fairbairn agreed on the decrease of splitting in the later phase of whole-object integration, but he elaborated a scheme of "transitional" ways of relating to objects in the path from infantile dependence to mature dependence, providing ideas about specific handling of the object and ego in varying psychological organizations. Thus, while all three writers agreed about the shift from the predominance of splitting to the possibility of integration, they elaborated on the process in different ways.

This paper is Klein's first description of projective identification and of the interaction between projective processes and introjection. Projective identification forms the basis for the interactive way in which the inner world is organized in response to external object relations. Her description of the inner-world ramifications is more vivid and detailed than her description of the effects of actual behaviors of the parents that influence the child. That emphasis was later supplied by Winnicott, while Bion developed the idea of projective and introjective identification as the basis for unconscious communication with the external object and made the behavior of the external object a dynamic part of his theory in the idea of the container/contained (see Chapters 32 and 33).

In this first description of projective identification, Klein elaborated on its role in narcissistic object relations, that a person treats others as though they were part of oneself, and on obsessional mechanisms of control of others as a way of trying to control the parts of the self that have, through projective identification, been lodged in the other person.

At the outset it will be useful to summarize briefly the conclusions regarding the earliest phases of development which I have already put forward (Klein 1932, 1935).

In early infancy anxieties characteristic of psychosis arise which drive the ego to develop specific defence mechanisms. In this period the fixation points for all psychotic disorders are to be found. This hypothesis led some people to believe that I regarded all infants as psychotic; but I have already dealt sufficiently with this misunderstanding on other occasions. The psychotic anxieties, mechanisms, and ego defences of infancy have a profound influence on development in all its aspects, including the development of the ego, superego, and object relations.

I have often expressed my view that object relations exist from the beginning of life, the first object being the mother's breast, which to the child becomes split into a good (gratifying) and bad (frustrating) breast; this splitting results in a severance of love and hate. I have further suggested that the relation to the first object implies its introjection and projection, and thus from the beginning object relations are moulded by an interaction between introjection and projection, between internal and external objects and situations. These processes participate in the building up of the ego and superego and prepare the ground for the onset of the Oedipus complex in the second half of the first year.

From the beginning the destructive impulse is turned against the object and is first expressed in phantasied oral-sadistic attacks on the mother's breast, which soon develop into onslaughts on her body by all sadistic means. The persecutory fears arising from the infant's oral-sadistic impulses to rob the mother's body of its good contents, and from the anal-sadistic impulses to put his excrements into her (including the desire to enter her body in order to control her from within) are of great importance for the development of paranoia and schizophrenia.

I enumerated various typical defences of the early ego, such as the mechanisms of splitting the object and the impulses, idealization, denial of inner and outer reality, and the stifling of emotions. I also mentioned various anxiety contents, including the fear of being poisoned and devoured. Most of these phenomena—prevalent in the first few months of life—are found in the later symptomatic picture of schizophrenia.

This early period (first described as the *persecutory phase*) I later termed *paranoid position*,[1] and held that it precedes the depressive position. If persecutory fears are very strong, and for this reason (among others) the infant cannot work through the paranoid-schizoid position,

1. When this paper was first published in 1946, I was using my term *paranoid position* synonymously with W. R. D. Fairbairn's *schizoid position*. On further deliberation I decided to combine Fairbairn's term with mine and throughout the present book [*Developments in Psycho-Analysis*, 1952, in which this paper was first published] I am using the expression *paranoid-schizoid position*.

the working through of the depressive position is in turn impeded. This failure may lead to a regressive reinforcing of persecutory fears and strengthen the fixation points for severe psychoses (that is to say, the group of schizophrenias). Another outcome of serious difficulties arising during the period of the depressive position may be manic-depressive disorders in later life. I also concluded that in less severe disturbances of development the same factors strongly influence the choice of neurosis.

While I assumed that the outcome of the depressive position depends on the working through of the preceding phase, I nevertheless attributed to the depressive position a central role in the child's early development. For with the introjection of the object as a whole the infant's object relation alters fundamentally. The synthesis between the loved and hated aspects of the complete object gives rise to feelings of mourning and guilt, which imply vital advances in the infant's emotional and intellectual life. This is also a crucial juncture for the choice of neurosis or psychosis. To all these conclusions I still adhere.

SOME NOTES ON FAIRBAIRN'S RECENT PAPERS

In a number of papers W. R. D. Fairbairn (1941, 1944, 1946) has given much attention to the subject matter with which I am now dealing. I therefore find it helpful to clarify some essential points of agreement and disagreement between us. It will be seen that some of the conclusions which I shall present in this paper are in line with Fairbairn's conclusions, while others differ fundamentally. Fairbairn's approach was largely from the angle of ego development in relation to objects, while mine was predominantly from the angle of anxieties and their vicissitudes. He called the earliest phase the *schizoid position:* he stated that it forms part of normal development and is the basis for adult schizoid and schizophrenic illness. I agree with this contention and consider his description of developmental schizoid phenomena as significant and revealing, and of great value for our understanding of schizoid behaviour and of schizophrenia. I also think that Fairbairn's view that the group of schizoid or schizophrenic disorders is much wider than has been acknowledged is correct and important, and the particular emphasis he laid on the inherent relation between hysteria and schizophrenia deserves full attention. His term *schizoid position* would be appropriate if it is understood to cover both persecutory fear and schizoid mechanisms.

I disagree—to mention first the most basic issues—with his revision of the theory of mental structure and instincts. I also disagree with his view that to begin with only the bad object is internalized—a view which seems to me to contribute to the important differences between us regarding the development of object relations as well as of ego development. For I hold that the introjected good breast forms a vital part of the ego, exerts from the beginning a fundamental influence on the process of ego development, and affects both ego structure and object relations. I also differ from Fairbairn's (1941) view that "the great problem of the schizoid individual is how to love without destroying by love, whereas the great problem of the depressive individual is how to love without destroying by hate." This conclusion is in line not only with his rejecting Freud's concept of primary instincts but also with his underrating the role which aggression and hatred play from the beginning of life. As a result of this approach, he does not give enough weight to the importance of early anxiety and conflict and their dynamic effects on development.

CERTAIN PROBLEMS OF THE EARLY EGO

. . . . So far, we know little about the structure of the early ego. Some of the recent suggestions on this point have not convinced me: I have particularly in mind Glover's concept of ego nuclei and Fairbairn's theory of a central ego and two subsidiary egos. More helpful in my view is Winnicott's (1945) emphasis on the unintegration of the early ego.[2] I would also say that the early ego largely lacks cohesion, and a tendency towards integration alternates with a tendency towards disintegration, a falling into bits.[3] I believe that these fluctuations are characteristic of the first few months of life.

We are, I think, justified in assuming that some of the functions which we know from the later ego are there at the beginning. Prominent amongst these functions is that of dealing with anxiety. I hold that anxiety arises

---

2. In this paper Winnicott also described the pathological outcome of states of unintegration, for instance the case of a woman patient who could not distinguish between her twin sister and herself.

3. The greater or lesser cohesiveness of the ego at the beginning of postnatal life should be considered in connection with the greater or lesser capacity of the ego to tolerate anxiety which, as I have previously contended (Klein 1932 particularly p. 49), is a constitutional factor.

from the operation of the death instinct within the organism, is felt as fear of annihilation (death) and takes the form of fear of persecution. The fear of the destructive impulse seems to attach itself at once to an object—or rather it is experienced as the fear of an uncontrollable overpowering object. Other important sources of primary anxiety are the trauma of birth (separation anxiety) and frustration of bodily needs, and these experiences too are from the beginning felt as being caused by objects. Even if these objects are felt to be external, they become through introjection internal persecutors and thus reinforce the fear of the destructive impulse within.

The vital need to deal with anxiety forces the early ego to develop fundamental mechanisms and defences. The destructive impulse is partly projected outwards (deflection of the death instinct) and, I think, attaches itself to the first external object, the mother's breast. As Freud has pointed out, the remaining portion of the destructive impulse is to some extent bound by the libido within the organism. However, neither of these processes entirely fulfils its purpose, and therefore the anxiety of being destroyed from within remains active. It seems to me in keeping with the lack of cohesiveness, that under the pressure of this threat the ego tends to fall to pieces.[4] This falling to pieces appears to underlie states of disintegration in schizophrenics.

The question arises whether some active splitting processes within the ego may not occur even at a very early stage. As we assume, the early ego splits the object and the relation to it in an active way, and this may imply some active splitting of the ego itself. In any case, the result of splitting is a dispersal of the destructive impulse which is felt as the source of danger. I suggest that the primary anxiety of being annihilated by a destructive force within, with the ego's specific response of falling to pieces or splitting itself, may be extremely important in all schizophrenic processes.

SPLITTING PROCESSES IN RELATION TO THE OBJECT

The destructive impulse projected outwards is first experienced as oral aggression. I believe that oral-sadistic impulses towards the mother's

4. Ferenczi (1930) suggests that most likely every living organism reacts to unpleasant stimuli by fragmentation, which might be an expression of the death instinct. Possibly, complicated mechanisms (living organisms) are only kept as an entity through the impact of external conditions. When these conditions become unfavourable the organism falls to pieces.

breast are active from the beginning of life, though with the onset of teething the cannibalistic impulses increase in strength—a factor stressed by Abraham.

In states of frustration and anxiety the oral-sadistic and cannibalistic desires are reinforced, and then the infant feels that he has taken in the nipple and the breast *in bits*. Therefore in addition to the divorce between a good and a bad breast in the young infant's phantasy the frustrating breast—attacked in oral-sadistic phantasies—is felt to be in fragments; the gratifying breast, taken in under the dominance of the sucking libido, is felt to be complete. This first internal good object acts as a focal point in the ego. It counteracts the processes of splitting and dispersal, makes for cohesiveness and integration, and is instrumental in building up the ego.[5] The infant's feeling of having inside a good and complete breast may, however, be shaken by frustration and anxiety. As a result, the divorce between the good and bad breast may be difficult to maintain, and the infant may feel that the good breast too is in pieces.

I believe that the ego is incapable of splitting the object—internal and external—without a corresponding splitting taking place within the ego. Therefore the phantasies and feelings about the state of the internal object vitally influence the structure of the ego. The more sadism prevails in the process of incorporating the object, and the more the object is felt to be in pieces, the more the ego is in danger of being split in relation to the internalized object fragments.

The processes I have described are, of course, bound up with the infant's phantasy life, and the anxieties which stimulate the mechanism of splitting are also of a phantastic nature. It is in phantasy that the infant splits the object and the self, but the effect of this phantasy is a very real one, because it leads to feelings and relations (and later on, thought processes) being in fact cut off from one another.[6]

---

5. D. W. Winnicott (1945) referred to the same process from another angle: he described how integration and adaptation to reality depend essentially on the infant's experience of the mother's love and care.

6. In the discussion following the reading of this paper, W. C. M. Scott referred to another aspect of splitting. He stressed the importance of the breaks in continuity of experiences, which imply a splitting in time rather than in space. He referred as an instance to the alternation between states of being asleep and states of being awake. I fully agree with his point of view.

SPLITTING IN CONNECTION WITH PROJECTION AND INTROJECTION

So far, I have dealt particularly with the mechanism of splitting as one of the earliest ego mechanisms and defences against anxiety. Introjection and projection are from the beginning of life also used in the service of this primary aim of the ego. Projection, as Freud described, originates from the deflection of the death instinct outwards and in my view it helps the ego to overcome anxiety by ridding it of danger and badness. Introjection of the good object is also used by the ego as a defence against anxiety.

Closely connected with projection and introjection are some other mechanisms. Here I am particularly concerned with the connection between splitting, idealization, and denial. As regards splitting of the object, we have to remember that in states of gratification love feelings turn towards the gratifying breast, while in states of frustration hatred and persecutory anxiety attach themselves to the frustrating breast.

Idealization is bound up with the splitting of the object, for the good aspects of the breast are exaggerated as a safeguard against the fear of the persecuting breast. While idealization is thus the corollary of persecutory fear, it also springs from the power of the instinctual desires which aim at unlimited gratification and therefore create the picture of an inexhaustible and always bountiful breast—an ideal breast.

We find an instance of such a cleavage in infantile hallucinatory gratification. The main processes which come into play in idealization are also operative in hallucinatory gratification, namely, splitting of the object and denial both of frustration and of persecution. The frustrating and persecuting object is kept widely apart from the idealized object. However, the bad object is not only kept apart from the good one but its very existence is denied, as is the whole situation of frustration and the bad feelings (pain) to which frustration gives rise. This is bound up with denial of psychic reality. The denial of psychic reality becomes possible only through strong feelings of omnipotence—an essential characteristic of early mentality. Omnipotent denial of the existence of the bad object and of the painful situation is in the unconscious equal to annihilation by the destructive impulse. It is, however, not only a situation and an object that are denied and annihilated—*it is an object relation* which suffers this fate, and therefore a part of the ego, from which the feelings towards the object emanate, is denied and annihilated as well.

In hallucinatory gratification, therefore, two interrelated processes take place: the omnipotent conjuring up of the ideal object and situation, and the equally omnipotent annihilation of the bad persecutory object and the painful situation. These processes are based on splitting both the object and the ego.

In passing I would mention that in this early phase splitting, denial and omnipotence play a role similar to that of repression at a later stage of ego development. In considering the importance of the processes of denial and omnipotence at a stage which is characterized by persecutory fear and schizoid mechanisms, we may remember the delusions both of grandeur and of persecution in schizophrenia.

So far, in dealing with persecutory fear, I have singled out the oral element. However, while the oral libido still has the lead, libidinal and aggressive impulses and phantasies from other sources come to the fore and lead to a confluence of oral, urethral, and anal desires, both libidinal and aggressive. Also the attacks on the mother's breast develop into attacks of a similar nature on her body, which comes to be felt as it were as an extension of the breast, even before the mother is conceived of as a complete person. The phantasied onslaughts on the mother follow two main lines: one is the predominantly oral impulse to suck dry, bite up, scoop out, and rob the mother's body of its good contents. (I shall discuss the bearing of these impulses on the development of object relations in connection with introjection.) The other line of attack derives from the anal and urethral impulses and implies expelling dangerous substances (excrements) out of the self and into the mother. Together with these harmful excrements, expelled in hatred, split-off parts of the ego are also projected on to the mother or, as I would rather call it, *into* the mother.[7] These excrements and bad parts of the self are meant not only to injure but also to control and to take possession of the object. Insofar as the mother comes to contain the bad parts of the self, she is not felt to be a separate individual but is felt to be *the* bad self.

Much of the hatred against parts of the self is now directed towards the mother. This leads to a particular form of identification which establishes the prototype of an aggressive object relation. I suggest for these pro-

---

7. The description of such primitive processes suffers from a great handicap, for these phantasies arise at a time when the infant has not yet begun to think in words. In this context, for instance, I am using the expression "to project *into* another person" because this seems to me the only way of conveying the unconscious process I am trying to describe.

cesses the term *projective identification*. When projection is mainly derived from the infant's impulse to harm or to control the mother,[8] he feels her to be a persecutor. In psychotic disorders this identification of an object with the hated parts of the self contributes to the intensity of the hatred directed against other people. As far as the ego is concerned the excessive splitting off and expelling into the outer world of part of itself considerably weaken it. For the aggressive component of feelings and of the personality is intimately bound up in the mind with power, potency, strength, knowledge, and many other desired qualities.

It is, however, not only the bad parts of the self which are expelled and projected, but also good parts of the self. Excrements then have the significance of gifts, and parts of the ego which, together with excrements, are expelled and projected into the other person represent the good, i.e., the loving parts of the self. The identification based on this type of projection again vitally influences object relations. The projection of good feelings and good parts of the self into the mother is essential for the infant's ability to develop good object relations and to integrate his ego. However, if this projective process is carried out excessively, good parts of the personality are felt to be lost, and in this way the mother becomes the ego ideal; this process too results in weakening and impoverishing the ego. Very soon such processes extend to other people,[9] and the result may be an over-strong dependence on these external representatives of one's own good parts. Another consequence is a fear that the capacity to love has been lost because the loved object is felt to be loved predominantly as a representative of the self.

The processes of splitting off parts of the self and projecting them into objects are thus of vital importance for normal development as well as for abnormal object relations.

---

8. M. G. Evans, in a short unpublished communication (read to the British Psycho-Analytical Society, January 1946) gave some instances of patients in whom the following phenomena were marked: lack of sense of reality, a feeling of being divided, and parts of the personality having entered the mother's body in order to rob and control her; as a consequence the mother and other people similarly attacked came to represent the patient. Evans related these processes to a very primitive stage of development.

9. W. C. M. Scott in an unpublished paper (read to the British Psycho-Analytical Society) described three interconnected features which he came upon in a schizophrenic patient: a strong disturbance of her sense of reality, her feeling that the world round her was a cemetery, and the mechanism of putting all good parts of herself into another person—Greta Garbo—who came to stand for the patient.

The effect of introjection on object relations is equally important. The introjection of the good object, first of all the mother's breast, is a precondition for normal development. I have already described that it comes to form a focal point in the ego and makes for cohesiveness of the ego. One characteristic feature of the earliest relation to the good object—internal and external—is the tendency to idealize it. In states of frustration or increased anxiety, the infant is driven to take flight to his internal idealized object as a means of escaping from persecutors. From this mechanism various serious disturbances may result: when persecutory fear is too strong, the flight to the idealized object becomes excessive, and this severely hampers ego development and disturbs object relations. As a result the ego may be felt to be entirely subservient to and dependent on the internal object—only a shell for it. With an unassimilated idealized object there goes a feeling that the ego has no life and no value of its own.[10] I would suggest that the condition of flight to the unassimilated idealized object necessitates further splitting processes within the ego. For parts of the ego attempt to unite with the ideal object, while other parts strive to deal with the internal persecutors.

The various ways of splitting the ego and internal objects result in the feeling that the ego is in bits. This feeling amounts to a state of disintegration. In normal development, the states of disintegration which the infant experiences are transitory. Among other factors, gratification by the external good object[11] again and again helps to break through these schizoid states. The infant's capacity to overcome temporary schizoid states is in keeping with the strong elasticity and resilience of the infantile mind. If states of splitting and therefore of disintegration, which the ego is unable to overcome, occur too frequently and go on for too long, then in my view they must be regarded as a sign of schizo-

10. Paula Heimann (1942) described a condition in which the internal objects act as foreign bodies embedded in the self. Whilst this is more obvious with regard to the bad objects, it is true even for the good ones, if the ego is compulsively subordinated to their preservation. When the ego serves its good internal objects excessively, they are felt as a source of danger to the self and come close to exerting a persecuting influence. Paula Heimann introduced the concept of the assimilation of the internal objects and applied it specifically to sublimation. As regards ego development, she pointed out that such assimilation is essential for the successful exercise of ego functions and for the achievement of independence.

11. Looked at in this light, the mother's love and understanding of the infant can be seen as the infant's greatest standby in overcoming states of disintegration and anxieties of a psychotic nature.

phrenic illness in the infant, and some indications of such illness may already be seen in the first few months of life. In adult patients, states of depersonalization and of schizophrenic dissociation seem to be a regression to these infantile states of disintegration.[12] . . .

I have so far described some effects of excessive introjection and projection on object relations. I am not attempting to investigate here in any detail the various factors which in some cases make for a predominance of introjective and in other cases for a predominance of projective processes. As regards normal personality, it may be said that the course of ego development and object relations depends on the degree to which an optimal balance between introjection and projection in the early stages of development can be achieved. This in turn has a bearing on the integration of the ego and the assimilation of internal objects. Even if the balance is disturbed and one or the other of these processes is excessive, there is some interaction between introjection and projection. For instance the projection of a predominantly hostile inner world which is ruled by persecutory fears leads to the introjection—in taking-back—of a hostile external world, and vice versa—the introjection of a distorted and hostile external world reinforces the projection of a hostile inner world.

Another aspect of projective processes, as we have seen, concerns the forceful entry into the object and control of the object by parts of the self. As a consequence, introjection may then be felt as a forceful entry from the outside into the inside, in retribution for violent projection. This may lead to the fear that not only the body but also the mind is controlled by other people in a hostile way. As a result there may be a severe disturbance in introjecting good objects—a disturbance which would impede all ego functions as well as sexual development and might lead to an excessive withdrawal to the inner world. This withdrawal is, however, caused not only by the fear of introjecting a dangerous external world but also by the fear of internal persecutors and an ensuing flight to the idealized internal object.

---

12. Herbert Rosenfeld (1947) has presented case material to illustrate how the splitting mechanisms which are bound up with projective identification were responsible both for a schizophrenic state and for depersonalization. In Rosenfeld (1950) he also pointed out that a confusional state comes about if the subject loses the capacity to differentiate between good and bad objects, between aggressive and libidinal impulses, and so on. He suggested that in such states of confusion splitting mechanisms are frequently reinforced for defensive purposes.

I have referred to the weakening and impoverishment of the ego resulting from excessive splitting and projective identification. This weakened ego, however, becomes also incapable of assimilating its internal objects, and this leads to the feeling that it is ruled by them. Again, such a weakened ego feels incapable of taking back into itself the parts which it projected into the external world. These various disturbances in the interplay between projection and introjection, which imply excessive splitting of the ego, have a detrimental effect on the relation to the inner and outer world and seem to be at the root of some forms of schizophrenia.

Projective identification is the basis of many anxiety situations, of which I shall mention a few. The phantasy of forcefully entering the object gives rise to anxieties relating to the dangers threatening the subject from within the object. For instance, the impulses to control an object from within it stir up the fear of being controlled and persecuted inside it. By introjecting and reintrojecting the forcefully entered object, the subject's feelings of inner persecution are strongly reinforced; all the more since the reintrojected object is felt to contain the dangerous aspects of the self. The accumulation of anxieties of this nature, in which the ego is, as it were, caught between a variety of external and internal persecution-situations, is a basic element in paranoia.[13]

SCHIZOID OBJECT RELATIONS

To summarize now some of the disturbed object relations which are found in schizoid personalities: the violent splitting of the self and excessive projection have the effect that the person towards whom this process is directed is felt as a persecutor. Since the destructive and hated part of the self which is split off and projected is felt as a danger to the loved object and therefore gives rise to guilt, this process of projection in some ways also implies a deflection of guilt from the self on to the other

13. Herbert Rosenfeld (1947, 1949) discussed the clinical importance of those paranoid anxieties which are connected with projective identification in psychotic patients. In the two schizophrenic cases he described, it became evident that the patients were dominated by the fear that the analyst was trying to force himself into the patient. When these fears were analysed in the transference situation, improvement could take place. Rosenfeld has further connected projective identification (and the corresponding persecutory fears) with female sexual frigidity on the one hand and on the other with the frequent combination of homosexuality and paranoia in men.

person. Guilt has, however, not been done away with, and the deflected guilt is felt as an unconscious responsibility for the people who have become representatives of the aggressive part of the self.

Another typical feature of schizoid object relations is their narcissistic nature, which derives from the infantile introjective and projective processes. For, as I suggested earlier, when the ego ideal is projected into another person, this person becomes predominantly loved and admired because he contains the good parts of the self. Similarly, the relation to another person on the basis of projecting bad parts of the self into him is of a narcissistic nature, because in this case as well the object strongly represents one part of the self. Both these types of a narcissistic relation to an object often show strong obsessional features. The impulse to control other people is, as we know, an essential element in obsessional neurosis. The need to control others can to some extent be explained by a deflected drive to control parts of the self. When these parts have been projected excessively into another person, they can only be controlled by controlling the other person. One root of obsessional mechanisms may thus be found in the particular identification which results from infantile projective processes. This connection may also throw some light on the obsessional element which so often enters into the tendency for reparation. For it is not only an object about whom guilt is experienced but also parts of the self which the subject is driven to repair or restore. . . .

THE DEPRESSIVE POSITION IN RELATION TO THE PARANOID-SCHIZOID POSITION

I now wish to consider further steps in the infant's development. So far I have described the anxieties, mechanisms, and defences which are characteristic of the first few months of life. With the introjection of the complete object in about the second quarter of the first year marked steps in integration are made. This implies important changes in the relation to objects. The loved and hated aspects of the mother are no longer felt to be so widely separated, and the result is an increased fear of loss, states akin to mourning and a strong feeling of guilt, because the aggressive impulses are felt to be directed against the loved object. The depressive position has come to the fore. The very experience of depressive feelings in turn has the effect of further integrating the ego, because it makes for an increased understanding of psychic reality and better perception of the external world, as well as for a greater synthesis between inner and external situations.

The drive to make reparation, which comes to the fore at this stage, can be regarded as a consequence of greater insight into psychic reality and of growing synthesis, for it shows a more realistic response to the feelings of grief, guilt, and fear of loss resulting from the aggression against the loved object. Since the drive to repair or protect the injured object paves the way for more satisfactory object relations and sublimations, it in turn increases synthesis and contributes to the integration of the ego.

During the second half of the first year the infant makes some fundamental steps towards working through the depressive position. However, schizoid mechanisms still remain in force, though in a modified form and to a lesser degree, and early anxiety situations are again and again experienced in the process of modification. The working through of the persecutory and depressive positions extends over the first few years of childhood and plays an essential part in the infantile neurosis. In the course of this process, anxieties lose in strength; objects become both less idealized and less terrifying, and the ego becomes more unified. All this is interconnected with the growing perception of reality and adaptation to it.

If development during the paranoid-schizoid position has not proceeded normally and the infant cannot—for internal or external reasons—cope with the impact of depressive anxieties a vicious circle arises. For if persecutory fear, and correspondingly schizoid mechanisms, are too strong, the ego is not capable of working through the depressive position. This forces the ego to regress to the paranoid-schizoid position and reinforces the earlier persecutory fears and schizoid phenomena. Thus the basis is established for various forms of schizophrenia in later life, for when such a regression occurs, not only are the fixation points in the schizoid position reinforced, but there is a danger of greater states of disintegration setting in. Another outcome may be the strengthening of depressive features.

External experiences are, of course, of great importance in these developments. For instance, in the case of a patient who showed depressive and schizoid features, the analysis brought up with great vividness his early experiences in babyhood, to such an extent that in some sessions physical sensations in the throat or digestive organs occurred. The patient had been weaned suddenly at four months of age because his mother fell ill. In addition, he did not see his mother for four weeks. When she returned, she found the child greatly changed. He had been a lively baby, interested in his surroundings, and he seemed to have lost this interest. He had become apathetic. He had accepted the substitute food fairly easily and in fact never refused food. But he did not thrive on it any more, lost weight, and had a good deal of digestive trouble. It was only at the end of the first year, when other food was introduced, that he again made good physical progress.

Much light was thrown in the analysis on the influence these experiences had on his whole development. His outlook and attitudes in adult life were based on the patterns established in this early stage. For instance, we found again and again a tendency to be influenced by other people in an unselective way—in fact to take in greedily whatever was offered—together with great distrust during the process of introjection. This process was constantly disturbed by anxieties from various sources, which also contributed to an increase of greed.

Taking the material of this analysis as a whole, I came to the conclusion that at the time when the sudden loss of the breast and of the mother occurred, the patient had already to some extent established a relation to a complete good object. He had no doubt already entered the depressive position but could not work through it successfully and the paranoid-schizoid position became regressively reinforced. This expressed itself in the "apathy" which followed a period when the child had already shown a lively interest in his surroundings. The fact that he had reached the depressive position and had introjected a complete object showed in many ways in his personality. He had actually a strong capacity for love and a great longing for a good and complete object. A characteristic feature of his personality was the desire to love people and trust them, unconsciously to regain and build up again the good and complete breast which he had once possessed and lost.

CONNECTION BETWEEN SCHIZOID AND MANIC-DEPRESSIVE PHENOMENA

Some fluctuations between the paranoid-schizoid and the depressive positions always occur and are part of normal development. No clear division between the two stages of development can therefore be drawn; moreover, modification is a gradual process and the phenomena of the two positions remain for some time to some extent intermingled and interacting. In abnormal development this interaction influences, I think, the clinical picture both of some forms of schizophrenia and of manic-depressive disorders. . . .

SOME SCHIZOID DEFENCES

It is generally agreed that schizoid patients are more difficult to analyse than manic-depressive types. Their withdrawn, unemotional attitude, the narcissistic elements in their object relations (to which I referred earlier), a kind of detached hostility which pervades the whole relation to the analyst create a very difficult type of resistance. I believe that it is largely the splitting processes which account for the patient's failure in contact with the analyst and for his lack of response to the analyst's interpretations. The patient himself feels estranged and far away, and this feeling corresponds to the analyst's impression that considerable parts of the patient's personality and of his emotions are not available. Patients with schizoid features may say: "I hear what you are saying. You may be right, but it has no meaning for me." Or again they say they feel they are not there. The expression "no meaning" in such cases does not imply an active rejection of the interpretation but suggests that parts of the personality and of the emotions are split off. These patients can, therefore, not deal with the interpretation; they can neither accept it nor reject it.

I shall illustrate the processes underlying such states by a piece of material taken from the analysis of a man patient. The session I have in mind started with the patient's telling me that he felt anxiety and did not know why. He then made comparisons with people more successful and fortunate than himself. These remarks also had a reference to me. Very strong feelings of frustration, envy, and grievance came to the fore. When I interpreted—to give here again only the gist of my interpretations—that these feelings were directed against the analyst and that he wanted to destroy me, his mood changed abruptly. The tone of his voice became flat, he spoke in a slow, expressionless way, and he said that he felt detached from the whole situation. He added that my interpretation seemed correct, but that it did not matter. In fact, he no longer had any wishes, and nothing was worth bothering about.

My next interpretations centred on the causes for this change of mood. I suggested that at the moment of my interpretation the danger of destroying me had become very real to him and the immediate consequence was the fear of losing me. Instead of feeling guilt and depression, which at certain stages of his analysis followed such interpretations, he now attempted to deal with these dangers by a particular method of splitting. As we know, under the pressure of ambivalence, conflict, and guilt, the patient often splits the figure of the analyst; then the analyst may at certain moments be loved, at other moments hated. Or the relations to the analyst may be split in such a way that he remains the good (or bad) figure while somebody else becomes the opposite figure. But this was not the kind of splitting which occurred in this particular instance. The patient split off those parts of himself, i.e., of his ego, which he felt to be dangerous and hostile towards the analyst. He turned his destructive impulses from his object *towards his ego,* with the result that parts of his ego temporarily went out of existence. In unconscious phantasy this amounted to annihilation of part of his personality. The particular mechanism of turning the destructive impulse against one part of his personality, and the ensuing dispersal of emotions, kept his anxiety in a latent state.

My interpretation of these processes had the effect of again altering the patient's mood. He became emotional, said he felt like crying, was depressed, but felt more integrated; then he also expressed a feeling of hunger.[14]

The violent splitting off and destroying of one part of the personality under the pressure of anxiety and guilt is in my experience an important schizoid mechanism. To refer briefly to another instance: a woman patient had dreamed that she had to deal with a wicked girl child who was determined to murder somebody. The patient tried to influence or control the child and to extort a confession from her which would have been to the child's benefit; but she was unsuccessful. I also entered into the dream and the patient felt that I might help her in dealing with the child. Then

14. The feeling of hunger indicated that the process of introjection had been set going again under the dominance of the libido. While to my first interpretation of his fear of destroying me by his aggression he had responded at once with the violent splitting off and annihilation of parts of his personality, he now experienced more fully the emotions of grief, guilt and fear of loss, as well as some relief of these depressive anxieties. The relief of anxiety resulted in the analyst again coming to stand for a good object which he could trust. Therefore the desire to introject me as a good object could come to the fore. If he could build up again the good breast inside himself, he would strengthen and integrate his ego, would be less afraid of his destructive impulses; in fact he could then preserve himself and the analyst.

the patient strung up the child on a tree in order to frighten her and also prevent her from doing harm. When the patient was about to pull the rope and kill the child, she woke. During this part of the dream the analyst was also present but again remained inactive.

I shall give here only the essence of the conclusions I arrived at from the analysis of this dream. In the dream the patient's personality was split into two parts: the wicked and uncontrollable child on the one hand, and on the other hand the person who tried to influence and control her. The child, of course, stood also for various figures in the past, but in this context she mainly represented one part of the patient's self. Another conclusion was that the analyst was the person whom the child was going to murder, and my role in the dream was partly to prevent this murder from taking place. Killing the child—to which the patient had to resort—represented the annihilation of one part of her personality. . . .

Changes of mood, of course, do not always appear as dramatically within a session as in the first instance I have given in this section. But I have repeatedly found that advances in synthesis are brought about by interpretations of the specific causes for splitting. Such interpretations must deal in detail with the transference situation at that moment, including of course the connection with the past, and must contain a reference to the details of the anxiety situations which drive the ego to regress to schizoid mechanisms. The synthesis resulting from interpretations on these lines goes along with depression and anxieties of various kinds. Gradually such waves of depression—followed by greater integration—lead to a lessening of schizoid phenomena and also to fundamental changes in object relations. . . .

Interpretations which tend towards synthesizing the split in the self, including the dispersal of emotions, make it possible for the anxiety gradually to be experienced as such, though for long stretches we may in fact only be able to bring the ideational contents together but not to elicit the emotions of anxiety.

I have also found that interpretations of schizoid states make particular demands on our capacity to put the interpretations in an intellectually clear form in which the links between the conscious, preconscious and unconscious are established. This is, of course, always one of our aims, but it is of special importance at times when the patient's emotions are not available and we seem to address ourselves only to his intellect, however much broken up.

SUMMARY AND CONCLUSIONS

I will now summarize some of the conclusions presented in this paper. One of my main points was the suggestion that in the first few months of life anxiety is predominantly experienced as fear of persecution and that this contributes to certain mechanisms and defences which are significant for the paranoid-schizoid position. Outstanding among these defences are the mechanisms of splitting internal and external objects, emotions, and the ego. These mechanisms and defences are part of normal development and at the same time form the basis for later schizophrenic illness. I described the processes underlying identification by projection as a combination of splitting off parts of the self and projecting them on to another person, and some of the effects this identification has on normal and schizoid object relations. The onset of the depressive position is the juncture at which by regression schizoid mechanisms may be reinforced. I also suggested a close connection between the manic-depressive and schizoid disorders, based on the interaction between the infantile paranoid-schizoid and depressive positions.

REFERENCES

Fairbairn, W. R. D. (1941). A revised psychopathology of the psychoses and neuroses. *International Journal of Psycho-Analysis* 22.

——(1944). Endopsychic structure considered in terms of object-relationships. *International Journal of Psycho-Analysis* 25.

——(1946). Object relationships and dynamic structure. *International Journal of Psycho-Analysis* 27.

Ferenczi, S. (1930). Notes and fragments. In *Final Contributions to the Problems and Methods of Psycho-Analysis*. London: Hogarth.

Heimann, P. (1942). Sublimation and its relation to the processes of internalization. *International Journal of Psycho-Analysis* 23.

Klein, M. (1932). *The Psycho-Analysis of Children*. London: Hogarth.

——(1935). A contribution to the psychogenesis of manic-depressive states. *International Journal of Psycho-Analysis* 16.

Rosenfeld, H. (1947). Analysis of a schizophrenic state with depersonalization. In *Psychotic States*. London: Hogarth, 1965.

——(1949). Remarks on the relation of male homosexuality to paranoia. In *Psychotic States*. London: Hogarth, 1965.

——(1950). A note on the psychopathology of confusional states in chronic schizophrenia. In *Psychotic States*. London: Hogarth, 1965.

Winnicott, D. W. (1945). Primitive emotional development. In *Collected Papers*. London: Hogarth, 1958.

13

"The Origins of Transference" (1952)

In this paper, Klein linked the importance of object relations from the beginning of life, with her view of transference as a vehicle for understanding patients' early experience. The paper draws together aspects of her earlier writing in emphasizing the interplay of relations to internal and external objects, and describes a new view of the importance of working with transference as a "total situation." By this she means that the whole pattern of the patient's relationship to all past objects and the complex inner relationships between them are lived out in relationship to the analyst, and are used to understand patients' object relations before words. She includes the internal worlds built on this foundation, and the relationships with external objects that have been subsequently determined by the internal organization.

This paper is seminal to modern views of the role of transference. It is a useful complement to the one published by Fairbairn in 1958 on the nature of analytic treatment (excerpted in Chapter 9), which emphasized the central role of the relationship with the analyst as a potentially curative new relationship, not only as an opportunity to understand the totality of the transference. Both points of view are necessary for a synthesized view of transference as a dynamic relationship between ego and object, patient and therapist.

I hold that transference originates in the same processes which in the earliest stages determine object relations. Therefore we have to go back again and again in analysis to the fluctuations between objects, loved and hated, external and internal, which dominate early infancy. We can fully appreciate the interconnection between positive and negative transferences only if we explore the early interplay between love and hate, and the vicious circle of aggression, anxieties, feelings of guilt and increased aggression, as well as the various aspects of objects towards whom these conflicting emotions and anxieties are directed. On the other hand, through exploring these early processes I became convinced that the analysis of the negative transference, which had received relatively little attention[1] in psychoanalytic technique, is a precondition for analysing the deeper layers of the mind. The analysis of the negative as well as of the positive transference and of their interconnection is, as I have held for many years, an indispensable principle for the treatment of all types of patients, children and adults alike. I have substantiated this view in most of my writings from 1927 onwards.

This approach, which in the past made possible the psychoanalysis of very young children, has in recent years proved extremely fruitful for the analysis of schizophrenic patients. Until about 1920 it was assumed that schizophrenic patients were incapable of forming a transference and therefore could not be psychoanalysed. Since then the psychoanalysis of schizophrenics has been attempted by various techniques. The most radical change of view in this respect, however, has occurred more recently and is closely connected with the greater knowledge of the mechanisms, anxieties, and defences operative in earliest infancy. Since some of these defences, evolved in primal object relations against both love and hatred, have been discovered, the fact that schizophrenic patients are capable of developing both a positive and a negative transference has been fully understood; this finding is confirmed if we consistently apply in the treatment of schizophrenic patients[2] the principle that it is as necessary to analyse the negative as the positive transference—that in fact the one cannot be analysed without the other.

Retrospectively it can be seen that these considerable advances in technique are supported in psychoanalytic theory by Freud's discovery of the life and death instincts, which has fundamentally added to the understanding of the origin of ambivalence. Because the life and death instincts, and therefore love and hatred, are at bottom in the closest interaction, negative and positive transference are basically interlinked.

1. This was largely due to the undervaluation of the importance of aggression.

2. This technique is illustrated in Segal (1950) and Rosenfeld (1952a, b).

The understanding of earliest object relations and the processes they imply has essentially influenced technique from various angles. It has long been known that the psychoanalyst in the transference situation may stand for mother, father, or other people, that he is also at times playing in the patient's mind the part of the superego, at other times that of the id or the ego. Our present knowledge enables us to penetrate to the specific details of the various roles allotted by the patient to the analyst. There are in fact very few people in the young infant's life, but he feels them to be a multitude of objects because they appear to him in different aspects. Accordingly, the analyst may at a given moment represent a part of the self, of the superego or any one of a wide range of internalized figures. Similarly it does not carry us far enough if we realize that the analyst stands for the actual father or mother, unless we understand which aspect of the parents has been revived. The picture of the parents in the patient's mind has in varying degrees undergone distortion through the infantile processes of projection and idealization, and has often retained much of its phantastic nature. Altogether, in the young infant's mind every external experience is interwoven with his phantasies and on the other hand every phantasy contains elements of actual experience, and it is only by analysing the transference situation to its depth that we are able to discover the past both in its realistic and phantastic aspects. It is also the origin of these fluctuations in earliest infancy which accounts for their strength in the transference, and for the swift changes—sometimes even within one session—between father and mother, between omnipotently kind objects and dangerous persecutors, between internal and external figures. Sometimes the analyst appears simultaneously to represent both parents—in that case often in a hostile alliance against the patient, whereby the negative transference acquires great intensity. What has then been revived or has become manifest in the transference is the mixture in the patient's phantasy of the parents as one figure, the "combined parent figure" as I described it elsewhere (Klein 1932). This is one of the phantasy formations characteristic of the earliest stages of the Oedipus complex and which, if maintained in strength, is detrimental both to object relations and sexual development. The phantasy of the combined parents draws its force from another element of early emotional life—i.e., from the powerful envy associated with frustrated oral desires. Through the analysis of such early situations we learn that in the baby's mind when he is frustrated (or dissatisfied from inner causes) his frustration is coupled with the feeling that another object (soon represented by the father) receives from the mother the coveted gratification and love denied to himself at that moment. Here is one root of the phantasy that the parents are combined in an everlasting mutual gratification of an oral, anal, and genital nature. And this is in my view the prototype of situations of both envy and jealousy.

There is another aspect of the analysis of transference which needs mentioning. We are accustomed to speak of the transference *situation* But do we always keep in mind the fundamental importance of this concept? It is my experience that in unravelling the details of the transference it is essential to think in terms of *total situations* transferred from the past into the present as well as of emotions, defences, and object relations.

For many years—and this is up to a point still true today—transference was understood in terms of direct references to the analyst in the patient's material. My conception of transference as rooted in the earliest stages of development and in deep layers of the unconscious is much wider and entails a technique by which from the whole material presented the *unconscious elements* of the transference are deduced. For instance, reports of patients about their everyday life, relations, and activities not only give an insight into the functioning of the ego, but also reveal—if we explore their unconscious content—the defences against the anxieties stirred up in the transference situation. For the patient is bound to deal with conflicts and anxieties reexperienced towards the analyst by the same methods he used in the past. That is to say, he turns away from the analyst as he attempted to turn away from his primal objects; he tries to split the relation to him, keeping him either as a good or as a bad figure; he deflects some of the feelings and attitudes experienced towards the analyst on to other people in his current life, and this is part of "acting out."[3]

In keeping with my subject matter, I have predominantly discussed here the earliest experiences, situations, and emotions from which transference springs. On these foundations, however, are built the later object relations and the emotional and intellectual developments which necessitate the analyst's attention no less than the earliest ones; that is to say, our

3. The patient may at times try to escape from the present into the past rather than realize that his emotions, anxieties, and phantasies are at the time operative in full strength and focused on the analyst. At other times, as we know, the defences are mainly directed against reexperiencing the past in relation to the original objects.

field of investigation covers *all* that lies between the current situation and the earliest experiences. In fact it is not possible to find access to earliest emotions and object relations except by examining their vicissitudes in the light of later developments. It is only by linking again and again (and that means hard and patient work) later experiences with earlier ones and vice versa, it is only by consistently exploring their interplay, that present and past can come together in the patient's mind. This is one aspect of the process of integration which, as the analysis progresses, encompasses the whole of the patient's mental life. When anxiety and guilt diminish and love and hate can be better synthesized, splitting processes—a fundamental defence against anxiety—as well as repressions lessen while the ego gains in strength and coherence; the cleavage between idealized and persecutory objects diminishes; the phantastic aspects of objects lose in strength; all of which implies that unconscious phantasy life—less sharply divided off from the unconscious part of the mind—can be better utilized in ego activities, with a consequent general enrichment of the personality. I am touching here on the *differences*—as contrasted with the similarities—between transference and the first object relations. These differences are a measure of the curative effect of the analytic procedure.

I suggested above that one of the factors which bring about the repetition compulsion is the pressure exerted by the earliest anxiety situations. When persecutory and depressive anxiety and guilt diminish, there is less urge to repeat fundamental experiences over and over again, and therefore early patterns and modes of feelings are maintained with less tenacity. These fundamental changes come about through the consistent analysis of the transference; they are bound up with a deep-reaching revision of the earliest object relations and are reflected in the patient's current life as well as in the altered attitudes towards the analyst.

REFERENCES

Klein, M. (1932). *The Psycho-Analysis of Children*. London: Hogarth.

Rosenfeld, H. (1952a). Notes on the psycho-analysis of the super-ego conflict of an acute schizophrenic patient. *International Journal of Psycho-Analysis* 33.

—— (1952b). Transference phenomena and transference analysis in an acute catatonic schizophrenic patient. *International Journal of Psycho-Analysis* 33:457–464.

Segal, H. (1950). Some aspects of the analysis of a schizophrenic. *International Journal of Psycho-Analysis* 31.

14

"A Study of Envy and Gratitude" (1956)

Klein read a paper on envy and gratitude at the 19th International Congress in Geneva in 1955, of which this is an expanded lecture given to the British Society of Psychoanalysis in 1956. She later expanded it into a short book (Klein 1957). These papers introduce her last major theoretical contributions. She argued that unconscious envy is present from the beginning as an attitude toward the mother and her breast for the possession of all that the infant needs and desires. This implies, she stated, that there is a rudimentary ego present from the beginning. Klein had been arguing for many years that this was the case, in agreement with what Fairbairn had written from the early 1940s. She also described the processes of nonintegration and integration in early ego organization, which Winnicott was exploring in a similar vein at about the same time in material contained later in this volume. The three original contributors to object relations theory were not in fundamental disagreement about these process of early ego organization. In this paper, for instance, Klein was explicit about the way the Oedipus complex is built on the early relation to the mother, which she called the oral relation to the breast. To her explicit agreement with Fairbairn on this point, she added the rich set of ideas about envy and gratitude that form the heart of this paper.

Envy is an early attitude of the infant in a two-person situation, felt toward the mother for possessing what it needs, and is, according to Klein, a hostile attitude of attack and spoiling projected into the breast, which is therefore felt to fill the breast itself with aggression toward the infant in return. Greed is an allied affect having to do with introjecting, or desiring to take in, all the envied breast possesses, while jealousy is felt in a three-person situation toward a third party who has the love of someone also desired by the child.

Perhaps the most overlooked point made in this paper and in Klein's writing in general, is the countervailing importance of gratitude, the positive force of love which is part of the infant's constitutional endowment, which, from the beginning, balances the destructive forces of envy and spoiling. Gratitude is the basis of sustenance of good object relations, which lead to feelings of generosity. Klein included a persuasive discussion of the importance of good early object relations in the development of the ego and later relationships, contrasting these with persecutory relationships on the one hand and idealization on the other. Klein's description of idealization as a defense against persecutory anxiety was once again close to Fairbairn's description of the exciting object and its dynamic relationship to the rejecting object, another aspect of the consonance of the two theories. Her statement that a strongly loving attitude lessens the need for idealization was close to his contention that good early experiences contribute to a lessening of ego splitting into libidinal and anti-libidinal structures. Winnicott's discussion of the role of good early experience, as we shall see, also emphasized that it supported the nurturing to minimize the exaggerated splitting of false self from true self.

In another part of her discussion, Klein emphasized envy's role not only toward the mother, but toward the parental couple, and the way the early envy of the mother comes to include envy for her possession of the father and his penis. This extension of her consideration of the child's attitude toward, and internalization of, the couple is a further contribution to modern ideas about the oedipal situation. Her discussion of the role of envy in the development of both girls and boys significantly modified Freud's early ideas of development and provided a basis of understanding consistent with modern views.

Klein concluded with comments on the treatment of envy in analysis, underscoring its role in understanding early life. Her mention of the recovery of *memories in feelings,* which we now refer to as *implicit memories,* furthered the analytic understanding of early life for those patients whose difficulties are rooted in experiences before the development of words.

REFERENCE

Klein, M. (1957). *Envy and Gratitude: A Study of Unconscious Sources.* London: Tavistock.

In this paper I wish to draw attention to a particular aspect of earliest object relations and internalization processes. I am referring to the effects of envy on the development of the capacity for gratitude and happiness. The contention I wish to put forward is that envy contributes to the infant's difficulties, in that he feels that the gratification he was deprived of has been kept for itself by the breast which frustrated him.

A distinction should be drawn between envy, jealousy, and greed. Envy is the angry feeling that another person possesses and enjoys something desirable—the envious impulse being to take it away or to spoil it. Moreover, envy implies the subject's relation to one person only and goes back to the earliest exclusive relation with the mother. Jealousy is based on envy, but it involves the subject's relation to at least two people. Jealousy is mainly concerned with love which the subject feels is his due and which has been taken away, or is in danger of being taken away from him. In the everyday conception of jealousy, a man or a woman feels deprived of the person they love by somebody else.

Greed is an impetuous and insatiable craving, exceeding what the subject needs and what the object can and wishes to give. At the unconscious level, greed aims primarily at completely scooping out, sucking dry, and devouring the breast, that is to say, its aim is destructive introjection, whereas envy not only aims at robbing in this way, but also at putting badness, primarily bad excrements and bad parts of the self, into the mother—first of all into her breast—in order to spoil and destroy her; in the deepest sense this means destroying her creativeness. This process I have defined elsewhere as a destructive aspect of projective identification which starts from the beginning of life. The difference between greed and envy, although no rigid dividing line can be drawn since they are so closely associated, would accordingly be that greed is mainly bound up with introjection and envy with projection.

My work has shown me that the first object to be envied is the feeding breast, for the infant feels that it possesses everything that he desires and that it has an unlimited flow of milk and love which it keeps for its own gratification. This feeling adds to his sense of grievance and hatred. If envy is excessive—which would indicate that paranoid and schizoid features are strong—the result is a disturbed relation to the mother.

We find this primitive envy revived in the transference situation. For instance: the analyst has just given an interpretation which brought the patient relief and produced a change of mood from despair to hope and trust. With some patients, or with the same patient at other times, this helpful interpretation may soon become the object of criticism. It is then no longer felt to be something good he has received and which he has experienced as an enrichment. The envious patient grudges the analyst the success of his work, and if his envious criticism has the effect of making him feel that the analyst and the help he is giving have become spoilt, the patient cannot introject the analyst sufficiently as a good object and cannot accept his interpretations with real conviction. He may also feel, because of guilt about devaluing the help given, that he is unworthy to benefit by analysis.

In these ways, envy plays an important part in the negative therapeutic reaction, in addition to the factors discovered by Freud and further developed by Joan Riviere. Needless to say, our patients criticize us for a variety of reasons, sometimes with justification. But a patient's need to devalue the very help he has experienced is the expression of envy. This applies particularly to paranoid patients, who indulge in the sadistic pleasure of disparaging the analyst's work even though it has given them relief. On the other hand, some of our patients try to avoid criticism and are, up to a point, very cooperative. And yet we find that their doubts and uncertainties about the value of the analysis persist. In my experience the slow progress we make in such cases has also to do with envy. The patient has split off the envious and hostile part of his self; nevertheless it is bound to influence fundamentally the course of the analysis. Other patients try to avoid criticism by becoming confused. This confusion is not only a defence but also expresses the uncertainty as to whether the analyst is still a good figure, or whether he and the help he is giving have become bad because he has been spoilt by criticism.

All these attitudes are part of the negative therapeutic reaction because they interfere with the gradual building up of a good object in the transference situation and therefore—just as in the earliest situation the good food and the primal good object could not be assimilated—in the transference situation the result of the analysis is impaired.

Thus in the context of the analytic material we can sometimes gather how the patient felt as a baby towards the mother's breast. For instance, the infant may have a grievance that the milk comes too quickly or too slowly, or that he was not given the breast when he most craved for it, and therefore when it is offered, he does not want it any more. He turns away from it and sucks his fingers instead. When he accepts the breast he may not drink enough, or the feed is disturbed. Some infants obviously have great difficulty in overcoming such grievances. With others these feelings, even though based on actual frustrations, are soon overcome: the breast is taken and the feed is fully enjoyed.

It is in the nature of envy that it spoils the primal good object and gives added impetus to sadistic attacks on the breast, which I have often described in other connections. Excessive envy increases the intensity of such attacks and their duration, and thus makes it more difficult for the infant to regain the lost good object, whereas sadistic attacks on the breast which are less determined by envy pass more quickly and therefore do not, in the infant's mind, so strongly and lastingly destroy the goodness of the object; the breast which returns is felt as an evidence that it is not injured and that it is still good.

When envy is excessive, the infant does not sufficiently build up a good object, and therefore cannot preserve it internally. Hence, somewhat later he is unable to establish firmly other good objects in his inner world.

The contrary situation holds in children with a strong capacity for love. The relation to the good object is deeply rooted and can, without being fundamentally damaged, withstand temporary states of envy, hatred, and grievance—which arise even in children who are loved and well mothered. Thus, when these negative states are transient, the good object is regained time and again. This is an essential factor in establishing the good object and in laying the foundations for stability and a strong ego.

The emotions and attitudes I have referred to arise in the earliest stage of infancy when for the baby the mother is the one and only object. How far this exclusive relation remains undisturbed depends partly on external factors. But the feelings which underlie it—above all, the capacity for love—appear to be innate. I have repeatedly put forward the hypothesis that the primal good object, the mother's breast, forms the core of the ego and vitally contributes to its growth and integration. We find in the analysis of our patients that the breast in its good aspects is the prototype of maternal goodness and generosity, as well as of creativeness. All this is felt by the infant in much more primitive ways than language can express it.

Strong envy of the feeding breast interferes with the capacity for complete gratification which is of vital importance for the infant's development. For if the *undisturbed* enjoyment in being fed is *frequently* experienced, the introjection of the mother's breast as a good object comes about with relative security. The capacity to fully enjoy gratification at the breast forms the foundation for all later happiness, as well as for pleasure from various sources. It is significant that Freud attributed so much importance to the pleasure–pain principle.

A full gratification at the breast means that the infant feels he has received from his loved object a unique gift, which he wants to keep. This is the basis of gratitude. Gratitude includes belief in good objects and trust in them. It includes also the ability to assimilate the loved object—not only as a source of food—and to love it without envy interfering. The more often this gift received is fully accepted, the more often the feeling of enjoyment and gratitude—implying the wish to return pleasure—is experienced. Gratitude is closely bound up with generosity. For inner wealth derives from having assimilated the good object, and this enables the individual to share its gifts with others.

To clarify my argument, a reference to my views on the early ego is necessary. I believe that it exists in a rudimentary form from the beginning of postnatal life, and performs a number of important functions. It might well be that this early ego is identical with the unconscious part of the ego which Freud postulated. Though he did not assume that an ego exists from the beginning, he attributed to the organism a function which, as I see it, can only be performed by the ego. The threat of annihilation by the death instinct within is, in my view—which differs from Freud's on this point—the primordial anxiety and it is the ego which, in the services of the life instinct, possibly even called into operation by the life instinct, deflects to some extent that threat outwards. This fundamental defence against the death instinct Freud attributed to the organism, whereas I regard this process as the primary activity of the ego.

There are other primary activities of the ego which in my view derive from the imperative need to deal with the struggle between life and death instincts. One of these functions is gradual integration. The opposite tendency of the ego to split itself and its object is partly due to the ego lacking cohesion at birth, and partly it is a defence against the primordial anxiety. I have, for many years, attributed great importance to one particular process of splitting, the division of the breast into a good and bad object. I took this to be an expression of the innate conflict between love and hate and the ensuing anxieties. However, coexisting with this division there appear to be various processes of splitting, such as fragmenting the ego and its objects, whereby a dispersal of the destructive impulses is achieved. This is one of the characteristic defences during the paranoid-schizoid position which I believe normally extends over the first three or four months of life. . . .

To return to the splitting process which I take to be a precondition for the young infant's relative stability: during the first few months he predominantly keeps the good object apart from the bad one and thus, in a fundamental way, preserves it. This primal division only succeeds if there is adequate capacity for love. Excessive envy, a corollary of destructive impulses, interferes with the building up of a good object and the primal split between the good and bad breast cannot be sufficiently achieved. The result is that later the differentiation between good and bad is disturbed in various connections. On the other hand, if the split between the two aspects of the object is too deep, the all-important processes of ego integration and object synthesis, as well as of mitigation of hatred by love, are impaired and the depressive position cannot be worked through. A very deep and sharp division between loved and hated objects indicates that destructive impulses, envy, and persecutory anxiety are very strong and serve as a defence against these emotions.

I am touching here on the problem of idealization. This is an early process which I take to be universal, but the motive power behind it varies individually. As I discovered many years ago in my work with young children, idealization is a corollary to persecutory anxiety—a defence against it—and the ideal breast is the counterpart of the devouring breast. But I also found that idealization derives from the innate feeling that an extremely good breast exists, a feeling which leads to the longing for a good object. Infants whose capacity for love is strong have less need for idealization than those in whom destructive impulses and persecutory anxiety are paramount. Excessive idealization denotes that persecution is the main driving force. It becomes also an important defence against envy, because if the object is exalted so much that comparison with it becomes impossible, envy is counteracted. The idealized object, which largely replaces the good one, is much less integrated in the ego since it stems predominantly from persecution.

While people who have been able to establish the primal good object with relative security are capable of retaining their love for it in spite of its shortcomings, with others idealization is a characteristic of their love relations and friendships. This tends to break down and then one loved object may have to be frequently exchanged for another; for no such person can fully come up to expectations. The former idealized person is then often felt as a persecutor (which shows the origin of idealization as a counterpart to persecution) and on to him is projected the subject's envious and critical attitude.

There is a direct link between the envy experienced towards the mother's breast and the development of jealousy. Jealousy is based on the suspicion of and rivalry with the father, who is accused of having taken away the mother's breast, and the mother. This rivalry marks the early stages of the positive and negative Oedipus complexes which arise concurrently with the depressive position in the second quarter of the first year. The importance of the combined parent figure, expressed in such phantasies as the mother or the mother's breast containing the penis of the father, or the father containing the mother, have been elaborated by me in earlier writings. The influence of this combined parent figure on the infant's ability to differentiate between the parents and to establish good relations with each of them, is affected by the strength of envy and the ensuing jealousy. For the feeling that the parents are always getting sexual gratification from one another reinforces the phantasy—derived from various sources—that they are always combined. The consequence may be a lasting disturbance in the relation to both parents.

During the period characterized by the depressive position, when the infant progressively integrates his feelings of love and hatred and synthesizes the good and bad aspects of the mother, he goes through states of mourning bound up with feelings of guilt. He also begins to understand more of the external world and realizes that he cannot keep his mother to himself as his exclusive possession. Jealousy is, as we know, inherent in the Oedipus situation and is accompanied by hate and death wishes. Normally, however, the gain of new objects who can be loved—the father and siblings—and other compensations which the developing ego derives from the external world, mitigate jealousy and grievance to some extent. If paranoid and schizoid mechanisms are strong, jealousy—and, at bottom, envy—remains unmitigated.

All this has an essential bearing on the development of the Oedipus complex. Freud has shown how vital the relation of the girl to the mother is in her subsequent relations to men. I believe that if her first oral gratifications have been disturbed, mainly by internal factors such as strong envy, greed, and hatred, her turning away from the breast towards the penis is largely a flight mechanism. If this is so, the relation to the father, and later on to other men, may suffer in different ways.

Freud's discovery of penis envy in women, and its link with aggressive impulses, was a basic contribution to the understanding of envy.

When penis envy and castration wishes are strong, the envied object, the penis, is to be destroyed, and the man who owns it deprived of it. There are a number of factors contributing to penis envy which are, however, not relevant to my thesis. In this context I wish to consider the woman's penis envy only in so far as it is of oral origin. As we know, under the dominance of oral desires, the penis is strongly equated with the breast (as Abraham has shown) and in my experience penis envy can be traced back to envy of the mother's breast.

Much in the girl's relation to the father depends on whether envy of the mother's possession of the father prevails, or whether she is mainly intent on gaining his love entirely for herself. If envy is the main factor, her desire to spoil the father for the mother makes him into a valueless or bad object, undermines her relation to men and may express itself in frigidity. If jealousy about the father's love predominates, she may combine some hatred against the mother with love for the father.

In men, the envy of the mother's breast is also a very important factor. If it is strong and oral gratification thereby impaired, hatred and anxieties are transferred to the female genital. Whereas normally the genital development enables the boy to retain his mother as a love object, a deep disturbance in the oral relation opens the way for severe difficulties in the genital relation to women. Excessive envy of the breast is likely to extend to all feminine attributes, in particular to the woman's capacity to bear children.

At bottom, envy is directed against creativeness: what the envied breast has to offer is unconsciously felt as the prototype of creativeness, because the breast and the milk it gives is felt to be the source of life. In both men and women this envy plays a major part in the desires to take away the attributes of the other sex, as well as to possess or spoil those of the parent of the same sex. It follows that paranoid jealousy and rivalry in the direct and inverted Oedipus situations are in both the male and female, however divergent their development, based on excessive envy towards the primal object: the mother and her breast.

I shall now illustrate some of my conclusions by clinical material. My first instance is taken from the analysis of a woman patient. She had been breast-fed, but circumstances had otherwise not been favourable and she was convinced that her babyhood and feeding had been wholly unsatisfactory. Her grievance about the past linked with hopelessness about the present and future. Envy of the feeding breast, and the ensuing difficulties in object relations, had already been extensively analysed prior to the material to which I am going to refer.

The patient telephoned and said that she could not come for treatment because of a pain in her shoulder. On the next day she rang me to say that she was still not well but expected to see me on the following day. When, on the third day, she actually came, she was full of complaints. She had been looked after by her maid, but nobody else had taken an interest in her. She described to me that at one moment her pain had suddenly increased, together with a sense of extreme coldness. She had felt an impetuous need for somebody to come at once and cover up her shoulder so that it should get warm, and go away again as soon as that was done. It occurred to her at that moment that this must be how she had felt as a baby when she wanted to be looked after and nobody came.

It was characteristic of the patient's attitude to people and threw light on her earliest relation to the breast that she desired to be looked after but at the same time repelled the very object which was to gratify her. The suspicion of the gift received, together with her impetuous need to be cared for, which ultimately meant a desire to be fed, expressed her ambivalent attitude towards the breast. I have referred to infants whose response to frustration is to make insufficient use of the gratification which even the delayed feed could give them. I would assume that though they do not give up their desire for a gratifying breast, they cannot enjoy it and therefore repel it. The case under discussion illustrates some of the reasons for this attitude: suspicion of the gift she wished to receive because the object was already spoilt by envy and hatred, and therefore deep resentment about every frustration. We also have to remember—and this applies to other adults in whom envy is marked—that many disappointing experiences, no doubt partly due to her own attitude, had even beforehand made her feel that the desired care would not be satisfactory.

In the course of this session the patient reported a dream: she was in a restaurant, sat down at a table, but nobody came to serve her. She decided to join a queue and fetch herself something to eat. In front of her was a woman who took two or three little cakes and went away with them. The patient also took two or three little cakes. From her associations I am selecting the following: the woman seemed very determined, and her figure reminded her of mine. There was a sudden doubt about the name of the cakes (actually *petits fours*) which she first thought were *petit fru*, which reminded her of *petit frau* and thus of *Frau Klein*.[1] The gist of my interpretations was that her grievance about the missed analytic sessions

1. *Klein* = little.

related to the unsatisfactory feeds and unhappiness in babyhood. The two cakes out of the "two or three" stood for the breast which she felt she had been twice deprived of by missing analytic sessions. The fact that the woman was "determined" and that the patient followed her example in taking the cakes pointed both to her identification with the analyst and at her projection of her greed on to her. In the context of this paper, one aspect of the dream is most relevant. The woman who went away with the two or three *petits fours* stood not only for the breast which was withheld, but also for the breast which was going to feed itself. (Taken together with the other material, the "determined" analyst did not only represent a breast but a person with whose qualities, good or bad, the patient identified herself.)

To frustration was thus added envy of the breast. This envy gave rise to bitter resentment, for the mother was felt to be selfish and mean, feeding and loving herself rather than her baby. In this analytic situation I was suspected of having enjoyed myself during the time when she was absent, or of having given the time to other patients whom I preferred. The queue which the patient had to join referred to other more favoured rivals.

The response to the analysis of the dream was a striking change in the emotional situation. The patient now experienced a feeling of happiness and gratitude more vividly than in previous analytic sessions. She had tears in her eyes, which was unusual, and said that she felt as if now she had had an entirely satisfactory feed.

It also occurred to her that her breast-feeding and her infancy might have been happier than it appeared to her in retrospect. Moreover, she felt more hopeful about the future and about the result of her analysis. The patient had more fully realized one part of herself which was by no means unknown to her in other connections. She was fully aware that she was envious and jealous of various people but had not been able to recognize it sufficiently in the relation to the analyst because it was too painful to acknowledge that she was grudging me the success of the analysis on which her hopes were centered. In this session, after the interpretation of it, her envy had lessened; the capacity for enjoyment and gratitude had come to the fore, and she was able to experience a happy feed. This emotional situation had to be worked through over and over again, both in the positive and negative transference, until a more stable result was achieved.

We find that some patients are even quite able to express their dislike and criticism of the analyst, but this differs fundamentally from the realization that at bottom it was they who by their envy spoilt the analyst and his work. The envious part of the self is split off, but exerts its power and contributes to the negative therapeutic reaction.

To come back to the patient under discussion, it was by enabling her gradually to bring the split-off parts of her self together in relation to the analyst, and by her recognizing how envious and therefore suspicious she was of me, and in the first place of her mother, that the experience of that happy feed came about. This was bound up with feelings of gratitude. In the course of the analysis envy was diminished and feelings of gratitude became much more frequent and lasting.

In passing I would say that it is not only in children but also in adults that a full revival of the emotions felt during the earliest feeding experiences can come about in the transference situation. For instance, a feeling of hunger or thirst comes up very strongly during the session and has gone after the interpretation which was felt to have satisfied it. One of my patients, overcome by such feelings, got up from the couch and put his arms round one section of the arch which separated one part of my consulting room from the other. I have repeatedly heard the expression at the end of such a session, "I have been well nourished." The good object, in its earliest primitive form as the mother who takes care of the baby and feeds him, had been regained. . . .

I can only touch here on the fluctuation and difficulties we encounter when we analyse the splitting processes which are bound up with the analysis of envy. For instance, the patient has experienced gratitude for and appreciation of the analyst's skill, but this very skill becomes the cause of the transformation of admiration into envy. Envy may be counteracted by pride in having a good analyst. But if this pride stirs up possessiveness and greed, there is a return to the baby's greedy attitude which could be described in the following terms: "I have everything I want, the good mother belongs only to me." Such a greedy and controlling attitude is liable to spoil the relation to the good object. Guilt about destructive greed might soon lead to another defence, such as, "I do not want to injure the analyst (mother); I rather refrain from accepting her gifts." Such an attitude in turn may easily give rise to guilt about not accepting the analyst's help.

Each of the changes I have just enumerated has to be analysed as it comes up in the transference situation. It is by working through a multitude of defences and the emotions which underlie these defences that we can in time help the patient to achieve a better balance. With this end in view we have again and again to analyse the splitting processes, which I now think is the most difficult part of the analytic procedure. Since no anxiety can be experienced without the ego using whatever defences are available, these splitting processes play an important role as defences against persecutory and depressive anxieties. It appears to me that the realization of envy and the harm done by it to the loved object, and the deep anxieties to which this realization gives rise, contributes to the strong resistance we meet in attempting to undo the split and to bring about steps in integration. It is of the greatest importance to observe every detail in the transference situation which throws light on the earliest difficulties. In this way we sometimes discover that even a strong positive transference may be deceptive for it may be based on idealization and a covering up of the hatred and envy which are split off.

I have described how painful it is for the patient to realize his harmful and spoiling envy against the loved mother, and why there is such a strong resistance against such insight. When the patient nevertheless, through the analytic procedure, comes face to face with this split-off hated and despised part of his personality, this is often experienced as a shock and leads to depression. The feeling of guilt resulting from the realization of destructive envy may lead to the patient temporarily inhibiting his own capacities. We encounter a very different line when the undoing of the split is felt as unbearable and the consequence is an increase of omnipotent and even megalomaniac phantasies. This can be a critical stage because the patient may take refuge in increasing his hostile attitudes. Thus he feels justified in hating the analyst and in thinking that he, the patient, is superior to him and undervalued by him. He feels that everything so far achieved in the analysis was his own doing. To go back to the early situation, the patient as an infant sometimes felt superior to the parents; I have also met with the phantasies that he or she created, as it were, the mother or gave birth to her and possessed the mother's breasts. It was thus the mother who robbed the patient of the breast and not the patient who robbed her. Projection, omnipotence, and persecution are then at their highest. . . .

The insight gained in the process of integration leads step by step to the patient recognizing that there are dangerous parts in his self; he becomes able to accept this because with growing integration the capacity for love increases and envy and hatred are mitigated. The pain which the patient goes through during these processes is gradually diminished by improvements bound up with integration. For instance, patients become able to make decisions which they were previously unable to come to make, and in general to use their gifts more freely. This is linked up with a lessening inhibition of their capacity to make reparation. Their powers of enjoyment may increase in many ways and hope comes up again and again.

The enrichment of the personality by integrating split-off parts of the self is a vital process. Together with hatred, envy, and destructiveness, other important parts of the personality had been lost and are regained in the course of the analysis. . . .

I have found that whenever integration has come about more fully and the patient has been able up to a point to accept the hating and hated part of his personality, he has also in retrospect established the primal good object more securely than he had done in infancy. We can, therefore, look from another angle at the aspects of technique which I am trying to convey. From the beginning all emotions attach themselves to the first object. If destructive impulses, envy, and paranoid anxiety are excessive, the infant grossly distorts and magnifies every frustration from external sources which he experiences, and the mother's breast turns externally and internally predominantly into a persecutory object. Then even actual gratifications cannot be sufficiently accepted and cannot sufficiently counteract persecutory anxiety. In taking the analysis back to earliest infancy, we enable the patient to revive fundamental situations—a revival which I have often spoken of as "memories in feelings." This implies that in retrospect the patient lives more successfully through early frustrations. The means by which this is achieved is the analysis of the negative and positive transference which takes us back to earliest object relations. If we succeed, the patient realizes his own destructive impulses and projections, revises therefore his first object relations and establishes, in retrospect, his good object more securely, in particular by establishing the analyst as a good object in the transference. This can only come about if splitting processes, which have been largely used as a defence against persecution and guilt, lose in strength as a result of analysis. Thus the more integrated ego becomes capable of experiencing guilt and feelings of responsibility which it was unable to face in infancy; object synthesis and therefore a mitigation of hatred by love becomes possible, and greed and envy, which are corollaries of destructive impulses, lose in power. It is on these lines that also the psychoanalysis of psychotics can succeed.

To put it differently: by the consistent analysis of the negative as well as the positive transference, persecutory anxiety and schizoid mechanisms are diminished and the patient can work through the depressive position. When his initial inability to establish a good object is to some extent overcome, his capacity for enjoyment and the appreciation of the gifts received from the good object increase step by step and envy is diminished and gratitude becomes possible. These changes extend to many aspects of the patient's personality and range from earliest emotional life to adult experiences and relations. In the analysis of the effects of early disturbances on the whole development lies, I believe, our greatest hope of helping our patients.

V

D. W. WINNICOTT

15

"Primitive Emotional Development" (1945)

Donald Winnicott, a pediatrician turned analyst, was the third major contributor to object relations in Britain. Winnicott was supervised by Klein and was thought of as one of her supporters in the 1940s during the "Controversial Discussions." Later he came to think of himself as influenced by but independent of Klein (Winnicott 1962).

His pediatric grounding in the close observation of babies and children with their mothers gave him an independent perspective that fit his idiosyncratic attitude. His contributions draw on an intense and intuitive understanding of the meaning of the relationships to children, and to a lesser extent, on their meaning for mothers. He is a theorist on whose observations we can draw to bridge the gap between Klein's emphasis on the infant's contribution to its own development, and Fairbairn's observations about the internalization and reorganization of experience with the mother during the period of infantile dependency.

In a 1941 paper, "The Observation of Infants in a Set Situation," which I have not reprinted here, Winnicott described observations of infants with their mothers that characterize much of his contribution. He described the period of hesitation, its relationship to anxieties connected with the baby's wish to explore, and even the transmission of anxiety from the mother to the infant. This observation set the stage for his later description of the psychosomatic partnership between mother and infant as the vehicle for the building up of the infant's inner world modeled on the mother's psychology, as transmitted through her physical handling of the infant and her responses to the infant's needs and anxieties.

"Primitive Emotional Development" characterizes the qualities of the child's object relationships during the first few years in different terms from those used in earlier analytic discussion. Nevertheless, it is possible to discern links to Klein and Fairbairn in Winnicott's discussion of the process of integration of the early ego from a state of unintegration. All three theoreticians were concerned with learning how the baby achieved a progressive integration during the earliest months of life, and all three assumed the existence of an ego that strove toward integration. Klein voiced her agreement with Winnicott's formulation of an early state of non-integration in her "Schizoid Mechanisms" paper in 1946, excerpted in Chapter 12.

Winnicott described integration as a process that must be supported by the mother, but that is also driven by the child. He centered his discussion on the infant's *moment of illusion* that the infant has created an object or a situation that in reality has been offered by the mother. This paradox remained a cornerstone of Winnicott's view of the pairing of the processes of internalization and discovery, both of which were needed for successful development. The paradox is discussed more fully in his paper on transitional objects, which is excerpted in Chapter 18. Winnicott led the way in this examination of the process of the baby's internalizing of external experience with the mother and other important people. Stephen Mitchell (Chapter 55) later drew on Winnicott in making this paradox of discovery and invention the cornerstone of his ideas of development which, he said, must occur in a "relational matrix."

In "Primitive Emotional Development," Winnicott also described a stage of the infant's preconcern in object relating, characterized by an attitude of "primitive ruthlessness" toward the mother, to be later developed in his paper "The Use of an Object" (excerpted in Chapter 24). He led us to see how the mother must be available to be used by the infant, without feeling abused by the way the infant takes her for granted.

REFERENCE

Winnicott, D. W. (1962). "A personal view of the Kleinian contribution." In *The Maturational Processes and the Facilitating Environment*, pp. 171–178. London: Hogarth, 1965.

The main object of this paper is to present the thesis that the early emotional development of the infant, before the infant knows himself (and therefore others) as the whole person he is (and they are), is vitally important: indeed that here are the clues to the psychopathology of psychoses.

PRIMARY PROCESSES

There are three processes which seem to me to start very early: (1) integration, (2) personalization, and (3), following these, the appreciation of time and space and other properties of reality—in short, realization. . . .

It may be assumed that at the theoretical start the personality is unintegrated, and that in regressive disintegration there is a primary state to which regression leads. We postulate a primary unintegration.

Disintegration of personality is a well-known psychiatric condition, and its psychopathology is highly complex. Examination of these phenomena in analysis, however, shows that the primary unintegrated state provides a basis for disintegration, and that delay or failure in respect of primary integration predisposes to disintegration as a regression, or result of failure in other types of defence.

In any case, integration starts right away at the beginning of life, and in our work we can never take it for granted. We have to account for it and watch its fluctuations.

An example of unintegration phenomena is provided by the very common experience of the patient who proceeds to give every detail of the weekend and feels contented at the end if everything has been said, though the analyst feels that no analytic work has been done. Sometimes we must interpret this as the patient's need to be known in all his bits and pieces by one person, the analyst. To be known means to feel integrated at least in the person who knows one. This is the ordinary stuff of infant life, and an infant who has had no one person to gather his bits together starts with a handicap in his own self-integrating task, and perhaps he cannot succeed, or at any rate cannot maintain integration with confidence.

The tendency to integrate is helped by two sets of experience: the technique of infant-care whereby an infant is kept warm, handled and bathed and rocked and named, and also the acute instinctual experiences which tend to gather the personality together from within. Many infants are well on the way toward integration during certain periods of the first 24 hours of life. In others the process is delayed or setbacks occur because of early inhibition of making greedy attacks. There are long stretches of time in a normal infant's life in which a baby does not mind whether he is many bits or one whole being, or whether he lives in his mother's face or in his own body, provided that from time to time he comes together and feels something. Later I will try to explain why disintegration is frightening, whereas unintegration is not.

In regard to environment, bits of nursing technique, faces seen and sounds heard, and smells smelt are only gradually pieced together into one being to be called mother. In the transference situation in analysis of psychotics we get the clearest proof that the psychotic states of unintegration had a natural place at a sufficiently primitive stage of the emotional development of the individual.

It is sometimes assumed that in health the individual is always integrated, as well as living in his own body, and able to feel that the world is real. There is, however, much sanity that has a symptomatic quality, being charged with fear or denial of madness, fear or denial of the innate capacity of every human being to become unintegrated, depersonalized, and to feel that the world is unreal. Sufficient lack of sleep produces these conditions in anyone.[1]

Equally important with integration is the development of the feeling that one's person is in one's body. Again it is instinctual experience and repeated quiet experiences of body-care that gradually build up what may be called satisfactory personalization. And as with disintegration so also the depersonalization phenomena of psychosis relate to early personalization delays.

Depersonalization is a common thing in adults and in children; it is often hidden for instance in what is called deep sleep and in prostration attacks with corpse-like pallor—"She's miles away," people say, and they're right.

A problem related to that of personalization is that of the imaginary companions of childhood. These are not simple phantasy constructions. Study of the future of these imaginary companions (in analysis) shows that they are sometimes other selves of a highly primitive type. I cannot here formulate a clear statement of what I mean, and it would be out of place for me to explain this detail at length now. I would say, however,

---

1. Through artistic expression we can hope to keep in touch with our primitive selves. It is from here that the most intense feelings and even fearfully acute sensations derive, and we are poor indeed if we are only sane.

that this very primitive and magical creation of imaginary companions is easily used as a defence, as it magically bypasses all the anxieties associated with incorporation, digestion, retention, and expulsion.

DISSOCIATION

Out of the problem of unintegration comes another, that of dissociation. Dissociation can usefully be studied in its initial or natural forms. According to my view there grows out of unintegration a series of what are then called dissociations, which arise owing to integration being incomplete or partial. Take the quiet and the excited states. I think an infant cannot be said to be aware at the start that while feeling this and that in his cot or enjoying the skin stimulations of bathing, he is the same as himself screaming for immediate satisfaction, possessed by an urge to get at and destroy something unless satisfied by milk. This means that he does not know at first that the mother he is building up through his quiet experiences is the same as the power behind the breasts that he has in his mind to destroy. . . .

REALITY ADAPTATION

Let us now assume integration. If we do, we reach another enormous subject, the primary relation to external reality. In ordinary analyses we can and do take for granted this step in emotional development, which is highly complex and which, when it is made, represents a big advance in emotional development, yet is never finally made and settled. Many cases that we consider unsuitable for analysis are unsuitable indeed if we cannot deal with the transference difficulties that belong to an essential lack of true relation to external reality. If we allow analysis of psychotics, we find that in some analyses this essential lack of true relation to external reality is almost the whole thing.

I will try to describe in the simplest possible terms this phenomenon as I see it. In terms of baby and mother's breast (I am not claiming that the breast is essential as a vehicle of mother-love) the baby has instinctual urges and predatory ideas. The mother has a breast and the power to produce milk, and the idea that she would like to be attacked by a hungry baby. These two phenomena do not come into relation with each other until the mother and child *live an experience together.* The mother being mature and physically able has to be the one with tolerance and understanding, so that it is she that produces a situation which may with luck result in the first tie the infant makes with an external object, that is external to self from the infant's point of view.

I think of the process as if two lines came from opposite directions, liable to come near each other. If they overlap there is a moment of *illusion*—a bit of experience which the infant can take as *either* his hallucination *or* a thing belonging to external reality.

In other language, the infant comes to the breast when excited, and ready to hallucinate something fit to be attacked. At that moment the actual nipple appears and he is able to feel it was that nipple that he hallucinated. So his ideas are enriched by actual details of sight, feel, smell, and next time this material is used in the hallucination. In this way he starts to build up a capacity to conjure up what is actually available. The mother has to go on giving the infant this type of experience. The process is immensely simplified if the infant is cared for by one person and one technique. It seems as if an infant is really designed to be cared for from birth by his own mother, or failing that by an adopted mother, and not by several nurses.

It is especially at the start that mothers are vitally important, and indeed it is a mother's job to protect her infant from complications that cannot yet be understood by the infant, and to go on steadily providing the simplified bit of the world which the infant, through her, comes to know. Only on such a foundation can objectivity be built, or a scientific attitude. All failure in objectivity at whatever date relates to failure in this stage of primitive emotional development. Only on a basis of monotony can a mother profitably add richness. . . .

Phantasy is not something the individual creates to deal with external reality's frustrations. This is only true of phantasying. Phantasy has more title to the word primary than has realization, and its enrichment with the world's riches depends on the moments of illusion that I have described. . . .

In the most primitive state, which may be retained in illness, and to which regression may occur, the object behaves according to magical laws, i.e., it exists when desired, it approaches when approached, it hurts when hurt. Lastly, it vanishes when not wanted.

This last is most terrifying, and is the only true annihilation. To not want, perhaps as a result of satisfaction, is to annihilate the object. This is one reason why infants are not always happy and contented after a satisfactory feed. One patient of mine carried this fear right on to adult life and only grew up from it in analysis, a man who had had an extremely good early experience with his mother and in his home.[2]

I realize that this is only the bare outline of the vast problem of the initial steps in the development of a relation to external reality, and the relation of phantasy to reality. Soon we must add ideas of incorporation, but at the start a simple *contact* with external or shared reality has to be made, by the infant's hallucinating and the world's presenting, with moments of illusion for the infant in which the two are taken by him to be identical, which they never in fact are.

For this illusion to be produced in the baby's mind a human being has to be taking the trouble all the time to bring the world to the baby in understandable form, and in a limited way, suitable to the baby's needs. For this reason a baby cannot exist alone, psychologically or physically, and really needs one person to care for him at first.

The subject of illusion is a very wide one that needs study; it will be found to provide the clue to a child's interest in bubbles and clouds and rainbows and all mysterious phenomena, and also to his interest in fluff, which is most difficult to explain in terms of instinct direct. Somewhere here, too, is the interest in breath, which never decides whether it comes primarily from within or without, and which provides a basis for the conception of spirit, soul, anima.

PRIMITIVE RUTHLESSNESS (STAGE OF PRECONCERN)

We are now in a position to look at the earliest kind of relationship between a baby and his mother.

If one assumes that the individual is becoming integrated and personalized and has made a good start in his realization, there is still a long way for him to go before he is related as a whole person to a whole mother, and concerned about the effect of his own thoughts and actions on her.

We have to postulate an early ruthless object relationship. This may again be a theoretical phase only, and certainly no one can be ruthless

2. I will just mention another reason why an infant is not satisfied with satisfaction. He feels fobbed off. He intended, one might say, to make a cannibalistic attack and he has been put off by an opiate, the feed. At best he can postpone the attack.

after the concern stage except in a dissociated state. But ruthless dissociation states are common in early childhood, and emerge in certain types of delinquency, and madness, and must be available in health. The normal child enjoys a ruthless relation to his mother, mostly showing in play, and he needs his mother because only she can be expected to tolerate his ruthless relation to her even in play, because this really hurts her and wears her out. Without this play with her he can only hide a ruthless self and give it life in a state of dissociation.[3]

I can bring in here the great fear of disintegration as opposed to the simple acceptance of primary unintegration. Once the individual has reached the stage of concern he cannot be oblivious to the result of his impulses, or to the action of bits of self such as biting mouth, stabbing eyes, piercing yells, sucking throat, etc., etc. Disintegration means abandonment of the whole person-object to his impulses, uncontrolled because acting on their own, and further this conjures up the idea of similarly uncontrolled (because dissociated) impulses directed towards himself.[4]

PRIMITIVE RETALIATION

To go back half a stage: it is usual, I think, to postulate a still more primitive object relationship in which the object acts in a retaliatory way. This is prior to a true relation to external reality. In this case the object, or the environment, is as much part of the self as the instinct is which conjures it up.[5] In introversion of early origin and therefore of primitive quality the individual lives in this environment which is himself, and a very poor life it is. There is no growth because there is no enrichment from external reality. . . .

---

3. There is in mythology a ruthless figure—Lilith—whose origin could be usefully studied.

4. Crocodiles not only shed tears when they do not feel sad—preconcern tears; they also readily stand for the ruthless primitive self.

5. This is important because of our relationship to Jung's analytic psychology. We try to reduce everything to instinct, and the analytic psychologists reduce everything to this part of the primitive self which looks like environment but which arises instantly out of instinct (archetypes). We ought to modify our view to embrace both ideas, and to see, if it is true, that in the earliest theoretical primitive state the self has its own environment self-created, which is as much the self as the instincts that produce it. This is a theme that requires development.

16

"Hate in the Countertransference" (1947)

This paper, read at a meeting of the British Psycho-Analytical Society in 1947 and published in 1949, was the first to suggest that analysts' responses to their patients should include what Winnicott called an "objective countertransference," that part of the analysts' affective response to their patients that is justified by the patients' treatment of them, and that corresponds to what patients would ordinarily stir up in other people. Most importantly, this includes the therapists' capacity to hate patients when hate is objectively justified, to bear that hate, and to work toward growth in the patient that can modify the aggression in the relationship and allow the emergence of positive feelings in the countertransference.

This is the first in a series of papers on transference that came from Klein's colleagues, including, as principal examples, those by Heimann, Racker, and Joseph, which are excerpted in this volume. They all grew out of Klein's close attention to the transference as a "total situation," and marked a radical departure in the use of the analysts' personal response as a therapeutic tool. Although Fairbairn did not work this way, his theory and ideas about the relationship as the instrument of change, especially as elaborated by Guntrip, are consistent with it. This paper also describes much of the way Winnicott himself worked, and is therefore important for understanding many of his later contributions.

In this paper I wish to examine one aspect of the whole subject of ambivalency, namely, hate in the countertransference. . . .

To help the general psychiatrist the psychoanalyst must not only study for him the primitive stages of the emotional development of the ill individual, but also must study the nature of the emotional burden which the psychiatrist bears in doing his work. What we as analysts call the countertransference needs to be understood by the psychiatrist too. However much he loves his patients, he cannot avoid hating them and fearing them, and the better he knows this the less will hate and fear be the motive determining what he does to his patients.

STATEMENT OF THEME

One could classify countertransference phenomena thus:

1. Abnormality in countertransference feelings, and set relationships and identifications that are under repression in the analyst. The comment on this is that the analyst needs more analysis, and we believe this is less of an issue among psychoanalysts than among psychotherapists in general.
2. The identifications and tendencies belonging to an analyst's personal experiences and personal development which provide the positive setting for his analytic work and make his work different in quality from that of any other analyst.
3. From these two I distinguish the truly objective countertransference, or if this is difficult, the analyst's love and hate in reaction to the actual personality and behaviour of the patient, based on objective observation.

I suggest that if an analyst is to analyse psychotics or antisocials he must be able to be so thoroughly aware of the countertransference that he can sort out and study his *objective* reactions to the patient. These will include hate. . . .

If the analyst is going to have crude feelings imputed to him he is best forewarned and so forearmed, for he must tolerate being placed in that position. Above all he must not deny hate that really exists in himself. Hate *that is justified* in the present setting has to be sorted out and kept in storage and available for eventual interpretation.

If we are to become able to be the analysts of psychotic patients we must have reached down to very primitive things in ourselves, and this is but another example of the fact that the answer to many obscure problems of psychoanalytic practice lies in further analysis of the analyst. (Psychoanalytic research is perhaps always to some extent an attempt on the part of an analyst to carry the work of his own analysis further than the point to which his own analyst could get him.)

A main task of the analyst of any patient is to maintain objectivity in regard to all that the patient brings, and a special case of this is the analyst's need to be able to hate the patient objectively.

Are there not many situations in our ordinary analytic work in which the analyst's hate is justified? A patient of mine, a very bad obsessional, was almost loathsome to me for some years. I felt bad about this until the analysis turned a corner and the patient became lovable, and then I realized that his unlikeableness had been an active symptom, unconsciously determined. It was indeed a wonderful day for me (much later on) when I could actually tell the patient that I and his friends had felt repelled by him, but that he had been too ill for us to let him know. This was also an important day for him, a tremendous advance in his adjustment to reality.

In the ordinary analysis the analyst has no difficulty with the management of his own hate. This hate remains latent. The main thing, of course, is that through his own analysis he has become free from vast reservoirs of unconscious hate belonging to the past and to inner conflicts. . . .

POSTPONEMENT OF INTERPRETATION

The analyst must be prepared to bear strain without expecting the patient to know anything about what he is doing, perhaps over a long period of time. To do this he must be easily aware of his own fear and hate. He is in the position of the mother of an infant unborn or newly born. Eventually, he ought to be able to tell his patient what he has been through on the patient's behalf, but an analysis may never get as far as this. There may be too little good experience in the patient's past to work on. What if there be no satisfactory relationship of early infancy for the analyst to exploit in the transference?

There is a vast difference between those patients who have had satisfactory early experiences which can be discovered in the transference, and those whose very early experiences have been so deficient or distorted that the analyst has to be the first in the patient's life to supply certain environmental essentials. In the treatment of the patient of the latter kind all sorts of things in analytic technique become vitally important that can be taken for granted in the treatment of patients of the former type. . . .

During the Second World War a boy of 9 came to a hostel for evacuated children, sent from London not because of bombs but because of truancy. I hoped to give him some treatment during his stay in the hostel, but his symptom won and he ran away as he had always done from everywhere since the age of 6 when he first ran away from home. However, I had established contact with him in one interview in which I could see and interpret through a drawing of his that in running away he was unconsciously saving the inside of his home and preserving his mother from assault, as well as trying to get away from his own inner world which was full of persecutors.

I was not very surprised when he turned up in the police station very near my home. This was one of the few police stations that did not know him intimately. My wife very generously took him in and kept him for three months, three months of hell. He was the most lovable and most maddening of children, often stark staring mad. But fortunately we knew what to expect. We dealt with the first phase by giving him complete freedom and a shilling whenever he went out. He had only to ring up and we fetched him from whatever police station had taken charge of him.

Soon the expected changeover occurred, the truancy symptom turned round, and the boy started dramatizing the assault on the inside. It was really a whole-time job for the two of us together, and when I was out the worst episodes took place.

Interpretation had to be made at any minute of day or night, and often the only solution in a crisis was to make the correct interpretation, as if the boy were in analysis. It was the correct interpretation that he valued above everything.

The important thing for the purpose of this paper is the way in which the evolution of the boy's personality engendered hate in me, and what I did about it.

Did I hit him? The answer is no, I never hit. But I should have had to have done so if I had not known all about my hate and if I had not let him know about it too. At crises I would take him by bodily strength, and without anger or blame, and put him outside the front door, whatever the weather or the time of day or night. There was a special bell he could ring, and he knew that if he rang it he would be readmitted and no word said about the past. He used this bell as soon as he had recovered from his maniacal attack.

The important thing is that each time, just as I put him outside the door, I told him something; I said that what had happened had made me hate him. This was easy because it was so true.

I think these words were important from the point of view of his progress, but they were mainly important in enabling me to tolerate the situation without letting out, without losing my temper and every now and again murdering him.

This boy's full story cannot be told here. He went to an Approved School. His deeply rooted relation to us has remained one of the few stable things in his life. This episode from ordinary life can be used to illustrate the general topic of hate justified in the present; this is to be distinguished from hate that is only justified in another setting but which is tapped by some action of a patient (child).

A MOTHER'S LOVE AND HATE

Out of all the complexity of the problem of hate and its roots I want to rescue one thing, because I believe it has an importance for the analyst of psychotic patients. I suggest that the mother hates the baby before the baby hates the mother, and before the baby can know his mother hates him.

Before developing this theme I want to refer to Freud's remarks. In *Instincts and their Vicissitudes* (1915) (where he says so much that is original and illuminating about hate), Freud says: "we might at a pinch say of an instinct that it 'loves' the objects after which it strives for purposes of satisfaction, but to say that it 'hates' an object strikes us as odd, so we become aware that the attitudes of love and hate cannot be said to characterize the relation of instincts to their objects, but are reserved for the relations of the ego as a whole to objects."

This I feel is true and important. Does this not mean that the personality must be integrated before an infant can be said to hate? However early integration may be achieved—perhaps integration occurs earliest at the height of excitement or rage—there is a theoretical earlier stage in which whatever the infant does that hurts is not done in hate. I have used the term *ruthless love* in describing this stage. Is this acceptable? As the infant becomes able to feel a whole person, so does the word *hate* develop meaning as a description of a certain group of his feelings.

The mother, however, hates her infant from the word go. I believe Freud thought it possible that a mother may under certain circumstances have only love for her boy baby; but we may doubt this. We know about a mother's love and we appreciate its reality and power. Let me give some of the reasons why a mother hates her baby, even a boy.

1. The baby is not her own (mental) conception.
2. The baby is not the one of childhood play, father's child, brother's child, etc.

3. The baby is not magically produced.
4. The baby is a danger to her body in pregnancy and at birth.
5. The baby is an interference with her private life, a challenge to preoccupation.
6. To a greater or lesser extent a mother feels that her own mother demands a baby, so that her baby is produced to placate her mother.
7. The baby hurts her nipples even by suckling, which is at first a chewing activity.
8. He is ruthless, treats her as scum, an unpaid servant, a slave.
9. She has to love him, excretions and all, at any rate at the beginning, till he has doubts about himself.
10. He tries to hurt her, periodically bites her, all in love.
11. He shows disillusionment about her.
12. His excited love is cupboard love, so that having got what he wants he throws her away like orange peel.
13. The baby at first must dominate, he must be protected from coincidences, life must unfold at the baby's rate and all this needs his mother's continuous and detailed study. For instance, she must not be anxious when holding him, etc.
14. At first he does not know at all what she does or what she sacrifices for him. Especially he cannot allow for her hate.
15. He is suspicious, refuses her good food, and makes her doubt herself, but eats well with his aunt.
16. After an awful morning with him she goes out, and he smiles at a stranger, who says: "Isn't he sweet!"
17. If she fails him at the start she knows he will pay her out for ever.
18. He excites her but frustrates—she mustn't eat him or trade in sex with him.

I think that in the analysis of psychotics, and in the ultimate stages of the analysis, even of a normal person, the analyst must find himself in a position comparable to that of the mother of a newborn baby. When deeply regressed the patient cannot identify with the analyst or appreciate his point of view any more than the fetus or newly born infant can sympathize with the mother.

A mother has to be able to tolerate hating her baby without doing anything about it. She cannot express it to him. If, for fear of what she may do, she cannot hate appropriately when hurt by her child she must fall back on masochism, and I think it is this that gives rise to the false theory of a natural masochism in women. The most remarkable thing about a mother is her ability to be hurt so much by her baby and to hate so much without paying the child out, and her ability to wait for rewards that may or may not come at a later date. . . .

It seems to me doubtful whether a human child as he develops is capable of tolerating the full extent of his own hate in a sentimental environment. He needs hate to hate.

If this is true, a psychotic patient in analysis cannot be expected to tolerate his hate of the analyst unless the analyst can hate him.

PRACTICAL PROBLEM OF INTERPRETATION

If all this is accepted there remains for discussion the question of the interpretation of the analyst's hate to the patient. This is obviously a matter fraught with danger, and it needs the most careful timing. But I believe an analysis is incomplete if even towards the end it has not been possible for the analyst to tell the patient what he, the analyst, did unbeknown for the patient whilst he was ill, in the early stages. Until the interpretation is made the patient is kept to some extent in the position of infant, one who cannot understand what he owes to his mother.

SUMMARY

An analyst has to display all the patience and tolerance and reliability of a mother devoted to her infant, has to recognize the patient's wishes as needs, has to put aside other interests in order to be available and to be punctual, and objective, and has to seem to want to give what is really only given because of the patient's needs.

There may be a long initial period in which the analyst's point of view cannot be (even unconsciously) appreciated by the patient. Acknowledgment cannot be expected because at the primitive root of the patient that is being looked for there is no capacity for identification with the analyst, and certainly the patient cannot see that the analyst's hate is often engendered by the very things the patient does in his crude way of loving. . . .

REFERENCE

Freud, S. (1915). Instincts and their vicissitudes. *Standard Edition* 14:109–140.

17

"Aggression in Relation to Emotional Development" (1950)

This brief excerpt develops the theory of aggression in normality and pathology, expanding Winnicott's theory of the place of hate in development and in therapy. It also relates the role of aggression to the use of schizoid defenses described ten years earlier by Fairbairn and Klein, elaborating on patients' defensive retreat to a schizoid inner world to avoid projecting aggression onto external objects.

PRECONCERN

It is necessary to describe a theoretical stage of unconcern or ruthlessness in which the child can be said to exist as a person and to have purpose, yet to be unconcerned as to results. He does not yet appreciate the fact that what he destroys when excited is the same as that which he values in quiet intervals between excitements. His excited love includes an imaginative attack on the mother's body. Here is aggression as a part of love.[1]

One can see some degree of this appearing as a dissociation between quiet and excited aspects of the personality, so that children who are ordinarily nice and lovable will "act out of character" and do aggressive things to people they love, not feeling fully responsible for their actions.

1. This has been called "preambivalent," but this term avoids the issue of the integration of part-object and whole object, breast and mother who holds and cares.

If aggression is lost at this stage of emotional development there is also some degree of loss of capacity to love, that is to say, to make relationships with objects.

STAGE OF CONCERN

Now comes the stage described by Melanie Klein as the *depressive position* in emotional development. For my purpose I will call this the *stage of concern.* The individual's ego integration is sufficient for him to appreciate the personality of the mother figure, and this has the tremendously important result that he is concerned as to the results of his instinctual experience, physical and ideational.

The stage of concern brings with it the capacity to feel guilty. Henceforth some of the aggression appears clinically as grief or a feeling of guilt or some physical equivalent, such as vomiting. The guilt refers to the damage which is felt to be done to the loved person in the excited relationship. In health the infant can hold the guilt, and so with the help of a personal and live mother (who embodies a time factor) is able to discover his own personal urge to give and to construct and to mend. In this way much of the aggression is transformed into the social functions, and appears as such. In times of helplessness (as when no person can be found to accept a gift or to acknowledge effort to repair) this transformation breaks down, and aggression reappears. *Social activity cannot be satisfactory* except it be based on a feeling of *personal* guilt in respect of aggression.

ANGER

In my description there now comes a place for anger at frustration. Frustration, which is inevitable in some degree in all experience, encourages the dichotomy: (1) innocent aggressive impulses towards frustrating objects, and (2) guilt-productive aggressive impulses towards good objects. Frustration acts as a seduction away from guilt and fosters a defence mechanism, namely, the direction of love and hate along separate lines. If this splitting of objects into good and bad[2] takes place, there is an easing of

2. I should now say "idealized and bad" instead of "good and bad" (1957). [Winnicott added this footnote when he gathered his collected papers for publication in 1958. D. E. S.]

guilt feeling; but in payment the love loses some of its valuable aggressive component, and the hate becomes the more disruptive. . . .

In health the child's interest is directed both towards external reality and towards the inner world, and he has bridges between the one world and the other (dreams, play, etc.). In ill-health the child may rearrange his relationships so that the good is concentrated within and the bad is projected. He now lives in his inner world. He may be said to have become introverted (or pathologically introverted).

A recovery from pathological introversion involves a new turning out into what is for such a child an external world full of persecutors, *and at this point in his recovery the child regularly becomes aggressive.* This is an important source of aggressive *behaviour.* If in a child's recovery from introversion the attack-in-defence is mishandled by those in charge, the child easily slips back into introversion. Apart from illness, some degree of this state of affairs is met daily in the life of any small child, and the concept is by no means a purely theoretical one. An individual is in a sensitive state on coming round after a period of concentration on a personal task.

18

"Transitional Objects and Transitional Phenomena" (1951)

This best known of Winnicott's contributions ties together his studies of infants and of psychic development. The paper's creative ambiguity embodies the paradox Winnicott saw at the heart of development of mind, at the center of each individual's need to reconcile inner and outer realities. His use of the term *transitional* has a rich set of references. In his opening footnote, he acknowledges Fairbairn's use of the term, by which Fairbairn signified the transition from infantile dependence to adult dependence. For Winnicott, however, the term implies the potential space and phenomena that lie between self and object, mother and baby, the baby's inner and outer worlds, and the world of things and of fantasy. Winnicott's exploration of transitional phenomena was to continue over the next twenty years, but already in this first paper he stated that these phenomena are the progenitors of cultural and artistic phenomena. It is in the space between inner and outer worlds, which is also the space between people—the transitional space—that intimate relationships and creativity occur.

A STUDY OF THE FIRST *NOT-ME* POSSESSION

It is well known that infants as soon as they are born tend to use fist, fingers, thumbs in stimulation of the oral erotogenic zone, in satisfaction of the instincts at that zone, and also in quiet union. It is also well known that after a few months infants of either sex become fond of playing with dolls, and that most mothers allow their infants some special object and expect them to become, as it were, addicted to such objects.

There is a relationship between these two sets of phenomena that are separated by a time interval, and a study of the development from the earlier into the later can be profitable, and can make use of important clinical material that has been somewhat neglected.

The First Possession[1]

Those who happen to be in close touch with mothers' interests and problems will be already aware of the very rich patterns ordinarily displayed by babies in their use of the first *Not-Me* possession. These patterns, being displayed, can be subjected to direct observation.

There is a wide variation to be found in a sequence of events which starts with the newborn infant's fist-in-mouth activities, and that leads eventually on to an attachment to a teddy, a doll or soft toy, or to a hard toy.

It is clear that something is important here other than oral excitement and satisfaction, although this may be the basis of everything else. Many other important things can be studied, and they include:

The nature of the object.
The infant's capacity to recognize the object as *Not-Me*.
The place of the object—outside, inside, at the border.
The infant's capacity to create, think up, devise, originate, produce an object.
The initiation of an affectionate type of object relationship.

I have introduced the terms *transitional object* and *transitional phenomena* for designation of the intermediate area of experience, between the thumb and the teddy bear, between the oral erotism and true object relationship, between primary creative activity and projection of what has already been introjected, between primary unawareness of indebtedness and the acknowledgement of indebtedness ("Say: ta!").

1. It is necessary to stress that the word used here is *possession* and not *object*. In the typed version distributed to members I did in fact use the word *object* (instead of *possession*) in one place by mistake, and this led to confusion in the discussion. It was pointed out that the first *Not-Me object* is usually taken to be the breast. The reader's attention is drawn to the use of the word *transitional* in many places by Fairbairn (1952).

By this definition an infant's babbling or the way an older child goes over a repertoire of songs and tunes while preparing for sleep comes within the intermediate area as transitional phenomena, along with the use made of objects that are not part of the infant's body yet are not fully recognized as belonging to external reality.

It is generally acknowledged that a statement of human nature is inadequate when given in terms of interpersonal relationships, even when the imaginative elaboration of function, the whole of fantasy both conscious and unconscious, including the repressed unconscious, is allowed for. There is another way of describing persons that comes out of the researches of the past two decades, that suggests that of every individual who has reached to the stage of being a unit (with a limiting membrane and an outside and an inside) it can be said that there is an *inner reality* to that individual, an inner world which can be rich or poor and can be at peace or in a state of war.

My claim is that if there is a need for this double statement, there is need for a triple one; there is the third part of the life of a human being, a part that we cannot ignore, an intermediate area of *experiencing*, to which inner reality and external life both contribute. It is an area which is not challenged, because no claim is made on its behalf except that it shall exist as a resting-place for the individual engaged in the perpetual human task of keeping inner and outer reality separate yet interrelated.

It is usual to refer to *reality-testing*, and to make a clear distinction between apperception and perception. I am here staking a claim for an intermediate state between a baby's inability and growing ability to recognize and accept reality. I am therefore studying the substance of *illusion*, that which is allowed to the infant, and which in adult life is inherent in art and religion. We can share a respect for *illusory experience*, and if we wish we may collect together and form a group on the basis of the similarity of our illusory experiences. This is a natural root of grouping among human beings. Yet it is a hallmark of madness when an adult puts too powerful a claim on the credulity of others, forcing them to acknowledge a sharing of illusion that is not their own.

I hope it will be understood that I am not referring exactly to the little child's teddy bear nor to the infant's first use of the fist (thumb, fingers). I am not specifically studying the first object of object relationships. I am concerned with the first possession, and with the intermediate area between the subjective and that which is objectively perceived.

Development of a Personal Pattern

There is plenty of reference in psychoanalytic literature to the progress from "hand to mouth" to "hand to genital," but perhaps less to progress leading to the handling of truly "*Not-Me*" objects. Sooner or later in an infant's development there comes a tendency on the part of the infant to weave other-than-me objects into the personal pattern. To some extent these objects stand for the breast, but it is not especially this point that is under discussion.

In the case of some infants the thumb is placed in the mouth while fingers are made to caress the face by pronation and supination movements of the forearm. The mouth is then active in relation to the thumb, but not in relation to the fingers. The fingers caressing the upper lip, or some other part, may be or may become more important than the thumb engaging the mouth. Moreover this caressing activity may be found alone, without the more direct thumb-mouth union (Freud 1905, Hoffer 1949).

In common experience one of the following occurs, complicating an autoerotic experience such as thumb-sucking:

1. with the other hand the baby takes an external object, say a part of a sheet or blanket, into the mouth along with the fingers; or
2. somehow or other the bit of cloth[2] is held and sucked, or not actually sucked. The objects used naturally include napkins and (later) handkerchiefs, and this depends on what is readily and reliably available; or
3. the baby starts from early months to pluck wool and to collect it and to use it for the caressing part of the activity.[3] Less commonly, the wool is swallowed, even causing trouble; or
4. mouthing, accompanied by sounds of "mum-mum," babbling, anal noises, the first musical notes, and so on.

One may suppose that thinking, or fantasying, gets linked up with these functional experiences.

---

2. An example is the blanket-doll of the child in the film *A Two-year-old Goes to Hospital* by James Robertson (Tavistock Clinic).

3. Here there could possibly be an explanation for the use of the term *wool-gathering*, which means inhabiting the transitional or intermediate area.

All these things I am calling *transitional phenomena.* Also, out of all this (if we study any one infant) there may emerge some thing or some phenomenon—perhaps a bundle of wool or the corner of a blanket or eiderdown, or a word or tune, or a mannerism, which becomes vitally important to the infant for use at the time of going to sleep, and is a defence against anxiety, especially anxiety of depressive type (Illingworth 1951). Perhaps some soft object or cot cover has been found and used by the infant, and this then becomes what I am calling a *transitional object.* This object goes on being important. The parents get to know its value and carry it round when travelling. The mother lets it get dirty and even smelly, knowing that by washing it she introduces a break in continuity in the infant's experience, a break that may destroy the meaning and value of the object to the infant.

I suggest that the pattern of transitional phenomena begins to show at about 4–6–8–12 months. Purposely I leave room for wide variations.

Patterns set in infancy may persist into childhood, so that the original soft object continues to be absolutely necessary at bedtime or at time of loneliness or when a depressed mood threatens. In health, however, there is a gradual extension of range of interest, and eventually the extended range is maintained, even when depressive anxiety is near. A need for a specific object or a behaviour pattern that started at a very early date may reappear at a later age when deprivation threatens.

This first possession is used in conjunction with special techniques derived from very early infancy, which can include or exist apart from the more direct autoerotic activities. Gradually in the life of an infant teddies and dolls and hard toys are acquired. Boys to some extent tend to go over to use hard objects, whereas girls tend to proceed right ahead to the acquisition of a family. It is important to note, however, that *there is no noticeable difference between boy and girl in their use of the original Not-Me possession,* which I am calling the transitional object.

As the infant starts to use organized sounds (mum, ta, da) there may appear a "word" for the transitional object. The name given by the infant to these earliest objects is often significant, and it usually has a word used by the adults partly incorporated in it. For instance, "baa" may be the name, and the "b" may have come from the adult's use of the word *baby* or *bear.*

I should mention that sometimes there is no transitional object except the mother herself. Or an infant may be so disturbed in emotional development that the transition state cannot be enjoyed, or the sequence of objects used is broken. The sequence may nevertheless be maintained in a hidden way.

Summary of Special Qualities in the Relationship

1. The infant assumes rights over the object, and we agree to this assumption. Nevertheless some abrogation of omnipotence is a feature from the start.
2. The object is affectionately cuddled as well as excitedly loved and mutilated.
3. It must never change, unless changed by the infant.
4. It must survive instinctual loving, and also hating, and, if it be a feature, pure aggression.
5. Yet it must seem to the infant to give warmth, or to move, or to have texture, or to do something that seems to show it has vitality or reality of its own.
6. It comes from without, from our point of view, but not so from the point of view of the baby. Neither does it come from within; it is not an hallucination.
7. Its fate is to be gradually allowed to be decathected, so that in the course of years it becomes not so much forgotten as relegated to limbo. By this I mean that in health the transitional object does not "go inside" nor does the feeling about it necessarily undergo repression. It is not forgotten and it is not mourned. It loses meaning, and this is because the transitional phenomena have become diffused, have become spread out over the whole intermediate territory between "inner psychic reality" and "the external world as perceived by two persons in common," that is to say, over the whole cultural field.

At this point my subject widens out into that of play, and of artistic creativity and appreciation, and of religious feeling, and of dreaming, and also of fetishism, lying and stealing, the origin and loss of affectionate feeling, drug addiction, the talisman of obsessional rituals, etc.

Relationship of the Transitional Object to Symbolism

It is true that the piece of blanket (or whatever it is) is symbolical of some part-object, such as the breast. Nevertheless, the point of it is not its symbolic value so much as its actuality. Its not being the breast (or the mother) is as important as the fact that it stands for the breast (or mother).

When symbolism is employed the infant is already clearly distinguishing between fantasy and fact, between inner objects and external objects, between primary creativity and perception. But the term *transitional object,* according to my suggestion, gives room for the process of becoming able to accept difference and similarity. I think there is use for a term for the root of symbolism in time, a term that describes the infant's journey from the purely subjective to objectivity, and it seems to me that the transitional object (piece of blanket, etc.) is what we see of this journey of progress towards experiencing. . . .

CLINICAL DESCRIPTION OF A TRANSITIONAL OBJECT

Two Brothers: Contrast in Early Use of Possessions

Distortion in Use of Transitional Object

X, now a healthy man, has had to fight his way towards maturity. The mother "learned how to be a mother" in her management of X when he was an infant and she was able to avoid certain mistakes with the other children because of what she learned with him. There were also external reasons why she was anxious at the time of her rather lonely management of X when he was born. She took her job as a mother very seriously and she breast-fed X for seven months. She feels that in his case this was too long and he was very difficult to wean. He never sucked his thumb or his fingers and when she weaned him "he had nothing to fall back on." He had never had the bottle or a dummy or any other form of feeding. He had a very strong and early *attachment to the mother herself,* as a person, and it was her actual person that he needed.

From twelve months he adopted a rabbit which he would cuddle and his affectionate regard for the rabbit eventually transferred to real rabbits. This particular rabbit lasted till he was 5 or 6 years old. It could be described as a *comforter,* but it never had the true quality of a transitional object. It was never, as a true transitional object would have been, more important than the mother, an almost inseparable part of the infant. In the case of this particular boy the kind of anxieties which were brought to a head by the weaning at seven months later produced asthma, and only gradually did he conquer this. It was important for him that he found employment far away from the home town. His attachment to his mother is still very powerful. He comes within the wide definition of the term *normal* or *healthy*. This man has not married.

Typical Use of Transitional Object

X's younger brother, Y, has developed in quite a straightforward way throughout. He now has three healthy children of his own. He was fed at the breast for four months and then weaned without difficulty.[4] Y sucked his thumb in the early weeks and this again "made weaning easier for him than for his older brother." Soon after weaning at five to six months he adopted the end of the blanket where the stitching finished. He was pleased if a little bit of the wool stuck out at the corner and with this he would tickle his nose. This very early became his "Baa"; he invented this word for it himself as soon as he could use organized sounds. From the time when he was about a year old he was able to substitute for the end of the blanket a soft green jersey with a red tie. This was not a "comforter," as in the case of the depressive older brother, but a "soother." It was a sedative which always worked. This is a typical example of what I am calling a *transitional object.* When Y was a little boy it was always certain that if anyone gave him his "Baa" he would immediately suck it and lose anxiety, and in fact he would go to sleep within a few minutes if the time for sleep were at all near. The thumb-sucking continued at the same time, lasting until he was 3 or 4 years old, and he remembers thumb-sucking and a hard place on one thumb which resulted from it. He is now interested (as a father) in the thumb-sucking of his own children and their use of "Baas."

THEORETICAL STUDY

There are certain comments that can be made on the basis of accepted psychoanalytic theory.

4. The mother had "learned from her first child that it was a good idea to give one bottle feed while breast feeding," that is, to allow for the positive value of substitutes for herself, and by this means she achieved easier weaning than with X.

1. The transitional object stands for the breast, or the object of the first relationship.
2. The transitional object antedates established reality-testing.
3. In relation to the transitional object the infant passes from (magical) omnipotent control to control by manipulation (involving muscle erotism and coordination pleasure).
4. The transitional object may eventually develop into a fetish object and so persist as a characteristic of the adult sexual life. . . .
5. The transitional object may, because of anal-erotic organization, stand for faeces (but it is not for this reason that it may become smelly and remain unwashed).

Relationship to Internal Object (Klein)

It is interesting to compare the transitional object concept with Melanie Klein's concept of the internal object. The transitional object is *not an internal object* (which is a mental concept) – it is a possession. Yet it is not (for the infant) an external object either.

The following complex statement has to be made. The infant can employ a transitional object when the internal object is alive and real and good enough (not too persecutory). But this internal object depends for its qualities on the existence and aliveness and behaviour of the external object (breast, mother figure, general environmental care). Badness or failure of the latter indirectly leads to deadness or to a persecutory quality of internal object. After a persistence of failure of the external object fails to have meaning to the infant, and then, and then only, does the transitional object become meaningless too. The transitional object may therefore stand for the "external" breast, but *indirectly* so, through standing for an "internal" breast.

The transitional object is never under magical control like the internal object, nor is it outside control as the real mother is.

Illusion–Disillusionment

There is no possibility whatever for an infant to proceed from the pleasure principle to the reality principle or towards and beyond primary identification (see Freud 1921, 1923), unless there is a good-enough mother.[5] The good-enough "mother" (not necessarily the infant's own mother) is one who makes active adaptation to the infant's needs, an active adaptation that gradually lessens, according to the infant's growing ability to account for failure of adaptation and to tolerate the results of frustration. Naturally the infant's own mother is more likely to be good enough than some other person, since this active adaptation demands an easy and unresented preoccupation with the one infant; in fact, success in infant care depends on the fact of devotion, not on cleverness or intellectual enlightenment.

The good-enough mother, as I have stated, starts off with an almost complete adaptation to her infant's needs, and as time proceeds she adapts less and less completely, gradually, according to the infant's growing ability to deal with her failure. . . .

Illusion and the Value of Illusion

The mother, at the beginning, by an almost 100 percent adaptation affords the infant the opportunity for the *illusion* that her breast is part of the infant. It is, as it were, under magical control. The same can be said in terms of infant care in general, in the quiet times between excitements. Omnipotence is nearly a fact of experience. The mother's eventual task is gradually to disillusion the infant, but she has no hope of success unless at first she has been able to give sufficient opportunity for illusion.

In another language, the breast is created by the infant over and over again out of the infant's capacity to love or (one can say) out of need. A subjective phenomenon develops in the baby which we call the mother's breast.[6] The mother places the actual breast just there where the infant is ready to create, and at the right moment.

---

5. One effect, and the main effect, of failure of the mother in this respect at the start of an infant's life, is discussed clearly (in my view) by Marion Milner (1952). She shows that because of the mother's failure there is brought about a premature ego development, with precocious sorting out of a bad from a good object. The period of illusion (or my transitional phase) is disturbed. In analysis or in various activities in ordinary life an individual can be seen to be going on seeking the valuable resting-place of illusion. Illusion in this way has its positive value. See also Freud (1950).

6. I include the whole technique of mothering. When it is said that the first object is the breast, the word *breast* is used, I believe, to stand for the technique of mothering as well as for the actual flesh. It is not impossible for a mother to be a good-enough mother (in my way of putting it) with a bottle for the actual feeding. If this wide meaning of the word *breast* is

From birth, therefore, the human being is concerned with the problem of the relationship between what is objectively perceived and what is subjectively conceived of, and in the solution of this problem there is no health for the human being who has not been started off well enough by the mother. *The intermediate area to which I am referring is the area that is allowed to the infant between primary creativity and objective perception based on reality testing.* The transitional phenomena represent the early stages of the use of illusion, without which there is no meaning for the human being in the idea of a relationship with an object that is perceived by others as external to that being.

The idea illustrated in Figure 18–1 is this: that at some theoretical point early in the development of every human individual an infant in a certain setting provided by the mother is capable of conceiving of the idea of something which would meet the growing need which arises out of instinctual tension. The infant cannot be said to know at first what is to be created. At this point in time the mother presents herself. In the ordinary way she gives her breast and her potential feeding urge. The mother's adaptation to the infant's needs, when good enough, gives the infant the *illusion* that there is an external reality that corresponds to the infant's own capacity to create. In other words, there is an overlap between what the mother supplies and what the child might conceive of. To the observer the child perceives what the mother actually presents, but this is not the whole truth. The infant perceives the breast only insofar as a breast could be created just there and then. There is no interchange between the mother and the infant. Psychologically the infant takes from a breast that is part of the infant, and the mother gives milk to an infant that is part of herself. In psychology, the idea of interchange is based on an illusion.

In Figure 18–2 a shape is given to the area of illusion, to illustrate what I consider to be the main function of the transitional object and of transitional phenomena. The transitional object and the transitional phenomena start each human being off with what will always be important for them, i.e., a neutral area of experience which will not be challenged. *Of the transitional object it can be said that it is a matter of*

---

kept in mind, and maternal technique is seen to be included in the total meaning of the term, then there is a bridge forming between the wording of Melanie Klein's statement of early history and that of Anna Freud. The only difference left is one of dates, which is in fact an unimportant difference which will automatically disappear in the course of time.

agreement between us and the baby that we will never ask the question "Did you conceive of this or was it presented to you from without?" The important point is that no decision on this point is expected. The question is not to be formulated.

Figure 18–1

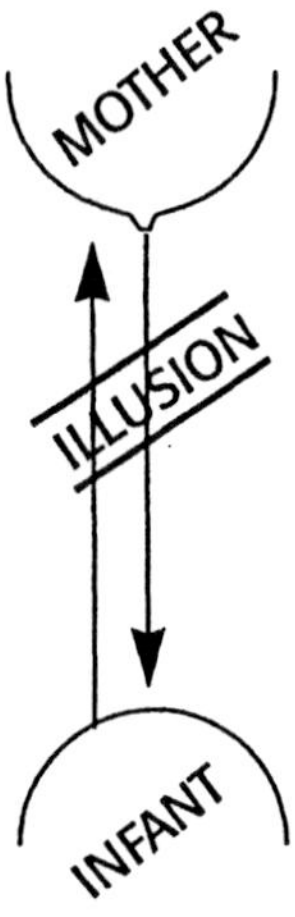

Figure 18–2

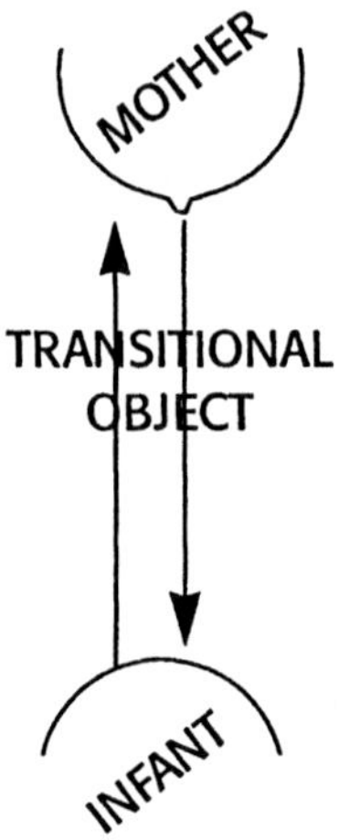

This problem, which undoubtedly concerns the human infant in a hidden way at the beginning, gradually becomes an obvious problem on account of the fact that the mother's main task (next to providing opportunity for illusion) is disillusionment. This is preliminary to the task of weaning, and it also continues as one of the tasks of parents and educators. In other words, this matter of *illusion* is one which belongs inherently to human beings and which no individual finally solves for himself or herself, although a *theoretical* understanding of it may provide a *theoretical* solution. If things go well, in this gradual disillusionment process, the stage is set for the frustrations that we gather together under the word *weaning;* but it should be remembered that when we talk about the phenomena (which Klein has specifically illuminated) that cluster around weaning we are assuming the underlying process, the process by which opportunity for illusion and gradual disillusionment is provided. If illusion-disillusionment has gone astray the infant cannot attain to so normal a thing as weaning, nor to a reaction to weaning, and it is then absurd to refer to weaning at all. The mere termination of breast-feeding is not a weaning. . . .

In infancy this intermediate area is necessary for the initiation of a relationship between the child and the world, and is made possible by good-enough mothering at the early critical phase. Essential to all this is continuity (in time) of the external emotional environment and of particular elements in the physical environment such as the transitional object or objects.

The transitional phenomena are allowable to the infant because of the parents' intuitive recognition of the strain inherent in objective perception, and we do not challenge the infant in regard to subjectivity or objectivity just here where there is the transitional object.

Should an adult make claims on us for our acceptance of the objectivity of his subjective phenomena we discern or diagnose madness. If, however, the adult can manage to enjoy the personal intermediate area without making claims, then we can acknowledge our own corresponding intermediate areas, and are pleased to find examples of overlapping, that is to say common experience between members of a group in art or religion or philosophy. . . .

SUMMARY

Attention is drawn to the rich field for observation provided by the earliest experiences of the healthy infant as expressed principally in the relationship to the first possession.

This first possession is related backwards in time to autoerotic phenomena and fist- and thumb-sucking, and also forwards to the first soft animal or doll and to hard toys. It is related both to the external object (mother's breast) and to internal objects (magically introjected breast), but is distinct from each.

The transitional objects and transitional phenomena belong to the realm of illusion which is at the basis of initiation of experience. This early stage in development is made possible by the mother's special capacity for making adaptation to the needs of her infant, thus allowing the infant the illusion that what the infant creates really exists.

This intermediate area of experience, unchallenged in respect of its belonging to inner or external (shared) reality, constitutes the greater part of the infant's experience and throughout life is retained in the intense experiencing that belongs to the arts and to religion and to imaginative living, and to creative scientific work.

A positive value of illusion can therefore be stated.

An infant's transitional object ordinarily becomes gradually decathected, especially as cultural interests develop.

In psychopathology:

Addiction can be stated in terms of regression to the early stage at which the transitional phenomena are unchallenged.

Fetishism can be described in terms of a persistence of a specific object or type of object dating from infantile experience in the transitional field, linked with the delusion of a maternal phallus.

Pseudologia fantastica and thieving can be described in terms of an individual's unconscious urge to bridge a gap in continuity of experience in respect of a transitional object.

REFERENCES

Fairbairn, W. (1952). *Psychoanalytic Study of the Personality.* London: Tavistock.

Freud, S. (1905). The case of Dora. *Collected Papers* 3:63–64.

——. (1921). Group psychology and the analysis of the ego. *Standard Edition* 18:65–143.

——. (1923). The ego and the id. *Standard Edition* 19:3–66.

——. (1950 [1954]). *The Origins of Psychoanalysis.* London: Imago.

Hoffer, W. (1949). Mouth, hand and ego-integration. *Psychoanalytic Study of the Child* 3-4:51. New York: International Universities Press.

Illingworth, R. S. (1951). Sleep disturbances in young children. *British Medical Journal,* April 7.

Milner, M. (1952). Aspects of symbolism in comprehension of the not-self. *International Journal of Psycho-Analysis* 33:181.

19

"Metapsychological and Clinical Aspects of Regression within the Psychoanalytical Setup" (1954)

This paper and the following one introduce Winnicott's ideas on the treatment of patients who have experienced significant privation during early development, many of whom look as though they are intact to therapists not attuned to deeper levels of hurt and inner disturbance. Winnicott's description of the "freezing of the failure situation" continues to be a useful conceptualization in cases of the traumatic arrest of development.

I group cases according to the technical equipment they require of the analyst. I divide cases into the following three categories. First, there are those patients who operate as whole persons and whose difficulties are in the realm of interpersonal relationships. The technique for the treatment of these patients belongs to psychoanalysis as it developed in the hands of Freud at the beginning of the century.

Then second there come the patients in whom the wholeness of the personality only just begins to be something that can be taken for granted; in fact one can say that analysis has to do with the first events that belong to and inherently and immediately follow not only the achievement of wholeness but also the coming together of love and hate and the dawning recognition of dependence. This is the analysis of the stage of concern, or of what has come to be known as the *depressive position.* These patients require the analysis of mood. The technique for this work is not different from that needed by patients in the first category; nevertheless some new management problems do arise on account of the increased range of clinical material tackled. Important from our point of view here is the idea of the *survival of the analyst* as a dynamic factor.

In the third grouping I place all those patients whose analyses must deal with the early stages of emotional development before and up to the establishment of the personality as an entity, before the achievement of space-time unit status. The personal structure is not yet securely founded. In regard to this third grouping, the accent is more surely on management, and sometimes over long periods with these patients ordinary analytic work has to be in abeyance, management being the whole thing.

To recapitulate in terms of environment, one can say that in the first grouping we are dealing with patients who develop difficulties in the ordinary course of their home life, assuming a home life in the prelatency period, and assuming satisfactory development at the earlier infantile stages. In the second category, the analysis of the depressive position, we are dealing with the mother–child relationship especially around the time that weaning becomes a meaningful term. The mother holds a situation in time. In the third category there comes primitive emotional development, that which needs the mother actually holding the infant. . . .

For me, the word *regression* simply means the reverse of progress. This progress itself is the evolution of the individual, psyche-soma, personality, and mind with (eventually) character formation and socialization. Progress starts from a date certainly prior to birth. There is a biological drive behind progress. It is one of the tenets of psychoanalysis that health implies continuity in regard to this evolutionary progress of the psyche and that health is maturity of emotional development appropriate to the age of the individual, maturity that is to say in regard to this evolutionary process.

On closer examination one observes immediately that *there cannot be a simple reversal of progress*. For this progress to be reversed there has to be in the individual an organization which enables regression to occur.

We see:

> A failure of adaptation on the part of the environment that results in the development of a false self.

> A belief in the possibility of a correction of the original failure represented by a latent capacity for regression which implies a complex ego organization.
>
> Specialized environmental provision, followed by actual regression.
>
> New forward emotional development, with complications that will be described later. . . .

One has to include in one's theory of the development of a human being the idea that it is normal and healthy for the individual to be able to defend the self against specific environmental failure by a *freezing of the failure situation.* Along with this goes an unconscious assumption (which can become a conscious hope) that opportunity will occur at a later date for a renewed experience in which the failure situation will be able to be unfrozen and reexperienced, with the individual in a regressed state, in an environment that is making adequate adaptation. The theory is here being put forward of regression as part of a healing process, in fact, a normal phenomenon that can properly be studied in the healthy person. In the very ill person there is but little hope of new opportunity. In the extreme case the therapist would need to go to the patient and actively present good mothering, an experience that could not have been expected by the patient. . . .

It seems to me that it is only lately in the literature that *regression to dependence* has taken its rightful place in clinical descriptions. The reason for this must be that it is only recently that we have felt strong enough in our understanding of individual psyche-soma and mental development to be able to allow ourselves to examine and allow for the part that environment plays. . . .

My thesis up to this point can be stated thus:

> Psychotic illness is related to environmental failure at an early stage of the emotional development of the individual. The sense of futility and unreality belongs to the development of a false self which develops in protection of the true self.
>
> The setting of analysis reproduces the early and earliest mothering techniques. It invites regression by reason of its reliability.
>
> The regression of a patient is an organized return to early dependence or double dependence. The patient and the setting merge into the original success situation of primary narcissism.

> Progress from primary narcissism starts anew with the true self able to meet environmental failure situations without organization of the defences that involve a false self protecting the true self.
>
> To this extent psychotic illness can only be relieved by specialized environmental provision interlocked with the patient's regression.
>
> Progress from the new position, with the true self surrendered to the total ego, can now be studied in terms of the complex processes of individual growth.

In practice there is a sequence of events:

1. The provision of a setting that gives confidence.
2. Regression of the patient to dependence, with due sense of the risk involved.
3. The patient feeling a new sense of self, and the self hitherto hidden becoming surrendered to the total ego. A new progression of the individual processes which had stopped.
4. An unfreezing of an environmental failure situation.
5. From the new position of ego strength, anger related to the early environmental failure, felt in the present and expressed.
6. Return from regression to dependence, in orderly progress towards independence.
7. Instinctual needs and wishes becoming realizable with genuine vitality and vigour.

All this repeated again and again. . . .

It is proper to speak of the patient's *wishes*, the wish (for instance) to be quiet. With the regressed patient the word wish is incorrect; instead we use the word *need*. If a regressed patient *needs* quiet, then without it nothing can be done at all. If the need is not met the result is not anger, only a reproduction of the environmental failure situation which stopped the processes of self growth. The individual's capacity to "wish" has become interfered with, and we witness the reappearance of the original cause of a sense of futility.

The regressed patient is near to a reliving of dream and memory situations; an acting out of a dream may be the way the patient discovers what is urgent, and talking about what was acted out follows the action but cannot precede it.

Or take the detail of being on time. The analyst is not one who keeps patients waiting. Patients dream about being kept waiting and all the other variations on the theme, and they can be angry when the analyst is late. This is all part of the way the material goes. But patients who regress are different about the initial moment. There come phases when everything hangs on the punctuality of the analyst. If the analyst is there ready waiting, all is well—if not, well then both analyst and patient may as well pack up and go home, since no work can be done. Or, if one considers the patient's own unpunctuality, a neurotic patient who is late may perhaps be in a state of negative transference. A depressive patient is more likely by being late to be giving the analyst a little respite, a little longer for other activities and interests (protection from aggression, greed).

The psychotic (regressive) patient is probably late because there is not yet established any hope that the analyst will be on time. It is futile to be on time. So much hangs on this detail that the risk cannot be taken, so the patient is late; therefore no work gets done. . . .

On recovery from regression the patient, with the self now more fully surrendered to the ego, needs ordinary analysis as designed for the management of the depressive position and of the Oedipus complex in interpersonal relationships. For this reason, if for no other, the student should acquire proficiency in the analysis of the carefully chosen non-psychotic before proceeding to the study of regression. Preliminary work can be done by a study of the setting in classical psychoanalysis.

20

"Clinical Varieties of Transference" (1955–56)

In "Mind and its Relation to the Psyche-Soma," Winnicott (1954) wrote of the early psychological organization developed from the mind dwelling in a body, the *psyche-soma.* He described the way in which the mother's handling of the infant gave birth to the psyche, which originated out of body experience. Later, in his book *Playing and Reality* (Winnicott 1971), he added the term *psychosomatic partnership* for the relationship between mother and infant in which the bodily partnership through which the mother held and handled the child's body and bodily needs formed the original basis for their psychological partnership, and in which her experience and mental processes form the basis for the infant's emerging psyche.

In "Psychoses and Child Care" (Winnicott 1953) he had first discussed the development of a false self, to be elaborated on in later papers, including the paper on regression excerpted in Chapter 19, and "Ego Distortion in Terms of True and False Self," which is excerpted in Chapter 23. In Winnicott's thinking, the true self is a core being that relates to inner potential, needs, and self-expression; the false self is layered around the true self, takes care of it, shelters it from harm or extinction, and relates to the demands of outer reality, thereby also being vulnerable to distortion by the demands of others.

In this paper, he employed these two concepts in discussing clinical regression as an opportunity to make up for what was missing, severely distorted, or traumatized in early development. The discussion of the handling of transference reactions to failures by the analyst continues to have immediate relevance to therapeutic practice.

REFERENCES

Winnicott, D. W. (1953). Psychoses and child care. *British Journal of Medical Psychology* 26.
——(1954). Mind and its relation to the psyche-soma. *British Journal of Medical Psychology* 27.
——(1971). *Playing and Reality.* London: Tavistock.

There may be extreme cases in which there is no more than a collection of reactions to environmental failures of adaptation at the critical stage of emergence from primary identification. I am sure this condition is compatible with life, and with physical health. In the cases on which my work is based there has been what I call a true self hidden, protected by a false self. This false self is no doubt an aspect of the true self. It hides and protects it, and it reacts to the adaptation failures and develops a pattern corresponding to the pattern of environmental failure. In this way the true self is not involved in the reacting, and so preserves a continuity of being. However, this hidden true self suffers an impoverishment that derives from lack of experience.

The false self may achieve a deceptive false integrity, that is to say a false ego-strength, gathered from an environmental pattern, and from a good and reliable environment; for it by no means follows that early maternal failure must lead to a general failure of child care. The false self cannot, however, experience life or feel real.

In the favourable case the false self develops a fixed maternal attitude towards the true self, and is permanently in a state of holding the true self as a mother holds a baby at the very beginning of differentiation and of emergence from primary identification.

In the work that I am reporting the analyst follows the basic principle of psychoanalysis, that the patient's unconscious leads and is alone to be pursued. In dealing with a regressive tendency the analyst must be prepared to follow the patient's unconscious process if he is not to issue a directive and so step outside the analyst's role. I have found that it is not necessary to step outside the analyst's role and that it is possible to follow the patient's unconscious lead in this type of case as in the analysis of neurosis. There are differences, however, in the two types of work.

Where there is an intact ego and the analyst can take for granted these earliest details of infant care, then the setting of the analysis is unimportant relative to the interpretative work. (By *setting,* I mean the summation of all the details of management.) Even so there is a basic ration of management in ordinary analysis which is more or less accepted by all analysts.

In the work I am describing the setting becomes more important than the interpretation. The emphasis is changed from the one to the other.

The behaviour of the analyst, represented by what I have called the setting, by being good enough in the matter of adaptation to need, is gradually perceived by the patient as something that raises a hope that the true self may at last be able to take the risks involved in its starting to experience living.

Eventually the false self hands over to the analyst. This is a time of great dependence, and true risk, and the patient is naturally in a deeply regressed state. (By *regression* here I mean regression to dependence and to the early developmental processes.) This is also a highly painful state because the patient is aware, as the infant in the original situation is not aware, of the risks entailed. In some cases so much of the personality is involved that the patient must be in care at this stage. The processes are better studied, however, in those cases in which these matters are confined, more or less, to the time of the analytic sessions.

One characteristic of the transference at this stage is the way in which we must allow the patient's past to *be* the present. This idea is contained in Sechehaye's book and in her title *Symbolic Realization.* Whereas in the transference neurosis the past comes into the consulting room, in this work it is more true to say that the present goes back into the past, and *is* the past. Thus the analyst finds himself confronted with the patient's primary process in the setting in which it had its original validity.

Good-enough adaptation by the analyst produces a result which is exactly that which is sought, namely, a shift in the patient of the main site of operation from a false to a true self. There is now for the first time in the patient's life an opportunity for the development of an ego, for its integration from ego nuclei, for its establishment as a body ego, and also for its repudiation of an external environment with the initiation of a relatedness to objects. For the first time the ego can experience id impulses, and can feel real in so doing, and also in resting from experiencing. And from here there can at last follow an ordinary analysis of the ego's defences against anxiety.

There builds up an ability of the patient to use the analyst's limited successes in adaptation, so that the ego of the patient becomes able to begin to recall the original failures, all of which were recorded, kept ready. These failures had a disruptive effect at the time, and a treatment of the kind I am describing has gone a long way when the patient is able to take an example of original failure and to be angry about it. Only when the patient reaches this point, however, can there be the beginning of reality testing. It seems that something like primary repression overtakes these recorded traumata once they have been used in the treatment.

The way that this change comes about from the experience of being disrupted to the experience of anger is a matter that interests me in a special way, as it is at this point in my work that I found myself surprised. *The patient makes use of the analyst's failures.* Failures there must be, and indeed there is no attempt to give perfect adaptation; I would say that it is less harmful to make mistakes with these patients than with neurotic patients. Others may be surprised, as I was, to find that while a gross mistake may do but little harm, a very small error of judgment may produce a big effect. The clue is that the analyst's failure is being used and must be treated as a *past* failure, one that the patient can perceive and encompass, and be angry about now. The analyst needs to be able to make use of his failures in terms of their meaning for the patient, and he must if possible account for each failure even if this means a study of his unconscious countertransference.

In these phases of analytic work that which would be called resistance in work with neurotic patients always indicates that *the analyst has made a mistake,* or in some detail has behaved badly; in fact, the resistance remains until the analyst has found out the mistake and has tried to account for it, and has used it. If he defends himself, the patient misses the opportunity for being angry about a past failure just where anger was becoming possible for the first time. Here is a great contrast between this work and the analysis of neurotic patients with intact ego. It is here that we can see the sense in the dictum that every failed analysis is a failure not of the patient but of the analyst.

This work is exacting partly because the analyst has to have a sensitivity to the patient's needs and a wish to provide a setting that caters for these needs. The analyst is not, after all, the patient's natural mother.

It is exacting, also, because of the necessity for the analyst to look for his own mistakes whenever resistances appear. Yet it is only by using his own mistakes that he can do the most important part of the treatment in these phases, the part that enables the patient to become angry for the first time about the details of failure of adaptation that (at the time when they happened) produced disruption. It is this part of the work that frees the patient from dependence on the analyst.

In this way the negative transference of "neurotic" analysis is replaced by objective anger about the analyst's failures, so there again is an important difference between the transference phenomena in the two types of work.

We must not look for an awareness of our adaptation successes, since these are not felt as such at a deep level. Although we cannot work without the theory that we build up in our discussions, this work inevitably finds us out if our understanding of our patient's need is a matter of the mind rather than of the psyche-soma.

In my clinical work I have proved, at least to myself, that one kind of analysis does not preclude the other. I find myself slipping over from one to the other and back again, according to the trend of the patient's unconscious process. When work of the special kind I have referred to is completed it leads naturally on to ordinary analytic work, the analysis of the depressive position and of the neurotic defences of a patient with an ego, an intact ego, an ego that is able to experience id impulses and to take the consequences. What needs to be done now is the study in detail of the criteria by which the analyst may know *when to work with the change of emphasis*, how to see that a need is arising which is of the kind that I have said must be met (at least in a token way) by active adaptation, the analyst keeping the concept of primary identification all the time in mind.

21

"Primary Maternal Preoccupation" (1956)

This paper describes the mother–infant relationship from the standpoint of the mother's state of mind. Winnicott alluded often to the necessity that the mother be capable of this reciprocal state of mind as a fundamental quality of providing for her infant. With this paper, he began to develop concepts concerning the reciprocal mental qualities in mother and infant which determine the progress of early development. The following three papers continue this theme.

It is my thesis that in the earliest phase we are dealing with a very special state of the mother, a psychological condition which deserves a name, such as *primary maternal preoccupation.* I suggest that sufficient tribute has not yet been paid in our literature, or perhaps anywhere, to a very special psychiatric condition of the mother, of which I would say the following things:

> It gradually develops and becomes a state of heightened sensitivity during, and especially towards the end of, the pregnancy.
>
> It lasts for a few weeks after the birth of the child.
>
> It is not easily remembered by mothers once they have recovered from it.
>
> I would go further and say that the memory mothers have of this state tends to become repressed.

This organized state (that would be an illness were it not for the fact of the pregnancy) could be compared with a withdrawn state, or a dissociated state, or a fugue, or even with a disturbance at a deeper level such as a schizoid episode in which some aspect of the personality takes over temporarily. I would like to find a good name for this condition and to put it forward as something to be taken into account in all references to the earliest phase of infant life. I do not believe that it is possible to understand the functioning of the mother at the very beginning of the infant's life without seeing that she must be able to reach this state of heightened sensitivity, almost an illness, and to recover from it. (I bring in the word *illness* because a woman must be healthy in order both to develop this state and to recover from it as the infant releases her. If the infant should die, the mother's state suddenly shows up as illness. The mother takes this risk.)

I have implied this in the word *devoted* in the term *ordinary devoted mother* (Winnicott 1949). There are certainly many women who are good mothers in every other way and who are capable of a rich and fruitful life but who are not able to achieve this "normal illness" which enables them to adapt delicately and sensitively to the infant's needs at the very beginning; or they achieve it with one child but not with another. Such women are not able to become preoccupied with their own infant to the exclusion of other interests, in the way that is normal and temporary. It may be supposed that there is a "flight to sanity" in some of these people. Some of them certainly have very big alternative concerns which they do not readily abandon or they may not be able to allow this abandonment until they have had their first babies. When a woman has a strong male identification she finds this part of her mothering function most difficult to achieve, and repressed penis envy leaves but little room for primary maternal preoccupation. . . .

The mother who develops this state that I have called *primary maternal preoccupation* provides a setting for the infant's constitution to begin to make itself evident, for the developmental tendencies to start to unfold, and for the infant to experience spontaneous movement and become the owner of the sensations that are appropriate to this early phase of life. The instinctual life need not be referred to here because what I am discussing begins before the establishment of instinct patterns.

I have tried to describe this in my own language, saying that if the mother provides a good-enough adaptation to need, the infant's own line of life is disturbed very little by reactions to impingement. (Naturally, it is the *reactions* to impingement that count, not the impingements themselves.) Maternal failures produce phases of reaction to impingement and these reactions interrupt the "going on being" of the infant. An excess of this reacting produces not frustration but a *threat of annihilation*. This in my view is a very real primitive anxiety, long antedating any anxiety that includes the word *death* in its description.

In other words, the basis for ego establishment is the sufficiency of "going on being," uncut by reactions to impingement. A sufficiency of "going on being" is only possible at the beginning if the mother is in this state that (I suggest) is a very real thing when the healthy mother is near the end of her pregnancy, and over a period of a few weeks following the baby's birth.

Only if a mother is sensitized in the way I am describing can she feel herself into her infant's place, and so meet the infant's needs. These are at first body needs, and they gradually become ego needs as a psychology emerges out of the imaginative elaboration of physical experience.

There comes into existence an ego-relatedness between mother and baby, from which the mother recovers, and out of which the infant may eventually build the idea of a person in the mother. From this angle the recognition of the mother as a person comes in a positive way, normally, and not out of the experience of the mother as the symbol of frustration. The mother's failure to adapt in the earliest phase does not produce anything but an annihilation of the infant's self.

What the mother does well is not in any way apprehended by the infant at this stage. This is a fact according to my thesis. Her failures are not felt as maternal failures, but they act as threats to personal self-existence.

In the language of these considerations, the early building up of the ego is therefore silent. The first ego organization comes from the experience of threats of annihilation which do not lead to annihilation and from which, repeatedly, there is *recovery*. Out of such experiences confidence in recovery begins to be something which leads to an ego and to an ego capacity for coping with frustration. . . .

According to this thesis a good-enough environmental provision in the earliest phase enables the infant to begin to exist, to have experience, to build a personal ego, to ride instincts, and to meet with all the difficulties inherent in life. All this feels real to the infant who becomes able to have a self that can eventually even afford to sacrifice spontaneity, even to die.

On the other hand, without the initial good-enough environmental provision, this self that can afford to die never develops. The feeling of real is absent and if there is not too much chaos the ultimate feeling is of futility. The inherent difficulties of life cannot be reached, let alone the satisfactions. If there is not chaos, there appears a false self that hides the true self, that complies with demands, that reacts to stimuli, that rids itself of instinctual experiences by having them, but that is only playing for time.

It will be seen that, by this thesis, constitutional factors are more likely to show up in the normal, where the environment in the first phase has been adaptive. By contrast, when there has been failure at this first phase, the infant is caught up in primitive defence mechanisms (false self, etc.) which belong to the threat of annihilation, and constitutional elements tend to become overridden (unless physically manifest).

It is necessary here to leave undeveloped the theme of the infant's introjection of illness patterns of the mother, though this subject is of great importance in consideration of the environmental factor in the next stages, after the first stage of absolute dependence.

In reconstructing the early development of an infant there is no point at all in talking of instincts, except on a basis of ego development.

There is a watershed:

Ego maturity—instinctual experiences strengthen ego.
Ego immaturity—instinctual experiences disrupt ego.

Ego here implies a summation of experience. The individual self starts as a summation of resting experience, spontaneous motility, and sensation, return from activity to rest, and the gradual establishment of a capacity to wait for recovery from annihilations; annihilations that result from reactions to environmental impingement. For this reason the individual needs to start in the specialized environment to which I have here referred to as primary maternal preoccupation.

REFERENCE

Winnicott, D.W. (1949). *The Ordinary Devoted Mother and Her Baby.* Nine Broadcast Talks. Reprinted in *The Child and the Family.* London: Tavistock, 1957.

22

"The Theory of the Parent–Infant Relationship" (1960)

"The Capacity to Be Alone" (Winnicott 1958), which is not reprinted here, describes the quality of *ego-relatedness*, which enables an infant to develop a capacity to be alone. Paradoxically, this capacity has to arise from the ability to be at rest and alone in the presence of the mother. Eventually this capacity can be taken in so that the mature individual can be alone, reassured only by its own internal objects. Winnicott's 1958 paper thematically paves the way for these excerpts from "The Theory of the Parent–Infant Relationship."

This description of the reciprocity of processes in infant growth and maternal care is another landmark in analytic thought. In this paper, Winnicott fleshed out a famous comment he had made some years earlier, contained in a footnote with which I have begun the selection: "There is no such thing as an infant." The gloss on this aphorism is that "whenever one finds an infant one finds maternal care, and without maternal care there would be no infant." The mother must be there for the infant and learn to react to the specific needs and signals of her particular infant, and to the needs of each moment in order for the infant to become itself.

REFERENCE

Winnicott, D. W. (1958). The capacity to be alone. *International Journal of Psycho-Analysis* 39:416–420.

I once said: "There is no such thing as an infant," meaning, of course, that whenever one finds an infant one finds maternal care, and without maternal care there would be no infant. (Discussion at a Scientific Meeting of the British Psycho-Analytical Society, circa 1940.)

One half of the theory of the parent–infant relationship concerns the infant, and is the theory of the infant's journey from absolute dependence, through relative dependence, to independence, and, in parallel, the infant's journey from the pleasure principle to the reality principle, and from autoerotism to object relationships. The other half of the theory of the parent–infant relationship concerns maternal care, that is to say, the qualities and changes in the mother that meet the specific and developing needs of the infant towards whom she orientates.

THE INFANT

The key word in this part of the study is *dependence*. Human infants cannot start to *be* except under certain conditions. These conditions are studied below, but they are part of the psychology of the infant. Infants come into *being* differently according to whether the conditions are favourable or unfavourable. At the same time conditions do not determine the infant's potential. This is inherited, and it is legitimate to study this inherited potential of the individual as a separate issue, *provided always that it is accepted that the inherited potential of an infant cannot become an infant unless linked to maternal care.*

The inherited potential includes a tendency towards growth and development. All stages of emotional growth can be roughly dated. Presumably all developmental stages have a date in each individual child. Nevertheless, not only do these dates vary from child to child, but also, *even if they were known in advance* in the case of a given child, they could not be used in predicting the child's actual development because of the other factor, maternal care. If such dates could be used in prediction at all, it would be on the basis of assuming a maternal care that is adequate in the important respects. (This obviously does not mean adequate only in the physical sense; the meaning of adequacy and inadequacy in this context is discussed below.)

The Inherited Potential and its Fate

It is necessary here to attempt to state briefly what happens to the inherited potential if this is to develop into an infant, and thereafter into a child, a child reaching towards independent existence. Because of the complexities of the subject such a statement must be made on the assumption of satisfactory maternal care, which means parental care. Satisfactory parental care can be classified roughly into three overlapping stages:

1. Holding.
2. Mother and infant living together. Here the father's function (of dealing with the environment for the mother) is not known to the infant.
3. Father, mother, and infant, all three living together.

The term *holding* is used here to denote not only the actual physical holding of the infant, but also the total environmental provision prior to the concept of *living with.* In other words, it refers to a three-dimensional or space relationship with time gradually added. This overlaps with, but is initiated prior to, instinctual experiences that in time would determine object relationships. It includes the management of experiences that are inherent in existence, such as the *completion* (and therefore the *noncompletion*) of processes, processes which from the outside may seem to be purely physiological but which belong to infant psychology and take place in a complex psychological field, determined by the awareness and the empathy of the mother. (This concept of holding is further discussed below.)

The term *living with* implies object relationships, and the emergence of the infant from the state of being merged with the mother, or his perception of objects as external to the self.

This study is especially concerned with the holding phase of maternal care, and with the complex events in infants' psychological development that are related to this holding phase. It should be remembered, however, that a division of one phase from another is artificial, and merely a matter of convenience, adopted for the purpose of clearer definition.

Infant Development During the Holding Phase

In the light of this some characteristics of infant development during this phase can be enumerated. It is at this stage that

primary process
primary identification

autoerotism
primary narcissism

are living realities.

In this phase the ego changes over from an unintegrated state to a structured integration, and so the infant becomes able to experience anxiety associated with disintegration. The word *disintegration* begins to have a meaning which it did not possess before ego integration became a fact. In healthy development at this stage the infant retains the capacity for reexperiencing unintegrated states, but this depends on the continuation of reliable maternal care or on the buildup in the infant of memories of maternal care beginning gradually to be perceived as such. The result of healthy progress in the infant's development during this stage is that he attains to what might be called *unit status*. The infant becomes a person, an individual in his own right.

Associated with this attainment is the infant's psychosomatic existence, which begins to take on a personal pattern; I have referred to this as the psyche indwelling in the soma.[1] The basis for this indwelling is a linkage of motor and sensory and functional experiences with the infant's new state of being a person. As a further development there comes into existence what might be called a limiting membrane, which to some extent (in health) is equated with the surface of the skin, and has a position between the infant's "me" and his "not-me." So the infant comes to have an inside and an outside, and a body-scheme. In this way meaning comes to the function of intake and output; moreover, it gradually becomes meaningful to postulate a personal or inner psychic reality for the infant.[2]

During the holding phase other processes are initiated; the most important is the dawn of intelligence and the beginning of a mind as something distinct from the psyche. From this follows the whole story of the secondary processes and of symbolic functioning, and of the organization of a personal psychic content, which forms a basis for dreaming and for living relationships.

At the same time there starts in the infant a joining up of two roots of impulsive behaviour. The term *fusion* indicates the positive process whereby diffuse elements that belong to movement and to muscle erotism

1. For an earlier statement by me on this issue see my paper, "Mind and its Relation to the Psyche-Soma" (1949).

2. Here the work on primitive fantasy, with whose richness and complexity we are familiar through the teachings of Melanie Klein, becomes applicable and appropriate.

become (in health) fused with the orgiastic functioning of the erotogenic zones. This concept is more familiar as the reverse process of defusion, which is a complicated defence in which aggression becomes separated out from erotic experience after a period in which a degree of fusion has been achieved. All these developments belong to the environmental condition of *holding,* and without a good-enough holding these stages cannot be attained, or once attained cannot become established.

A further development is in the capacity for object relationships. Here the infant changes from a relationship to a subjectively conceived object to a relationship to an object objectively perceived. This change is closely bound up with the infant's change from being merged with the mother to being separate from her, or to relating to her as separate and "not-me." This development is not specifically related to the holding, but is related to the phase of "living with."

Dependence

In the holding phase the infant is maximally dependent. One can classify dependence thus:

1. *Absolute dependence.* In this state the infant has no means of knowing about the maternal care, which is largely a matter of prophylaxis. He cannot gain control over what is well and what is badly done, but is only in a position to gain profit or to suffer disturbance.
2. *Relative dependence.* Here the infant can become aware of the need for the details of maternal care, and can to a growing extent relate them to personal impulse, and then later, in a psychoanalytic treatment, can reproduce them in the transference.
3. *Towards independence.* The infant develops means for doing without actual care. This is accomplished through the accumulation of memories of care, the projection of personal needs and the introjection of care details, with the development of confidence in the environment. Here must be added the element of intellectual understanding with its tremendous implications.

Isolation of the Individual

Another phenomenon that needs consideration at this phase is the hiding of the core of the personality. Let us examine the concept of a central or true self. The central self could be said to be the inherited potential which is experiencing a continuity of being, and acquiring in its own way and at its own speed a personal psychic reality and a personal body-scheme.[3] It seems necessary to allow for the concept of the isolation of this central self as a characteristic of health. Any threat to this isolation of the true self constitutes a major anxiety at this early stage, and defences of earliest infancy appear in relation to failures on the part of the mother (or in maternal care) to ward off impingements which might disturb this isolation.

Impingements may be met and dealt with by the ego organization, gathered into the infant's omnipotence and sensed as projections.[4] On the other hand they may get through this defence in spite of the ego support which maternal care provides. Then the central core of the ego is affected, and this is the very nature of psychotic anxiety. In health the individual soon becomes invulnerable in this respect, and if external factors impinge there is merely a new degree and quality in the hiding of the central self. In this respect the best defence is the organization of a false self. Instinctual satisfactions and object relationships themselves constitute a threat to the individual's personal going-on-being. *Example:* a baby is feeding at the breast and obtains satisfaction. This fact by itself does not indicate whether he is having an ego-syntonic id experience or, on the contrary, is suffering the trauma of a seduction, a threat to personal ego continuity, a threat by an id experience which is not ego-syntonic, and with which the ego is not equipped to deal.

In health, object relationships can be developed on the basis of a compromise, one which involves the individual in what later would be called cheating and dishonesty, whereas a direct relationship is possible only on the basis of regression to a state of being merged with the mother.

Annihilation

Anxiety in these early stages of the parent–infant relationship relates to the *threat of annihilation,* and it is necessary to explain what is meant by this term.

---

3. In "The Capacity to Be Alone" (Winnicott 1958) I have tried to discuss another aspect of this developmental phase as we see it in adult health. (Cf. Greenacre 1958.)

4. I am using the term *projections* here in its descriptive and dynamic and not in its full metapsychological sense. The function of primitive psychic mechanisms, such as introjection, projection, and splitting, falls beyond the scope of this paper.

In this place which is characterized by the essential existence of a holding environment, the *inherited potential* is becoming itself a *continuity of being*. The alternative to being is reacting, and reacting interrupts being and annihilates. Being and annihilation are the two alternatives. The holding environment therefore has as its main function the reduction to a minimum of impingements to which the infant must react with resultant annihilation of personal being. Under favourable conditions the infant establishes a continuity of existence and then begins to develop the sophistications which make it possible for impingements to be gathered into the area of omnipotence. At this stage the word *death* has no possible application, and this makes the term *death instinct* unacceptable in describing the root of destructiveness. Death has no meaning until the arrival of hate and of the concept of the whole human person. When a whole human person can be hated, death has meaning, and close on this follows that which can be called maiming; the whole hated and loved person is kept alive by being castrated or otherwise maimed instead of killed. These ideas belong to a phase later than that characterized by dependence on the holding environment. . . .

THE ROLE OF THE MATERNAL CARE

I shall now attempt to describe some aspects of maternal care, and especially holding. In this paper the concept of *holding* is important, and a further development of the idea is necessary. The word is here used to introduce a full development of the theme contained in Freud's (1911, p. 220) phrase, ". . . when one considers that the infant—provided one includes with it the care it receives from its mother—does almost realize a psychical system of this kind." I refer to the actual state of the infant-mother relationship at the beginning when the infant has not separated out a self from the maternal care on which there exists absolute dependence in a psychological sense.[5]

At this stage the infant needs and in fact usually gets an environmental provision which has certain characteristics:

---

5. Reminder: to be sure of separating this off from object relationships and instinct-gratification I must *artificially* confine my attention to the body needs of a general kind. A patient said to me: "A good analytic hour in which the right interpretation is given at the right time *is* a good feed."

It meets physiological needs. Here physiology and psychology have not yet become distinct, or are only in the process of doing so; and

It is reliable. But the environmental provision is not mechanically reliable. It is reliable in a way that implies the mother's empathy.

Holding:

Protects from physiological insult.

Takes account of the infant's skin sensitivity—touch, temperature, auditory sensitivity, visual sensitivity, sensitivity to falling (action of gravity) and of the infant's lack of knowledge of the existence of anything other than the self.

It includes the whole routine of care throughout the day and night, and it is not the same with any two infants because it is part of the infant, and no two infants are alike.

Also it follows the minute day-to-day changes belonging to the infant's growth and development, both physical and psychological.

It should be noted that mothers who have it in them to provide good-enough care can be enabled to do better by being cared for themselves in a way that acknowledges the essential nature of their task. Mothers who do not have it in them to provide good-enough care cannot be made good enough by mere instruction.

Holding includes especially the physical holding of the infant, which is a form of loving. It is perhaps the only way in which a mother can show the infant her love. There are those who can hold an infant and those who cannot; the latter quickly produce in the infant a sense of insecurity, and distressed crying.

All this leads right up to, includes, and coexists with the establishment of the infant's first object relationships and his first experiences of instinctual gratification.[6] . . .

Examination of One Detail of Maternal Care

I will give an example to illustrate subtlety in infant care. An infant is merged with the mother, and while this remains true the nearer the

6. For further discussion of this aspect of the developmental processes see my paper, "Transitional Objects and Transitional Phenomena" (excerpted in Chapter 18).

mother can come to an exact understanding of the infant's needs the better. A change, however, comes with the end of merging, and this end is not necessarily gradual. As soon as mother and infant are separate, from the infant's point of view, then it will be noted that the mother tends to change in her attitude. It is as if she now realizes that the infant no longer expects the condition in which there is an almost magical understanding of need. The mother seems to know that the infant has a new capacity, that of giving a signal so that she can be guided towards meeting the infant's needs. It could be said that if now she knows too well what the infant needs, this is magic and forms no basis for an object relationship. . . . At the end of merging, when the child has become separate from the environment, an important feature is that the infant has to give a signal.[7] We find this subtlety appearing clearly in the transference in our analytic work. It is very important, except when the patient is regressed to earliest infancy and to a state of merging, that the analyst shall *not* know the answers except insofar as the patient gives the clues. The analyst gathers the clues and makes the interpretations, and it often happens that patients fail to give the clues, making certain thereby that the analyst can do nothing. This limitation of the analyst's power is important to the patient, just as the analyst's power is important, represented by the interpretation that is right and that is made at the right moment, and that is based on the clues and the unconscious cooperation of the patient who is supplying the material which builds up and justifies the interpretation. In this way the student analyst sometimes does better analysis than he will do in a few years' time when he knows more. When he has had several patients he begins to find it irksome to go as slowly as the patient is going, and he begins to make interpretations based not on material supplied on that particular day by the patient but on his own accumulated knowledge or his adherence for the time being to a particular group of ideas. This is of no use to the patient. The analyst may appear to be very clever, and the patient may express admiration, but in the end the correct interpretation is a trauma, which the patient has to reject, because it is not his. He complains that the analyst attempts to hypnotize him, that is to say, that the analyst is inviting a severe regression to dependence, pulling the patient back to a merging in with the analyst.

The same thing can be observed with the mothers of infants; mothers who have had several children begin to be so good at the technique of

7. Freud's later (1926) theory of anxiety as a signal to the ego.

mothering that they do all the right things at the right moments, and then the infant who has begun to become separate from the mother has no means of gaining control of all the good things that are going on. The creative gesture, the cry, the protest, all the little signs that are supposed to produce what the mother does, all these things are missing, because the mother has already met the need just as if the infant were still merged with her and she with the infant. In this way the mother, by being a seemingly good mother, does something worse than castrate the infant. The latter is left with two alternatives: either being in a permanent state of regression and of being merged with the mother, or else staging a total rejection of the mother, even of the seemingly good mother.

We see therefore that in infancy and in the management of infants there is a very subtle distinction between the mother's understanding of her infant's need based on empathy, and her changeover to an understanding based on something in the infant or small child that indicates need. This is particularly difficult for mothers because of the fact that children vacillate between one state and the other; one minute they are merged with their mothers and require empathy, while the next they are separate from her, and then if she knows their needs in advance she is dangerous, a witch. It is a very strange thing that mothers who are quite uninstructed adapt to these changes in their developing infants satisfactorily and without any knowledge of the theory. This detail is reproduced in psychoanalytic work with borderline cases, and in all cases at certain moments of great importance when dependence in transference is maximal. . . .

The important thing, in my view, is that the mother through identification of herself with her infant knows what the infant feels like and so is able to provide almost exactly what the infant needs in the way of holding and in the provision of an environment generally. Without such an identification I consider that she is not able to provide what the infant needs at the beginning, which is *a live adaptation to the infant's needs.* The main thing is the physical holding, and this is the basis of all the more complex aspects of holding, and of environmental provision in general. . . .

With the care that it receives from its mother each infant is able to have a personal existence, and so begins to build up what might be called a *continuity of being.* On the basis of this continuity of being the inherited potential gradually develops into an individual infant. If maternal care is not good enough then the infant does not really come into existence, since there is no continuity of being; instead the personality becomes built on the basis of reactions to environmental impingement.

All this has significance for the analyst. Indeed it is not from direct observation of infants so much as from the study of the transference in the analytic setting that it is possible to gain a clear view of what takes place in infancy itself. This work on infantile dependence derives from the study of the transference and countertransference phenomena that belong to the psychoanalyst's involvement with the borderline case. In my opinion this involvement is a legitimate extension of psychoanalysis, the only real alteration being in the diagnosis of the illness of the patient, the etiology of whose illness goes back behind the Oedipus complex, and involves a distortion at the time of absolute dependence. . . .

REFERENCES

Freud, S. (1911). Formulations on the two principles of mental functioning. *Standard Edition* 12.

—— (1926). Inhibitions, symptoms and anxiety. *Standard Edition* 20.

Greenacre, P. (1958). Early physical determinants in the development of the sense of identity. *Journal of the American Psychoanalytic Association* 6:4.

Winnicott, D. W. (1948). Reparation in respect of mother's organized defence against depression. In *Collected Papers: Through Paediatrics to Psycho-Analysis*, pp. 91–96. London: Tavistock.

—— (1949). Mind and its relation to the psyche-soma. *British Journal of Medical Psychology* 27 (1954).

—— (1951). Transitional objects and transitional phenomena. *International Journal of Psycho-Analysis* 34 (1953).

—— (1958). The capacity to be alone. *International Journal of Psycho-Analysis* 39:416–420.

23

"Ego Distortion in Terms of True and False Self" (1960)

Winnicott's division of personality into true and false selves relates to Klein and Fairbairn's description of the schizoid personality and schizoid processes. Although schizoid phenomena and the concept of the split between true and false self are rarely discussed in the same context, Winnicott's version of a developmental split in personality adds a dimension to Klein and Fairbairn's ideas. The splits to be considered are not only those between good and bad experience, but also between those that validate the infant's core personality and those that require a compliance through which potentially frustrating experience can be potentially satisfying, although at the risk of falsifying the expression of the self. Winnicott's description of the false self also extends the sense of internal dynamic beyond Fairbairn's postulation of dynamic interaction between parts of ego and object. The dynamic here is between aspects of the self, seeking trueness to a sense of inner self, and accommodation to the mother and the wider world of external objects. We will see further elaboration of this set of issues in the work of Guntrip, whose idea of the *repressed libidinal ego* that seeks an object that cannot be found relates partly to Winnicott's *true self* and partly to Fairbairn's *libidinal ego.*

This paper depicts the origin of the true self in innate qualities of the infant, but its nurture and safekeeping rest with the behavior of the mother. Winnicott referred briefly to the required *primary maternal preoccupation* he had written about earlier (see Chapter 21), describing the state of mind of the *good-enough mother.* Winnicott thought that true development required good care. He states paradoxically that the achievement of symbolic representation comes about not only by the infant's action in separating words from things, but by the mother's making real the things for which the infant searches. Thus, the growth of symbolic thought is linked to the interpersonal world. At the same time, Bion was writing a series of papers (excerpted below) demonstrating that the growth of symbolic thought is dependent on interpersonal encounter. Winnicott describes these processes from the observable transactions, while Bion does so in terms of internal processes.

One recent development in psychoanalysis has been the increasing use of the concept of the false self. This concept carries with it the idea of a true self. . . .

HISTORY

It would appear to me that the idea of a false self, which is an idea which our patients give us, can be discerned in the early formulations of Freud. In particular I link what I divide into a true and a false self with Freud's division of the self into a part that is central and powered by the instincts (or by what Freud called sexuality, pregenital and genital), and a part that is turned outwards and is related to the world. . . .

EGO NEEDS AND ID NEEDS

It must be emphasized that in referring to the meeting of infant needs I am not referring to the satisfaction of instincts. In the area that I am examining the instincts are not yet clearly defined as internal to the infant. The instincts can be as much external as can a clap of thunder or a hit. The infant's ego is building up strength and in consequence is getting towards a state in which id demands will be felt as part of the self, and not as environmental. When this development occurs, then id satisfaction becomes a very important strengthener of the ego, or of the true self; but id excitements can be traumatic when the ego is not yet able to include them, and not yet able to contain the risks involved and the frustrations experienced up to the point when id satisfaction becomes a fact.

A patient said to me: "Good management [ego care] such as I have experienced during this hour is a feed [id satisfaction]. He could not have said this the other way around, for if I had fed him he would have complied and this would have played into his false self defence, or else he would have reacted and rejected my advances, maintaining his integrity by choosing frustration . . .

Example

The best example I can give is that of a middle-aged woman who had a very successful false self but who had the feeling all her life that she had not started to exist, and that she had always been looking for a means of getting to her true self. She still continues with her analysis, which has lasted many years. In the first phase of this research analysis (this lasted two or three years), I found I was dealing with what the patient called her "caretaker self." This "caretaker self":

1. found psychoanalysis;
2. came and sampled analysis, as a kind of elaborate test of the analyst's reliability;
3. brought her to analysis;
4. gradually after three years or more handed over its function to the analyst (this was the time of the depth of the regression, with a few weeks of a very high degree of dependence on the analyst);
5. hovered round, resuming caretaking at times when the analyst failed (analyst's illness, analyst's holidays, etc.).

Its ultimate fate will be discussed later.

From the evolution of this case it was easy for me to see the defensive nature of the false self. Its defensive function is to hide and protect the true self, whatever that may be. Immediately it becomes possible to classify false self organizations:

1. At one extreme: the false self sets up as real and it is this that observers tend to think is the real person. In living relationships, work relationships, and friendships, however, the false self begins to fail. In situations in which what is expected is a whole person the false self has some essential lacking. At this extreme the true self is hidden.
2. Less extreme: the false self defends the true self; the true self is, however, acknowledged as a potential and is allowed a secret life.

Here is the clearest example of clinical illness as an organization with a positive aim, the preservation of the individual in spite of abnormal environmental conditions. This is an extension of the psychoanalytic concept of the value of symptoms to the sick person.

3. More towards health: the false self has as its main concern a search for conditions which will make it possible for the true self to come into its own. If conditions cannot be found then there must be reorganized a new defence against exploitation of the true self, and if there be doubt then the clinical result is suicide. Suicide in this context is the destruction of the total self in avoidance of annihilation of the true self. When suicide is the only defence left against betrayal of the true self, then it becomes the lot of the false self to organize the suicide. This, of course, involves its own destruction, but at the same time eliminates the need for its continued existence, since its function is the protection of the true self from insult.
4. Still further towards health: the false self is built on identifications (as for example that of the patient mentioned, whose childhood environment and whose actual nannie gave much colour to the false self organization).
5. In health: the false self is represented by the whole organization of the polite and mannered social attitude, a "not wearing the heart on the sleeve," as might be said. Much has gone to the individual's ability to forgo omnipotence and the primary process in general, the gain being the place in society which can never be attained or maintained by the true self alone. . . .

THE MIND AND THE FALSE SELF

A particular danger arises out of the not infrequent tie-up between the intellectual approach and the false self. When a false self becomes organized in an individual who has a high intellectual potential there is a very strong tendency for the mind to become the location of the false self, and in this case there develops a dissociation between intellectual activity and psychosomatic existence. (In the healthy individual, it must be assumed, the mind is not something for the individual to exploit in escape from psychosomatic being. I have developed this theme at some length in "Mind and its Relation to the Psyche-Soma" (Winnicott 1949a).

When there has taken place this double abnormality, (1) the false self organized to hide the true self, and (2) an attempt on the part of the individual to solve the personal problem by the use of a fine intellect, a clinical picture results which is peculiar in that it very easily deceives. The world may observe academic success of a high degree, and may find it hard to believe in the very real distress of the individual concerned, who feels "phoney" the more he or she is successful. When such individuals destroy themselves in one way or another, instead of fulfilling promise, this invariably produces a sense of shock in those who have developed high hopes of the individual.

AETIOLOGY . . .

To get to a statement of the relevant developmental process it is essential to take into account the mother's behaviour and attitude, because in this field dependence is real, and near absolute. It is not possible to state what takes place by reference to the infant alone.

In seeking the aetiology of the false self we are examining the stage of first object relationships. At this stage the infant is most of the time unintegrated, and never fully integrated; cohesion of the various sensorimotor elements belongs to the fact that the mother holds the infant, sometimes physically, and all the time figuratively. Periodically the infant's gesture gives expression to a spontaneous impulse; the source of the gesture is the true self, and the gesture indicates the existence of a potential true self. We need to examine the way the mother meets this infantile omnipotence revealed in a gesture (or a sensorimotor grouping). I have here linked the idea of a true self with the spontaneous gesture. Fusion of the motility and erotic elements is in process of becoming a fact at this period of development of the individual.

THE MOTHER'S PART

It is necessary to examine the part played by the mother, and in doing so I find it convenient to compare two extremes; by one extreme the mother *is a good-enough mother* and by the other the mother *is not a good-enough mother.* The question will be asked: what is meant by the term good-enough?

The good-enough mother meets the omnipotence of the infant and to some extent makes sense of it. She does this repeatedly. A true self begins to have life, through the strength given to the infant's weak ego by the mother's implementation of the infant's omnipotent expressions.

The mother who is not good enough is not able to implement the infant's omnipotence, and so she repeatedly fails to meet the infant gesture; instead she substitutes her own gesture which is to be given sense by the compliance of the infant. This compliance on the part of the infant is the earliest stage of the false self, and belongs to the mother's inability to sense her infant's needs.

It is an essential part of my theory that the true self does not become a living reality except as a result of the mother's repeated success in meeting the infant's spontaneous gesture or sensory hallucination. (This idea is closely linked with Sechehaye's [1951] idea contained in the term *symbolic realization.* This term has played an important part in modern psychoanalytic theory, but it is not quite accurate since it is the infant's *gesture or hallucination* that is made real, and the capacity of the infant *to use a symbol* is the result.)

There are now two possible lines of development in the scheme of events according to my formulation. *In the first case* the mother's adaptation is *good enough* and in consequence the infant begins to believe in external reality, which appears and behaves as by magic (because of the mother's relatively successful adaptation to the infant's gestures and needs), and which acts in a way that does not clash with the infant's omnipotence. On this basis the infant can gradually abrogate omnipotence. The true self has a spontaneity, and this has been joined up with the world's events. The infant can now begin to enjoy the *illusion* of omnipotent creating and controlling, and then can gradually come to recognize the illusory element, the fact of playing and imagining. Here is the basis for the symbol which at first is both the infant's spontaneity or hallucination, and also the external object created and ultimately cathected.

In between the infant and the object is some thing, or some activity or sensation. Insofar as this joins the infant to the object (viz. maternal part-object) so far is this the basis of symbol formation. On the other hand, insofar as this something separates instead of joins, so is its function of leading on to symbol-formation blocked.

In the second case, which belongs more particularly to the subject under discussion, the mother's adaptation to the infant's hallucinations and spontaneous impulses is deficient, *not good enough.* The process that leads to the capacity for symbol usage does not get started (or else it becomes broken up, with a corresponding withdrawal on the part of the infant from advantages gained).

When the mother's adaptation is not good enough at the start the infant might be expected to die physically, because cathexis of external objects is not initiated. The infant remains isolated. But in practice the infant lives, but lives falsely. The protest against being forced into a false existence can be detected from the earliest stages. The clinical picture is one of general irritability, and of feeding and other function disturbances which may, however, disappear clinically, only to reappear in serious form at a later stage.

In this second case, where the mother cannot adapt well enough, the infant gets seduced into a compliance, and a compliant false self reacts to environmental demands and the infant seems to accept them. Through this false self the infant builds up a false set of relationships, and by means of introjections even attains a show of being real, so that the child may grow to be just like mother, nurse, aunt, brother, or whoever at the time dominates the scene. The false self has one positive and very important function: to hide the true self, which it does by compliance with environmental demands.

In the extreme examples of false self development, the true self is so well hidden that spontaneity is not a feature in the infant's living experiences. Compliance is then the main feature, with imitation as a speciality. When the degree of the split in the infant's person is not too great there may be some almost personal living through imitation, and it may even be possible for the child to act a special role, that of the true self *as it would be if it had had existence.*

In this way it is possible to trace the point of origin of the false self, which can now be seen to be a defence, a defence against that which is unthinkable, the exploitation of the true self, which would result in its annihilation. (If the true self ever gets exploited and annihilated this belongs to the life of an infant whose mother was not only "not good enough" in the sense set out above, but was good and bad in a tantalizingly irregular manner. The mother here has as part of her illness a need to cause and to maintain a muddle in those who are in contact with her. This may appear in a transference situation in which the patient tries to make the analyst mad [Bion 1959, Searles 1959]. There may be a degree of this which can destroy the last vestiges of an infant's capacity to defend the true self.) . . .

Primary maternal preoccupation enables the mother to know about her infant's earliest expectations and needs, and makes her personally satisfied insofar as the infant is at ease. It is because of this identification with her infant that she knows how to hold her infant, so that the infant starts by existing and not by reacting. Here is the origin of the true self which cannot become a reality without the mother's specialized relationship, one which might be described by a common word: devotion.[1]

THE TRUE SELF

The concept of a false self needs to be balanced by a formulation of that which could properly be called the true self. At the earliest stage the true self is the theoretical position from which come the spontaneous gesture and the personal idea. The spontaneous gesture is the true self in action. Only the true self can be creative and only the true self can feel real. Whereas a true self feels real, the existence of a false self results in a feeling unreal or a sense of futility.

The false self, if successful in its function, hides the true self, or else finds a way of enabling the true self to start to live. Such an outcome may be achieved by all manner of means, but we observe most closely those instances in which the sense of things being real or worth while arrives during a treatment. My patient to whose case I have referred has come near the end of a long analysis *to the beginning of her life.* She contains no true experience, she has no past. She starts with fifty years of wasted life, but at last she feels real, and therefore she now wants to live.

The true self comes from the aliveness of the body tissues and the working of body functions, including the heart's action and breathing. It is closely linked with the idea of the primary process, and is, at the beginning, essentially not reactive to external stimuli, but primary. There is but little point in formulating a true self idea except for the purpose of trying to understand the false self, because it does no more than collect together the details of the experience of aliveness.

Gradually the degree of sophistication of the infant becomes such that it is more true to say that the false self hides the infant's inner reality than to say that it hides the true self. By this time the infant has an established

1. On account of this I called my series of talks to mothers, "The Ordinary Devoted Mother and Her Baby" (Winnicott, 1949b).

limiting membrane, has an inside and an outside, and has become to a considerable extent disentangled from maternal care.

It is important to note that according to the theory being formulated here the concept of an individual inner reality of objects applies to a stage later than does the concept of what is being termed the true self. The true self appears as soon as there is any mental organization of the individual at all, and it means little more than the summation of sensorimotor aliveness.

The true self quickly develops complexity, and relates to external reality by natural processes, by such processes as develop in the individual infant in the course of time. The infant then comes to be able to react to a stimulus without trauma because the stimulus has a counterpart in the individual's inner, psychic reality. The infant then accounts for all stimuli as projections, but this is a stage that is not necessarily achieved, or that is only partially achieved, or it may be reached and lost. This stage having been achieved, the infant is now able to retain the sense of omnipotence even when reacting to environmental factors that the observer can discern as truly external to the infant. All this precedes by years the infant's capacity to allow in intellectual reasoning for the operation of pure chance.

Every new period of living in which the true self has not been seriously interrupted results in a strengthening of the sense of being real, and with this goes a growing capacity on the part of the infant to tolerate two sets of phenomena: These are:

1. Breaks in continuity of true self living. (Here can be seen a way in which the birth process might be traumatic, as for instance when there is delay without unconsciousness.)
2. Reactive or false self experiences, related to the environment on a basis of compliance. This becomes the part of the infant which can be (before the first birthday) taught to say "Ta," or, in other words, can be taught to acknowledge the existence of an environment that is becoming intellectually accepted. Feelings of gratitude may or may not follow.

THE NORMAL EQUIVALENT OF THE FALSE SELF

In this way, by natural processes, the infant develops an ego organization that is adapted to the environment, but this does not happen automatically and indeed it can only happen if first the true self (as I call it) has become a living reality, because of the mother's good-enough adaptation to the infant's living needs. There is a compliant aspect to the true self in healthy living, an ability of the infant to comply and not to be exposed. The ability to compromise is an achievement. The equivalent of the false self in normal development is that which can develop in the child into a social manner, something which is adaptable. In health this social manner represents a compromise. At the same time, in health, the compromise ceases to become allowable when the issues become crucial. When this happens the true self is able to override the compliant self. Clinically this constitutes a recurring problem of adolescence. . . .

CONSEQUENCES FOR THE PSYCHOANALYST

If these considerations prove to have value, then the practising psychoanalyst must be affected in the following ways:

1. In analysis of a false personality the fact must be recognized that the analyst can only talk to the false self of the patient about the patient's true self. It is as if a nurse brings a child, and at first the analyst discusses the child's problem, and the child is not directly contacted. Analysis does not start until the nurse has left the child with the analyst, and the child has become able to remain alone with the analyst and has started to play.
2. At the point of transition, when the analyst begins to get into contact with the patient's true self, there must be a period of extreme dependence. Often this is missed in analytic practice. The patient has an illness, or in some other way gives the analyst a chance to take over the false self (nursemaid) function, but the analyst at that point fails to see what is happening, and in consequence it is others who care for the patient and on whom the patient becomes dependent in a period of disguised regression to dependence, and the opportunity is missed.
3. Analysts who are not prepared to go and meet the heavy needs of patients who become dependent in this way must be careful in choosing their cases that they do not include false self types.

In psychoanalytic work it is possible to see analyses going on indefinitely because they are done on the basis of work with the false self. In one case, a man patient who had had a considerable amount of analysis before coming to me, my work really started with him when I made it clear to him that I recognized his nonexistence. He made the remark that over the years all the good work done with him had been futile because it had been done on the basis that he existed, whereas he had only existed falsely. When I had said that I recognized his nonexistence he felt that he had been communicated with for the first time. What he meant was that his true self that had been hidden away from infancy had now been in communication with his analyst in the only way which was not dangerous. This is typical of the way in which this concept affects psychoanalytic work. . . .

A principle might be enunciated, that in the false self area of our analytic practice we find we make more headway by recognition of the patient's nonexistence than by a long-continued working with the patient on the basis of ego defence mechanisms. The patient's false self can collaborate indefinitely with the analyst in the analysis of defences, being so to speak on the analyst's side in the game. This unrewarding work is only cut short profitably when the analyst can point to and specify an absence of some essential feature: "You have no mouth," "You have not started to exist yet," "Physically you are a man, but you do not know from experience anything about masculinity," and so on. These recognitions of important fact, made clear at the right moments, pave the way for communication with the true self. A patient who had had much futile analysis on the basis of a false self, cooperating vigorously with an analyst who thought this was his whole self, said to me: "The only time I felt hope was when you told me that you could see no hope, and you continued with the analysis."

On the basis of this one could say that the false self (like the multiple projections at later stages of development) deceives the analyst if the latter fails to notice that, regarded as a whole functioning person, the false self, however well set up, lacks something, and that something is the essential central element of creative originality. . . .

REFERENCES

Bion, W. (1959). Attacks on linking. *International Journal of Psycho-Analysis* 40:308–315.

Searles, H. F. (1959). The effort to drive the other person crazy—an element in the aetiology and psychotherapy of schizophrenia. *British Journal of Medical Psychology* 32:1–18.

Sechehaye, M. (1951). *Symbolic Realization.* New York: International Universities Press.

Winnicott, D. W. (1949a). Mind and its relation to the psyche-soma, pp. 243–254. In *Collected Papers: From Paediatrics to Psycho-Analysis*. London: Tavistock, 1958.

——(1949b). *The Ordinary Devoted Mother and Her Baby.* Nine Broadcast Talks. Republished in *The Child and the Family.* London: Tavistock, 1957.

24

"The Use of an Object and Relating through Identifications" (1969)

Winnicott differentiated between aggression that is reactive to environmental failure, and aggression that is essential to the child's capacity to apprehend and use the external world. Applying this principle to the clinical situation, he argued that it is essential for the therapist to know the difference in the intention of the patient, and to survive without retaliation the attacks that are part of the patient's coming into being. The capacity of the mother and the therapist to be used in this way provides an environment that facilitates development, and sets the stage for the growth of the child's (or patient's) use of the mother (or therapist) as a specific object relationship. There is nothing in Fairbairn, Klein, or Freud that directly anticipates this unique area of Winnicott's understanding of the positive aspects of aggression from the beginning, although the most compatible and complementary ideas are Bion's formulation of the container/contained, which elaborates on the mother's internal processes that make it possible to tolerate being used as an object.

What I have to say in this present paper is extremely simple. Although it comes out of my psychoanalytical experience I would not say that it could have come out of my psychoanalytical experience of two decades ago, because I would not then have had the technique to make possible the transference movements that I wish to describe. For instance, it is only in recent years that I have become able to wait and wait for the natural evolution of the transference arising out of the patient's growing trust in the psychoanalytic technique and setting, and to avoid breaking up this natural process by making interpretations. It will be noticed that I am talking about the making of interpretations and not about interpretations as such. It appals me to think how much deep change I have prevented or delayed in patients *in a certain classification category* by my personal need to interpret. If only we can wait, the patient arrives at understanding creatively and with immense joy, and I now enjoy this joy more than I used to enjoy the sense of having been clever. I think I interpret mainly to let the patient know the limits of my understanding. The principle is that it is the patient and only the patient who has the answers. We may or may not enable him or her to be able to encompass what is known or become aware of it with acceptance.

By contrast with this comes the interpretative work which the analyst must do and which distinguishes analysis from self-analysis. This interpreting by the analyst, if it is to have effect, must be related to the patient's ability *to place the analyst outside the area of subjective phenomena.* What is then involved is the patient's ability to use the analyst, which is the subject of this paper. In teaching, as in the feeding of a child, the capacity to use objects is taken for granted, but in our work it is necessary for us to be concerned with the development and the establishment of the capacity to use objects and to recognize a patient's inability to use objects, where this is a fact. . . .

In object relating the subject allows certain alterations in the self to take place, of a kind that has caused us to invent the term *cathexis*. The object has become meaningful. Projection mechanisms and identifications have been operating, and the subject is depleted to the extent that something of the subject is found in the object, though enriched by feeling. Accompanying these changes is some degree of physical involvement (however slight) towards excitement, in the direction of the functional climax of an orgasm. (In this context I deliberately omit reference to the very important aspect of relating that is an exercise in cross-identifications. This must be omitted here because it belongs to a phase of development that is subsequent to and not prior to the phase of development with which I am concerned in this paper, that is to say, the move from self-containment and relating to subjective objects into the realm of object usage) (Winnicott 1968).

Object relating is an experience of the subject that can be described in terms of the subject as an isolate (Winnicott 1958, 1963). When I speak of the use of an object, however, I take object relating for granted, and add new features that involve the nature and the behaviour of the object. For instance, the object, if it is to be used, must necessarily be real in the sense of being part of shared reality, not a bundle of projections. It is this, I think, that makes for the world of difference that exists between relating and usage. . . .

In clinical terms: two babies are feeding at the breast; one is feeding on the self in the form of projections, and the other is feeding on (using) milk from a woman's breast. Mothers, like analysts, can be good or not good enough; some can and some cannot carry the baby over from relating to usage.

I would like to put in a reminder here that the essential feature in the concept of transitional objects and phenomena (according to my presentation of the subject) is *the paradox, and the acceptance of the paradox:* the baby creates the object but the object was there waiting to be created and to become a cathected object. I tried to draw attention to this aspect of transitional phenomena by claiming that in the rules of the game we all know that we will never challenge the baby to elicit an answer to the question: did you create that or did you find it? . . .

To use an object the subject must have developed a *capacity* to use objects. This is part of the change to the reality principle.

This capacity cannot be said to be inborn, nor can its development in an individual be taken for granted. The development of a capacity to use an object is another example of the maturational process as something that depends on a facilitating environment.

In the sequence one can say that first there is object relating, then in the end there is object use; in between, however, is the most difficult thing, perhaps, in human development, or the most irksome of all the early failures that come for mending. This thing that there is in between relating and use is the subject's placing of the object outside the area of the subject's omnipotent control, that is, the subject's perception of the object as an external phenomenon, not as a projective entity, in fact recognition of it as an entity in its own right.

This change (from relating to use) means that the subject destroys the object. From here it could be argued by an armchair philosopher that there is therefore no such thing in practice as the use of an object; if the object be external, then the object is destroyed by the subject. Should the philosopher come out of his chair and sit on the floor with his patient, however, he will find that there is an intermediate position. In other words, he will find that after "subject relates to object" comes "subject destroys object" (as it becomes external); and then may come "*object survives* destruction by the subject." But there may or may not be survival. A new feature thus arrives in the theory of object relating. The subject says to the object: "I destroyed you," and the object is there to receive the communication. From now on the subject says: "Hullo object!" "I destroyed you." "I love you." "You have value for me because of your survival of my destruction of you." "While I am loving you I am all the time destroying you in (unconscious) *fantasy.*" Here fantasy begins for the individual. The subject can now use the object that has survived. It is important to note that it is not only that the subject destroys the object because the object is placed outside the area of omnipotent control. It is equally significant to state this the other way round and to say that it is the destruction of the object that places the object outside the area of the subject's omnipotent control. In these ways the object develops its own autonomy and life, and (if it survives) contributes-in to the subject, according to its own properties.

In other words, because of the survival of the object, the subject may now have started to live a life in the world of objects, and so the subject stands to gain immeasurably; but the price has to be paid in acceptance of the ongoing destruction in unconscious fantasy relative to object relating.

Let me repeat. This is a position that can only be arrived at by the individual in early stages of emotional growth through the actual survival of cathected objects that are at the time in process of becoming destroyed because real, becoming real because destroyed (being destructible and expendable).

From now on, this stage having been reached, projective mechanisms assist in the act of *noticing what is there,* but are not *the reason why the object is there.* In my opinion this is a departure from orthodox psychoanalytic theory, which tends to think of external reality only in terms of the individual's projective mechanisms.

I have now nearly made my whole statement. Not quite, however, because it is not possible for me to take for granted an acceptance of the fact that the first impulse in the subject's relation to the object (objectively perceived, not subjective) is destructive.

The central postulate in this thesis is that whereas the subject does not destroy the subjective object (projection material), destruction turns up and becomes a central feature insofar as the object is objectively perceived, has autonomy, and belongs to "shared" reality. This is the difficult part of my thesis, at least for me.

It is generally understood that the reality principle involves the individual in anger and reactive destruction, but my thesis is that the destruction plays its part in making the reality, placing the object outside the self. For this to happen, favourable conditions are necessary. . . .

In psychoanalytic practice the positive changes that come about in this area can be profound. They do not depend on interpretative work. They do depend on the analyst's survival of the attacks, which includes the idea of absence of a change to retaliation. These attacks may be very difficult for the analyst to stand, especially when they are expressed in terms of delusion or through manipulation which makes the analyst actually do things that are technically bad. (I refer to such a thing as unreliability at moments when reliability is all that matters, as well as to survival in terms of keeping alive and the absence of the quality of retaliation.)

The analyst feels like interpreting, but this can spoil the process and for the patient can seem like a kind of self-defence, the analyst parrying the patient's attack. Better to wait until after the phase is over, and then discuss with the patient what has been happening. This is surely legitimate, for as analyst one has one's own needs; but verbal interpretation at this point is not the essential feature and brings its own dangers. The essential feature is the analyst's survival and the intactness of the psychoanalytic technique. Imagine how traumatic can be the actual death of the analyst when this kind of work is in process, although even the actual death of the analyst is not as bad as the development in the analyst of a change towards retaliation. These risks simply must be taken by the patient. Usually the analyst lives through these phases of movement in the transference, and after each phase there comes reward in terms of love, reinforced by the fact of the backcloth of unconscious destruction.

It appears to me that the idea of a developmental phase involving survival of object does affect the theory of the roots of aggression. It is no good saying that a baby of a few days old envies the breast. It is legitimate, however, to say that at whatever age a baby begins to allow the breast an external position (outside the area of projection) then this means that destruction of the breast has become a feature. I mean the actual impulse to destroy. It is an important part of what a mother does, to be the first person to take the baby through this first version of the many that will be encountered, of attack that is survived. This is the right moment in the child's development, because of the child's relative feebleness, so that destruction can fairly easily be survived. Even so it is a very tricky matter; it is only too easy for a mother to react moralistically when her baby bites and hurts.[1] But this language involving the breast is jargon. The whole area of development and of management is involved in which adaptation is related to dependence, apart, that is, from the important detail of relating to the breast.

It will be seen that, although *destruction* is the word I am using, this actual destruction belongs to the object's failure to survive. Without this failure, destruction remains potential. The word *destruction* is needed, not because of the baby's impulse to destroy, but because of the object's liability not to survive.

The way of looking at things that belongs to my presentation of this paper makes possible a new approach to the whole subject of the roots of aggression. For instance, it is not necessary to give inborn aggression more than that which is its due in company with everything else that is inborn. Undoubtedly inborn aggression must be variable in a quantitative sense in the same way that everything else that is inherited is variable as between individuals. The variations in inborn aggression are slight as compared with the total inheritance of that which can lead to aggressiveness. By contrast, the variations are great that arise out of the differences in the experiences of various newborn babies according to whether they are or are not seen through this very difficult phase. Such variations in the field of experience are indeed immense. Moreover, the babies that have been seen through this phase well are likely to be more aggressive *clinically* than the ones who have not been seen through the phase well, and for whom aggression is not something that can be encompassed (become ego-syntonic), or can be retained only in the form of a liability to be the object of attack.

This involves a rewriting of the theory of the roots of aggression since most of that which has already been written by analysts has been formulated without reference to that which is being discussed in this paper. The assumption is always there, in orthodox theory, that aggression is reactive to the encounter with the reality principle, whereas here it is the destructive drive that creates the quality of externality.

Let me look for a moment at the exact place of this attack and survival in the hierarchy of relationships. More primitive and quite different is annihilation. Annihilation means "no hope"; cathexis withers up because no result completes the reflex to produce conditioning. Attack in anger

1. In fact, the baby's development is immensely complicated if he or she should happen to be born with a tooth, so that the gum's attack on the breast can never be tried out.

relative to the encounter with the reality principle is a more sophisticated concept, postdating the destruction that I postulate here. In the destruction of the object to which I am referring *there is no anger.* There could be said to be joy at the object's survival. From this moment, or arising out of this phase, the object is *in fantasy* always being destroyed. This quality of "always being destroyed" makes the reality of the surviving object felt as such, strengthens the feeling tone, and contributes to object constancy. The object can now be used.

I wish to conclude with a note on using and usage. By "use" I do not mean "exploitation." As analysts, we know what it is like to be used, which means that we can see the end of the treatment, be it several years away. Many of our patients come with this problem already solved—they can use objects and they can use us and can use analysis, just as they have used their parents and their siblings and their homes. However, there are many patients who need us to be able to give them a capacity to use us. In meeting the needs of such patients, we shall need to know what I am saying here about our survival of their destructiveness. A backcloth of unconscious destruction of the analyst is set up and we survive it or, alternatively, we shall become involved in yet another analysis interminable.

SUMMARY

Object relating can be described in terms of the experience of the subject. Description of object usage involves consideration of the nature of the object. I am offering for discussion the reasons why, in my opinion, a capacity to use an object is more sophisticated than a capacity to relate to objects; and relating may be to a subjective object, but usage implies that the object is part of external reality.

This sequence can be observed: (1) Subject *relates* to object. (2) Object is in process of being found instead of placed by the subject in the world. (3) Subject *destroys* object. (4) Object survives destruction. (5) Subject can *use* object.

The object is always being destroyed. This destruction becomes the unconscious backcloth for love of a real object; that is, an object outside the area of the subject's omnipotent control.

Study of this problem involves a statement of the positive value of destructiveness. The destructiveness plus the object's survival of the destruction places the object outside the area in which projective mental mechanisms operate, so that a world of shared reality is created which the subject can use and which can feed back into the subject.

REFERENCES

Winnicott, D. W. (1958). The capacity to be alone. In *The Maturational Processes and the Facilitating Environment*, pp. 29–36. London: Hogarth, 1965.

——(1963). Communicating and not communicating leading to a study of certain opposites. In *The Maturational Processes and the Facilitating Environment*, pp. 179–192. London: Hogarth, 1965.

——(1968). Interrelating in terms of cross-identifications. In *Playing and Reality*, pp. 129–137. London: Tavistock, 1971.

25

"Playing: Its Theoretical Status in the Clinical Situation" (1971)

This paper ties together Winnicott's examination of the developmental importance of playing and the meaning of interchange in psychotherapy. The word and concept of *play* extends beyond its meaning for childhood play to include the play between people at any age, and the back and forth of emotional engagement between inside and outside and between one person and another. The words *play* and *playing* came to occupy a central role in Winnicott's thinking.

Psychotherapy takes place in the overlap of two areas of playing, that of the patient and that of the therapist. Psychotherapy has to do with two people playing together. The corollary of this is that where playing is not possible then the work done by the therapist is directed towards bringing the patient from a state of not being able to play into a state of being able to play. . . .

PLAYING IN TIME AND SPACE

In order to give a place to playing I postulated a *potential space* between the baby and the mother. This potential space varies a very great deal according to the life experiences of the baby in relation to the mother or mother figure, and I contrast this potential space (a) with the inner world (which is related to the psychosomatic partnership) and (b) with actual, or external, reality (which has its own dimensions, and which can be studied objectively, and which, however much it may seem to vary according to the state of the individual who is observing it, does in fact remain constant).

I can now restate what I am trying to convey. I want to draw attention away from the sequence psychoanalysis, psychotherapy, play material, playing, and to set this up again the other way round. In other words, *it is play that is the universal,* and that belongs to health: playing facilitates growth and therefore health; playing leads into group relationships; playing can be a form of communication in psychotherapy; and, lastly, psychoanalysis has been developed as a highly specialized form of playing in the service of communication with oneself and others. . . .

THEORY OF PLAY

It is possible to describe a sequence of relationships related to the developmental process and to look and see where playing belongs.

A. Baby and object are merged in with one another. Baby's view of the object is subjective and the mother is oriented towards the making actual of what the baby is ready to find.

B. The object is repudiated, re-accepted, and perceived objectively. This complex process is highly dependent on there being a mother or mother figure prepared to participate and to give back what is handed out.

This means that the mother (or part of mother) is in a "to and fro" between being that which the baby has a capacity to find and (alternatively) being herself waiting to be found.

If the mother can play this part over a length of time without admitting impediment (so to speak) then the baby has some *experience* of magical control, that is, experience of that which is called "omnipotence" in the description of intrapsychic processes.

In the state of confidence that grows up when a mother can do this difficult thing well (not if she is unable to do it), the baby begins to enjoy experiences based on a "marriage" of the omnipotence of intrapsychic processes with the baby's control of the actual. Confidence in the mother makes an intermediate playground here, where the idea of magic originates, since the baby does to some extent experience omnipotence. All this bears closely on Erikson's (1950) work on identity formation. I call this a playground because play starts here. The playground is a potential space between the mother and the baby or joining mother and baby.

Play is immensely exciting. It is exciting not primarily because the instincts are involved, be it understood! The thing about playing is always the precariousness of the interplay of personal psychic reality and the experience of control of actual objects. This is the precariousness of magic itself, magic that arises in intimacy, in a relationship that is being found to be reliable. To be reliable the relationship is necessarily motivated by the mother's love, or her love-hate, or her object relating, not by reaction formations. When a patient cannot play, the therapist must attend to this major symptom before interpreting fragments of behaviour.

C. The next stage is being alone in the presence of someone. The child is now playing on the basis of the assumption that the person who loves and who is therefore reliable is available and continues to be available when remembered after being forgotten. This person is felt to reflect back what happens in the playing.[1]

D. The child is now getting ready for the next stage, which is to allow and to enjoy an overlap of two play areas. First, surely, it is the mother who plays with the baby, but she is rather careful to fit in with the baby's play activities. Sooner or later, however, she introduces her own playing, and she finds that babies vary according to their capacity to like or dislike the introduction of ideas that are not their own.

Thus the way is paved for a playing together in a relationship. . . .

PSYCHOTHERAPY

Here in this area of overlap between the playing of the child and the playing of the other person there is a chance to introduce enrichments. The teacher aims at enrichment. By contrast, the therapist is concerned specifically with the child's own growth processes, and with the removal of blocks to development that may have become evident. It is psychoanalytic theory that has made for an understanding of these blocks. At the same time it would be a narrow view to suppose that psychoanalysis is the only way to make therapeutic use of the child's playing.

---

1. I have discussed a more sophisticated aspect of these experiences in my paper "The Capacity to be Alone" (1958).

It is good to remember always that playing is itself a therapy. To arrange for children to be able to play is itself a psychotherapy that has immediate and universal application, and it includes the establishment of a positive social attitude towards playing. This attitude must include recognition that playing is always liable to become frightening. Games and their organization must be looked at as part of an attempt to forestall the frightening aspect of playing. Responsible persons must be available when children play; but this does not mean that the responsible person need enter into the children's playing. When an organizer must be involved in a managerial position then the implication is that the child or the children are unable to play in the creative sense of my meaning in this communication.

The essential feature of my communication is this, that playing is an experience, always a creative experience, and it is an experience in the space-time continuum, a basic form of living.

The precariousness of play belongs to the fact that it is always on the theoretical line between the subjective and that which is objectively perceived.

It is my purpose here simply to give a reminder that children's playing has everything in it, although the psychotherapist works on the material, the content of playing. Naturally, in a set or professional hour a more precise constellation presents than would present in a timeless experience on the floor at home; but it helps us to understand our work if we know that the basis of what we do is the patient's playing, a creative experience taking up space and time, and intensely real for the patient.

Also, this observation helps us to understand how it is that psychotherapy of a deep-going kind may be done without interpretative work. . . . [I]n reporting what I call "therapeutic consultations" [I make the point] that the significant moment is that at which *the child surprises himself or herself.* It is not the moment of my clever interpretation that is significant (Winnicott 1971).

Interpretation outside the ripeness of the material is indoctrination and produces compliance (Winnicott 1960). A corollary is that resistance arises out of interpretation given outside the area of the overlap of the patient's and the analyst's playing together. Interpretation when the patient has no capacity to play is simply not useful, or causes confusion. When there is mutual playing, then interpretation according to accepted psychoanalytic principles can carry the therapeutic work forward. This playing has to be spontaneous, and not compliant or acquiescent, if psychotherapy is to be done.

SUMMARY

(a) To get to the idea of playing it is helpful to think of the *preoccupation* that characterizes the playing of a young child. The content does not matter. What matters is the near-withdrawal state, akin to the *concentration* of older children and adults. The playing child inhabits an area that cannot be easily left, nor can it easily admit intrusions.

(b) This area of playing is not inner psychic reality. It is outside the individual, but it is not the external world.

(c) Into this play area the child gathers objects or phenomena from external reality and uses these in the service of some sample derived from inner or personal reality. Without hallucinating the child puts out a sample of dream potential and lives with this sample in a chosen setting of fragments from external reality.

(d) In playing, the child manipulates external phenomena in the service of the dream and invests chosen external phenomena with dream meaning and feeling.

(e) There is a direct development from transitional phenomena to playing, and from playing to shared playing, and from this to cultural experiences.

(f) Playing implies trust, and belongs to the potential space between (what was at first) baby and mother figure, with the baby in a state of near-absolute dependence, and the mother figure's adaptive function taken for granted by the baby.

(g) Playing involves the body:
- (i) because of the manipulation of objects;
- (ii) because certain types of intense interest are associated with certain aspects of bodily excitement.

(h) Bodily excitement in erotogenic zones constantly threatens playing, and therefore threatens the child's sense of existing as a person. The instincts are the main threat to play as to the ego; in seduction some external agency exploits the child's instincts and helps to annihilate the child's sense of existing as an autonomous unit, making playing impossible (cf. Khan 1964).

(i) Playing is essentially satisfying. This is true even when it leads to a high degree of anxiety. There is a degree of anxiety that is unbearable and this destroys playing.

(j) The pleasurable element in playing carries with it the implication that the instinctual arousal is not excessive; instinctual arousal beyond a certain point must lead to:

(i) climax;
(ii) failed climax and a sense of mental confusion and physical discomfort that only time can mend;
(iii) alternative climax (as in provocation of parental or social reaction, anger, etc.).

Playing can be said to reach its own saturation point, which refers to the capacity to contain experience.

(k) Playing is inherently exciting and precarious. This characteristic derives not from instinctual arousal but from the precariousness that belongs to the interplay in the child's mind of that which is subjective (near-hallucination) and that which is objectively perceived (actual, or shared reality).

REFERENCES

Axline, V. (1947). *Play Therapy.* Cambridge, MA. Houghton Mifflin.

Erikson, E. (1950). Growth and crisis of the healthy personality. In *Identity and the Life Cycle.* New York: International Universities Press.

Khan, M. M. R. (1964). The function of intimacy and acting out in sexual perversions. In *Sexual Behavior and the Law,* ed. Slovenko. Springfield, IL: Thomas.

Winnicott, D. W. (1958). The capacity to be alone. *International Journal of Psycho-Analysis* 39. Republished in *The Maturational Processes and the Facilitating Environment.* London: Hogarth, 1965.

——(1960). Ego distortion in terms of true and false self. In *The Maturational Processes and the Facilitating Environment.* London: Hogarth, 1965.

——(1971). *Therapeutic Consultations in Child Psychiatry.* London: Hogarth.

26

"The Location of Cultural Experience" (1967)

Winnicott thought the potential space between infant and mother where play occurred was the beginning of personal expression and creativity. By extension, it is the location of the space for all man's creativity, the place where man in society creates a culture by a process derivative of play in the same way that the interplay between patient and therapist is the area of their therapeutic creativity. This idea has been influential in the study of literature and the arts as it has been in psychotherapy.

Play is in fact neither a matter of inner psychic reality nor a matter of external reality. . . .

If play is neither inside nor outside, where is it? . . .

I have claimed that when we witness an infant's employment of a transitional object, the first not-me possession, we are witnessing both the child's first use of a symbol and the first experience of play. An essential part of my formulation of transitional phenomena is that we agree never to make the challenge to the baby: did you create this object, or did you find it conveniently lying around? That is to say, an essential feature of transitional phenomena and objects is a quality in our attitude when we observe them.

The object is a symbol of the union of the baby and the mother (or part of the mother). This symbol can be located. It is at the place in space and time where and when the mother is in transition from being (in the baby's mind) merged in with the infant and alternatively being experienced as an object to be perceived rather than conceived of. The use of an object symbolizes the union of two now separate things, baby and mother, at the point in time and space of the initiation of their state of separateness.[1] . . .

The place where cultural experience is located is in the *potential space* between the individual and the environment (originally the object). The same can be said of playing. Cultural experience begins with creative living first manifested in play.

For every individual the use of this space is determined by *life experiences* that take place at the early stages of the individual's existence.

From the beginning the baby has maximally intense experiences in the potential space between the subjective object and the object objectively perceived, between me-extensions and the not-me. This potential space is at the interplay between there being nothing but me and there being objects and phenomena outside omnipotent control.

Every baby has his or her own favourable or unfavourable experience here. Dependence is maximal. The potential space happens only *in relation to a feeling of confidence* on the part of the baby, that is, confidence related to the dependability of the mother figure or environmental elements, confidence being the evidence of dependability that is becoming introjected.

In order to study the play and then the cultural life of the individual one must study the fate of the potential space between any one baby and the human (and therefore fallible) mother figure who is essentially adaptive because of love.

It will be seen that if this area is to be thought of as part of the ego organization, here is a part of the ego that is not a body ego, that is not founded on the pattern of body *functioning* but is founded on body *experiences*. These experiences belong to object relating of a nonorgiastic kind, or to what can be called ego relatedness, at the place where it can be said that *continuity* is giving place to *contiguity*. . . .

I suggest that the time has come for psychoanalytic theory to pay tribute to a *third area*, that of cultural experience which is a derivative of play. Psychotics insist on our knowing about it, and it is of great importance in our assessment of the lives rather than the health of human

1. It is necessary to simplify matters by referring to the use of objects, but the title of my original paper was "Transitional Objects and Transitional Phenomena" (1951).

beings. . . . this third area has been contrasted with inner or personal psychic reality and with the actual world in which the individual lives, which can be objectively perceived. I have located this important area of experience in the potential space between the individual and the environment, that which initially both joins and separates the baby and the mother when the mother's love, displayed or made manifest as human reliability, does in fact give the baby a sense of trust or of confidence in the environmental factor. . . .

The potential space between baby and mother, between child and family, between individual and society or the world, depends on experience which leads to trust. It can be looked upon as sacred to the individual in that it is here that the individual experiences creative living.

By contrast, exploitation of this area leads to a pathological condition in which the individual is cluttered up with persecutory elements of which he has no means of ridding himself.

It may perhaps be seen from this how important it can be for the analyst to recognize the existence of this place, the only place where play can start, a place that is at the continuity-contiguity moment, where transitional phenomena originate.

REFERENCE

Winnicott, D.W. (1951). Transitional objects and transitional phenomena. In *Collected Papers*, pp. 229–242. London: Tavistock, 1958.

27

"Mirror-Role of Mother and Family in Child Development" (1967)

This paper carries Winnicott's conception of the environmental provision by the mother to another level in exploring the mirroring role of the mother who enables the baby to find its own self in her face. In a suggestive allusion, he extends this function beyond the role played by the mother alone to that of the whole family, suggesting that family members carry out this function for each other throughout life. Although this is one of the few places in which Winnicott mentioned the role of the wider family, his intuitive sense has been useful in extending object relations concepts to the family and to family therapy.

In individual emotional development *the precursor of the mirror is the mother's face.* I wish to refer to the normal aspect of this and also to its psychopathology.

Jacques Lacan's paper "Le Stade du Miroir" (1949) has certainly influenced me. He refers to the use of the mirror in each individual's ego development. However, Lacan does not think of the mirror in terms of the mother's face in the way that I wish to do here.

I refer only to infants who have sight. The wider application of the idea to cover infants with poor sight or no sight must be left over until the main theme is stated. The bare statement is this: in the early stages of the emotional development of the human infant a vital part is played by the environment which is in fact not yet separated off from the infant by the infant. Gradually the separating-off of the not-me from the me takes place, and the pace varies according to the infant and according to the environment. The major changes take place in the separating-out of the mother as an objectively perceived environmental feature. If no one person is there to be mother the infant's developmental task is infinitely complicated.

Let me simplify the environmental function and briefly state that it involves:

1. Holding
2. Handling
3. Object presenting.

The infant may respond to these environmental provisions, but the result in the baby is maximal personal maturation. By the word *maturation* at this stage I intend to include the various meanings of the word *integration,* as well as psychosomatic interrelating and object relating.

A baby is held, and handled satisfactorily, and with this taken for granted is presented with an object in such a way that the baby's legitimate experience of omnipotence is not violated. The result can be that the baby is able to use the object, and to feel as if this object is a subjective object, and created by the baby.

All this belongs to the beginning, and out of all this come the immense complexities that comprise the emotional and mental development of the infant and child.[1]

Now, at some point the baby takes a look around. Perhaps a baby at the breast does not look at the breast. Looking at the face is more likely to be a feature (Gough 1962). What does the baby see there? To get to the answer we must draw on our experience with psychoanalytic patients who reach back to very early phenomena and yet who can verbalize (when they feel they can do so) without insulting the delicacy of what is preverbal, unverbalized, and unverbalizable except perhaps in poetry.

What does the baby see when he or she looks at the mother's face? I am suggesting that, ordinarily, what the baby sees is himself or herself. In other words the mother is looking at the baby and *what she looks like is related to what she sees there.* All this is too easily taken for granted. I am asking that this, which is naturally done well by mothers who are caring for their babies, shall not be taken for granted. I can make my point by

---

1. For further and detailed discussion of these ideas the reader can consult my paper "The Theory of the Parent–Infant Relationship" (1960a).

going straight over to the case of the baby whose mother reflects her own mood or, worse still, the rigidity of her own defences. In such a case what does the baby see?

Of course nothing can be said about the single occasions on which a mother could not respond. Many babies, however, do have to have a long experience of not getting back what they are giving. They look and they do not see themselves. There are consequences. First, their own creative capacity begins to atrophy, and in some way or other they look around for other ways of getting something of themselves back from the environment. They may succeed by some other method, and blind infants need to get themselves reflected through other senses than that of sight. Indeed, a mother whose face is fixed may be able to respond in some other way. Most mothers can respond when the baby is in trouble or is aggressive, and especially when the baby is ill. Second, the baby gets settled in to the idea that when he or she looks, what is seen is the mother's face. The mother's face is not then a mirror. So perception takes the place of apperception, perception takes the place of that which might have been the beginning of a significant exchange with the world, a two-way process in which self-enrichment alternates with the discovery of meaning in the world of seen things.

Naturally, there are halfway stages in this scheme of things. Some babies do not quite give up hope and they study the object and do all that is possible to see in the object some meaning that ought to be there if only it could be felt. Some babies, tantalized by this type of relative maternal failure, study the variable maternal visage in an attempt to predict the mother's mood, just exactly as we all study the weather. The baby quickly learns to make a forecast: "Just now it is safe to forget the mother's mood and to be spontaneous, but any minute the mother's face will become fixed or her mood will dominate, and my own personal needs must then be withdrawn otherwise my central self may suffer insult."

Immediately beyond this in the direction of pathology is predictability, which is precarious, and which strains the baby to the limits of his or her capacity to allow for events. This brings a threat of chaos, and the baby will organize withdrawal, or will not look except to perceive, as a defence. A baby so treated will grow up puzzled about mirrors and what the mirror has to offer. If the mother's face is unresponsive, then a mirror is a thing to be looked at but not to be looked into.

To return to the normal progress of events, when the average girl studies her face in the mirror she is reassuring herself that the mother image is there and that the mother can see her and that the mother is *en rapport* with her. When girls and boys in their secondary narcissism look in order to see beauty and to fall in love, there is already evidence that doubt has crept in about their mother's continued love and care. So the man who falls in love with beauty is quite different from the man who loves a girl and feels she is beautiful and can see what is beautiful about her.

I will not try to press home my idea, but instead I will give [an] example so that the idea I am presenting can be worked over by the reader.

ILLUSTRATION

I refer to a woman of my acquaintance who married and brought up three fine sons. She was also a good support to her husband who had a creative and important job. Behind the scenes this woman was always near to depression. She seriously disturbed her marital life by waking every morning in a state of despair. She could do nothing about it. The resolution of the paralysing depression came each day when at last it was time to get up and, at the end of her ablutions and dressing, she could "put on her face." Now she felt rehabilitated and could meet the world and take up her family responsibilities. This exceptionally intelligent and responsible person did eventually react to a misfortune by developing a chronic depressive state which in the end became transformed into a chronic and crippling physical disorder.

Here is a recurring pattern, easily matched in the social or clinical experience of everyone. What is illustrated by this case only exaggerates that which is normal. The exaggeration is of the task of getting the mirror to notice and approve. The woman had to be her own mother. If she had had a daughter she would surely have found great relief, but perhaps a daughter would have suffered because of having too much importance in correcting her mother's uncertainty about her own mother's sight of her. . . .

I see that I am linking apperception with perception by postulating a historical process (in the individual) which depends on being seen:

When I look I am seen, so I exist.
I can now afford to look and see.
I now look creatively and what I apperceive I also perceive.
In fact I take care not to see what is not there to be seen (unless I am tired).

This glimpse of the baby's and child's seeing the self in the mother's face, and afterwards in a mirror, gives a way of looking at analysis and at the psychotherapeutic task. Psychotherapy is not making clever and apt interpretations; by and large it is a long-term giving the patient back what the patient brings. It is a complex derivative of the face that reflects what is there to be seen. I like to think of my work this way, and to think that if I do this well enough the patient will find his or her own self, and will be able to exist and to feel real. Feeling real is more than existing; it is finding a way to exist as oneself, and to relate to objects as oneself, and to have a self into which to retreat for relaxation.

But I would not like to give the impression that I think this task of reflecting what the patient brings is easy. It is not easy, and it is emotionally exhausting. But we get our rewards. Even when our patients do not get cured they are grateful to us for seeing them as they are, and this gives us a satisfaction of a deep kind.

This to which I have referred in terms of the mother's role of giving back to the baby the baby's own self continues to have importance in terms of the child and the family. Naturally, as the child develops and the maturational processes become sophisticated, and identifications multiply, the child becomes less and less dependent on getting back the self from the mother's and the father's face and from the faces of others who are in parental or sibling relationships (Winnicott 1960b). Nevertheless, when a family is intact and is a going concern over a period of time each child derives benefit from being able to see himself or herself in the attitude of the individual members or in the attitudes of the family as a whole. We can include in all this the actual mirrors that exist in the house and the opportunities the child gets for seeing the parents and others looking at themselves. It should be understood, however, that the actual mirror has significance mainly in its figurative sense.

This could be one way of stating the contribution that a family can make to the personality growth and enrichment of each one of its individual members.

REFERENCES

Gough, D. (1962). The behaviour of infants in the first year of life. *Proceedings of the Royal Society of Medicine* 55.

Lacan, J. (1949). Le stade du miroir comme formateur de la fonction de je, telle qu'elle nous est révelée dans l'expérience psychoanalytique. *Ecrits.* Paris: Editions du Seuil, 1966.

Winnicott, D. W. (1960a). The theory of the parent–infant relationship. In *The Maturational Processes and the Facilitating Environment*, pp. 37–55. London: Hogarth, 1965.
——(1960b). Ego distortion in terms of true and false self. In *The Maturational Processes and the Facilitating Environment*, pp. 140–152. London: Hogarth, 1965.

28

Therapeutic Consultations in Child Psychiatry (1971)

This selection comes from a book, published posthumously, that documented Winnicott's method of brief therapeutic consultation to children, a technique that drew on his entire theory of emotional development and of therapy—letting children or adults speak for themselves, creating a situation that set up the potential space for shared creative play and communication, and allowing the child to make the interpretations insofar as possible. The squiggle game embodies Winnicott's valuing of the spontaneous gesture as the expression of the true self, as well as illustrating that therapy takes place in the overlap of the two areas of play—that of the patient and that of the therapist. In many ways, the invention of the squiggle technique is the culmination of Winnicott's therapeutic attitude.

My technique in these reported cases usually takes the form of what could be called the "squiggle game." There is nothing original of course about the squiggle game and it would not be right for somebody to learn how to use the squiggle game and then to feel equipped to do what I call a therapeutic consultation. The squiggle game is simply one way of getting into contact with a child. What happens in the game and in the whole interview depends on the use made of the child's experience, including the material that presents itself. In order to use the mutual experience one must have in one's bones a theory of the emotional development of the child and of the relationship of the child to the environmental factors. In my cases described here an artificial link is made between the squiggle game and the psychotherapeutic consultation, and this arises out of the fact that from the drawings of the child, and of the child and myself, one can find one way of making the case come alive. It is almost as if the child, through the drawings, is alongside me, and to some extent taking part in describing the case, so that the reports of what the child and the therapist said tend to ring true. There is also a practical significance of the squiggle or drawing material in that there can be a gain from taking the parents into one's confidence and letting them know what their child was like in the special circumstances of the therapeutic consultation. This is more real for them than if I report what the child said. They recognise the types of drawing that adorn the nursery wall or that the child brings home from school, but often they are amazed when they see the drawings in sequence, drawings which display personality qualities and perceptive abilities which may not have been evident in the home setting. In several of the cases given here this aspect of the matter will come up for discussion, and naturally it is not always good to give parents this insight (that can be so useful). Parents might perhaps abuse the confidence that the therapist has placed in them, and so undo the work that depends on a kind of intimacy between child and therapist. . . .

In some of the cases reported there are dramatic changes following one or two therapeutic consultations. These have to be taken not only as evidence of the work done but also as evidence of the parents' attitude. . . . I wish to emphasise, however, that my aim in presenting these consultations is not to give a series illustrating symptomatic cure. I am rather aiming to report examples of communication with children. . . .

In some of the cases presented in this series it will be seen that the child's symptomatology reflects illness in one or both of the parents or in the social situation, and that it is this which needs attention. Nevertheless it may be the child who best puts us in touch with the principal defect in the environment. The series as a whole does, however, according to my claim, show that in many cases the child who is brought by parents who are concerned about their child's condition is in fact the ill member of the group, and it is the child then who needs primary attention. Every child or grown-up has a problem, and it is this problem as it is causing tensions at the moment that will appear in the consultation material. When several problems appear at once in a first interview then this is evidence of a need for work of a more prolonged kind so that the various problems may be sorted out and be dealt with separately, and perhaps in various ways. . . .

ROSEMARY AT 10 YEARS

This child was seen once, and in her personal interview she found a clue to her symptoms. She was brought because of "black fits of depression." She also had blinding headaches, nausea, and photophobia, lasting two or three days and sending her to bed. She had lately become withdrawn. Along with this was a bad temper in the morning.

All these symptoms cleared up when she arrived at the drawing of the dream in which her mother got run over.

Rosemary is one of two children in a good working-class family.

The interview was as follows. There were two visitors and two psychiatric social workers present. This was a routine clinic case.

Rosemary started drawing and showed some ability.

(1) She drew a girl.
(2) We then played squiggles and she turned my squiggle into a head.

1

2

(3) Hers, which I turned into a landscape.

3

4) She and I together turned her squiggle into Bruno, which is a *transitional object* of hers.

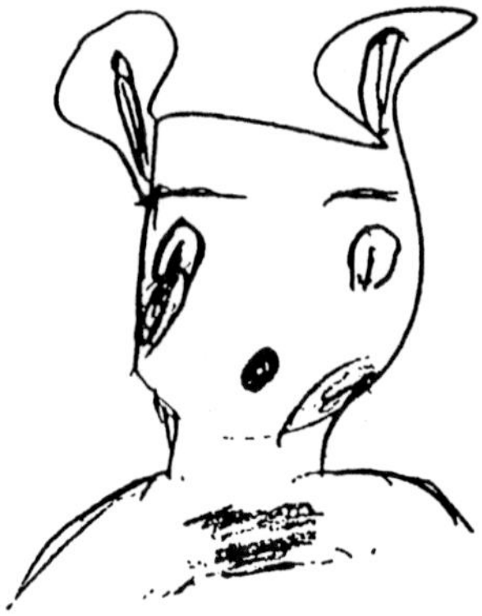

4

5

(5) She followed this up by drawing an earlier transitional object, called Doggie; it is broken, and the drawing shows this.
She said her brother took her teddy. Her brother is nice and very naughty. She doesn't hate him but she gets very cross with him. She wanted a sister.

6

(6) Is her drawing of the brother?
Apparently her father draws cartoons with her, and some of her drawing technique is influenced in this way by her father.
She talked about nice dreams but she said: "Last night I and two friends were in the tower waiting to be executed."

7

8

(7) Is a bad dream of this kind?
She said at 5 years old (when her brother was 3) she had a horrible dream, which she drew.

(8) Her drawing. It was a wicked stepmother who broke the glass slipper, herself being Cinderella.

9

(9) Gives a picture of Cinderella. To some extent she is the Prince, although she would not want actually to be a man.
A sad dream would be a nightmare of mother getting killed.

10

(10) Her drawing. She drew this with great intensity of feeling and very quickly, showing mother being run over by father's car.

I made an interpretation here about the hate between her mother and herself which makes sense in the context of the triangular situation with the father.

After this she was able to tell me about a weird dream.

11

(11) Her drawing of a weird dream, showing bubbles coming at her, making a funny noise like an earache noise; they are white. This dream is somewhat influenced by science fiction and links with the idea of comets and meteors which presumably are met with in space.

I suggest that these white bubbles that make a funny noise give a picture of a coming alive "inside," following a phase of deadness "inside" which is represented here by the dead mother of the dream.

In this case the girl's depressive mood was the clinical manifestation of the death wish towards her mother which was under repression. This death wish was experienced in the context of strong positive feeling towards both parents, who together built and maintained the good home that she lived in.

VI

WILFRED BION

29

Experiences in Groups: "Group Dynamics: A Re-View" (1952)

Wilfred Bion is a Kleinian whose work is respected by all who look to British object relations theory. His writing is the most enigmatic and difficult of all the theorists included in this volume, but *Experiences in Groups*, the earliest work for which Bion is remembered, is an exception in that the writing is clear. It has continued to be seminal for group therapy and group relations. Those who know only his writing about groups may not understand the roots of this work in the thought of Freud and Klein, or the way this set of ideas extends analytic thought beyond the field of individual development by examining the group context of individual development. *Experiences in Groups* is a classic for the fields of group therapy and group relations, but its importance for individual psychoanalytic theory has been underrated. Bion's concern with elaborating the meanings of projective identification as a mode of communication during development and in treatment began with the publication of this part of the book in a 1952 article, and continued through the rest of his writing during the next thirty years.

THE WORK GROUP

In any group there may be discerned trends of mental activity. Every group, however casual, meets to "do" something; in this activity, according to the capacities of the individuals, they cooperate. This cooperation is voluntary and depends on some degree of sophisticated skill in the individual. Participation in this activity is possible only to individuals with years of training and a capacity for experience that has permitted them to develop mentally. Since this activity is geared to a task, it is related to reality, its methods are rational, and, therefore, in however embryonic a form, scientific. Its characteristics are similar to those attributed by Freud (1911) to the ego. This facet of mental activity in a group I have called the *work group*. The term embraces only mental activity of a particular kind, not the people who indulge in it.

When patients meet for a group therapy session it can always be seen that some mental activity is directed to the solution of the problems for which the individuals seek help. Here is an example of a passing phase in such a group:

Six patients and I are seated round a small room. Miss A suggests that it would be a good idea if members agreed to call each other by their Christian names.[1] There is some relief that a topic has been broached, glances are exchanged, and a flicker of synthetic animation is momentarily visible. Mr. B ventures that it is a good idea, and Mr. C says it would "make things more friendly." Miss A is encouraged to divulge her name but is forestalled by Miss D who says she does not like her Christian name and would rather it were not known. Mr. E suggests pseudonyms; Miss F examines her fingernails. Within a few minutes of Miss A's suggestion, the discussion has languished, and its place has been taken by furtive glances, an increasing number of which are directed towards me. Mr. B rouses himself to say that we must call each other something. The mood is now a compound of anxiety and increasing frustration. Long before I am mentioned it is clear that my name has become a preoccupation of the group. Left to its own devices the group promises to pass into apathy and silence.

For my present purposes I shall display such aspects of the episode as illustrate my use of the term *work group*. In the group itself I might well do the same, but that would depend on my assessment of the significance of the episode in the context of the group mental life, as far as it had then emerged. First, it is clear that if seven people are to talk together it would help the discussion if names were available. Insofar as the discussion has arisen through awareness of that fact it is a product of work-group activity. But the group has gone further than to propose a step that would be helpful in any group no matter what its task might be. The proposal

1. See also the discussion of taboo on names in *Totem and Taboo* (Freud 1913).

has been made that Christian names should be used because that would make for friendliness. In the group of which I am speaking it would have been accurate to say that the production of friendliness was regarded as strictly relevant to therapeutic need. At the point in its history from which the example is taken, it would also be true to say that both Miss D's objection and Mr. E's proposed solution would be regarded as dictated by therapeutic need, and in fact I pointed out that the suggestions fitted in with a theory, not yet explicitly stated, that our diseases would be cured if the group could be conducted in such a way that only pleasant emotions were experienced. It will be seen that the demonstration of work-group function must include the development of thought designed for translation into action; the theory, in this instance the need for friendliness, on which it is based; the belief in environmental change as in itself sufficient for cure without any corresponding change in the individual; and finally a demonstration of the kind of fact that is believed to be "real."

It so happened, in the instance I have given, that I was subsequently able to demonstrate that work-group function, though I did not call it that, based on the idea that cure could be obtained from a group in which pleasant feelings only were experienced, did not appear to have produced the hoped-for cure, and indeed was being obstructed by some sort of difficulty in achieving a limited translation into the apparently simple act of assigning names. Before passing to the discussion of the nature of the obstructions to work-group activity, I would mention here a difficulty, which must already be evident, in the exposition of my theories. For me to describe a group episode, such as the one I have been discussing, and then to attempt the deduction of theories from it, is only to say that I have a theory that such-and-such took place and that I can say it again only in different language. The only way in which the reader can deliver himself from the dilemma is to recall to himself the memory of some committee or other gathering in which he has participated and consider to what extent he can recall evidence that could point to the existence of what I call work-group function, not forgetting the actual administrative structure, chairman and so forth, as material to be included in his review.

THE BASIC ASSUMPTIONS

The interpretations in terms of work-group activity leave much unsaid; is the suggested use of pseudonyms motivated only with a view to meeting the demands of reality? The furtive glances, the preoccupation with the correct mode for addressing the analyst, which became quite overt subsequently, cannot profitably be interpreted as related to work-group function.

Work-group activity is obstructed, diverted, and on occasion assisted, by certain other mental activities that have in common the attribute of powerful emotional drives. These activities, at first sight chaotic, are given a certain cohesion if it is assumed that they spring from basic assumptions common to all the group. In the example I have given it was easy to recognize that one assumption common to all the group was that they were met together to receive some form of treatment from me. But exploration of this idea as part of work-group function showed that ideas existed invested with reality by force of the emotion attached to them, that were not in conformity even with the somewhat naïve expectation consciously entertained by the less sophisticated members. Furthermore, even sophisticated individuals, one member for example being a graduate in science, showed by their behaviour that they shared these ideas.

The first assumption is that the group is met in order to be sustained by a leader on whom it depends for nourishment, material and spiritual, and protection. Stated thus, my first basic assumption might be regarded as a repetition of my remark, above, that the group assumed that they were met together to receive some form of treatment from me, only differing from it in being couched in metaphorical terms. But the essential point is that the basic assumption can only be understood if the words in which I have stated it are taken as literal and not metaphorical.

Here is a description of a therapeutic group in which the dependent assumption, as I shall call it, is active.

Three women and two men were present. The group had on a previous occasion shown signs of work-group function directed towards curing the disability of its members; on this occasion they might be supposed to have reacted from this with despair, placing all their reliance on me to sort out their difficulties while they contented themselves with individually posing questions to which I was to provide the answers. One woman had brought some chocolate, which she diffidently invited her right-hand neighbour, another woman, to share. One man was eating a sandwich. A graduate in philosophy, who had in earlier sessions told the group he had no belief in God, and no religion, sat silent, as indeed he often did, until one of the women with a touch of acerbity in her tone, remarked that he had asked no questions. He replied, "I do not need to talk because I know that I only have to come here long enough and all my questions will be answered without my having to do anything."

I then said that I had become a kind of group deity, that the questions were directed to me as one who knew the answers without need to resort to work, that the eating was part of a manipulation of the group to give substance to a belief they wished to preserve about me, and that the philosopher's reply indicated a disbelief in the efficacy of prayer but seemed otherwise to belie earlier statements he had made about his disbelief in God. When I began my interpretation I was not only convinced of its truth but felt no doubt that I could convince the others by confrontation with the mass of material—only some of which I can convey in this printed account. By the time I had finished speaking I felt I had committed some kind of gaffe; I was surrounded by blank looks; the evidence had disappeared. After a time, the man, who had finished his sandwich and placed the carefully folded paper in his pocket, looked round the room, eyebrows slightly raised, interrogation in his glance. A woman looked tensely at me, another with hands folded gazed meditatively at the floor. In me a conviction began to harden that I had been guilty of blasphemy in a group of true believers. The second man, with elbow draped over the back of his chair, played with his fingers. The woman who was eating, hurriedly swallowed the last of her chocolate. I now interpreted that I had become a very bad person, casting doubts on the group deity, but that this had been followed by an increase of anxiety and guilt as the group had failed to dissociate itself from the impiety.

In this account I have dwelt on my own reactions in the group for a reason which I hope may become more apparent later. It can be justly argued that interpretations for which the strongest evidence lies, not in the observed facts in the group but in the subjective reactions of the analyst, are more likely to find their explanation in the psychopathology of the analyst than in the dynamics of the group. It is a just criticism, and one which will have to be met by years of careful work by more than one analyst, but for that very reason I shall leave it on one side and pass on to state now a contention that I shall support throughout this paper. It is that in group treatment many interpretations, and amongst them the most important, have to be made on the strength of the analyst's own emotional reactions. It is my belief that these reactions are dependent on the fact that the analyst in the group is at the receiving end of what Melanie Klein (1946) has called projective identification, and that this mechanism plays a very important role in groups. Now the experience of counter-transference appears to me to have quite a distinct quality that should enable the analyst to differentiate the occasion when he is the object of a projective identification from the occasion when he is not. The analyst feels he is being manipulated so as to be playing a part, no matter how difficult to recognize, in somebody else's phantasy—or he would do if it were not for what in recollection I can only call a temporary loss of insight, a sense of experiencing strong feelings and at the same time a belief that their existence is quite adequately justified by the objective situation without recourse to recondite explanation of their causation. From the analyst's point of view, the experience consists of two closely related phases: in the first there is a feeling that whatever else one has done, one has certainly not given a correct interpretation; in the second there is a sense of being a particular kind of person in a particular emotional situation. I believe ability to shake oneself out of the numbing feeling of reality that is a concomitant of this state is the prime requisite of the analyst in the group; if he can do this he is in a position to give what I believe is the correct interpretation, and thereby to see its connection with the previous interpretation, the validity of which he has been caused to doubt.

I must return to consider the second basic assumption. Like the first, this also concerns the purpose for which the group has met. My attention was first aroused by a session in which the conversation was monopolized by a man and woman who appeared more or less to ignore the rest of the group. The occasional exchange of glances amongst the others seemed to suggest the view, not very seriously entertained, that the relationship was amatory, although one would hardly say that the overt content of the conversation was very different from other interchanges in the group. I was, however, impressed with the fact that individuals, who were usually sensitive to any exclusion from supposedly therapeutic activity, which at that time had come to mean talking and obtaining an "interpretation" from me or some other member of the group, seemed not to mind leaving the stage entirely to this pair. Later it became clear that the sex of the pair was of no particular consequence to the assumption that pairing was taking place. There was a peculiar air of hopefulness and expectation about these sessions which made them rather different from the usual run of hours of boredom and frustration. It must not be supposed that the elements to which I would draw attention, under the title of pairing group, are exclusively or even predominantly in evidence.

In fact there is plenty of evidence of states of mind of the kind we are familiar with in psychoanalysis; it would indeed be extraordinary, to take one example, if one did not see in individuals evidence of reaction to a group situation that could approximate to an acting out of the primal scene. But, in my opinion, to allow one's attention to be absorbed by these reactions is to make difficult any observation of what is peculiar to the group; furthermore I think such concentration at worst can lead to a debased psychoanalysis rather than an exploration of the therapeutic possibilities of the group. The reader must, then, assume that in this, as in other situations, there will always be a plethora of material familiar in a psychoanalysis, but still awaiting its evaluation in the situation of the group; this material I propose for the present to ignore, and I shall now turn to a consideration of the air of hopeful expectation that I have mentioned as a characteristic of the pairing group. It usually finds expression verbally in ideas that marriage would put an end to neurotic disabilities; that group therapy would revolutionize society when it had spread sufficiently; that the coming season, spring, summer, autumn, or winter, as the case may be, will be more agreeable; that some new kind of community—an improved group—should be developed, and so on. These expressions tend to divert attention to some supposedly future event, but for the analyst the crux is not a future event but the immediate present—the feeling of hope itself. This feeling is characteristic of the pairing group and must be taken by itself as evidence that the pairing group is in existence, even when other evidence appears to be lacking. It is itself both a precursor of sexuality and a part of it. The optimistic ideas that are verbally expressed are rationalizations intended to effect a displacement in time and a compromise with feelings of guilt—the enjoyment of the feeling is justified by appeal to an outcome supposedly morally unexceptionable. The feelings thus associated in the pairing group are at the opposite pole to feelings of hatred, destructiveness, and despair. For the feelings of hope to be sustained it is essential that the "leader" of the group, unlike the leader of the dependent group and of the fight-flight group, should be unborn. It is a person or idea that will save the group—in fact from feelings of hatred, destructiveness, and despair, of its own or of another group—but in order to do this, obviously, the messianic hope must never be fulfilled. Only by remaining a hope does hope persist. The difficulty is that, thanks to the rationalization of the dawning sexuality of the group, the premonition of sex which obtrudes as hope, there is a tendency for the work group to be influenced in the direction of producing a messiah, be it person, idea, or utopia. Insofar as it succeeds, hope is weakened, for obviously nothing is then to hope for, and, since destructiveness, hatred, and despair have in no way been radically influenced, their existence again makes itself felt. This in turn accelerates a further weakening of hope. If, for purposes of discussion, we accept the idea that the group should be manipulated in order to compass hopefulness in the group, then it is necessary that those who concern themselves with such a task, either in their capacity as members of a specialized work group such as I shall describe shortly, or as individuals, should see to it that messianic hopes do not materialize. The danger, of course, is that such specialized work groups will either suffer through excess of zeal and thereby interfere with innocent, creative work-group function or alternatively allow themselves to be forestalled and so put to the troublesome necessity of liquidating the messiah and then recreating the messianic hope. In the therapeutic group the problem is to enable the group to be consciously aware of the feelings of hope, and its affiliations, and at the same time tolerant of them. That it is tolerant of them in the pairing group is a function of the basic assumption and cannot be regarded as a sign of individual development.

The third basic assumption is that the group has met to fight something or to run away from it. It is prepared to do either indifferently. I call this state of mind the fight-flight group; the accepted leader of a group in this state is one whose demands on the group are felt to afford opportunity for flight or aggression and if he makes demands that do not do so, he is ignored. In a therapeutic group the analyst is the work-group leader. The emotional backing that he can command is subject to fluctuation according to the active basic assumption and the extent to which his activities are felt to fit in with what is required of a leader in these differing states of mind. In the fight-flight group the analyst finds that attempts to illuminate what is taking place are obstructed by the ease with which emotional support is obtained for such proposals as express either hatred of all psychological difficulty or alternatively the means by which it can be evaded. In this context I would remark that the proposal to use Christian names, in the first example I gave, might well have been interpreted as an expression of the desire for flight in a fight-flight group though, in fact, for reasons connected with the stage of development that the group had reached, I interpreted it in terms of work-group function. . . .

I think that the central position in group dynamics is occupied by the more primitive mechanisms that Melanie Klein has described as peculiar to the paranoid-schizoid and depressive positions. In other words I feel, but would not like to be challenged with my limited experience to prove, that it is not simply a matter of the incompleteness of the illumination provided by Freud's discovery of the family group as the prototype of all groups, but the fact that this incompleteness leaves out the source of the main emotional drives in the group.

It may be, of course, that this is an artifact produced by the frustration of the individual's desire to be alone with me in the group. I do not wish to minimize the importance of this, but in fact I do not believe that the phenomena I have witnessed are peculiar to a therapeutic group. All groups stimulate and at the same time frustrate the individuals composing them, for the individual is impelled to seek the satisfaction of his needs in his group and is at the same time inhibited in this aim by the primitive fears that the group arouses.

To recapitulate: any group of individuals met together for work shows work-group activity, that is, mental functioning designed to further the task in hand. Investigation shows that these aims are sometimes hindered, occasionally furthered, by emotional drives of obscure origin. A certain cohesion is given to these anomalous mental activities if it is assumed that emotionally the group acts as if it had certain basic assumptions about its aims. These basic assumptions, which appear to be fairly adequately adumbrated by three formulations, dependence, pairing, and fighting or flight, are, on further investigation, seen to displace each other, as if in response to some unexplained impulse. They appear, furthermore, to have some common link, or, perhaps, even to be different aspects of each other. Further investigation shows that each basic assumption contains features that correspond so closely with extremely primitive part-objects that sooner or later psychotic anxiety, appertaining to these primitive relationships, is released. These anxieties, and the mechanisms peculiar to them, have been already displayed in psychoanalysis by Melanie Klein, and her descriptions tally well with the emotional states that find an outlet in mass action of the group in behaviour that seems to have coherence if it is considered to be the outcome of a basic assumption. Approached from the angle of sophisticated work-group activity, the basic assumptions appear to be the source of emotional drives to aims far different either from the overt task of the group or even from the tasks that would appear to be appropriate to Freud's view of the group as based on the family group. But approached from the angle of psychotic anxiety associated with phantasies of primitive part-object relationships, described by Melanie Klein and her co-workers, the basic-assumption phenomena appear far more to have the characteristics of defensive reactions to psychotic anxiety, and to be not so much at variance with Freud's views as supplementary to them. In my view, it is necessary to work through both the stresses that appertain to family patterns and the still more primitive anxieties of part-object relationships. In fact I consider the latter to contain the ultimate sources of all group behaviour.

REFERENCES

Freud, S. (1911). Formulations on the two principles of mental functioning. *Standard Edition*, 12.

——(1913). *Totem and taboo. Standard Edition*, 13.

Klein, M. (1946). Notes on some schizoid mechanisms. In Klein et al., eds. *Developments in Psycho-Analysis*. London: Hogarth, 1952.

30

Second Thoughts: "The Development of Schizophrenic Thought" (1956) and "Attacks on Linking" (1959)

A number of Bion's early papers that were originally published in the *International Journal of Psycho-Analysis* were reprinted in 1967 in a volume called *Second Thoughts,* where he also elaborated on the papers by appending his reconsiderations. Taken together, they give a theory of mind that extends ideas of Freud and Klein on the nature of mind as an apparatus for thinking, for incorporating, and for relating to reality, and on the role of projective identification in the development of the capacity to think, to allay anxiety, and to communicate. Since projective identification is an interpersonal concept, involving the interaction of two people, his model is essentially one of the development of mind in an interpersonal context and through interpersonal influence, but this did not become explicit until Bion developed his idea of the mother as the container of the infant's projected anxieties, published in *Learning from Experience* in 1962. It is useful to read the early papers while keeping that later development in mind.

In his 1956 paper "The Development of Schizophrenic Thought," Bion described schizophrenic thinking as a process that involves the projection of parts of the mental apparatus for experiencing conscious awareness, with a resulting lack of an awareness of internal and external reality.

He used these ideas to differentiate between the psychotic and non-psychotic parts of personality, but the term *psychotic* refers not to a technical, descriptive diagnosis, as we commonly think of psychosis, but to the states of primitive, early anxieties that disrupt thinking and organization, and had already been used for many years by the Kleinians to apply to such primitive anxieties in everyone.

In this paper, Bion described how parts of the ego are, in unconscious phantasy, projected into things in the outside world, where they take the form of bizarre fragments. External objects are, he said, encapsulated in these fragments of the personality which come to control them. Bion linked this process to that previously described by Segal (1957, Chapter 35) as symbolic equation, in which the patient equates things to ideas but cannot symbolize them. In this way, patients use objects as ideas, now moving "not in a world of dreams, but in a world of objects which are ordinarily the furniture of dreams" (see p. 293 below). Bion thought the psychotic patient (or the neurotic person employing psychotic functions) used projective identification where the neurotic would use repression. By using projective identification, the patient put unacceptable ideas and affects outside the self instead of burying them inside through repression, all because of a hatred of reality, which motivates a phantasied sadistic attack on it.

Schizophrenic disturbance springs from an interaction between (1) the environment, and (2) the personality. In this paper I ignore the environment and focus attention on four essential features of schizophrenic personality. First is a preponderance of destructive impulses so great that even the impulses to love are suffused by them and turned to sadism. Second is a hatred of reality, which, as Freud pointed out, is extended to all aspects of the psyche that make for awareness of it. I add hatred of internal reality and all that makes for awareness of it. Third, derived from these two, is an unremitting dread of imminent annihilation. Fourth is a precipitate and premature formation of object relations, foremost amongst which is the transference, whose thinness is in marked contrast to the tenacity with which it is maintained. The prematurity, thinness, and tenacity are pathognomonic and are alike derived from dread of annihilation by the death instincts. The schizophrenic is preoccupied with the conflict, never finally resolved, between destructiveness on the one hand and sadism on the other.

TRANSFERENCE

The relationship with the analyst is premature, precipitate, and intensely dependent. When the patient broadens it under pressure of his life or death instincts two concurrent streams of phenomena become manifest: First projective identification, with the analyst as object, becomes overactive with the resulting painful confusional states such as Rosenfeld has described. Second, the mental and other activities by which the dominant impulse, be it life instincts or death instincts, strives to express itself, are at once subjected to mutilation by the temporarily subordinated impulse. Driven by the wish to escape the confusional states and harassed by the mutilations, the patient strives to restore the restricted relationship; the transference is again invested with its characteristic featurelessness. Whether the patient walks straight past me into the consulting room as if scarcely aware of my presence, or whether he displays an effusive, mirthless bonhomie, the restricted relationship is unmistakable. Restriction and expansion alternate throughout the analysis.

THE DIVERGENCE

To sum up, ignoring the effect of the external environment, the schizophrenic personality depends on the existence in the patient of four features: (1) a conflict that is never decided between life and death instincts; (2) a preponderance of destructive impulses; (3) hatred of external and internal reality; (4) a tenuous but tenacious object relationship. This peculiar endowment makes it certain that the schizophrenic patient's progression through the paranoid-schizoid and depressive positions is markedly different from that of the nonpsychotic personality. This difference hinges on the fact that this combination of characteristics leads to a massive resort to projective identification. It is therefore to projective identification that I now turn, but my examination of it is restricted to its deployment by the schizophrenic against all that apparatus of awareness that Freud described as being called into activity by the demands of the reality principle.

DIVERGENCE OF PSYCHOTIC FROM NONPSYCHOTIC PERSONALITY

I spoke of Melanie Klein's picture of the paranoid-schizoid position and the important part played in it by the infant's phantasies of sadistic attacks on the breast. Identical attacks are directed against the apparatus of perception from the beginning of life. This part of his personality is cut up, split into minute fragments, and then, using the projective identification, expelled from the personality. Having thus rid himself of the apparatus of conscious awareness of internal and external reality, the patient achieves a state which is felt to be neither alive nor dead.

This apparatus of conscious awareness is intimately connected with verbal thought and all that provides, at the early stage of which I speak, the foundations of its inchoation.

Projective identification of conscious awareness and the associated inchoation of verbal thought is the central factor in the differentiation of the psychotic from the nonpsychotic personality. I believe it takes place at the outset of the patient's life. These sadistic attacks on the ego and on the foundations of inchoate verbal thought, and the projective identification of the fragments, makes certain that from this point on there is an ever-widening divergence between the psychotic and nonpsychotic parts of the personality until at last the gulf is felt to be unbridgeable.

FATE OF THE EXPELLED FRAGMENTS

Insofar as the destruction is successful, the patient experiences a failure in his capacity for perception. All his sense impressions appear to have suffered mutilation of a kind which would be appropriate had they been attacked as the breast is felt to be attacked in the sadistic phantasies of the infant. The patient feels imprisoned in the state of mind he has achieved and unable to escape from it because he feels he lacks the apparatus of awareness of reality, which is both the key to escape and the freedom itself to which he would escape. This sense of imprisonment is intensified by the menacing presence of the expelled fragments within whose planetary movements he is contained. The nature of this imprisonment will become clearer with the discussion of the fate of these expelled fragments, to which I now turn.

In the patient's phantasy the expelled particles of ego lead to an independent and uncontrolled existence outside the personality, but either containing or contained by external objects, where they exercise their functions as if the ordeal to which they have been subjected has served only to increase their number and to provoke their hostility to the psyche that ejected them. In consequence the patient feels himself to be surrounded by bizarre objects whose nature I shall now describe.

THE PARTICLES

Each particle is felt to consist of a real external object which is incapsulated in a piece of personality that has engulfed it. The character of this complete particle will depend partly on the character of the real object, say a gramophone, and partly on the character of the particle of personality that engulfs it. If the piece of the personality is concerned with sight, the gramophone when played is felt to be watching the patient. If with hearing, then the gramophone when played is felt to be listening to the patient. The object, angered at being engulfed, swells up, so to speak, and suffuses and controls the piece of personality that engulfs it; to that extent the particle is felt to have become a thing. Since these particles are used by the patient as if they were prototypes of ideas—later to become words—this suffusion of the piece of personality by the contained, but controlling, object leads the patient to feel that words are the actual things they name, and so to the confusions, described by Segal, that arise because the patient equates, but does not symbolize.

CONSEQUENCES FOR THE PATIENT

The patient now moves, not in a world of dreams, but in a world of objects which are ordinarily the furniture of dreams. These objects, primitive yet complex, partake of qualities which in the nonpsychotic are peculiar to matter, anal objects, senses, ideas, superego, and the remaining qualities of personality. One result is that the patient strives to use real objects as ideas and is baffled when they obey the laws of natural science and not those of mental functioning.

Associated with projective identification is the psychotic personality's inability to introject. If he wishes to take in an interpretation, or bring back these objects I have been describing, he does so by projective identification reversed, and by the same route. This situation was neatly summed up by the patient who said he used his intestine as a brain. When I said he had swallowed something, he replied, "The intestine doesn't swallow." Dr. Segal (1957) has described . . . some of the patient's vicissitudes in the depressive position; I would now add that, thanks to this employment of projective identification, he cannot synthesize his objects: he can only agglomerate and compress them. Further, whether he feels he has had something put into him, or whether he feels he has introjected it, he feels the ingress as an assault, and a retaliation by the object for his violent intrusion into it.

REPRESSION

It will be clear that where the nonpsychotic personality, or part of the personality, employs repression, the psychotic has employed projective identification. Therefore there is no repression, and what should be his unconscious is replaced by the world of dream furniture in which I have described him as moving.

VERBAL THOUGHT

The inception of verbal thought which I described as appertaining to the depressive position is gravely disturbed because it is that which synthesizes and articulates impressions and thus is essential to awareness of internal and external reality; for that reason it is subject to continuing attacks such as I have described.

Further, excessive projective identification in the paranoid-schizoid position prevented smooth introjection and assimilation of sense impressions and consequently the establishment of the firm base of good objects on which the inception of verbal thought depends.

An attempt to think involves bringing back to control, and therefore to his personality, the expelled particles and their accretions. Projective identification is therefore reversed and the concomitant agglomeration and compression lead to highly compact speech, the construction of which is more appropriate to music than the articulation of words as used for nonpsychotic communication.

Moreover, since, as we have seen, these particles share the qualities of things, the patient can feel he is being split by their reentry. Again, since these particles include pieces of conscious awareness of sense impressions, the senses are felt to become painfully compressed and acute to an intolerable degree. The patient can be seen to be in the grip of extremely painful, tactile, auditory, or visual hallucinations. Depression and anxiety being subject to the same mechanism are similarly intensified until the patient is compelled to deal with these emotions in the way that Segal has described (1957).

CONCLUSION

Experience of these theories in practice has convinced me that the treatment of psychotic personality will not be successful until the patient's destructive attacks on his ego, and his substitution of projective identification for repression and introjection, have been worked through. I further consider that even in the severe neurotic there is a psychotic personality that has to be dealt with in the same way before success is achieved.

"Attacks on Linking" (1959)

In "Attacks on Linking," Bion continued the theme of sadistic attacks on the external object motivated by envy and carried out through massive projective identification. Here he elaborated on attacks on the link between the breast and the baby, between the analyst and patient, and between the parents. This paper gives clinical examples of the type Bion used in establishing his interpretations, and proceeds to establish the connection between the attacks on patients' mental apparatus and attacks on the object that stands for and constitutes the environment—that is, the mother or the therapist. In passing, Bion refers to a triad of personality characteristics of "curiosity, arrogance, and stupidity" seen as a constellation in patients who have suffered an internal "disaster" in which a primitive superego has been established that denies the patient the ordinary use of projective identification to create links with the object, substituting stupidity for knowledge and arrogance for the usual sense of self-respect. The triad was described in the paper "On Arrogance," which also appeared in *Second Thoughts* but is not reprinted here.

This paper offers the first differentiation between projective identification as normal unconscious communication and projective identification as pathological defense, thus forming a bridge to the later growth of Bion's ideas on thinking and containment.

I shall discuss phantasied attacks on the breast as the prototype of all attacks on objects that serve as a link and projective identification as the mechanism employed by the psyche to dispose of the ego fragments produced by its destructiveness. . . .

The examples are drawn from the analysis of two patients and are taken from an advanced stage of their analyses. To preserve anonymity I shall not distinguish between the patients and shall introduce distortions of fact which I hope do not impair the accuracy of the analytic description.

Observation of the patient's disposition to attack the link between two objects is simplified because the analyst has to establish a link with the patient and does this by verbal communication and his equipment of psychoanalytical experience. Upon this the creative relationship depends and therefore we should be able to see attacks being made upon it. . . .

> These are the examples:
>
> (1) I had reason to give a patient an interpretation making explicit his feelings of affection and his expression of them to his mother for her ability to cope with a refractory child. The patient attempted to express his agreement with me, but although he needed to say only a few words his expression of them was interrupted by a very pronounced stammer which had the effect of spreading out his remark over a period of as much as a minute and a half. The actual sounds emitted bore resemblance to gasping for breath; gaspings were interspersed with gurgling sounds as if he were immersed in water. I drew his attention to these sounds and he agreed that they were peculiar and himself suggested the descriptions I have just given.
>
> (2) The patient complained that he could not sleep. Showing signs of fear, he said, "It can't go on like this." Disjointed remarks gave the impression that he felt superficially that some catastrophe would occur, perhaps akin to insanity, if he could not get more sleep. Referring to material in the previous session I suggested that he feared he would dream if he were to sleep. He denied this and said he could not think because he was wet. I reminded him of his use of the term wet as an expression of

contempt for somebody he regarded as feeble and sentimental. He disagreed and indicated that the state to which he referred was the exact opposite. From what I knew of this patient I felt that his correction at this point was valid and that somehow the wetness referred to an expression of hatred and envy such as he associated with urinary attacks on an object. I therefore said that in addition to the superficial fear which he had expressed he was afraid of sleep because for him it was the same thing as the oozing away of his mind itself. Further associations showed that he felt that good interpretations from me were so consistently and minutely split up by him that they became mental urine which then seeped uncontrollably away. Sleep was therefore inseparable from unconsciousness, which was itself identical with a state of mindlessness which could not be repaired. He said, "I am dry now." I replied that he felt he was awake and capable of thought, but that this good state was only precariously maintained. . . .

(3) In the first twenty minutes of the session the patient made three isolated remarks which had no significance for me. He then said that it seemed that a girl he had met was understanding. This was followed at once by a violent, convulsive movement which he affected to ignore. It appeared to be . . . [a] stabbing attack. . . . I tried to draw his attention to the movement, but he ignored my intervention as he ignored the attack. He then said that the room was filled with a blue haze. A little later he remarked that the haze had gone, but said he was depressed. I interpreted that he felt understood by me. This was an agreeable experience, but the pleasant feeling of being understood had been instantly destroyed and ejected. I reminded him that we had recently witnessed his use of the word blue as a compact description of vituperative sexual conversation. If my interpretation was correct, and subsequent events suggested that it was, it meant that the experience of being understood had been split up, converted into particles of sexual abuse and ejected. Up to this point I felt that the interpretation approximated closely to his experience. Later interpretations, that the disappearance of the haze was due to reintrojection and conversion into depression, seemed to have less reality for the patient, although later events were compatible with its being correct. . . .

FEATURES COMMON TO THE ABOVE ILLUSTRATIONS

These episodes have been chosen by me because the dominant theme in each was the destructive attack on a link. In the first the attack was expressed in a stammer which was designed to prevent the patient from using language as a bond between him and me. In the second sleep was felt by him to be identical with projective identification that proceeded unaffected by any possible attempt at control by him. Sleep for him meant that his mind, minutely fragmented, flowed out in an attacking stream of particles.

The examples I give here throw light on schizophrenic dreaming. The psychotic patient appears to have no dreams, or at least not to report any, until comparatively late in the analysis. My impression now is that this apparently dreamless period is a phenomenon analogous to the invisible visual hallucination. That is to say, that the dreams consist of material so minutely fragmented that they are devoid of any visual component. When dreams are experienced which the patient can report because visual objects have been experienced by him in the course of the dream, he seems to regard these objects as bearing much the same relationship to the invisible objects of the previous phase as faeces seem to him to bear to urine. The objects appearing in experiences which we call dreams are regarded by the patient as solid and are, as such, contrasted with the contents of the dreams which were a continuum of minute, invisible fragments.

At the time of the session the main theme was not an attack on the link but the consequences of such an attack, previously made, in leaving him bereft of a state of mind necessary for the establishment of a satisfying relationship between him and his bed. Though it did not appear in the session I report, uncontrollable projective identification, which was what sleep meant to him, was thought to be a destructive attack on the state of mind of the coupling parents. There was therefore a double anxiety: one arising from his fear that he was being rendered mindless, the other from his fear that he was unable to control his hostile attacks, his mind providing the ammunition, on the state of mind that was the link between the parental pair. Sleep and sleeplessness were alike inacceptable. . . .

In my third example, the report of the understanding girl and the haze, my understanding and his agreeable state of mind have been felt as a link between us which could give rise to a creative act. The link had been regarded with hate and transformed into a hostile and destructive sexuality rendering the patient–analyst couple sterile. . . .

CURIOSITY, ARROGANCE, AND STUPIDITY

In the paper I presented at the International Congress of 1957 I suggested that Freud's analogy of an archaeological investigation with a psycho-analysis was helpful if it were considered that we were exposing evidence not so much of a primitive civilization as of a primitive disaster. The value of the analogy is lessened because in the analysis we are confronted not so much with a static situation that permits leisurely study, but with a catastrophe that remains at one and the same moment actively vital and yet incapable of resolution into quiescence. This lack of progress in any direction must be attributed in part to the destruction of a capacity for curiosity and the consequent inability to learn, but before I go into this I must say something about a matter that plays hardly any part in the illustrations I have given.

Attacks on the link originate in what Melanie Klein (1948) calls the paranoid-schizoid phase. This period is dominated by part-object relationships. If it is borne in mind that the patient has a part-object relationship with himself as well as with objects not himself, it contributes to the understanding of phrases such as "it seems" which are commonly employed by the deeply disturbed patient on occasions when a less disturbed patient might say "I think" or "I believe." When he says "it seems" he is often referring to a feeling—an "it seems" feeling—which is a part of his psyche and yet is not observed as part of a whole object. The conception of the part-object as analogous to an anatomical structure, encouraged by the patient's employment of concrete images as units of thought, is misleading because the part-object relationship is not with the anatomical structures only but with function, not with anatomy but with physiology, not with the breast but with feeding, poisoning, loving, hating. This contributes to the impression of a disaster that is dynamic and not static. The problem that has to be solved on this early, yet superficial, level must be stated in adult terms by the question, "What is something?" and not the question "Why is something?" because "why" has, through guilt, been split off. Problems, the solution of which depends upon an awareness of causation, cannot therefore be stated, let alone solved. This produces a situation in which the patient appears to have no problems except those posed by the existence of analyst and patient. His preoccupation is with what is this or that function, of which he is aware though unable to grasp the totality of which the function is a part. It follows that there is never any question why the patient or the analyst is there, or why something is said or done or felt, nor can there be any question of attempting to alter the causes of some state of mind. . . . Since "what?" can never be answered without "how?" or "why?" further difficulties arise. . . .

DENIAL OF NORMAL DEGREES OF PROJECTIVE IDENTIFICATION

I employ the term *link* because I wish to discuss the patient's relationship with a function rather than with the object that subserves a function; my concern is not only with the breast, or penis, or verbal thought, but with their function of providing the link between two objects.

In her "Notes on Some Schizoid Mechanisms" Melanie Klein (1946) speaks of the importance of an excessive employment of splitting and projective identification in the production of a very disturbed personality. She also speaks of the "introjection of the good object, first of all the mother's breast" as a "precondition for normal development." I shall suppose that there is a normal degree of projective identification, without defining the limits within which normality lies, and that associated with introjective identification this is the foundation on which normal development rests.

This impression derives partly from a feature in a patient's analysis which was difficult to interpret because it did not appear to be sufficiently obtrusive at any moment for an interpretation to be supported by convincing evidence. Throughout the analysis the patient resorted to projective identification with a persistence suggesting it was a mechanism of which he had never been able sufficiently to avail himself; the analysis afforded him an opportunity for the exercise of a mechanism of which he had been cheated. I did not have to rely on this impression alone. There were sessions which led me to suppose that the patient felt there was some object that denied him the use of projective identification. In the illustrations I have given, particularly in the first, the stammer, and the third, the understanding girl and the blue haze, there are elements which indicate that the patient felt that parts of his personality that he wished to repose in me were refused entry by me, but there had been associations prior to this which led me to this view. . . .

In the analysis a complex situation may be observed. The patient feels he is being allowed an opportunity of which he had hitherto been cheated; the poignancy of his deprivation is thereby rendered the more acute and so are the feelings of resentment at the deprivation. Gratitude for the opportunity coexists with hostility to the analyst as the person who will not understand and refuses the patient the use of the only method of communication by which he feels he can make himself understood. Thus the link between patient and analyst, or infant and breast, is the mechanism of projective identification. The destructive attacks upon this link originate in a source external to the patient or infant, namely the analyst or breast. The result is excessive projective identification by the patient and a deterioration of his developmental processes. . . .

Before I discuss this consequence for the patient's development, I must refer to the inborn characteristics and the part that they play in producing attacks by the infant on all that links him to the breast, namely, primary aggression and envy. The seriousness of these attacks is enhanced if the mother displays the kind of unreceptiveness which I have described, and is diminished, but not abolished, if the mother can introject the infant's feelings and remain balanced (Klein 1957); the seriousness remains because the psychotic infant is overwhelmed with hatred and envy of the mother's ability to retain a comfortable state of mind although experiencing the infant's feelings. This was clearly brought out by a patient who insisted that I must go through it with him, but was filled with hate when he felt I was able to do so without a breakdown. Here we have another aspect of destructive attacks upon the link, the link being the capacity of the analyst to introject the patient's projective identifications. Attacks on the link, therefore, are synonymous with attacks on the analyst's, and originally the mother's, peace of mind. The capacity to introject is transformed by the patient's envy and hate into greed devouring the patient's psyche; similarly, peace of mind becomes hostile indifference. At this point analytic problems arise through the patient's employment (to destroy the peace of mind that is so much envied) of acting out, delinquent acts and threats of suicide. . . .

CONCLUSIONS

The main conclusions of this paper relate to that state of mind in which the patient's psyche contains an internal object which is opposed to, and destructive of, all links whatsoever from the most primitive (which I have suggested is a normal degree of projective identification) to the most sophisticated forms of verbal communication and the arts.

In this state of mind emotion is hated; it is felt to be too powerful to be contained by the immature psyche, it is felt to link objects and it gives reality to objects which are not self and therefore inimical to primary narcissism.

The internal object which in its origin was an external breast that refused to introject, harbour, and so modify the baneful force of emotion, is felt, paradoxically, to intensify, relative to the strength of the ego, the emotions against which it initiates the attacks. These attacks on the linking function of emotion lead to an overprominence in the psychotic part of the personality of links which appear to be logical, almost mathematical, but never emotionally reasonable. Consequently the links surviving are perverse, cruel, and sterile.

The external object which is internalized, its nature, and the effect when so established on the methods of communication within the psyche and with the environment, are left for further elaboration later.

REFERENCES

Bion, W. R. (1957). On arrogance. Paper presented at International Psycho-Analytic Congress. *International Journal of Psycho-Analysis* 39, 1958.

Klein, M. (1946). Notes on some schizoid mechanisms. *International Journal of Psycho-Analysis* 27.

——(1948). The theory of anxiety and guilt. *International Journal of Psycho-Analysis* 29.

——(1957). *Envy and Gratitude*. London: Tavistock.

Segal, H. (1957). Notes on symbol formation. *International Journal of Psycho-Analysis* 38:391–397.

31

Summary of "The Differentiation of the Psychotic from the Non-Psychotic Personalities" (1957) and "A Theory of Thinking" (1962)

These papers are so complex and enigmatic that I have decided to summarize them here in lieu of excerpts. "Differentiation of Psychotic and Non-Psychotic Personalities" is part of a series of papers on the psychotic aspect of personality—a part Bion accepts as a ubiquitous part of infantile functioning that complements the non-psychotic part of the personality. It is an aspect of mental functioning, not part of any diagnostic schema.

Psychotic mechanisms concern an attack on the apparatus of thinking, with a splintering of experience into minute particles or bizarre objects because of a hatred of internal and external reality. These mental fragments are, in phantasy, evacuated outside the mind where they enter into and engulf external objects (that is, the world of things) so that parts of the mind (ego, superego) are felt to reside in external things. Objects that the normal person imbues with meaning through symbol formation and employs symbolically in dreams are now felt to control the process of thinking and the personality itself. Bion says that, as a result, the psychotic person moves not in the non-psychotic person's "world of dreams," but in a world of bizarre objects that corresponds to the non-psychotic personality's "furniture of dreams."

"A Theory of Thinking" presupposes the material of the "Psychotic/Non-Psychotic" paper in constructing an analytic theory of thinking. The enigmatic quality of the "Thinking" paper in particular rests partly in the way Bion used ordinary words to mean something new. His theory proposes that *thinking* is a sense organ designed to take care of *thoughts,* which are composed of *preconceptions*—empty, anticipations by the infant of finding something it is searching for—*conceptions,* and *concepts.* A conception occurs when the infant's search meets an object and a preconception meets with a *realization.* As an example: the infant searching meets a breast and realizes a concept—*breast.* In the infant who does not suffer too much frustration, not meeting the breast also results in a concept of *no breast. Concepts* are classes of thoughts or conceptions.

According to Bion, the individual experiences *beta elements,* which are something like unorganized sensations or emotions, perceptions that have not acquired meaning. For these elements to acquire meaning, the individual has to acquire an *alpha process,* which can transform them into meaningful and tolerable sensations or feelings. This develops through a cycle of projection and introjection with the mother.

In this paper, Bion described the role of the mother in enabling this to happen. Through projective identification, the infant puts unmanageable anxiety into her, which she can tolerate. She does so in an unconscious process that Bion called her *reverie,* which is her internal "organ" for sensing and containing her baby's anxieties, then feeding them back for the baby to introject in more tolerable form. This set of activities together forms what Bion later called the *container/contained,* the projection by the infant of primitive, unmanageable anxieties into the mother, her reception and modification of them through her reverie, and the reintrojection of the now-modified anxieties and elements by the baby. If the mother's reverie fails to modify them, or if she blocks the projective identification, the infant takes back a *nameless dread*—a much worse form of anxiety based in the failure of the object relationship.

With this theory of thinking and the model of the container/contained, the attacks on linking within the individual's mind and between the individual and the object, as elaborated in the previous chapter, can now be seen to constitute attacks on the process of thinking and of the relationship required to build the capacity for thinking during development. The mother can contribute to blocking the process of thinking by blocking the cycle of projective and introjective identification—that is, by refusing to accept the projection of aspects of the baby's anxiety.

This revolutionary interpersonal model for the establishment of the capacity to think, the tolerance of strong affects and ideas, and the growth of mind elaborates Klein's model of projective identification as a process originating with the baby for the purpose of communication and emotional growth. It adds considerable power to Fairbairn's proposal that introjection is the first activity in the establishment of mind. It offers a model that links the differing emphases of Klein and Fairbairn in constructing a cycle of projective and introjective identification between mother and baby.

It is also useful to contrast Bion's model of the *container/contained* with Winnicott's concept of the interaction between infant and mother as transacted through *transitional phenomena* supported by the mother's "environmental" function. Winnicott focused mainly on the *externally observable* aspects of the mother–infant interaction through which the baby uses *external objects and interactions* to make something of the relationship with the mother, and of the things she offers the baby. Bion had nothing to say theoretically about the actual interactions through which containment and reverie occur, and focused on the internal processes exclusively, leaving the details to our imagination. Synthesizing the two sets of ideas allows us to move toward a comprehensive understanding of the relevance of both external and internal interaction in the growth of the self and of thinking. Unconscious communication of the sort Bion considered is carried out through a complex pattern of external interaction and speech, so that the matters that occur as transitional phenomena between mother and child constitute the vehicle through which unconscious internal matters are also conveyed. Some of the most interesting work on this sort of interaction has appeared in the recent writing of Bollas, Symington, and Ogden, excerpted in the final sections of this volume.

32

Learning from Experience (1962): "The K-Link"

The following section from Bion's book *Learning from Experience* (1962) first introduces one of Bion's best known formulations: the *container* and the *contained,* and the use of *L, H, K* to stand for love, hate, knowledge. The qualities L and H are not in themselves opposites, but do have opposites termed $-L$ and $-H$, which have a rough representation as the absence or love or the absence of hate. *K,* knowledge, or perhaps the ability to learn about the truth in derivative form, has as its opposite $-K$—the evasion of learning or knowledge. Although he had not yet coined these terms when he wrote the papers that appeared together in *Second Thoughts,* it was the inability to form *K*—that is, the quality of $-K$—that Bion had explored in attacks on linking and in the formation of thought.

The selection here introduces the container/contained. In it, the infant's primitive anxieties are located in the mother through projective identification. She tolerates and modifies them through a process he calls her *reverie,* enabling the infant to reabsorb them from her in detoxified form. In this revolutionary model, the process of the growth of tolerance and thinking capacity is seen as having an interpersonal origin.

Melanie Klein has described an aspect of projective identification concerned with the modification of infantile fears: the infant projects a part of its psyche, namely its bad feelings, into a good breast. Thence in due course they are removed and re-introjected. During their sojourn in the good breast they are felt to have been modified in such a way that the object that is re-introjected has become tolerable to the infant's psyche.

From the above theory I shall abstract for use as a model the idea of a container into which an object is projected and the object that can be projected into the container: the latter I shall designate by the term contained. The unsatisfactory nature of both terms points the need for further abstraction.

Container and contained are susceptible of conjunction and permeation by emotion. Thus conjoined or permeated or both they change in a manner usually described as growth. When disjoined or denuded of emotion, they diminish in vitality, that is, approximate to inanimate objects. Both container and contained are models of abstract representations of psychoanalytic realizations.

The next step in abstraction is dictated by the need for designation. I shall use the sign ♀ for the abstraction representing the container and ♂ for the contained.

These signs both denote and represent. They are variables or unknown in that they are replaceable. They are constants in that they are only replaceable by constants. For syntactical purposes they are functors.

Reconsidering K in the light of previous discussion although K is essentially a function of two objects it can be considered as a function of one.

The earliest and most primitive manifestation of K occurs in the relationship between mother and infant. As a part object relationship it may be stated as a relationship between mouth and breast. In abstract terms it is between ♂ and ♀ (as I have proposed the use of these signs).

In K, L and H being factors and therefore subordinate, ♂ is projected into ♀ and abstraction, of a type that I shall use the term commensal to describe, follows. By commensal I mean ♂ and ♀ are dependent on each other for mutual benefit and without harm to either. In terms of a model the mother derives benefit and achieves mental growth from the experience: the infant likewise abstracts benefit and achieves growth.

The activity that I have here described as shared by two individuals becomes introjected by the infant so that the ♂ ♀ apparatus becomes installed in the infant as part of the apparatus of alpha-function. A model is provided by the idea of the infant who explores an object by putting it into his mouth. What talking was originally done by the mother, possibly a rudimentary designatory function, is replaced by the infant's own baby talk. Using this as a model from which to abstract a theory to represent the realization of the development of thoughts, I propose the following terms: (a) Preconception. This term represents a state of expectation. The term is the counterpart of a variable in mathematical logic or an unknown in mathematics. It has the quality that Kant ascribes to an empty thought in that it can be thought but cannot be known. (b) Conception. Conception is that which results when a preconception mates with the appropriate sense impressions. I have used a phrase in which the implied model is obvious. The abstraction from the relationship of preconception to sense impressions is ♀ to ♂ (NOT ♂ to ♀).

To summarize. The relationship between mother and infant described by Melanie Klein as projective identification is internalized to form an apparatus for regulation of a preconception with the sense data of the appropriate realization. This apparatus is represented by a model: the mating of preconception with sense impressions to produce a conception. The model is in turn represented by ♂ ♀.

The repetition of mating of preconception and sense data, that results in commensal abstraction, promotes growth in ♂ and ♀. That is to say the capacity for taking in sense impressions develops together with the capacity for awareness of sense data.

33

Attention and Interpretation (1970)

In the book *The Elements of Psycho-Analysis* Bion (1963) elaborated a quasi-mathematical "grid" for categorizing elements and forms of action in psychoanalysis, and discussed his concepts of beta elements and alpha functioning at length. While Bion wrote extensively about the grid as a method for increasing the level of scientific study of psychoanalysis, most students of his work have not shared his enthusiasm for it. I have not excerpted any of the exceedingly dense writing from this book.

Bion continued to refer to the grid in *Transformations* (1965) and *Attention and Interpretation* (1970). Because the grid is so complex, and because the benefits to be obtained from its study are elusive, I have eliminated all references to it in the following excerpts from *Attention and Interpretation*. Even so, the writing in these excerpts is among Bion's most complex and enigmatic, verging on the mystical. Nevertheless, the contributions contained in them are too important to omit.

In *Attention and Interpretation*, Bion presented his aphorism that therapists should be "without memory and desire." That is to say, a therapist should not desire something for patients that imposes on them, and should approach each session without the burden of preformed ideas, even those from a previous session, since such memories distort finding what is there to be discovered in the current session. While the advice to be without memory or desire, taken alone, would distort the process of coming to know a patient or of supporting the patient's growth, it provides a revolutionary corrective to the idea that therapists know where patients should go, any more than mothers should know the kind of person their babies will grow up to be.

In advocating this state of mind, Bion introduced the term *O*—the unknowable ultimate truth—of which *K* is a only an approximation, a tangible embodiment necessary to the endeavor of the attempt to know the truth of *O,* but also, necessarily and always, a deceptive falsification. He also introduces the term *F* for the "act of faith" that Bion feels must accompany the analytic endeavor, and the term *at-one-ment*, which is the desirable but unattainable state of being at one with *O.*

The concept *negative capability*, introduced in the closing pages of *Attention and Interpretation*, summarizes the attitude that should support the analytic endeavor. The term was coined by Keats who wrote about a quality of Shakespeare's poetic character as a capacity for "being in uncertainties, mysteries, doubts, without any irritable reaching after fact and reason." (Murray 1955, p. 261). Negative capability describes the analyst's attitude of suspended, non-expectation that allows the patient's self, and the relationship between patient and analyst to evolve without imposition from the analyst.

This fully involved openness is an elaboration of Freud's description of the basic analytic attitude:

> The most successful cases are those in which one proceeds, as it were, without any purpose in view, allows oneself to be taken by surprise by any new turn in them, and always meets them with an open mind, free from any suppositions. . . . [S]o the doctor's unconscious is able, from the derivatives of the unconscious which are communicated to him, to reconstruct that unconscious which has determined the patient's free associations. [Freud, 1912, pp. 114–115].

REFERENCES

Bion, W. R. (1963). *Elements of Psycho-Analysis*. London: Heinemann.
—— (1965). *Transformations*. London: Heinemann.
—— (1970). *Attention and Interpretation*. London: Tavistock.
Freud, S. (1912). Recommendations to physicians practising psycho-analysis. *Standard Edition* 12: 114–115.
Murray, J. M. (1955). *Keats*. New York: Noonday.

"Reality Sensuous and Psychic"

Psychoanalytical events cannot be stated directly, indubitably, or incorrigibly any more than can those of other scientific research. I shall use the sign O to denote that which is the ultimate reality represented by terms such as ultimate reality, absolute truth, the godhead, the infinite, the thing-in-itself. O does not fall in the domain of knowledge or learning save incidentally; it can be "become," but it cannot be "known." It is darkness and formlessness but it enters the domain K when it has evolved to a point where it can be known, through knowledge gained by experience, and formulated in terms derived from sensuous experience; its existence is conjectured phenomenologically. . . .

It is impossible to undergo an analysis without learning about psychoanalysis as practised by one particular psychoanalyst; this is a misfortune rather than an advantage. Furthermore, established beliefs and conventions, hardened habits of thought, unless subjected to vigilance, reestablish themselves and encroach upon the freedom the psychoanalyst has won by being psychoanalysed and lead to deterioration of his efficiency. . . .

The analyst must focus his attention on O, the unknown and unknowable. The success of psychoanalysis depends on the maintenance of a psychoanalytic point of view; the point of view is the psychoanalytic vertex; the psychoanalytic vertex is O. With this the analyst cannot be identified: he must *be* it.

Every object known or knowable by man, including himself, must be an evolution of O. It is O when it has evolved sufficiently to be met by K capacities in the psychoanalyst. He does not know the "ultimate reality" of a chair or anxiety or time or space, but he knows a chair, anxiety, time, and space. Insofar as the analyst becomes O he is able to know the events that are *evolutions* of O.

Restating this in terms of psychoanalytic experience, the psychoanalyst can know what the patient says, does, and appears to be, but cannot know the O of which the patient is an evolution: he can only "be" it. He knows phenomena by virtue of his senses but, since his concern is with O, events must be regarded as possessing either the defects of irrelevancies obstructing, or the merits of pointers initiating, the process of "becoming" O. Yet interpretations depend on "becoming" (since he cannot know O). The interpretation is an actual event in an evolution of O that is common to analyst and analysand.

A fallacious but helpful description in A is that the practising analyst must wait for the analytic session to "evolve." He must wait not for the analysand to talk or to be silent or to gesture, or for any other occurrence that is an actual event, but for an evolution to take place so that O becomes manifest in K through the emergence of actual events. Similarly, the reader must disregard what I say until the O of the experience of reading has evolved to a point where the actual events of reading issue in his interpretation of the experiences. Too great a regard for what I have written obstructs the process I represent by the term *he becomes the O that is common to himself and myself.*

The reasons for this are as follows: There can be no genuine outcome that is based on falsity. Therefore the outcome depends on the closeness with which the interpretative appraisal approximates to truth. The psychoanalyst and his analysand are alike dependent on the senses, but psychic qualities, with which psychoanalysis deals, are not perceived by the senses but, as Freud says, by some mental counterpart of the sense organs, a function that he attributed to consciousness. Without wishing to discard this possibility I prefer to consider it as an open question and substitute a more general postulate which I represent by O. To put it in more popular terms, I would say the more "real" the psychoanalyst is the more he can be at one with the reality of the patient. Conversely, the more he depends on actual events the more he relies on thinking that depends on a background of sense impression.

In the primitive phase, which Freud regards as dominated by the pleasure principle and from which he excludes the operation of memory, this last being dependent on the prior development of a capacity for thought, the prototype of memory appears to reside in one of the aspects of projective identification. This mechanism, employed to fulfil the duties of thought until thought takes over, appears as an interchange first between mouth and breast and then between introjected mouth and introjected breast. This I regard as reaction between container ♀ and contained ♂. ♀ seems to be the element which is nearest in this phase to the memory. . . .

The impulse to be rid of painful stimuli gives the "content" of the memory (♀) an unsatisfactory quality when one is engaged in the pursuit of truth O. The more successful the memory is in its accumulations the more nearly it approximates to resembling a saturated element saturated with saturated elements. An analyst with such a mind is one who is incapable of learning because he is satisfied. Furthermore, because of its primitive nature, his memory is believed to be filled only with objects giving rise to feelings of pleasure and to be empty of unpleasure components, or vice versa. The attitude towards the "memory" or "unconscious" depends on the idea that it is a container for the "evacuations" of projective identification. Such a "memory" is no equipment for an analyst whose aim is O, as may be seen by considering what is represented by this sign.

It stands for the absolute truth in and of any object; it is assumed that this cannot be known by any human being; it can be known about, its presence can be recognized and felt, but it cannot be known. It is possible to be at one with it. That it exists is an essential postulate of science but it cannot be scientifically discovered. No psychoanalytic discovery is possible without recognition of its existence, at-one-ment with it and evolution. The religious mystics have probably approximated most closely to expression of experience of it. Its existence is as essential to science as to religion. Conversely, the scientific approach is as essential to religion as it is to science and is as ineffectual until a transformation from K → O takes place.

In order to know about the analysand the analyst has recourse to K. Memory is a part of K. Notation (Freud 1911), in the wide sense of the term, is its servant. But memory depends on the senses. It is limited by the limitations of the senses and their subordination to the pleasure–pain principle; memories are therefore fallacious and memory has the defects of its origin in functions of possessiveness and evacuation.

The psychoanalyst is concerned with O, which is incommunicable save through K activity. O may appear to be attainable by K through phenomena, but in fact that is not so. K depends on the evolution of O → K. At-one-ment with O would seem to be possible through the transformation K → O, but it is not so. The transformation O → K depends on ridding K of memory and desire. I turn accordingly to consider "desire." . . .

The desires that can be represented verbally are relatively simple to deal with. For example, the thought occurs that one would like to go abroad for the annual holiday; this can be followed by further ideas, more or less detailed elaborations of the main theme. These thoughts are typical "desires"; they are extremely common and can be harboured almost unaware; they may be reminiscences or anticipations.

The "memories" and "desires" to which I wish to draw attention have the following elements in common: they are ready formulated and therefore require no formulation; they derive from experience gained through the senses; they are evocations of feelings of pleasure or pain; they are formulations "containing" pleasure or pain. . . . [T]heir function is to prevent transformation of the K → O order.

The above characteristics cannot be indulged by the psychoanalyst without impairment of analytic capacity. For any who have been used to remembering what patients say and to desiring their welfare, it will be hard to entertain the harm to analytic intuition that is inseparable from any memories and *any* desires.

The first point is for the analyst to impose on himself a positive discipline of eschewing memory and desire. I do not mean that "forgetting" is enough; what is required is a positive act of refraining from memory and desire.

It may be wondered what state of mind is welcome if desires and memories are not. A term that would express approximately what I need to express is faith—faith that there is an ultimate reality and truth—the unknown, unknowable, "formless infinite." This must be believed of every object of which the personality can be aware; the evolution of ultimate reality (signified by O) has issued in objects of which the individual can be aware. The objects of awareness are aspects of the "evolved" O and are such that the sensuously derived mental functions are adequate to apprehend them. For them faith is not required; for O it is. The analyst is not concerned with such sensuously apprehended objects or with knowledge of such objects. Memories and desires are worthless but inevitable features that he encounters in himself as he works. He is concerned with these objects in his analysand because he is concerned with the working of the analysand's mind. His analysand will express his awareness of O in people and things by formulations representing the intersection of evolutions of O with the evolution of his awareness.

It is not possible to say that such formulations by the analysand are not to be interpreted; no such rule can be laid down far from the situation in which it is to be applied because the criteria for it do not exist. Nor can the criteria be established in the situation of the analysis, for they are part of an ineffable experience. There can be no rules about the nature of the emotional experience that will show that the emotional experience is ripe for interpretation. Instead I can only suggest rules for the analyst that will help him to achieve the frame of mind in which he is receptive to O of the analytic experience. If he is able to be receptive to O, then he may feel impelled to deal with the intersection of the evolution of O with the domain of objects of sense or of formulations based on the senses. Whether he does so or not cannot depend on *rules* for O, or O → K, but only on his ability to be at one with O.

My last sentence represents an "act" of what I have called "faith." It is in my view a scientific statement because for me faith is a scientific state of mind and should be recognized as such. But it must be faith unstained by any element of memory or desire. If it reveals an aspect of O which has to be formulated, then the *transformation* will require the operation of memory and desire. . . .

The discipline that I propose for the analyst, namely avoidance of memory and desire, in the sense in which I have used those terms, increases his ability to exercise acts of faith. An act of faith is peculiar to scientific procedure and must be distinguished from the religious meaning with which it is invested in conversational usage; it becomes apprehensible when it can be represented in and by thought. It must "evolve" before it can be apprehended and it is apprehended when it is a thought just as the artist's O is apprehensible when it has been transformed into a work of art. . . .

Receptiveness achieved by denudation of memory and desire (which is essential to the operation of acts of faith) is essential to the operation of psychoanalysis and other scientific proceedings.

"Opacity of Memory and Desire"

The act of faith (F) depends on disciplined denial of memory and desire. A bad memory is not enough; what is ordinarily called forgetting is as bad as remembering. It is necessary to inhibit dwelling on memories and desires. They are two facets of the same thing: both are composed of elements based on sense impressions; both imply the absence of immediate sensual satisfaction; one supposes a store of sensual objects, the memory being the container, and the other a conjunction of sensually satisfying objects. The invariants are an inside and an outside composed of objects which are sensible. The more the psychoanalyst occupies himself with memory and desire the more his facility for harbouring them increases and the nearer he comes to undermining his capacity for

F. For consider: if his mind is preoccupied with what is or is not said, or with what he does or does not hope, it must mean that he cannot allow the experience to obtrude, particularly that aspect of it which is more than the sound of the patient's voice or the sight of his postures. What sounds the patient makes, or what spectacle he presents, relates to O only insofar as O has evolved into the K domain.

"Container and Contained Transformed"

The discussion of the configuration of container and contained has occupied a considerable space in this book. It may, therefore, seem surprising if, at this stage and in relatively few sentences, I describe what is perhaps the most important mechanism employed by the practising psychoanalyst. It requires less description and is relatively more easily grasped. It is for these reasons only that it occupies what may appear to be an insignificant place in this book. It is derived from Melanie Klein's descriptions of the paranoid-schizoid and depressive positions, and to these the reader should refer.

Here, briefly, is my formulation of this matter as it concerns the practising analyst: In every session the psychoanalyst should be able, if he has followed what I have said in this book, particularly with regard to memory and desire, to be aware of the aspects of the material that, however familiar they may seem to be, relate to what is unknown both to him and to the analysand. Any attempt to cling to what he knows must be resisted for the sake of achieving a state of mind analogous to the paranoid-schizoid position. For this state I have coined the term *patience* to distinguish it from paranoid-schizoid position, which should be left to describe the pathological state for which Melanie Klein used it. I mean the term to retain its association with suffering and tolerance of frustration.

Patience should be retained without "irritable reaching after fact and reason" until a pattern "evolves." This state is the analogue to what Melanie Klein has called the depressive position. For this state I use the term *security.* This I mean to leave with its association of safety and diminished anxiety. I consider that no analyst is entitled to believe that he has done the work required to give an interpretation unless he has passed through both phases—patience and security. The passage from the one to the other may be very short, as in the terminal stages of analysis, or it may be long. Few, if any, psychoanalysts should believe that they are likely to escape the feelings of persecution and depression commonly associated with the pathological states known as the paranoid-schizoid and depressive positions. In short, a sense of achievement of a correct interpretation will be commonly found to be followed almost immediately by a sense of depression. I consider the experience of oscillation between patience and security to be an indication that valuable work is being achieved.

"Prelude to or Substitute for Achievement"

> I had not a dispute but a disquisition with Dilke on various subjects; several things dove-tailed in my mind, and at once it struck me what quality went to form a Man of Achievement, especially in Literature, and which Shakespeare possessed so enormously—I mean Negative Capability, that is, when a man is capable of being in uncertainties, mysteries, doubts, without any irritable reaching after fact and reason.
> John Keats[1]

A number of aspects of the practice of psychoanalysis must now be discussed; I group them under the "Language of Achievement." The quotation from Keats will serve as an introduction to the area to be covered. Language is loosely and widely defined to include behaviour of which it is sometimes said "actions speak louder than words." Set over against and in contrast with the language of achievement I consider the language that is a substitute for, and not a prelude to, action. Language of achievement includes language that is both prelude to action and itself a kind of action; the meeting of psychoanalyst and analysand is itself an example of this language. This discussion is centred on the problem of bringing attention to bear on the realizations to which Freud's theories approximate.

Any session should be judged by comparison with the Keats formulation so as to guard against one commonly unobserved fault leading to

1. Letter to George and Thomas Keats, December 21, 1817 (Murray 1955, p. 261).

analysis "interminable." The fault lies in the failure to observe and is intensified by the inability to appreciate the significance of observation. I have rarely failed to experience hatred of psychoanalysis and its reciprocal, sexualization of psychoanalysis. . . . The human animal has not ceased to be persecuted by his mind and the thoughts usually associated with it—whatever their origin may be. Therefore I do not expect any psychoanalysis properly done to escape the odium inseparable from the mind. Refuge is sure to be sought in mindlessness, sexualization, acting out, and degrees of stupor. The psychoanalyst's attention must not wander from areas of material characterized either by the Language of Substitution or by the Language of Achievement; he must remain sensitive to both. I do not claim that sensitivity can be achieved easily; the mental space available to the analysand and the material observed are subject to so many transformations that such a claim suggests inexperience of the practice of psychoanalysis. The experienced analysand finds dreams a useful standby because psychoanalysts are rightly expected to want to hear them. Current events can be transformed to expression in sadomasochistic terms or near psychopathological jargon; there is no limit to the forms of transformation. Experience leads to an extension of the area over which the language of achievement operates and therefore an extension of the area in which its operation can be recognized.

REFERENCES

Freud, S. (1911). Formulations on two principles of mental functioning. *Standard Edition* 12.
Murray, J. M. (1955). *Keats*. New York: Noonday Press.

VII

KLEIN'S THEORY ELABORATED

The next three authors—Isaacs, Segal, and Rosenfeld—were part of Klein's group whose papers elaborating essential parts of her theory and practice have become cornerstones of Kleinian theory. Betty Joseph was an equally influential member of this group, writing on pathological development, as in her paper, "Addiction to Near Death," but I have chosen to excerpt one of her papers on transference in a later section rather than a theoretical contribution that could well accompany this group. Together, the four were contemporaries of Bion and were involved in a creative exchange of ideas with him and with Klein.

Susan Isaacs's "The Nature and Function of Phantasy" (1948) was written as a chapter for the 1952 book *Developments in Psychoanalysis* by Klein and her colleagues, but was first published in the *International Journal of Psycho-Analysis* in 1948. While the word "phantasy" has the connotation of "not real," what Klein and Isaacs meant was the unconscious thought or organization of feelings that give form to the underlying instinct. The spelling of the word with "ph" was a deliberate device used by Klein to denote this meaning, and her practice became standard among her followers.

This paper gives the classic Kleinian formulation of unconscious phantasy as the link between instinct and object, closely bound up with the process of symbol formation as originally spelled out by Klein in her 1930 paper and as later elaborated by Segal in the paper that follows. The concept is basic to Klein's work, but she never spelled out its formulation in the detail and clarity that Isaacs brings to her discussion. Therefore, this paper has remained as the classic description of unconscious phantasy. The concept of unconscious phantasy as the link between inner and outer reality is necessary in order to follow all subsequent Kleinian lines of thought.

This paper and the following one by Segal together capture the heart of Kleinian conceptualization of the development of thought, the growth in the processes of symbolization and linkage as the mind develops. These ideas are complementary to Bion's contribution, presented in the previous section.

REFERENCE

Joseph, B. (1982). Addiction to near death. *International Journal of Psycho-Analysis* 63:449–456.

34

Susan Isaacs's "The Nature and Function of Phantasy" (1948)

COMMON USAGES OF THE TERM *PHANTASY*

Among psychoanalytic writers, the term has sometimes referred (in line with everyday language) only to *conscious* fantasies, of the nature of daydreams. But Freud's discoveries soon led him to recognize the existence of *unconscious* phantasies. This reference of the word is indispensable. The English translators of Freud adopted a special spelling of the word *phantasy,* with the *ph,* in order to differentiate the psychoanalytical significance of the term, i.e., predominantly or entirely unconscious phantasies, from the popular word *fantasy,* meaning conscious day dreams, fictions, and so on. The psychoanalytical term *phantasy* essentially connotes *unconscious* mental content, which may or may not become conscious.

This meaning of the word has assumed a growing significance, particularly in consequence of the work of Melanie Klein on the early stages of development.

Again, the word *phantasy* has often been used to mark a contrast to *reality,* the latter word being taken as identical with "external" or "material" or "objective" facts. But when external reality is thus called "objective" reality, this makes an implicit assumption which denies to psychical reality its *own objectivity as a mental fact.* Some analysts tend to contrast phantasy with reality in such a way as to undervalue the dynamic importance of phantasy. A related usage, very common in patients, is to think of phantasy as something merely or only imagined, as something unreal, in contrast with what is actual, what *happens* to one. This kind of attitude tends towards a depreciation of psychical reality and of the significance of mental processes as such. . . .

A further point, of importance in our general thesis, is that unconscious phantasy is fully active in the normal, no less than in the neurotic mind. . . . The difference between normal and abnormal lies in the way in which the unconscious phantasies are dealt with, the particular mental processes by means of which they are worked over and modified, and the degree of direct or indirect gratification in the real world and adaptation to it, which these favoured mechanisms allow. . . .

A study of the conclusions arising from the analysis of young children leads to the view that phantasies are the primary content of unconscious mental processes. . . .

Freud has said that ". . . everything conscious has a preliminary unconscious stage. . . ." (1932, p. 562). All mental processes originate in the unconscious and only under certain conditions become conscious. They arise either directly from instinctual needs or in response to external stimuli acting upon instinctual impulses. "We suppose that it (the id) is somewhere in direct contact with somatic processes and takes over from them instinctual needs and gives them *mental expression.*" . . . (1933, p. 98). (My italics.)

Now in the view of the present writer, this mental expression of instinct *is* unconscious phantasy. Phantasy is (in the first instance) the mental corollary, the psychic representative, of instinct. There is no impulse, no instinctual urge or response which is not experienced as unconscious phantasy. . . .

The first mental processes, the psychic representatives of bodily impulses and feelings, i.e., of libidinal and destructive instincts, are to be regarded as the earliest beginning of phantasies. In the mental development of the infant, however, phantasy soon becomes also a means of defence against anxieties, a means of inhibiting and controlling instinctual urges and an expression of reparative wishes as well. The relation between phantasy and wish-fulfilment has always been emphasized, but our experience has shown, too, that most phantasies (like symptoms) also serve various other purposes as well as wish-fulfilment, e.g., denial, reassurance, omnipotent control, reparation, etc. It is, of course, true that, in a wider sense, all these mental processes which aim at diminishing instinctual tension, anxiety, and guilt also serve the aim of wish-fulfilment, but it is useful to discriminate the specific modes of these different processes and their particular aims.

All impulses, all feelings, all modes of defence are experienced in phantasies which give them *mental* life and show their direction and purpose.

A phantasy represents the particular content of the urges or feelings (for example, wishes, fears, anxieties, triumphs, love or sorrow) dominating the mind at the moment. In early life, there is indeed a wealth of unconscious phantasies which take specific form in conjunction with the cathexis of particular bodily zones. . . .

On the basis of those principles of observation and interpretation, which have already been described and are well established by psychoanalytic work, we are able to conclude that when the child shows his desire for his mother's breast, he *experiences* this desire as a specific phantasy—"I want to suck the nipple." If desire is very intense (perhaps on account of anxiety), he is likely to feel: "I want to eat her all up." Perhaps to avert the repetition of loss of her, or for his pleasure, he may feel: "I want to keep her inside me." If he is feeling fond, he may have the phantasy: "I want to stroke her face, to pat and cuddle her." At other times, when he is frustrated or provoked, his impulses may be of an aggressive character: he will experience these as, e.g., "I want to bite the breast; I want to tear her to bits." Or if, e.g., urinary impulses are dominant, he may feel: "I want to drown and burn her." If anxiety is stirred by such aggressive wishes, he may phantasy: "I myself shall be cut or bitten up by mother"; and when his anxiety refers to his internal object, the breast which has been eaten up and kept inside, he may want to eject her and feel: "I want to throw her out of me." . . .

Not merely do these phantasies appear and disappear according to changes in the instinctual urges stirred up by outer circumstances, they also exist together, side by side in the mind, even though they be contradictory; just as in a dream, mutually exclusive wishes may exist and be expressed together.

Not only so: these early mental processes have an omnipotent character. Under the pressure of instinct-tension, the child in his earliest days not only feels, "I want to," but implicitly phantasies, "I *am* doing" this and that to his mother: "I *have* her inside me," when he wants to. The wish and impulse, whether it be love or hate, libidinal or destructive, tends to be felt as actually fulfilling itself, whether with an external or an internal object. This is partly because of the overwhelmingness of his desires and feelings. In these earliest days, his own wishes and impulses fill the whole world at the time when they are felt. It is only slowly that he learns to distinguish between the wish and the deed, between external facts and his feelings about them. The degree of differentiation partly depends upon the stage of development reached at the time, and partly upon the momentary intensity of the desire or emotion. . . .

Many of the familiar difficulties of the young infant (e.g., in feeding and excreting, or his phobias of strangers and anxiety of being left alone, etc.) can best be integrated with well-established analytic views, and their significance more fully understood, if they are seen as manifestations of early phantasy. . . .

PHANTASIES AND WORDS

We must now consider very briefly the relation between phantasies and words.

The primary phantasies, the representatives of the earliest impulses of desire and aggressiveness, are expressed in and dealt with by mental processes far removed from words and conscious relational thinking, and determined by the logic of emotion. At a later period, they may under certain conditions (sometimes in children's spontaneous play, sometimes only in analysis) become capable of being expressed in words.

There is a wealth of evidence to show that phantasies are active in the mind long before language has developed, and that even in the adult they continue to operate alongside and independently of words. Meanings, like feelings, are far older than speech, alike in racial and in childhood experience. . . .

We . . . can occasionally gather quite direct evidence from a young child that a particular phantasy may dominate his mind long before its content can be put into words.

As an example: a little girl of one year and eight months, with poor speech development, saw a shoe of her mother's from which the sole had come loose and was flapping about. The child was horrified, and screamed with terror. For about a week she would shrink away and scream if she saw her mother wearing any shoes at all, and for some time could only tolerate her mother's wearing a pair of brightly coloured house shoes. The particular offending pair was not worn for several months. The child gradually forgot about the terror, and let her mother wear any sort of shoes. At two years and eleven months, however (fifteen months later), she suddenly said to her mother in a frightened voice,

"Where are Mummy's broken shoes?" Her mother hastily said, fearing another screaming attack, that she had sent them away, and the child then commented: "They might have eaten me right up."

The flapping shoe was thus *seen* by the child as a threatening mouth, and responded to as such, at one year and eight months, even though the phantasy could not be put into words. Here, then, we have the clearest possible evidence that a phantasy can be felt, and felt as real, long before it can be expressed in words.

PHANTASIES AND SENSORY EXPERIENCE

Words, then, are a late development in our means of expressing the inner world of our phantasy. By the time a child can use words—even primitive words such as "Baby o-o-oh"—he has already gone through a long and complicated history of psychic experience. . . .

INSTINCT, PHANTASY, AND MECHANISM

We must now consider another important aspect of our problem, that of the relation between instincts, phantasies and mechanisms. . . . To consider *introjection* and *projection*, in particular: these are abstract terms, the names of certain fundamental mechanisms or methods of functioning in the mental life. They refer to such facts as that ideas, impressions, and influences are often taken into the self and become part of it; or that aspects or elements of the self may be disowned and attributed to some person or group of persons, or some part of the external world. These common mental processes . . . are intimately related to certain pervasive phantasies. The phantasies of incorporating (devouring, absorbing, etc.) loved and hated objects, persons or parts of persons, into ourselves are amongst the earliest and most deeply unconscious phantasies, fundamentally oral in character since they are the psychic representatives of the oral impulses. Some of these oral phantasies have been described above, for example: "I want to take and I am taking her (mother or breast) into me." The distinction should be kept clear between a specific phantasy of incorporating an object and the general mental mechanism of introjection. The latter has a far wider reference than the former, although so intimately related to it. To understand the relationship between phantasies and mechanisms, we must look more closely at the relation of both to instinct. In our view, phantasy is the operative link between instinct and ego mechanism.

An instinct is conceived of as a borderline psychosomatic process. It has a bodily aim, directed to concrete external objects. It has a representative in the mind which we call a "phantasy." Every human activity derives from some instinct; it is only through the phantasy of what would fulfil our instinctual needs that we are enabled to attempt to realize them in external reality.

Although themselves psychic phenomena, phantasies are primarily about bodily aims, pains, and pleasures, directed to objects of some kind. When contrasted with external and bodily realities, the phantasy, like other mental activities, is a figment, since it cannot be touched or handled or seen; yet it is real in the experience of the subject. It is a true mental function and it has real effects, not only in the inner world of the mind but also in the external world of the subject's bodily development and behaviour, and hence of other people's minds and bodies. . . .

How does anyone—whether psychologist or other person—come . . . to realize that what he has actually "taken inside," his internal object, is an image and not a bodily concrete object? By a long and complex process of development. This, in broad outline, must include the following steps, among others:

1. The earliest phantasies are built mainly upon oral impulses, bound up with taste, smell, touch (of the lips and mouth), kinaesthetic, visceral, and other somatic sensations; these are at first more closely linked with the experience of "taking things in" (sucking and swallowing) than with anything else. The visual elements are relatively small.
2. These sensations (and images) are a bodily experience, at first scarcely capable of being related to an external, spatial object. (The kinaesthetic, genital, and visceral elements are not usually so referred.) They give the phantasy a concrete bodily quality, a "me-ness," experienced *in* the body. On this level, images are scarcely if at all distinguishable from actual sensations and external perceptions. The skin is not yet felt to be a boundary between inner and outer reality.
3. The visual element in perception slowly increases, becoming suffused with tactile experience and spatially differentiated. The early

visual images remain largely "eidetic" in quality—probably up to 3 or 4 years of age. They are intensely vivid, concrete, and often confused with perceptions. Moreover, they remain for long intimately associated with somatic responses: they are very closely linked with emotions and tend to immediate action. (Many of the details referred to here so summarily have been well worked out by psychologists.)

4. During the period of development when the visual elements in perception (and in corresponding images) begin to predominate over the somatic, becoming differentiated and spatially integrated, and thus making clearer the distinction between the inner and the outer worlds, the concrete bodily elements in the total experience of perceiving (and phantasying) largely undergo *repression.* The visual, externally referred elements in phantasy become relatively de-emotionalized, de-sexualized, independent, in consciousness, of bodily ties. They become "images" in the narrower sense, representations "in the mind" (but not, consciously, incorporations in the body) of external objects recognized to be such. It is "realized" that the objects are outside the mind, but their images are "in the mind."
5. Such images, however, draw their power to affect the mind by being "in it," i.e., their influence upon feelings, behaviour, character, and personality, upon the mind as a whole, is founded upon *their repressed unconscious somatic associates* in the unconscious whole of wish and phantasy, which *form the link with the id,* and which do mean, in unconscious phantasy, that the objects to which they refer are believed to be inside the body, to be incorporated. . . .

PHANTASY, MEMORY-IMAGES, AND REALITY

[T]he intellectual functions of judgment and reality testing "are derived from the interplay of the primary instinctual impulses" (Freud 1925). If, then, phantasy be the "language" of these primary instinctual impulses, it can be assumed that phantasy enters into the earliest development of the ego in its relation to reality, and supports the testing of reality and the development of knowledge of the external world.

We have already seen that the earliest phantasies are bound up with sensations and affects. These sensations, no matter how selectively overemphasized they may be under the pressure of affect, bring the experiencing mind into contact with external reality, as well as expressing impulses and wishes.

The external world forces itself upon the attention of the child, in one way or another, early and continuously. The first psychical experiences result from the massive and varied stimuli of birth and the first intake and expulsion of breath—followed presently by the first feed. These considerable experiences during the first twenty-four hours must already evoke the first mental activity, and provide material for both phantasy and memory. Phantasy and reality-testing are both in fact present from the earliest days.[1]

External perceptions begin to influence mental processes at a certain point (actually from birth on, though at first they are not appreciated as external). At first the psyche deals with most external stimuli, as with the instinctual ones, by means of the primitive mechanisms of introjection and projection. Observation of the infant during the first few weeks shows that insofar as the external world does not satisfy our wishes, or frustrates or interferes with us, it is at once hated and rejected. We may then fear it and watch it and attend to it, in order to defend ourselves against it; but not until it is in some degree libidinized through its connections with oral satisfactions, and thus receives some measure of love, can it be played with and learnt about and understood.

We conclude with Freud that the disappointingness of hallucinatory satisfaction is the first spur to some degree of adaptation to reality. . . .

In their developed forms, phantasy thinking and reality thinking are distinct mental processes, different modes of obtaining satisfaction. The fact that they have a distinct character when fully developed, however, does not necessarily imply that reality thinking *operates* quite independently of unconscious phantasy. It is not merely that they "blend and interweave"; their relationship is something less adventitious than this. In our view, *reality-thinking cannot operate without concurrent and supporting unconscious phantasies*, e.g., we continue to "take things in"

1. An appreciation of what external facts, e.g., the way he is fed and handled in the very beginning, and later the emotional attitudes and conduct of both his parents, or his actual experience of loss or change, mean to the child in terms of his phantasy life gives a greater weight to real experiences than would usually be accorded by those who have no understanding of their phantasy value to the child. Such actual experiences in early life have a profound effect upon the character of his phantasies as they develop, and therefore upon their ultimate outcome in his personality, social relationships, intellectual gifts or inhibitions, neurotic symptoms, etc.

with our ears, to "devour" with our eyes, to "read, mark, learn, and inwardly digest" throughout life.

These conscious metaphors represent unconscious psychic reality. It is a familiar fact that all early learning is based upon the oral impulses. The first seeking and mouthing and grasping of the breast is gradually shifted on to other objects, the hand and eye only slowly attaining independence of the mouth, as instruments of exploration and of knowing the outer world. . . .

In her papers "Infant Analysis" (1926) and "The Importance of Symbol Formation in the Development of the Ego" (1930), Klein took up Ferenczi's view that (primary) identification, which is the forerunner of symbolism, "arises out of the baby's endeavour to rediscover in every object his own organs and their functioning" (Klein 1930), and also Ernest Jones's view that the pleasure principle makes it possible for two separate objects to be equated because of an affective bond of interest. Klein showed, by means of illuminating clinical material, how the primary symbolic function of external objects enables phantasy to be elaborated by the ego, allows sublimations to develop in play and manipulation, and builds a bridge from the inner world to interest in the outer world and knowledge of physical objects and events. His pleasurable interest in his body, his discoveries and experiments in this direction, are clearly shown in the play of an infant of three or four months. In this play he manifests (among other mechanisms) this process of symbol formation, bound up with those phantasies which we later discover in analysis to have been operating at the time. *The external physical world is in fact libidinized largely through the process of symbol-formation.* . . .

In particular, observation made it clear that spontaneous make-believe play creates and fosters the first forms of "as if" thinking. In such play, the child re-creates selectively those elements in past situations which can embody his emotional or intellectual need of the present, and adapts the details moment-by-moment to the present play situation. This ability to evoke the *past* in imaginative play seems to be closely connected with the growth of the power to evoke the *future* in constructive hypothesis, and to develop the consequences of "ifs." The child's make-believe play is thus significant not only for the adaptive and creative intentions which when fully developed mark out the artist, the novelist and the poet, but also for the sense of reality, the scientific attitude, and the growth of hypothetical reasoning.

The argument of this paper may now be summarized. The concept of *phantasy* has gradually widened in psychoanalytic thought. It now requires clarification and explicit expansion in order to integrate all the relevant facts.

Phantasies are the primary content of unconscious mental processes. Unconscious phantasies are primarily about bodies, and represent instinctual aims towards objects. These phantasies are, in the first instance, the psychic representatives of libidinal and destructive instincts; early in development they also become elaborated into defences, as well as wish-fulfilments and anxiety contents.

Freud's postulated *hallucinatory wish-fulfilment* and his *primary introjection* and *projection* are the basis of the phantasy life.

Through external experience, phantasies become elaborated and capable of expression, but they do not depend solely upon external experience for their existence. Phantasies are not dependent upon words, although they may under certain conditions be capable of expression in words. The earliest phantasies are experienced in sensations; later, they take the form of plastic images and dramatic representations.

Phantasies have both psychic and bodily effects, e.g., in conversion symptoms, bodily qualities, character and personality, neurotic symptoms, inhibitions, and sublimations.

Unconscious phantasies form the operative link between *instincts* and *mechanisms*. When studied in detail, every variety of ego mechanism can be seen to arise from specific sorts of phantasy, which in the last resort have their origin in instinctual impulses. "The ego is a differentiated part of the id." A mechanism is an abstract general term describing certain mental processes which are experienced by the subject as unconscious phantasies.

Adaptation to reality and reality thinking require the support of concurrent unconscious phantasies. Observation of the ways in which knowledge of the external world develops shows how the child's phantasy contributes to his learning.

Unconscious phantasies exert a continuous influence throughout life, both in normal and neurotic people, the differences lying in the specific character of the dominant phantasies, the desire or anxiety associated with them and their interplay with each other and with external reality.

REFERENCES

Freud, S. (1925). Negation. *International Journal of Psycho-Analysis* 6:369.
——(1932). *The Interpretation of Dreams.* Revised English translation. George Allen and Unwin.
——(1933). *New Introductory Lectures on Psycho-Analysis.* London: Hogarth.
Klein, M. (1926). Infant analysis. *International Journal* of *Psycho-Analysis* 7.
——(1930). The importance of symbol formation in the development of the ego. *International Journal of Psycho-Analysis* 11.

35

Hanna Segal's "Notes on Symbol Formation" (1957)

This paper is an elaboration and clarification of Klein's 1930 contribution on symbol formation as an activity of the ego essential to development. The outstanding clarity of this paper also makes it useful in summarizing the developmental sequence in the move from the paranoid-schizoid position to the depressive position, and the change in the quality of projective identification and communication that occurs in normality but fails to occur when growth is blocked.

The understanding and interpretation of unconscious symbolism is one of the main tools of the psychologist. Often he is faced with the task of understanding and recognizing the meaning not only of a particular symbol but also of the whole process of symbol formation. This applies particularly to work with patients who show a disturbance or inhibition in the formation or free use of symbols, as for instance, psychotic or schizoid patients.

To give a very elementary example from two patients. One—whom I will call A—was a schizophrenic in a mental hospital. He was once asked by his doctor why it was that since his illness he had stopped playing the violin. He replied with some violence: "Why? do you expect me to masturbate in public?"

Another patient, B, dreamt one night that he and a young girl were playing a violin duet. He had associations to fiddling, masturbating, etc., from which it emerged clearly that the violin represented his genital and playing the violin represented a masturbation phantasy of a relation with the girl.

Here then are two patients who apparently use the same symbols in the same situation—a violin representing the male genital, and playing the violin representing masturbation. The way in which the symbols function, however, is very different. For A, the violin had become so completely equated with his genital that to touch it in public became impossible. For B, playing the violin in his waking life was an important sublimation. We might say that the main difference between them is that for A the symbolic meaning of the violin was conscious, for B unconscious. I do not think, however, that this was the most important difference between the two patients. In the case of B, the fact that the meaning of the dream became completely conscious had in no way prevented him from using his violin. In A, on the other hand, there were many symbols operating in his unconscious in the same way in which the violin was used on the conscious level. . . .

The main difference between the first and second patient quoted in their use of the violin as the symbol for the male genital was not that in the one case the symbol was conscious and in the other unconscious, but that in the first case it was felt to *be* the genital, and in the second to *represent* it. . . .

In 1930, Melanie Klein raised the problem of inhibition in symbol formation. She described an autistic little boy of 4, Dick, who could not talk or play; he showed no affection or anxiety, and took no interest in his surroundings apart from door handles, stations, and trains, which seemed to fascinate him. His analysis revealed that the child was terrified of his aggression towards his mother's body, and of her body which he felt had turned bad because of his attacks on it: because of the strength of his anxieties he had erected powerful defences against his phantasies about her. There resulted a paralysis of his phantasy life and of symbol formation. He had not endowed the world around him with any symbolic meaning and therefore took no interest in it. Melanie Klein came to the conclusion that if symbolization does not occur, the whole development of the ego is arrested.

If we accept this view it follows that the processes of symbolization require a new and more careful study. To begin with, I find it helpful, following Morris (1938), to consider symbolizing as a *three*-term relation, i.e., a relation between the thing symbolized, the thing functioning as a symbol, and a *person* for whom the one represents the other. In psychological terms, symbolism would be a relation between the ego, the object, and the symbol.

Symbol formation is an activity of the ego attempting to deal with the anxieties stirred by its relation to the object. That is primarily the fear of bad objects and the fear of the loss or inaccessibility of good objects. Disturbances in the ego's relation to objects are reflected in disturbances of symbol formation. In particular, disturbances in differentiation between ego and object lead to disturbances in differentiation between the symbol and the object symbolized and therefore to concrete thinking characteristic of psychoses.

Symbol formation starts very early, probably as early as object relations, but changes its character and functions with the changes in the character of the ego and object relations. Not only the actual content of the symbol, but the very way in which symbols are formed and used seem to me to reflect very precisely the ego's state of development and its way of dealing with its objects. If symbolism is seen as a three-term relation, problems of symbol formation must always be examined in the context of the ego's relation with its objects.

I shall try to describe briefly some basic attitudes of the ego to the objects, and the way in which I think they influence the processes of symbol formation and the functioning of symbolism. My description is based here on Melanie Klein's (1930) concept of the paranoid-schizoid position and of the depressive position. According to her, the oral stage of development falls into two phases, the earlier being the point of fixation of the schizophrenic group of illnesses, the later that of the manic-depressive. In my description, which will of necessity be very schematic, I shall select only those points which are directly relevant to the problem of symbol formation.

The chief characteristics of the infant's first object relations are the following. The object is seen as split into an ideally good and a wholly bad one. The aim of the ego is total union with the ideal object and total annihilation of the bad one, as well as of the bad parts of the self. Omnipotent thinking is paramount and reality sense intermittent and precarious. The concept of absence hardly exists. Whenever the state of union with the ideal object is not fulfilled, what is experienced is not absence; the ego feels assailed by the counterpart of the good object—the bad object, or objects. It is the time of the hallucinatory wish-fulfilment, described by Freud, when the thought creates objects which are then felt to be available. According to Melanie Klein, it is also the time of the bad hallucinosis when, if the ideal conditions are not fulfilled, the bad object is equally hallucinated and felt as real.

A leading defence mechanism in this phase is projective identification. In projective identification, the subject in phantasy projects large parts of himself into the object, and the object becomes identified with the parts of the self that it is felt to contain. Similarly, internal objects are projected outside and identified with parts of the external world which come to represent them. These first projections and identifications are the beginning of the process of symbol formation.

The early symbols, however, are not felt by the ego to be symbols or substitutes, but to be the original object itself. They are so different from symbols formed later that I think they deserve a name of their own. In my paper of 1950 I suggested the term *equation*. This word, however, differentiates them too much from the word *symbol* and I would like to alter it here to *symbolic equation*.

The symbolic equation between the original object and the symbol in the internal and the external world is, I think, the basis of the schizophrenic's concrete thinking where substitutes for the original objects, or parts of the self, can be used quite freely, but, as in the two examples of schizophrenic patients which I quoted, they are hardly different from the original object: they are felt and treated as though they were *identical* with it. This nondifferentiation between the thing symbolized and the symbol is part of a disturbance in the relation between the ego and the object. Parts of the ego and internal objects are projected into an object and identified with it. The differentiation between the self and the object is obscured. Then, since a part of the ego is confused with the object, the symbol—which is a creation and a function of the ego—becomes, in turn, confused with the object which is symbolized.

Where such symbolic equations are formed in relation to bad objects, an attempt is made to deal with them as with the original object, that is by total annihilation and scotomization. In Melanie Klein's paper (1930) quoted above, it seemed as though Dick had formed no symbolic relations to the external world. The paper was written very early on in Dick's analysis, and I wonder, on the basis of my own experience with schizophrenics, whether it did not, perhaps, subsequently transpire that Dick had formed numerous symbolic equations in the external world. If so, then these would have carried the full anxiety experienced in relation to the original persecutory or guilt-producing object: his mother's body, so that he had had to deal with them by annihilation, that is by total withdrawal of interest. Some of the symbols which he had formed as his analysis progressed, and he started to show an interest in certain objects in the consulting room, seemed to have had the characteristics of such symbolic equations. For instance, when he saw some pencil shavings he said: "Poor Mrs. Klein." To him the shavings were Mrs. Klein cut into bits. . . .

The development of the ego and the changes in the ego's relation to its objects are gradual, and so is the change from the early symbols, which I called symbolic equations, to the fully formed symbols in the depressive position. It is therefore only for the sake of clarity that I shall make here a very sharp differentiation between the ego's relations in the paranoid-schizoid position and in the depressive position respectively, and an equally sharp differentiation between the symbolic equations and the symbols which are formed during and after the depressive position.

When the depressive position has been reached, the main characteristic of object relation is that the object is felt as a whole object. In connexion with this there is a greater degree of awareness and differentiation of the separateness between the ego and the object. At the same time, since the object is recognized as a whole, ambivalence is more fully experienced. The ego in this phase is struggling with its ambivalence and its relation to the object is characterized by guilt, fear of loss or actual experience of loss and mourning, and a striving to re-create the object. At the same time, processes of introjection become more pronounced than those of projection, in keeping with the striving to retain the object inside as well as to repair, restore, and re-create it.

In favourable circumstances of normal development, after repeated experiences of loss, recovery, and re-creation, a good object is securely established in the ego. Three changes in relation to the object, as the ego develops and integrates, affect fundamentally the ego's reality sense. With an increased awareness of ambivalence, the lessening of the intensity of projection, and the growing differentiation between the self and the object, there is a growing sense of reality both internal and external. The internal world becomes differentiated from the external world. Omnipotent thinking, characteristic of the earlier phase, gradually gives way to more realistic thinking. Simultaneously, and as part of the same process, there is a certain modification of the primary instinctual aims. Earlier on, the aim was to possess the object totally if felt as good, or to annihilate it totally if felt as bad. With the recognition that the good and the bad objects are one, both these instinctual aims are gradually modified. The ego is increasingly concerned with saving the object from its aggression and possessiveness. And this implies a certain degree of inhibition of the direct instinctual aims, both aggressive and libidinal.

This situation is a powerful stimulus for the creation of symbols, and symbols acquire new functions which change their character. The symbol is needed to displace aggression from the original object, and in that way to lessen the guilt and the fear of loss. The symbol is here not an equivalent of the original object, since the aim of the displacement is to save the object, and the guilt experienced in relation to it is far less than that due to an attack on the original object. The symbols are also created in the *internal* world as a means of restoring, re-creating, recapturing, and owning again the original object. But in keeping with the increased reality sense, they are now felt as created by the ego and therefore never completely equated with the original object.

Freud (1923) postulates that a modification of instinctual aims is the basic precondition of sublimation. In my view the formation of symbols in the depressive position necessitates some inhibition of direct instinctual aims in relation to the original object and therefore the symbols become available for sublimation. The symbols, created internally, can then be reprojected into the external world, endowing it with symbolic meaning.

The capacity to experience loss and the wish to re-create the object within oneself gives the individual the unconscious freedom in the use of symbols. And as the symbol is acknowledged as a creation of the subject, unlike the symbolic equation, it can be freely used by the subject.

When a substitute in the external world is used as a symbol it may be used more freely than the original object, since it is not fully identified with it. Insofar, however, as it is distinguished from the original object it is also recognized as an object in itself. Its own properties are recognized, respected, and used, because no confusion with the original object blurs the characteristics of the new object used as a symbol.

In an analysis we can sometimes follow very clearly the changes in the symbolic relations in the patient's attitude to his faeces. On the schizoid level the patient expects his faeces to be the ideal breast; if he cannot maintain this idealization his faeces become persecutory, they are ejected as a bitten-up, destroyed, and persecuting breast. If the patient tries to symbolize his faeces in the external world the symbols in the external world are felt to be faeces—persecutors. No sublimation of anal activities can occur under these conditions.

On the depressive level, the feeling is that the introjected breast has been destroyed by the ego and can be re-created by the ego. The faeces may then be felt as something created by the ego out of the object and can be valued as a symbol of the breast and at the same time as a good product of the ego's own creativity.

When this symbolic relation to faeces and other body products has been established a projection can occur on to substances in the external world such as paint, plasticine, clay, etc., which can then be used for sublimation.

When this stage of development has been achieved, it is of course not irreversible. If the anxieties are too strong, a regression to a paranoid-schizoid position can occur at any stage of the individual's development and projective identification may be resorted to as a defence against anxiety. Then symbols which have been developed and have been functioning as symbols in sublimation, revert to concrete symbolic equations. This is mainly due to the fact that in massive projective identification the ego becomes again confused with the object, the symbol becomes confused with the thing symbolized and therefore turns into an equation. . . .

I should like at this point to summarize what I mean by the terms *symbolic equation* and *symbol,* respectively, and the conditions under which they arise. In the symbolic equation, the symbol substitute is felt to *be* the original object. The substitute's own properties are not recognized or admitted. The symbolic equation is used to deny the absence of the ideal object, or to control a persecuting one. It belongs to the earliest stages of development.

The symbol proper, available for sublimation and furthering the development of the ego, is felt to *represent* the object; its own characteristics are recognized, respected, and used. It arises when depressive feelings predominate over the paranoid-schizoid ones, when separation from the object, ambivalence, guilt, and loss can be experienced and tolerated. The symbol is used not to deny but to overcome loss. When the mechanism of projective identification is used as a defence against depressive anxieties, symbols already formed and functioning as symbols may revert to symbolic equations.

Symbol formation governs the capacity to communicate, since all communication is made by *means* of symbols. When schizoid disturbances in object relations occur, the capacity to communicate is similarly disturbed, first because the differentiation between the subject and the object is blurred, second because the means of communication are lacking since symbols are felt in a concrete fashion and are therefore unavailable for purposes of communication. One of the ever-recurring difficulties in the analysis of psychotic patients is this difficulty of communication. Words, for instance, whether the analyst's or the patient's, are felt to be objects or actions, and cannot be easily used for purposes of communication.

Symbols are needed not only in communication with the external world, but also in internal communication. Indeed, it could be asked what is meant when we speak of people being well in touch with their unconscious. It is not that they have consciously primitive phantasies, like those which become evident in their analyses, but merely that they have some awareness of their own impulses and feelings. However, I think that we mean more than this; we mean that they have actual *communication* with their unconscious phantasies. And this, like any other form of communication, can only be done with the help of symbols. So that in people who are "well in touch with themselves" there is a constant free symbol-formation, whereby they can be consciously aware and in control of *symbolic expressions* of the underlying primitive phantasies. The difficulty of dealing with schizophrenic and schizoid patients lies not only in that they cannot communicate with us, but even more in that they cannot communicate with themselves. Any part of their ego may be split off from any other part with no communication available between them. . . .

And this takes me to the last point of my paper. I think that one of the important tasks performed by the ego in the depressive position is that of dealing not with depressive anxieties alone, but also with unresolved earlier conflicts. A new achievement belonging to the depressive position, the capacity to symbolize and in that way to lessen anxiety and resolve conflict is used in order to deal with the *earlier* unresolved conflicts by symbolizing them. Anxieties, which could not be dealt with earlier on because of the extreme concreteness of the experience with the object and the object substitutes in symbolic equations, can gradually be dealt with by the more integrated ego by symbolization, and in that way they can be integrated. In the depressive position and later, symbols are formed not only of the whole destroyed and re-created object characteristic of the depressive position, but also of the split object—extremely good and extremely bad—and not only of the whole object but also of part-objects. Some of the paranoid and ideal object relations and anxieties may be symbolized as part of the integrative process in the depressive position. . . .

The word *symbol* comes from the Greek term for throwing together, bringing together, integrating. The process of symbol formation is, I think, a continuous process of bringing together and integrating the internal with the external, the subject with the object, and the earlier experiences with the later ones.

REFERENCES

Freud, S. (1923). The ego and the id. *Standard Edition* 19.

Klein, M. (1930). On the Importance of symbol formation in the development of the ego. *Contributions to Psycho-Analysis*, 1921–45, pp. 219–232. London: Hogarth.

Morris, C. (1938). Foundations of the theory of signs. *International Encyclopedia of Unified Science*. Chicago: University of Chicago Press.

Segal, H. (1950). Some aspects of the analysis of a schizophrenic. *International Journal of Psycho-Analysis* 31.

36

Herbert Rosenfeld's "A Clinical Approach to the Psychoanalytic Theory of the Life and Death Instincts: An Investigation into the Aggressive Aspects of Narcissism" (1971)

Herbert Rosenfeld's early work concentrated on the elucidation of Klein's ideas on primitive mental mechanisms in the treatment of severely disturbed patients, including those hospitalized for psychosis. He also investigated the role of the death instinct in destructive narcissism based on perverse idealization of the bad self, and the kind of confusional states and impasse that can develop between patient and therapist as a result of chronic misunderstanding or collusion in the interplay of transference and countertransference. Rosenfeld and other Kleinians (for instance, Joseph and Steiner, whose work is excerpted later in this volume) have explored the importance of these primitive mechanisms both in severe pathology and in the treatment of higher level neurotic patients.

The following excerpt from Rosenfeld's landmark 1971 paper contains his contribution on destructive narcissism. This paper explores a theme many Kleinians have pursued concerning defensive or pathological organizations. John Steiner extends this tradition in his contribution, which outlines a modern formulation of these states in which pathological organizations represent a problematic position lodged between paranoid-schizoid and depressive positions.

In my previous work on narcissism (1964) I stressed the projective and introjective identification of self and object (fusion of self and object) in narcissistic states, which act as a defence against any recognition of separateness between the self and objects. Awareness of separation immediately leads to feelings of dependence on an object and therefore to inevitable frustrations. However, dependence also stimulates envy, when the goodness of the object is recognized. Aggressiveness towards objects therefore seems inevitable in giving up the narcissistic position and it appears that the strength and persistence of omnipotent narcissistic object relations is closely related to the strength of the envious destructive impulses.

In studying narcissism in greater detail it seems to me essential to differentiate between the libidinal and the destructive aspects of narcissism. In considering narcissism from the libidinal aspect one can see that the over-valuation of the self plays a central role, based mainly on the idealization of the self. Self-idealization is maintained by omnipotent introjective and projective identifications with good objects and their qualities. In this way the narcissist feels that everything that is valuable relating to external objects and the outside world is part of him or is omnipotently controlled by him.

Similarly, when considering narcissism from the destructive aspect, we find that again self-idealization plays a central role, but now it is the idealization of the omnipotent destructive parts of the self. They are directed both against any positive libidinal object relationship and any libidinal part of the self which experiences need for an object and the desire to depend on it. The destructive omnipotent parts of the self often remain disguised or they may be silent and split off, which obscures their existence and gives the impression that they have no relationship to the external world. In fact they have a very powerful effect in preventing dependent object relations and in keeping external objects permanently devalued, which accounts for the apparent indifference of the narcissistic individual towards external objects and the world.

In the narcissism of most patients libidinal and destructive aspects exist side by side but the violence of the destructive impulses varies. In the narcissistic states where the libidinal aspects predominate destructiveness becomes apparent as soon as the omnipotent self-idealization is threatened by contact with an object which is perceived as separate from the self. The patient feels humiliated and defeated by the revelation that it is the external object which, in reality, contains the valuable qualities which he had attributed to his own creative powers. In analysis one observes that when the patient's feelings of resentment and revenge at being robbed of his omnipotent narcissism diminish, envy is consciously experienced, since it is then that he becomes aware of the analyst as a valuable external person.

When the destructive aspects predominate, the envy is more violent and appears as a wish to destroy the analyst as the object who is the real source of life and goodness. At the same time violent self-destructive impulses appear, and these I want to consider in more detail. In terms of the infantile situation the narcissistic patient wants to believe that he has given life to himself and is able to feed and look after himself. When he is faced with the reality of being dependent on the analyst, standing for the parents, particularly the mother, he would prefer to die, to be nonexistent, to deny the fact of his birth, and also to destroy his analytic progress and insight representing the child in himself, which he feels the analyst, representing the parents, has created. Frequently at this point the patient wants to give up the analysis but more often he acts out in a self-destructive way by spoiling his professional success and his personal relations. Some of these patients become suicidal and the desire to die, to disappear into oblivion, is expressed quite openly and death is idealized as a solution to all problems.

As the individual seems determined to satisfy a desire to die and to disappear into nothing which resembles Freud's description of the "pure" death instinct, one might consider that we are dealing in these states with the death instinct in complete defusion. However, analytically one can observe that the state is caused by the activity of destructive envious parts of the self which become severely split off and defused from the libidinal caring self which seems to have disappeared. The whole self becomes temporarily identified with the destructive self, which aims to triumph over life and creativity represented by the parents and the analyst by destroying the dependent libidinal self experienced as the child.

The patient often believes that he has destroyed his caring self, his love, for ever and there is nothing anybody can do to change the situation. When this problem is worked through in the transference and some libidinal part of the patient is experienced as coming alive, concern for the analyst, standing for the mother, appears, which mitigates the destructive impulses and lessens the dangerous defusion.

There are some narcissistic patients where defused destructive impulses seem to be constantly active and dominate the whole of their personality and object relations. They express their feelings in an only slightly disguised way by devaluing the analyst's work with their persistent indifference, tricky repetitive behaviour and sometimes open belittlement. In this way they assert their superiority over the analyst representing life and creativity by wasting or destroying his work, understanding and satisfaction. They feel superior in being able to control and withhold those parts of themselves which want to depend on the analyst as a helpful person. They behave as if the loss of any love object including the analyst would leave them cold and even stimulate a feeling of triumph. Such patients occasionally experience shame and some persecutory anxiety but only minimal guilt, because very little of their libidinal self is kept alive. It appears that these patients have dealt with the struggle between their destructive and libidinal impulses by trying to get rid of their concern and love for their objects by killing their loving dependent self and identifying themselves almost entirely with the destructive narcissistic part of the self which provides them with a sense of superiority and self-admiration.

One narcissistic patient, who kept relations to external objects and the analyst dead and empty by constantly deadening any part of his self that attempted object relations, dreamt of a small boy who was in a comatose condition, dying from some kind of poisoning. He was lying on a bed in the courtyard and was endangered by the hot midday sun which was beginning to shine on him. The patient was standing near to the boy but did nothing to move or protect him. He only felt critical and superior to the doctor treating the child, since it was he who should have seen that the child was moved into the shade. The patient's previous behaviour and associations made it clear that the dying boy stood for his dependent libidinal self which he kept in a dying condition by preventing it from getting help and nourishment from the analyst. I showed him that even when he came close to realizing the seriousness of his mental state, experienced as a dying condition, he did not lift a finger to help himself or to help the analyst to make a move towards saving him, because he was using the killing of his infantile dependent self to triumph over the analyst and to show him up as a failure. The dream illustrates clearly that the destructive narcissistic state is maintained in power by keeping the libidinal infantile self in a constant dead or dying condition.

Occasionally the analytic interpretations penetrated the narcissistic shell and the patient felt more alive. He then admitted that he would like to improve but soon he felt his mind drifting away from the consulting room and became so detached and sleepy that he could scarcely keep awake. There was an enormous resistance, almost like a stone wall, which prevented any examination of the situation, but gradually it became clear that the patient felt pulled away from any closer contact with the analyst, because as soon as he felt helped there was not only the danger that he might experience a greater need for the analyst but he feared that he would attack him with sneering and belittling thoughts. Contact with the analyst meant a weakening of the narcissistic omnipotent superiority of the patient and the experience of a conscious feeling of overwhelming envy which was strictly avoided by the detachment.

The destructive narcissism of these patients appears often highly organized, as if one were dealing with a powerful gang dominated by a leader who controls all the members of the gang to see that they support one another in making the criminal destructive work more effective and powerful. However, the narcissistic organization not only increases the strength of the destructive narcissism, but it has a defensive purpose to keep itself in power and so maintain the *status quo*. The main aim seems to be to prevent the weakening of the organization and to control the members of the gang so that they will not desert the destructive organization and join the positive parts of the self or betray the secrets of the gang to the police, the protecting superego, standing for the helpful analyst, who might be able to save the patient. Frequently when a patient of this kind makes progress in the analysis and wants to change he dreams of being attacked by members of the Mafia or adolescent delinquents and a negative therapeutic reaction sets in. This narcissistic organization is in my experience not primarily directed against guilt and anxiety, but seems to have the purpose of maintaining the idealization and superior power of the destructive narcissism. To change, to receive help, implies weakness and is experienced as wrong or as failure by the destructive narcissistic organization which provides the patient with his sense of superiority. In cases of this kind there is a most determined chronic resistance to analysis and only the very detailed exposure of the system enables analysis to make some progress. . . .

I shall now briefly report some case material from a narcissistic neurotic patient to illustrate the existence of a split-off, omnipotent, destructive part of himself which became more conscious during analysis and lost some of its violence. The patient is an unmarried business man of 37, who has been in treatment for several years. He came to analysis because of character problems and was consciously very determined to have analysis and to cooperate in it. However, there was a chronic resistance to the analysis, which was very elusive and repetitive. The patient had to leave London occasionally for short business trips and he often returned too late on Mondays and so missed either part or the whole of his session. He frequently met women during these trips and brought to analysis many of the problems which arose with them. It was, of course, clear from the beginning that some acting out was taking place but only when he regularly reported murderous activities in his dreams after such weekends did it become apparent that violently destructive attacks against the analysis and the analyst were hidden in the acting-out behaviour. The patient was at first reluctant to accept that the acting out of the weekend was killing and therefore blocking the progress of the analysis, but gradually he changed his behaviour and the analysis became more effective and he reported considerable improvement in some of his personal relationships and his business activities. At the same time he began to complain that his sleep was frequently disturbed and that he woke up during the night with violent palpitations which kept him awake for several hours. During these anxiety attacks he felt that his hands did not belong to him; they seemed violently destructive as if they wanted to destroy something by tearing it up, and were too powerful for him to control so that he had to give in to them. He then dreamt of a very powerful arrogant man who was nine feet tall and who insisted that he had to be absolutely obeyed. His associations made it clear that this man stood for a part of himself and related to the destructive overpowering feelings in his hands which he could not resist. I interpreted that he regarded the omnipotent destructive part of himself as a superman who was nine feet tall and much too powerful for him to disobey. He had disowned this omnipotent self, which explained the estrangement of his hands during the nightly attacks. I further explained this split-off self as an infantile omnipotent part which claimed that it was not an infant but stronger and more powerful than all the adults, particularly his mother and father and now the analyst. His adult self was so completely taken in and therefore weakened by this omnipotent assertion that he felt powerless to fight the destructive impulses at night. The patient reacted to the interpretation with surprise and relief and reported after some days that he felt more able to control his hands at night. He became gradually more aware that the destructive impulses at night had some connection with analysis because they increased after any success which could be attributed to it. Thus he saw that the wish to tear at himself was related to a wish to tear out and destroy a part of himself which depended on the analyst and valued him. Simultaneously the aggressive narcissistic impulses which had been split off became more conscious during analytic sessions and he sneered saying: "Here you have to sit all day wasting your time." He felt that he was the important person and he should be free to do anything he wanted to do, however cruel and hurting this might be to others and himself. He was particularly enraged by the insight and understanding which the analysis gave him. He hinted that his rage was related to wanting to reproach me for helping him, because this interfered with his omnipotent acting-out behaviour. He then reported a dream, that he was running a long-distance race and he was working very hard at it. However, there was a young woman who did not believe in anything that he was doing. She was unprincipled, nasty, and did everything to interfere and mislead him. There was a reference to the woman's brother, who was called "Mundy." He was much more aggressive than his sister and he appeared in the dream snarling like a wild beast, even at her. It was reported in the dream that this brother had had the task of misleading everybody during the previous year. The patient thought that the name "Mundy" referred to his frequent missing of the Monday sessions a year ago. He realized that the violent uncontrolled aggressiveness related to himself but he felt the young woman was also himself. During the last year he had often insisted in his analytic sessions that he felt he was a woman, and was very contemptuous of and superior to the analyst. Lately, however, he occasionally dreamt of a little girl who was receptive and appreciative of her teachers, which I had interpreted as a part of him which wanted to show more appreciation of the analyst, but was prevented from coming into the open by his omnipotence. In the dream the patient admits that the aggressive omnipotent part of himself, represented as male, which had dominated the acting out until a year ago, had now become quite conscious. His identification with the analyst is expressed in the dream as a determination to work hard at his analysis. The dream, however, is also a warning that he would continue his aggressive acting out in analysis by asserting in a misleading way that he could present himself omnipotently as a grown-up woman instead of allowing himself to respond to the work of the analysis with receptive feelings relating to a more positive infantile part of himself. In fact the patient was moving in the analysis towards a strengthening of his positive dependence, which enabled him to expose openly the opposition of the aggressive narcissistic omnipotent parts of his personality; in other words, the patient's severe instinctual defusion is gradually developing into normal fusion.

SUMMARY

I have attempted in this paper to investigate clinical conditions where aggressive impulses predominate and examine their relation to Freud's theory of the defusion and fusion of the life and death instincts. I have found that even in the most severe states of defusion of the instinct clinical states which resemble Freud's description of the death instinct in its original form reveal on detailed analysis that it is the destructive aspect of the death instinct which is active in paralysing, or psychically killing, the libidinal parts of the self derived from the life instinct. I therefore think that it is not possible to observe an unfused death instinct in the clinical situation.

Some of these destructive states cannot be described as defusions because they are really pathological fusions, in which the psychic structure dominated by a destructive part of the self succeeds in imprisoning and overpowering the libidinal self, which is completely unable to oppose the destructive process.

It seems that certain omnipotent, narcissistic states are dominated by the most violent destructive processes, so that the libidinal self is almost completely absent or lost. Clinically it is therefore essential to find access to the libidinal dependent self, which can mitigate the destructive impulses. In analysing the omnipotent structure of the narcissistic state the infantile nature of the process has to be exposed in order to release these dependent parts which can form good object relations leading to the introjection of libidinal objects which are the basis of normal fusion.

REFERENCE

Rosenfeld, H. (1964). On the psychopathology of narcissism. *International Journal of Psycho-Analysis* 45:332–337.

VIII

EARLY CONTRIBUTIONS OF THE INDEPENDENT GROUP

The "independent" or "middle group" of the British Psycho-Analytic Society consisted of those analysts who wished to identify with neither Anna Freud's nor Melanie Klein's positions during and following the so-called controversial discussions that took place in the Society in the 1940s (King and Steiner 1991). Instead, this group was characterized by an independence of mind and loyalty, taking ideas from both sides of the Freud–Klein split, and from elsewhere as it suited them. Indeed, they cannot properly be called a group, since they did not fit neatly into any theoretical grouping and did not work together in any regular way as the Freud and Klein groups did. So their principal shared feature has continued to be their independence from other groups and, most often, from each other. Fairbairn and Winnicott are considered ideologically as members of this nongroup, as are the three contributors considered in this section, Balint, Bowlby, and Guntrip. Guntrip was not a member of the Psycho-Analytical Society at all, having trained originally as a minister. Prominent later contributors considered to be part of what has more lately and officially been called the "group of independent analysts" are Sutherland, Coltart, Casement, Bollas, and Symington, whose works are excerpted in this collection, and such other members of the British Society as Enid Balint, Masud Khan, John Padel, Charles Rycroft, Margaret Little, Eric Rayner, Harold Stewart, John Klauber, Juliet Mitchell, and Adam Limentani.

Michael Balint was one of the major early contributors to analytic theory and therapy. In addition, his application of analytic understanding to psychosomatic diseases, to the practice of medicine, and to the work of the practicing doctor has been widely used in medical education. He assembled groups of general practitioners, and later of medical students, to discuss cases together and used the power of the group to promote understanding of the case in enough depth to significantly improve doctors' management of the case under discussion and of their work in general. These groups have come to be known as "Balint groups." He and his wife Enid Balint were also interested in the application of analytic understanding to the institution of marriage, which resulted in her founding the Family Discussion Bureau at the Tavistock Institute of Human Relations, still in operation as the Tavistock Marital Studies Institute.

Here, we can only focus on Balint's views of early infancy and their implications for therapy. Balint wrote that under certain circumstances of severe pathology, treatment should promote a regression that could, late in a thoroughgoing treatment, provide for a "new beginning" supported by developmental provisions previously unavailable to the patient. Study of these states of therapeutic regression enabled Balint to make highly original formulations about early development. He did so in idiosyncratic language, which may be one of the reasons that his contributions to analytic theory have been little understood and largely underrated, while his innovations to medical education and the application of groups to learning the complexities of development and pathology have long been acknowledged.

In the following excerpts from his best-known book, *The Basic Fault,* Balint describes a process of development beginning in the area of the "basic fault"–an area akin to a geological fault running to the core. The emotional basic fault begins with a primary mix-up between self and environment, which Balint felt existed in the beginning. It continues as a two-person relationship with the strains between self and others that have their origins before oedipal development. Here he was exploring territory that was close to Winnicott's description of the mother–infant relationship in the beginning that leads later to a creative capacity to be alone. Balint describes this as the "area of creation," the capacity to be alone that parallels the later capacity to enter three-person oedipal relationships. It is this area of the formation of the self that also concerned Guntrip in his extension of Fairbairn's work, as conveyed in the selections that follow those of Balint. More recently, these concerns about the formation of the self have come back into focus in Kohut's self psychology, and in the work of object relations theorists Ogden, Bollas, and Sutherland.

Balint also described two important concepts whose difficult terminology has kept them from being better appreciated: *ocnophilism* and *philobatism.* The ocnophil values primarily objects and ignores or fears the spaces between them, whereas the philobat values the spaces between and devalues or fears the objects. This conceptual offering is, I believe, related to Winnicott's description of the potential space, or transitional space between mother and baby. It offers a new language for describing the vicissitudes of object relating and the need for separation from the object, and for describing the fit or lack of fit between mothers and babies that occupied Winnicott's interest. It also provides an avenue for exploring Fairbairn's description of the relation between ego and object, and complements Guntrip's descriptions of the schizoid personality, excerpted in Chapter 38, which could be said to seek the "space between" rather than the object.

These are the concepts that underlie Balint's therapeutic idea of the "new beginning" to which he alludes at the end of this excerpt, a notion that for severely disturbed and deprived patients, the analyst can provide the support and tolerance that eventually allows the patient to regress to the area of the basic fault where the trouble initially began, offering an opportunity for a new start.

REFERENCE

King, P., and Steiner, R., eds. (1991). *The Freud-Klein Controversies 1941–45.* London: Routledge.

37

Michael Balint's *The Basic Fault* (1968)

[A]nalytical work proceeds on at least two different levels, one familiar and less problematic, called the oedipal level, and the other, for the description of which terms like preoedipal, pregenital, and preverbal are in use. . . .

Just as the oedipal level possesses its own name derived from one of its main characteristics, so the other level should have its own, and should not be called pre-something else—certainly not preoedipal, because it may coexist with the oedipal level, at any rate as far as our clinical experiences go. For the moment I wish to leave open the question whether or not there are periods when the mind knows only the one level and not the other. On the other hand it must be emphasized that this other level is definitely simpler, more primitive, than the oedipal level. I propose to call it the level of the *basic fault,* and I wish to stress that it is described as a fault, not as a situation, position, conflict, or complex.

The chief characteristics of the level of the basic fault are (a) all the events that happen in it belong to an exclusively two-person relationship—there is no third person present; (b) this two-person relationship is of a particular nature, entirely different from the well-known human relationships of the oedipal level; (c) the nature of the dynamic force operating at this level is not that of a conflict; and (d) adult language is often useless or misleading in describing events at this level, because words have not always an agreed conventional meaning. . . .

First about the nature of the primitive two-person relationship at this level. In the first approach this can be considered as an instance of primary object relationship or of primary love, which I have described on several occasions (M. Balint 1932, 1934, 1937, 1959). Any third party interfering with this relationship is experienced as a heavy burden or as an intolerable strain. A further important quality of this relationship is the immense difference of intensity between the phenomena of satisfaction and frustration. Whereas satisfaction—the "fitting in" of the object with the subject—brings about a feeling of quiet tranquil well-being which can be observed only with difficulty as it is so natural and soft, frustration—the lack of fitting in of the object—evokes highly vehement and loud symptoms. . . .

THE AREA OF THE BASIC FAULT

Accepting theoretically the existence of the level of the basic fault, we have to ask what kind of events in the course of analytic treatment have to be considered as signals that this level has been reached. Taking a fairly normal case, let us suppose that the treatment has been proceeding smoothly for some time, patient and analyst have understood each other, while the strains and demands on either of them, but especially on the analyst, were only reasonable and, in particular, at all times intelligible. Then at some point, suddenly or insidiously, the atmosphere of the analytic situation changes profoundly. With some patients this might happen after a very short period, or even right from the start. . . .

Interpretations given by the analyst are not experienced any longer by the patient as interpretations. Instead he may feel them as an attack, a demand, a base insinuation, an uncalled-for rudeness or insult, unfair treatment, injustice, or at least as a complete lack of consideration, and so on; on the other hand, it is equally possible that the analyst's interpretations may be experienced as something highly pleasing and gratifying, exciting or soothing, or as a seduction; in general as an irrefutable sign of consideration, affection, and love. It may also happen that common words which until then have had an agreed conventional "adult" meaning and could be used without any great consequence, become immensely important and powerful, either in a good or a bad sense. At such times, in fact, the analyst's every casual remark, every gesture or movement, may matter enormously and may assume an importance far beyond anything that could be realistically intended.

Moreover—and this is not so easy to admit—the patient somehow seems able to get under the analyst's skin. He begins to know much too much about his analyst. This increase in knowledge does not originate from any outside source of information but apparently from an uncanny talent that enables the patient to "understand" the analyst's motives and to "interpret" his behaviour. This uncanny talent may occasionally give the impression of, or perhaps even amount to, telepathy or clairvoyance (see M. Balint 1955). The analyst experiences this phenomenon as if the patient could see inside him, could find out things about him. The things thus found out are always highly personal, in some ways always concerned with the patient, and are in a way absolutely correct and true, and at the same time utterly out of proportion, and thus untrue—at least this is how the analyst feels them.

If now the analyst fails to "click in," that is, to respond as the patient expects him to do, no reaction of anger, rage, contempt, or criticism will appear in the transference as one would expect it at the oedipal level. The only thing that can be observed is a feeling of emptiness, being lost, deadness, futility, and so on, coupled with an apparently lifeless acceptance of everything that has been offered. In fact everything is accepted without much resistance but nothing makes any sense. Another reaction to the analyst's failure to "click in" might have the appearance of persecutory anxieties. Leaving on one side that in these states anxiety—in its common-sense clinical form—is usually very slight, hardly existent, the fact remains that at any frustration these patients feel that it was intentionally inflicted upon them. They cannot accept that there exists any other cause for a frustration of their desires than malice, evil intention, or at least, criminal negligence. Good things may happen by chance, but frustrations are unchallengeable proofs of evil and hostile sentiments in their environment.

Remarkably, all this is simply accepted as a painful fact and it is most surprising how little anger, still less a willingness to fight, is mobilized by it. It is still more surprising that a feeling of hopelessness hardly ever develops; it seems that despair and hopelessness belong to the oedipal level; they are probably postdepressive. Though feelings of emptiness and deadness (cf. E. Balint 1963) may be very strong, behind them there is usually an earnest, quiet determination to see things through. This queer mixture of profound suffering, absence of cheap pugnacity, and an unshakeable determination to get on makes these patients truly appealing—an important diagnostic sign that the work has reached the level of the basic fault.

The analyst's reaction also is characteristic, and is utterly different from his reaction to a resistance at the oedipal level. . . . Everything touches him much more closely; he finds it rather difficult to maintain his usual attitude of sympathetic, objective passivity; in fact, he is in constant danger of subjective emotional involvement. Some analysts allow, or even elect, to be carried away by this forceful current and must then change their techniques accordingly. Others carefully and cautiously stick to their well-proven guns and consistently avoid any risk of becoming involved. There are also those who, in face of this threat, adopt—perhaps as a reaction formation against it—a somewhat omnipotent confidence, constantly reassuring themselves that their technique of interpretation is capable of dealing with any situation.

Another important group of phenomena is centred upon what may be called appreciation of, and gratitude for, the analyst's work. On the oedipal level, provided the analyst's work has been up to professional standards, these two sentiments—appreciation and gratitude—are powerful allies and, especially during bleak periods, may help considerably. At the level of the basic fault one cannot be certain at all that the patient will bear in mind, still less that he will appreciate, that his analyst was skilful and understanding in the past, whether remote or recent. One reason for this profound change is that at that level patients feel that it is their due to receive what they need. I shall return presently to this important feature.

Thus, if the analyst provides what is needed, this fact is taken for granted and loses all its value as proof of professional skill, of exceptional gift, or of favour, and in due course more and more demands will be produced. In present-day analytical literature this syndrome is called greediness, or even oral greed. I have no objection to calling it greed, but strong objection to calling it oral because this is misleading. It is not the relationship to the oral component instinct that is relevant for the understanding of this syndrome but the fact that it originates in a primitive two-person relationship which may or may not be oral. To cite the range of addictions in which greediness is a most important feature, there are very numerous and unquestionably oral addictions, foremost among them nicotine and alcohol; but there are many that are non-oral, such as morphinism, sniffing cocaine, and not forgetting the various forms of scratching as in pruritus.

At the oedipal level the analyst is hardly ever tempted out of his sympathetic passivity; if he abandons his passivity at the level of the basic fault, he may start on a dangerous spiral of addiction—because of the peculiar lack of gratitude, or presence of greed; if he remains adamant either the treatment will be broken off by the patient as hopeless, or after a long forlorn struggle the patient will be forced to identify himself with the aggressor, as the analyst is felt to be, i.e., as I heard it described in one of my seminars—the patient is made to acquire an everlasting internal long-playing record. . . .

All these events belong essentially to the field of two-person psychology and are more elementary than those belonging to the three-person oedipal level. Moreover, they lack the structure of a conflict. This was one of the reasons why I proposed to call them "basic." But why *fault?* First, because this is exactly the word used by many patients to describe it. The patient says that he feels there is a fault within him, a fault that must be put right. And it is felt to be a fault, not a complex, not a conflict, not a situation. Second, there is a feeling that the cause of this fault is that someone has either failed the patient or defaulted on him; and third, a great anxiety invariably surrounds this area, usually expressed as a desperate demand that this time the analyst should not—in fact must not—fail him.

The term *fault* has been in use in some exact sciences to denote conditions that are reminiscent of that which we are discussing. Thus, for instance, in geology and in crystallography the word *fault* is used to describe a sudden irregularity in the overall structure, an irregularity which in normal circumstances might lie hidden but, if strains and stresses occur, may lead to a break, profoundly disrupting the overall structure.

We are accustomed to think of every dynamic force operating in the mind as having the form either of a biological drive or of a conflict. Although highly dynamic, the force originating from the basic fault has the form neither of an instinct nor of a conflict. It is a fault, something wrong in the mind, a kind of deficiency which must be put right. It is not something dammed up for which a better outlet must be found, but something missing either now, or perhaps for almost the whole of the patient's life. An instinctual need can be satisfied, a conflict can be solved, a basic fault can perhaps be merely healed provided the deficient ingredients can be found; and even then it may amount only to a healing with defect, like a simple, painless scar.

The adjective *basic* in my new term not only means that it relates to simpler conditions than those characterizing the Oedipus complex, but also that its influence extends widely, probably over the whole psychobiological structure of the individual, involving in varying degrees both his mind and his body. In this way the concept of the basic fault allows us to understand not only the various neuroses (perhaps also psychoses), character disorders, psychosomatic illnesses, etc., as symptoms of the same etiological entity, but also—as the experiences of our research into general medical practice have shown—a great number of ordinary "clinical" illnesses as well (M. Balint 1957, Greco and Pittenger 1966, Lask 1966). By this I mean that under the influence of various emotional experiences, among them medical treatment, a "clinical" illness may disappear to give way to a specific psychological disorder and vice versa.

In my view the origin of the basic fault may be traced back to a considerable discrepancy in the early formative phases of the individual between his biopsychological needs and the material and psychological care, attention, and affection available during the relevant times. This creates a state of deficiency whose consequences and aftereffects appear to be only partly reversible. The cause of this early discrepancy may be congenital, i.e., the infant's biopsychological needs may have been too exacting (there are nonviable infants and progressive congenital conditions, like Friedreich's ataxia or cystic kidneys), or may be environmental, such as care that is insufficient, deficient, haphazard, overanxious, overprotective, harsh, rigid, grossly inconsistent, incorrectly timed, overstimulating, or merely un-understanding or indifferent.

As may be seen from my description, I put the emphasis on the lack of "fit" between the child and *the people* who represent his environment. Incidentally, we started with a similar lack of fit—between the analyst's otherwise correct technique and a particular patient's needs; this is very likely to be an important cause of difficulties, and even failures, experienced by analysts in their practice. . . .

Returning now to our main theme, I wish the reader to be aware of my personal bias, under the influence of which my description of the processes, which eventually may result in some basic fault, will be couched in terms of object relationship. In my view, all these processes happen within a very primitive and peculiar object relationship, fundamentally different from those commonly observed between adults. It is definitely a two-person relationship in which, however, only one of the partners matters; his wishes and needs are the only ones that count and must be attended to; the other partner, though felt to be immensely powerful, matters only insofar as he is willing to gratify the first partner's needs and desires or decides to frustrate them; beyond this his personal interests, needs, desires, wishes, etc., simply do not exist. . . .

THE AREA OF CREATION

Until now I have discussed two possible levels, or areas, in the mind: those of the Oedipus conflict and of the basic fault. To complete the picture I have to mention . . . a third area. . . . Whereas the area of the Oedipus conflict is characterized by the presence of at least two objects, apart from the subject, and the area of the basic fault by a very peculiar, exclusively two-person relationship, the third area is characterized by the fact that in it there is no external object present. The subject is on his own and his main concern is to produce something out of himself; this something to be produced may be an object, but is not necessarily so. I propose to call this the *level* or *area of creation*. . . .

Despite many attempts, very little indeed is understood of these processes. One obvious reason for this paucity of knowledge is the fact that throughout this whole area there is no external object present, and thus no transference relationship can develop. Where there is no transference, our analytic methods are powerless, and thus we are restricted to inferences from observations obtained after the individual has left the boundaries of this area. . . .

We know that there are no "objects" in the area of creation, but we know also that for most—or some—of the time the subject is not entirely alone there. The trouble is that our language has no words to describe, or even to indicate, the "somethings" that are there when the subject is not completely alone; in order to be able to talk about them at all, I propose to use the term *preobject;* "object-embryo" would be too definite; in German *Objekt-Anlage* may prove a good term. If I understood Bion (1962, 1963), he was faced with the same difficulty; his proposition for this special case was to call them α and β elements, and α function.

. . . [T]he preobjects existing in the area of creation must be so primitive that they cannot be considered as organized or whole. Only after the work of creation has succeeded in making them organized or whole, can a proper verbal or oedipal interaction between them and external objects take place. It is probable that more primitive interactions—congenial to the levels of the basic fault and of creation—take place all the time; these, however, are difficult to observe and still more difficult to describe adequately (M. Balint 1959).

The only thing we know is that the process of creation—transforming the preobject into a proper object—is unpredictable. . . . Perhaps, if we can change our own approach from that of considering [a patient's] silence as a symptom of resistance to studying it as a possible source of information, we may learn something about this area of the mind. . . .

Thus we arrive at a sequence: first, the level of creation, then the level of the basic fault, and last, the level of the Oedipus complex. As we know from embryology, it often happens that during development an early complex structure is gradually simplified or even completely lost at a later stage (cf. M. Balint 1959). Thus it is thinkable that the earliest level might be that of primary love and with it the level of the basic fault, out of which, on the one hand, the level of the Oedipus conflict develops in differentiation,. and, on the other hand, the level of creation by simplification. . . .

PRIMARY LOVE

According to my theory, the individual is born in a state of intense relatedness to his environment, both biologically and libidinally. Prior to birth, self and environment are harmoniously "mixed up," in fact, they interpenetrate each other. In this world, as has been mentioned, there are as yet no objects, only limitless substances or expanses.

Birth is a trauma that upsets this equilibrium by changing the environment radically and enforces—under a real threat of death—a new form of adaptation. This starts off or, at any rate considerably accelerates, the separation between individual and environment. Objects, including the ego, begin to emerge from the mix-up of substances and from the breaking up of the harmony of the limitless expanses. The objects have—in contrast to the friendlier substances—firm contours and sharp boundaries which henceforth must be recognized and respected. Libido is no longer in a homogeneous flux from the id to the environment; under the influence of the emerging objects, concentrations and rarefactions appear in its flow.

Wherever the developing relationship to a part of the environment or to an object is in painful contrast to the earlier undisturbed harmony, libido may be withdrawn to the ego, which starts or accelerates developing—perhaps as a consequence of the enforced new adaptation—in an attempt to regain the previous feeling of "oneness" of the first stages. This part of the libido would be definitely narcissistic, but secondary to the original environment cathexis. Accordingly the libidinal cathexes observed in early infancy would be of four sorts: (a) remnants of the original environment cathexis transferred to the emerging objects, (b) other remnants of the original environment cathexis withdrawn to the ego as secondary comforters against frustration, i.e., narcissistic and autoerotic cathexes, and (c) re-cathexes emanating from the secondary narcissism of the ego. In addition to these three fairly well-studied forms of cathexis, there is a fourth which results in the development of the ocnophilic and the philobatic structures of the world (M. Balint 1959). In the ocnophilic world the primary cathexis, though mixed with a great deal of anxiety, seems to adhere to the emerging objects; these are felt to be safe and comforting while the spaces between them are threatening and horrid. In the philobatic world the objectless expanses retain the original primary cathexis and are experienced as safe and friendly, while the objects are felt as treacherous hazards.

The ocnophil's reaction to the emergence of objects is to cling to them, to introject them, since he feels lost and insecure without them; apparently he chooses to *overcathect his object relationships*. The other type, the philobat, *overcathects his own ego functions* and develops skills in this way, in order to be able to maintain himself alone with very little, or even no, help from his objects. Ocnophilia and philobatism are probably instances of the basic fault, certainly not the only ones. It is upon this foundation that, on the one hand, the Oedipus complex is built and on the other, possibly the area of the creation. This latter may entail as a first step a regressive *withdrawal from objects* found too harsh and frustrating, to the harmonious mix-up of earlier states, which is then followed by *an attempt to create something better,* kinder, more understandable, more beautiful, and above all, more consistent and more harmonious than the real objects proved to be. Unfortunately this attempt does not succeed each time; much too often the creation is no better—even worse—than the bitter reality.

At first most of the objects are possibly indifferent or even frustrating, but some of them prove to be sources of gratification; provided the infant care is not too deficient or insensitive, parts of the environment may retain some of its original *primary cathexis,* they become what I called *primary objects,* and one's relationship to them and to their derivatives in later life will always be different, that is, more primitive than the relationship to anything else in the world. Such primary objects are, first of all, one's mother and, remarkably, for many people most of the four elements which are archaic mother symbols: water, earth, air, and, less frequently, fire. . . . during certain phases of a satisfactory analytic treatment the analyst assumes, in fact must assume, the qualities of a primary object. . . .

For many years I thought that there was only one type of this primitive two-person relationship, the type that I now call ocnophilia. In this relationship, as just described, the object is felt as a vitally important support. Any threat of being separated from it creates intense anxiety and the most frequently used defence against it is clinging. On the other hand, the object inherits so much cathexis from the primary substances that it becomes so important that no concern or consideration can be given to it, it must have no separate interests from the individual's, it must simply be there and, in fact, it is taken for granted. The consequences of this kind of object relationship are (a) an overvaluation of the object—which is thus not necessarily due to an overcathexis by narcissistic libido, and (b) a comparative inhibition against developing personal skills which might make the individual independent from his objects.

During the past fifteen years or so I have discovered a second type of primitive relationship to objects or, perhaps more correctly, to the environment. I proposed for it the term *philobatism.* In this, objects are considered as indifferent, or even as deceitful and untrustworthy hazards, better to be avoided. To achieve this, the individual must develop some personal skills—that is, his ego—in order to retain, or regain, the freedom of movement in, and harmony, with, the objectless expanses, such as mountains, deserts, sea, air, etc., all of which belong to the class of potentially primary objects—or more correctly, primary substances—but *pari passu* his object relationships may become thwarted.

A common feature of all these primitive forms of object relationship is that in it the object is taken for granted; the idea that an indifferent object exists and that it should be changed into a cooperative partner by the "work of conquest" has not yet arisen. In this harmonious two-person relationship only one partner may have wishes, interests, and demands on his own; without any further need for testing, it is taken for granted that the other partner, the object, or the friendly expanse, will automatically have the same wishes, interests, and expectations. This explains why this is so often called the state of omnipotence. This description is somewhat out of tune; there is no feeling of power, in fact, no need for either power or effort, as all things *are* in harmony.

If any hitch or disharmony between subject and object occurs, the reaction to it will consist of loud and vehement symptoms suggesting processes either of a highly aggressive and destructive, or profoundly disintegrated, nature, i.e., either as if the whole world, including the self, would have been smashed up, or as if the subject would have been flooded with pure and unmitigated aggressive-destructive impulses. On the other hand, if the harmony is allowed to persist without much disturbance from outside, the reaction amounts to a feeling of tranquil, quiet well-being which is rather inconspicuous and difficult to observe.

This difference expressed in adult language would run somewhat like this: "I must be loved and looked after in every respect by everyone and everything important to me, without anyone demanding any effort or claiming any return for this. It is only my own wishes, interests, and needs that matter; none of the people who are important to me must have any interests, wishes, needs different from mine, and if they have any at all, they must subordinate theirs to mine without any resentment or strain; in fact, it must be their pleasure and their enjoyment to fit in with my wishes. If this happens I shall be good, pleased, and happy, but that is all. If this does not happen, it will be horrifying both for the world and for me."

If we bear in mind that the ongoing harmonious relationship in this phase between subject and object or expanse is as important as the ongoing supply of air, we understand that loud, vehement, and aggressive symptoms appear when the harmony between the subject and its primary object or substance is disturbed. This primary relationship is so important to the subject that he cannot tolerate any interference with it from outside, and if anything contrary to his needs or wishes happens, he simply must resort to desperate methods.

How does hatred enter into this relationship? Hatred is the perpetuation of the unconditional dependence on primary love, with the one difference that its sign has been changed into negative. As I pointed out in my paper "On Love and Hate" (1951), to liberate the individual from the fixation to his hate, the cooperation of his environment is indispensable, internal changes only are hardly ever sufficient. In rare cases external events may by chance provide the required changes in the environment, but conditions for this are so exacting that the probability is very small indeed. The only situation in which the environment can be expected to comply intentionally and systematically with these exacting requirements is the analytic situation, especially during the phase of "new beginning." If the analyst succeeds in responding in the right way to the primitive, unrealistic wishes, the patient may be helped to reduce the oppressive inequality between himself and his object. With the waning of this inequality, the patient's dependence on his primary object, which was reenacted in the new beginning phase of the analytic process, may decrease considerably, or even disappear altogether. When the inequality, and with it the dependence, has been reduced, there will be no more need for any defence against them; hatred can then be largely given up, and with it the intensity of the aggressive, destructive urges.

If my theory is correct, then we must expect to come across all these three types of object relationships—the most primitive harmonious interpenetrating mix-up, the ocnophilic clinging to objects, and the philobatic preference for objectless expanses—in every analytic treatment that is allowed to regress beyond a certain point. In fact, I arrived at my theory the other way around, through observing in my analytic practice these three types of relationship to me and to the environment in general, and then building up my theory from these observations.

Where is the place of narcissism in this theory? In my opinion *all narcissism is secondary* to the most primitive of these relationships, that of the harmonious interpenetrating mix-up; its immediate cause is always a disturbance between the individual and his environment; this leads to frustration as a consequence of which the individual comes to differentiate what was until then the harmonious fusion of self and environment, withdraws part of his cathexis from the environment, and invests it in his developing ego.

REFERENCES

Balint, E. (1963). On being empty of oneself. *International Journal of Psycho-Analysis* 44:470.

Balint, M. (1932). Character analysis and new beginning. In *Primary Love and Psycho-Analytic Technique.* London: Hogarth, 1952.

——(1934). The final goal of psycho-analytic treatment. In *Primary Love and Psycho-Analytic Technique.* London: Hogarth, 1952.

——(1937). Early developmental states of the ego. Primary object-love. In *Primary Love and Psycho-Analytic Technique.* London: Hogarth, 1952.

——(1951). On love and hate. In *Primary Love and Psycho-Analytic Technique.* London: Hogarth, 1952.

——(1952). *Primary Love and Psycho-Analytic Technique.* London: Hogarth.

——(1955). Notes on parapsychology and parapsychological healing. *International Journal of Psycho-Analysis* 36.

——(1956). Pleasure, object, and libido. *British Journal of Medical Psychology* 29:162.

——(1957). *The Doctor, His Patient and the Illness.* London: Pitman; New York: International Universities Press. Second edition, 1964.

——(1959). *Thrills and Regressions.* London: Hogarth; New York: International Universities Press.

Bion, W. R. (1962). *Learning from experience.* London: Heinemann.

——(1963). *Elements of psychoanalysis.* London: Heinemann.

Greco, R. S., with Pittenger, R. A. (1966). *One man's practice.* London: Tavistock; Philadelphia: Lippincott.

Lask, A. (1966). *Asthma, attitude and milieu.* London: Tavistock; Philadelphia: Lippincott.

38

Harry Guntrip's "The Schizoid Problem, Regression, and the Struggle to Preserve an Ego" (1961)

Harry Guntrip was a minister, a psychotherapist, and a disciple of Fairbairn and Winnicott who investigated territory similar to Balint's basic fault and new beginning. Unlike the idiosyncratic originality of Balint, Guntrip's new ideas grew out of close, reasoned study of the contributions of Freud, Fairbairn, Klein, and Winnicott and of the scientific tradition. Consequently, his writing offers a unique critical review and integration of their contributions as preparation for Guntrip's own additions.

Guntrip suggested, with Fairbairn's agreement, that where Fairbairn had used the term *ego*, the concept of *self* would be more appropriate. In this paper, Guntrip tackles the problem of the locus of defensive retreat of the self in severe schizoid states, furthering Fairbairn's original area of inquiry. His description of a retreat to a phantasied womb can also be understood in Winnicott's terms as an overidealization of the environment mother who is, in phantasy, installed inside where the true self can be put in cold storage.

Guntrip's principal contribution in this paper is his description of a further split of Fairbairn's *libidinal ego* into an oral sadistic component maintaining a forlorn tie to the object, and a withdrawn passive part of the ego. This splitting leads to the retreat of a part of the ego (the *repressed libidinal ego,* in his terminology) to the interior with an ultimate threat of loss of the ego or self in a futile search for a sustaining object. This occurs in situations of severe privation of early parental support. In this selection, Guntrip described the fear of the self, ringed around by the threat of persecution from the bad objects and of smothering imprisonment by good objects, feeling there is nowhere to turn, and finally, unable to find any object, fearing the loss of the ego itself and becoming depersonalized in the process.

The description contained in this article and in Guntrip's books *Personality Structure and Human Interaction* (1961) and *Schizoid Phenomena, Object Relations and the Self* (1969) was Guntrip's single most original contribution. Alongside it, his theoretical scholarship, his understanding of the importance of the child's actual experience, and the corresponding importance of the relationship between therapist and patient to build effective psychotherapy, constitute his legacy. His work has been widely appreciated by psychotherapists, but as a minister, he was also able to build bridges of understanding to clergy and to pastoral counselors, allowing them to apply object relations to pastoral counseling and to their everyday work.

CAUSES AND STAGES OF SCHIZOID WITHDRAWAL

Fear and Flight from External Reality

The most pathological schizoid withdrawal takes place astonishingly early, in the first year of life. It can, of course, occur at any time of life as a generalized reaction, but the more it is found to be structurally embedded in the personality the earlier it originally occurred. It can then, certainly, be intensified and consolidated all through later childhood and evoked by pressures in real life at any time, but there is little doubt that in the beginning it is associated with what Melanie Klein called "persecutory anxiety" and "the infantile anxiety situations." It is a "fear and flight" reaction in the face of danger. The view of the later Freud and of Mrs. Klein that the ultimate source of the danger is wholly internal, a "death instinct," innate active aggression working inwardly, threatening destruction against the primary psyche, has found no general acceptance. It would be unscientific to fall back on such a speculative idea when satisfactory clinical analysis is available. The view of the earlier Freud that psychopathological development began, not with innate aggression but with the libidinal drives of the sexual instinct aiming at erotic pleasure and proving to be incompatible with social reality, at least implied that the source of the trouble was more in the environment than in the infant. The world into which the infant was born could not tolerate his nature and his needs and he came up against painful frustrations. However, this view does not cover all the facts.

Fairbairn (1952) takes a wider view of libidinal need as not limited to the sexual but embracing all that is involved in the need for personal relationships, on however simple and primitive a level at the beginning: the goal of libidinal need is not pleasure but the object (at first the breast and the mother). The frustration of libidinal need for good object relations both arouses aggression and intensifies libidinal needs till the infant fears his love needs as destructive towards his objects. In the later "depressive position" which Winnicott calls the stage of "ruth" or "concern for the object" this would lead to guilt. But at this earliest stage it leads to the schizoid withdrawal, a simple fear reaction, away from the danger of devouring and therefore losing the love object. Schizoid persons have given up the outward expression of needs, while also being haunted by the fear of losing love objects. One patient says: "I can't make moderate demands so I don't make any at all," and another insists "I lose everyone I love." Yet the schizoid fear is not so much on behalf of the object as on behalf of the ego and the consequences to it of losing the object. Here lies the difference between the moral and the pre-moral level of development. The schizoid personality is basically on a pre-moral level; hence the horrifying callousness schizoid people can manifest. It is not in accordance with Fairbairn's psychodynamic outlook to treat these libidinal needs as discrete entities demanding satisfaction in and for themselves. They are the needs of an ego. Since the need for an object arises from the fact that without object relations no strong ego development is possible, we must conclude that the satisfaction of libidinal needs is not an end in itself but is an experience of good object relationships in which the infant discovers himself as a person, and his ego development proceeds firmly and self-confidently. Fairbairn's view brings out the question of ego growth in weakness or in strength as the background of all problems arising out of fears, conflicts, and withdrawals over frustrated needs.

Deprivation of needs is, however, not the only cause of schizoid withdrawal, and Winnicott emphasizes what seems to be an even more primitive situation. Not only must the mother meet the infant's needs when he feels them, but she must not force herself on him in ways and at times that he does not want. That constitutes "impingement" on the as yet weak, immature, and sensitive ego of the infant. He cannot stand this and shrinks away into himself. There are many other sources of impingement in loveless, authoritarian, and quarrelsome families, and often sheer fear is aroused in the tiny child. Fairbairn has also recently stressed in private conversation that trouble arises not only over the child's needs for the parents, but also over the parents' pressures on the child who is often exploited in the interests of the parents' needs, not the baby's. The startle reaction to sudden loud noise is perhaps the simplest case of fear at impingement, and such impingement experiences, particularly at the hands of parents, begin the building up of basic impressions that the whole outer world is not supporting but hostile.

Judging by the reflexion of these early events in the psychopathology of adults, this factor of impingement and pressure of a hostile environment, bearing to an intolerable degree on the tender infant mind, is the true source of "persecutory anxiety," of fear of annihilation, and of flight back inside, of withdrawal of the emotionally traumatized infant libidinal ego into itself out of reach of the dangerous outer world. What an adult may do consciously, as in the case of a wife who felt that her husband was inconsiderate and said, "I built a wall around myself so that I should not be hurt," the infant does instinctively. He takes flight inwards from the outer world. Fear of deprived and therefore dangerous active oral-sadistic libidinal needs belongs to a higher level, that of the struggle to remain in object relationships. It precipitates withdrawal in two ways, however, through fear of devouring and losing the object, and through fear of retaliation and of being devoured by the object. This latter fear may develop into guilt and the fear of punishment. Withdrawal from direct frightening impingement by the object in the first place is more primitive. Deep fear-enforced withdrawal from object relations is then to a regressed passive level of a womb-like state inside. Severe schizoid states disclose a total fear of the entire outer world, and deprivation and impingement combine. The world is a frightening emptiness when it does not respond and meet the infant's needs, and a frightening persecutor when it actively and hurtfully impinges. The infant cannot develop a secure and strong ego sense either in a vacuum or under intolerable pressure and he seeks to return to a vaguely remembered earlier safe place, even though in fact he can only withdraw into isolation within himself. . . .

Impingement and rejection or deprivation of needs for object relationships must be bracketed together as defining the traumatic situation which drives the infant into a retreat within himself in search of a return to the womb. Probably deprivation in the sense of "tantalizing refusal" leads to *active* oral phenomena while impingement and deprivation as "desertion" lead to shrinking away inside into a passive state.

A Two-Stage Withdrawal, from External and Internal Bad Objects

The previous section describes the origins of the first stage of what appears to be a two-stage retreat from bad object relationships. This initial escape is from the outer material world into an inner mental one. But contact with the object world cannot be given up, especially at this early age, without threatening to lead to loss or emptying of the ego. Thus part of the total self must be left to function on the conscious level and keep touch with the world of real external objects. If that were not done, and relationship with outer reality were wholly given up, the infant would presumably die. Thus a "splitting" of the hitherto unitary, pristine ego occurs, into a part dealing with the outer world (Freud's "reality ego" and Fairbairn's "central ego") and a part that has withdrawn into the inner mental world.

The withdrawn part of the total self must also, however, keep in object relationships if it is to maintain its experience of itself as a definite ego. the "mind," instead of being simply an active function dealing with the outer world, becomes a place to live in. As Melanie Klein has shown, the infant internalizes his objects and builds up an inner world of object relations. Fairbairn regards the infant as internalizing his unsatisfying objects in an effort to master them in inner reality because he cannot master them in the outer world. In the result, however, they are felt to be as powerful and terrifying in inner reality as in outer, a "fifth column" of internal persecutors or saboteurs who have infiltrated into the inner world where the infant has sought relief inside himself from pressure. A serious predicament has arisen. On the face of it no further retreat seems possible and a series of fresh manoeuvres are made. Fairbairn has described these in terms of "object splitting" and "ego splitting" processes, which build up the structure of the inner world in terms of endopsychic object relations. The internal unsatisfying object is split into its three main aspects, libidinally exciting, libidinally rejective, and emotionally neutral or good and undisturbing. The last or "ideal object" is projected back into the real object and what has all the appearance of an external object relationship is maintained with it by the central ego, the ordinary ego of everyday living. Nevertheless, this is not a properly objective relation, for the object is not fully realistically perceived but only experienced in the light of a partial image projected from inner reality. Thus, once some measure of schizoid withdrawal has been set up, such contact with the outer world as is maintained is defective and governed by the projection of partial and oversimplified images of the object, a fact constantly demonstrated by the poor judgement of others, the over- or underestimation of either good or bad qualities, commonly displayed by people.

Then, while the real object (the actual parent) is unrealistically idealized, his or her exciting and rejective aspects remain as distinguishable and separated phantasied objects of the infant's need for relationships in the inner world. Thus, the unity of that part of the ego which has withdrawn inside away from outer reality becomes split into an ego attached to the exciting object and an ego attached to the rejective object. Just as the exciting object arouses libidinal needs while the rejective object denies them, so the attachment to the exciting object results in a *libidinal ego* characterized by ever-active and unsatisfied desires which come to be felt in angry and sadistic ways; and the attachment to the rejective object results in an *anti-libidinal ego* based on an identification which reproduces the hostility of the rejecting object to libidinal needs. Inevitably the libidinal ego is hated and persecuted by the anti-libidinal ego as well as by the rejective object, so that the infant has now become divided against himself. This is easy to recognize in the contempt and scorn shown by many patients of their own needs to depend for help on other people or on the analyst. It is seen also in the fear and hate of weakness that is embedded in our cultural attitudes. The internal persecution of the libidinal ego by the anti-libidinal ego is vividly seen in the dream of a male patient. He was sitting in an armchair in my room wanting to relax, but at the same time he was also standing behind the chair looking down on the "him" that was sitting in the chair, with an expression of hate and hostility and raising a dagger to kill the needy weak self.

At this stage, the part of the ego which has withdrawn from outer reality has now created for itself a complex inner world of objects both exciting and persecuting. The existence of these internal objects enables the parts of the ego which maintain relations with them to retain ego sense. It seems evident that the real need which dictates the creation of Melanie Klein's world of internal objects, good and bad, and the processes of ego splitting described by Fairbairn, is not simply the urge to master the object but the vital need of the psyche to retain an ego sense. This can only be done by maintaining object relations at least in the inner mental world, after withdrawing in that part of one's personal life from the outer material one. So long as a continuing phantasy life can be kept going by the libidinal and anti-libidinal egos, the ego is kept in being though cut off from outer reality. At one time the libidinal ego is sadistically phantasying the incorporation of its exciting object in inner reality, at another the anti-libidinal ego has possessed itself of the sadism and along with the rejective object phantasies crushing or slave-driving the masochistically suffering libidinal ego. (According to Fairbairn, internal objects are psychic structures just as much as partial egos are. The total psychic self "impersonates" objects to itself in the inner world so as to retain ego sense in phantasied relations.) Though this kind of inner life results in states of acute "persecutory anxiety," the ego is still in being; it has not succumbed to depersonalization after breaking off emotional rapport with objects in real life. This is indeed the rationale of the creation and maintenance of the Kleinian internal objects world: it is a defence against ego-loss, which shows why it is so hard for the patient to give it up.

Yet the position of the withdrawn ego is little bettered, for its enemies have infiltrated into its safe retreat where they are even harder to get away from than before. Freud realized that when, in the early days of psychoanalysis, the sources of internal dangers were thought to be "instinct derivatives." He stressed that the ego cannot escape from what is actually a part of internal reality. This, however, turns out not to be entirely true; or at least it is indubitably true that the ego makes one further attempt to escape from the intolerable internal pressures put upon it by its postnatal world of bad objects. It is the libidinal ego which is the part of the originally whole and now split ego in which the persecutory pressure is felt; and clinical facts have suggested to me that it repeats, in face of the *internal* bad object world, the same manoeuvre that was made by the whole ego when it sought to withdraw from the *external* bad object world. It leaves parts of itself to carry on such relations as are possible, in sadomasochistic terms, with the exciting and rejecting objects of the internal phantasy world, while the traumatized, sensitive, and exhausted heart of it withdraws deeper still. The evidence provided by regressive behaviour, regressive symptoms, and regressive dreams and phantasies shows that this most deeply withdrawn ego feels and phantasies a return to the womb, safe inside the "fortress" from which it probably still has some dim memory of having emerged. Only thus can the clinical facts be conceptualized, facts of the distinct and separate functioning of an active oral infantile libidinal ego tied to a terrifying world of internal bad object relations, and of a passive regressed libidinal ego concerned only with an imperative need to escape and be "safe inside" and giving up all definite object relations in favour of an enclosing protective environment. It is the irresistible pull of this regressed ego under certain circumstances that precipitates the schizoid breakdown in the most extreme cases, but its powerful pull manifested in the teeth of stubborn resistance and defence accounts for all the tensions and illnesses that arise out of this desperate struggle to possess and to retain an ego.

I first made this suggestion of a final split in the libidinal ego itself in an article, "Ego Weakness and the Hard Core of the Problem of Psychotherapy" (1960) and traced out some of its consequences in the closing section of a book, *Personality Structure and Human Interaction* (1961). Here I have sought to give fuller clinical evidence for this view. In addition to the two levels of ego splitting which Fairbairn describes, namely, first that between the central ego in touch with the outer world and a withdrawn ego in the inner world, and second the further splitting of this withdrawn ego into the libidinal ego and the anti-libidinal ego, there is a third and ultimate split in the libidinal ego itself. It divides into an active sadomasochistic oral ego which continues to maintain internal bad object relations, and a passive regressed ego which seeks to return to the antenatal state of absolute passive dependent security; here in quietude, repose, and immobility it may find the opportunity to recuperate and grow to a rebirth, as Winnicott (1955) holds. I suggest that this regressed ego is identical with what Winnicott calls the "true self" put into cold storage to await the chance of rebirth in better conditions. I do not, however, feel sure whether the regressed ego feels itself to be "frozen in cold storage" (frozen in fear probably) or whether it feels hidden in the deepest unconscious in the warmth of an hallucinated intrauterine condition. Some patients appear to feel one way and others the other.

The dream of a university lecturer which shows how little his academic life had touched his deeper mentality, illustrates this two-stage retreat: "I was on a tropical South Seas island and thought I was all alone. Then I found it was full of white people who were very hostile to me and surged at me. I found a little hut on the shore and rushed into it and barred the door and windows and got into bed." He has retreated from civilization to his lonely island (his internal world) only to find that his bad objects, white people, are still with him. So he makes a second retreat which is a complete regression. In defence against this he had twice succumbed to a manic psychosis followed by a depressed, apathetic state. The fact that this manoeuvre involves a splitting of the withdrawn libidinal ego into two is seen in another dream in which the patient was in the consulting room of the analyst. There were two little boys in the room whom he wanted to send out, but the analyst was looking after them and wished them to remain. They sat together on chairs; one was unnaturally alert and watchful, keeping in touch with everything that went on, while the other had a dull expressionless face and took no notice of anything at all, but was completely withdrawn. Here are the active oral ego and the passive regressed ego, along with the central ego, i.e., the patient in his familiar everyday self, sitting apart in an armchair. But his anti-libidinal ego was in concealed partnership with the central ego and hostile to the children. . . .

The *regressed ego* denotes, not a freely available generalized "fear and flight" reaction but the deepest structurally specific part of the complex personality, existing in a settled attitude of fear, weakness, withdrawal, and absolute dependence not in the active postnatal infantile sense but in a passive antenatal sense. It represents the most profoundly traumatized part of the personality and is the hidden cause of all regressive phenomena from conscious escapist phantasies to complete schizoid apathy, unless its need is understood and met; but there lies the greatest difficulty and challenge to therapy. In a letter to the writer dated 1 January 1960, Fairbairn accepted this extension of his structural theory. He wrote: "I consider your concept of the splitting of the libidinal ego into two parts—an oral needy libidinal ego and a regressed libidinal ego—as an original contribution of considerable explanatory value. It solves a problem which I had not hitherto succeeded in solving." Winnicott wrote on 31 October, 1960: "Your split in the libidinal ego seems to have a lot in common with my 'hidden true self' and the 'false self built upon a compliance basis' (a defence in illness, and in health simply the polite self that does not wear its heart on its sleeve). I do think that research can usefully be based on these ideas that are in the air and which you are developing in your own way." It is a pleasure to quote these two writers to whose pioneering work in theory and therapy I owe most for stimulus. I would, however, think that Winnicott's "false compliant self in health" corresponds to the central ego of Fairbairn and his "false compliant self as a defence in illness" corresponds to Fairbairn's anti-libidinal ego, especially in its function of hating weakness. This to me especially seems to warrant the term false self. . . .

THE FIGHT AGAINST REGRESSION

The Determined Drive Backwards

We have stated that, left to himself, the individual can only either provide for his regressed ego in the extreme case by illness, owing to the practical difficulties of providing for it in any other way, or else seek to suppress it as an internal danger threatening to undermine his adjustment to real life in the outer world. The vague influence of a regressed part of the total self is easy to recognize in many people as an attitude of getting through life with as little trouble as possible, getting out of things if they can, and having to push themselves to do what they must. Generally a sustained if automatic effort is made over the years to stave off regression in any more definite sense, though many people have a history of periodic breakdowns say every four or five years, with minor signs of nervous strain and tension in between. In many cases, however, very vigorous defences of an anti-libidinal nature (anti-libidinal towards the self even when apparently libidinal towards others) are built into the personality and direct very energetic if overtense drives into real life. . . .

The ultimate characteristic of the regressed ego is dependent passivity, the vegetative passivity of the intrauterine state which fostered original growth and can foster recuperation. Nature heals in a state of rest. That is the goal. Nevertheless, the regressed ego shows great energy and activity in pursuit of its goal, an activity in reverse that carries it not into life but out of it. There is a great deal of research to be done on various aspects of regression for, clinically, the picture presented is confusing. One comes across states which suggest that there is a regressed ego which feels to be already "in the womb" and oblivious to all else, or if not in a warm safe hiding place then completely withdrawn, immobilized in fear, and having never emerged since the first drastic schizoid retreat in infancy. Some patients, after long analysis, can find themselves suddenly totally "cut off" and living in the deepest, most hidden schizoid part of their total self which they have at last contacted and must live in and with till they regain emotional rapport with the outer world at that deep level. Again, a regressed ego, which in itself seems quite dissociated, exerts a powerful pull on the rest of the personality, drawing it down while it resists frantically. Yet again, at times the whole self seems to have become a regressing ego showing great energy in a drive backwards towards the goal not as yet reached; and sometimes the regressed ego is phantasied as in the womb and resisting every effort to force it to a premature rebirth. . . .

Once the regressed ego feels to have reached its goal of retreat deep inside the hidden, womb-like state of the deepest unconscious, the central ego seems to have little success in drawing it out again. Thus an unmarried woman in middle life dreamed that she was watching a childbirth, but the baby could not be got out. Its head emerged but then it stuck fast, and even ropes tied on to it and passed through the window and fastened to horses who were driven to pull failed to drag it out. This patient was telling herself that she could not force her regressed ego to a rebirth. In this state some patients manage to carry on routine living in a de-emotionalized, cold, mechanical way. This patient felt exhausted with the fight to keep her central ego functioning. Some patients exhibit more the determined drive backwards into regression or the pull of their regressed ego on the rest of their personality, others give the impression that a part of their personality has for long been inaccessible and hidden away quite out of touch with outer life. I am inclined to feel that in every case there is a deepest part of the original ego split off and hidden in a state of regression, corresponding to what Winnicott calls the "true self" hidden away in safe storage to await a favourable chance of rebirth. The more active phenomena of the "pull and drive" to regression may represent the conflicts set up in the psyche over the effects on the whole, of the existence of a profound regressed ego originating in very early life. This creates, from the point of view of external living, a struggle between longings for, fears of, and resistances against breakdown. The "struggle to preserve an ego" has two aspects: the struggle to preserve the central ego of everyday life from being undermined by regression, and the struggle to preserve the basic libidinal ego, the core of the personality, from being crushed by overpowering outer reality or lost irretrievably when it withdraws deep within out of reach of being hurt.

This latter aspect of the problem emerges in tragic self-contradictoriness in the problem of schizoid suicide. The longing to die represents the schizoid need to withdraw the ego from a world that is too much for it to cope with. Whereas depressive suicide is the result of an angry destructive impulse, schizoid suicide is the result of apathy towards real life which cannot be accepted any longer. All available energy goes into a quiet but tenacious determination to fade out into oblivion, by means of gas, hypnotic pills or drowning. One patient expressed the longing to die at a time of great stress and I suggested that what she wanted was not destruction, nonexistence, but escape into warmth, comfort and being almost but not quite unconscious. She said, "That's it; just conscious enough to be aware of being warm and safe," like having gas at the dentist's to escape pain, which appeared to her "like a very pleasant way of dying." Unfortunately, in practice, more is achieved than is intended and the patient may die.

The Need to Save the Ego by Internal Object Relations

Once the fear-dictated retreat from outer reality has been set up, the schizoid individual has two opposed needs both of which must be met unless death is to supervene; the need to withdraw from intolerable reality and the need to remain in touch with it, to save the ego in both cases. This is what enforces the final ego split into an active suffering and a passive regressed libidinal ego. The flight into regression begets a counterflight back into object relations again. But this return to objects must still compromise with fear and the need to remain withdrawn, and this leads to the creation of an object world that enables the ego to be both withdrawn, yet not "in the womb," the Kleinian world of "internal objects," dream, and phantasy, a world of object relationships which is also withdrawn "inside" out of the external world. This, *par excellence* is the world of psychoneurotic and psychotic experience. Sometimes the flight back from deep regression to objects in the sense of "internal objects" appears to go further and become a return to the external world itself. But close inspection shows this to be illusory. It is not a return to the actual reality of external objects as such in their own right, but a projection on to them of the internal world of phantasy objects, which accounts for the unrealistic reactions of psychotic and psychoneurotic patients to real people. Living in the internal phantasy world and the projected phantasy world both constitute a defence against loss of the ego by too complete regression and depersonalization, while remaining in varying degrees withdrawn from external reality which is still felt to be hostile.

This type of defence, however, has its own dangers. Over and above the ultimate danger of ego loss by schizoid depersonalization, there are three further dangers of ego loss that arise in this mid-region of defensive activities. The flight back to objects is at first a return to the bad objects from whom escape was originally sought. Bad object relations at first safeguard the separate identity of the ego by setting it in clear opposition to its object, a defence much used. The frightened person becomes quarrelsome, but this may go too far and get out of control, mounting up to persecutory anxiety in the inner world and the schizophrenic fear of being torn to pieces. There appear to be two ways of escape from this schizophrenic terror of disintegration of the ego under persecution by internal bad objects or under the pressures of real life experienced in the internal persecutory setup. The flight to good objects gives rise to another perilous situation for the ego. The basic attitude to good objects is already fixed as a panic-stricken flight inside for safety. Even short of that, the relation to a good object is so much one of fear-enforced infantile dependence that it feels smothering, as already noted. Thus *claustrophobic* anxiety arises, to be distinguished from the schizoid fear of ego loss by depersonalization, the typical state to which the central ego in touch with the outer world is reduced when all vitality has been drained out of it by too complete regression. This could lead to death and total ego loss. The claustrophobic fear of being stifled by being shut in is the price to be paid for seeking safety through flight back inside. The active ego is in danger of being lost by reduction to a state of passivity in which no self-expression is now possible.

Thus *no objects* involve the fear of ego loss by depersonalization, *bad objects* involve the fear of ego loss by disintegration under destructive persecution, *good objects* involve the fear of the loss of the active ego by imprisonment in smothering passivity. One further possibility remains, a compromise between bad and good objects. If one hates good objects instead of bad ones, there will not be the same danger of retaliation by the object and also smothering is avoided. But now a fourth danger appears.

If one hates a good object the ego feels fear, not primarily for itself but for the object. Guilt will arise and with it Mrs. Klein's "depressive anxiety" in place of the more primitive "persecutory anxiety." *Ambivalent object relations* involve fear of loss of the ego for all practical purposes through the paralysis of depression, in which state the ego dare not do anything at all for fear of doing wrong. The good object becomes an accusatory object and the ego feels morally persecuted. We may thus grade the dangers to which the ego feels exposed. The ultimate and worst danger is that of total ego loss, represented in consciousness by depersonalization, and by such profound apathy through schizoid withdrawal and regression that death would ensue. Against this danger the defence of resort to bad object relations tends to overdevelop, and leads either to schizophrenic terror of disintegration under violent persecution, or depressive paralysis under merciless accusation and pathological guilt. Nevertheless these two psychotic dangers arise out of the operation of the defence of bad object relations against the ultimate schizoid danger. . . .

The hope and possibility of the rebirth of the regressed ego is the obvious final problem raised in the interests of psychotherapy. I cannot see that we know very much about it as yet. Winnicott has opened a pathway that many research workers will tread before the problem is mastered. I hope to be able to report clinical data on this matter. At this stage I feel only able to say that I have found encouraging results with several patients who each in his or her own different way, have been able to find security for their regressed ego in the psychotherapeutic relationship. There appear to be two aspects of the problem. The first is the slow growth out of their anti-libidinal (Freudian sadistic superego) persecution of themselves; they need to unlearn their ruthless driving of themselves by ceaseless inner mental pressure to keep going as "forced pseudo-adults" and to acquire the courage to adopt more of the understanding attitude of the therapist to the hard-pressed and frightened child within. Simultaneously with this there goes on a second process, the growth of a constructive faith that if the needs of the regressed ego are met, first in the relation to the therapist who protects it in its need for an initial passive dependence, this will mean not collapse and loss of active powers for good and all, but a steady recuperation from deep strain, diminishing of deep fears, revitalization of the personality, and rebirth of an active ego that is spontaneous and does not have to be forced and driven, what Balint calls the "new beginning."

REFERENCES

Fairbairn, W. R. D. (1952). *Psychoanalytic Studies of the Personality.* London: Tavistock.

Guntrip, H. (1960). Ego-weakness and the hard core of the problem of psychotherapy. *British Journal of Medical Psychology* 33:163.

——(1961). *Personality Structure and Human Interaction.* London: Hogarth.

——(1969). *Schizoid Phenomena, Object Relations and the Self.* New York: International Universities Press.

Winnicott, D. W. (1955). Metapsychological and clinical aspects of regression within the psychoanalytical set-up. *International Journal of Psycho-Analysis* 36:16.

39

John Bowlby's "The Role of Attachment in Personality Development" (1988)

John Bowlby was a child psychiatrist and psychoanalyst who headed the Tavistock Clinic's Department of Children and Parents. His research approach to problems of early loss and deprivation in the development of personality and psychopathology grew into his major contribution, that of attachment theory, which drew heavily on ethology and other forms of observational science. Attachment theory has been one of the major sources for modern infant research, whose lessons have in turn offered so much to the continuing evolution of psychoanalysis and object relations theory, and the allied fields of family therapy, education, and social policy concerning child rearing. The culmination of Bowlby's work is contained in the three-volume work *Attachment and Loss,* which includes *Attachment* (1969), *Separation* (1973), and *Loss* (1980); The work on attachment is summarized here in a paper published in 1988.

Bowlby is unique in the analytic world in the attention he focused on the experience of children's tie to their mothers and families, which corrected many years of analytic focus on the formative influence of the child's inner world without considering family influence. His analytic derivation, he once told me, was chiefly from Fairbairn, whose emphasis on the lifelong need for relationships was at the heart of his own work. He disagreed, however, with the Fairbairn's use of the term *dependence* to describe the quality of relationship of the child to the mother, feeling it had acquired a perjorative connotation, preferring always to use the term *attachment* to describe that condition required by everyone throughout the life span.

REFERENCES

Bowlby, J. (1969). *Attachment*, vol. 1 of *Attachment and Loss* (2nd edition 1982). London: Hogarth Press; New York: Basic Books; Harmondsworth: Penguin, 1971.

——(1973). *Separation: Anxiety and Anger*, vol. 2 of *Attachment and Loss*. London: Hogarth Press; New York: Basic Books; Harmondsworth: Penguin, 1975.

——(1980). *Loss: Sadness and Depression*, vol. 3 of *Attachment and Loss*. London: Hogarth Press; New York: Basic Books; Harmondsworth: Penguin, 1981.

THE PRIMACY OF INTIMATE EMOTIONAL BONDS

Attachment theory regards the propensity to make intimate emotional bonds to particular individuals as a basic component of human nature, already present in germinal form in the neonate and continuing through adult life into old age. During infancy and childhood bonds are with parents (or parent substitutes) who are looked to for protection, comfort, and support. During healthy adolescence and adult life these bonds persist, but are complemented by new bonds, commonly of a heterosexual nature. Although food and sex sometimes play important roles in attachment relationships, the relationship exists in its own right and has a key survival function of its own, namely protection. Initially the only means of communication between infant and mother is through emotional expression and its accompanying behaviour. Although supplemented later by speech, emotionally mediated communication nonetheless persists as a principal feature of intimate relationships throughout life.

Within the attachment framework, therefore, intimate emotional bonds are seen as neither subordinate to nor derivative from food and sex. Nor is the urgent desire for comfort and support in adversity regarded as childish, as dependency theory implies. Instead the capacity to make intimate emotional bonds with other individuals, sometimes in the careseeking role and sometimes in the caregiving one, is regarded as a principal feature of effective personality functioning and mental health.

As a rule careseeking is shown by a weaker and less experienced individual towards someone regarded as stronger and/or wiser. A child, or older person in the careseeking role, keeps within range of the caregiver, the degree of closeness or of ready accessibility depending on circumstances: hence the concept of attachment behaviour.

Caregiving, the major role of parents and complementary to attachment behaviour, is regarded in the same light as careseeking, namely as a basic component of human nature.

Exploring the environment, including play and varied activities with peers, is seen as a third basic component and one antithetic to attachment behaviour. When an individual (of any age) is feeling secure he is likely to explore away from his attachment figure. When alarmed, anxious, tired, or unwell he feels an urge towards proximity. Thus we see the typical pattern of interaction between child and parent known as exploration from a secure base, first described by Ainsworth (1967). Provided the parent is known to be accessible and will be responsive when called upon, a healthy child feels secure enough to explore. At first these explorations are limited both in time and space. Around the middle of the third year, however, a secure child begins to become confident enough to increase time and distance away—first to half-days and later to whole days. As he grows into adolescence, his excursions are extended to weeks or months, but a secure home base remains indispensable nonetheless for optimal functioning and mental health. Note that the concept of secure base is a central feature of the theory of psychotherapy proposed.

During the early months of life an infant shows many of the component responses of what will later become attachment behaviour, but the organized pattern does not develop until the second half of the first year. From birth onwards he shows a germinal capacity to engage in social interaction and pleasure in doing so (Stern 1985): thus there is no autistic or narcissistic phase. Within days, moreover, he is able to distinguish between his mother-figure and others by means of her smell and by hearing her voice, and also by the way she holds him. Visual discrimination is not reliable until the second quarter. Initially crying is the only means available to him for signalling his need for care, and contentment the only means for signalling that he has been satisfied. During the second month, however, his social smile acts strongly to encourage his mother in her ministrations and his repertoire of emotional communications rapidly extends (Izard and Read 1982; Emde 1983).

The development of attachment behaviour as an organized system, having as its goal the keeping of proximity or of accessibility to a discriminated mother-figure, requires that the child should have developed the cognitive capacity to keep his mother in mind when she is not present: this capacity develops during the second six months of life. Thus from 9 months onwards the great majority of infants respond to being left with a strange person by protest and crying, and also by more or less prolonged fretting and rejection of the stranger. These observations demonstrate that during these months an infant is becoming capable of representation and that his working model of his mother is becoming available to him for purposes of comparison during her absence and for recognition after her return. Complementary to his model of his mother, he develops a working model of himself in interaction with her; likewise for father.

A major feature of attachment theory is the hypothesis that attachment behaviour is organized by means of a control system within the central nervous system, analogous to the physiological control systems that maintain physiological measures such as blood pressure and body temperature within set limits. Thus the theory proposes that, in a way analogous to physiological homeostasis, the attachment control system maintains a person's relation to his attachment figure between certain limits of distance and accessibility, using increasingly sophisticated methods of communication for doing so. As such, the effects of its operation can be regarded as an example of what can usefully be termed environmental homeostasis (Bowlby 1969, 1982). By postulating a control system of this sort (with analogous systems controlling other forms of behaviour) attachment theory contains within itself a theory of motivation that can replace traditional theories which invoke a postulated build-up of energy or drive. Among several advantages of control theory are that it gives as much attention to the conditions terminating a behavioural sequence as to those initiating it and is proving a fruitful framework for empirical research.

The presence of an attachment control system and its linkage to the working models of self and attachment figure(s) that are built in the mind during childhood are held to be central features of personality functioning throughout life.

PATTERNS OF ATTACHMENT AND CONDITIONS DETERMINING THEIR DEVELOPMENT

The second area to which attachment theory pays special attention is the role of a child's parents in determining how he develops. There is today impressive and mounting evidence that the pattern of attachment that an individual develops during the years of immaturity—infancy, childhood, and adolescence—is profoundly influenced by the way his parents (or other parent figures) treat him. This evidence derives from a number of systematic research studies, the most impressive being prospective studies of socio-emotional development during the first five years undertaken by developmental psychologists who are also clinically sophisticated. Pioneered by Ainsworth (Ainsworth, Blehar, Waters, and Wall 1978; Ainsworth 1985) and expanded, notably by Main (Main, Kaplan, and Cassidy 1985) and Sroufe (1983, 1985) in the United States and by Grossmann (Grossmann, Grossmann, and Schwan 1986) in Germany, these studies are now multiplying fast. Their findings are remarkably consistent and have the clearest of clinical significance.

Three principal patterns of attachment, first described by Ainsworth and her colleagues in 1971, are now reliably identified, together with the family conditions that promote them. These are first the pattern of secure attachment in which the individual is confident that his parent (or parent figure) will be available, responsive, and helpful should he encounter adverse or frightening situations. With this assurance, he feels bold in his explorations of the world. This pattern is promoted by a parent, in the early years especially by mother, being readily available, sensitive to her child's signals, and lovingly responsive when he seeks protection and/or comfort.

A second pattern is that of anxious resistant attachment in which the individual is uncertain whether his parent will be available or responsive or helpful when called upon. Because of this uncertainty he is always prone to separation anxiety, tends to be clinging, and is anxious about exploring the world. This pattern, in which conflict is evident, is promoted by a parent being available and helpful on some occasions but not on others, and by separations and, as clinical findings show, by threats of abandonment used as a means of control.

A third pattern is that of anxious avoidant attachment in which the individual has no confidence that, when he seeks care, he will be responded to helpfully but, on the contrary, expects to be rebuffed. When in marked degree such an individual attempts to live his life without the love and support of others, he tries to become emotionally self-sufficient and may later be diagnosed as narcissistic or as having a false self of the type described by Winnicott (1960). This pattern, in which conflict is more hidden, is the result of the individual's mother constantly rebuffing him when he approaches her for comfort or protection. The most extreme cases result from repeated rejections.

Although in most cases the pattern observed conforms fairly closely to one or another of the three well-recognized types, there have been puzzling exceptions. During the assessment procedure used in these studies (the Ainsworth Strange Situation), in which infant and mother are observed in interaction during a series of brief episodes, certain infants have appeared to be disoriented and/or disorganized. One infant appears dazed; another freezes immobile; a third engages in some stereotypy; a fourth starts a movement, then stops unaccountably. After much study Main and her colleagues have concluded that these peculiar forms of behaviour occur in infants who are exhibiting a disorganized version of one of the three typical patterns, more often than not the anxious resistant one (Main and Weston 1981; Main and Solomon 1990). Some instances are seen in infants known to have been physically abused and/or grossly neglected by the parent (Crittenden 1985). Others occur in dyads in which the mother is suffering from a severe form of bipolar affective illness and who treats her child in an erratic and unpredictable way (Radke-Yarrow et al. 1985). Yet others are shown by the infants of mothers who are still preoccupied with mourning a parental figure lost during the mother's childhood and by those of mothers who themselves suffered physical or sexual abuse as children (Main and Hesse 1990). Cases showing these deviant patterns are clearly of great clinical concern, and much attention is now being given to them.

Knowledge of the origins of these deviant patterns confirms in the clearest possible way the influence on a child's pattern of attachment of the parent's way of treating his or her child. Yet further confirmatory evidence comes from detailed observations of the way different mothers treat their children during a laboratory session arranged when the child is 2½ years old (Matas et al. 1978). In this study the child is given a small but difficult task for the solution of which he requires a little assistance, and his mother is free to interact with him. In this situation, it is found, the way she treats him correlates closely with the pattern of attachment her child showed towards her eighteen months earlier. Thus the mother of a child earlier assessed as securely attached is found to be attentive and sensitive to his performance and to respond to his successes and difficulties in a way that is helpful and encouraging. Conversely the mother of a child earlier assessed as insecure is found to be less attentive and/or less sensitive. In some cases her responses are ill-timed and unhelpful; in others she may take little notice of what he is doing or how he is feeling; in yet others she may actively discourage or reject his bids for help and encouragement. Note that the pattern of interaction adopted by the mother of a secure infant provides an excellent model for the pattern of therapeutic intervention advocated here.

In thus underlining the very great influence that a child's mother has on his development, it is necessary also to consider what has led a mother to adopt the style of mothering she does. One major influence on this is the amount of emotional support, or lack of it, she herself is receiving at the time. Another is the form of mothering that she herself received when a child. Once these factors are recognized, as they have been by many analytically oriented clinicians long since, the idea of blaming parents evaporates and is replaced by a therapeutic approach.

PATHWAYS TO PERSONALITY DEVELOPMENT

There is one further way in which attachment theory differs from traditional types of psychoanalytic theory, namely its rejection of the model of development in which an individual is held to pass through a series of stages in any one of which he may become fixated or to which he may regress, and its replacement by a model in which an individual is seen as progressing along one or another of an array of potential developmental pathways. Some of these pathways are compatible with healthy development; others deviate in one or another direction in ways incompatible with health.

All variants of the traditional model invoking phases of development are based on the assumption that, at some phase of normal development, a child shows psychological features that, in an older individual, would be regarded as signs of pathology. Thus a chronically anxious and clinging adult might be regarded as being fixated in or having regressed to a postulated phase of orality or of symbiosis; while a deeply withdrawn individual might be regarded as having regressed to a postulated phase of autism or of narcissism. Systematic and sensitive studies of human infants, such as those reported by Stern (1985), have now rendered this model untenable. Observations show that infants are socially responsive from birth onwards. Healthily developing toddlers do not show anxious clinging except when they are frightened or distressed; at other times they explore with confidence.

The model of developmental pathways regards an infant at birth as having an array of pathways potentially open to him, the one along which he will in fact proceed being determined at every moment by the interaction of the individual as he now is with the environment in which he happens then to be. Each infant is held to have his own individual array of potential pathways for personality development which, except for infants born with certain types of neurological damage, include many that are compatible with mental health and also many that are incompatible. Which particular pathway he proceeds along is determined by the environment he meets with, especially the way his parents (or parent substitutes) treat him, and how he responds to them. Children who have parents who are sensitive and responsive are enabled to develop along a healthy pathway. Those who have insensitive, unresponsive, neglectful, or rejecting parents are likely to develop along a deviant pathway which is in some degree incompatible with mental health and which renders them vulnerable to breakdown, should they meet with seriously adverse events. Even so, since the course of subsequent development is not fixed, changes in the way a child is treated can shift his pathway in either a more favourable direction or a less favourable one. Although the capacity for developmental change diminishes with age, change continues throughout the life cycle so that changes for better or for worse are always possible. It is this continuing potential for change that means that at no time of life is a person invulnerable to every possible adversity and also that at no time of life is a person impermeable to favourable influence. It is this persisting potential for change that gives opportunity for effective therapy.

REFERENCES

Ainsworth, M. D. S. (1967). *Infancy in Uganda: Infant Care and the Growth of Attachment.* Baltimore, MD: Johns Hopkins Press.

——(1985). I. Patterns of infant–mother attachment: antecedents and effects on development. II. Attachment across the life-span, *Bulletin of the New York Academy of Medicine* 61:771–791 and 791–812.

Ainsworth, M. D. S., Bell, S. M., and Stayton, D. J. (1971). Individual differences in strange situation behavior of one-year-olds. In *The Origins of Human Social Relations,* ed. H. R. Schaffer, pp. 17–57. London: Academic Press.

Ainsworth, M. D. S., Blehar, M. C., Waters, E., and Wall, S. (1978). *Patterns of Attachment: Assessed in the Strange Situation and at Home.* Hillsdale, N.J.: Lawrence Erlbaum.

Bowlby, J. (1969). *Attachment,* vol. 1 of *Attachment and Loss* (2nd edition 1982) London: Hogarth; New York: Basic Books; Harmondsworth: Penguin, 1971.

——(1982). *Attachment,* 2nd edition of vol. 1 of *Attachment and Loss.* London: Hogarth; New York: Basic Books.

Crittenden, P. (1985). Maltreated infants: vulnerability and resilience. *Journal of Child Psychology and Psychiatry* 26:85–96.

Emde, R. N. (1983). The pre-representational self and its affective core. *Psychoanalytic Study of the Child* 38:165–192. New Haven: Yale University Press.

Grossmann, K. E., Grossmann, K., and Schwan, A. (1986). Capturing the wider view of attachment: a reanalysis of Ainsworth's Strange Situation. In *Measuring Emotions in Infants and Children,* ed. C. E. Izard and P. B. Read. New York: Cambridge University Press.

Izard, C. E., and Read, P. B., eds. (1982). *Measuring Emotions in Infants and Children.* New York: Cambridge University Press.

Main, M., and Hesse, E. (1990). Lack of resolution of mourning in adulthood and its relationship to infant organization: some speculation rearding causal mechanisms. In *Attachment in the Preschool Years,* ed. M. Greenberg, D. Cichetti, and M. Cummings. Chicago: University of Chicago Press.

Main, M., Kaplan, N., and Cassidy, J. (1985). Security in infancy, childhood and adulthood: a move to the level of representation. In *Growing Points in Attachment: Theory and Research.,* ed. I. Bretherton and E. Waters. Monographs of the Society for Research in Child Development Serial 209:66–104. Chicago: University of Chicago Press.

Main, M., and Solomon, J. (1990). Procedure for identifying infants as disorganized/disoriented during the Ainsworth Strange Situation. In *Attachment in the Preschool Years,* ed. M. Greenberg, D. Cichetti, and M. Cummings. Chicago: University of Chicago Press.

Main, M., and Weston, D. (1981). Quality of attachment to mother and to father: related to conflict behaviour and the readiness for establishing new relationships. *Child Development* 52:932–940.

Matas, L., Arend, R. A., and Sroufe, L. A. (1978). Continuity of adaptation in the second year: the relationship between quality of attachment and later competence. *Child Development* 49:547–556.

Radke-Yarrow, M., Cummings, E. M., Kuczynski, L. and Chapman, M. (1985). Patterns of attachment in two- and three-year-olds in normal families and families with parental depression. *Child Development* 56:884–893.

Sroufe, L. A. (1983). Infant–caregiver attachment and patterns of adaptation in pre-school: the roots of maladaptation and competence. In *Minnesota Symoposium in Child Psychology,* 16:41–81. Minneapolis: University of Minnesota Press.

——(1985). Attachment-classification from the perspective of infant–caregiver relationships and infant temperament. *Child Development* 56:1–14.

Stern, D. N. (1985). *The Interpersonal World of the Infant.* New York: Basic Books.

Winnicott, D. W. (1960). Ego distortion in terms of true and false self. In *The Maturational Processes and the Facilitating Environment,* pp. 140–152. London: Hogarth; New York: International Universities Press.

IX

TRANSFERENCE AND COUNTERTRANSFERENCE

40

Paula Heimann's "On Countertransference" (1949)

Study of the implications of object relations theory for therapy pervades the writings of all major contributors, but nowhere are the implications more direct than in the study of transference and countertransference. The new directions in the use of the therapist's own reactions as a source of information about the patient's early experience, even before language, began with Klein's description of transference as a "total situation" (excerpted in Chapter 13) and Winnicott's landmark paper, "Hate in the Countertransference" (excerpted in Chapter 16).

The papers excerpted in this section were instrumental in the evolution of understanding and use of countertransference beyond Freud's original formulation. He first described it as the area of the analyst's unanalyzed neuroses and pathology, requiring supervision and personal analysis. But with Klein's changing emphasis, Winnicott's description of the objective hate in the work with some patients, and Paula Heimann's paper, a new direction was taken. Quickly, analysts began to study a wider, enriched view of the therapist's range of responses to the patient and the affective currents between them that re-create early relationships through the ubiquitous interplay of projective and introjective identification.

The work of these early clinicians on transference, countertransference, and on the mechanism projective identification which is the vehicle for them is continued in the writing of current contributors, represented later in this volume in selections from James Grotstein, Betty Joseph, Otto Kernberg, and David and Jill Scharff.

Paula Heimann's paper followed Winnicott's "Hate in the Countertransference" and a handful of others in the early literature in challenging the notion of strict analytic abstinence or "neutrality." Many analysts seemed to have taken Freud's admonition on the analyst's need to maintain neutrality—by which he meant primarily a position equidistant among the structures of personality—as an injunction to analysts against having feelings toward their patients. Freud and Klein had thought that countertransference was an interference to analysis because it stemmed from the analyst's unconscious, unanalyzed responses to patients. Heimann's paper, with its common sense and nearly telegraphic brevity, delivered a revolutionary message that analysts' responses were themselves signals of patients' unconscious issues and conflicts. This theoretical movement, together with Bion's work on projective identification and containment and Joseph's contribution on transference as a total situation were perhaps the major influences toward making countertransference a central aspect of technique in modern psychoanalysis and psychotherapy.

This short note on countertransference has been stimulated by certain observations I made in seminars and control analyses. I have been struck by the widespread belief amongst candidates that the countertransference is nothing but a source of trouble. Many candidates are afraid and feel guilty when they become aware of feelings towards their patients and consequently aim at avoiding any emotional response and at becoming completely unfeeling and "detached."

When I tried to trace the origin of this ideal of the detached analyst, I found that our literature does indeed contain descriptions of the analytic work which can give rise to the notion that a good analyst does not feel anything beyond a uniform and mild benevolence towards his patients, and that any ripple of emotional waves on this smooth surface represents a disturbance to be overcome. This may possibly derive from a misreading of some of Freud's statements, such as his comparison with the surgeon's state of mind during an operation, or his simile of the mirror. At least these have been quoted to me in this connection in discussions on the nature of the countertransference. . . .

For the purpose of this paper I am using the term *countertransference* to cover all the feelings which the analyst experiences towards his patient. It may be argued that this use of the term is not correct, and that countertransference simply means transference on the part of the analyst. However, I would suggest that the prefix *counter* implies additional factors. . . .

My thesis is that the analyst's emotional response to his patient within the analytic situation represents one of the most important tools for his work. The analyst's countertransference is an instrument of research into the patient's unconscious.

The analytic situation has been investigated and described from many angles, and there is general agreement about its unique character. But my impression is that it has not been sufficiently stressed that it is a *relationship* between two persons. What distinguishes this relationship from others is not the presence of feelings in one partner, the patient, and their absence in the other, the analyst, but above all the degree of the feelings experienced and the use made of them, these factors being interdependent. The aim of the analyst's own analysis, from this point of view, is not to turn him into a mechanical brain which can produce interpretations on the basis of a purely intellectual procedure, but to enable him, to *sustain* the feelings which are stirred in him, as opposed to discharging them (as does the patient), in order to *subordinate* them to the analytic task in which he functions as the patient's mirror reflection.

If an analyst tries to work without consulting his feelings, his interpretations are poor. I have often seen this in the work of beginners, who, out of fear, ignored or stifled their feelings.

We know that the analyst needs an evenly hovering attention in order to follow the patient's free associations, and that this enables him to listen simultaneously on many levels. . . .

I would suggest that the analyst along with this freely working attention needs a freely roused emotional sensibility so as to follow the patient's emotional movements and unconscious phantasies. Our basic assumption is that the analyst's unconscious understands that of his patient. This rapport on the deep level comes to the surface in the form of feelings which the analyst notices in response to his patient, in his countertransference. This is the most dynamic way in which his patient's voice reaches him. In the comparison of feelings roused in himself with his patient's associations and behaviour, the analyst possesses a most valuable means of checking whether he has understood or failed to understand his patient.

Since, however, violent emotions of any kind, of love or hate, helpfulness or anger, impel towards action rather than towards contemplation and blur a person's capacity to observe and weigh the evidence correctly, it follows that, if the analyst's emotional response is intense, it will defeat its object.

Therefore the analyst's emotional sensitivity needs to be extensive rather than intensive, differentiating, and mobile.

There will be stretches in the analytic work, when the analyst who combines free attention with free emotional responses does not register his feelings as a problem, because they are in accord with the meaning he understands. But often the emotions roused in him are much nearer to the heart of the matter than his reasoning, or, to put it in other words, his unconscious perception of the patient's unconscious is more acute and in advance of his conscious conception of the situation.

A recent experience comes to mind. It concerns a patient whom I had taken over from a colleague. The patient was a man in the forties who had originally sought treatment when his marriage broke down. Among his symptoms promiscuity figured prominently. In the third week of his analysis with me he told me, at the beginning of the session, that he was going to marry a woman whom he had met only a short time before.

It was obvious that his wish to get married at this juncture was determined by his resistance against the analysis and his need to act out his transference conflicts. Within a strongly ambivalent attitude the desire for an intimate relation with me had already clearly appeared. I had thus many reasons for doubting the wisdom of his intention and for suspecting his choice. But such an attempt to short-circuit analysis is not infrequent at the beginning of, or at a critical point in, the treatment and usually does not represent too great an obstacle to the work, so that catastrophic conditions need not arise. I was therefore somewhat puzzled to find that I reacted with a sense of apprehension and worry to the patient's remark. I felt that something more was involved in his situation, something beyond the ordinary acting out, which, however, eluded me.

In his further associations which centred round his friend, the patient, describing her, said she had had a "rough passage." This phrase again registered particularly and increased my misgivings. It dawned on me that it was precisely because she had had a rough passage that he was drawn to her. But still I felt that I did not see things clearly enough. Presently he came to tell me his dream: he had acquired from abroad a very good second-hand car which was damaged. He wished to repair it, but another person in the dream objected for reasons of caution. The patient had, as he put it, "to make him confused" in order that he might go ahead with the repair of the car.

With the help of this dream I came to understand what before I had merely felt as a sense of apprehension and worry. There was indeed more at stake than the mere acting out of transference conflicts.

When he gave me the particulars of the car—very good, second-hand, from abroad—the patient spontaneously recognized that it represented myself. The other person in the dream who tried to stop him and whom he confused, stood for that part of the patient's ego which aimed at security and happiness and for the analysis as a protective object.

The dream showed that the patient wished me to be damaged (he insisted on my being the refugee to whom applies the expression "rough passage" which he had used for his new friend). Out of guilt for his sadistic impulses he was compelled to make reparation, but this reparation was of a masochistic nature, since it necessitated blotting out the voice of reason and caution. This element of confusing the protective figure was in itself double-barrelled, expressing both his sadistic and his masochistic impulses; insofar as it aimed at annihilating the analysis, it represented the patient's sadistic tendencies in the pattern of his infantile anal attacks on his mother; insofar as it stood for his ruling out his desire for security and happiness, it expressed his self-destructive trends. Reparation turned into a masochistic act again engenders hatred, and, far from solving the conflict between destructiveness and guilt, leads to a vicious circle.

The patient's intention of marrying his new friend, the injured woman, was fed from both sources, and the acting out of his transference conflicts proved to be determined by this specific and powerful sado-masochistic system.

Unconsciously I had grasped immediately the seriousness of the situation, hence the sense of worry which I experienced. But my conscious understanding lagged behind, so that I could decipher the patient's message and appeal for help only later in the hour, when more material came up.

In giving the gist of an analytic session I hope to illustrate my contention that the analyst's immediate emotional response to his patient is a significant pointer to the patient's unconscious processes and guides him towards fuller understanding. It helps the analyst to focus his attention on the most urgent elements in the patient's associations and serves as a useful criterion for the selection of interpretations from material which, as we know, is always overdetermined.

From the point of view I am stressing, the analyst's countertransference is not only part and parcel of the analytic relationship, but it is the patient's *creation*, it is a part of the patient's personality. . . .

The approach to the countertransference which I have presented is not without danger. It does not represent a screen for the analyst's shortcomings. When the analyst in his own analysis has worked through his infantile conflicts and anxieties (paranoid and depressive), so that he can easily establish contact with his own unconscious, he will not impute to his patient what belongs to himself. He will have achieved a dependable equilibrium which enables him to carry the roles of the patient's id, ego, superego, and external objects which the patient allots to him or—in other words—projects on him, when he dramatizes his conflicts in the analytic relationship. In the instance I have given the analyst was predominantly in the roles of the patient's good mother to be destroyed and rescued, and of the patient's reality ego which tried to oppose his sadomasochistic impulses. In my view Freud's demand that the analyst must "recognize and master" his countertransference does not lead to the conclusion that the countertransference is a disturbing factor and that the analyst should become unfeeling and detached, but that he must use his emotional response as a key to the patient's unconscious. This will protect him from entering as a co-actor on the scene which the patient reenacts in the analytic relationship and from exploiting it for his own needs. At the same time he will find ample stimulus for taking himself to task again and again and for continuing the analysis of his own problems. This, however, is his private affair, and I do not consider it right for the analyst to communicate his feelings to his patient. In my view such honesty is more in the nature of a confession and a burden to the patient. In any case it leads away from the analysis. The emotions roused in the analyst will be of value to his patient, if used as one more source of insight into the patient's unconscious conflicts and defences; and when these are interpreted and worked through, the ensuing changes in the patient's ego include the strengthening of his reality sense so that he sees his analyst as a human being, not a god or demon, and the "human" relationship in the analytic situation follows without the analyst's having recourse to extra-analytical means.

Psychoanalytic technique came into being when Freud, abandoning hypnosis, discovered resistance and repression. In my view the use of countertransference as an instrument of research can be recognized in his descriptions of the way by which he arrived at his fundamental discoveries. When he tried to elucidate the hysterical patient's forgotten memories, he felt that a force from the patient opposed his attempts and that he had to overcome this resistance by his own psychic work.

He concluded that it was the same force which was responsible for the repression of the crucial memories and for the formation of the hysterical symptom.

The unconscious process in hysterical amnesia can thus be defined by its twin facets, of which one is turned outward and felt by the analyst as resistance, whilst the other works intrapsychically as repression.

Whereas in the case of repression countertransference is characterized by the sensation of a quantity of energy, an opposing force, other defence mechanisms will rouse other qualities in the analyst's response.

I believe that with more thorough investigation of countertransference from the angle I have attempted here, we may come to work out more fully the way in which the character of the countertransference corresponds to the nature of the patient's unconscious impulses and defences operative at the actual time.

41

Heinrich Racker's "The Meaning and Uses of Countertransference" (1957)

Heinrich Racker was born in Poland and trained in Vienna before fleeing the Nazis by moving to Argentina. When this article was published in an American journal, *The Psychoanalytic Quarterly* in 1957, it was influential in introducing the American analytic audience to the widening scope of transference and countertransference. Racker added his voice to those who argued for normalizing the functions of countertransference through examination of the identifications and reactions of the therapist. Racker suggested new terms to signify that responses can either be in identification with the patient's self—*concordant identification*—or in identification with the patient's objects—*complementary identification.* These concepts have increased therapists' capacity to specify their countertransference responses, thereby increasing understanding and improving their ability to formulate interpretations.

The fact that countertransference conflicts determine the deficiencies in the analysis of transference becomes clear if we recall that transference is the expression of the internal object relations; for understanding of transference will depend on the analyst's capacity to identify himself both with the analysand's impulses and defenses, and with his internal objects, and to be conscious of these identifications. This ability in the analyst will in turn depend upon the degree to which he accepts his countertransference, for his countertransference is likewise based on identification with the patient's id and ego and his internal objects. One might also say that transference is the expression of the patient's relations with the fantasied and real countertransference of the analyst. For just as countertransference is the psychological response to the analysand's real and imaginary transferences, so also is transference the response to the analyst's imaginary and real countertransferences. Analysis of the patient's fantasies about countertransference, which in the widest sense constitute the causes and consequences of the transferences, is an essential part of the analysis of the transferences. Perception of the patient's fantasies regarding countertransference will depend in turn upon the degree to which the analyst himself perceives his countertransference processes–on the continuity and depth of his conscious contact with himself.

To summarize, the repression of countertransference (and other pathological fates that it may meet) necessarily leads to deficiencies in the analysis of transference, which in turn lead to the repression and other mishandling of countertransference as soon as the candidate becomes an analyst. It is a heritage from generation to generation, similar to the heritage of idealizations and denials concerning the imagoes of the parents, which continue working even when the child becomes a father or mother. The child's mythology is prolonged in the mythology of the analytic situation,[1] the analyst himself being partially subject to it and collaborating unconsciously in its maintenance in the candidate.

Before illustrating these statements, let us briefly consider one of those ideals in its specifically psychoanalytic expression: the ideal of the analyst's objectivity. No one, of course, denies the existence of subjective factors in the analyst and of countertransference in itself; but there seems to exist an important difference between what is generally acknowledged in practice and the real state of affairs. The first distortion of truth in the "myth of the analytic situation" is that analysis is an interaction between a sick person and a healthy one. The truth is that it is an interaction between two personalities, in both of which the ego is under pressure from the id, the superego, and the external world; each personality has its internal and external dependencies, anxieties, and pathological defenses; each is also a child with its internal parents; and each of these whole personalities–

1. Little (1951) speaks, for instance, of the "myth of the impersonal analyst."

that of the analysand and that of the analyst—responds to every event of the analytic situation. Besides these similarities between the personalities of analyst and analysand, there also exist differences, and one of these is in "objectivity." The analyst's objectivity consists mainly in a certain attitude toward his own subjectivity and countertransference. The neurotic (obsessive) ideal of objectivity leads to repression and blocking of subjectivity and so to the apparent fulfilment of the myth of the "analyst without anxiety or anger." The other neurotic extreme is that of "drowning" in the countertransference. True objectivity is based upon a form of internal division that enables the analyst to make himself (his own countertransference and subjectivity) the object of his continuous observation and analysis. This position also enables him to be relatively "objective" toward the analysand.

The term *countertransference* has been given various meanings. They may be summarized by the statement that for some authors countertransference includes everything that arises in the analyst as psychological response to the analysand, whereas for others not all this should be called countertransference. Some, for example, prefer to reserve the term for what is infantile in the relationship of the analyst with his analysand, while others make different limitations (Gitelson 1952, A. Reich 1951). Hence efforts to differentiate from each other certain of the complex phenomena of countertransference lead to confusion or to unproductive discussions of terminology. Freud invented the term countertransference in evident analogy to transference, which he defined as reimpressions or re-editions of childhood experiences, including greater or lesser modifications of the original experience. Hence one frequently uses the term transference for the totality of the psychological attitude of the analysand toward the analyst. We know, to be sure, that real external qualities of the analytic situation in general and of the analyst in particular have important influence on the relationship of the analysand with the analyst, but we also know that all these present factors are experienced according to the past and the fantasy—according, that is to say, to a transference predisposition. As determinants of the transference neurosis and, in general, of the psychological situation of the analysand toward the analyst, we have both the transference predisposition and the present real and especially analytic experiences, the transference in its diverse expressions being the resultant of these two factors.

Analogously, in the analyst there are the countertransference predisposition and the present real, and especially analytic, experiences, and the countertransference is the resultant. It is precisely this fusion of present and past, the continuous and intimate connection of reality and fantasy, of external and internal, conscious and unconscious, that demands a concept embracing the totality of the analyst's psychological response, and renders it advisable, at the same time, to keep for this totality of response the accustomed term countertransference. Where it is necessary for greater clarity one might speak of total countertransference and then differentiate and separate within it one aspect or another. One of its aspects consists precisely in what is transferred in countertransference; this is the part that originates in an earlier time and that is especially the infantile and primitive part within total countertransference. Another of these aspects—closely connected with the previous one—*what is neurotic* in countertransference; its main characteristics are the unreal anxiety and the pathological defenses. Under certain circumstances one may also speak of a *countertransference neurosis* (Little 1951, Racker 1953). . . .

The intention to understand creates a certain predisposition, a predisposition to identify oneself with the analysand, which is the basis of comprehension. The analyst may achieve this aim by identifying his ego with the patient's ego or, to put it more clearly although with a certain terminological inexactitude, by identifying each part of his personality with the corresponding psychological part in the patient—his id with the patient's id, his ego with the ego, his superego with the superego, accepting these identifications in his consciousness. But this does not always happen, nor is it all that happens. Apart from these identifications, which might be called *concordant* (or *homologous) identifications,* there exist also highly important identifications of the analyst's ego with the patient's internal objects, for example, with the superego. Adapting an expression from Helene Deutsch, they might be calleα *complementary identifications.*[2] We will consider these two kinds of identification and their destinies later.

The concordant identification is based on introjection and projection, or, in other terms, on the resonance of the exterior in the interior, on recognition of what belongs to another as one's own ("this part of you is I") and on the equation of what is one's own with what belongs to another ("this part of me is you"). The processes inherent in the complementary identifications are the same, but they refer to the patient's objects. The

2. Deutsch (1926) speaks of the "complementary position" when she refers to the analyst's identifications with the object imagoes.

greater the conflicts between the parts of the analyst's personality, the greater are his difficulties in carrying out the concordant identifications in their entirety.

The complementary identifications are produced by the fact that the patient treats the analyst as an internal (projected) object, and in consequence the analyst feels treated as such; that is, he identifies himself with this object. The complementary identifications are closely connected with the destiny of the concordant identifications: it seems that to the degree to which the analyst fails in the concordant identifications and rejects them, certain complementary identifications become intensified. It is clear that rejection of a part or tendency in the analyst himself—his aggressiveness, for instance—may lead to a rejection of the patient's aggressiveness (whereby this concordant identification fails) and that such a situation leads to a greater complementary identification with the patient's rejecting object, toward which this aggressive impulse is directed.

Current usage applies the term *countertransference* to the complementary identifications only; that is to say, to those psychological processes in the analyst by which, because he feels treated as and partially identifies himself with an internal object of the patient, the patient becomes an internal (projected) object of the analyst. Usually excluded from the concept countertransference are the concordant identifications—those psychological contents that arise in the analyst by reason of the empathy achieved with the patient and that really reflect and reproduce the latter's psychological contents. Perhaps it would be best to follow this usage, but there are some circumstances that make it unwise to do so. In the first place, some authors include the concordant identifications in the concept of countertransference. One is thus faced with the choice of entering upon a terminological discussion or of accepting the term in this wider sense. I think that for various reasons the wider sense is to be preferred. If one considers that the analyst's concordant identifications (his "understandings") are a sort of reproduction of his own past processes, especially of his own infancy, and that this reproduction or reexperience is carried out as response to stimuli from the patient, one will be more ready to include the concordant identifications in the concept of countertransference. Moreover, the concordant identifications are closely connected with the complementary ones (and thus with countertransference in the popular sense), and this fact renders advisable a differentiation but not a total separation of the terms. Finally, it should be borne in mind that the disposition to empathy—that is, to concordant identification—springs largely from the sublimated positive countertransference, which likewise relates empathy with countertransference in the wider sense. All this suggests, then, the acceptance of countertransference as the totality of the analyst's psychological response to the patient. If we accept this broad definition of countertransference, the difference between its two aspects mentioned above must still be defined. On the one hand we have the analyst as subject and the patient as object of knowledge, which in a certain sense annuls the object relationship, properly speaking; and there arises in its stead the approximate union or identity between the subject's and the object's parts (experiences, impulses, defenses). The aggregate of the processes pertaining to that union might be designated, where necessary, *concordant countertransference.* On the other hand we have an object relationship very like many others, a real transference in which the analyst "repeats" previous experiences, the patient representing internal objects of the analyst. The aggregate of these experiences, which also exist always and continually, might be termed *complementary countertransference.*

A brief example may be opportune here. Consider a patient who threatens the analyst with suicide. In such situations there sometimes occurs rejection of the concordant identifications by the analyst and an intensification of his identification with the threatened object. The anxiety that such a threat can cause the analyst may lead to various reactions or defense mechanisms within him, for instance, annoyance with the patient. This—his anxiety and annoyance—would be contents of the complementary countertransference. The perception of his annoyance may, in turn, originate guilt feelings in the analyst and these lead to desires for reparation and to intensification of the "concordant" identification and "concordant" countertransference.

REFERENCES

Deutsch, H. (1926). Occult processes occurring during psychoanalysis. In *Psychoanalysis and the Occult,* ed. Devereux. New York: International Universities Press, 1953.

Gitelson, M. (1952). The emotional position of the analyst in the psychoanalytic situation. *International Journal of Psycho-Analysis* 33.

Little, M. (1951). Countertransference and the patient's response to it. *International Journal of Psycho-Analysis* 32.

Racker, H. (1953). Contribution to the problem of countertransference (1948). *International Journal of Psycho-Analysis* 34:313–324.

Reich, A. (1951). On countertransference. *International Journal of Psycho-Analysis* 32.

42

Joseph Sandler's "Countertransference and Role-Responsiveness" (1976)

Sandler has an analytic background as, and is a member of, the Freudian group of the British Psychoanalytical Society (now called the Contemporary Freudian Group), but he has maintained a role throughout his career as a broadly informed integrator of thought from all perspectives. In this paper, he added to our understanding of the action of transference and countertransference when he expanded the definition of countertransference to include not only the feeling responses of the analyst, but the analyst's unconsciously motivated enactments as well. He suggested that the analyst's role should include an attitude of *free-floating responsiveness* to the patient's unconscious initiatives, which is a counterpart of Freud's prescription of *free-floating attention*. In this way, Sandler suggested, therapists are open to an *actualization* of roles, which should no longer be considered to be simply a matter of the analyst's acting out but a vehicle that informs the therapist about the way patients influence others, now from inside a shared experience. The experience of actualization can therefore open the way to specific interpretations about object relations in current and past life.

This paper has had broad influence. In its wake, Spillius notes that "it is most useful to think of projective identification as the patient's phantasy, and to distinguish that phantasy from the patient's attempts to 'actualize' it by evoking appropriate responses in the analyst, which the analyst's role-responsiveness allows to occur, and which the analyst can use to understand his own response and the patient's phantasy and evocations" (personal communication).

No one can doubt the value of the analyst's continuing analysis of his countertransference. We can, I believe, start by assuming that the understanding of countertransference *is* important. My own interest in the subject has, in recent years, run parallel with an interest in the psychoanalytic psychology of object relationships, and what I present in the following is based on the assumption that a relationship or, to say the least, an interaction, develops between the two parties to the analytic process. We are all aware of the special features of the analytic situation, with its capacity to induce the regressive revival of the past in the present, in a way which is usually entirely unconscious in or rationalized by the patient. On the other hand, we have the use made by the analyst of his special skills, including the employment by him of such capacities as that for free-floating attention, for self-analysis and for the maintenance of what Winnicott (1960) has called the "professional attitude." By free-floating attention I do not mean the "clearing of the mind" of thoughts or memories, but the capacity to allow all sorts of thoughts, daydreams, and associations to enter the analyst's consciousness while he is at the same time listening to and observing the patient.

I have mentioned the interaction between the patient and the analyst, and this is in large part (though, of course, not wholly) determined by what I shall refer to as the intrapsychic role relationship which each party tries to impose on the other. One aspect of such a role relationship can be appropriate to the task in hand, i.e., to the work of analysis. Certainly from the side of the patient we may see a whole variety of very specific role relationships emerge. What I want to emphasize is that the role relationship of the patient in analysis at any particular time consists of a role in which he casts himself, and a complementary role in which he casts the analyst at that particular time. The patient's transference would thus represent an attempt by him to impose an interaction, an *interrelationship* (in the broadest sense of the word) between himself and the analyst. Nowadays many analysts must have the conviction (or at least the uneasy feeling) that the conceptualization of transference as the patient's libidinal or aggressive energic cathexis of a past object being transferred to the image of the analyst in the present is woefully inadequate. The patient's unconscious wishes and mechanisms with which we are concerned in our work are expressed intrapsychically in (descriptively) unconscious images or fantasies, in which both self and object in interaction have come to be represented in particular roles. In a sense the patient, in the transference, attempts to *actualize*[1] *these in a disguised way,* within the framework and limits of the analytic situation. In doing so, he resists becoming aware of any infantile relationship which he might be attempting to impose. I want to underline, at this point, the difference between the manifest content of what the patient brings and the latent unconscious content (in particular the infantile role relationships which he seeks to express or enact, as well as the defensive role relationships which he seeks to express or enact, as well as the defensive role relationships which he may have constructed). If the patient keeps to the rules he will report rather than enact, and our clues, as analysts, to the unconscious inner role relationship which the patient is trying to impose, come to us via our perceptions and the application of our analytic tools.

One could regard even the simplest instinctual wish as, from early in life, a wish to impose and to experience a role relationship as a vehicle of instinctual gratification. However, what I have to say here applies not only to unconscious instinctual wishes, but to the whole gamut of unconscious (including preconscious) wishes related to all sorts of needs, gratifications, and defences.

Parallel to the free-floating attention of the analyst is what I should like to call his *free-floating responsiveness.* The analyst is, of course, not a machine in absolute self-control, only experiencing on the one hand, and delivering interpretations on the other, although much of the literature might seem to paint such a picture. Among many other things he talks, he greets the patient, he makes arrangements about practical matters, he may joke and, to some degree, allow his responses to depart from the classical psychoanalytic norm. My contention is that in the analyst's overt reactions to the patient as well as in his thoughts and feelings what can be called his role-responsiveness shows itself, not only in his feelings but also in his attitudes and behaviour, as a crucial element in his "useful" countertransference.

---

1. I want to use the term *actualization* in the dictionary sense of the word, not in the specific technical senses in which it has been used by certain writers. The *Oxford English Dictionary* defines *actualization* as "a making actual; a realization in action or fact," and *actualize* as "to make actual, to convert into an actual fact, to realize in action."

Let me give an example to illustrate what I mean. This patient, aged 35, had not had any previous analysis and had very little knowledge of the analytic process. He was referred to me because of extreme anxiety about making public presentation of his work, although he felt absolutely competent and at ease in private and informal discussions. He had had a very narrow education, was the son of Eastern European immigrants, but because of his great financial and organizational skills had risen to a very high position in an extremely large financial organization. In the initial interview I found that he responded extremely well to trial interpretations, and I felt that work with him was going to be rewarding and a pleasure. During the first week or two of his analysis I found that I was talking very much more than I usually do. I should say that I am not an unduly silent analyst. After a little while I felt that something was making me anxious in regard to this patient, and some self-analytic reflexion on my part showed me that I was afraid that he would leave, that I was anxious to keep him, to lower his anxiety level so that he would stay in analysis and that I was talking more than usual in order to avoid the aggressive side of his ambivalent feelings. When I saw this, I felt relieved and reverted to my more usual analytic behaviour. However, I noticed at once the urge to talk during the session and became aware that the patient, by a slight inflexion of his voice, succeeded in ending every sentence with an interrogation, although he did not usually formulate a direct question. This gave me the opportunity to point out to him what he was doing (he was quite unaware of it, just as I had been unaware of it in him) and to show him how much he needed to have me reassure him by talking. He then recalled how he would feel extremely anxious as a child when his father returned home from work, and would compulsively engage his father in conversation, asking him many questions in order to be reassured that his father was not angry with him. His father had been a professional fighter, was very violent, and the patient was terrified of him but needed his father's admiration and love, to be the preferred child. (Later in the analysis we were, as one might expect, to see his fear of his own hostility to his father.) He told me that his father had the habit of not listening and not responding, and how frightening this was. The patient then realized that from early childhood onwards he had developed the trick of asking questions without directly asking them, and this had become part of his character, being intensified in situations where he feared disapproval and needed supplies of reassurance from authority figures.

The point I want to make here is that, apart from the "ordinary" elements in his analytic work, the analyst will often respond overtly to the patient in a way which he feels indicates only his own (the analyst's) problems, his own blind spots, and he may successfully resort to self-analysis in order to discover the pathology behind his particular response or attitude to behind his particular response or attitude to the patient. However, I want to suggest that very often the irrational response of the analyst, which his professional conscience leads him to see entirely as a blind spot of his own, may sometimes be usefully regarded as a compromise formation between his own tendencies and his reflexive acceptance of the role which the patient is forcing on him.

Naturally, some analysts will be more susceptible to certain roles than others, and also the proportion of the contribution from the side of the patient and from the side of the analyst will vary greatly from one instance to another. And, of course, not all the irrational actions and reactions of the analyst are reflexions of the role into which he is manoeuvred by the patient. What I wanted to show in this example was simply how the patient, by a rather subtle element in his behaviour, evoked an overt response from the analyst which, at first sight, seemed to be only irrational countertransference. Let me say emphatically that I am absolutely opposed to the idea that all countertransference responses of the analyst are due to what the patient has imposed on him. . . . I have suggested that the analyst has, within certain limits, a free-floating behavioural responsiveness in addition to his free-floating conscious attention.

Within the limits set by the analytical situation, he will, unless he becomes aware of it, tend to comply with the role demanded of him, to integrate it into his mode of responding and relating to the patient. Normally, of course, he can catch this counterresponse in himself, particularly if it appears to be in the direction of being inappropriate. However, he may only become aware of it through observing his own behaviour, responses, and attitudes, after these have been carried over into action. What I have been concerned with in this paper is the special case of the analyst regarding some aspect of his own behaviour as deriving entirely from within himself when it could more usefully be seen as a compromise between his own tendencies or propensities and the role relationship which the patient is unconsciously seeking to establish. I should add that I do not find the terms *projection, externalization, projective identification,* and *putting parts of oneself into the analyst* sufficient to explain and to understand the processes of dynamic interaction which occur in the transference and countertransference. It seems that a complicated system of unconscious cues, both given and received, is involved. This is the same sort of process that occurs not only in the aspects of transference and countertransference discussed here but in normal object relationships and in the process of temporary or permanent object choice as well.

REFERENCE

Winnicott, D. W. (1960). Countertransference. *British Journal of Medical Psychology* 33: 17–21.

43

Betty Joseph's "Transference: The Total Situation" (1985)

Betty Joseph was among those students of Klein who exerted an early influence on the understanding of pathological organization, but her principal contribution has been to technique. No one brings a more astute sensibility than she to the study of transference and countertransference, in her study of the here and now of the consulting room situation, the moment-to-moment shifts in atmosphere, intent, and content which flesh out Klein's meaning of "transference as the total situation." Joseph believes that close attention to these matters is more important in facilitating psychic change than any other single factor, including the verbal interpretation of transference and countertransference, or the linking of transference to its genetic origins. But in her close monitoring of these minute shifts in the atmosphere, the context of the work and the specifics of transference and countertransference material, Joseph is following an early lead of Klein's to make the intricacies of the relationship the primary focus of analytic study, outlined in Klein's 1952 paper "The Origins of Transference" (excerpted in Chapter 13). In the process of her study, Joseph defines the field of the relationship between patient and therapist as the operational heart of therapy and the chief agent of change.

Spillius believes that Joseph led the Kleinians to more caution about couching their interpretations in anatomical part-object terms, and spelled out the importance of what the patient does in contrast to the content of what he says (personal communication). This contrast is the starting point for understanding the way that early in their lives and again in the analytic situation patients attempt to control their unconscious expectations. Joseph's contribution complements Sandler's *role actualization,* focusing on the patient's enactments within sessions (Spillius 1994). She is operationally close to the more general dictum of Fairbairn and Guntrip that it is the therapeutic relationship itself which is the chief agent of change and growth.

REFERENCE

Spillius, E. (1994). Developments in Kleinian thought: overview and personal view. *Psychoanalytic Inquiry* 14(3).

Melanie Klein, through her continued work on early object relationships and early mental mechanisms, perhaps particularly projective identification, extended our understanding of the nature of transference and the process of transferring. In her paper "The Origins of Transference" (1952), she wrote: "It is my experience that in unravelling the details of the transference it is essential to think in terms of *total situations* transferred from the past into the present as well as emotion defences and object relations." She went on to describe how for many years transference had been understood in terms of direct references to the analyst, and how only later had it been realized that, for example, such things as reports about everyday life, etc., gave a clue to the unconscious anxieties stirred up in the transference situation. It seems to me that the notion of total situations is fundamental to our understanding and our use of the transference today, and it is this I want to explore further. By definition it must include everything that the patient brings into the relationship. What he brings in can best be gauged by our focusing our attention on what is going on within the relationship, how he is using the analyst, alongside and beyond what he is saying. Much of our understanding of the transference comes through our understanding of how our patients act on us to feel things for many varied reasons; how they try to draw us into their defensive systems; how they unconsciously act out with them; how they convey aspects of their inner world built up from infancy—elaborated in childhood and adulthood, experiences often beyond the use of words, which we can often only capture through the feelings aroused in us, through our countertransference, used in the broad sense of the word.

Countertransference, the feelings aroused in the analyst, like transference itself, was originally seen as an obstacle to the analytic work, but now, used in this broader sense, we would see it, too, no longer as an obstacle, but as an essential tool of the analytic process. Further, the notion of our being used and of something constantly going on, if only we can become aware of it, opens up many other aspects of transference, which I shall want to discuss later. For example, that movement and change is an essential aspect of transference—so that no interpretation can be seen as a pure interpretation or explanation but must resonate in the patient in a way which is specific to him and his way of functioning; that the level at which a patient is functioning at any given moment and the nature of his anxieties can best be gauged by trying to be aware of how the transference is actively being used; that shifts that become visible in the transference are an essential part of what should eventually lead to real psychic change. Such points emerge more clearly if we are thinking in terms of total situations being transferred.

I want to exemplify this by bringing a short piece of material in which we can see how the patient's immediate anxieties and the nature of her relationship with her internal figures emerge in the whole situation lived out in the transference, although individual associations and references to many people came up in the material as if asking to be interpreted. This material comes from the discussion of a case at a recent postgraduate seminar of mine. The analyst brought material from a patient who seemed very difficult to help adequately: schizoid, angry, an unhappy childhood with probably emotionally unavailable parents. The analyst was dissatisfied with the work of a particular session which she brought, and with its results. The patient had brought details of individual people and situations.

The seminar felt that many of the interpretations about this were sensitive and seemed very adequate. Then the seminar started to work very hard to understand more. Different points of view about various aspects were put forward, but no one felt quite happy about their own or other people's ideas. Slowly it dawned on us that probably this was the clue, that our problem in the transference, and that what was probably going on in the transference was a projection of the patient's inner world, in which she, the patient, could not understand and, more, could not make sense of what was going on. She was demonstrating what it felt like to have a mother who could not tune into the child and, we suspected, could not make sense of the child's feelings either, but behaved as if she could, as we, the seminar, were doing. So the patient had developed defences in which she argued or put forward apparently logical ideas, which really satisfied no one, but which silenced the experience of incomprehensibility and gave her something to hold on to. If the analyst actually struggles in such situations to give detailed interpretations of the meaning of individual associations, then she is living out the patient's own defensive system, making pseudosense of the incomprehensible, rather then trying to make contact with the patient's experience of living in an incomprehensible world. The latter can be very disturbing experience for the analyst, too. It is more comfortable to believe that one understands "material" than to live out the role of a mother who cannot understand the infant/patient.

I think that the clue to the transference here (assuming that what I am describing is correct) lay in our taking seriously the striking phenomenon in the seminar, of our struggling to understand and our desperate need to understand instead of getting stuck on the individual associations brought up by the patient, which in themselves would appear to make a lot of possible sense. This we got more through our countertransference of needing to guess, feeling pressurized to understand at all costs, which enabled us, we thought, to sense a projective identification of a part of the patient's inner world and the distress, of which we got a taste in the seminar.

I am assuming that this type of projective identification is deeply unconscious and not verbalized. If we work only with the part that is verbalized, we do not really take into account the object relationships being acted out in the transference; here, for example, the relationship between the uncomprehending mother and the infant who feels unable to be understood, and it is this that forms the bedrock of her personality. If we do not get through to this, we shall, I suspect, achieve areas of understanding, even apparent shifts in the material, but real psychic change, which can last beyond the treatment will, I think, not be possible. I suspect that what has happened in such cases is that something has gone seriously wrong in the patient's very early relationships, but that on top of this has been built up a character structure of apparent or pseudonormality, so that the patient has been able to get into adulthood without actually breaking down and apparently functioning more or less well in many areas of her life. Interpretations dealing only with the individual associations would touch only the more adult part of the personality, while the part that is really needing to be understood is communicated through the pressures brought on the analyst. We can sense here the living out in the transference of something of the nature of the patient's early object relationships, her defensive organization, and her method of communicating her whole conflict. . . .

The transference (is) the place where we can see not only the nature of the defences being used, but the level of psychic organization within which the patient is operating. To demonstrate this, I shall bring a fragment of material from a patient whom I shall call C., who is a somewhat obsessional personality, with severe limitations in his life, the extent of which he had not realized until he started treatment. I began to gain the impression that beneath the obsessional structure, controlling, superior, and rigid, there was a basically phobic organization. I shall try to reduce the piece of material that I am bringing to its bare bones.

C. had asked during the week to come a quarter of an hour earlier on the Friday, my first session in the day, in order to catch a train, as he had to go to Manchester for work. Then he described in great and obsessional detail on the Friday his worries about catching the train, getting through the traffic, etc., and how he had safeguarded these problems. He also discussed an anxiety about losing his membership in a club because of nonattendance, and spoke about a friend being slightly unfriendly on the phone. Detailed interpretations about his feeling unwanted related to the weekend, feeling shut out, and a need not to go away but rather to remain here or shut inside, did not seem to make real contact or to help him. But in relation to my showing him his need to be inside and safe he started to talk, now in a very different and smooth way, about how similar this problem was to his difficulty in changing jobs, moving his office, getting new clothes, how he stuck to the old ones, although by now he was short of clothes. Then there was the same problem about changing cars . . .

At this point I think that an interesting thing had occurred. While all that he was saying seemed accurate and important in itself, the thoughts were no longer being thought, they had become words, concrete analytic objects into which he could sink, get drawn in, as if they were the mental concomitant of a physical body into which he was withdrawing in the session. The question of separating off, mentally as physically, could be evaded since our ideas could now be experienced as completely in tune and he had withdrawn into them. When I pointed this out to C., he was shocked, saying: "When you said that, Manchester came into my mind, it was like sticking a knife into me." I thought that the knife that goes in was not just my pushing reality back into his mind, but a knife that goes in between himself and me, separating us off and making him aware of being different and outside, and this aroused immediate anxiety.

I bring this material to show how the interpretations about his obsessional control and his reassuring himself and me, then the interpretations about his needing to avoid separation, new things, etc., and to be inside, were not experienced as helpful explanations, but were used as concrete objects, as parts of myself that he could get inside defensively, warding off psychotic anxieties of a more agoraphobic type associated with separation. Thus the two levels of operating—obsessional defending against phobic—could be seen to be lived out in the transference, and when the deeper layer was tackled, when I showed him the smooth defensive use of my words, my interpretations were felt as knife-like, and the anxieties reemerged in the transference. In one sense this material is comparable with the case we discussed in the seminar. In such situations, if interpretations and understanding remain on the level of the individual associations, as contrasted with the total situation and the way that the analyst and his words are used, we shall find that we are being drawn into a pseudo-mature or more neurotic organization and missing the more psychotic anxieties and defences, which manifest themselves once we take into account the total situation—which is being acted out in the transference.

In this paper, I am concentrating on what is being lived in the transference and in this last example, as at the beginning, I tried to show how interpretations are rarely heard purely as interpretations, except when the patient is near to the depressive position. Then interpretations and the transference itself becomes more realistic and less loaded with fantasy meaning. Patients operating with more primitive defences of splitting and projective identification tend to "hear" our interpretations or "use" them differently and how they "use" or "hear" and the difference between these two concepts needs to be distinguished if we are to clarify the transference situation and the state of the patient's ego and the correctness or not of his perceptions. Sometimes our patients hear our interpretations in a more paranoid way, for example, as a criticism or as an attack. C., after getting absorbed in my thoughts, heard my interpretations about Manchester as a knife that cut into him—between us. Sometimes the situation looks similar, the patient seems disturbed by an interpretation, but has, in fact, heard it, understood it, correctly, but unconsciously used it in an active way, thus involving the analyst. . . .

C., having heard certain of my interpretations and their meaning correctly, used the words and thoughts not to think with, but unconsciously to act with, to get into and try to involve me in this activity, spinning words but not really communicating with them. Such activities not only colour but structure the transference situation and have important implications for technique.

I have tried in this paper to discuss how I think we are tending to use the concept of transference today. I have stressed the importance of seeing transference as a living relationship in which there is constant movement and change. I have indicated how everything of importance in the patient's psychic organization based on his early and habitual ways of functioning, his fantasies, impulses, defences and conflicts, will be lived out in some way in the transference. In addition, everything that the analyst is or says is likely to be responded to according to the patient's own psychic makeup, rather than the analyst's intentions and the meaning he gives to his interpretations. I have thus tried to discuss how the way in which our patients communicate their problems to us is frequently beyond their individual associations and beyond their words, and can often only be gauged by means of the countertransference. These are some of the points that I think we need to consider under the rubric of the total situations which are transferred from the past.

REFERENCE

Klein, M. (1952). The origins of transference. In *The Writings of Melanie Klein*, Vol. 3, pp. 48–56. London: Hogarth, 1975.

X

ADVANCES IN THEORY

44

John Steiner's "A Theory of Psychic Retreats" (1993)

We move now to consider a few themes chosen from recent contributions to object relations theory. The selection of which themes to follow must be arbitrary, since there is no possibility of completeness in such a rapidly expanding field. I have chosen, therefore, on the basis of a few central themes and from among a group of prominent contributors who fit together relatively well.

Beginning with the work of Joan Riviere, Bion, and Rosenfeld on narcissistic organization, and Edna O'Shaughnessy on defensive organization (1981), many Kleinians had been working on concepts of pathological developments in personality. (For instance, see Riviere 1936, Bion 1962 excerpted above, Money-Kyrle 1968, Rosenfeld 1971, excerpted above, Segal 1972, Joseph 1981, O'Shaughnessy 1981).

John Steiner is a consultant medical psychotherapist at the Tavistock Clinic, and a leading modern Kleinian. His book *Psychic Retreats* brings together the main currents of these developments in the concept of *pathological organizations* or *psychic retreats*. These organizations of the personality are lodged in an uneasy but staunchly defended equilibrium between the paranoid-schizoid and depressive positions, blocking further maturation.

REFERENCES

Bion, W. R. (1962). *Second Thoughts*. London: Heinemann.

Joseph, B. (1981). Towards the experiences of psychic pain. In *Psychic Equilibrium and Psychic Change: Selected Papers of Betty Joseph,* ed E. Spillius and M. Feldman. London: Routledge, 1989.

Money-Kyrle, R. E. (1968). Cognitive development. *International Journal of Psycho-Analysis* 49:691–698.
O'Shaughnessy, E. (1981). A clinical study of a defensive organization. *International Journal of Psycho-Analysis* 62:359–369.
Riviere, J. (1936). A contribution to the analysis of negative therapeutic reaction. *International Journal of Psycho-Analysis* 17:304–320.
Rosenfeld, H. (1971). A clinical approach to the psychoanalytic theory of the life and death instincts. *International Journal of Psycho-Analysis* 52:169–178.
Segal, H. (1972). A delusional system as a defence against the re-emergence of a catastrophic situation. *International Journal of Psycho-Analysis* 53:393–401.

A psychic retreat provides the patient with an area of relative peace and protection from strain when meaningful contact with the analyst is experienced as threatening. It is not difficult to understand the need for transient withdrawal of this kind, but serious technical problems arise in patients who turn to a psychic retreat, habitually, excessively, and indiscriminately. In some analyses, particularly with borderline and psychotic patients, a more or less permanent residence in the retreat may be taken up and it is then that obstacles to development and growth arise.

In my own clinical experience this type of withdrawal and the resultant failure to allow contact with the analyst takes many forms. An aloof type of schizoid superiority is expressed as a cold condescension in one patient and as a mocking dismissal of my work in another. Some patients are clearly reacting to anxiety, and their withdrawal appears to indicate that the analysis has touched on a sensitive topic which has to be avoided. Perhaps the most difficult type of retreat is that in which a false type of contact is offered and the analyst is invited to engage in ways which seem superficial, dishonest, or perverse. Sometimes these reactions can be seen to result from clumsy or intrusive behaviour on the part of the analyst, but it often happens that even careful analysis leaves the patients out of contact. They retreat behind a powerful system of defences which serve as a protective armour or hiding place, and it is sometimes possible to observe how they emerge with great caution like a snail coming out of its shell and retreat once more if contact leads to pain or anxiety.

We have come to understand that obstacles to contact and obstacles to progress and development are related, and that they both arise from the deployment of a particular type of defensive organization by means of which the patient hopes to avoid intolerable anxiety. I call such systems of defences pathological organizations of the personality and use this term to denote a family of defensive systems which are characterized by extremely unyielding defences and which function to help the patient to avoid anxiety by avoiding contact with other people and with reality. The pursuit of this approach has led me to examine in more detail the way defences operate and, in particular, how they interconnect to form complex, closely knit defensive systems.

The analyst observes psychic retreats as states of mind in which the patient is stuck, cut off, and out of reach, and he may infer that these states arise from the operation of a powerful system of defences. The patient's view of the retreat is reflected in the descriptions which he gives and also in unconscious phantasy as it is revealed in dreams, memories, and reports from everyday life which give a pictorial or dramatized image of how the retreat is unconsciously experienced. Typically it appears as a house, a cave, a fortress, a desert island, or a similar location which is seen as an area of relative safety. Alternatively, it can take an interpersonal form, usually as an organization of objects or part-objects which offers to provide security. It may be represented as a business organization, as a boarding school, as a religious sect, as a totalitarian government or a Mafia-like gang. Often tyrannical and perverse elements are evident in the description, but sometimes the organization is idealized and admired. . . .

Melanie Klein (1952) described the paranoid-schizoid and depressive positions in terms of a grouping of defences, and a pattern of anxieties and other emotions. Each is characterized also by typical mental structures and by typical forms of object relationship, both internal and external. It is in relationship to these positions that pathological organizations can most readily be understood, and indeed the retreat can also be thought of as a position with its own grouping of anxieties, its pattern of defences, its typical object relations and characteristic structure. I have previously referred to it as a "borderline position" because of its place on the border between the two basic positions (Steiner 1987, 1990).

The terminology of the positions can be confusing because of the inferred connection to particular types of clinical disorder. Klein had to emphasize that the paranoid-schizoid position did not imply paranoid psychosis in any simple way nor the depressive position, depressive illness. In the same way, the term "borderline position" is not confined to borderline patients, and although it is true that psychic retreats can be readily observed in borderline states they are also a prominent feature of psychotic patients at one extreme and of normal and neurotic individuals at times of stress, at the other. Klein herself occasionally spoke of a manic position and an obsessional position (Klein 1946), and these more organized defensive states have many features in common with psychic retreats. It is clear that not only the basic two positions but also the borderline position occur in all patients, and the notion of positions can help the analyst to consider where the patient is located at any particular time.

The patient can withdraw to a retreat at a borderline position where he is under the protection of a pathological organization from either of the two basic positions. This theme is elaborated later in the book, where use is made of a triangular equilibrium diagram to illustrate that as the patient emerges from the retreat he may find himself confronted with anxieties from either of the two basic positions.

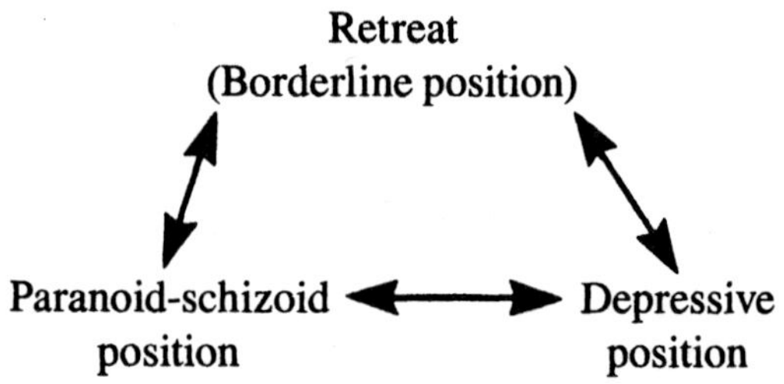

When the analysis is stuck there is very little, if any, movement discernible in this equilibrium, and the patient becomes firmly established in the retreat protected by the pathological organization and only rarely emerges to face either depressive or paranoid-schizoid anxieties. In less stuck situations, which of course occur in patients who may nevertheless be quite ill and even psychotic, more movement is discernible and shifts occur in which anxieties are at least transiently faced. Here the loss of equilibrium may give rise to severe anxiety and immediate return to the retreat, but it may also enable analytic development to take place. . . .

A particular type of relationship with reality which is characteristic of retreats plays an important role in preventing the move towards the depressive position which is necessary for development to occur. Freud, in his discussion of fetishism (Freud 1927), described how the patient adopts a stance in which reality is neither fully accepted nor fully disavowed, so that contradictory views are held simultaneously and are reconciled in a variety of ways. In my view, a central aspect of the perverse attitude is reflected in this kind of relation to reality. It is important in sexual perversions, where some of the basic "facts of life," such as the difference between the sexes and between the generations, are simultaneously accepted and disavowed, but it has a more general applicability to any aspect of reality which is difficult to accept. In particular, we see it prominent in the difficult task of facing the reality of aging and death to which a similarly perverse stance is often taken. A perverse pseudo-acceptance of reality is one of the factors which makes the retreat so attractive for the patient who can keep sufficient contact with reality to appear "normal" while at the same time evading its most painful aspects.

A second aspect of perversion is seen when the object relations which make up the organization are examined. The links which bind the organization together are often sadomasochistic and involve a cruel type of tyranny in which objects and the patient himself are controlled and bullied in a ruthless way. Sometimes the sadism is obvious, but often the tyranny is idealized and develops a seductive hold on the patient, who appears to become addicted to it, often gaining a masochistic gratification in the process.

It is only with long and painful work that the patient begins to feel he has the capacity to say "no" to the attractive pull of the perversion as alternative sources of help become available. He may then feel less entrapped by the organization and feel he only need turn to its protection at times of particular stress. As the addictive properties lessen he is able to free himself more and face psychic reality. Once this becomes even partially possible, mourning and loss lead to a partial recovery of parts of the self and the dependence on the organization is further loosened. It nevertheless always remains part of the personality where the patient can retreat when reality becomes unbearable. If it is recognized for what it is—namely, an area where perverse relationships and perverse thinking are sanctioned—the patient may accept an occasional need to adopt these methods without idealizing them. The protection of the retreat is then seen to offer a temporary respite from anxiety but no real security and no opportunity for development. Like other elements in the inner world, it can then be viewed more realistically and the patient can come to terms with it.

REFERENCES

Freud, S. (1927). Fetishism. *Standard Edition* 21:149–157.

Klein, M. (1946). Notes on some schizoid mechanisms. *International Journal of Psycho-Analysis* 27:99–110.

——(1952). Some theoretical conclusions regarding the emotional life of the infant in *Developments in Psychoanalysis*, ed. J. Riviere. Reprinted in *The Writings of Melanie Klein*, vol 3, pp. 61–93. London: Hogarth, 1975.

Steiner, J. (1987). The interplay between pathological organisations and the paranoid-schizoid and depressive positions. *International Journal of Psycho-Analysis* 68:69–80.

—— (1990). Pathological organisations as obstacles to mourning: the role of unbearable guilt. *International Journal of Psycho-Analysis* 71:87–94.

45

Elizabeth Bott Spillius's "Varieties of Envious Experience" (1993)

Elizabeth Spillius is the editor of the *New Library of Psychoanalysis.* Like Sutherland, she is a consummate editor with a thorough knowledge of analytic theory beyond the constraints of a single tradition. This is exemplified in the excerpts from this paper on envy in which she carefully traces Klein's concept of envy and its role in development and pathology. In the excerpt here, she defines its scope and then expands the concept to include the interpersonal field.

I used to think that envy was only destructive to the individual and to those around him when it was unconscious and split off, and that in analysis it would become conscious, arouse guilt, and gradually become integrated with more positive dispositions. I soon found, however, that this notion was too simple. In some patients envy appears to be very obvious, certainly to outside observers, and sometimes it appears to be conscious in some form or other to the envious individual, but without arousing his guilt or remorse. . . .

Envy may be felt, according to the *Oxford English Dictionary,* when the individual compares himself with someone superior in happiness, reputation, or in the possession of anything desirable. In my view, envy is especially likely to be felt when the individual has to *depend* on someone who is felt to be this sort of superior person, and all envious patients defend themselves to some extent against being aware of such dependence. The person whose envy is ego-dystonic directs defences against becoming aware that envy may be the basis of his behaviour, especially his various forms of attack on good objects. In the analysis of this sort of patient and this sort of envy, both analyst and patient have the same, or potentially the same, definition of envy: it is a destructive attack on a good object. The person whose envy is impenitent, however, does not suffer from conscious guilt and a sense of responsibility for his envy; he thinks it is the envied person's fault that he, the envier, feels so wretched. His defences are used to maintain and enhance what he regards as a legitimate grievance. In the analytic situation, such a patient's definition of envy is different from that of the analyst. The analyst, if he is using the Kleinian definition I have described above, thinks the patient is making a destructive attack on a good object; the patient thinks he is making a legitimate attack on an object who deserves to be hated. The patient may not jib at being told he is envious—should his analyst be so unwise as to tell him so directly—because the impenitently envious patient does not define envy in the same way as his Kleinian analyst does. . . .

A frequent aspect of the defensive arrangements of the person who suffers from impenitent envy is that he feels unconsciously that he is profoundly unlovable and inferior, qualities which he projects on to those towards whom he feels superior. Thus the person with impenitent envy and a persistent sense of grievance tends to find himself in a world in which some people are unfairly superior to him while others are justifiably inferior. In such a person character perversion is likely to play an important role—sadism and masochism are sometimes pronounced, and frequently there is a preoccupation with the issue of power. Such a person reminds one of Milton's Satan, with his abandoning of hope, good, and remorse, and his welcoming of evil and power:

> So farewell hope, and with hope farewell fear,
> Farewell remorse: all good to me is lost;
> Evil be thou my good;
> (*Paradise Lost*, Bk IV, 1, lines 108–10).

Like Carpy, however, I have found that in cases of grievance and impenitent experiencing of envy, defences are used not only to maintain and enhance the sense of grievance, but also to evade acknowledging the acute pain and sense of loss, sometimes fear of psychic collapse, that would come from realising that one wants a good object but really feels that one does not or has not had it. Feeling perpetual grievance and blame, however miserable, is less painful than mourning the loss of the relationships one wishes one had had. Grievance is thus a form of narcissistic defence. "Envy and narcissism," as Segal said at the Symposium on Envy and Jealousy in 1969, "can be seen as two sides of the same coin."

Defences against envy are multiple, and frequently reinforce one another to form what John Steiner (1985) has called a "pathological organization." This is especially likely in cases of impenitent envy, but is also found in severe cases of ego-dystonic envy. . . .

Rather than characterise the comparison between ego-dystonic and impenitent envy solely in terms of the paranoid-schizoid and depressive positions, however, I want to describe in greater detail a model that I have gradually constructed of the factors that I think mitigate or exacerbate envy. My model centres on the *perceived relation between giver and receiver,* partly because it is this relation that we see especially clearly in analysis, as in infancy, but also because it is the relation in which envy is particularly likely to be aroused.

One crucial factor seems to me to be the conscious and unconscious feelings of the giver about giving, and the way these feelings are perceived or misperceived, consciously and unconsciously, by the receiver. It must already be apparent that my model is potentially exceedingly complex. Presumably there is some "factual" reality about the nature of the giving and receiving, but this reality is complicated enormously by the conscious and unconscious feelings and perceptions of both giver and receiver, and it is these psychic realities that are especially important in the experience of envy.

Let us suppose that the giver takes pleasure in giving, and, further, that he is not, for example, giving in order to establish superiority over the receiver. Let us suppose, too, that the receiver is able to perceive this accurately and also to realise that the giver knows that he, the receiver, might resent being given to. . . . In this type of giving and this type of perception by the receiver, it is likely to be relatively easy for the receiver to acknowledge envy and to feel positive feelings as well; in particular, the receiver may feel able to give something back to the giver in the form of feeling pleasure as well as some resentment about being given to. If the giver can recognise and accept this return gift, this gratitude, a benign circle may be set up in which both parties give something of value to each other. The receiver's capacity to be given to is a return gift to the original giver. Goodness in the other becomes bearable, even enjoyable. The receiver introjects and identifies with an object who enjoys giving and receiving, and an internal basis for admiration can develop, and hence emulation of the generous giver becomes possible.

Let us suppose, in contrast, that the giver actually takes little pleasure in giving, that he is narcissistic and uninterested in the receiver, or that he is outright hostile or inconsistent towards the receiver, or that he feels, consciously or unconsciously, that the receiver is making unreasonable demands or draining his resources unfairly; or suppose that the giver gives eagerly and with pleasure, but only in order to demonstrate his superiority over the receiver. Or, further, let us suppose that he gives reluctantly and unwillingly because he is trying to conceal the fact that he feels what he gives is bad. And, still further, let us suppose that the giver's lack of genuine pleasure and generosity is accurately perceived by the receiver. In any of these examples, envy is likely to be exacerbated; pleasure in receiving cannot easily develop, and the receiver will not readily feel grateful. The receiver is likely to feel resentful and to give as little as possible back to the original giver. The original giver, deprived of gratitude, gives less, or more aggressively, and the deprivation/envy circle continues. So, somewhat paradoxically, envy is likely to be greatest when the giving object is felt to give little or badly. The receiver takes in and identifies with a giver-object who does not enjoy giving and receiving, and the vicious circle is perpetuated internally. Genuine emulation becomes very difficult, and is likely to involve splitting, projection, and a takeover of the giver's power. . . .

The contrast I have drawn so far is, of course, much too simple. It takes some account of the giver's motives and mode of giving, but it assumes that the receiver perceives and interprets these modes correctly. In reality, however, the receiver may make many types and degrees of misperception and misinterpretation. For example, the giver may give with pleasure and in good faith, yet the receiver may misinterpret the gift as an attempt by the giver to establish superiority. A giver may have a reasonable expectation of gratitude for a gift generously given, but the receiver may be so resentful that the giver has the capacity to give, whereas he, the receiver, cannot supply the good thing for himself, that he reacts with hatred, contempt, conventional politeness, or simply ignores that the gift has been given—all of these being forms of spoiling. Or the giver may give diffidently because of a conviction, conscious or unconscious, that what he has to give is really bad, and the receiver may misperceive this as stinginess, superiority, or indifference. . . .

Although my basic model of giving/receiving has become very complicated, I have found it essential to include the conscious and unconscious feelings, perceptions, and misperceptions of both giver and receiver. And, in spite of its complexity, I have found the model and its many variations useful in making a first step towards understanding the connections between giving, receiving, and envy in the inner worlds of my patients and in understanding their expectations of me and my reactions to them. I should like to emphasise, however, that I use my model to achieve more accurate *descriptions* of envious reactions. When it comes to attempts at causal explanations, I think one must be very cautious.

REFERENCES

Carpy, D. (no date given). Fantasy versus reality in childhood trauma: who's to blame? Unpublished paper.

Segal, H. (1969). Unpublished contribution to the discussion of the Symposium of the British Psycho-Analytical Society, on envy and jealousy.

Steiner, J. (1985). The interplay between pathological organizations and the paranoid-schizoid and depressive positions. *International Journal of Psycho-Analysis* 66:201–213. Also in *Melanie Klein Today, vol. 1, Mainly Theory,* ed. E. B. Spillius, pp. 324–342. London and New York: Routledge, 1988.

46

Esther Bick's "The Experience of the Skin in Early Object Relations" (1968)

The next four selections form a group in their emphasis on the move to early integration from the states of non-integration which Klein and Winnicott studied, and which elaborate on Fairbairn's idea of an original pristine, unsplit ego. Bick and Ogden also develop aspects of the notion of pathological organizations of the personality outlined by Rosenfeld and Steiner, as they move toward a third position which is in dynamic relationship to the two developmental positions described by Klein.

Following developments presented in papers by Esther Bick (reprinted below), Frances Tustin (1980, 1984) and Donald Meltzer and his colleagues (Meltzer 1975, Meltzer et al. 1975) on the development of the self in relationship to the mother through experiences at the level of the skin, Thomas Ogden proposed a new position which he called *the autistic-contiguous position.* He sees it as analogous to Klein's paranoid-schizoid and depressive positions. Although Klein believed that the paranoid-schizoid position was present from birth, Ogden believes that the autistic-contiguous position begins first, and that the paranoid-schizoid position begins sometime later. This development also follows the themes of work by Balint, Guntrip, and Winnicott concerning the early stage of origin of difficulties in the self and its integration.

Ogden's work on the early formation of the self leads us to Sutherland's extension of Fairbairn and Guntrip on the growth of an autonomous self as the goal of mature development. An important related development, excerpted in Chapter 56, is Christopher Bollas's proposal (1989) of a personal idiom in human development—an extension of Winnicott's ideas on the spontaneous gesture as the expression of the true self.

We begin this section with Esther Bick's paper written within the Kleinian tradition, reprinted here in its entirety. It can be seen to echo the themes of an early state of nonintegration, which also concerned Winnicott. Her contribution is grounded in close observation of infants and their mothers, published in another of her papers (1964), which became a mainstay of analytic research and training under the influence of Klein and Winnicott. Although the tradition of infant observation is not directly represented in this collection, it is a continuing source of information about development and a resource in training for the use of countertransference and observation in therapy. The book *Closely Observed Infants* (Miller et al. 1989) gives a good overview of the aims and processes involved in infant observation.

REFERENCES

Bick, E. (1964). Notes on infant observation in psychoanalytic training. *International Journal of Psycho-Analysis* 45:558–561.
Bollas, C. (1989). *Forces of Destiny: Psychoanalysis and the Human Idiom.* London: Free Association.
Meltzer, D. (1975). Adhesive identification. *Contemporary Psychoanalysis* 11:289–310.
Meltzer, D., Bremner, J., Hoxter, S., et al. (1975). *Explorations in Autism: A Psycho-Analytical Study.* Perthshire: Clunie.
Miller, L., Rustin, M., Rustin, M., and Shuttleworth, J. eds. (1989). *Closely Observed Infants.* London: Duckworth.
Tustin, F. (1980). Autistic objects. *International Review of Psycho-Analysis* 7:27–40.
—— (1984). Autistic shapes. *International Review of Psycho-Analysis* 11:279–290.

The central theme of this brief communication is concerned with the primal function of the skin of the baby and of its primal objects in relation to the most primitive binding together of parts of the personality not as yet differentiated from parts of the body. It can be most readily studied in psychoanalysis in relation to problems of dependence and separation in the transference.

The thesis is that in its most primitive form the parts of the personality are felt to have no binding force amongst themselves and must therefore be held together in a way that is experienced by them passively, by the skin functioning as a boundary. But this internal function of containing the parts of the self is dependent initially on the introjection of an external object, experienced as capable of fulfilling this function. Later, identification with this function of the object supersedes the unintegrated state and gives rise to the fantasy of internal and external spaces. Only then the stage is set for the operation of primal splitting and idealization of self and object as described by Melanie Klein. Until the containing functions have been introjected, the concept of a space within the self cannot arise. Introjection, i.e., construction of an object in an internal space is therefore impaired. In its absence, the function of projective identification will necessarily continue unabated and all the confusions of identity attending it will be manifest.

The stage of primal splitting and idealization of self and object can now be seen to rest on this earlier process of containment of self and object by their respective "skins."

The fluctuations in this primal state will be illustrated in case material, from infant observation, in order to show the difference between unintegration as a passive experience of total helplessness, and disintegration through splitting processes as an active defensive operation in the service of development. We are, therefore, from the economic point of view, dealing with situations conducive to catastrophic anxieties in the unintegrated state as compared with the more limited and specific persecutory and depressive ones.

The need for a containing object would seem, in the infantile unintegrated state, to produce a frantic search for an object—a light, a voice, a smell, or other sensual object—which can hold the attention and thereby be experienced, momentarily at least, as holding the parts of the personality together. The optimal object is the nipple in the mouth, together with the holding and talking and familiar-smelling mother.

Material will show how this containing object is experienced concretely as a skin. Faulty development of this primal skin function can be seen to result either from defects in the adequacy of the actual object or from fantasy attacks on it, which impair introjection. Disturbance in the primal skin function can lead to a development of a "second-skin" formation through which dependence on the object is replaced by a pseudo-independence, by the inappropriate use of certain mental functions, or perhaps innate talents, for the purpose of creating a substitute for this skin container function. The material to follow will give some examples of "second-skin" formation.

Here I can only indicate the types of clinical material upon which these findings are based. My present aim is to open up this topic for a detailed discussion in a later paper.

INFANT OBSERVATION: BABY ALICE

One year of observation of an immature young mother and her first baby showed a gradual improvement in the "skin-container" function up to twelve weeks. As the mother's tolerance to closeness to the baby increased, so did her need to excite the baby to manifestations of vitality lessen. A consequent diminution of unintegrated states in the baby could be observed. These had been characterized by trembling, sneezing, and disorganized movements. There followed a move to a new house in a still unfinished condition. This disturbed severely the mother's holding capacity and led her to a withdrawal from the baby. She began feeding whilst watching television, or at night in the dark without holding the baby. This brought a flood of somatic disturbance and an increase of unintegrated states in the baby. Father's illness at that time made matters worse and the mother had to plan to return to work. She began to press the baby into a pseudo-independence, forcing her onto a training cup, introducing a bouncer during the day, whilst harshly refusing to respond to the crying at night. The mother now returned to an earlier tendency to stimulate the child to aggressive displays which she provoked and admired. The result by 6½ months was a hyperactive and aggressive little girl, whom mother called "a boxer" from her habit of pummelling people's faces. We see here the formation of a muscular type of self-containment—"second-skin" in place of a proper skin container.

ANALYSIS OF A SCHIZOPHRENIC GIRL: MARY

Some years of analysis, since Mary was 3½, have enabled us to reconstruct the mental states reflected in the history of her infantile disturbance. The facts are as follows: a difficult birth, early clenching of the nipple but lazy feeding, bottle supplement in the third week but on breast until 11 months, infantile eczema at 4 months and scratching until bleeding, extreme clinging to mother, severe intolerance to waiting for feeds, delayed and atypical development in all areas.

In the analysis, severe intolerance to separation was reflected from the start as in the jaw-clenched systematic tearing and breaking of all materials after the first holiday break. Utter dependence on the immediate contact could be seen and studied in the unintegrated states of posture and motility on the one hand, and thought and communication on the other, which existed at the beginning of each session, improving during the course, to reappear on leaving. She came in hunched, stiff-jointed, grotesque, like a "sack of potatoes" as she later called herself, and emitting an explosive "SSBICK" for "Good morning, Mrs. Bick." This sack of potatoes seemed in constant danger of spilling out its contents partly due to the continual picking of holes in her skin representing the "sack" skin of the object in which parts of herself, the "potatoes," were contained (projective identification). Improvement from the hunched posture to an erect one was achieved, along with a lessening of her general total dependence, more through a formation of a second skin based on her own muscularity than on identification with a containing object.

ANALYSIS OF AN ADULT NEUROTIC PATIENT

The alternation of two types of experience of self—the "sack of apples" and "the hippopotamus"—could be studied in regard to quality of contact in the transference and experience of separation, both being related to a disturbed feeding period. In the "sack of apples" state, the patient was touchy, vain, in need of constant attention and praise, easily bruised and constantly expecting catastrophe, such as a collapse when getting up from the couch. In the "hippopotamus" state, the patient was aggressive, tyrannical, scathing, and relentless in following his own way. Both states were related to the "second-skin" type of organization, dominated by projective identification. The "hippopotamus" skin, like the "sack" were a reflection of the object's skin inside which he existed, whilst the thin-skinned, easily bruised, apples inside the sack, represented the state of parts of the self which were inside this insensitive object.

ANALYSIS OF A CHILD: JILL

Early in the analysis of a 5-year-old child, whose feeding period had been characterized by anorexia, skin-container problems presented themselves, as in her constant demand from mother during the first analytic holiday, that her clothes should be firmly fastened, her shoes tightly laced. Later material showed her intense anxiety and need to distinguish herself from toys and dolls, about which she said: "Toys are not like me, they break to pieces and don't get well. They don't have a skin. We have a skin!"

SUMMARY

In all patients with disturbed first-skin formation, severe disturbance of the feeding period is indicated by analytic reconstruction, though not always observed by the parents. This faulty skin-formation produces a general fragility in later integration and organizations. It manifests itself in states of unintegration as distinct from regression involving the most basic types of partial or total, unintegration of body, posture, motility, and corresponding functions of mind, particularly communication. The "second skin" phenomenon which replaces first skin integration, manifests itself as either partial or total type of muscular shell or a corresponding verbal muscularity.

Analytic investigation of the second skin phenomenon tends to produce transitory states of unintegration. Only an analysis which perseveres to thorough working-through of the primal dependence on the maternal object can strengthen this underlying fragility. It must be stressed that the containing aspect of the analytic situation resides especially in the setting and is therefore an area where firmness of technique is crucial.

47

Thomas Ogden's "On the Concept of an Autistic-Contiguous Position" (1989)

Ogden used Bick's work along with that of others in proposing a new developmental position analogous to Klein's paranoid-schizoid and depressive positions. He believes that the *autistic-contiguous position* begins earlier and is more fundamental than the other two, in that it involves the initial formation and maintenance of the body self and its extensions into the integration and coherence of an internal sense of self throughout life. Once each position has entered the child's development, it is in continuous interplay with the other positions throughout the rest of life. In the excerpts from this paper, Ogden examines the basic concept of the autistic-contiguous position and its interplay with the other two positions.

In a previous paper (Ogden 1988), I term the psychological organization generating the most primitive state of being the *autistic-contiguous position.* (I have used the term *position* because I view this psychological organization as a developing and ongoing mode of generating experience as opposed to a phase of development. I regard it as having equal organizing significance to the paranoid-schizoid and depressive positions and as contributing equally powerfully to the dialectic constituting human experience.) The elaboration of this primitive organization represents an integral part of normal development through which a distinctive mode of experience is generated. This mode of organizing experience is characterized by specific types of defence, forms of object relatedness, quality of anxiety, and degree of subjectivity that I shall describe and clinically illustrate. The state of being that is generated by this psychological organization stands in both a diachronic and a synchronic relationship to the paranoid-schizoid and depressive positions. Although the autistic-contiguous position has a period of primacy earlier than that of the two psychological organizations described by Klein, it coexists dialectically with the paranoid-schizoid and depressive positions from the beginning of psychological life (Ogden 1988). The concepts of the depressive, the paranoid-schizoid, and the autistic-contiguous positions constitute preserving and negating contexts for one another, just as the ideas of night and day, darkness and light, sound and silence, consciousness and unconsciousness each create, preserve, and negate the other. The delineation of the autistic-contiguous dimension of experience does not in any sense diminish the significance of the paranoid-schizoid and depressive dimensions. The present chapter represents an attempt to extend the concept of psychological "positions" or organizations to include the most primitive aspects of human experience.

PRIMITIVE ORGANIZATION OF EXPERIENCE

The autistic-contiguous organization is associated with a specific mode of attributing meaning to experience in which raw sensory data are ordered by means of forming presymbolic connections between sensory impressions that come to constitute bounded surfaces. It is on these surfaces that the experience of self has its origins: "The ego [the "I"] is first and foremost a bodily ego. . . . (Freud 1923, p. 26), i.e., the ego is ultimately derived from bodily sensations, chiefly from those springing from the surface of the body" (Freud 1923, p. 26, footnote added in 1927).

I have retained the word *autistic* in the designation of the most primitive psychological organization despite the fact that the term is usually associated with a pathologically closed psychological system that I do not feel is characteristic of the normal autistic-contiguous mode. I have done so because I believe that pathological forms of autism involve hypertrophied versions of the types of defense, the method of attributing meaning to experience, and the mode of object relatedness characterizing the normal autistic-contiguous organization.

I believe the word *contiguous* is particularly apt in further naming this organization since, as is later discussed, the experience of surfaces touching one another is a principal medium through which connections are made and organization achieved in this psychological mode. The word *contiguous* thus provides the necessary antithesis to the connotations of isolation and disconnectedness carried by the word *autistic*. . . .

The observational data of Bower (1977), Brazelton (1981), Eimas (1975), Stern (1985), Trevarthan (1979), and others have provided powerful evidence for the capacity of the infant from the first days and weeks of life to perceive, make discriminations among, and respond to external objects in a way that is inferred to reflect the infant's (at least sporadic) awareness of externality. . . . Ordinarily, the interplay of the experience of oneness and that of separateness within the early mother–infant relationship makes tolerable the infant's moments of awareness of his separateness. The normal elaboration of the autistic-contiguous organization depends upon the capacity of the mother and infant to generate forms of sensory experience that "heal" or "make bearable" the awareness of the separateness that is an intrinsic component of early infantile experience (Tustin 1986). When the mother–infant dyad is unable to function in a way that provides the infant a healing sensory experience, the holes in the fabric of the "emergent self" (Stern 1985) become a source of unbearable "awareness of bodily separateness [which results in] an agony of consciousness" (Tustin 1986, p. 43). Under such circumstances, the infant's development is skewed in the direction of pathological autism that involves the creation of a state of psychological deadness, which Meltzer and colleagues (1975) compares to the "absence" in a *petit mal* seizure and which I (Ogden 1980) have described as a state of "non-experience," a state in which there is a cessation or paralysis of the process of attributing meaning to experience.

THE NATURE OF SENSATION-DOMINATED EXPERIENCE

In an autistic-contiguous mode, it is experiences of sensation, particularly at the skin surface, that are the principal media for the creation of psychological meaning and the rudiments of the experience of self. Sensory contiguity of skin surface, along with the element of rhythmicity, are basic to the most fundamental set of infantile object relations: the infant's experience of being held, nursed, and spoken to by the mother. These early experiences are object-related in a specific sense of the word that is related to the nature of subjectivity in the autistic-contiguous position. In previous contributions (Ogden 1986), I have discussed Klein's concept of the depressive position as a psychological organization in which there is an interpreting subject mediating between symbol and symbolized, mediating between oneself and one's lived experience. In a paranoid-schizoid mode, there is very little sense of a mediating, interpreting "I"; instead, the self is to a large extent a self-as-object, a self that only minimally experiences itself as the author of its own thoughts, feelings, sensations, and perceptions. Instead, in a paranoid-schizoid mode, the individual experiences himself as buffeted by thoughts, feelings, and sensations as if they were forces or things that simply happen.

The nature of one's relationship to one's objects is determined to a large degree by the nature of the subjectivity (the form of "I-ness") that constitutes the context for those object relations. In the autistic-contiguous position, the relationship to objects is one in which the organization of a rudimentary sense of "I-ness" arises from relationships of sensory contiguity (i.e., *touching*) that over time generate the sense of a bounded sensory surface on which one's experience occurs (the beginnings of the feeling of "a place where one lives" [Winnicott 1971]). Examples of boundedness generated from relationships of contiguity include the sense of shape created by the impression of the infant's skin surface when he rests his cheek against the mother's breast; the sense of the continuity and predictability of shape derived from the rhythmicity and regularity of the infant's sucking activity (in the context of a maternally provided holding environment); the rhythm of the "dialogue" of cooing engaged in by mother and infant; the feeling of edgedness generated by the infant's pressing his gums tightly on the mother's nipple or finger.

The rudimentary beginnings of subjectivity in the autistic-contiguous position must be described from the perspective of two vertices simultaneously. On the one hand, the infant and mother are one: "There is no such thing as an infant" (Winnicott 1960, footnote on p. 39). From this perspective the infant's subjectivity can be thought of as being held in trust by the mother (more accurately, by the aspect of the mother–infant that an outside observer would view as the mother). At the same time, from another perspective, the infant and mother are never absolutely at one, and the infant's subjectivity in the autistic-contiguous position can be thought of as an extremely subtle, non-self-reflective sense of "going on being" (Winnicott 1956) in which sensory need is in the process of acquiring features of subjective desire (the sensory-level beginnings of a subject wishing for something). Sensory experience in an autistic-contiguous mode has a quality of rhythmicity that is becoming continuity of being; it has boundedness that is the beginning of the experience of a place where one feels, thinks, and lives; it has such features as shape, hardness, coldness, warmth, and texture, that are the beginnings of the qualities of who one is.

Tustin (1980, 1984) has described two types of experience with objects that constitute important means of ordering and defining experience in the autistic-contiguous position. (These means of organizing and delineating experience are secondarily enlisted in the construction of psychological defense.) The first of these forms of relatedness to objects (which again only an outside observer would recognize as a relationship to an external object) is the creation of "autistic shapes" (1984).[1] Shapes generated in an autistic-contiguous mode must be distinguished from what we ordinarily think of as the shape of an object. These early shapes are "'felt' shapes" (Tustin 1986, p. 280) arising from the experience of soft touching of surfaces, which makes a sensory impression. The experience of shape in an autistic-contiguous mode does not involve the conception of the "objectness" or "thingness" of that which is being felt. As Tustin (1984) puts it, we can attempt to create for ourselves the experience of an autistic shape if we reduce the chair we are sitting on to the sensation it makes on our buttocks. From this perspective there is no sense of the chair as an object aside from the sensation that is generated. The "shape" of that impression is idiosyncratic to each of us, and changes as we shift in our seats.

For the infant, the objects generating shapes in an autistic-contiguous mode include the soft parts of his own body and the body of the mother as well as soft bodily substances (including saliva, urine, and feces). Experiences of shape in an autistic-contiguous mode contribute to the sense of

1. Tustin (1980, 1984), following the lead of J. Anthony (1958), conceives of a phase of "normal autism" (which she more recently has designated the "auto-sensuous" [1986] phase of development). In this phase, the infant makes use of "shapes" in a way that resembles the shapes utilized by autistic children; however, the normal infantile utilization of shapes is not nearly as extensive or rigid, and does not serve to cut off relations with external objects, as is the case in pathological autism.

cohesion of self and also to the experience of perception of what is becoming the object. Much later in development, words like "comfort," "soothing," "safety," "connectedness," "holding," "cuddling," and "gentleness" will be attached to the experience of shapes in an autistic-contiguous mode. A second form of very early definition of sensory experience described by Tustin (1980), the experience of autistic objects, stands in marked contrast to the experience of autistic shapes. An autistic object is the experience of a hard, angular sensory surface that is created when an object is pressed hard against the infant's skin. In this form of experience, the individual experiences his surface (which in a sense is all there is of him) as a hard crust or armour that protects him against unspeakable dangers that only later will be given names. An autistic object is a safety-generating sensory impression of edgedness that defines, delineates, and protects one's otherwise exposed and vulnerable surface shell). As experience is increasingly generated in paranoid-schizoid and depressive modes, words like armour, shell, crust, danger, attack, separateness, otherness, invasion, rigidity, impenetrability, repulsion, are attached to the quality of sensory impressions created by autistic objects. . . .

AUTISTIC-CONTIGUOUS EXPERIENCE AND PATHOLOGICAL AUTISM

Although pathological autism can be thought of as constituting an "asymbolic" realm, the normal autistic-contiguous mode is "presymbolic" in that the sensory-based units of experience being organized are preparatory for the creation of symbols mediated by experience of transitional phenomena (Winnicott 1951). The developmental directionality of this process stands in contrast to the static nature of asymbolic experience in pathological autism wherein the effort is to maintain a perfectly insulated closed system (in which sensory experience does not lead anywhere except back to itself). Pathological autism aims at the absolute elimination of the unknown and the unpredictable.

The machine-like predictability of experiences with pathological autistic shapes and objects substitutes for experiences with inevitably imperfect and not entirely predictable human beings. No person can compete with the capacity of never-changing autistic shapes and objects to provide absolutely reliable comfort and protection.

Experience at the skin surface is critically important in that it constitutes an arena where there is a convergence of the infant's idiosyncratic, presymbolic world of sensory impressions and the interpersonal world made up of objects (which an outside observer would view as) having an existence separate from the infant and outside of his omnipotent control. It is on this stage that the infant will either elaborate a way of being in the world in relation to the mother and the rest of the object world or will elaborate sensory-dominated ways of being (more accurately a way of not-being) that are designed to insulate a potential self (that never comes into being) from all that lies outside of his sensory-dominated world. To the extent that the bodily system is closed off from mutually transforming experiences with human beings, there is an absence of "potential space" (Winnicott 1971; see also Ogden 1985, 1987) between oneself and the other (a potential psychological space between self-experience and sensory perception). This closed, bodily world is a world without room in which to create a distinction between symbol and symbolized and therefore a world in which there is no possibility for the coming into being of an interpreting subject; it is a world in which there is no psychological space between the infant and mother in which transitional phenomena might be created/discovered. . . .

THE NATURE OF AUTISTIC-CONTIGUOUS ANXIETY

Each of the three basic psychological organizations (the autistic-contiguous, the paranoid-schizoid, and the depressive) has associated with it its own characteristic form of anxiety. In each case, the nature of the anxiety is related to the experience of disconnectedness (disintegration) within that mode of experience, whether it be the disruption of whole object relations in the depressive position, the fragmentation of parts of self and object in the paranoid-schizoid position, or the disruption of sensory cohesion and boundedness in the autistic-contiguous position.

Depressive anxiety involves the fear that one has in fact or in phantasy harmed or driven away a person whom one loves; anxiety in a paranoid-schizoid mode is at core a sense of impending annihilation which is experienced in the form of fragmenting attacks on the self and one's objects; autistic-contiguous anxiety involves the experience of impending disintegration of one's sensory surface or one's "rhythm of safety" (Tustin 1986), resulting in the feeling of leaking, dissolving, disappearing or falling into shapeless unbounded space (cf. Bick 1968, Rosenfeld 1984).

Common manifestations of autistic-contiguous anxiety include terrifying feelings that one is rotting; the sensation that one's sphincters and other means of containing bodily contents are failing and one's saliva, tears, urine, faeces, blood, menstrual fluids, etc. are leaking; fear that one is falling, for example, anxiety connected with falling asleep for fear that one will fall into endless, shapeless space. Patients experiencing this form of insomnia often attempt to relieve their anxiety (their fear of "falling asleep") by tightly surrounding themselves in blankets and pillows, keeping bright lights on in their bedroom or by playing familiar music all night.

> Ms. K., a 25-year-old graduate student, began therapy because of her terror of the fog and of the sound of the ocean. The fog was frighteningly suffocating: "You can't see the horizon." The patient was terrified of "going crazy" without being aware that it was happening and frequently beseeched the therapist to inform her if the therapist should sense that the patient was losing touch with reality.
>
> Ms. K.'s mother contracted spinal meningitis when the patient was 4 months old and was hospitalized for fourteen months. From the time that the patient's mother returned home, Mrs. K. was confined to a wheelchair and tyrannically ruled the house from her metal chair. The patient's earliest memory (which seemed to her as much like a dream as a memory) was of reaching out to her mother in her wheelchair and being pushed away by her mother. At the same moment, the patient, in this memory, looked out of the window and saw a small child falling through the ice on the pond that was located just behind the patient's house. Mrs. K. said, "You'd better go save her."
>
> I view this "memory" as a vivid representation of the patient's experience of falling through the containing surface of self (initially created in the interaction of mother and infant). Ms. K. is both the small child falling through the ice and the older child who must try to pull the child out of the hole before she drowns. The metallic, wheelchair-mother is not felt to be capable of saving the child and in fact seems to be the one who is unconsciously being blamed for the child's fall through the hole (the mother's pushing the patient away).
>
> The ocean and the fog came to be experienced by Ms. K. as the ever-present danger of annihilating shapelessness into which she might fall. Because of the tenuousness of the patient's sense of cohesiveness of self,

she lived in constant fear of "going crazy" (losing "touch" with reality in a literal, sensory way). The patient lacked the feeling of sensory groundedness that is ordinarily provided by the interpersonal "touch" of common sense (a shared sensory experience of the world) which heavily contributes to our sense of being sane.

AUTISTIC-CONTIGUOUS MODES OF DEFENCE

Defences generated in an autistic-contiguous mode are directed at the reestablishment of continuity of the bounded sensory surface and ordered rhythmicity upon which the early integrity of self rests. Within the analytic hour, patients spanning the full range of psychological maturity commonly attempt to reconstitute a sensory "floor" (Grotstein 1987) of experience by means of activities like hair twirling; foot tapping (even while lying on the couch); stroking of the lips, cheek, or ear lobe; humming; intoning; picturing or repeating series of numbers; focusing on symmetrical geometric shapes on the ceiling or wall or using a finger to trace shapes on the wall next to the couch. Such activities can be thought of as self-soothing uses of autistic shapes.

Between analytic hours, patients commonly attempt to maintain or reestablish a failing sense of bodily cohesion by means of rhythmic muscular activities including long periods of bicycle riding, jogging, lap swimming, etc.; eating and purging rituals; rocking (sometimes in a rocking chair); head banging (often against a pillow); riding buses and subways or driving a car for hours; maintaining a system of numbers or geometric shapes in one's head or in computer programmes that are continually being worked on (i.e., "perfected"), etc. The absolute regularity of these activities is so essential to the process of allaying anxiety that the individual cannot/will not allow any other activity to take precedence over them.

Bick (1968, 1986) uses the phrase "second-skin formation" to describe the way in which the individual attempts to create a substitute for a deteriorating sense of the cohesiveness of skin surface. Often the individual attempts to use the sensory experience of adhering to the surface of the object in order to resurrect the integrity of his own surface. For example, one might attempt to adhere to an object by means of tenacious eye contact or a steady stream of chatter in a way that is "experienced . . . as holding the parts of the [sensory-dominated] personality together" (Bick 1968, p. 49).

Meltzer (Meltzer et al. 1975) has introduced the term *adhesive identification* to refer to the defensive adherence to the object in the service of allaying the anxiety of disintegration. Imitation and mimicry, for instance, are utilized in an effort to make use of the surface of the object as if it were one's own. Adhesive identification is a form of identification more primitive than either introjective or projective identification in that the latter two forms of identification involve a sense of inner space into which one can project an aspect of oneself or into which one can take an aspect of the object. In an autistic-contiguous mode, one attempts to defend against the anxiety of disintegration by sticking bits of the surface of the object to one's own failing surface.

Tustin (1986) correctly points out that the object utilized in "adhesive identification" is not experienced as a separate object and therefore the term *adhesive equation* better describes the way in which the individual is equated with (becomes the qualities of) the surface of the object being used in this form of defence. . . .

Psychopathology can be thought of as a collapse of the generative dialectical interplay of modes of experience (cf. Ogden 1985, 1987). Collapse in the direction of an autistic-contiguous mode results in a tyrannizing imprisonment in a closed system of bodily sensations that precludes the development of "potential space" (Winnicott 1971). Collapse in the direction of a paranoid-schizoid mode results in a sense of entrapment in a world of things-in-themselves wherein one does not experience oneself as the author of one's thoughts and feelings; rather, thoughts, feelings, and sensations are experienced as objects or forces bombarding, entering into or propelled from oneself. Collapse in the direction of a depressive mode results in the experience of a subject alienated from his bodily sensations and from the immediacy and spontaneity of lived experience. . . .

SUMMARY

The development of British object relations theory over the past twenty years can be viewed as containing the beginnings of an exploration of a realm of experience that lies outside of the states of being addressed by Klein, Winnicott, Fairbairn, and Bion. In this paper, the idea of an autistic-contiguous position is proposed as a way of conceptualizing a psychological organization more primitive than either the paranoid-schizoid or the depressive position. This mode of organizing experience stands in a dialectical relationship to the paranoid-schizoid and depressive modes: each creates, preserves, and negates the others. The autistic-contiguous mode is a sensory-dominated, presymbolic mode of generating experience which provides a good measure of the boundedness of human experience and the beginnings of a sense of the place where one's experience occurs. Anxiety in this mode consists of an unspeakable terror of the dissolution of boundedness resulting in feelings of leaking, falling or dissolving into endless, shapeless space.

REFERENCES

Anthony, J. (1958). An experimental approach to the psychopathology of childhood: autism. *British Journal of Medical Psychology* 31:211–225.

Bick, E. (1968). The experience of the skin in early object relations. *International Journal of Psycho-Analysis* 49:484–486.

—— (1986). Further considerations on the function of the skin in early object relations. *British Journal of Psychotherapy* 2:292–299.

Bower, T. G. R. (1977). The object in the world of the infant. *Scientific American* 225:30–48.

Brazelton, T. B. (1981). *On Becoming a Family: The Growth of Attachment.* New York: Delta/Seymour Lawrence.

Eimas, P. (1975). Speech perception in early infancy. In *Infant Perception: From Sensation to Cognition,* vol. 2, ed. L. B. Cohen and P. Salapatek, pp. 193–228. New York: Academic Press.

Freud, S. (1923). The ego and the id. *Standard Edition* 19:12–59.

Grotstein, J. (1987). *Schizophrenia as a disorder of self-regulation and interactional regulation.* Presented at the Boyer House Foundation Conference: The Regressed Patient, San Francisco, March 21.

Meltzer, D. et al. (1975). *Explorations in Autism.* Perthshire: Clunie.

Ogden, T. (1979). On projective identification. *International Journal of Psycho-Analysis* 60:357–373.

—— (1980). On the nature of schizophrenic conflict. *International Journal of Psycho-Analysis* 61:513–533.

—— (1985). On potential space. *International Journal of Psycho-Analysis* 66:129–141.

—— (1986). *The Matrix of the Mind: Object Relations and the Psychoanalytic Dialogue.* Northvale, NJ: Jason Aronson.

—— (1987). The transitional oedipal relationship in female development. *International Journal of Psycho-Analysis* 68:495–498.

—— (1988). On the dialectical structure of experience: some clinical and theoretical implications. *Contemporary Psychoanalysis* 23:17–45.

Rosenfeld, D. (1984). Hypochondrias, somatic delusion and body scheme in psychoanalytic practice. *International Journal of Psycho-Analysis* 65:377–388.
Stern, D. (1985). *The Interpersonal World of the Infant.* New York: Basic Books.
Trevarthan, C. (1979). Communication and cooperation in early infancy: a description of primary intersubjectivity. In *Before Speech,* ed. M. Bellowa. Cambridge: Cambridge University Press.
Tustin, F. (1980). Autistic objects. *International Review of Psycho-Analysis* 7:27–40.
—— (1984). Autistic shapes. *International Review of Psycho-Analysis* 11:279–290.
—— (1986). *Autistic Barriers in Neurotic Patients.* London: Karnac; New Haven: Yale University Press, 1987.
Winnicott, D. W. (1951). Transitional objects and transitional phenomena. In *Playing and Reality,* pp. 1–25. New York: Basic Books.
—— (1956). Primary maternal preoccupation. In *Through Paediatrics to Psycho-Analysis,* pp. 300–305. New York: Basic Books.
—— (1960). The theory of the parent infant relationship. In *The Maturational Processes and the Facilitating Environment,* pp. 37–55. New York: International Universities Press.
—— (1971). *Playing and Reality.* New York: Basic Books.

48

John D. Sutherland's "The Autonomous Self" (1993)

John Sutherland, who, along with Guntrip, was the major disciple of Fairbairn, became a towering figure in the psychoanalytic world in his own right. He was director of the Tavistock Clinic for 21 years of its heyday, and founded the Scottish Institute of Human Relations after his retirement from the Tavistock. He was also editor of many of the major analytic publications—the *International Journal of Psycho-Analysis*, the *British Journal of Medical Psychology,* and the *International Library of Psycho-Analysis.* In these roles, he acquired a comprehensive understanding of the major currents and issues in psychoanalysis.

Sutherland wrote a critical biography of Fairbairn (Sutherland 1989) as well as a series of papers supporting his conviction that object relations theory needed to develop a more through understanding of the nature of the self. Thus he followed Guntrip's lead in exploring the formation and function of the self throughout life. Sutherland brought to this study an unusual capacity to look at the growth of the self in relationship with the family and to the wider society. The contribution excerpted here continues the theme of Ogden's paper on the conditions for the development of the self, but also considers the social conditions and consequences of growth of an autonomous self.

REFERENCE

Sutherland, J. D. (1989). *Fairbairn's Journey to the Interior.* London: Free Association.

EARLY DEVELOPMENT OF THE SELF

The first preoccupying activity of the self is learning how to relate effectively with the mother. Feeding, of course, is dominant but not exclusively so. Sucking is mediated by a mother who, with the infant, fits the joint behavior into a successful pattern. The infant must be innately equipped to incorporate from the breast and to take in from the world, with a hunger originating from both sources, needs that can be recognized and responded to by the mother. At first, the self does not need to be conscious of itself in the manner of the adult. In an environment that is actively anticipating and providing for the needs of the self, the organization of experience can proceed by a sentience that monitors and distinguishes what feels "right" or "good" from what does not meet the tensions of need and so is affectively frustrating—that is, "bad" or "wrong." The growth of self-awareness, however, must begin early to develop the capacity to be alert to the attitudes of others by recognizing their emotional states.

The clinical evidence from disorders in the self strongly suggests that effective development of the self rests on a joyful, empathic responsiveness from the mother. Various limited frustrations of particular behaviors can be readily tolerated if the overall feelings communicated by the mother, and later by the father, come from a genuine joy in the baby as it is. Such an attitude puts no pressure on the baby's spontaneous maturational achievements to match preconceived images the parents may be using as molds into which, often unconsciously, the baby is to be fitted.

Good-enough mothering gives the first "layering" in the structuring of the self as a person. At this stage (I do not think we can be too specific in terms of age), the main achievement is a self that can feel secure and ready to explore and incorporate the world as physical and psychological capacities and talents emerge. From the start, an immense amount of experience with the social and physical worlds is rapidly acquired. A "person" seems to be being established at first without much differentiation of gender, even though babies are responded to somewhat differently according to their sex. The next main structuring is for this person to become more specifically a male or female. It would seem from disorders of the self that the relationship with the father now becomes of critical importance. The growing assertiveness of the boy must be responded to as before by the mother's joyful acceptance, but the father's acceptance now needs to be available as well for both the girl and boy infant. I have also concluded that, for the eventual integration of the self, the relationship between the parents and their joint attitudes toward the child are almost as critically important as that of each parent separately.

In the earliest months—the traditional oral stage—there seems to be no question that orality represents a more general incorporative need for which the alimentary function is the prototype. The infant needs to incorporate the mother in a personal way, that is, as having the significance of a whole object and not one confined to the feeding activity. The affective qualities of the physical and psychological incorporations, however, seem closely linked at this initial phase, if we are to explain how greed for food or drink is so often substituted later for personal deprivation. In addiction there is, of course, as the physiological result of the intake, the ensuing feeling of relaxation, of general loss of tension from frustrated social needs, and eventually of being in a state of some euphoria.

The question of how much the infant self is differentiated from the mother has tended to be regarded as settled by the assumption that there is a phase of nondifferentiation. This belief has been related to the phenomena of merging and identification, and also to the amount of differentiation or perception of a separate figure that would be possible with what is known of neurophysical development. Stern (1985) strongly advocates a recognized differentiation of the infant's own boundaries as present from birth, based partly on the grounds that it is difficult to see how two separate psyches could be undifferentiated, but mainly based on the findings from the infant–mother studies. From what we have stressed about the operation of an innate organizing principle, it would entail from the start in any organism a powerful assertion and maintenance of autonomy and of the integrity of its wholeness.

It is not at all fanciful to imagine such a powerful autonomy being present, yet covered over by the closeness of the attachment of the infant to the mother. When a self is postulated as the realization, from experience in relating to the mother, of a potential in the form of an innate gestalt that has the "shape" or "feel" of a person built into it, and that is strongly motivated to encounter this shape in the outer world, then a phase of undifferentiation is neither necessary nor conceivable. Such a gestalt would be activated not by energies external to it, but by its own nature to seek completion from the appropriate sources in the environment. This assumption implies nothing different in principle from the other innate behavioral systems, for example, seeking the breast and "knowing" when it is found. There is no doubt that the ordinary mother (and, indeed, adults in general) is highly and innately motivated to respond to the infant from the earliest stages as having this "potential person" quality.

We know, too, that sucking from the breast is not the action of a passive infant being supplied with all it needs. The infant shows a pronounced dynamic of its own to regulate the feeding process to match its own feelings, to train its mother, so to speak, in what is a relationship of mutual satisfaction. When things do not go well, there is marked disturbance in the infant's whole state. It is also well recognized that although various physical factors may cause difficulties, problems also commonly arise when the mother's attitude differs from that of the ordinarily spontaneously responding mother. Serious frustrations are then felt with great intensity, as witnessed in the infant's increasingly desperate signals that things should be put right. The self-feeling in these circumstances is undoubtedly one of disturbed security, with inhibitions in the readiness to relate to the external world socially and in instrumental inhibitions of various kinds. We also need to note Spitz's (1965) finding that meeting the bodily needs for food does not necessarily keep the baby alive. There is a hunger for stimulating exchanges with the caretakers that must be satisfied to foster a vital dynamic to go on living.

We cannot deal with all the specific features of the rapidly changing situation of the infant with its mother. I simply wish to indicate that autonomous reactions—either positive, in which case the dynamic of the self is encouraged, or negative, when it meets with varying degrees of deprivation, from the less intense to violent expressions of aggressive behavior—all point to affective experience and responses that constitute an independently operating infant self. The infant's recognition of the boundaries of its own body at quite an early age also suggests that this differentiated self is present then (as in Stern's striking data on Siamese twins).

INTENTIONALITY

The existence of a subjective sense of the self and its conscious intentionality is strongly suggested by the observational data on infants approaching the end of their first year. The infant also "understands" the mother's subjective state about this time (for instance, see Stern [1985] on infant and mother "pointing," and the "visual cliff" data). By the end of the second year, the subjective sense of self, and of the self as agent in creating imagined relationships to gratify fantasied relationships, is clearly established. Stern's account of the emergence of the core self, the subjective self, of each of these with "the other," and finally the verbal self and the narrative self presents a convincing picture. What I believe to be one of its most fundamental implications is the role of holistic patterns from the start. Particularly important is the discovery of the innate organization of transmodal perceptions with integrated modes of response. We cannot conceive of such integrated holistic activity without assuming an integrated whole that mediates it. Although not so confidently established, it seems to me of great importance that Stern virtually accepts Trevarthan's (1980) belief in the existence of an innate capacity for the shared awareness of human subjectivity. Moreover, I find highly plausible Trevarthan's view that this developmental leap represents the differentiation of a coherent field of intentionality.

Intentionality has recently become very much a focus of philosophical concern. Its existence is much more difficult to conceive and to establish when we do not take into account the evolutionary development of the self; and, of course, for the physically minded theorists, it is thought to be a vitalistic notion. Thus, assuming the absolute necessity of the organism to maintain interchanges with the environment—an assumption so obvious when bodily processes are considered—a necessary condition for the survival of homo sapiens, the social animal par excellence, is the constant outreach to grapple with and overcome the limitations of the environment, both social and physical. The cognitive explorations required here would alone make for a perpetual intentionality, but the innate dynamic of the person at all stages, apart from the need to relate to others, has this need to keep realizing the self through the incessant urge to know more. That was what the Romantic poets sensed in their appraisal of the pleasure from knowledge and the deep identity of truth and beauty. What evolution has created so far is this innate organization that, out of its experiences, evolves the personalization of the organizing principle in a creative interplay between the child and its family, and subsequently between individuals and their culture. The subjectivity of the person is an incredibly sensitive monitor for regulating personal well-being, a sense of being, and with the further sensing that this feeling is only "right" or "complete" when it incorporates the innate need for "being" to be always "becoming." This truth is proverbial in almost all cultures, and I shall mention only this saying in the Gaelic culture of Celtic Scotland: "Joy of seeking, joy of never finding!"

It is from the interplay of the self with its culture that Erikson's epigenetic phases evolved. Characteristically, his phases are not tied to libidinal zones, but to changes in the quality of the dominant self-feeling in its relationships with its society. The patterns of relatedness thought to be derived from the libidinal zones are there. As Stern stressed, these patterns do not constitute a succession of stages, with each replacing the predecessor. What we now see to be covered by "orality" is the behavior determined by the intense incorporative needs to secure the appropriate intake from the environment, bodily and personally, for the developments urged by the genic inheritance. The resultant oral structuring is one that maintains a permanent process in the continuing of the self-process. Our clinical work demonstrates daily the labile balance of the appropriate give and take in social relations. With the good-enough mothering experience, this balance is maintained from everyday transactions. Where this experience has been lacking, we see greed and infantile dependence reemerging as the regression to more primitive modes of "taking in" to make good the deficiency. Early stages never disappear but remain as modes of relating that can be reactivated by various environmental factors.

Intersubjective sharing is the means through which individuals can relate with rapid appraisals of intentions and affects in others. This sharing develops from the simultaneous acquisition of self-awareness and the knowledge of the self-states of others. In short, the person is created from interchanges with other persons. Infant development research shows the progressive gains and their extraordinary rapidity from the latter part of the first year onward. The period of the most intense socialization has been described by Bowlby and his colleagues in terms of bonding and attachment theory. The attachment phenomena are very real, but I do not think these terms are adequate for the ongoing inner processes. The period of intense closeness that lays the foundation for attachment is used by Mahler as the one for the symbiotic relationship from which individuation evolves. For myself, I find it clinically much more useful to see the closeness as necessary behavior for the gestation of the self. Far from being undifferentiated, the self is being formed steadily, and any interference with this self-determined dynamic elicits intense aggression. Not unexpectedly, the embryoniclike state of the self needs the closest contact with the mother's "self" as well as her care.

The concept of an *innate dynamic gestalt* underlying the formation of the person resembles Lichtenstein's organizing principle, which constitutes the potential self that is then personalized by the earliest relationships with the mother. Moreover, this potential being personalized by this specific experience becomes the unique identity of the person. I have suggested that this potential be conceptualized as an inherited gestalt that seeks to become a person by finding the "expected" encounters. (Such a possibility is fairly readily conceivable today with the discovery of such holistic fields of force in the organism as are revealed in holograms.) The fitting of a particular gestalt with its environment is a process going on all the time. Postulating a central agent implies a view of development proceeding from this center by differentiation, with the creation of various subsystems.

REFERENCES

Spitz (1965). *The First Year of Life.* New York: International Universities Press.

Stern, D. (1985). *The Interpersonal World of the Infant: A View from Psychoanalysis and Developmental Psychology.* New York: Basic Books.

Trevarthan, C. (1980) The foundations of inter-subjectivity. Development of interpersonal and co-operative understanding in infants. In *The Social Foundations of Language and Thought: Essays in Honor of J. S. Bruner,* ed. D. Olson. New York: Norton.

XI

ADVANCES IN CLINICAL CONCEPTS

Increasingly, there is a feeling that something new is created in the potential space between patient and therapist that is unique to their relationship, that was not there before, and that is entirely unlike anything else between each of them and any other person. The idiosyncrasies of such a relationship notwithstanding, this entirely personal joint construction contains echoes of a similar structure between mother and baby, and is the instrument of understanding, empathy, and growth for patient and therapist as it was for mother and infant. In my view, this idea, given different names and descriptions by various contributors, is the most important idea to emerge from current psychoanalytic thinking. It is an idea whose evolution draws on the work of the entire tradition we have been studying, from Freud, Fairbairn, Klein, Winnicott, Bion, Heimann, Racker, Balint, and Guntrip to the work of several of the most original current writers. I have used its evolution in the choice of the selections for this section on modern clinical concepts.

The contributors whose work is excerpted below are only a few of the many who are extending the object relations tradition. Along with writers like Joseph, Spillius, Sandler, Ogden, and Sutherland, who have already been presented, the writers presented here are among the current contributors whose ideas specifically extend the themes we have been following in the course of this volume.

I have arranged this collection of excerpts concerning the nature of the therapeutic relationship into three groups: those representing advances in the understanding of splitting and projective identification, advances in the analyst's work through intensive study of the clinical situation and increased self-awareness, and increased understanding of the structure of therapy as a joint creation of the patient and therapist.

Contributions to the Treatment of Splitting and Projective Identification

49

James Grotstein's *Splitting and Projective Identification* (1981)

James Grotstein is an American analyst profoundly steeped in the tradition of British object relations, especially the work of Fairbairn, Klein, and Bion. He was in analysis with Bion during Bion's years in Los Angeles, and has for many years coordinated a study group for the exploration of Bion's ideas. He organized a visit by Guntrip to the United States, and has edited a book on the significance of Fairbairn's legacy.

This excerpt discusses the meaning and uses of splitting and projective identification. It presents his original elaborations on these processes, particularly his notion of the *dual-track theory,* in which he proposed that there is a facilitating split in the way therapists relate to patients by giving themselves over to a full unconscious relationship, and by paradoxically separating out their powers of observation and understanding at the same time.

REFLECTIVE RECAPITULATIONS

Normal splitting and projective identification are the beneficent legacies of a series of self-objects which can now be seen as the harmonious cooperation of intrapsychic and interpersonal objects. In infancy it takes three people to lead one life, the life of the infant; in adulthood, it takes two—at least. Thus, mother and father are linked together in Siamese twinship with the infant who itself links up with this Siamese bond with its own inherent background object of primary identification.

Abnormal splitting and projective identification emerge from infantile mental catastrophe, disappointment, dissolution, and despair. Thus, the therapist who wishes to acknowledge the importance of splitting and projective identification must allow himself to become "pregnant" with his patient's material not only so as to be able to be receptive to the patient's preverbal, primitive *communication,* but also to be able to allow the patient the achievement of *autistic relatedness* guaranteed by a background object of primary identification, the achievement of *symbiotic relatedness* guaranteed by the interpersonal self-object, and the reasonable guarantee of the *hope of a future* by the reestablishment of a relationship with the object of destiny.

Thus, the therapist who treats a patient enters into an epigenetically predetermined sequence of relationships which I have called "Siamese bonding." These include autistic, symbiotic, and separated-individuated relatedness. By this I mean that the therapist engages in a dual-track relationship with the patient *and* in the understanding of the person's material insofar as the relationship is both real and in phantasy, and insofar as the patient is reporting his empathic failures in present and past realities which have both real and phantasy components. I am advising the therapist, in other words, to play two hands at the piano rather than one, so to speak. I hope I have demonstrated my reasons for this in the case histories of the psychotic patients. Although I believe it is very important to detail the patient's employment of defensive splitting and projective identification, I consider it even more important to help establish an autistic and symbiotic bonding with the patient so that the content of interpretations of splitting and projective identification can be seen as the "best possible solutions" that the patient could make under the circumstances (Pao 1979).

We see from the case histories that these patients invariably had to resort to the use of defensive splitting and projective identification because of their feelings of enfeeblement and helplessness. In their attempts to rescue themselves they have compounded their miseries by creating a double anxiety—the results of splitting and projective identification and the cost to ego cohesiveness that it betokens. The infant and the patient want their objects to be background objects which can be a backboard for the reflection of their thoughts and a transformative object who can "catch," sort out, and reflect upon the projections so as to give significance and meaning to the patient's productions. From another point of view, it can be said that the existence of projective identification ultimately depends upon the receiver of it. The more empathic the therapist object is with the patient's projective identifications, the less projective and identifying they are and the more they become communications which can have self-transcendent meaning for the patient. At the same time, projective identifications for which the patient is not ready for reflection must be contained within the domain of postponement by the therapist so that the patient does not have to resort to psychotic disavowal or eradication of his or her state of mind.

It must also be remembered that infants and patients are keenly susceptible to the projections of their parents and their therapist, as Langs has so beautifully pointed out. Thus, therapy is indeed a bipersonal field with the possibility of projective identifications and splitting going across the network in both directions. That is why we must be especially in touch with the patient's experience of us as therapists so as to be in tune with our own empathic failures which may have resulted in our own projective identifications into and onto the patient, which then reroute him from his own scenario onto ours.

Splitting and projective identification create the internal objects of the inner world as scaffoldings for the development of future psychic structures. The design of the creation follows the protocol of all the possible relationships between the parts of the infant's subjective self (mouth, anus, genital, skin, sense organs, mind, etc.) and the corresponding anatomy of the object's body. The linkages follow instinctual motivations or, as I prefer to call them, after Bion, L, H, and K functions, where L stands for love, nurture, slumber, etc.; H stands for hate, aggression, defense, preparation, repairing, and taking care of; and K stands for knowledge, stimulation, curiosity, and the desire to transcend oneself. Thus, the infant's mouth projectively identified with mother's breast can create, for instance, a hungry, biting breast, a kissing breast, a scooped-out breast, etc., the latter of which may then be reprojected onto mother as a damaged whole-vagina with teeth, for instance. The infant's hungry eyes can be projectively identified with daddy's penis and the reinternalized as a moralistically voyeuristic superego object. The projective identification of the infant's epistemophilic instinct into the eye of the object (or the reverse, the projective identification of the infant's eyes into mother's mind—then combined with the projective identification of the infant's destructive feelings) can finally cause the internalization of that phenomenon known as "the evil eye"—and so on, and so on.

By and large, the L, H, and K functions produce three normal internal objects: a nurturing object, a protective object (a boundary object or sphincter object: a gatekeeper), and a stimulating object. The pathological vicissitudes of these are many and have been listed. Mason (1981) has discussed the suffocating superego, which is a projective identification of the infant's possessiveness into a breast which is then internalized as a claustrophobia-inducing object which suffocates the life out of the patient's ego.

Internal objects formed by splitting and projective identification constitute, as I stated above, a scaffolding for primitive psychic structure. They correspond to self-objects. It could be said that they are like the baby teeth which await the development of permanent teeth, corresponding to object representations which take their place. Object representations are not internal objects, but rather are the imaginative portraitures of external persons who are no longer possessed by omnipotent desire plus the shadow of the former presence of internal objects. They constitute permanent psychic structures.

The dual-track bids that the therapist/parent extend safety and empathy to the infant/patient while at the same time encouraging the patient to extend amnesty toward him-/herself (self as object). Empathy toward the struggling authentic self must be tempered by vigilance, discipline, and rigor in protecting it from the other split-off, malevolent, but hapless subpersonalities within the psyche whose imaginative births owe their origins to unbearable experience once upon a time. The rigor and discipline with which the therapist and patient must detect and confront these splits must be tempered by the amnesty extended toward their rehabilitation back into psychic at-one-ment. All this is done so that the infant/patient can utilize his/her own dual-track in confronting the cafeteria of experience in order to locate and select those qualities from persons in this world of experience that are needed for survival and for the future, and to separate off those persons and experiences which are not relevant and meaningful to his/her scenario.

Splitting and projective identification have an epigenesis and eventually become sublimated functions within the mature psychic structure. Whereas splitting is to become discrimination and normal porous repression, projective identification not only participates in normal porous repression, but also becomes the means of communication between oneself and oneself and between oneself and the other. In the depressive position of separation-individuation with rapprochement, the infant learns projectively to identify in its mother the feeling of subjectivity so that mother now becomes not only an object but also a co-subject. This is the beginning of empathy in the capacity to tolerate another scenario in a cosmos vaster than the infant's own omnipotent cosmos.

Projective identification ultimately is the basis for thinking. We first become aware of thoughts and feelings as they emerge and/or irrupt into our awareness. Bion calls these "thoughts without a thinker." Freud designated them by a more mechanistic terminology as instinctual drives. I prefer the former. The "thoughts without a thinker" emerge into our awareness for our mind to think about. In order for them to emerge, they must experience a projective trajectory onto the surface of object representations which constitute a table for thought, having been honed from experience with a containing mother who can reflect, "catch," and sort out. This is the basis for a "thinking couple." Ultimately, projective identification in its most basic communicative form, is the cry of agony of the infant who must put its experience into the caretaking object so that that object can know how the infant feels.

Thus, projective identification has a significance beyond simple communication and can be likened to a spiritual experience. Every culture since the beginning of time has practiced one form or another of ritual sacrifice. The circumcision of the Jews and their kosher ceremonies reflect an even more ancient and more deadly origin. The Christian Eucharist is currently the most well-known ceremony commemorating the mystical need for human sacrifice where the one is chosen as a token to reflect and represent the sacrifices of the many. It seems we are still in that stage of evolution where human sacrifice is needed. The infant may need its mother, father, or sibling to be its own token sacrifice where it can project its agony into these objects so that they can "know" its agony and thereby relieve it. By the same token, parents do likewise with each other and with their children. It is as if all human beings, parents and children alike, are really children who wish someone to know their agony so that the tale can be told. The transmission of this message is projective identification. The capacity to "know" that message is the ability to tolerate suffering through this "exchange transfusion" between the sacred and the profane.

REFERENCES

Mason, A. (1981). The suffocating superego. In *Do I Dare Disturb the Universe? A Memorial for Wilfred R. Bion*, ed. J. S. Grotstein. Beverly Hills: Caesura.

Pao, P.-N. (1979). *Schizophrenic Disorders: Theory and Treatment from a Psychodynamic Point of View.* New York: International Universities Press.

50

Jill Savege Scharff's *Projective and Introjective Identification and the Use of the Therapist's Self* (1992)

Jill Savege Scharff was born in Scotland, and trained in Edinburgh with Sutherland and at the Tavistock Clinic in London before emigrating to the United States. Her experience in family and couple therapy as well as psychoanalysis spawned her investigation of projective and introjective identification. Her writing emphasizes the neglected introjective arm of a cybernetic cycle of continuous projective and introjective identification, which forms a continuous cycle of communication in healthy development, in the maintenance of intimate relationships, in pathology, and in therapy.

INTROJECTION, INTROJECTIVE IDENTIFICATION, PROJECTION, PROJECTIVE IDENTIFICATION

For simplicity, I refer to the person who is doing the projecting as the *projector.* The person receiving the projection will be called the *projectee.* The person initiating an introjective identification will be called the *introjector.* The person from whom the introjection is selected will be the *introjectee.*

The following steps characterize introjective identification.

1. Introjection

The introjector takes in a feeling, an idea, or a part of the self or object of another person, the introjectee. Introjection may be simply a way of perceiving the outside world or it may be the first step in the construction of an internal object in the realm of the ego or superego. Introjection is classically viewed as occurring by the oral route. I think that it also occurs through the eyes, ears, nose, skin, vagina, and anus.

2. Identification

The introjector now identifies with the introject. The self becomes like the part that has been taken in from the introjectee. In the course of development, the introjectee is most often a parent. The part taken in may be a loved, feared, or rivaled part of the other person. It may be accurate or distorted by feelings about the other person. It will form an amalgam with other introjections to form an internal object with which the self is in close relation and which represents both becoming like and reacting against the external object found in the introjectee. Introjective identification occurs in order to maintain a tie to the introjectee, to re-create a lost relationship, to possess something good that is admired or envied, to protect the other person from something bad, or to displace and become the other person.

3. Psychic Structure Formation

Introjective identification leads to the formation of the ego and the superego. Freud saw the superego as a superimposed censoring structure made up entirely of introjective identifications with the parents and reaction formations against them at the oedipal stage. In Fairbairn's object relations theory, in relation to objects experienced as bad, we see aggressively forbidding parts of the ego splitting off as subformations to preserve the central ego from intolerable aspects of its interaction with the parents. These ego parts are somewhat equivalent to superego structure described by Freud, but they develop long before the oedipal phase. In Kleinian theory, introjective identification contributes to the development of the superego in infancy. When the introjective identification is with a bad object, the self may act aggressively to that internal object and its representatives when it is re-projected in a relationship, or the self may be bombarded by the bad object found in a new relationship. If the introjected part is identified with by the superego and overvalued, the self may actually be denigrated. When the introjected object is a good object, it contributes to the formation of the ego ideal and colors the ego positively.

4. Reprojection and Projective Identification

Now the process ties in to the steps of projective identification.

Projection

In *projection,* a part of the self—either a part of the ego or its internal objects, or a feeling or an idea originally connected to the self or objects split off from them—is expelled from the intrapsychic domain and displaced to an external object during an unconscious mental process. The person doing the projecting (called the projector) has no awareness of the projection onto the other person (the projectee), and so has a feeling of separateness from the external object that possesses the expelled part of the self. The object is believed to be invested with qualities that it does not have. The only identification occurring is that of identifying or misrecognizing a quality in that object. Semantically, one might argue that the term *projective identification* applies because of the occurrence of identification in a form inherent in Segal's definition of projective identification. But technically it does not qualify as a projective identification because there is no feeling of oneness with the recipient of the projection. The projection does not necessarily fit. It may be a delusion as in paranoia, a misperception as in neurosis, or a normal momentary expulsion followed by reintrojection of an unaltered projection.

Projective Identification

In projective identification, a number of steps follow. The first step is always a projection. Whether it remains a projection or becomes a projective identification depends on whether the second step of identifying the object with the projection occurs. Here I mean the external or the internal object. If the only object affected is the internal object, then the process remains an intrapsychic one. Whether it remains a single projection- or a dual projection-projective identification depends on whether the object of the projection actively contributes to the process or not. When the external object of the projection contributes to the process, either actively by exciting and deserving the projection or passively by not refuting it, then projective identification has entered the interpersonal dimension. Then the object may simultaneously project parts of itself into the subject, thus creating a mutual process of projective identification. If all the steps are completed, the process of projective identification goes beyond description as a one-body or two-body phenomenon to a multi-part-and-object phenomenon, a description that does justice to the recruitment into the process of any number of parts of self and objects of one, two, or more personalities in unconscious communication during interaction in family life.

The following steps characterize *projective identification.*

1. *Projection.* The projector expels a part of the self or its objects into an external object and identifies the external object as if it were imbued with qualities that do not pertain to it; in fact, they pertain to the projector. (This is the original projection. Identification occurs only in the sense of naming or recognizing a quality.)
2. *Object induction.* The projector so convincingly identifies the projected part of the self in the external object that the feeling state corresponding to that part of the self is unconsciously evoked in the projectee.
3. *Introjective identification by the object.* At this point the projectee has identified with the projection of the projector through the process of introjective identification at the unconscious level. This feeling state may persist, affecting attitude and behavior toward the projector. Alternatively, it may be dis-identified with and shaken off as alien. Or the feeling state may be compared against other feeling states experienced in relation to the projector and modified by the discriminating and integrating functions of the projectee's personality in a process of transformation.
4. *Transformation by the object.* Since the projectee has his or her own personality, the projected part of the projector's self with which the

projectee identifies is not the same as the part was when still inside the intrapsychic arena of the projector. The part has been transformed by its temporary lodging in another host, its goodness or badness being confirmed, exaggerated or, diminished. This process has been described by Bion as containment of the anxious infant's projective identifications by the mother in her state of reverie.

5. *Types of introjective identification by the object.* The part of the self projected may be a part of the ego (part of the self-representation) or a part of the object. In other words, the introjective identification of the projectee may be, in Racker's terms, concordant or complementary to the projector's self (Racker 1968).
   a. Introjective identification of the *concordant* type. The projectee is induced to embody the projected part of the ego (in shorthand, the self) while the object remains located in the projector.
   b. Introjective identification of the *complementary* type. The projectee is induced to embody the projected object in relation to the projector's ego (self).

   The introjective identification is determined not only by which part of the self or object is actually projected but also by the projectee's valency (Bion 1959) to respond in identification with the projector's projected part of self or object.
6. *Valency of the object to receive a projection.* When the projectee has a valency for a certain projection, then the projectee will tend to accept that projection and identify with that part of the projector's self. Sometimes this valent part is actively seeking parts of another to identify with to the point of stealing part of another person's mind through "extractive introjection" (Bollas 1989, p. 5).
7. *Reintrojective identification by the self.* The self identifies with or assimilates itself to the reinternalized confirmed or modified part of the self that had been projected. Then psychic structure is "cemented" or slightly altered. Cementing can be a healthy process if accurately received projections are accurately returned by the external object, but it can be unhealthy by not permitting change. Alteration can be healthy if the modification is slight and based on the projectee's unconscious capacity to appreciate the otherness of the other person and to harbor and return the projected part of the projector in a detoxified form that calms anxiety and reduces the likelihood of future distortion because of it. Alteration can be unhealthy when it returns the projection in a totally distorted form which does nothing

to modify anxiety, may even aggravate it, or do violence to the integrity of the projector.

8. *Mutual projective identification.* The projector that projects into the projectee is at the same time receiving projections from the projectee. Projector–projectee pairs unconsciously match up based on valencies to identify with each other's projections. Because more than one person is present in a relationship, projective identification becomes a mutual process: for example, husband and wife connect according to unconscious complementarity of object relations, patient and analyst relate through the transference and countertransference. And projective identification is intimately tied to introjective identification.

I find a medical analogy helpful here. I see introjective processes working like osteoblasts, those cells that busily build bone without much thought to the final product. Osteoclasts break down the bone that the osteoblasts have built, but they do so precisely according to an architectural design that shapes the final bone form. Like osteoclasts, projective processes sculpt the final form of the introject. Working in parallel with introjective processes, projective processes also have a proactive role in shaping what is taken in. As the bone is subject to the strains imposed by the stronger pull of more developed muscles and by stimulation from growth hormone, the osteoblasts have to respond with more bone mass and the osteoclasts fine-tune the resulting bone formation. So at each developmental level in infancy and adulthood introjective and projective processes shape the growing personality.

REFERENCES

Bion, W. (1959). *Experiences in Groups.* New York: Basic Books.

Bollas, C. (1989). *Forces of Destiny: Psychoanalysis and Human Idiom.* London: Free Association Books.

Racker, H. (1968). *Transference and Countertransference.* New York: International Universities Press.

51

Otto Kernberg's "Transference and Countertransference in the Treatment of Borderline Patients" (1975)

Otto Kernberg has introduced ideas from British object relations theory to the American audience, and has produced notable developments himself, most particularly in the areas of the treatment of severely disturbed patients within the borderline and narcissistic classifications, as well as in exploring the application of object relations ideas to love relationships, groups, and institutions (Kernberg 1976). His work on the capacity for mature love extends the work of Freud, Balint, and Winnicott, blending their influence with the work of Americans Edith Jacobson and Margaret Mahler, thus integrating relational ideas with ego psychology, a trend that has remained a hallmark of the American object relations group.

This excerpt applies Kernberg's general principles for the treatment of patients with borderline personality, as elaborated in 1975. Kernberg has continued to advance the treatment of the severely disturbed patient throughout his career, as well as inspiring the adoption of object relations ideas in American psychoanalysis generally.

REFERENCE

Kernberg, O. F. (1976). *Object Relations Theory and Clinical Psychoanalysis.* New York: Jason Aronson.

An outline of my approach to the treatment of borderline patients (Kernberg 1975), together with clinical material, should illustrate the differences between the technique used with borderline patients and that used with other types of patients. I will have two points of emphasis. First is the difference between the particular psychotherapeutic approach proposed for borderline patients and that used in a standard psychoanalysis. The second is the common principles underlying standard psychoanalytic technique and technical interventions made in the course of any session with borderline patients. My therapeutic approach may be subsumed under two headings: (a) transference interpretation limited by the deployment of special parameters of technique (Eissler 1953), and (b) systematic resolution of the constellations of primitive object relations activated in the transference.

TRANSFERENCE INTERPRETATION LIMITED BY THE DEPLOYMENT OF SPECIAL PARAMETERS OF TECHNIQUE

The predominantly negative transference of borderline patients should be systematically elaborated only in the "here and now," without attempting to achieve full genetic reconstructions. The reason is that lack of differentiation of the self concept and lack of differentiation and individualization of objects interfere with the ability of these patients to differentiate present and past object relations, resulting in their confusing transference and reality and failing to differentiate the analyst from the transference object. Full genetic reconstructions, therefore, have to await advanced stages of the treatment.

The typical defensive constellations of these patients should be interpreted as they enter the transference; the implication is that the interpretation of the predominant, primitive defensive operations characteristic of borderline personality organization strengthens the patient's ego and brings about structural intrapsychic change which contributes to resolving this organization.

Limits should be set in order to block acting out of the transference, with as much structuring of the patient's life outside the hours as necessary to protect the neutrality of the therapist. The implications are that, although interventions in the patient's external life may sometimes be needed, the technical neutrality of the therapist is essential for the treatment; moreover, it is important to avoid allowing the therapeutic relationship, with its gratifying and sheltered nature, to replace ordinary life, lest primitive pathological needs be gratified in the acting out of the transference during and outside the hours.

The less primitively determined, modulated aspects of the positive transference should not be interpreted. This fosters the gradual development of the therapeutic alliance; however, the primitive idealizations that reflect the splitting of "all good" from "all bad" object relations need to be interpreted systematically as part of the effort to work through these primitive defenses.

Interpretations should be formulated so that the patient's distortions of the therapist's interventions and of present reality (especially of the patient's perceptions in the hour) can be systematically clarified. One implication is that the patient's magical utilization of the therapist's interpretations needs to be interpreted.

The highly distorted transferences (at times, of an almost psychotic nature), reflecting fantastic internal object relations related to early ego disturbances, should be worked through *first* in order to reach *later* the transferences related to actual childhood experiences. All transferences, of course, recapitulate childhood fantasies, actual experiences, and defensive formations against them, and it is often difficult to sort out fantasies from reality. However, the extreme nature of the fantasied relationships reflecting very early object relations gives the transference of borderline patients special characteristics—our next point.

SYSTEMATIC RESOLUTION OF THE CONSTELLATIONS OF PRIMITIVE OBJECT RELATIONS ACTIVATED IN THE TRANSFERENCE

A predominant characteristic of the transference of borderline patients, particularly in early stages of treatment, is the presence of overwhelming chaos, meaninglessness or emptiness, or conscious suppression or distortion. The most general reason for this state of affairs is the predominance of "primitive transferences," that is, the activation in the transference of part-object relations—units of early self- and object-images and the primitive affects linking them—which do not represent the characteristic developments of internal object relations of neurotic patients and of normal people. The ordinary transference neurosis is characterized by the activation of the patient's infantile self or aspects of that infantile self linked to or integrated with his infantile self in general, while the patient reenacts emotional conflicts of this infantile self with parental objects that are, in turn, integrated and reflect the parental figures as experienced in infancy and childhood. In contrast, the nonintegrated self- and object-representations of borderline patients are activated in the transference in ways that do not permit the reconstruction of infantile conflicts with the parental objects as perceived in reality. Rather, the transference reflects a multitude of internal object relations of dissociated or split-off self aspects with dissociated or split-off object-representations of a highly fantastic and distorted nature.

The basic cause of these developments in borderline patients is their failure to integrate the libidinally and aggressively determined self- and object-images. Such a lack of integration derives from the pathological predominance of aggressively determined self- and object-images and a related failure to establish a sufficiently strong ego core around the (originally nondifferentiated) good self- and object-images. The problem with borderline patients is that the intensity of aggressively determined self- and object-images and of defensively idealized, "all good" self- and object-images makes integration impossible. Because of the implicit threat to the good object relations, bringing together extreme loving and hateful images of the self and of significant others would trigger unbearable anxiety and guilt; therefore, there is an active defensive separation of such contradictory self- and object-images. In other words, primitive dissociation or splitting becomes a major defensive operation.

The overall strategical aim in working through the transference developments of borderline patients is to resolve these primitive dissociations of the self- and object-representations and thus to transform primitive transferences—that is, the primitive level of internalized object relations activated in the transference—into the transference reactions of the higher level or integrated, more realistic type of internalized object relations related to real childhood experiences. Obviously, this requires intensive, long-term treatment along the lines I have suggested (Kernberg 1975)—usually not less than three sessions a week over a number of years. The strategy of interpretation of the transference may be divided into three steps.

These three steps represent, in essence, the sequence involved in the working through of primitive transference developments in patients with borderline personality organization. In this process, the dissociated or generally fragmented aspects of the patient's intrapsychic conflicts are gradually integrated into significant units of primitive internalized object relations. Each unit is constituted by a certain self-image, a certain object-image, and a major affect disposition linking them. The units of internalized object relations become activated in the transference, and when they can be interpreted and integrated with other related or contradictory units (particularly when libidinally and aggressively invested units can be integrated), the process of working through the transference and of the resolution of primitive constellations of defensive operations characteristic of borderline conditions has begun.

The first step consists in the psychotherapist's efforts to reconstruct, on the basis of his gradual understanding of what is emotionally predominant in the chaotic, meaningless, empty, distorted, or suppressed material, the nature of the primitive or part-object relation that has become activated in the transference. He needs to evaluate what, at any point in the contradictory bits of verbal and behavioral communication, in the confused and confusing thoughts and feelings and expressions of the patient, is of predominant emotional relevance in the patient's present relation with him and how this predominant material can be understood in the context of the patient's total communications. In other words, the therapist by his interpretative efforts transforms the prevalent meaningless or futility in the transference (which dehumanizes the therapeutic relationship) into an emotionally significant, although highly distorted, fantastic transference relationship.

In the second step, the therapist must evaluate this crystallizing, predominant object relation in the transference in terms of the self-image and the object-image involved and clarify the affect of the corresponding interaction of self and object. The therapist may represent one aspect of the patient's dissociated self and/or one aspect of the primitive object-representation, and patient and therapist may interchange their enactment of self- and object-images. These aspects of the self- and object-representations need to be interpreted and the respective internal object relations clarified in the transference.

In the third step, this particular part-object relation activated in the transference has to be integrated with other, related and opposite, defensively dissociated part-object relations until the patient's real self and his internal conception of objects can be integrated and consolidated.

Integration of self and objects, and thus of the entire world of internalized object relations, is a major strategic aim in the treatment of patients with borderline personality organization. Integration of affects with their related fantasied or real human relations involving the patient and the significant object is another aspect of this work. The patient's affect dispositions reflect the libidinal or aggressive investment of certain internalized object relations, and the integration of split-off, fragmented affect states is a corollary of the integration of split-off, fragmented internalized object relations.

REFERENCES

Eissler, K. R. (1953). The effect of the structure of the ego on psychoanalytic technique. *Journal of the American Psychoanalytic Association* 1:104–143.

Kernberg, O. (1975). *Borderline Conditions and Pathological Narcissism.* New York: Jason Aronson.

Advances in Understanding the Role of the Therapist in Promoting Growth

52

Nina Coltart's " 'Slouching Towards Bethlehem . . .' or Thinking the Unthinkable in Psychoanalysis" (1982)

The next three contributors examine the therapeutic action of analysis and analytic psychotherapy. Each of them, in a highly personal way, calls attention to the importance of taking in the total experience with the patient and working to become aware of the meaning of its effect on the analyst and on the therapeutic action by the analyst that follows. Part of this expanded awareness also includes an increased awareness of the effect of the therapist on the patient. The result is a heightened understanding of the reciprocity of the relationship and viscissitudes of the constant interplay of personalities.

Nina Coltart is a senior member of the Group of Independent Analysts in London, the so-called middle group that did not choose sides in the controversy between psychoanalysts loyal to Anna Freud and to Melanie Klein in the mid-1940s. This group has maintained a staunch independence of mind throughout the ensuing years, drawing ideas and orientation from any source that made sense, in the tradition of Balint, Fairbairn, and Winnicott. In this article, Coltart's exploration of the concept of openness extends Bion's use of *acts of faith* and *negative capability,* the giving up of memory and desire, as she examines the struggles of the therapist striving to maintain an open mind in the midst of challenging work.

And what rough beast, its hour come round at last,
Slouches towards Bethlehem to be born?
—W. B. Yeats, "The Second Coming"

It is of the essence of our impossible profession that in a very singular way we do not know what we are doing. Do not be distracted by random associations to this idea. I am not undermining our deep, exacting training; nor discounting the ways in which—unlike many people who master a subject and then just *do* it, or teach it—we have to keep *at* ourselves, our literature, and our clinical cross talk with colleagues. All these daily operations are the efficient, skillful, and thinkable tools with which we constantly approach the heart of our work, which is a mystery.

The day that one qualifies as an analyst, the analyst that one is *going to be* is a mystery. Ten years later, we may just about be able to look back and discern the shape of the rough beast—ourselves as analysts in embryo—as it slouched along under the months and years until, its hour come round at last, there is some clearer sense of ourselves as analysts. The process of doing analysis has slowly given birth to an identity which we now more or less recognize as an analyst, or at least the identity which we have become, and are still becoming, which for us approximates to the notion of "being an analyst." This may be very different from that which we long ago had visualized or hoped for.

It is my belief that something very similar obtains also for our work with our patients. However much we gain confidence, refine our technique, decide more creatively when and how and what to interpret, each hour with each patient is also in its way an act of faith; faith in ourselves, in the process, and faith in the secret, unknown, *unthinkable* things in our patients which, in the space which is the analysis, are slouching towards the time when their hour comes round at last. When that hour comes, by dint of all our long, thoughtful, interpretative attempts to familiarize ourselves with the patient's inner world, we begin to see shaping up things that we may have guessed at; or predicted, or theoretically constructed or relied on; or even, almost like by-products of months of careful, steady work, things that take us by surprise. We have been waiting attentively, in Freud's own words, "for the pattern to emerge." Those of us who were fortunate enough to be taught by the late Dr. Bion value the stress which he laid on the need to develop the ability to tolerate not knowing, the capacity to sit it out with a patient, often for long periods, without any real precision as to where we are, relying on our regular tools and our faith in the process, to carry us through the obfuscating darkness of resistance, complex defences, and the sheer *unconsciousness* of the unconscious. . . .

To return to the *act of faith,* Bion uses this phrase and by it intends to signify the most highly desirable stance of the psychoanalyst. He says that the act of faith is peculiar to scientific procedure and must be distinguished from the religious meaning with which it is invested in common usage. The essence of its creation—and Bion sees it, as do I, as a positive, willed act—is refraining from memory and desire, a phrase which many people *do* loosely associate with what they know of Bion. He says in *Attention and Interpretation* (1970, p. 30): "It may be wondered what state of mind is welcome if desires and memories are not. A term that would express approximately what I need to express is 'faith'—faith that there is an ultimate reality and truth—the unknown, unknowable, 'formless infinite' " which can become at least partly known through evolution into objects of which the individual personality can become aware. The channel for this evolution and the transformation of the apprehension of the ultimate reality, or a bit of it, is the analyst's direct attention and perception, and his capacity to bring together hitherto meaningless fragments of the patient's mental and verbal elements into a thinking process, and communicate this back to the patient.

Bion says that this form of attention, this act of faith, must be what he calls "unstained by any elements of memory or desire or sensation." He means in the analyst, of course. "The more the psycho-analyst occupies himself with memory and desire the more his facility for harbouring them increases and the nearer he comes to undermining his capacity for F [the act of faith]. For consider: if his mind is preoccupied with what is or is not said, or with what he does or does not hope, it must mean that he cannot allow the experience to obtrude" (1970, p. 41). No one who learns to denude himself of memory and desire, he goes on to say, and of all those elements of sense impression ordinarily present, can have any doubt of the reality of psychoanalytical experience which remains ineffable. It will be seen that Bion has intuition very high in his hierarchy of the tools at our disposal, and is advocating a constant sternly self-disciplined practice. Indeed, at one point, he actually equates intuition with "analytic observations."

It must be emphasized, however, in case it is not clear enough already, that Bion is not advocating random speculative commentary unrooted in a huge reservoir of experience, thought, theoretical knowledge, and the capacity to draw upon and correlate all these in the intervals *between* the dark experiencing of the act of faith, and in the interests of making the *evolution* of the total experience comprehensively available to the patient. The philosopher Immanuel Kant (1781) said: "Intuition without concept is blind: concept without intuition is empty." It seems to me that Bion, and I in my way in this paper, are striving for the merging of the two.

Before I move on from this section on Bion's thought, I just want to quote from a question-answer seminar recorded when Bion was in São Paulo in 1973. It says with such simplicity so much that elsewhere in his writings Bion goes over repetitively at length and in a complex way; the questioner asks: "How did you come to realize the advantages of suppressing memory and desire during an analytic session?" and Bion replies: "I found I could experience a flash of the obvious. One is usually so busy looking for something out of the ordinary that one ignores the obvious as if it were of no importance." Whereas, again in *Attention and Interpretation*, he says, unhelpfully if challengingly, "There can be no *rules* about the nature of the emotional experience that will show that it is ripe for interpretation." Here I would add that faith and self-reliance are indeed needed!

The crucial thing about our technical development is that it hinges on a paradox. There is a delicate balance between our reliance on our theories and on our knowledge of human nature in many of its dimensions—and experience tells us that human nature continually reveals similar patterns which generates good theory—the balance, I repeat, is between this *reliance*, and our willingness to be continually open to the emergence of the unexpected. *Plus ça change, plus c'est la même chose* may be a good truism for analysts, but it is only true in a restricted sense; it is the changes that are rung that are the essentials of individual humanity. There is a grim stage when we are *learning to be* analysts when we are endangered by our own templates, our theories, and our teachers. We may detect the faint shuffle of the slouching beast, and be tempted to throw a set of grappling irons into the darkness, seize him, label him, hang him round with words, and haul him prematurely to birth. We may then often be stuck with a deformed monster that we have largely created by our own precipitate verbosity; we may then proceed laboriously onwards with a sort of analytic mistake, while the true creature who is not yet ready for the light of day retreats backwards into the darkness again.

The use of the metaphor of the poem here says what I want to say, but perhaps I should explain it a little, and less poetically. The seductive impulse to use the power of one's thinking and theorizing to take possession of the patient too soon can be great, but will, as suggested, be of little ultimate value to him. Precipitate control of the material may lead to a sense of satisfaction in the analyst, and often to quite conscious layers of the patient, whose resistance to exposing his true unknown reality to the light will have been served by it. . . .

The special interest of psychosomatic symptoms, to pick up the main metaphor of this paper, is that the rough beast whose hour is not yet come is holed up in the body. There is a lovely quotation from the poet John Donne which refers to the nonpathological aspect of this:

> The blood spoke in her cheek,
> as if her body thought.

The beast has crossed that mysterious barrier whose location eludes us, and moved over into a stronghold from which it is only on rare occasions easy to deliver him. Mostly, he seems inaccessible, and we perceive that part of the mind has lodged on a psychotic island in the body. This image arises from a paper by Herbert Rosenfeld (1985), which sheds light on the treatment of women who not infrequently select the uterus as their psychotic island. We could say that a psychosomatic symptom represents that which is determined to remain unconscious, or unknowable, but which at the same time has actually made itself conscious in a very heavy disguise; it is speakable about only in a dense and enigmatic code. In terms of the metaphor of my paper, we have to ask what is the unthinkable content slouching along in the darkness of the psychosomatic symptom? How do we build a bridge which *really holds* over the secret area of the body–mind divide? Can the unthinkable become thinkable? Can we possibly devise words which have enough compatibility with the physical track chosen by the mind, so that we can send some sort of message down back along that same track via the body to the mind? By ordinary, careful analysis laced with inspiration one may at length interpret the psychosomatic symptom so irresistibly that it yields. A rush of new affects may appear. The now more verbal material may be enriched by new-old memories. Or the symptom may just quietly fade away. Nevertheless, there is a certain mystery which we do well not to ignore. It would be unwise to conclude that because we have apparently cured a genuine psychosomatic symptom by dynamic interpretation we actually know how it was done. We may be able to derive further theory from it. We may even be able to repeat the performance with another patient with a similar problem. But we do not quite know how it was done. Where and how did our laboriously evolved words and thoughts meet and capture the resolutely unthinkable beast in the unconscious process?

There is a way of visualizing analysis as a spiral process. The seemingly same ground is ploughed over and over again. And yet there is always something new about it. I refer to this spiral effect here because it has a special relevance to our work with psychosomatic symptoms. We may have undermined such a symptom to the point of its yielding. The patient may be in completely different territory, a long way up the spiral. Suddenly the symptom returns. It requires investigation all over again. The original understanding does not influence it in the same way. The mind is so protean that it can colonize the body in a new spirit and skilfully enlist the symptom under a new banner in the ongoing war of resistance in the transference.

Perhaps I may end here by saying that patients with such symptoms, and silent patients, teach us most vividly and memorably that there is always in our work a dimension that is beyond words. Some people suffer more from the unthinkable than others, and for these we have to do all in our power to help towards the therapeutic transformation, to bring thoughts to the unthinkable and words to the inexpressible. Gradually the rough beast may, within the framework of the analytic relationship, slouch towards being born, and the new creature emerging from the birth is the increased happiness and peace of mind of the patient. But in all of us there are some things which will never be within our reach; there is always a mystery at the heart of every person, and therefore in our job as analysts.

REFERENCES

Bion, W. (1970). *Attention and Interpretation.* London: Tavistock.

——(1973). *Brazilian Lectures 1.* Rio de Janeiro: Imago Editora, 1974.

Kant, I. (1781). *Critique of Pure Reason.* London: Dent Everyman Library, 1934.

Rosenfeld, H. (1985). The relationship between psychosomatic symptoms and psychotic states. In *Yearbook of Psychoanalytic Psychotherapy,* vol. 1. Emerson, NJ: New Concept.

53

Patrick Casement's *On Learning from the Patient* (1985): "The Internal Supervisor"

Patrick Casement is a member of the independent group who has closely studied the process of the monitoring of the analyst's self in the conduct of therapy. His original concept of the *internal supervisor* evolves out of the work of Winnicott, Fliess, Money-Kyrle, Bion, and others, but has, at the same time, a decidedly individual stamp.

Support from a supervisor or analyst can offer *hindsight* on what has been missed in an earlier session; it can also offer *foresight* in relation to what may be yet encountered. Therapists still need to develop a capacity to function with more immediate (but not instant) *insight* within the momentum of the analytic process. Not even that which is sometimes called the "internalized supervisor" meets all that is required here.

As a counterbalance to the many pressures upon a therapist in a session, I have found it useful to think in terms of an internal supervisor (Casement 1973). I first began to articulate the need for this in supervising others. I noticed that trainees in supervision often lean too heavily upon the advice or comments of a supervisor, which creates a barrier between the social worker or therapist and the client or patient. The effect of this becomes evident in the trainee's subsequent clinical work. I therefore came to see that formal supervision alone does not adequately prepare a student to deal with the immediacy of the therapeutic present. . . .

SUPERVISING OTHERS

When therapists have an opportunity to supervise others, they can enter into a further phase of growth that recapitulates much of what has gone before. The sequence is like a spiral in which they can find themselves back at a beginning, the beginning of training or the beginning of a treatment. They are back where they have been before, but also where they have never been before.

Just as we can see our own errors more clearly in others, so too in supervising others. Here there are endless opportunities for therapists to reexamine their own work, when looking closely at the work of the person being supervised. Not infrequently, supervisors will be seeing reflections of their own difficulties with technique. We do not always do as we teach others to do, but we can learn a lot by trying to do so.

When I have followed the work of my supervisees from an interactional point of view it has brought home to me how closely patients follow the work of their therapists, monitoring their moods, noticing their timing, wondering about the unconscious implications of their comments (what clues these may give the patient beyond the attempted inscrutability of the therapist). I had not realized before how much I too must give away of myself in the manner of my own interventions, or the mode of my responses to a patient.

RENEWED REFLECTION

Once I had come to recognize this unintentional manoeuvring of the patient by those I supervise, it became imperative for me to monitor my own work more closely. Some therapists might be surprised by how often they could be falling into modes of intervention that they have questioned when supervising someone else. This realization can stir into life a renewed cycle of learning about technique, and about our own contribution to the responses that we see in our patients.

TRIAL IDENTIFICATION

As a part of the internal supervision that I am suggesting, I often find it helpful to use trial identification (Fliess 1942). This can also be thought of as related to empathy in seeking to understand a patient. Reik (1937) pointed out that we develop empathy as a capacity to share in the experience of others, not just *like* our own but *as* our own.

Money-Kyrle (1956) linked this to the analyst's familiarity with his own unconscious:

> It is just because the analyst can recognize his early self which has already been analysed, in the patient, that he can analyse the patient. His empathy and insight, as distinct from his theoretical knowledge, depend on this kind of partial identification. Identification can take two forms—introjective and projective. We may therefore expect to find both forms in the analyst's partial identification with his patient. As the patient speaks, the analyst will as it were become introjectively identified with him, and having understood him inside, will reproject him and interpret. What I think the analyst is most aware of is the projective phase—that is to say, the phase in which the patient is the representative of a former immature or ill part of himself, including his damaged objects, which he can now understand and therefore treat by interpretation, in the external world. [pp. 360–361]

It is therefore not just the patient who needs to develop the capacity for a therapeutic dissocation within his ego, such as Sterba (1934) describes. The therapist also has to be able to maintain this benign split within himself, whereby his experiencing ego is free to move between himself and the patient, between thinking and feeling. Kris (1950) refers to this as "regression in the service of the ego." The analyst uses a controlled regression within himself in order to cross the boundary between his conscious (rational) thinking and his unconscious (primary-process/irrational) thinking. Allowing himself this freedom to enter a state of listening reverie, alongside the patient, he can monitor what it may feel like to be the patient (in whichever context).

Now, when I use trial identification I do so in a number of different ways. I may, for example, think or feel myself into whatever experience is being described by a patient. I may also put myself into the shoes of the other person being referred to. From each of these viewpoints it is possible to pick up elements of the patient's object relating that might otherwise be missed.

In addition to these more usual ways of monitoring a patient through trial identification, I also try to put myself into the patient's shoes in his or her relationship to me. I try to listen (as the patient might) to what it crosses my mind to say, silently trying out a possible comment or interpretation. This helps me to recognize when a patient could mis-hear what I wish to say, because of its ambiguity or due to an unfortunate choice of words. Or, I put myself into the patient's position and reflect upon my own last comment. Frequently this will alert me to the unintentional, and unconscious, communications that a patient could read into what I have just said. Then, when I listen to the patient's subsequent response, it becomes easier to see when this has been actually provoked by me, by my timing or manner of interpreting.

I first learned to monitor the therapeutic interaction in this way by trial-identifying with the patient when following the clinical presentations of people whom I supervised. With practice it becomes possible to use these two viewpoints simultaneously, the patient's and one's own, rather like following the different voices in polyphonic music.

This capacity to be in two places at once, in the patient's shoes and in one's own simultaneously, can only be encompassed if therapists can develop a capacity to synthesize these apparently paradoxical ego states. It is here, I believe, that the processing function of the internal supervisor comes to the fore. It is more than self-analysis and it is more than self-supervision.

REFERENCES

Casement, P. (1973). The supervisory viewpoint. In *Family Therapy in Social Work: Conference Papers*, ed. W. F. Finn. London: Family Welfare Association.

Fliess, R. (1942). The metapsychology of the analyst. *Psychoanalytic Quarterly* 11:211–227.

Kris, E. (1950). On preconscious mental processes. *Psychoanalytic Quarterly* 19:540–560.

Money-Kyrle, R. (1956). Normal counter-transference and some of its deviations. *International Journal of Psycho-Analysis* 37:360–366.

Reik, T. (1937). *Surprise and the Psychoanalyst.* New York: E. P. Dutton.

Sterba, R. (1934). The fate of the ego in analytic therapy. *International Journal of Psycho-Analysis* 15:117–126.

54

Neville Symington's "The Analyst's Act of Freedom as Agent of Therapeutic Change" (1983)

Neville Symington is a member of the group of independent analysts whose comprehensive understanding of theory and the therapeutic process is captured in his book, *The Analytic Experience* (1986), which sets down the lecture series given at the Tavistock Clinic in London for many years before he emigrated to Australia. The excerpt given here is from a journal article in which he discussed his realization of the constraint patients often visit on their therapists without either patient or therapist being aware of it, and of the facilitation of the therapy at the moment of recognition. This insight draws on a contribution of Bion's (included in Symington's excerpt) about an attitude of constraint imposed by a collusion in an unconscious attitude.

Symington approached the relationship between patient and therapist at the opposite pole from that used by Casement, who in the preceding excerpt looked at the therapist's effect on the patient—the *patient's* introjection of the *therapist*. Symington began by looking at the therapist's dawning awareness of the effect of the patient on him—the *therapist's* introjection of the *patient*. He then considered their mutuality in arriving at an understanding of unconscious processes.

REFERENCE

Symington, N. (1986). *The Analytic Experience*. New York: St. Martin's.

In this paper I intend to explore a phenomenon with which all analysts are familiar. I will first describe it and then examine what its implications are for theory. I shall refer to it as the *x-phenomenon*. I shall start with some clinical examples.

I was charging Miss M. a little more than half what my other patients were paying. She had been a clinic patient and I used to sigh to myself and say inwardly, "Poor Miss M., £X is the most that I can charge her."

I did not in fact articulate it so clearly as that. In my mind it was like an acknowledged fact that everyone knows, like the unreliability of the English weather. It was part of the furniture of my mind and I had resigned myself to it in the same way as I reluctantly resign myself to the English weather. So the analysis went on and on with that assumption as its unquestioned concomitant until one day a startling thought occurred to me: "Why can't Miss M. pay the same as all my other patients?"

Then I remembered the resentment she frequently expressed towards her boss who always called her "*Little* Mary." A certainty began to grow in me that I was the prisoner of an illusion about the patient's capacities. I had been lassoed into the patient's self-perception and I was just beginning to extricate myself from it. I then brought up the question of her fee and in the course of a discussion she said, "If I *had* to pay more then I know I would."

She had now clearly told me that she had the capacity in her to pay more and that this could be mobilized if I changed my inner attitude towards her. A few sessions later I said to her, "I have been thinking over our discussion about the fee. I charge most of my other patients £X and in our discussion I have not heard anything that makes me think that I should not charge you the same."

For two sessions she cried rather pitifully but then became resolved that she would meet the challenge. Soon she found a job that paid her one third more than her previous salary. In moving job she extricated herself from the patronizing tutelage of the boss who called her "Little Mary." She had been able to do this because she had first been freed from the patronizing attitude of her analyst. Shortly after this she finally gave the push to a parasitic boyfriend. Again I think she had been able to do this because she had been able to give the push to a parasitic analyst. These two events were soon followed by other favourable developments. I think the source of these beneficial changes was in that moment of inner freedom when I had the unexpected thought: "Why can't Miss M pay the same as my other patients?" I am calling this act of inner freedom the "x-phenomenon."

Now I want to take another example. This patient was an obsessional man who used to hesitate sometimes in the middle of telling me something, usually as he was about to tell me some thought he had had since the previous session. As he had often expressed his apprehension that I would think him pathetic I would say to him something like, "I think you are afraid that if you tell me about the incident in your mind I shall think you are pathetic."

Of course I was thereby clearly inferring that I would not think him pathetic. With this assurance he would then obligingly tell me the thought in his mind. Then one day I was reading the following passage from *Four Discussions with W. R. Bion* (Bion 1978):

> Q. . . . She wouldn't be put off by what you suggest; she would get irritated with your reply and insist that you call her by her first name.
> B. Why not the second one? Why not whore? Or prostitute? If she isn't one, then what's the trouble? Is she wanting to be called a prostitute or a whore? If not, what is the point of the story? What convinced her that her father was right?
> Q. She wants sex with other men besides her husband, therefore in her view, she must be a whore. She's afraid that if she got a divorce from her husband she would run around and have sex with all sorts of men—behave like a free whore.
> B. In view of what you are saying I think I would try to draw her attention to the way in which she wishes to limit my freedom about what I call her. It is just as much a limitation if the patient wants you to give the correct interpretation. Why shouldn't I be free to form my own opinion that she's a whore or that she is something quite different? Why be angry with me because in fact I am free to come to my own conclusions?
> Q. Her fear is that your own conclusion will be that she is a whore.
> B. But why shouldn't I be allowed to come to that conclusion?
> Q. So you conclude she is a whore—now where are you?
> B. But I haven't said that I do. The point I want to show is that there is a wish to limit my freedom of thought. [pp. 15–16]

As I read this I had a moment of illumination about my obsessional patient. I had been a prisoner of this patient's controlling impulses and at the moment of reading this passage from Bion I had a new understanding in which I felt freed inwardly (though this had outward concomitants). The next time he expressed his apprehension that I would think him pathetic I said to him quietly, "But I am quite free to think that."

He was much taken aback. It was possible then to see how much he operated by controlling my thoughts and the thoughts of others. A great fear was that if he allowed me to think my own thoughts then I might have the thought: "How nice it would be to get away from Mr X."

Then on to his feeling that no one ever *wanted* to be with him. This was linked to childhood experiences where his parents never wanted to be with him but farmed him out with child minders while they pursued their business interests in various parts of the world. We were able to look at his need to wind himself around me like a boa constrictor and try to substitute my thinking and feeling for his, to make me into his ego, as it were. It was then possible to link his failure to be able to think and feel with the absence of a mother or analyst who wanted to be with him. The foundation of the thinking capacity seems to lie in the internalization of this maternal desire. Again the source of all this interpretive work and insight started from the moment of my own inner act of freedom. So this was another case of the x-phenomenon. . . .

Now, in the psychoanalytical situation . . . the patient's communications and the analyst's feelings and thoughts become the raw material out of which understanding arises. The analyst does not only have his own false ideas to clear away but needs to be passive to the analytical process and combating the resistance that he and the patient are locked into. The attempt to understand is being continually sabotaged by a parallel process that stimulates and fosters false ideas. Received theoretical positions may be used by the resistant process, as they also may be used by the benign psychoanalytical process. The patient and analyst as a corporate entity are involved in these two processes. Belief in the psychoanalytical process seems to be the essential ingredient for both parties. However, it seems that it may be the special role of the analyst to carry this belief for the patient as well as for himself, specially early on in treatment. . . .

In order to separate, the patient needs to get access to the analyst's core feelings. His interpretations need to flow from here to as great an extent as possible if the patient is to be able to separate. This is most especially true for the psychotic patient whose fusion at the superego level is greatest and whose need for ego to ego contact is also greatest. It greatly concerned one patient whether what I said to him was what I thought or felt or was just a received dictum of the psychoanalytical tradition and therefore just a superego content. Each time a resistance was overcome it was then possible to reach further into what I truly thought or felt and then he was able to separate himself a bit more from that mother glue. He became more able to separate himself from the analyst and from his maternal object intrapsychically. My greatest problem in his analysis was to reach those feelings which were most truly mine. In the case of that patient the problem was particularly acute but on reflection I think this may be a central problem in every analysis.

The psychoanalytical setting is concerned to foster a particular type of communication which is demonstrated most clearly in those moments which I have called the x-phenomenon. This level of communication occurs from the very first moment when the patient enters the consulting room and with it a certain patterning of unconscious knowledge. The goal of the interpretive work is to make this conscious. At the same time there is another process at work, in both the analyst and the patient, whose goal is to sabotage the analysis. This process is located in the superego and makes use of illusions and cultural myths as its instrument. We call this process resistance but I have wanted to emphasize that this is a system in which both analyst and patient are involved, not something that is just located in the patient. The x-phenomenon implies that there is a knowledge that is preverbal and that it is anterior to speech and therefore to interpretation. At this level of knowledge the patient knows unconsciously the analyst's internal attitudes. If, for example, the analyst is unconsciously envious of the patient in some particular way then the patient perceives it and only a change in the analyst's inner attitude will enable the patient to move forward psychically. The moment the analyst becomes aware of his or her attitude and is freed from it then the patient perceives it. That is to say he or she perceives a change within the self and may make declarations to that effect without knowing the cause. The interpretations that follow the x-phenomen become conscious articulations of a change that has already occurred unconsciously at the ego to ego level. The interpretations help them to reestablish the superego so that its myths and values change and become tuned into the changes that have occurred within the ego.

With the exception of Winnicott I think that most analysts operate on the assumption that people are separate entities. I think that the x-phenomenon and the particular form of knowledge that it must imply means that people are individuals and yet part of a corporate entity. Because we are parts of a corporate entity then as soon as analyst and patient come together in the same room there is an immediate adaptation and fusing. The corporate entity instantly establishes itself. Socially this occurs when two people meet but in this case ego to ego contact is kept to a minimum, so also the joint-illusion is kept to a minimum. In psychoanalysis the latter is enhanced but only, so to speak, so as to hypercathect it and work through it and give place to the personal.

REFERENCE

Bion, W. R. (1978). *Four Discussions with W. R. Bion*. Perthshire: Clunie.

The Relational Matrix of Growth and Change

55

Stephen A. Mitchell's *Relational Concepts in Psychoanalysis: An Integration* (1988) and "Contemporary Perspectives on the Self: Toward an Integration" (1991)

The last group of contributors has struggled with a new area of growth and change, one that they find to be uniquely interpersonal and relational. In the view that emerges from a study of their work, the process of change comes not from any single aspect of technique such as genetic or transference interpretation, or the taking back of projective identification and the reduction of splitting. Rather it comes from growth that occurs in a transitional potential space between patient and therapist, a growth of something that is their unique, shared creation.

This development in theory can be seen to follow Fairbairn and Guntrip's emphasis on the therapeutic relationship, and to make sense of the way Joseph's focus on the totality of the transference and countertransference and Spillius's new thoughts on envy as an interpersonal situation move conceptualization from a focus on one person in a relationship—the baby or the patient—to a focus on both persons at the same time, or at least in rapid alternation. We can also see the beginnings of this idea in the writings of the three contributors of the previous section: Coltart, Casement, and Symington. Each of the following writers has a different way of describing this creation.

Stephen Mitchell, an American affiliated with the William Alanson White Institute in New York and the New York University Postdoctoral Program in Psychoanalysis, is steeped in the traditions of object relations, as well as interpersonal analysis, which began with the work of Sullivan and Fromm. With Jay Greenberg, he wrote a widely hailed text (1983) exploring the sources of relational concepts in psychoanalysis. The breadth of his scholarship is also evident in this excerpt from his own later book, which offers a view of development and therapy based on an integrated relational model. It is intrinsic to his model that individuals are seen as simultaneously self-creating and created by the environmental forces that shape them. The process grows out of the paradox of Winnicott's transitional phenomena, in which it can never be clear whether the infant created something or merely found what the mother placed there. Personality and growth are created in the potential space between the infant and the mother, between any two people in intimate relationships, between analyst and patient. Whose creation personality is can never be determined. It belongs to both the individual and to the pair in the relationship (and by extension, to the wider family or group.)

In the first excerpt given here, Mitchell examines the various relational theories, including those of developmentalists drawing on infant research, Kohutian self psychologists, and object relations, to contrast the differing aspects of the relationship of self and object that each theory emphasizes in constructing the complex pattern that, all together, goes to make up what he calls a "relational-conflict model" of psychoanalysis. In the second selection, he applies this perspective to the emergence of the self in analytic treatment.

REFERENCE

Greenberg, J., and Mitchell, S. (1983). *Object Relations in Psychoanalytic Theory*. Cambridge, MA: Harvard University Press.

A RELATIONAL-CONFLICT MODEL

The integrated relational perspective on the therapeutic action of psychoanalysis represents a convergence of interpersonal psychoanalysis, object relations theories such as those of Fairbairn and Racker, and certain currents of both self psychology and existential psychoanalysis. . . . In the relational-conflict view disturbances in early relationships with caretakers are understood to seriously distort subsequent relatedness, not by freezing infantile needs in place, but by setting in motion a complex process through which the child builds an interpersonal world (a world of object relations) from what is available. . . .

This model locates the central mechanism of analytic change in an alteration in the basic structure of the analysand's relational world. . . .

From the point of view of self-organization, the analytic situation allows the analysand to recover, reconnect with, and fully experience aspects of himself previously disclaimed, hidden, disavowed. . . .

Other relational-model theorists (Fairbairn and Racker, for instance) describe the same process in terms of alterations in internal object relations. The self here also is formed in complementarity with the character structures of significant others. . . . Early object ties are maintained as powerful internal presences; current object relations are experienced projectively in terms of those internal object relations and subsequently structured through a reintegration of new experiences into never-changing old configurations. Analytic change entails an alteration of these internal structures and relationships. . . .

Other relational-model theorists, particularly those in the interpersonal tradition, have focused on the way in which the analytic process facilitates changes in the analysand's transactional patterns. Anxiety about anxiety has forced the analysand into repetitive, constricted patterns in his interactions with others. From this angle, it is the ritualized action that delimits the experience of *both* self and other, because the continual repetition of stereotyped integrations makes it impossible for the analysand to experience himself or anyone else in other than collapsed, unidimensional ways. . . . The analytic process encourages the analysand to try something different, to put himself in a different interpersonal situation in which richer experiences of self and other are possible. . . .

I regard each of these formulations as useful. The analysand does not know any other way to be, and does not want to know any other way, because of the object loss and guilt, the fear of self-loss and loneliness, that behaving and experiencing oneself differently implies. These approaches enrich one another in illuminating the tenacity and complexity of psychopathology. . . .

Mitchell has continued to elaborate on the implications for psychoanalysis of his relational conflict model. In the following selection from "Contemporary Perspectives on the Self: Toward an Integration" he explores the emergence of the self in analytic treatment.

New forms of experience of self . . . are learned only by being lived in, through participation in the psychoanalytic process in a variety of different ways: through analysts' interpretations, curiosity, and other features of a distinctly analytic presence; through the atmosphere created by the structure of the analytic situation; through the model of the analyst's sense of himself or herself, in the countertransference, as a container of multiple versions of self, providing a vehicle for understanding the manifold intricacies of relatedness; and through the profound form of intimacy created and protected by the structure of the analytic relationship.

The inadequacy of the medical model approach to psychoanalysis is no more apparent than when one considers the experience of self that is generated by the analytic process, which is not a return to "normality," some premorbid standard of health, but rather a form of being that has its own unique qualities. Nor do I think it sufficient to designate what the analysand gains in terms to a particular function, like a capacity for self-observation or self-reflection or self-analysis. Rather, psychoanalysis, at its best, makes possible a more variegated experience of self: past and present, fantasy and actuality interpenetrate each other; the phenomenology of the self as independent and separable is illuminated by an awareness of the self's embeddedness within a relational matrix; the experience of the self as layered in space is expanded by an appreciation of the self as continually regenerated in time; and an appreciation of the multiplicity within the integrity of self-organizations enriches the tapestry of subjective experience.

In some respects, the patient is actually less known at the end of an analysis than at the beginning. Early on, the patient's sense of who he is is reductively collapsed and stereotyped: the self as heroic, the self as monstrous, and so on. Much of the analysis involves a slow and painstaking revelation and articulation of these configurations, in the process of which the patient comes to feel very deeply and profoundly known indeed. At the end of analysis, the patient's ways of representing himself to himself tend to be much more fluid, complex, subtly textured. . . . He becomes aware of how highly selective the presentation of self within analysis really is, and the freedom and loneliness to that realization that are an important part of termination.

56

Christopher Bollas's *Forces of Destiny: Psychoanalysis and Human Idiom* (1989) and *Being a Character: Psychoanalysis and Self Experience* (1992): "Psychic Genera"

Christopher Bollas is a contemporary writer whose work has explored some of the most interesting areas of difficult interaction between patients and analysts. His notion of *extractive introjection* (Bollas 1987), in which one person in an intimate relationship acts, in effect, to rob the other of aspects of their experience or personality, has opened new ways of understanding the activity of introjective identification, a neglected counterpart of projective identification. In the following excerpt taken from his book *Forces of Destiny*, Bollas proposes an extension of Winnicott's notion of the role of the spontaneous gesture in the elaboration of the "true self," thereby adding to our capacity to understand a person's drive to become him or her self throughout the life cycle.

REFERENCE

Bollas, C. (1987). *Shadow of the Object: Psychoanalysis of the Unthought Known*. New York: Columbia University Press.

By sustaining the infant's illusion that he creates his world, the mother, from Winnicott's point of view, enables the infant to experience his objects as subjective in origin. Thus object orientation and subsequent object relating emerge from this primary experience that objects derive from one's creativity. Naturally the infant will actually be disillusioned, both by the mother's ordinary failures and by the many lessons culled from reality, but the illusion of primary subjectivity will not completely disappear. In my view, it simply means that the infant, the child, and then the adult will carry an internal sense of creating his own life, even if the structures of society, the laws of one's culture, and the course of events cannot possibly be said to evolve out of the subject's true self. But the maternal provision of an illusion of creativity, which sponsors an experience but not a sense of omnipotence, marries up with the destiny drive which we can think of as an internal sense of personal evolution through space and time. After all, in some ways, this is what developmental theory is about: an evolution that traces the progressive maturation of the individual.

A sense of destiny, then, would be a feeling that the person is fulfilling some of the terms of his inner idiom through familial, social, cultural, and intellectual objects. I believe that this sense of destiny is the natural course of the true self through the many types of object relations and that the destiny drive emerges, if it does, out of the infant's experience of the mother's facilitation of true self movement. The true self, as Winnicott suggested, can evolve through maternal adaptation and responds to the quality of care the child receives from the mother and the father, as well as from the school and the peer world. Does the object world, in other words, provide the right conditions for the child to evolve his idiom, to establish his personality in such a way as to feel both personally real and alive, and to articulate the many elements of his true self?

Bollas followed the book on human idiom with a book entitled Being a Character, *in which he proposed the idea of* psychic genera *as healing nuclei that are the counterpart of psychic trauma. In this excerpt, he focuses on the growth of genera in the individual, but throughout the piece there is an overtone of the necessity of a healing or growth-promoting relationship as the requisite condition for the promotion of psychic genera.*

Bollas's consideration of genera grows out of his thinking about the treatment of traumatized individuals. The idea of genera enables us to view in a positive way the human and interpersonal structures that promote and embody healing.

In this chapter I shall put forward the view that trauma has an opposite—genera[1]—which is the psychic incubation of libidinal cathexes of the object world. The sense of how to gather psychic investments to an inner area of work derives from the individual's experience of elaborating his own idiom, a process that involves the selection of specific objects which release idiom to its expression. As we are born with our idiom and as it is elaborated through parental provision, the individual develops a belief in psychic dissemination, which leads him to assume that he can articulate his idiom through the psychic freedom of object representation and the liberty of object choice.

Naturally, as this freedom to evolve the self is facilitated and influenced by the mother and the father, any sense a person has of the nature of personal elaboration will bear the marks of maternal and paternal provi-

---

1. Heretofore "genera" has been the plural form of the noun "genus," which means class or kind. But a different noun structure has always been hidden within it, based on the Latin origin of the word, "gignere," which means to give birth. The Aryan root, "gen," also means to beget. In *Creative Evolution* Henri Bergson almost transformed "genera" into a verbal noun when he linked it to reproductivity and to his concept of vital energy. In the late nineteenth century, perhaps "genera" still carried within it the notion of a dynamically moving structure, but twentieth-century thought has denuded the word of its dynamic origins, and it is now used only to refer to classes of objects, although it would be allowed that such classes do evolve. I think it is within the spirit of the original base of this word (to give birth, to reproduce) to use "genera" as both a singular and a plural noun, simply because the word "genus"—its theoretically proper singular form—now definitely refers to a a single class or species, and does not contain in English a sensible verbal noun meaning. I also find that I cannot say "a genus" when referring to the dynamic organization of an evolving psychic structure. So I suggest that we create a contemporary, though restricted usage, in which "genera" also refers to a particular type of psychic organization of lived experience that will result in creative new envisionings of life, either in psychoanalysis or in other walks of life. In the psychoanalytic context it matches exactly with trauma. The plural noun was "traumata," but this is rarely used. Sometimes writers use "traumas" for the plural form, but increasingly "trauma" is used for both singular and plural noun forms. As the entire aim of my neologistic use of "genera" is to pair it with "trauma," in order to clarify complex issues having to do with the nature of mental development, I feel justified in this small act of linguistic violence.

sion. In fact, what we might think of as primal genera—specific nascent factors of the infant's idiom that sponsor early aesthetic cohesions of the object world—are met by another organizing intelligence: the logics of parental provision. The question is, can the idiom of the child elicit generative parenting so that the articulations of subjectivity use the materials of reality to promote elaboration?

If genera develop through the successional elaboration of idiom, trauma leads to the person's binding of the self, which sponsors a type of psychic pain and leads to a very different kind of unconscious work. Thus these two principles, of trauma and genera, begin as fundamental ego dispositions toward reality, derived from the infant's and child's experience of the mother and the father. Children whose parents are impinging or acutely traumatizing collect such trauma into an internal psychic area which is intended to bind and limit the damage to the self, even though it will nucleate into an increasingly sophisticated internal complex as resonant trauma are unconsciously "referred" to such an area for linked containment. Children who experience parents as contributing to the elaborative dissemination of their personal idiom will subsequently develop an open-mindedness to the contributing effects of the object world. . . .

Perhaps it is possible to see how trauma-developed psychic processes will be conservative, fundamentally aiming to control the psychic damage, desensitizing the self to further toxic events. Thus, trauma can be seen as allied to the indigenous inner principle of the death instinct, which aims to preserve a constant state by ridding the subject of excitation; only in the beginning trauma is the effort to rid the self of excitation sponsored by the external object (or actual other) rather than in the more classical and Kleinian formulations which emphasize the death work's effort to rid the subject of the disturbing effects of instinctual urgency. The trauma-evolving child is already a self developing along very particular lines, such as those conceptualized by Fairbairn in his theory of the infant's internalization of the bad object, where the aim is to control the negative effect of bad parenting by taking the negating objects into oneself.

The child who internalizes fundamentally generative parents—who contribute to the evolution of his personal idiom—aims to develop such inner processes and to seek excitation and novelty as means of triggering personal growth. As such, genera link up with the life instincts which aggressively seek the procreative combinings of self with object.

The child who establishes inner psychic holding areas for the containment of disturbed parental communications or shocking events seeks to break links between the referred contents and their preconscious derivatives. To use Bion's language: he attacks the linking function that is vital to K (knowledge) and works to devitalize the pain of its meaning by transforming it into −K, thereby giving to such inner experiences an empty or vacuous feel. Pain is thereby transferred into nothingness. In the child's cultivation of internal possibilities for creative revisioning of self and reality, links between inner areas of such work and the data of life that seem related to it are sought, thereby establishing a valorization of unconscious work informed by the K function.

REFERENCES

Bergson, H. (1911). *Creative Evolution.* Lanham, MA: University Press of America, 1983.
Bollas, C. (1989). *Forces of Destiny.* London: Free Association.

57

Thomas Ogden's *Subjects of Analysis* (1994)

Thomas Ogden is a San Francisco analyst who spent a year at the Tavistock Clinic in London, and who has subsequently explored many aspects of the British tradition. In a previous excerpt in this volume, he described the autistic-contiguous position. In this excerpt, drawn from the introductory chapter of his 1994 book *Subjects of Analysis*, the influences of Bion and Winnicott are evident in the emphasis on the processes of negation and destruction in the creation of analytic understanding, and of Lacan, in the description of the need for confrontation with the other.

This excerpt expresses the theme that the creation of growth and development in therapy is a joint creation of patient and therapist. The exploration of this theme conveys the excitement at the leading edge of object relations theory and therapy today.

The subjects of analysis bear a dialectical relationship to one another. From the elements of the dialectic of subject and object, a new whole begins to emerge that almost immediately reveals itself to be a new source of dialectical tension. The analytic process, which creates analyst and analysand, is one in which the analysand is not simply the subject *of* analytic inquiry; the analysand at the same time must be the subject *in* that inquiry (that is, creating that inquiry) since his self-reflection is fundamental to the enterprise of psychoanalysis. Similarly, the analyst cannot simply be the observing subject of this endeavor since his subjective experience *in* this endeavor is the only possible avenue through which he gains knowledge of the relationship he is attempting to understand.

Having said something of the interdependence of analyst and analysand (as subjects creating and created, destroying and destroyed by one another), we must introduce a third term, for without it we will not have adequately described the psychoanalytic process in which the analyst and analysand as subjects of analysis create one another. The nature of the third term is that which defines the nature of psychoanalytic experience and differentiates it from all other intersubjective human events. (There exist innumerable forms of human intersubjectivity, but none involves the form of intersubjectivity that is distinctive to psychoanalysis.)

In the same moment that analyst and analysand are created, a third subject is generated that I refer to as the *analytic third,* since it is a middle term sustaining and sustained by the analyst and analysand as two separate subjects. More accurately, analyst and analysand come into being in the process of the creation of the analytic subject. The analytic third, although created jointly by (what is becoming) the analyst and analysand, is not experienced identically by analyst and analysand since each remains a separate subject in dialectical tension with the other. Moreover, although the analytic third is constituted in the process of the mutual negation/recognition of analyst and analysand, it does not reflect each of its creators *in the same way* any more than the third created in the experience of reading reflects the reader and writer in the same way. In other words, the transference and countertransference reflect one another, but are not mirror images of one another.

The analytic third is not only a form of experience participated in by analyst and analysand, it is at the same time a form of experiencing I-ness (a form of subjectivity) in which (through which) analyst and analysand become other than who they had been to that point. The analyst gives voice to and participates in the creation of experience that is the living past of the analysand and in this way not only hears about the analysand's experience, but *experiences his own creation of it.* The analyst does not experience the past of the analysand; rather, the analyst experiences his own creation of the past of the analysand as generated in his experience of the analytic third.

At the same time, the analysand experiences his own living past as created intersubjectively in the third. The analysand does not reexperience his past; the analysand experiences his past as it is being created for the first time in the process of its being lived in and through the analytic third. (It is therefore a past that could be created only by this particular analytic pair through this particular analytic third.) As an experience lived in (and through) the analytic third, one is never completely alone with oneself (and one's past experience), since one's experience is being created with another person. This feature of the analytic situation creates the conditions for a fundamental recontextualization of formerly unintegrable, split off, unutilizable experience of the analysand.

To conclude (or better, to begin), psychoanalysis can be thought of as an effort to experience, understand, and describe the shifting nature of the dialectic generated by the creation and negation of the analyst by the analysand and of the analysand by the analyst *within the context of the roles constituting the analytic setup*. The dialectical tension generated by this creative negation and recognition does not present a question to be answered, a riddle to be solved. It is fitting that the riddle of the Sphinx (taken as the paradigm of the analytic mystery of subjectivities confronting one another) does not have an answer. In the myth of Oedipus, there is momentary victory for Oedipus (and for us as audience in identification with Oedipus) in Oedipus's capacity to answer the riddle of the Sphinx and thereby overcome the power of the Sphinx to block entry to Thebes. But the answer to the riddle (more accurately, the very fact that an answer was offered and was accepted) quickly comes to strike us as a disappointing trivialization of the question (just as Oedipus's victory over the Sphinx is ultimately revealed in the narrative to be still another reflection of Oedipus's subjugation to the Other).

The question posed by the Sphinx in the form of a riddle concerning a creature that walks on four legs in the morning, two at midday and three in the evening, is a question about the nature of the human condition in its multiform possibilities (represented by fourness that becomes twoness that becomes threeness). The answer to the riddle of the Sphinx must include all possible answers to the question of what it is to be human in a community of historically rooted human beings. We must attempt not to allow the fundamental psychoanalytic questions about the nature of human experience generated in the confrontation of subjectivities in the analytic situation to be trivialized with answers that pretend to offer more than an effort to describe a moment in time that is disappearing and becoming something different as we are attempting to recognize what it is.

XII

TREATING GROUPS, FAMILIES, AND INSTITUTIONS

58

Henry Ezriel's "A Psychoanalytic Approach to Group Treatment" (1950)

From the beginning, object relations theory has been applied well beyond psychoanalysis. Many of the major contributors were involved in widening the scope of application of these ideas, beginning with Freud's consideration of group psychology, literature, and culture, and continuing with Fairbairn's consideration of social policy, social movements such as communism, education, and the psychology of art, and Winnicott's interest in applying what he had learned in pediatrics and psychoanalysis to child rearing and cultural questions.

The selections in this part can only hint at the richness of this area of study. Included are three of the early contributors, and a selection from work carried out by Jill Savege Scharff and myself that draws on these early contributions in order to apply object relations theory to the study and treatment of families and couples.

Henry Ezriel was a consultant psychiatrist at the Tavistock Clinic who published little after his early papers on group therapy and on a rigorous experimental approach to interpretation in psychoanalytic treatment. His work on groups developed after experience in one of Bion's early therapy groups at the Tavistock Clinic. His subsequent influence on the group therapy movement was extensive because of his teaching. The ideas in this excerpt were seminal in establishing the Tavistock Clinic's preeminence in the group therapy movement. This influence also extended to the Tavistock's role in studying group relations whose proponents included A. Kenneth Rice, Eric Miller, Pierre Turquet, and, in America, Margaret Rioch. A separate tradition of group analysis developed in Britain following the leadership of S. H. Foulkes. That tradition is not represented here because it did not derive in the first instance from object relations theory; however, over the years its practitioners have shared many ideas with object relations. Many of them, such as E. James Anthony, Malcolm Pines, Lionel Kreeger, and Earl Hopper, have been analysts who worked in both traditions.

Following Bion's work (1948, 1949) at the Tavistock Clinic,[1] a few members of the staff have tried to apply a strictly psychoanalytic technique to the treatment of patients in groups. So far we have not had an opportunity to compare our techniques directly, e.g., by sitting in at each other's groups, but discussions suggest that much of what we do is based on common principles. There are, however, some differences, hence the following description, although representative in many parts, has features which are specific to myself. . . .

One often gets the impression that group therapy has been taken up mainly in order to make psychotherapy accessible to a larger number of patients and thus to make this time-consuming treatment less expensive. I doubt, however, whether this was the main factor driving towards the development of group treatment. I think the reason why psychoanalysts became interested in the application of their method to groups of patients was that the development of psychoanalytic theory and practice had reached a point where such a step was a logical consequence.

I shall now list the hypotheses upon which my approach to groups is based and then raise some technical problems that arise from them.

(1) The "transference situation" is not something peculiar to treatment but occurs whenever one individual meets another. A person's manifest behaviour contains (in addition to any consciously motivated pattern) features which represent an attempt to solve any conscious tension arising from this person's relations with unconscious phantasy objects in the residues of unresolved infantile conflicts.

1. I wish to take this opportunity of thanking Dr. W.R. Bion, in whose first patients' group at the Tavistock Clinic in 1945 I had the good fortune of participating. Though my present technique is in various points different from what I learned there, Bion's basic principle of strictly adhering to "here and now" interpretations is also characteristic of my own, and, I think, also of the group-approach of other psychoanalysts at the Tavistock Clinic.

(2) When several people meet in a group each member projects his unconscious phantasy objects upon various other group members and then tries to manipulate them accordingly. Each member will stay in a role assigned to him by another only if it happens to coincide with his own unconscious phantasy and if it allows him to manipulate others into appropriate roles. Otherwise he will try to twist the discussion *until the real group does correspond to his phantasy group.* The result of each member doing this is that there will soon be established a "common denominator," a common group tension, out of each member's individual dominant unconscious tension. This unconscious group tension will lead to manifest interactions between the various group members, actions which aim at resolving or at least diminishing that aspect of their individual unconscious tension which is contained in the common group tension. Each member of the group adopts a particular role within the group, which corresponds to his or her specific way of defending himself or herself against unconscious fears set up by this group problem.

(3) It seems more effective to adhere strictly to a techniqué which uses *only* transference interpretations, i.e., interpretations of what is going on in the group *here and now.* In using such a technique it appears best to follow the practice instituted by many English[2] analysts in recent years of leaving the patient free from rules and regulations. Instead, the unconscious meaning of everything brought into the consulting room, verbalized or expressed in action, both in the session and with regard to his plans for outside activities, is interpreted. Such injunctions as not to read books about psychoanalysis, or not marrying, or not making important decisions during treatment, are not laid down before treatment; but when these topics come up, their unconscious significance is interpreted. What usually happens then is that the patient loses the unconscious need that is being gratified by the particular behaviour that formerly analysts would have tried to deal with by making rules. I think that such rules in fact lead to the evasion of the analysis of the unconscious determinants of the patient's intentions. By allowing him through a nondirective technique to display these in the transference, we get into the position of freeing him from the unconscious phantasies which determine, or at least contribute to, his behaviour in outside situations. We thus enable him to make a decision based on an assessment of the real situation free from the

2. I am using "English" here to denote the fact that this technique has been developed mainly by analysts in England.

influences of unconscious fears. For these reasons I do not give any advice and, indeed, I consider that every instance of reassurance or active interference in his so-called real, outside problems arises from faulty technique, due to my inadequacy in giving transference interpretations as consistently and as well as I should like to do.

It is in keeping with such a technique that I no longer ask any patient to tell me what comes to his mind in connexion with any particular item but, on the contrary, take it for granted that all he displays are his "free" associations. Whenever I think that he is holding back something I try to free his associations by means of interpretations. With one exception I therefore started all my groups without any explanation, even though I was seeing them for the first time at the first group session. (The patients had had the general purpose of group therapy mentioned at the time of their individual consultations with other colleagues at the clinic.) The initial tensions felt in such a group in which the individual members have not been introduced to one another, silences, embarrassments, and so on, are the first material to be interpreted and these interpretations lead to the unfolding of the individual difficulties and differences in a group. In one of my groups I saw the majority of the patients for a short individual interview before the group met, introduced them to one another at the start and made a few introductory remarks. I cannot say that this had any particularly beneficial effect, an experience shared by several colleagues at the Tavistock Clinic.

(4) In carrying out such a rigorous here-and-now technique, interpretations are directed primarily to the "common denominator," the common group tension, and any particular patient's reactions are only referred to insofar as two things can be shown to him: (a) that his behaviour represents his specific way of coping with this common group tension; (b) *why* he acts in this way in preference to other ways of dealing with this group problem. A patient in a group may, for instance, often try to obtain a "private interview" within the group session by offering "tempting" material to the analyst. He may recount a dream or some outside experience or his symptoms in great detail. On such occasions I pick out of this material only what seems to me to be relevant to the common group tension. A female patient, for instance, once reported an anxiety dream in which a train going through a tunnel had an accident. She mentioned many more details of this dream. In my interpretation I referred to this accident only, as representing in symbolic terms a wish to destroy a couple in intercourse, namely myself and a female patient who

she thought was flirting with me. All the other details of the dream, the particular content of which did not seem to have a direct bearing on the group situation, were remarked upon as an attempt to seduce me into a private relationship with her to the exclusion of the rest of the group and especially of the other female patient. The essence of her recounting the dream in all its details seemed to be part of her reaction to a jealousy-arousing situation in that particular session when she felt that another female patient got on too well with me. To give another example, a male patient who in preceding sessions felt rejected by the women of the group gave a long narrative of difficulties with his wife. He then asked me to do something about it outside the group since this was a "real" problem. In interpreting this material, I pointed out to him only those features that seemed to me relevant with regard to the interpersonal relations prevailing in the whole group at that moment, namely, that he was trying to secure my help against the supposedly overpowering female members of the group. I did not refer to various other things that he had mentioned on this occasion. Several difficulties which he had with his children, if reported in an individual session, would no doubt have had to be interpreted as signifying something quite different, since they would then represent material elicited in a "two-person transference" relationship. I only took them up in the group session as demonstrating his wife's "badness." I think that in this respect this technique differs from that of many other group workers and also from the technique followed by many analysts who, as far as one can father from published accounts of their group work, tend to interpret a patient's remarks independently of the common group tension. I use material only insofar as it finds expression in the here-and-now relations of the group members towards one another, i.e., as it forms part of the general group tension; I do not go beyond that.

Analysts experienced in individual psychoanalysis sometimes raise the question of what happens to the "tension" which a patient is supposed to feel in a group when he expresses some problem of his in great detail without getting from the group therapist an interpretation referring to these details. I think that his question misses the meaning of transference in a group (and for that matter sometimes even in individual psychoanalysis). In my opinion it would be a misunderstanding of the transference situation if the analyst took the verbalized material at face value, i.e., as the essential indicator of the tension which the patient experiences in the here and now. I have tried to explain before that, for instance, the verbalized *content* of various details of my patient's dream did not indicate her tension but that by enumerating them she was trying to capture my attention in an attempt to cope with her jealousy.

(5) From my experience I believe that as long as we strictly adhere to the rule only to interpret what becomes apparent in the interpersonal relations of group members in the here-and-now situation, it is not only safe but essential to make conscious the symbolic or otherwise veiled sexual meaning of the manifest material. Analysts without group experience often doubt whether patients could express intimate sexual problems or that the therapist could give "deep" interpretations in the presence of other patients. Such a statement is even made by group therapists who do not follow a rigorous transference technique. I have seen anxiety reactions on the part of patients (like leaving the room or staying away from one or more sessions, or staying away and writing to me for an individual interview or prolonged silence in many subsequent sessions) in the early months of my group work when I hesitated to give such interpretations and I have seen only beneficial results from doing the opposite.

REFERENCES

Bion, W.R. (1948). Experiences in groups. *Human Relations* 1.

——(1949). Experiences in groups. *Human Relations* 2.

Ferenczi, S. (1926). On the technique of psychoanalysis, In *Further Contributions to the Theory and Technique of Psycho-Analysis* p. 177. London: Hogarth.

59

Henry V. Dicks' *Marital Tension: Clinical Studies Towards a Psychological Theory of Interaction* (1967)

Henry Dicks was one of the early pioneers of object relations who worked for many years at the Tavistock Clinic, as well as chairing the Department of Psychiatry at the University of Leeds where he fostered the work of Harry Guntrip. At Tavistock, he was consultant to the marital studies program in the Adult Department, whose work paralleled that of Enid Balint's Family Discussion Bureau in the adjacent Tavistock Institute of Human Relations. His 1967 book, *Marital Tensions,* perhaps more than any other single publication, established the application of object relations theory to the study of marriage, and by implication, to that of the family. He was the first to conceptualize the power of Fairbairn's formulation to understand marital relationships, and to extend Klein's theory of projective identification by combining it with Fairbairn's theory of endopsychic structure and developing the concept of mutual projective identification as the basis for normality and pathology in marriage. These contributions are explicit in his book but are not clearly delineated in this excerpt, which summarizes another formulation—his concept of the three subsystems that together constitute the overall psychological system of marriage.

Marriage as a social institution continues to be the expression of the culture's aspiration to ensure the stability, security, and dignity of relational needs between the sexes and of its children. This is accepted by our clients at conscious level.

Marriage as a system of interpersonal relations is stable and durable to the degree that it achieves the qualities of a compound or integrated dyad from being at its start a sum of 1 + 1. The strength and stability of this integrate depends on an overall positive balance of satisfactions over dissatisfactions for both partners, for which the term positive feedback is appropriate. This is not to be taken as implying freedom from conflict, or even "happiness."

In this interaction we can, in theory and in practice, discern three major levels or subsystems, which are internally related to each other, but can vary independently, and have changing importance in maintaining the cohesion of the dyad over different phases.

The first and most "public" subsystem is that of sociocultural values and norms. Although in our society selection for marriage has tended towards the valuation of autonomous commitment of the partners to each other on the principle of expected satisfaction of mutual needs, there remain the traditional norms of selection on the basis (as well as the opportunities) of social homogeneity or "homogamy." Homogamy operates by subculture affinities of class, religion, education, race, etc., in which prospective spouses may be united by shared identifications through the parents' social status and values. Though of decreasing importance in a mobile society, homogamy at social level is a factor for initial cohesion in a certain proportion of marriages.

The second subsystem is that of the central egos, which operates at the level of the personal norms, conscious judgments, and expectations also derived from the developmental background of object relations and social learning preceding the marriage. At this level the subculture element can be enriched or diluted by individual variances (even in a socially homogamous partnership) of such factors as conscious differentiation from parent-generation models; habits and tastes; deeper rebellion, countercathexes, and counteridentifications vis-á-vis parental figures and values. At this point the "heterogamy" of free choice becomes possible, and with it potential conflict in one or both partners between subculture pressures (now operating intrapersonally) and the individuals' contrary norms and role expectations. The latter may be more or less adult than the subculture's norms, but will always be dynamically linked to the earlier object relations by which the subculture's norms came to be in the individuals' field of interaction.

It is within this second subsystem of interaction that the ongoing pulls and pushes of demands of the partners on each other for role performance are continually testing the consistency or inconsistencies of the consciously held ego attitudes in actual behaviour. In terms of object relations theory these personal norms result from the vicissitudes of successive phases of personality development. As such they may be expressions of a relatively unimpeded maturation of emotional and rational capacities through the incorporation of predominantly good objects whose norms and attitudes have been uncomplicatedly identified with. This would also result in an uncomplicated personal adherence to the major social and cultural values of the first subsystem. Thus the conscious norms and role models may be consistent with the "inner world" of object relations and consequent behaviour towards the love object.

The mating of persons with this degree of integration is likely to reveal few important contradictions between the initially attributed expectations from and towards the potential mate and the actual role behaviour unfolding in daily action after marriage. They will be "really like" what the surface ego presaged. We can visualize such a marriage as being stable and offering satisfactions either by reason of absence of major role-demand conflicts, or by reason of the whole-person cathexis in the mode of conflict resolution over emerging role divergencies. Within this concept there is room for both the complementarity and the similarity hypotheses of satisfactory mate selection.

It is here that such qualities of character as flexibility and tolerance of ambivalence of self's and partner's conations and attitudes are the essential equipment for meeting the other partner's manifestations of individual identity and divergent maturation. These divergencies may be the sources of crises in adaptation and loyalty springing from ego levels (e.g., over one spouse's diverging religious or political convictions that were an important element of shared subcultural heritage). Sufficient falloff in satisfaction at this level may theoretically give rise to "reasoned" partings, which do not result in calls for help from therapeutic services. In such cases the dyadic integration had not been completed.

The second subsystem, insofar as it works well, would correspond to Fairbairn's mature dependence, "characterized by a capacity on the part of differentiated individuals for co-operative relationships with differentiated objects." (1952, pp. 145–146)

The interferences with the satisfactory interaction at this level necessitates attention to the third subsystem. This is the area which I have called the unconscious forces flowing between the partners, forming bonds of a "positive" and "negative" kind, often referred to as transactions. It is topologically the field in which we locate the drives towards satisfaction of object relational needs which have undergone exclusion from awareness in the course of transition from primary towards more differentiated object seeking. According to the intensity of conflict during this development, the pathways of dynamic flow from self to object are more or less open along that developmental line, or are deflected into segregated channels or blind alleys at various phases along the line. These are the "repressed" or "split-off" internal ego-object relations, as envisaged by object relations theory. Their dynamic presence influences the integrity or potential contradictoriness of the central ego's perception of its own object needs and the directness with which it can perform its psychosocial roles in seeking the object and maintaining gratifying relation with it. I hold that it is the "mix" of the more or less unconscious interaction of object relations in this third subsystem which governs the longer-term quality of marriages.

In this conceptual framework, it is possible to assess the contributions from each subsystem of each partner towards the dyadic integrate. These contributions will vary in accordance with the degree of consistency or conflict between the explicit social and personal value norms and role expectations which the partners bring to the marriage, and their two "inner worlds" of object relations which require satisfaction or feedback within the dyad.

Within the great variety of permutations of interaction at the levels of the three subsystems and congruence or divergence between subsystems, I discern certain recurring patterns of dyadic adaptation to ambivalent investment of the partners ("tensions"), which in varying degree "threaten" the stability of the relationship. It is my contention that this dyadic adaptation or homoeostasis depends on the two partners' ability to deal with the pressures in the third subsystem in one of the following ways:

1. By congruence of all three subsystems—including the perception of each by the other as a whole person with consequent "benign" conflict-resolution.
2. By the successful use of shared cultural and personal-conscious norms and values as defences against the deeper impulsions from the libidinal and anti-libidinal primary object relation levels. This is collusive defence by idealization, convention, rationality, moral con-

sensus, etc. Conflict is not allowed to arise. The defences are effective for a greater or lesser time.

3. Contrariwise, by the collusive use of the cultural marital norms and values as a facade behind which to permit and act out the expression towards each other of elements in the primary libidinal and anti-libidinal object relational potentials by means of projective and introjective mechanisms, for which the partners share a need. These may come into operation at once or replace the failure of defensive collusion after a time, and give rise to what the external observer might term paranoid or depressive dyadic systems, in which the satisfactions are mainly, or at least episodically, at primary, fiercely ambivalent object relational levels. Here the "negative" or aggression-expressing bonds of the primary object relational attributions are often more emotionally rewarding than the "positive" or love-expressing bonds. The first and second subsystems in this situation are maintained because in themselves supportive to the dyad, or as an arena sanctioned by the "outside world," where the conflict (itself the satisfying feedback for the partners) can be conducted. We do not know by what pathway or mechanism mate selection for this type of interaction operates.

Finally, a theoretical conjecture on the failed marriage ending in permanent separation or divorce, which has, so far, been hardly mentioned. Marriages may prove unviable at any of the three subsystem levels. It would seem necessary for at least two of the three subsystems postulated to function with credit balances of satisfaction over dissatisfaction to both partners. Social affinity plus congruence of deep object relations can withstand strong divergencies of personal norms and tastes. Strong agreements over personal norms and values plus deeper object relations can override large cultural and social distance and incongruities. Even social homogamy and good overlap of personal norms and values can endure, provided their defensive efficacy against "unwelcome" confrontation at deeper object levels holds. But if reality testing proves to one or both partners that the relationship was based on nothing but social affinity or meeting ground, on nothing but some shared personal interests, or on nothing but seeing a potential parent figure or an exciting libidinal object as a guarantee against essentially infantile loneliness, then it is only a question of time before the need for a broader-based merging of lives will become felt, and, in due course, acted upon in one way or another. It is usually the case that, at this stage, the emotional content of the relationship is one of boredom, indifference, and withdrawal of investment. Nothing of the self is any longer projected into the other. The institutional aspects of the cohabitation may be continued for rational or social advantages, but the marriage as interpersonal relation will be dead. The opposite to love is not hate. These two always coexist so long as there is a live relationship. The opposite to love is indifference.

REFERENCE

Fairbairn, W. R. D. (1952). *Psychoanalytic Studies of the Personality.* London: Routledge & Kegan Paul.

60

David E. Scharff and Jill Savege Scharff's *Object Relations Family Therapy* (1987)

The work Jill Savege Scharff and I have undertaken to apply object relations to marital and family therapy has drawn on many of the sources presented in this volume—Freud, Fairbairn, Klein, Winnicott, Bion, and most directly on the synthesis Dicks presented in *Marital Tensions.* A complete object relations view of family development and family therapy draws on a full view of the development and pathology of individuals, of the group, and marriage, as well as those qualities unique to the family as a special group in society and in the consulting room. Similarly, techniques of psychodynamic treatment draw from all the modalities of individual and group treatment. This excerpt outlines a theory of therapy that contrasts individual therapy with that for families and couples.

We can use the elements of the early relations between mother and child to build a model of the relationship between the actions of individual therapy and those of the conjoint therapies (family therapy and couple therapy). As each derives from aspects of the early parent–child relationship, these forms of therapy have their influence through the particular echoes of it that they recall.

[Previously] we explored the origins of contextual holding and centered relating and holding.[1] In the beginning these grew out of the psychosomatic partnership between mother and baby. Each of the early holding situations corresponds to a later level of interaction between adults, or between an adult and an older child. Let us locate the experience and function of the therapist with the individual patient, and with families and couples.

A MODEL OF INDIVIDUAL THERAPY

The internal object life of the patient is communicated to the therapist through conscious communications and through the medium of direct communication by the central ego. What is communicated overtly contains all the material needed for the understanding of the unconscious, split-off, and repressed internal object life. In this unconscious realm, the relationship between parts of the self and the object are out of awareness but are communicated indirectly along with what is intended to be consciously communicated. This is familiar to psychoanalytic psychotherapists as lying squarely in the realm of transference. To family therapists it is the realm of metacommunication: those things that are relatively clear to the trained therapist as part of the message but that are outside of awareness or avowed intent of the patient, to one degree or another. The communication that we care about in any therapy that goes beyond being purely supportive and problem-solving in the most limited sense, involves the patient's capacity to communicate with the interior of the therapist. The therapist has an internal object system whose organization corresponds to that of the patient, although we rely on its being less split, less rigid, and less thoroughly repressed.

Therapists should have better access to these repressed areas that consist (just as the patients' do) of repressed objects and repressed parts of themselves. We rely on the relative maturity of the therapist, and on his or her more flexible self-understanding, to have these internal object relationships more available. Being more comfortable with them, the therapist can feel their activation when something happens with the patient, and being able to work with them, he or she can begin by

1. Contextual holding is that derived from the functions of Winnicott's environmental mother. Centered relating and holding derive from those of the object mother.

first appreciating the patient's experience. That is, the therapist can empathize and then can feed back a digested or metabolized internal experience to the patient. In accepting the "projection" of the patient's internal objects and acknowledging it, the therapist is performing the eye-to-eye function, like the mother who validates the baby's experience. This has been broadly discussed as "mirroring" by several writers (Kohut 1977, Pines 1982, 1985, Scharff 1982, Winnicott 1971). In the words we are using to describe these interactions, this goes on in the zone of centered or core relating. It is in this zone that communication between aspects of repressed inner object relations of therapist and patient can occur. It is in this zone that internal object relations can be modified by direct influence.

The fundamental building blocks of these crucial communications are projective and introjective identifications, for it is through these that each partner is able to allow the other into his or her interior space. As these accumulate over time, they constitute the transference/countertransference interaction that is the heart of psychoanalytic psychotherapy. We can note, therefore, that the kind of transference we are highlighting is the focused transference between the interior of each person, and that there is another transference we have not yet discussed. It is the transference of the patient to the therapist's ability to provide a holding environment, the contextual holding that is analogous both to the mother's holding and protecting of the baby and to the father's holding of the nursing couple.

In the discussion of individual therapy or psychoanalysis, differentiating between these aspects of transference has great potential. We do not yet have a language for the difference in the use of the transference of psychoanalytic psychotherapy and that of psychoanalysis proper. In the absence of such a language, the difference may be felt to be distinct, but it cannot always be described. This is especially true at the blurred edges of the boundary between the two, when psychotherapy becomes quite intense, or when psychoanalysis has not yet produced a transference neurosis or is making progress by using supposedly "nonanalytic" techniques that Eissler (1953) has called "parameters." The differentiation of transference into two distinct types deriving from these separate parts of primary relationships allows us to call the transference to the mother's and father's holding capacity the *contextual transference,* and the transference to the mother's centered relating the *focused transference.*

The Contextual Transference

The contextual transference is directed at the therapist as the provider of a holding environment that contains the patient's anxiety. The therapist creates the space in which the patient can mature and develop new psychological strength, where formerly the patient would have been blocked or incapacitated. When we discuss the way the therapist provides a holding context, we are discussing one function that is included in Bion's (1967) larger concept of "containment." This concept of containment is one of the most helpful of Bion's contributions. Sally Box (1984) has explored containment as one of the fundamental growth-promoting processes in families of adolescents. As Box shows, the whole process of containment includes both the provision of a container to the infant's or patient's anxiety, and the capacity for reverie—the absorption of the anxiety and fantasy that are unmanageable for the baby or patient. Thus, the concept of containment includes contextual holding, centered holding, and centered relating. The contextual transference is the transference only to the contextual holding aspect of containment. It can be differentiated from the focused transference, which emanates from the patient's early experience of both centered holding and centered relating. Elements of transference to the therapist's holding function that contribute to the contextual transference are:

1. To mother's holding of the baby
2. To father's holding of the baby
3. To father's holding of mother
4. To father's holding of mother and baby
5. To father and mother's sexual holding of each other
6. To father and mother's united holding of the family, including siblings
7. To the family's holding of father, mother, and the children
8. To the previous generation and its holding of the current family

In the early part of a psychotherapy or an analysis, it is the contextual transference that is activated, as the patient tells the therapist or analyst about his life and travails. Failures of understanding are due not to therapist inadequacy in internally processing the received experience of the patient's inner world but, rather, to the failure of the therapist to provide the holding context, which the patient relies on but is unsure of at the beginning. In this phase, the therapist has not become an internal object for the patient but is more like a fond relative with whom the internal objects can be discussed, just as the patient might tell a relative about his or her nuclear family. In the therapist's understanding presence the patient can explore his or her internal objects. The therapist's role is crucial, and it can catalyze internal reorganization, even including the remodeling of internal objects and self. But the therapist is not yet installed as a major internal figure.

The Focused Transference

The moment that the therapist does become a permanent internal figure, the patient is hit with the realization that a major shift has occurred in the therapeutic relationship. In a therapeutic setting, the impact of this shift is analogous to falling in love. This shift does not ordinarily occur in psychotherapy, but in analytic work this is the moment of the crystallization of the transference neurosis. And once this unique kind of attachment to the analyst has cemented, a new kind of work is possible because the therapist, previously only an external object, has now become a fully formed, new internal object for the patient. It is now possible for the therapist to become the internal object that reorganizes the whole history of internal objects. The principal components of the focused transference are:

1. To the centered relationship with mother
2. To the centered relationship with father
3. To the relationship with mother and father as a couple
4. To the centered relationships with siblings
5. To the relationships with extended family members, grandparents, and to any other primary caretakers

A brief example will illustrate the two kinds of transference in operation.

An Example of Focused and Contextual Transference from Individual Analysis

Miss Harvey came into her analytic session in her third year of analysis, lay down, and began to argue with the analyst. "Say something to me.

> Don't you know this is no way to do this with me? You're so stubborn." On this occasion, the analyst tried to ask her a question, but she burst out, "No, that's not it. You just interrupted me again. You never ask at the right time." The analyst said he felt silenced. He asked what this reminded her of from her early life. Although Miss Harvey could not always answer such questions, on this day she said, "You know goddamned well it's my mother. So what else?" He said he had not thought she yelled like this when she was little. "No, I never yelled. I couldn't speak. But she yelled at me, and I just felt worse and worse." Now the analyst could say that he felt she was acting like her mother and treating him the way she felt treated then, and that their job was to understand the reason she had to act this way now.

In this example, the patient complains about the contextual transference, but in fact she works openly and trustingly within it. It is actually part of her trust in what has been called the "therapeutic alliance" that lets her go on to enact the transference (Greenson 1965, Zetzel 1958). This is in marked contrast to the early part of the analysis, when she was too fearful of the treatment relationship to allow this kind of material to emerge. At that point, she hid the most painful parts of her internal world because her contextual transference to the contextual holding provided by the analyst was pervaded by distrust derived from her early experience. Now that she can convey the substance of her internal world, she reenacts an edition of the core relationship, and the therapist becomes the recipient of the transference from the internal representation of a part of herself while she acts like the internal part-object based on her experience of her mother.

The study of which kind of transference is the predominant one operating at a given time in individual therapy can extend our understanding of the differential actions of psychotherapy and psychoanalysis. An examination of the contextual transference will do much to clarify the progress of a patient in psychotherapy.

However, the use we wish to make here of the focused and contextual transferences is in family therapy. Individual psychotherapy cannot ordinarily take full advantage of the focused transference, and psychoanalysis must wait for a long time (at least a year) before the focused transference becomes crystallized into the transference neurosis. But the family brings the entire set of already installed transferences into the therapist's office, and these focused transferences to each other are available for study and modification. This does not mean that family members each develop a focused transference to the therapist, but it does mean that the focused transferences already active in the family are in the room with the therapist, rather than being only reported on as in individual psychotherapy.

A MODEL OF FAMILY THERAPY

When the family comes to the family therapist, it brings its contextual transference, just as individual patients do. The family is concerned about the therapist's capacity to listen, observe, understand, and provide for their emotional safety. The family therapist works with this contextual transference, and it is here that the work primarily stays. Although the individual therapist also has the contextual transference to frame the work, interest is focused on the patient's internal object world, even though its contents are not yet matters of the individual patient's transference to the individual therapist.

Not so for the family therapist whose view is primarily on the family as a group and on its capacity to offer holding to the family members. The transference that corresponds to this perspective is the family's shared transference to the therapist's holding capacity for the family members as a group. This constitutes the family's shared contextual transference.

SHARED FAMILY HOLDING

The family's overall shared holding corresponds most simply to the combination of the mother's arms-around holding of her baby, the father's support of that, and the parental marital relationship. Within this envelope, mother and baby have their eye-to-eye centered relationship, out of which the baby first builds internal objects. In the more complex situation of the family, the family-as-a-whole provides the envelope within which to foster the growth of multiple centered relationships—between all the children, parents, and any close grandparents or babysitters. Within this space, the family members provide the material and experience for each others' internal objects. What makes the family a unique group is this ongoing process of both contributing to each other's internal objects and living in intimate relation to them. This means that in treatment the family always brings these internal object relationship sets as many focused transferences.

Individual therapy works early on with individual transference manifestations that, in analysis, crystallize later into the transference neurosis, which is a re-edition of the original object relationships. In the family, however, we find various multiple re-editions of the original object relationships transferred onto the others—parents, siblings, or even pets. While the family therapist understands the vitality and importance of the multiple focused transferences, they are too complex to be clear as clinical transferences that can be used in the early stages of family therapy.

The attitude the family shares toward the therapist is pooled in the contextual transference to the therapist and to the therapeutic situation. As family therapists, we should primarily consider the transference from the family-as-a-whole because this is the most powerful way of organizing our understanding and intervention.

When we examine in detail the family's holding capacity for its members, we find that it is more complex than we have so far described, since it also includes the sum of the several dyads' holding of each other and of the ways the dyads support or undermine each other's holding. Clinically we will eventually be interested in this complex tapestry of transferences, but we begin with the family group's shared contextual holding capacity. This shared envelope provides a boundary within which the members maintain the private space in which to be a family and across which they transact business with other groups, including ourselves. The combined holding capacity can be sensed through the countertransference as we encounter the family at this boundary.

The way the therapist relates to the family in psychoanalytic family therapy is derived just as much from understanding of transference as it is in individual psychotherapy or analysis. . . . But as we have seen, the source of the transference is different here. While the individual therapist gets information from the internal object world of the patient, the family therapist gets transference information from the interactions in the shared holding space of the family. Family members in therapy interact mainly with each other, and their difficulties are understood as difficulties in the function they all contribute to, providing the holding for each other. We can recall here that it quickly becomes baby's job to provide holding to mother in her job as mother, just as she has from the beginning provided holding for her baby. In just the same way, the children provide their share of the holding for their parents, and although we could say that the child's is the minor share, this is not a useful way of approaching the situation. The children, and all family members, provide their own contributions to the shared holding function in the manner appropriate to their ages and development. And anyone's incapacity to do so becomes a deficit for the family as a whole and must be compensated for.

The source of the transference that is the business part of family therapy is, therefore, the contextual holding transference. It is here that we become affectively aware of the family's difficulty in providing holding for its members, and it is this failure that we consult to in doing family therapy. At a practical level, this means that we should begin by being emotionally equidistant from each of the family members, with an overall notion that we are really on the side of the family as a unit in its job of helping each of the members to grow, to love, and to work. Helm Stierlin (1977) stated this nicely when he said that when the family therapist finds himself on the side of or against one of the members, it is a countertransference signal that there is something wrong. Of course, this happens constantly in the family therapy setting, but on each occasion, it is a sign of a strain in the family's shared holding, and that is the useful point for our attention.

In organizing our understanding of the family at this level, we in turn provide an envelope around the family and around its presumably flawed holding capacity. Within the safety of the holding we provide, the family can begin to risk relaxing its own holding function in order to attempt new holding patterns.

The building blocks for these new holding patterns are the daily minute transactions that occur among the individuals and influence the whole group. In our therapeutic setting, we see samples of these within the container we provide. When we do so, we absorb and try to understand the anxieties the family shares, and to feed back our understanding of these. While we may do so by speaking to one individual, our primary focus is on the way that one individual speaks for the shared anxieties of the whole family group. Our ability to help them with the shared difficulty will help them to hold each other and help each other.

The interactions in family therapy come in many forms, however. At any one time the therapist and the family may be focusing on one person, or on a subgroup of two or three people. This means that the individual and the subgroups, not simply some theoretical action of the family group as a whole, form the sources of information. But in each of these transactions between subgroups, the family as a whole is affected and reacts or fails to react in some way. Some of these family-wide reactions are helpful for the overall holding function, and some are not. The most useful transference is the one at this level, and it is this level of organization that helps us determine where to intervene. When we do so, it is with an awareness that even if we speak momentarily to an individual family member or to a subgroup, any effect will immediately have consequences for the whole family.

REFERENCES

Bion, W. (1967). *Second Thoughts.* London: Heinemann.

Box, S. (1984). *Containment and countertransference.* Paper presented at the Washington School of Psychiatry, Fifth Annual Symposium on Psychoanalytic Family Therapy, Bethesda, MD, April.

Eissler, K. (1953). The effect of the structure of the ego on psychoanalytic technique. *Journal of the American Psychoanalytic Association* 1:104–143.

Greenson, R. (1965). The problem of working through. In *Drives, Affects and Behavior,* vol. 2, ed. M. Schur, pp. 217–314. New York: International Universities Press.

Kohut, H. (1977). *The Analysis of the Self.* New York: International Universities Press.

Pines, M. (1982). *Mirroring and group analysis: an illustration with reference to the group treatment of borderline and narcissistic disorders.* Presented at Washington School of Psychiatry Symposium on the British Group-Analytic Approach to Group and Family Treatment, Washington, DC, February.

—— (1985). Mirroring and child development. *Psychoanalytic Inquiry* 5:211–231.

Scharff, D. E. (1982). *The Sexual Relationship: An Object Relations View of Sex and the Family.* London: Routledge & Kegan Paul.

Stierlin, H. (1977). *Psychoanalysis and Family Therapy.* New York: Jason Aronson.

Winnicott, D. (1971). *Playing and Reality.* London: Tavistock.

Zetzel, E. (1958). Therapeutic alliance in the analysis of hysteria. In *The Capacity for Emotional Growth.* New York: International Universities Press, 1970.

61

Elliott Jaques' "Social Systems as Defence Against Persecutory and Depressive Anxiety" (1955)

Elliott Jaques applied Klein's concepts of deep anxiety and the paranoid-schizoid and depressive positions to adult development, social systems, and institutions. Like Ezriel, Jaques has acknowledged a debt to Bion in elaborating concepts that have fertilized the work of many analysts and analytically informed workers. In addition to later work of Jaques himself, the work at the Tavistock Institute of Human Relations carried out by Isabel Menzies Lyth, Eric Miller, Eric Trist, A. Kenneth Rice, and Harold Bridger stand out particularly in the application of object relations theory to institutions, social issues, and group relations training.

Jaques also published a seminal work on adult development, "Death and the Mid-Life Crisis" (1965), which used the life patterns of creative artists to illustrate the need to rework the depressive position during critical adult stages of development. This final selection is the theoretical starting place for the widening scope of object relations to the institutions and social organizations in which all individuals function throughout life. Jaques has continued to study the relationship of individuals to institutions throughout a long and productive career in applied social science.

REFERENCE

Jaques, E. (1965). Death and the mid-life crisis. *International Journal of Psycho-Analysis* 46:502–514.

In the present paper . . . I hope to illustrate and define how the mechanisms of projective and introjective identification operate in linking individual and social behaviour.

The specific hypothesis I shall consider is that one of the primary cohesive elements binding individuals into institutionalized human association is that of defence against psychotic anxiety. In this sense individuals may be thought of as externalizing those impulses and internal objects that would otherwise give rise to psychotic anxiety, and pooling them in the life of the social institutions in which they associate. This is not to say that the institutions so used thereby become "psychotic." But it does imply that we would expect to find in group relationships manifestations of unreality, splitting, hostility, suspicion, and other forms of maladaptive behaviour. These would be the social counterpart of—although not identical with—what would appear as psychotic symptoms in individuals who have not developed the ability to use the mechanism of association in social groups to avoid psychotic anxiety.

If the above hypothesis holds true, then observation of social process is likely to provide a magnified view of the psychotic mechanisms observable in individuals, while also providing a setting in which more than one observer can share. Moreover, many social problems—economic and political—which are often laid at the door of human ignorance, stupidity, wrong attitudes, selfishness, or power seeking, may become more understandable if seen as containing unconsciously motivated attempts by human beings to defend themselves in the best way available at the moment against the experience of anxieties whose sources could not be consciously controlled. And the reasons for the intractability to change of many social stresses and group tensions may be more clearly appreciated if seen as the "resistances" of groups of people unconsciously clinging to the institutions that they have, because changes in social relationships threaten to disturb existing social defences against psychotic anxiety. . . .

Freud has argued that two main processes operate in the formation of what he calls artificial groups, like the Army and the Church; one is identification by introjection, and the other is replacement of the ego-ideal by an object. I have suggested that this latter process implicitly contains the concept, formulated by Melanie Klein, of identification by projection. Further, Melanie Klein states explicitly that in the interaction between introjective and projective identification lies the basis of the infant's earliest relations with its objects. The character of these early relations is determined by the way in which the infant attempts to deal with its paranoid and depressive anxieties, and by the intensity of these anxieties.

Taking these conceptions of Freud and Melanie Klein, the view has here been advanced that one of the primary dynamic forces pulling individuals into institutionalized human association is that of defence against paranoid and depressive anxiety; and, conversely, that all institutions are unconsciously used by their members as mechanisms of defence against these psychotic anxieties. Individuals may put their internal conflicts into persons in the external world, unconsciously follow the course of the conflict by means of projective identification, and re-internalize the course and outcome of the externally perceived conflict by means of introjective identification. Societies provide institutionalized roles whose occupants are sanctioned, or required, to take into themselves the projected objects or impulses of other members. The occupants of such roles may absorb the objects and impulses—take them into themselves and become either the good or bad object with corresponding impulses; or, they may deflect the objects and impulses—put them into an externally perceived ally, or enemy, who is then loved, or attacked. The gain for the individual in projecting objects and impulses and introjecting their careers in the external world, lies in the unconscious cooperation with other members of the institution or group who are using similar projection mechanisms. Introjective identification then allows more than the return of the projected objects and impulses. The other members are also taken inside, and legitimize and reinforce attacks upon internal persecutors, or support manic idealization of loved objects, thereby reinforcing the denial of destructive impulses against them.

The unconscious cooperation at the phantasy level among members of an institution is structured in terms of what is here called the phantasy social form and content of institutions. The form and content of institutions may thus be considered from two distinct levels: that of the manifest and consciously agreed form and content (including structure and function, which, although possibly unrecognized, are nevertheless in the preconscious of members of the institution, and hence are relatively accessible to identification by means of conscious study); and that of the phantasy form and content, which are unconsciously avoided and denied, and, because they are totally unconscious, remain unidentified by members of the institution.

A case study is presented to illustrate how within one department in a factory a subinstitution, a committee of managers and elected workers' representatives, was used at the phantasy level for segregating hostile relations from good relations, which were maintained in the day-to-day production work of the department. When, however, the committee was charged with a serious and conscious negotiating task, its members encountered great difficulties because of the socially sanctioned phantasy content of their relationships with each other.

Some observations are made on the dynamics of social change. Change occurs where the phantasy social relations within an institution no longer serve to reinforce individual defences against psychotic anxiety. The institution may be restructured at the manifest and phantasy level, or the manifest structure may be maintained but the phantasy structure modified. Individuals may change roles or leave the institution altogether. Or, apparent change at the manifest level may often conceal the fact that no real change has taken place, the phantasy social form and content of the institution being left untouched. Imposed social change which does not take account of the use of institutions by individuals, to cope with unconscious psychotic anxieties, is likely to be resisted.

Finally, if the mechanisms herein described have any validity, then at least two consequences may follow. First, observation of social processes may provide one means of studying, as through a magnifying glass, the operation of paranoid and depressive anxieties and the defences built up against them. Unlike the psychoanalytical situation, such observations can be made by more than one person at the same time. And second, it may become more clear why social change is so difficult to achieve, and why many social problems are so intractable. For from the point of view here elaborated, changes in social relationships and procedures call for a restructuring of relationships at the phantasy level, with a consequent demand upon individuals to accept and tolerate changes in their existing pattern of defences against psychotic anxiety. Effective social change is likely to require analysis of the common anxieties and unconscious collusions underlying the social defences determining phantasy social relationships.

XIII

SUGGESTIONS FOR FURTHER READING

Here are the major sources of some of the contributors excerpted in this volume, annotated to guide the interested reader into their ideas. I have selected this list with an eye to accessibility; any of the readings included here will point the way to further works of interest to the reader. In addition to the books and collections included here, the major journals contain a wealth of readings and are generally the source of new material. In addition to the *International Journal of Psycho-Analysis*, I enjoy the British journal *Free Association* and the relative newcomers *Psychoanalytic Inquiry* and *Psychoanalytic Dialogues* as sources of new ideas and spirited investigation.

FREUD

The literature by and about Freud is so vast that I will not try here to give much guidance. Virtually the entire body of Freud's work, except for a few recently discovered items, is contained in *The Standard Edition of the Complete Psychological Works of Sigmund Freud, Volumes 1–24,* under the general editorship of James Strachey (London: Hogarth and the Institute of Psycho-Analysis, 1955).

Freud's reach was enormous, but some of the most readable papers are the case histories contained in *Studies on Hysteria* (*Standard Edition,* vol. 2); "Dora" ("Fragment of an Analysis of a Case of Hysteria," *Standard Edition* 7), "Little Hans" ("Analysis of a Phobia in a 5-year-old Boy," *Standard Edition* 10), "The Wolfman" ("An Infantile Neurosis," *Standard*

Edition 17), and "The Ratman" ("Notes upon a Case of Obsessional Neurosis," *Standard Edition* 10). Freud's recommendations on practice are examined in *Freud's Technique Papers: A Contemporary Perspective* by Steven Ellman (Northvale, NJ: Jason Aronson, 1991). Since Freud is the beginning point for all psychoanalytic thinking, the object relations elements are interwoven with the beginnings of all the analytic traditions.

Two books that begin with Freud to give an excellent overview of the origins and ramifications of object relations are Judith Hughes's *Reshaping the Psychoanalytic Domain: The Work of Melanie Klein, W. R. D. Fairbairn, and D. W. Winnicott* (Berkeley, CA: University of California Press, 1989) for a well-integrated and readable version of the historical context of the ideas, and J. R. Greenberg and S. A. Mitchell's *Object Relations in Psychoanalytic Theory* (Cambridge, MA: Harvard University Press, 1983) for a scholarly and comprehensive treatment of the evolution of the ideas and their implications.

FAIRBAIRN

Fairbairn's principal writings were published in his only book published in his lifetime, *Psychoanalytic Studies of the Personality* (London: Tavistock, 1952). This is now reprinted in softcover by Routledge with an introduction by David E. Scharff and Ellinor Fairbairn Birtles. The other major papers, published later, are contained in volume 1 of *From Instinct to Self: The Selected Papers of W. R. D. Fairbairn*, edited by David E. Scharff and Ellinor Fairbairn Birtles (Northvale, NJ: Jason Aronson, 1994). Volume 2 of that work contains his early papers, which study and often question Freud, and his applications of object relations to other fields, social concerns, and to the psychology of art.

For further reading about Fairbairn, I recommend J. D. Sutherland's biography, *Fairbairn's Journey into the Interior* (London: Free Association, 1989), Harry Guntrip's writing (see below), and J. Grotstein and D. Rinsley's *Fairbairn and the Origins of Object Relations* (New York: Guilford, 1993).

KLEIN

Virtually all of Klein's work is contained in the four volumes of her *Collected Works* (London: Hogarth, 1975; republished by Delacorte).

An excellent place to begin a more selected reading, and a book whose guidance I used in constructing this volume, is Juliet Mitchell's selection, *The Selected Melanie Klein* (London: Hogarth; New York: Free Press, 1986).

The best introduction, and the easiest access, to the ideas contained in Klein's work is Hanna Segal's *Introduction to the Work of Melanie Klein* (London: Hogarth, 1963, revised 1975). Robin Anderson's edited collection *Clinical Lectures on Klein and Bion* (London: Routledge, 1992) is an excellent and readable collection. The most comprehensive updating of Kleinian ideas to date is the collection edited by Elizabeth Spillius, *Melanie Klein Today,* Volumes 1 and 2 (London: Routledge, 1988).

WINNICOTT

Winnicott's major papers are contained in three collections: *Collected Papers: Through Pediatrics to Psycho-Analysis* (London: Hogarth, 1958 and 1975), with an excellent introduction and overview written by Winnicott's student and collaborator Masud Khan; *The Maturational Processes and the Facilitating Environment* (London: Hogarth, 1965); and *Playing and Reality* (London: Tavistock, 1971), which is the best integrated of the three and can be read through to acquire a good overview of Winnicott's thought. While several early books, such as *The Child, the Family and the Outside World* (a collection of radio talks) and *Individual and Family Development,* are of interest, four posthumous books elaborate more on his central ideas. *Therapeutic Consultations in Child Psychiatry* (London: Hogarth, 1971), gives the only detailed case histories illustrative of his consultative process, especially the squiggle technique. His short book, *The Piggle: An Account of the Psychoanalytic Treatment of a Little Girl* (New York: International Universities Press, 1977), and *Holding and Interpretation: Fragment of an Analysis* (London: Hogarth, 1986), illustrate his therapeutic style and thinking with a child and an adult, respectively. His final volume, *Human Nature* (New York: Schocken, 1988), which was revised over 15 years and was still incomplete at the time of his death, was his attempt to construct a comprehensive view of development.

There are several useful books about Winnicott. Those that stand out are Adam Phillips's *Winnicott* (Cambridge, MA: Harvard, 1988), Simon Grolnick's *The Work and Play of Winnicott* (Northvale, NJ: Jason

Aronson, 1990), *Boundary & Space: An Introduction to the Work of D. W. Winnicott,* by Madeleine Davis and David Wallbridge (London: Karnac, 1981), and *In Search of the Real: the Origins and Originality of D. W. Winnicott,* by Dodi Goldman (Northvale, NJ: Jason Aronson, 1993).

BION

Bion's papers have not to date been collected in a comprehensive way, but most are available in reprints. The major sources for the mainstay of his ideas are *Experiences in Groups* (London: Tavistock, 1961), *Second Thoughts* (London: Heinemann, 1967, reprinted by Karnac, 1984), *Attention and Interpretation* (London: Tavistock, 1970), and *Learning from Experience* (London: Heinemann, 1962; reprinted by Karnac, 1984). There are two useful explications of Bion: *The Work of Wilfred Bion* by L. Grinberg, D. Sor, and E. Tabak de Bianchedi (revised edition, Northvale, NJ: Jason Aronson, 1993) and *Wilfred Bion: The Life and Work* by G. Bléandonu, translated by C. Pajaczkowska (London: Free Association, 1994).

READING BEYOND THE ORIGINS: KLEINIAN WRITING

Hanna Segal, who wrote the most accessible book on Klein's work, has two collections of her own, *The Work of Hanna Segal* (New York: Jason Aronson, 1981) and *Dream, Phantasy and Art* (London: Routledge, 1991). Herbert Rosenfeld, whose work is underrepresented in this volume, explored the treatment of psychosis more than any other Kleinian. His last book, *Impasse and Interpretation* (London: Routledge, 1987), contains a summary of his thinking and a guide to his earlier contributions.

Elizabeth Spillius edited two volumes entitled *Melanie Klein Today,* which contain a general updating of Kleinian thinking, including such authors not yet mentioned as Meltzer, Joseph, Bick, Brenman, Sohn, O'Shaughnessy, Steiner, Pick, Money-Kyrle, Riesenberg-Malcolm, Jaques, and Menzies-Lyth. Robin Anderson's *Clinical Lectures on Klein and Bion* (London: Routledge, 1992) is an excellent introduction to the clinical application of Klein and Bion. A book that focuses on the modern Kleinian view of the Oedipus complex is *The Oedipus Complex Today:*

Clinical Implications, by R. Britton, M. Feldman, and E. O'Shaughnessy (London: Karnac, 1989). Heinrich Racker's book, *Transference and Countertransference* (New York: International Universities Press, 1968) remains a classic, to be read by all interested in applying theory to clinical technique. R. D. Hinshelwood's *A Dictionary of Kleinian Thought, 2nd ed.* (Northvale, NJ: Jason Aronson, 1991) gives formulations of all the major Kleinian ideas.

Among the contributions to child development and child therapy, the work of Frances Tustin, a Kleinian child psychotherapist, on autism and on the use of autistic objects stands out. Among her many publications, I recommend *Autistic Barriers in Neurotic Patients* (London: Karnac, 1986). There are two writers on infantile development, both Italian who have been important to the Kleinians: Eugenio Gaddini, *A Psychoanalytic Theory of Infantile Experience* (London: Routledge, 1992), and Alessandra Piontelli, *From Fetus to Child: An Observational and Psychoanalytic Study* (London: Routledge, 1992).

THE INDEPENDENT TRADITION

Michael Balint's writing is contained in several books. His contribution to medicine and the mind-body continuum is contained in a book he co-edited, *The Doctor, His Patient and the Illness* (London: Pitman, 1957). Two of his major books, *The Basic Fault* (London: Tavistock, 1958) and *Thrills and Regressions* (London: Tavistock, 1959), contain the heart of his contribution. Harold Stewart's *Psychic Experience and Problems of Technique* (London: Routledge, 1992) brings a number of these ideas forward, in addition to containing Stewart's own significant contribution.

Harry Guntrip wrote three books on analytic theory, which together with the collection of his essays constitute his opus. He was a scholar of object relations, so that his books lead the reader through the logic of the field as it evolved. They are *Schizoid Phenomena, Object Relations and the Self* (New York: International Universities Press, 1969), *Psychoanalytic Theory, Therapy and the Self* (London: Hogarth, 1971; reprinted by Karnac, 1977), and *Personality Structure and Human Interaction* (London: Hogarth, 1961). In addition, his papers are collected in *Personal Relations Therapy* edited by Jeremy Hazell (Northvale, NJ: Jason Aronson, 1994), which also contains an excellent critical and biographical introduction by Hazell, who is working on a Guntrip biography taken from Guntrip's unpublished 1,000-page autobiography and from unpublished letters.

John Bowlby's masterpiece is his three volume, *Attachment and Loss: Volume 1: Attachment* (1969), *Volume II: Separation: Anxiety and Anger* (1973), *Volume III: Loss: Sadness and Depression* (1980) (London: Hogarth). These books have become the starting point for modern infant research, and are well worth studying as the seminal contribution to an ethological view of human nature in psychoanalysis.

Two books capture the breadth of contributions to psychoanalysis from the independent tradition: Gregorio Kohon's collection *The British School of Psychoanalysis: The Independent Tradition* (London: Free Association, 1986) and Eric Rayner's synthesis of major ideas and themes *The Independent Mind in British Psychoanalysis* (Northvale, NJ: Jason Aronson, 1991). Neville Symington's *The Analytic Experience* (New York: St. Martin's, 1986) is an excellent history of psychoanalysis from the vantage point of the independent tradition. Then, I would urge the reader to pursue the writings of any of the authors included in this volume, and I would add the work of Masud Khan, *The Privacy of the Self* (London: Hogarth, 1974) and *Alienation in Perversion* (London: Hogarth, 1979), of Harold Stewart, *Psychic Change and Problems of Technique* (London: Routledge, 1992), as well as that of John Klauber, Juliet Mitchell, Adam Limentani, Enid Balint, Paula Heimann, and Charles Rycroft.

MODERN CONTRIBUTIONS

There can be no single list of authors writing today that would satisfy anyone. Nevertheless, here are some of my personal favorites.

Christopher Bollas: *Shadow of the Object: Psychoanalysis of the Unthought Known* (New York: Columbia, 1987), *Forces of Destiny: Psychoanalysis and the Human Idiom* (London: Free Association, 1989), *Being a Character: Psychoanalysis and Self Experience* (New York: Hill and Wang, 1992), *Cracking Up* (New York: Hill and Wang, 1995).

Patrick Casement: *Learning from the Patient* (New York: Guilford, 1991).

Nina Coltart: *Slouching Towards Bethlehem . . .* (London: Free Association; New York: Guilford, 1992).

James Grotstein: *Splitting and Projective Identification* (New York: Jason Aronson, 1981).

Betty Joseph: *Psychic Equilibrium and Psychic Change: Selected Papers of Betty Joseph,* edited by E. B. Spillius and M. Feldman (London: Routledge, 1989).

Otto Kernberg: *Object Relations Theory and Clinical Psychoanalysis* (New York: Jason Aronson, 1976).

Stephen Mitchell: *Relational Concepts in Psychoanalysis* (Cambridge, MA: Harvard, 1988) and *Hope and Dread in Psychoanalysis* (New York: Basic Books, 1993).

Thomas Ogden: *The Matrix of the Mind* (Northvale, NJ: Jason Aronson, 1986), *The Primitive Edge of Experience* (Northvale, NJ: Jason Aronson, 1989), and *Subjects of Analysis* (Northvale, NJ: Jason Aronson, 1994).

Harold Stewart: *Psychic Experience and Problems of Technique* (London: Routledge, 1992).

John Steiner: *Psychic Retreats* (London: Routledge, 1993).

Neville Symington: *Narcissism: A New Theory* (London: Karnac, 1993).

GROUPS, FAMILIES, AND INSTITUTIONS

Henry Dick's 1967 *Marital Tensions* (London: Routledge, reprinted by Karnac 1994) remains the starting place for object relations' view of the family, followed by Robin Skynner's *Systems of Marital and Family Psychotherapy* (New York: Brunner/Mazel, 1976), and Sam Slipp's *Object Relations: A Dynamic Bridge Between Individual and Family Treatment* (New York: Jason Aronson, 1984). *Crisis at Adolescence: Object Relations Therapy with the Family,* edited by S. Box with B. Copley, J. Magagna, and E. Moustaki Smilansky (Northvale, NJ: Jason Aronson, 1994), outlines the application to family therapy of the Tavistock Clinic's Adolescent Department. *Psychotherapy with Couples,* edited by S. Ruszczynski (London: Karnac, 1993) and *Intrusiveness and Intimacy in the Couple,* edited by S. Ruszczynski and J. Fisher (London: Karnac, 1995) give a survey of modern contributions by the Tavistock Marital Studies Institute. The two books by D. Scharff and J. S. Scharff, *Object Relations Family Therapy* (Northvale, NJ: Jason Aronson, 1987) and *Object Relations Couple Therapy* (Northvale, NJ: Jason Aronson, 1992) are probably the most comprehensive application of theory to technique in this area.

In group therapy, *Bion and Group Psychotherapy,* edited by Malcolm Pines (London: Routledge & Kegan Paul, 1985), is a collection of essays that extends the specific ideas put forth by Bion. An edited volume, *Handbook of Contemporary Group Psychotherapy: Contributions from Object Relations, Self Psychology and Social Systems Theories,* R. H. Klein, H. S. Bernard, and D. L. Singer, editors (Madison, CT: International Universities Press, 1992), contains three chapters on object relations thinking in group therapy and an extensive bibliography.

In the application of object relations theory to institutions, I recommend Isabel Menzies Lyth, whose papers have been collected as *Containing Anxiety in Institutions: Selected Essays,* Vol. 1 (1988) and *The Dynamics of the Social: Selected Essays,* Vol. 2. (1989) (London: Free Association), as well as A. K. Rice's *The Enterprise and its Environment: A System Theory of Management Organization* (London: Tavistock, 1963), and E. J. Miller and A. K. Rice's *Systems of Organization: The Control of Task and Sentient Boundaries* (London: Tavistock, 1967). The works of Eric Miller, Eric Trist, and Harold Bridger are central to this tradition. A recent important contribution is E. A. Shapiro and A. W. Carr's *Lost in Familiar Places: Creating New Connections between the Individual and Society* (New Haven: Yale, 1991). A readable, stimulating compendium is *The Unconscious at Work: Individual and Organizational Stress in the Human Services,* edited by A. Obholzer and V. Z. Roberts (London: Routledge, 1994).

Finally, the tradition of dynamic group relations is represented in Kenneth Rice's work, *Learning For Leadership* (London: Tavistock, 1965). The tradition of group relations conferences begun by Rice and his colleagues is summarized in many articles in *The Group Relations Reader,* Vol. 1, A. Coleman and W. Bexton, editors (Sausalito, CA: GREX, 1975). This volume includes a reprint of a particularly good summary article, Margaret Rioch's "Group Relations: Rationale and Technique," originally in *International Journal of Group Psychotherapy* (1970; 20:340]ND355). Lionel Kreeger's edited volume *The Large Group: Dynamics and Therapy* (London: Karnac, 1975) explores the dynamics of large groups.

Credits

The excerpts in this volume come from the following sources, for which the editor gratefully acknowledges permission from the authors, publishers, various author estates, the *International Journal of Psycho-Analysis* and the Institute of Psycho-Analysis London, and other journals of original publication as listed.

Part II: Sigmund Freud

From: *The Standard Edition of the Complete Works of Sigmund Freud,* translated and edited by J. Strachey. Hogarth Press and the Institute of Psycho-Analysis, 1955. By permission of the Sigmund Freud Copyrights.

"Three Essays on a Theory of Sexuality," *SE* 7: pp. 125–243. Also by permission, Basic Books.

"Mourning and Melancholia," *SE* 14: pp. 243–258. Also by permission, Basic Books.

"The Ego and the Id," *SE* 19: pp. 12–59. Also by permission, W. W. Norton & Co.

Part III: W. R. D. Fairbairn (By permission, the Fairbairn family)

"Schizoid Factors in the Personality," written in 1940 and published in *Psychoanalytic Studies of the Personality* (*PSOP*), pp. 3–27, 1952, Routledge & Kegan Paul. By permission of the publisher.

"A Revised Psychopathology of the Psychoses and Psychoneuroses," first published in the *International Journal of Psycho-Analysis,* vol. 22, pp. 252–279, 1941. Reprinted with minor amendments in *PSOP,* pp. 28–58. By permission.

"Endopsychic Structure Considered in Terms of Object Relationships," first published in the *International Journal of Psycho-Analysis,* vol. 25, 1944. Reprinted in *PSOP,* pp. 82–136. By permission.

"Observations on the Nature of Hysterical States," first published in the *British Journal of Medical Psychology,* vol. 27 (3), pp. 106–125, 1954. Reprinted in *From Instinct to Self: Volume I. Selected Papers of W. R. D. Fairbairn,* ed. D. E. Scharff and E. F. Birtles, pp. 3–40, 1994. By permission.

"The Nature and Aims of Psychoanalytic Treatment," first published in the *International Journal of Psycho-Analysis,* vol. 39, pp. 374–385, 1958. Reprinted in *From Instinct to Self: Volume I,* pp. 74–92. By permission.

Part IV: Melanie Klein (By permission, the Melanie Klein Trust, Hogarth Press and the Institute of Psycho-Analysis, and the *International Journal of Psycho-Analysis)*

"The Psycho-analytic Play Technique: Its History and Significance," originally published in *New Directions in Psycho-Analysis,* London: Tavistock, 1955. Reprinted in *The Writings of Melanie Klein* (*Collected Works*), vol. 3: *Envy and Gratitude and Other Works: 1946–1963,* pp. 122–140. Hogarth Press and the Institute of Psycho-Analysis, 1975. By permission, the editors, the Melanie Klein Trust, and Tavistock Publications.

"Notes on Some Schizoid Mechanisms," in the *International Journal of Psycho-Analysis,* vol. 27, pp. 99–110, 1946. Reprinted in *Collected Works,* volume 3, pp. 1–24.

"Some Theoretical Conclusions Regarding the Emotional Life of the Infant," from *Developments in Psycho-Analysis,* ed. M. Klein et al., pp. 198–236, 1952. London: Hogarth. Also in *Collected Works,* vol. III, pp. 61–93.

"The Origins of Transference," in the *International Journal of Psycho-Analysis,* vol. 33, pp. 433–438, 1952. Reprinted in *Collected Works,* vol. 3, pp. 48–56.

"A Study of Envy and Gratitude," from *The Selected Melanie Klein,* ed. J. Mitchell, pp. 211–229. London: Hogarth Press; New York: The Free Press, Macmillan, 1986.

Part V: D. W. Winnicott (By permission, Mark Paterson on behalf of the Winnicott Trust and the various publishers)

From: D. W. Winnicott: *Collected Papers: Through Paediatrics to Psycho-Analysis*. London: Hogarth Press and the Institute of Psycho-Analysis, 1958 and 1975.

"Aggression in Relation to Emotional Development," pp. 204–218.

"Primary Maternal Preoccupation," pp. 301–305.

The following of Winnicott's papers reprinted in his *Collected Papers* were first published in the *International Journal of Psycho-Analysis*. By permission.

"Primitive Emotional Development," vol. 26, pp. 137–143, 1945. In *Collected Papers,* pp. 145–156.

"Hate in the Counter-Transference," vol. 30, pp. 69–74, 1949. In *Collected Papers,* pp. 194–203.

"Transitional Objects and Transitional Phenomena," vol. 34, pp. 89–97, 1953. In *Collected Papers,* pp. 229–242.

"Metapsychological and Clinical Aspects of Regression within the Psycho-analytical Set-up," vol. 36, pp. 16–26, 1955. In *Collected Papers,* pp. 278–294.

"On Transference," vol. 37, pp. 386–388, 1956. In *Collected Papers* as "Clinical Varieties of Transference," pp. 295–299.

The following papers appeared in Winnicott's second volume of collected papers *The Maturational Processes and the Facilitating Environment,* London: Hogarth Press and the Institute of Psycho-Analysis, 1965.

"The Theory of the Parent–Infant Relationship" was first published in the *International Journal of Psycho-Analysis,* vol. 41, pp. 585–595,

1960. Reprinted in *The Maturational Processes and the Facilitating Environment,* pp. 37–55. London: Hogarth, 1965. By permission.

"Ego Distortions in Terms of True and False Self" first published in *The Maturational Processes and the Facilitating Environment,* pp. 140–152, 1960. London: Hogarth. By permission, Hogarth Press and the Institute of Psycho-Analysis, and International Universities Press.

The following papers appeared in Winnicott's *Playing and Reality*. London: Tavistock, 1971. The first three appeared originally in the *International Journal of Psycho-Analysis*. By permission.

"The Location of Cultural Experience," *International Journal of Psycho-Analysis,* vol. 48, pp. 368–372, 1969. *Playing and Reality* pp. 95–103.

"Playing: Its Theoretical Status in the Clinical Situation," *International Journal of Psycho-Analysis,* vol. 49, pp. 591–599, 1968. *Playing and Reality* pp. 38–52.

"The Use of an Object," *International Journal of Psycho-Analysis,* vol. 50, pp. 711–716, 1969. *Playing and Reality* pp. 86–94.

"Mirror Role of Mother and Family in Child Development," in *Playing and Reality* pp. 111–118, 1967. Originally published in *Predicament of the Family,* ed. P. Lomas, pp. 26–33, 1967. By permission, Tavistock Publications.

From D. W. Winnicott: *Therapeutic Consultations in Child Psychiatry,* 1971. London: Hogarth Press and the Institute of Psycho-Analysis. By permission.

Selection from "Introductory Comments," pp. 3–8 and the case of "Rosemary, 10 Years Old," pp. 105–109, including drawings. Originally published in *St. Mary's Hospital Gazette,* Jan/Feb. 1962, under the title "A Child Psychiatry Interview."

Part VI: Wilfred Bion (All by permission, Francesca Bion)

From *Experiences in Groups*. Also by permission, the *International Journal of Psycho-Analysis* and the Institute of Psycho-Analysis,

London, except where otherwise indicated.

"Group Dynamics: A Re-View," first published in the *International Journal of Psycho-Analysis,* vol. 33, 1952. This volume uses the significantly revised version published in *Experiences in Groups and Other Papers,* pp. 143–153 and 188–189, 1961. London: Tavistock. By permission, Tavistock Publications.

"Development of Schizophrenic Thought," in the *International Journal of Psycho-Analysis,* vol. 37, pp. 344–356, 1956. Also in *Second Thoughts,* 1967. London: Heinemann. Reprinted: London: Karnac, pp. 36–42, 1984.

"Attacks on Linking," in the *International Journal of Psycho-Analysis,* vol. 40, pp. 308–315, 1959. Also in *Second Thoughts,* pp. 93–109.

From: *Learning from Experience,* pp. 90–91, 1962, London: Heinemann. Reprinted by Karnac 1984, "The K-link," pp. 89–94. By permission, Karnac Books.

From *Attention and Interpretation*: "Reality Sensuous and Psychic," pp. 26–40; "Opacity of Memory and Desire," pp. 41–54; "Container and Contained Transformed," pp. 72–82; "Prelude to or Substitute for Achievement," pp. 125–129. London: Tavistock, 1970. By permission, Tavistock Publications.

Part VII: Klein's Theory Elaborated (All by permission, the authors or their estates, the *International Journal of Psycho-Analysis* and the Institute of Psycho-Analysis, London.

Susan Isaacs, "The Nature and Function of Phantasy," in the *International Journal of Psycho-Analysis,* vol. 29, pp. 73–97, 1948. Also in *New Developments in Psycho-Analysis,* ed. M. Klein et al., pp. 67–121, 1952. London: Hogarth Press and the Institute of Psycho-Analysis.

Hanna Segal, "Notes on Symbol Formation," in the *International Journal of Psycho-Analysis,* vol. 38, pp. 391–397, 1957. Also in *The Work of Hanna Segal: A Kleinian Approach to Clinical Practice,* pp. 49–65, 1981. New York: Jason Aronson.

Herbert Rosenfeld, "A Clinical Approach to the Psychoanalytic Theory of Life and Death Instincts: An Investigation into the Aggressive Aspects of Narcissism," in the *International Journal of Psycho-Analysis,* vol. 52, pp. 169–178, 1971. Also reprinted in *Melanie Klein Today, Volume I: Mainly Theory,* ed. E. Spillius, pp. 246–249, 1988. London: Routledge.

Part VIII: Early Contributions of the Independent Group

Michael Balint, *The Basic Fault: Therapeutic Aspects of Regression,* pp. 15–30 and 67–72, 1968. London: Tavistock. By permission.

Harry Guntrip, "The Schizoid Problem, Regression, and the Struggle to Preserve an Ego," in the *British Journal of Medical Psychology,* vol. 34, pp. 223–244, 1961. Reprinted in *Personal Relations Therapy: The Collected Papers of H. J. S. Guntrip,* ed. J. Hazell. Chapter 6: "The Appalling Risk of the Loss of Definite Selfhood and the Struggle to Retain a 'Familiar Self,' " pp. 157–186, 1994. Northvale, NJ: Jason Aronson. By permission, the *British Journal of Medical Psychology.*

John Bowlby, "The Role of Attachment in Personality Development," in *A Secure Base,* pp. 119–136, 1988. London: Routledge. By permission, Routledge.

Part IX: Transference and Countertransference (all by permission the *International Journal of Psycho-Analysis* or the *International Review of Psycho-Analysis,* and the Institute of Psycho-Analysis, London, except as indicated.

Paula Heimann, "On Countertransference," in the *International Journal of Psycho-Analysis,* vol. 31, pp. 81–84, 1950.

Heinrich Racker, "The Meanings and Uses of Countertransference," in the *Psychoanalytic Quarterly,* vol. 26, pp. 303–357, 1957. Reprinted in *Transference and Countertransference,* pp. 127–173, 1968. New York: International Universities Press. By permission, *Psychoanalytic Quarterly.*

Joseph Sandler, "Countertransference and Role-Responsiveness," in the *International Review of Psycho-Analysis,* vol. 3, pp. 43–47, 1976.

Betty Joseph, "Transference: The Total Situation," in the *International Journal of Psycho-Analysis,* vol. 66, pp. 447–454, 1985. Also in *Psychic Equilibrium and Psychic Change: Selected Papers of Betty Joseph,* ed. E. Spillius and M. Feldman, pp. 156–167, 1989. London: Routledge.

Part X: Advances in Theory

Esther Bick, "The Experience of the Skin in Early Object Relations," in the *International Journal of Psycho-Analysis,* vol. 49, pp. 484–486, 1969. By permission.

Thomas Ogden, "On the Concept of an Autistic-Contiguous Position," in the *International Journal of Psycho-Analysis,* vol. 70, pp. 127–140, 1989. Also in *The Primitive Edge of Experience,* pp. 47–81, 1989. Northvale, NJ: Jason Aronson. By permission.

John D. Sutherland, "The Autonomous Self," in *Bulletin of the Menninger Clinic,* vol. 57(1), pp. 3–32. Also in *The Autonomous Self: The Work of John D. Sutherland,* ed. J. S. Scharff, pp. 303–330, 1994. Northvale, NJ: Jason Aronson. By permission, *Bulletin of the Menninger Clinic.*

E. B. Spillius, "Varieties of Envious Experience," in the *International Journal of Psycho-Analysis,* vol. 74, pp. 1199–1212, 1993. By permission.

John Steiner, "A Theory of Psychic Retreats," from *Psychic Retreats: Pathological Organizations in Psychotic, Neurotic, and Borderline Patients,* pp. 1–2 and 10–13, 1993. London: Routledge. By permission, Routledge.

Part XI: Advances in Clinical Concepts

James Grotstein, "On Splitting and Projective Identification," from *Splitting and Projective Identification,* pp. 205–210, 1981. New York: Jason Aronson. By permission.

Jill Savege Scharff, "A Model of Projective and Introjective Identification," from *Projective and Introjective Identification and the Use of the Therapist's Self,* pp. 87–92. Northvale, NJ: Jason Aronson. By permission.

Otto Kernberg, "Transference and Countertransference in the Treatment of Borderline Patients," in *Journal of the National Association of Private Psychiatric Hospitals,* winter 1975. Also published in *Object Relations Theory and Clinical Psychoanalysis,* pp. 161–184, 1976. New York: Jason Aronson. By permission, *Journal of the National Association of Private Psychiatric Hospitals*.

Nina Coltart, "Slouching Towards Bethlehem . . . or Thinking the Unthinkable in Psychoanalysis," in *Slouching Towards Bethlehem . . . ,* pp. 1–14, 1992. London: Free Association and New York: Guilford. By permission, Free Association Books.

Patrick Casement, "The Internal Supervisor," from *On Learning from the Patient,* pp. 29–57, 1985. London: Routledge. By permission, Routledge and Guilford Press.

Neville Symington, "The Analyst's Act of Freedom as Agent of Therapeutic Change," in the *International Review of Psycho-Analysis,* vol. 10, pp. 283–291, 1983. Also in *The British School of Psychoanalysis: The Independent Tradition,* ed. G. Kohon, pp. 253–270, 1986. London: Free Association. By permission.

Stephen A. Mitchell, "Psychopathology and the Analytic Process," from *Relational Concepts in Psychoanalysis: An Integration,* pp. 289–291, 1988. Cambridge, MA: Harvard University Press.

Stephen A. Mitchell, "Contemporary Perspectives on the Self: Toward an Integration," in *Psychoanalytic Dialogues,* vol. 1, pp. 121–148, 1991.

Christopher Bollas, "The Destiny Drive," from *Forces of Destiny: Psycho-Analysis and the Human Idiom,* p. 35, 1989. London: Free Association Books. By permission.

Christopher Bollas, "Psychic Genera," from *Being a Charachter: Psycho-Analysis and Self Experience,* pp. 66–100, 1992. New York: Hill and Wang. By permission, Hill and Wang, and Routledge.

Thomas Ogden, "On Becoming a Subject," *from Subjects of Analysis,* pp. 1–11, 1994. Northvale, NJ: Jason Aronson. By permission.

Part XII: Treating Groups and Families

Henry Ezriel, "A Psycho-analytic Approach to Group Treatment," in the *British Journal of Medical Psychology,* vol. 23, pp. 59–74, 1950. By permission.

Henry V. Dicks, "A Model of Marriage," from *Marital Tensions: Clinical Studies Towards a Psychological Theory of Interaction*, pp. 129–134, 1967. London: Routledge & Kegan Paul. By permission.

David E. Scharff and Jill Savege Scharff, "Models of Individual and Family Therapy," from *Object Relations Family Therapy*, pp. 65–83, 1987. Northvale, NJ: Jason Aronson. By permission.

Elliott Jaques, "Social Systems as Defence against Persecutory and Depressive Anxiety," in *New Directions in Psychoanalysis*, ed. M. Klein et al., pp. 478–498, 1955. London: Tavistock. By permission.

Index